Public Relations Theory III

This important book chronicles, responds to, and advances the leading theories in the public relations discipline.

Taking up the work begun by the books *Public Relations Theory* and *Public Relations Theory II*, this volume offers completely original material reflecting public relations as practiced today. It features contributions by leading public relations researchers from around the world who write about new developments in the field. Important subjects include: a turn to more humanistic, social, dialogic, and cocreational perspectives on public relations; changes in the capacity and use of new information technologies; a greater emphasis on non-Western international and intercultural public relations that considers an increasingly politically polarized culture; and issues of ethics that look beyond how clients and the traditional mass media are treated and into much broader questions of voice, agency, race, identity, and the economic and political status of publics.

This book is a touchstone for advanced undergraduate and graduate courses in public relations theory and a key reference for researchers.

Carl H. Botan is Emeritus Professor of Communication at George Mason University, USA.

Erich J. Sommerfeldt is Associate Professor at the Hubbard School of Journalism and Mass Communication, University of Minnesota, USA.

Routledge Communication Series
Jennings Bryant/Dolf Zillmann, Series Editors

Selected titles include:

African American Communication, 3rd Edition
Exploring Identity and Culture
Edited by Ronald L. Jackson II, Amber L. Johnson, Michael L. Hecht and Sidney A. Ribeau

Handbook of Visual Communication, 2nd Edition
Theory, Methods, and Media
Edited by Sheree Josephson, James D. Kelly and Ken Smith

The Dynamics of Persuasion, 7th Edition
Communication and Attitudes in the 21st century
Richard M. Perloff

The Routledge Handbook of Health Communication, 3rd Edition
Edited by Teresa L. Thompson and Nancy Grant Harrington

The Routledge Handbook of Family Communication, 3rd Edition
Edited by Anita L. Vangelisti

The Media Handbook, 8th Edition
A Complete Guide to Advertising Media Selection, Planning, Research, and Buying
Helen Katz

Public Relations Theory III
In the Age of Publics
Edited by Carl H. Botan and Erich J. Sommerfeldt

For a full list of titles please visit:
www.routledge.com/Routledge-Communication-Series/book-series/RCS.

Public Relations Theory III

In the Age of Publics

Edited by Carl H. Botan
and Erich J. Sommerfeldt

NEW YORK AND LONDON

Designed cover image: © Cundra/Getty

First published 2023
by Routledge
605 Third Avenue, New York, NY 10158

and by Routledge
4 Park Square, Milton Park, Abingdon, Oxon, OX14 4RN

Routledge is an imprint of the Taylor & Francis Group, an informa business

Library of Congress Cataloging-in-Publication Data
Names: Botan, Carl H., editor. | Sommerfeldt, Erich J., editor.
Title: Public relations theory III: in the age of publics/[edited by]
    Carl H. Botan, Erich J. Sommerfeldt.
Other titles: Public relations theory three
Description: New York, NY: Routledge, 2023. | Includes
    bibliographical references and index.
Identifiers: LCCN 2022037900 (print) | LCCN 2022037901 (ebook) |
    ISBN 9780367683313 (paperback) | ISBN 9780367693282
    (hardback) | ISBN 9781003141396 (ebook)
Subjects: LCSH: Public relations.
Classification: LCC HM1221. P826 2023 (print) | LCC HM1221
    (ebook) | DDC 659.2—dc23/eng/20220829
LC record available at https://lccn.loc.gov/2022037900
LC ebook record available at https://lccn.loc.gov/2022037901

ISBN: 978-0-367-69328-2 (hbk)
ISBN: 978-0-367-68331-3 (pbk)
ISBN: 978-1-003-14139-6 (ebk)

DOI: 10.4324/9781003141396

Typeset in Bembo
by Apex CoVantage, LLC

Contents

Acknowledgements

The authors wish to acknowledge and thank the following:

Carl H. Botan—A special thanks to Dr. Vincent Hazleton, who co-authored the first two *PRT* books but chose to enjoy his fairly recent retirement from Radford University. In fact, Vince did far more than just co-author the first two *PRT* books. The original idea for a first conference on public relations theory held at Illinois State University in the spring of 1987 was Vince's (who then chaired the department at ISU), as was the original idea for a first book on public relations theory. That book emerged from rigorous revisions of the papers presented—and discussed at length and/or contested—over the three days of that conference. I dedicate this book to my patient wife, Jennifer.

Erich J. Sommerfeldt—First, my thanks to Carl H. Botan for his guidance and partnership through the editing process. Second, I'd like to offer thanks to the incredible roster of authors who contributed to this volume. Their work printed within is excellent and will, no doubt, make a substantial impact on the field. Finally, a special thanks to a lifelong friend and mentor, Maureen Taylor.

Organization of the Book

Public Relations Theory III divides 30 chapters into an introduction and four sections. Each section includes chapters by leading scholars from around the world who offer their most current understandings of how theory in the field has, and should, advance. This broad question is addressed in four sections: 1) new understandings and theories addressing the central role of publics, 2) new understandings of theories, 3) new understandings of how race, gender, and culture play out in public relations, 4) examples of how theories can be applied in practice. Most chapters cross the lines between sections in one or more ways.

1 Introduction

Carl H. Botan and Erich J. Sommerfeldt

The professional practice of public relations continues to grow, with an estimated global market value of over $129 billion by the year 2025—representing a significant increase from $88 billion in 2020 (Guttman, 2021). Accurate data about this growth in individual nations is hard to come by, but anecdotal evidence is plentiful. For example, in India, "The growth of public relations in India has been outstanding. . . . Public relations is burgeoning" (Value360 Communications, 2014), and in the United Kingdom, "The public relations and communications activities industry's revenue is expected to grow at a compound annual rate of 1.9% over the five years through 2022–23" (Ibis World, 2022, May 5). In the United States, the government's *Occupational Outlook Handbook* predicts 11% growth in public relations specialists and 13% growth for public relations and fundraising managers between 2020 and 2030 (Bureau of Labor Statistics, 2022). This kind of growth leads to increasing demands for public relations education and academic research in many areas, although what is taught and researched varies widely. Given the exponential growth in practice and the contemporaneous development of public relations research, this book faces a broader, more complicated, and international task than its predecessors, *Public Relations Theory I and II*.

While the growth of the public relations industry has spurred contemporaneous global development in public relations education and the academic study of its practice, at the same time, to borrow a phrase from an influential—and now classic—article by Dozier and Lauzen (2000), the intellectual domain of public relations continues to be "liberated" from the practice. While there remains a strong research focus on the professional activity of public relations, the discipline has continued to embrace a wider range of research questions and has tackled more complex social issues and the role of public relations within them. The slog toward disciplinary maturity has been characterized by scholars asking deeper and more critical questions about the problematic influence of public relations on society or, conversely, the capacity for public relations in making communities and societies a better place in which to live. This evolution in thinking and theory development is reflected in the content of the previous iterations of this book and is continued in this new volume.

DOI: 10.4324/9781003141396-1

The Evolution of Thought

Public Relations Theory I *to* III

Public Relations Theory I was published in 1989, a time in which the field was still in its academic nascency. At that time, the editors claimed only that it should be possible to study:

> Public relations as an instance of applied communication. As empha-sized in the book, scholars should be able to apply communication theory to explain and to predict public relations practice, and to use public relations practice as a site for the development of communica-tion theory.
>
> (Botan & Hazleton, 1989, p. xiii)

Public relations theory, at this point in the history of the discipline, was largely a matter of borrowing and adapting theories from more developed fields—or more developed areas of the larger communication field such as rhetoric—to public relations. As Botan (1989) in *Public Relations Theory I* explicitly said, "This book addresses one emerging view [of public relations] by examining public relations as an applied social science based in commu-nication" (p. 99). Thus, the first iteration of this book helped in the estab-lishment of public relations as a legitimate academic field—albeit one almost exclusively focused on understanding the function and mechanics of public relations practices within organizations and their resulting effects on publics.

Public Relations Theory II was published 17 years later in 2006 and, as writ-ten in the introduction by Botan and Hazelton, sought:

> Directly to confront major theoretical issues that now characterize the field, including actual theories of public relations. [The book] includes discussions of two important new areas: international/intercultural public relations and the role of new information technology in public relations.
>
> (2006, p. ix)

By 2006, the field showed signs of maturing. *Public Relations Theory II* helped to codify major theoretical perspectives within the field that had gained prominence in the 1990s, such as the Excellence Theory and Relationship Management. Furthermore, *Public Relations Theory II* provided theoretical direction to relatively new areas of scholarship within public relations studies like public diplomacy, corporate social responsibility, and crisis communication— the last of which would soon become a disciplinary behemoth, and some say a discipline of its own. Little could we know back in 2006 how the field would develop in the subsequent 17 years. We have chosen to highlight three areas of this growth.

A Turn From Managerial Research to Public Relations Role in Society

Public Relations Theory II began to observe a turn from almost exclusively management-focused public relations theories to more humanistic, social, dialogic, and co-creational (publics as creators of their own meanings, a process they may allow public relations clients to participate in, thus co-creating new meanings) perspectives on public relations. The trend toward co-creational and societally oriented theory has continued to the present day, though by no means does this mean the importance of functional or managerial research diminished. Today, management-centered models remain central to the scholarly literature and are far from "dying out" in relevance—particularly to those scholars dedicated to informing the practitioner community inthe ever-growing professional practice of public relations. Indeed, the development of managerial theory is essential if the discipline is to keep pace with the expansion of the practice and ensure the rigor of public relations undergraduate and graduate professional education.

The growth of co-creational theory as pertains to public relations' role in building and maintaining communities, societies, and nations is remarkable. One important aspect of this evolution is the ever-growing role of research with and on publics—and the expansion of the research methods and outcome variables employed into more qualitative, critical, and humanist paths. New theories and models have also emerged as central themes in the field. Moreover, broad questions of the ethics of public relations practices continue to challenge the field. Questions of identity, race, and agency have also been brought to the fore. Put simply, scholars have continued to examine what public relations "means" alongside what it "does," to whom and with what effect.

New Information Technologies

By the turn of the century, it was still considered noteworthy for public relations practitioners to utilize Internet-enabled technologies for public relations purposes. Indeed, many practitioners regarded the Internet and other digital communication technology as a distraction and were skeptical as to their strategic value (Hill & White, 2000). Much has changed. The question today is not whether, but when and how, to employ digital communication technology in public relations practice. The exponential growth in digital communication technology and its impact on the professional practice of public relations is unquestionable and deep. Changes in the capabilities and use of new information technologies have dwarfed what we thought we knew about the topic in 2006, helping to substantially reshape our understanding of the role of publics in public relations. These technologies have also changed what many thought we knew about publics even as late as 2006, in part because they help extend relationships across borders, time zones, and peoples. The integral role of digital communication is reflected throughout this book, particularly in several chapters that specifically work to build public relations theory in the digital realm.

Internationalization and Diversification

In the latter part of the 20th century, the scholarly conversation in public relations was dominated by North American and Western European scholars who were either unaware of, ignored, or did not have access to discourse from public relations scholars across the world. Because of this isolation, the study of international and intercultural public relations was often largely characterized by how American and Western European views and models could be applied in other countries and cultures. The representation of scholars not from the North American continent in *Public Relations Theory I* and *II* was admittedly poor. The representation of the global scholarly community in the academic journals of our field and their resulting influence on theory development has dramatically increased since the publication of the second iteration of this book. Today, contexts outside the United States are recognized to employ their own unique practices and, increasingly, unique views on theory. Additionally, Western theorists, practitioners, and academics are increasingly acknowledging the importance of challenges and questions long faced in other countries and cultures, including communication between cultures, between the haves and the have-nots, and how to practice, teach, and theorize about public relations in increasingly politically polarized societies.

Although this *Public Relations Theory III* book, like its predecessors, still seeks to chronicle and help advance theory development in the field of public relations, it has entirely different content and organization, and features a very different and more inclusive set of authors and approaches.

Organization

Public Relations Theory III divides 30 chapters into four sections, plus an introduction and concluding chapters. Each section is characterized by a central question that leading public relations authors and researchers from around the world respond to with their most current understandings. The final chapter of this book, by Taylor, explains how individual chapters fit into theoretic views and relate to each other, so this chapter will explain only the sections of the book and the importance of each.

Section 1: Publics Take Center Stage

Section 1 of this book focuses primarily on the question of how our understanding of publics and their ever more central role in public relations research is leading to a new conceptualization of public relations as an essentially publics-driven profession. Reflecting the general lack of research and scholarship addressing public relations—the first academic journal in the field *Public Relations Review* had only been founded in 1975—*Public Relations Theory I* reflected the focus of public relations scholarship in 1970s and 1980s. Although several chapters mentioned publics, the focus was primarily on how to adapt existing theories and models from other areas of communication (e.g., rhetoric, persuasion, or organizational communication), and even from other fields such as business, psychology, and economics, to be useful to public relations.

By 2006 the topics covered in *Public Relations Theory II* had evolved to include ever more sophisticated efforts in some of these same areas, but one chapter (Walker, 2006) began to address the internal functioning of publics by using a theory already established in Communication studies. With a few important exceptions, theoretic work in public relations by 2006 had largely ignored the internal functioning of publics, their motives, and values as well as how they exchange views and make their own decisions. "Success" in both books largely meant increasing the odds of getting publics to do whatever the campaign sponsor or client wanted and a general lack of concern with how, or whether, publics sought to bring about changes in the organization.

Public Relations Theory III has not answered all these challenges regarding publics but has swung the needle from a somewhat myopic focus on just what the organization wants toward a strong acknowledgement that publics are an independent force in publics relations. Publics are perhaps the most independent, and thus the primary, force in public relations with the most freedom to think and act. Public relations theorists, teachers, students, and practitioners may be at the beginning of what might be called a new *age of publics* when it comes to thinking about how publics function, internally and collectively, to decide the importance of specific issues, the outcomes of campaigns, and the worth of investments in public relations work—the things publics decide beyond simple compliance or non-compliance with campaign goals. This is a lesson one major public relations firm, Edelman (2022), may have been trying to teach us for more than two decades with their annual Trust Barometer, reporting on how and what various publics trust or do not trust.

Section 2: The Development and Augmentation of Theory

Section 2 examines major new or augmented theories in public relations and how some older theories are being understood in new, or sometimes more sophisticated, ways. Theoretical development in public relations has expanded over the years to cover many new topics and questions. Thus, Section 2 can be understood as addressing the broad question, "What new, or revised, theories characterize current public relations scholarship?" The authors in this section offer important overviews as well as expansions of major theories in the discipline.

Section 3: The Internationalization and Diversification of Public Relations

Section 3 considers how changes in our understandings of race, gender, and culture/nationality affect how public relations should be theorized and practiced in the 2020s and 2030s as a multicultural endeavor that must welcome, and make room for, more minority and female scholars, researchers, and practitioners. The practice (and study) of public relations was once predominantly White, mostly male, and largely restricted to Western cultural views from North America and Europe (mostly Germany and the U.K.). As those of us who started to practice (sometimes with other job titles that would be acknowledged as part of public relations today) in the mid-to-late 1960s can attest, reliable data about race, gender, or culture from that era is hard to find. By 2019, however:

> Compared to U.S. demographics, people of color are under-represented in the public relations profession. Whites make up 76.5 percent of the population, 2019 Census data show, but 83.6 percent of public relations specialists . . . reported the Bureau of Labor Statistics (BLS). . . . Regarding people of color, the latest Census figures show Latinos at 15.9 percent, blacks (sic) at 13.4 percent, and Asians at 5.9 percent [of the population]. However, for public relations specialists, the numbers show 13.6 percent Hispanics or Latinos, 9.9 percent blacks (sic), and 5.8 percent Asians, according to BLS.
>
> (Arthur W. Page Center, n.d.)

Public Relations Theory III is more publics-focused, international, intercultural, and inclusive than its two predecessors reflecting, we believe, the stunning growth of new public relations theory around the globe in a bit over a third of a century. Specifically, unlike in the public relations workforce, where women are still underrepresented in leadership roles, occupying 71.4% of all practitioners but only 30% of executive positions (Toth, 2023; Chapter 17 in this book), nearly two-thirds or the authors in this book are women. Equally notable is that close to half (27 or 46%) of the authors in this book are currently or originally from outside the United States, reflecting the international and intercultural growth of publics relations scholarship, with one important caveat. Note that some authors counted here as from outside the U.S. are faculty or graduate students in the U.S. at the time of writing but nevertheless are thought to inform their contribution to this book with cultural thought and values not indigenous to the U.S.

Section 4: Reinforcing Theoretical Bridges to the Practice

Section 4 focuses on how leading researchers in public relations have worked to bridge the gap between theory and practice. Such gaps are to be expected in most, maybe all, fields of professional practice that also have academic components, and public relations is primarily an applied field with an academic branch. The idea to have chapters that explain how a theory has been applied is not new to *Public Relations Theory III*. In fact, both earlier books have some chapters that addressed applications of theories to one extent or another. In this book, however, we chose to emphasize this kind of practical-theory link by grouping the chapters that would most probably help answer some of the kinds of questions practitioner-readers and scholar-readers might ask about applying theory to practice.

Like its two predecessors, we hope that *PRT III* will serve readers' needs by providing a sense of having an intellectual tradition to build upon. Such a feeling might be particularly important in applied fields like public relations because their academic home departments (or schools) may not think of public relations as an integral and important part of the intellectual life of the department. A sense of an intellectual tradition, and the ability to talk about it, may become increasingly useful in an era in which colleges and universities appear to be hiring more and more adjunct or term faculty to staff lower division and "applied" courses, reserving tenure track and tenured posts for those teaching topics with a demonstrable intellectual tradition. This is not a good historical period in which to allow university administrators, campus colleagues, or taxpayers to forget about the intellectual traditions within public relations.

References

Arthur W. Page Center. (n.d.). *Race and ethnicity in the U. S. and PR workplace*. Penn State University. www.pagecentertraining.psu.edu/public-relations-ethics/introduction-to-diversity-and-public-relations/lesson-2-how-to-reach-diverse-stakeholders/key-concepts-and-approaches/

Botan, C. H., & Hazleton, V. (1989). *Public relations theory*. Lawrence Erlbaum Associates.

Botan, C. H., & Hazleton, V. (2006). *Public relations theory II*. Lawrence Erlbaum Associates.

Bureau of Labor Statistics. (2022). *U.S. department of labor, occupational outlook handbook, public relations and fundraising managers*. Retrieved April 19, 2022, from www.bls.gov/ooh/management/public-relations-managers.htm

Dozier, D. M., & Lauzen, M. M. (2000). Liberating the intellectual domain from the practice: Public relations, activism, and the role of the scholar. *Journal of Public Relations Research, 12*(1), 3–22. https://doi.org/10.1207/S1532754XJPRR1201_2

Edelman. (2022). *2022 Edelman trust barometer: The cycle of distrust*. www.edelman.com/trust/2022-trust-barometer

Guttman, A. (2021, November 8). Public relations (PR) market value worldwide 2020, 2021, 2025. *Statista*. www.statista.com/statistics/645836/public-relations-pr-revenue/#:~:text=PR%20industry%20market%20size%20worldwide

%202020%2D2025&text=It%20was%20calculated%20that%20the,a%20CAGR%20 of%207.4%20percent

Hill, L. N., & White, C. (2000). Public relations practitioners' perception of the world wide web as a communications tool. *Public Relations Review, 26*(1), 31–51. https://doi. org/10.1016/S0363-8111(00)00029-1

Ibis World. (2022). *Public relations & communication activities in the UK—market research report.* www.ibisworld.com/united-kingdom/market-research-reports/public-relations-communication-activities-industry/

Value 36 Communications. (2014, November 27). *Public relations in India and its growth.* www.value360india.com/public-relations-in-india-growth/

Walker, G. (2006). Sense-making methodology: A theory of method for public relations. In C. Botan & V. Hazleton (Eds.), *Public relations theory II* (pp. 393–414). Lawrence Erlbaum Associates.

Section 1

Publics Take Center Stage

2 In the Age of Publics

Evolving Understandings of Theory and Publics

Carl H. Botan

Introduction: A Maturing Field

This intentionally short chapter seeks to introduce readers of this book to current understandings of *theory* and *publics* that are both appropriate to public relations and can serve the reader in other contexts. These terms, like many others, get some of their meaning from use in a field, job, or institutional role and some of their meaning from critical examination in scholarship. These differences would seem to make agreement on a single definition challenging, and that is exactly what we find. There are many different definitions of theory, just as there are of publics.

Some evaluate theories by how complex they are or how universally they apply. For example, some may think of very complex ideas (think of astrophysics explaining both the creation and end of our galaxy) or ones that affect nearly all aspects of our lives as theories but do not accept anything below that level as being a "real" theory. On the other hand, more applied fields, including public relations, may include as theory lessons learned from many past experiences. In this sense a theory can also be a plan based on extensive practitioner experience about what specific practices are most likely to lead to a positive campaign outcome and which practices lead to a less desired outcome. When translated into theory-speak this might look something like: In the absence of confounding variables, treatment A (independent variable condition one—an emotional appeal) will lead to higher donations to client's charity (dependent variable) than will treatment B (independent variable condition two—a scare appeal). Experienced practitioners make this kind of theory-argument regularly; they just use the language of application rather than that of academia. It is fair to think of the campaign plans used in public relations as mini theories under the practice-based theories heading on Table 2.1.

Of course, astrophysicists might think the practitioner is using the term *theory* too simply, and the practitioner might think the academic view of the astrophysicist as too abstract to be of much use to daily practice in the "real world." Neither is entirely right or wrong; they just face different questions, and different kinds of theories are needed to address different questions.

DOI: 10.4324/9781003141396-3

Table 2.1 Kinds of Theory

Kinds of Theory			
Common Sense Theories	Lay/Naïve Theories	Practice-Based Theory	Scientific/ Formal
Sample Citations			
Wellman & Lagutta, 2004; Astington, Harris & Olson, 1988	Sloutsky & Spino, 2004.	Gabriel, 2011, Marshall et al., 2007; Reckwitz, 2007	Hazleton & Botan, 1989, p. 10; Wacker, 1998, p. 361
Examples			
Hair of the dog that bit you, for hangovers	"Law" of averages when coin flipping	Nursing practice/ theory, e.g., how person, health, and care interact	Explain and predict role of gravity
Common Sources				
Personal experience, Single event, Superstition	Culture, Social upbringing	Mass media, Social media	Practice, work training, and education	Scholarship/ Research

Similarly, there is little agreement on what a public is, which is addressed in chapters throughout this book, particularly the second section. In the case of publics, practitioners might snicker at an astrophysicist simple understanding while astrophysics might be bewildered by the many dimensions, functions, and kinds of publics experienced public relations practitioners have learned to work with.

The following discussion of different kinds of theory in the first section, particularly the idea of a continuum of theories, is intended to help the reader decide where the contents of this book fit into their own views of theory and publics. It may also help lay a foundation for using another continuum in the second section of this chapter to help explain differing views of publics common in public relations scholarship and practice, and that are emphasized in several chapters, including the last chapter.

These views of publics range from static personal and organization-centered views to more evolved and dynamic views of publics. These go from merely asking, "How can we get what we need out of publics?" and the latter, instead asking, "How can our organization fit into the complex internal and external functioning of publics?" In other words, should we think of publics as existing primarily to meet the needs of our clients, or do our clients exist primarily to meet the needs of publics? Are publics just groups we identify as important to our clients meeting their own needs, as suggested when we label publics as target, primary, secondary, etc., or do publics have their own motivations and organize themselves to act in pursuit of their own goals?

Ironically, simpler more organization-centric views of publics can be harder to turn into successful guides for a campaign because they typically do not consider the values and internal dynamics through which publics develop their own motivations, understanding, and behaviors. While more complex theories of publics that often account for ongoing internal dynamics of publics may be harder to understand and use in a campaign, they also may promise much more sophisticated understanding of publics' direction and rate of change than do organization-centric views of publics.

A continuum implies a kind of progression—in this case, a progression of how understandings of publics have changed over time, although all terms for publics continue to be used. Viewing theories about publics on a continuum also helps set the stage for Chapter 3 in this book (Sommerfeldt & Innacone), which goes more deeply into publics.

Theory and Practice

Put in non-academic terms, a theory is usually thought of as something like a well-thought-through body of knowledge about relationships, such as between ideas or things. In defining theory for the first *Public Relations Theory* book in 1989, Hazleton and Botan sought to offer the simplest possible academic definition that still includes the necessary components of a theory—in other words, the minimal definition of a theory. We said that, at a minimum, "a theory consists of at least two concepts and a statement explaining or predicting the relationship between those concepts" (p. 7). Concepts can be ideas or things. Frey et al. (2000) wrote, "A theory is simply a generalization about a phenomenon, an explanation of how or why something occurs" (p. 30). Thus, theories are the way we make sense of our experiences by organizing them to explain how and why things happen. These minimum definitions of theories guide the discussion of theories in this chapter.

There are certainly more complex definitions of theory available in the literature, particularly if one seeks to develop a "good" theory. For example, Wacker (1998) says,

> By definition, theory must have four basic criteria: conceptual definitions, domain limitations, relationship-building, and predictions . . . To be good theory, a theory must follow the virtues (criteria) for "good" theory, including uniqueness, parsimony, conservation, generalizability, fecundity, internal consistency, empirical riskiness, and abstraction. . . .

> Theory-building research seeks to find similarities across many different domains to increase its abstraction level and its importance.
>
> (p. 361)

Remember, however, that even the relationship between darkness and a sense of danger for early humans, such as, "It is dangerous to be away from the fire at night because the big predators hunt then" probably served as a lay/naïve or even a practice-based theory. It addressed concepts with conceptual definitions, had a limited domain, addressed a relationship between the two things (fire and danger from predators), and made a testable prediction.

It may be best to think of theory as on a continuum with at least four different kinds (with many different terms for them, and more kinds, discussed in the literature), each kind more sophisticated, complex, and testable than the ones before it, as depicted in Table 2.1.

Theory is in constant use throughout public relations, and in personal lives, whether in practice, scholarship, or teaching. For example, every public relations plan contains a theory at some level because a plan is an attempt to predict what strategies and tactics will maximize the likelihood of a successful outcome, whether that is winning votes, educating about a public health practice, or promoting a product or service.

Kinds of Theories and Their Use in Public Relations

Even a cursory review of the kinds of theories used in public relations over the last 50 to 100 years, let alone how they are related to each other and are used in practice, would require far more space than this chapter affords. Instead, this section organizes these issues into Table 2.2 to help understanding of: 1) common names for kinds of theory, 2) one or two citations where these terms have been used, 3) examples of how each kind of theory is commonly used, and 4) what the source or foundation of each kind of theory might be. The bottom section of Table 2.1 may be particularly useful because it gives commonly used sources or kinds of support and justification for each kind of theory. For example, where some see a common sense theory, others may not see what they would call a theory at all but only a personal experience or prejudice (think conspiracy theories and prejudices about gender, race, or religion).

It is here that the great difference between what some call "common sense" theories and, for example, scientific or formal theories can be seen. A theory based on so-called common sense might have only one personal experience cited to support it, while a formal scientific theory might have dozens of peer-reviewed articles using double-blind experiments to support it. Practice-based theories often draw on years, or centuries, of successful practice by many people in different situations as their support, which

Table 2.2 Schools of Thought in Public Relations

Instrumental	*Modern/Social Scientific*	*Self-Organizing/Motivated (Cocreational)*
←		→
Focused solely on organization's goals. Publics as target/audience. Publics only a means to organizational ends. Often overtly manipulative claiming to be "objective."	Focus on message construction, social science research for targeting, and how publics interpret messages. Often use social science theory to be persuasive, tailoring campaigns to publics makes research for planning important.	Focus on the meanings publics construct, changing senders and messages to meet the needs of publics. Right of publics to free and fully informed decision making paramount. Research about publics drives campaigns.

is what many public relations theories and practices represent. Like other applied fields with an academic/scholarly branch, public relations theory has typically evolved from practice or been adapted from other fields or subfields. The public relations theories discussed in this book would fall into either the far right, scientific/formal column of Table 2.1, or the third column, actual public relations practice.

THEORY AND PRACTICE

As discussed, valid theories can be developed from practice, but there is a distinction between theory and practice (praxis). Practice is usually understood to include the practical *application* of knowledge, such as a theory, and can also be a kind of test of a theory. For example, Smith says:

> Where theory seeks to connect cause and effect in the mind, praxis endeavours to link means and ends in the real world. Where theory deals in categories of cases, praxis focuses on the case in hand . . . Clausewitz emphasized the constant interaction between theory and practice, regarding the boundary between them as in permanent flux. Theory must be tested against reality—either by applying it to history or by applying it in practice . . . In turn, praxis in both past and present provides raw material that can be used to modify existing theories or develop new ones.
>
> (2004, p. 185)

The terms *theory* and *practice* should not be used as though they are opposites, because they are complementary. As Smith says, practice often provides the raw material to build theories, as well as a proving ground for testing theories. On the other hand, theory often compiles and synthesizes sometimes large masses of experience. This relationship between theory and practice is not just complementary, but it also makes knowledge much more portable and sharable by facilitating the transfer of knowledge from one concrete situation or practice to another, or even from one time or generation to another.

Just as it takes effort to apply the knowledge summarized in a theory, it also takes some effort of reasoning to develop a new theory from practices. Indeed, many—perhaps most—theories have resulted from systematic review of practices or natural occurrences. The final section of this chapter shifts out of the discussion of theory in public relations to define and discuss publics and their roles. Publics are, as the title of this book and the contents of many of the chapters suggest, the dominant single concept in public relations, a position developed from practice, work, training and education, or public relations scholarship.

Publics

As the title of this book and many of its chapters suggest, increasingly sophisticated scholarly understandings of the active role of publics in public relations are emerging, sometimes aided by social media. The roughly 20 years that the author has served as a judge for the Public Relations Society of America's (PRSA) national Silver Anvil awards for the top practitioner campaigns also suggest that the practitioner community is going down a similar path, albeit at a somewhat more deliberate pace. This section, and several chapters in the book, covers the primary change in our understanding of publics more theoretically by focusing on how the field is moving from seeing publics as primarily just targets to seeing publics as having agency, the topic of Chapter 3.

Instrumental Views of Publics

Publics were once widely understood as just groups/masses of people whom organizations and skillful practitioners could influence, or even sometimes manipulate, to meet an organization's needs, most often through use of the mass media. This view of publics as mere instruments with which to meet corporate or political needs was epitomized by the famous quote from the robber baron Cornelius Vanderbilt, "The public be damned" (Longman, 2015). In fact, Cho (2012) used this quote to label one of the eras of public relations as "the public be damned era" in public relations.

The largely one-way orientation of mass media may well have contributed to this view of public as just instruments to meet organizational needs. Illustrated by using labels ranging from "hostile publics" (Kim & Krishna, 2015; Read, 2007) to "target publics" (Barrault-Stella & Weill, 2018), which suggest that practitioners and their clients were interested in publics only, or primarily, insofar as those publics might be instruments to serve the needs of a client. This might be fairly called the *instrumental* view of publics (e.g., Botan, 2018; Schultz et al., 2013; Taylor & Botan, 2006).

In this period, planning and assessing campaigns often betrayed a lack of interest in what individual members or publics were thinking or how they relate to each other internally while out of sight of both the organization and practitioners, as discussed in the next subsection. Gradually, this led to the somewhat more sophisticated, but still relatively simplistic, demographic analysis of groups, such as how males and females differed as groups, how youths differed from older people, or how urban dwellers differed from rural residents. Final reports and billing statements using such demographic studies were often quite professional-looking with statistics and colored graphs, while failing to address important differences within demographic groups such as women. Two other kinds of research were popular in this period, *exposure* to messages and advertising equivalency. Most practitioners in this period, including the author, thought it a best practice to use these procedures in planning, final reports, and billing statements.

Audience exposure or how many people ("eyeballs") have been exposed to the client's message was thought to be very important, particularly when using mass media. One person seeing or hearing a message one time counts as one exposure. Once again, all exposures are counted equally regardless of how members of the public assessed the message; so, for example, hundreds of people seeing a political ad and responding very negatively were counted as exposures equally with hundreds who responded positively. This often-reported number counted on circulation figures for newspapers; likely number of people viewing billboards, signs, television ads, and the like; and listener figures for radio. These circulation and exposure figures were conveniently publicized by each media in their sales pitches for advertising.

Circulation statistics often resulted in very large numbers about those publics who might have been exposed to messages, whether they paid attention or not, and whether they agreed or disagreed. However, they were merely imperfect measures of a particular medium and told us little or nothing about publics that might be important to for strategy.

Nevertheless, circulation figures were considered important with, for example, a story or ad in the *New York Times* worth many times more than the same story or ad in a small-town weekly paper. Then there was the possibility with stories of being picked up by other outlets, maybe even one of the wire-services, which could lead to important national and even international coverage for a client. For example, some of the publicity efforts of the author for the Detroit region's Air Traffic Controller's Union strike, which snarled air traffic across the U.S. in 1981, were picked up and ended up as multiple newspaper, television, and radio stories nationwide in the U.S. and in Canada.

One statistic, the much-loved and ridiculed *pass-along rate*, allowed speculation about how many additional readers or viewers saw each copy (Vials, 2006) of a magazine, newspaper, or the like. Again, however, pass-along rates were also typically reported as though all members of exposed publics attended to a message and the exposures were somehow a positive thing, whether individuals responded to their exposure positively or negatively.

Pass-along rates were usually reported for periodical publications like magazines but could be talked about whenever an outlet reported the estimated number of people who read, saw, or heard each copy of something, most commonly a magazine. These rates were typically reported by combining or multiplying the total circulation, viewership, or listenership of that media by the number of times each copy was passed along to a second reader or more.

Advertising equivalency was a still more ingenious (and misleading) statistic that also made assumptions about publics. Again, how readers viewed and valued the *different kinds* of content was ignored. Rather, this was an attempt to explain why budgeting for public relations was wiser financially than paying for advertising time or space. Equivalency simply expressed the value of earned public relations coverage by computing how much an equivalent amount of advertising time or space would have cost. How publics evaluated these different contents was ignored, such as whether publics thought of paid ads the same way as they thought of regular news content.

To be fair, however, advertising equivalency was usually used just to provide clients with the kind of hard data about a campaign that they so often want, in this case dollars and cents. Some, possibly many, practitioners who used equivalency figures did point out that the news coverage from news releases should not be valued the same as an equal amount of advertising because news content was much more believable and valued by readers, listeners, and viewers. Thus, news generated by public relations efforts was worth much more because it had been vetted by an outside authority (the media and its editors) for accuracy, they argued. However, this difference was usually not quantified, so the figures clients often used were the raw equivalency data.

Overall mid- and even many late-20th-century public relations campaigns *instrumentalized publics* because they were essentially one-way focused. Moving beyond this era in which publics were treated as instruments would require two more steps: movement into a modern or social scientific view of publics and finally into understanding the agency (self-control, self-motivation, power, influence, etc.) of publics, sometimes called the cocreational view of publics.

Social Scientific and Modern Views

In 1989 Hazleton and Botan said: "We should be able to apply communication theory to explain and to predict public relations practice and use public relations practice as a site for the development of communication theory" (p. xiii). *Public Relations Theory I* was dedicated to this view. Clearly, the move to a more social scientific view, which often focused on studying publics and what they were thinking or feeling had started before 1989 for there to be authors and chapters available for that book. Indeed, a vice-president of one of the major national public relations firms told the author in the early 1990s that their firm's default standard was that research should make up at least 10% of the total cost of each contract.

The underlying perception of the importance of publics was still based very heavily on what publics could do for the client, but here the meanings publics created about clients and their messages assumed an importance largely unheard of in public relations in earlier times. And in turn, these thoughts and feelings began to have an important role in both campaign planning and evaluation. Interviews (e.g., Wright, 1998), focus groups (e.g., Aldoory & Toth, 2002; Sallot, 1996), and other means of assessing how publics feel, such as attending community meetings and the like, were among the techniques used for both campaign planning and evaluation.

Message testing research (e.g., White & Raman, 1999; Novelli, 1982) is still used to help avoid misjudgments in increasingly expensive television campaigns and large-scale political, public health, safety, and marketing campaigns. However, message testing has been mostly conducted for planning campaigns rather than for evaluating them, so it often does not provide quality information about the active, even leading, role of publics in public relations relationships.

Humanism, Agency, and Self-Organizing and Motivated Publics

Public relations efforts today are adopting more humanistic views of publics as self-organizing and self-motivated (think activist groups), constantly changing (think political campaigns), with an independent sense of right and wrong (think about organizational crises). This is not actually a new view of publics, just one largely ignored for almost a hundred years since Dewey (1927; see also Sommerfeldt and Iannacone's chapter for more in-depth discussion of Dewey, 1927) said a public is "a group of people who *see themselves* as having a common interest with respect to an organization" and "*endeavor to act* through suitable structures and thus to *organize itself* [emphasis added] for oversight and regulation" (p. 29.) This theme of public's being self-organizing and endeavoring to achieve their own internal goals is still being argued today by many authors, including the author who defined a cocreational view of a public as "an interpretive community engaged in an ongoing process of developing a shared understanding of its relationship with a group or organization that can differ substantially from that of the organization" (Botan, 2018, p. 59).

The author previously explained the evolution of our understanding of publics across all strategic communication fields, of which public relations is the leading example, using a continuum (Botan, 2018). That information is updated and reproduced here with the permission of the publisher.

Social Media and the Age of Publics. Practitioners today may manifest this most recent view of publics as groups of interacting and self-motivated groups of individuals when they feel the need to "see what social media is saying" about some issue, product, or organization as a first step to assessing what a client may be facing just as much as when they use focus groups or surveys of individuals to make these same assessments. Such acts are implicit acknowledgement that today's publics are often actively involved in thinking out how they feel about an organizational practice or product and sharing this with other like-minded individuals and groups, before either the mass media (and clipping services) and the organization even becomes aware of all this is taking place.

To be clear, this chapter is not an argument for an expanding role of social media (see Chapters 4, 8, 12, and others). Rather, it is an argument for the expanding self-organizing role of publics that are making increased use of social media to facilitate construction and advancement of their own agendas. Both practitioners and scholars have already argued for this self-organizing and self-motivated view of publics extensively. For example, Zas (2018, November) says,

> Before the Internet, Public Relations audiences were anonymous masses of people categorised under generic titles. An audience we were look-ing to impact through mass media. However, everything changed with Facebook . . . The expansion of social networks has turned each indi-vidual within those anonymous masses into potential micro-influencers with an exponential capacity to affect the reputation and positioning of any brand.
>
> (Para 3)

Many practitioners used to buy, or do their own, clipping services to see what messages publics might be exposed to about their organization long before social media existed. Nevertheless, social media helps extend this practice into what publics themselves are thinking and saying about what they may or may not have seen and heard, not just in the mass media but also from other publics in social media. These changes are helping substantially reshape our understanding of the role of publics in public relations. This, as much as anything else, is leading to what we think may be the beginning of *the age of publics* in public relations, in which the focus of both public rela-tions practice and theory turns to a self-motivated and self-organized role for publics in determining their relationships with organizations and institutions.

The actual role of social media in this process may not be just positive, however, because "about two-thirds of Americans (64%) say social media have a mostly negative effect on the way things are going in the country today" (Auxier, 2020). Thus, public relations practitioners should not view social media as a solely positive or solely negative force, but one that fits well with a cocreational or self-motivating/organizing view of publics.

Conclusion

In 2018 the author defined a public as "an interpretive community engaged in an ongoing process of developing a shared understanding of its relationship with a group or organization, which can differ substantially from that of the organization" (Botan, 2018). Acknowledging publics as self-organizing creators of their own strategy and content has been addressed by numerous academics in recent years. Ranging from "ways that publics frame(d) their key messages" (Ban & Lovari, 2021, June 23) to Pieczka's (2019) call for the creation of "a more complex understanding of the formation of the public . . . in relation to processes of co-creation and circulation of a wide range of texts" (p. 1), this thread of understanding the increasingly important role of publics is picked up and expanded by Sommerfeldt in Chapter 3.

Sources

Aldoory, L., & Toth, E. (2002). Gender discrepancies in a gendered profession: A developing theory of public relations. *Journal of Public Relations Research*, *14*(2), 103–126. www.tandfonline.com/doi/abs/10.1207/s1532754xjprr1402_2?casa_token=iyWKN C8kJDUAAAAA%3AXTNrz868kNmcqmokkUS7fs-PrO1ZzdoZ5

Astington, J. W., Harris, P. L., & Olson, D. R. (1988). *Developing theories of mind*. Cambridge University Press.

Auxier, B. (2020). *64% of Americans say social media have a mostly negative effect on the way things are going in the U.S. today*. Pew Research Center. www.pewresearch.org/fact-tank/2020/10/15/64-of-americans-say-social

Ban, Z., & Lovari, A. (2021, June 23). Rethinking crisis dynamics from the perspective of online publics: A case study of Dolce & Gabbana's China crisis. *Public Relations Inquiry*, *10*(3), 311–331. https://journals.sagepub.com/doi/full/10.1177/20461 47X211026854

Barrault-Stella, L., & Weill, P. (Eds.). (2018). *Creating target publics for welfare policies*. Springer International. https://doi.org/10.1007/978-3-319-89596-3

Botan, C. (2018). *Strategic communication theory and practice: The cocreational model*. Wiley Blackwell.

Cho, S. (2012, March 27). *Four models of public relations*. https://sites.google.com/site/fourmodelsofpublicrelations/home/the-public-be-damned-era

Dewey, T. (1927). *The public and its problems*. Henry Holt.

Frey, L., Botan, C., & Kreps, G. (2000). *Investigating communication* (2nd ed.). Allyn & Bacon.

Gabriel, R. (2011). A practice-based theory of professional education: Teach for America's professional development model. *Urban Education*, *46*(5), 975–986. http://doi.org/10.1177/0042085911400324

Hazleton, V., & Botan, C. H. (1989). The role of theory in public relations. In C. Botan & V. Hazleton (Eds.), *Public relations theory* (pp. 3–15). Lawrence Erlbaum Associates. www.matternow.com/blog/3-ways-social-media-has-changed-public-relations/

Kim, S., & Krishna, A. (2015). *Bridging strategy for public engagement: Understanding the effects of bridging strategy on staunch and hostile publics' behavioral and relational outcomes*. Singapore Management University. www.Home>Schools>LKCSB>_SMU>193

Longman, M. (2015, January 23). Tor corporate law, the public be damned. *Washington Monthly*. https://washingtonmonthly.com/2015/01/23/for-corporate-law-the-public-be-damned/

Marshall, G. W., Michaels, C. E., & Mulki, J. P. (2007). Workplace isolation: Exploring the construct and its measurement. *Psychology & Marketing, 24*(3), 195–223.

Novelli, W. D. (1982). You can produce effective PSA's. *Public Relations Journal.* http://www1. psaresearch.com/images/YOU%20CAN%20PRODUCE%20EFFECTIVE%20 PSAs.pdf

Pieczka, M. (2019). Looking back and going forward: The concept of the *public* in public relations theory. *Public Relations Inquiry, 8*(3), 225–244.

Read, K. (2007). "Corporate pathos": New approaches to quell hostile publics. *Journal of Communication Management, 11*(4), 332–347.

Reckwitz, A. (2007). Practice theory. *The Blackwell Encyclopedia of Sociology* (online). https://doi.org/10.1002/9781405165518.wbesop125

Sallot, L. M. (1996). Using a public relations course to build university relationships. *Journalism and Mass Communication Educator, 51*(1), 51–60. https://doi.org/10.1177/107769589605100107

Schultz, F., Castello, I., & Morsing, M. (2013). The construction of corporate social responsibility in network societies: A communication view. *Journal of Business Ethics, 115*, 682–692. https://link.springer.com/article/10.1007/s10551-013-1826-8

Sloutsky, V. M., & Spine, M. A. (2004). Naïve theory and transfer of learning: When less is more and more is less. *Psychonomic Bulletin & Review, 11*, 528–535.

Smith, H. (2004). Praxis. In *On Clausewitz.* Palgrave Macmillan. https://doi.org/10.1057/9780230513679_15

Taylor, M., & Botan, C. (2006, March). Global public relations: Application of a cocreational approach. In M. Watson (Ed.), *Proceedings of the 9th international public relations research conference: Changing roles and functions in public relations* (pp. 484–491). University of Miami Institute for Public Relations. www.instituteforpr.org/files/uploads 9th_IPRRC_Proceedings.pdf

Vials, C. (2006). The popular front in the American century: "Life" magazine, Margaret Bourke-White, and consumer realism, 1936–1941. *American Periodicals, 16*(1), 74–102. www.jstor.org/stable/20770947

Wacker, J. G. (1998). A definition of theory: Research guidelines for different theory-building research methods in operations management. *Journal of Operations Management, 16*, 361–385.

Wellman, H. M., & Lagutta, K. H., (2004). Theory of mind for learning and teaching: The nature and role of explanation. *Cognitive Development, 19*, 479–497. http://dx.doi.org/10.1016/j.cogdev.2004.09.003

White, C., & Raman, N. V. (1999). The world wide web as a public relations medium: The use of research, planning, and evaluation in web site development. *Public Relations Review, 25*(4), 405–419.

Wright, D. K. (1998). Validating credibility measures of public relations and communications: Interviews with senior-level managers and executives from other corporate disciplines. *Journal of Communication Management, 3*(2), 105–118. www.memerald.com/insight/content/doi/10.1108/eb023488/full/html

Zas, I. P. (2018, November 6). The evolution of the public relations industry in the era of modern digital media. *Audience: Resources.* https://resources.audiense.com/blog/the-evolution-of-the-public-relations-industry-in-the-era-of-modern-digital-medians

3 A "Public" by Any Other Name

Reclaiming Publics Theory, and Liberating Publics From "OPR"

Erich J. Sommerfeldt and Jeannette Iannacone

Many important words in the public relations literature are manifestly "primitive terms"—undefined notions that appeal to an assumed common knowledge or generally understood meaning. A primitive term is one that everyone assumes they understand—a term so self-evident it requires no definition or explication (Chaffee, 1991). For example, in a seminal article on defining relationships in public relations, Broom et al. (1997) argued that *relationship*, to that point in time, had been treated as a primitive term in the public relations literature, lacking clear meaning and focus. As a representative example of this failing, Grunig and Huang (2000) recalled a humorous incident at a doctoral dissertation defense where a scholar outside public relations blunted asked: "Just what do you people mean by relationship?" (p. 26). The concept of dialogue has been similarly misunderstood in innumerable studies in the public relations literature for more than two decades. Indeed, the term *dialogue* is so rampantly misapplied in the literature that scholars who were early to introduce dialogue to the discipline have devoted nearly as many pages to correcting misinterpretations of the concept as they have in explicating its actual dimensions and appropriate applications (e.g., Kent & Theunissen, 2016; Paquette et al., 2015).

Of the primitive terms in the literature, we would suggest there is perhaps no other word so badly misunderstood in public relations than *publics*. Despite being one of two christening terms that—quite literally—define the discipline, the word *publics* is used by scholars with little ontological or methodological consistency. Frequently, the word *publics* is treated as synonymous with other common terms like *audiences* and *stakeholders*. Any distinctions among the terms (if distinctions are even recognized) are often dismissed as superficial or unworthy of detailed consideration. Indeed, widely cited pieces have ignored any differences among the terms or will vacillate between their use in writing. For example, as Rawlins (2006) wrote:

> "Publics" is the term used for stakeholders in the public relations litera-
> ture. Because the public relations profession evolved from journalism,
> the term has frequently been related to the recipients of messages from
> organizations. These publics, or more accurately, "audiences," become

DOI: 10.4324/9781003141396-4

segmented into more homogenous subsets that help communicators choose appropriate channels for reaching them. For example, publics can be employees, shareholders, political leaders, consumers, etc.

(p. 2)

Rawlins' suggestion that publics can be more accurately described as audiences reflects a gross misunderstanding of the term. Rawlins does go on to explain how stakeholders may be different than publics, but the implication that the terms might be the same, or even that one may be superior to the other, was made clear.

Precision in terminology can be difficult without an understanding of a word's etymology or theoretical history. That said, the way publics are conceptualized, operationalized, and measured in research is fundamental to understanding public relations' outcomes. For example, the organization-public relationships literature—often abbreviated as OPR—has consistently measured *individual* attitude and behaviors, with little regard for how such individuals might form a *public* by any definition. As written by Goertz and Mahoney (2012), "Most concepts are intended to represent phenomena in the empirical world as they actually exist" (p. 207), meaning public relations scholars should be describing the nature of reality when they use a certain term—providing an accurate articulation of the substance of a thing.

Given the inconsistent usage of the term *publics*, this chapter attempts to accomplish three things. The first aim is to provide a brief historical overview of *publics* and its relevance to the discipline. Only a few such synopses exist in the literature, and this chapter works to complement those efforts (e.g., Pieczka, 2019; Sommerfeldt, 2013; Vasquez & Taylor, 2001). Second, the chapter provides an overview of the differing ontological treatments of publics within the literature—specifying what has been meant by "publics" and what has been important in their empirical representation. Finally, we engage in a critique of the OPR literature, before suggesting avenues by which scholars can more thoughtfully engage with the theoretical construct of publics.

The Public

In 2001, Vasquez and Taylor authored a seminal chapter on explicating publics in public relations. As they noted: "For all the importance placed on the creation, maintenance, and adaptation of organization–public relationships, the term *public* is one of the most ambiguous concepts in the field's vocabulary" (p. 139). The ambiguity in understanding and treatment continues more than 20 years later. Hallahan (2000) lamented the inconsistency in the term's usage and clarified the definition of other terms with which publics are sometimes confused:

> Researchers and practitioners often use the term *public* when referring to a variety of other, closely related concepts. Public is used to refer to

potential or actual *audiences*, that is, receivers of messages. Public also is used to describe *segments*, such as a market segment, that is, a group of people who share particular demographic, psychographic or geodemographic characteristics and thus are likely to behave or respond to organizational actions or messages in a similar way.

(p. 501)

Hallahan further explained how *stakeholders* has been confused as synonymous with *publics*, in that they are simply people who may be impacted by the actions of an organization—stakeholders, in general, are thought to be more passive, whereas publics are more aware and active.

The irony, of course, in *publics* being so primitive a term in our literature is that practically no word used in public relations jargon has an older conceptual history than the word *public*. To adequately grapple with the notion of publics in public relations, one must first recognize and interrogate the obvious root of the term *the public*. The concept is intimately linked with the development of democratic theory and thinking. Pieczka (2019) provided an elegant chronicling of the history of *the* public. To briefly summarize her review, Pieczka noted how the very idea of the public as "a collective noun for the rational and autonomous citizens of a modern polity" (p. 227) originated with Enlightenment philosophers and was taken up by several prominent 20th-century political theorists whose work remains influential in public relations scholarship to this day (e.g., Dewey, 1927; Habermas, 1989; Lippmann, 1927). The work of American philosopher John Dewey in particular has been broadly accepted as fundamental to current understandings of publics, though we (and others) argue that his work has been grossly misunderstood by most public relations scholars (cf. Rakow, 2018b).

Contemporary thinking on publics in public relations can be directly traced back to classical notions of democracy and what it means to be an informed and engaged citizen (Sommerfeldt, 2013). Vasquez and Taylor (2001) described these treatments of the public as the "mass perspective," articulating the public as a "single population of aggregate individuals with enduring characteristics" (p. 140). To be a member of the public meant that one consumed enough information to have an informed opinion on matters of common concern or widely shared consequences. As recounted by Rakow (2018b), John Dewey argued that rational discussion can only occur when the public is informed enough through *publicity*, a neutral press: "a method for members of society to understand the whole of which they are a part and for the formation of intelligent public opinion" (p. 319). The informed, rational-critical discussion among people resulting in shared issue interpretations constitutes the public and "[serves] as a counterweight to the state" (Fraser, 1990, p. 75). As Vasquez and Taylor (2001) put it: "A public is responsible for identifying civic concerns, gathering information from events and debates, and articulating its judgment to government officials by some method of expression. In this manner, a public participates in the process of self-rule" (p. 141). Individuals process information, recognize a shared concern, organize and publicly express their views to solve problems.

The notion of the well-informed public engaging in discussion that creates the "will of the people" about political matters was at the root of the famed Dewey-Lippman "debate," and the contrast between their two perspectives sets the stage for later understandings of publics in public relations (cf. Rakow, 2018a). Prominent political writer Walter Lippman, in his landmark book *The Phantom Public* (1927) and elsewhere, took issue with Dewey's idealized version of an engaged, informed citizen, capable of expressing rational views on issues of most areas of public concern, writing:

> I think it is a false ideal. I do not mean an undesirable ideal. I mean an unattainable ideal, bad only in the sense that it is bad for a fat man to try to be a ballet dancer. . . . The ideal of the omnicompetent, sovereign citizen is, in my opinion, such a false ideal
>
> (p. 29)

In Lippman's more pessimistic view, public opinion does not arise from public discussion, it is instead created for the public by better-resourced special interests—and enacted through means like public relations.

Dewey's ideal of the informed, deliberative, and engaged public coming together to solve collective problems in the "great society" was, as Dewey himself admitted, never fully realized. To crudely summarize his arguments, the public was "eclipsed" by increasing economic pressures, the distraction of mass entertainment at the expense of political engagement, and a loss of a sense of community. Unlike Lippman, who felt that to expect more of the disinterested public was futile, Dewey believed the ultimate problem was not public disinterest or incompetence, but a lack of sufficient publicity; that is, public communication about important issues. Without such publicity and the engagement that results, citizens may become fragmented, isolated, and incapable of organizing for collective action and problem solving.

From the Public to Publics

As noted earlier, Dewey called the inability of the public to come together and solve problems the "eclipse of the public"—largely blaming communication industries like public relations for manipulating public opinion (Rakow, 2018b). Ironically, Dewey's conceptualization of publics organizing around common problems is central to most contemporary definitions of publics. Yet, it is precisely in this conceptualization that Dewey's explicit connections to public relations ends, for while his definition of the public is connected to common problem recognition, nowhere in Dewey's philosophy is the connection made of publics to organizations. Indeed, the rise of large organizations and corporate power was noted by Dewey as a hindrance for the public to effectively organize. As Rakow (2018b) convincingly argued, the use of Dewey in defining publics in relation to organizations represents a fundamental perversion of his philosophy. As she stated: "[Dewey] has been selectively invoked while the most significant aspects of his position ignored" (p. 322).

Rakow (2018b) traced the introduction of Dewey's thinking to the public relations discipline to an early undergraduate textbook by Cutlip and Center (1952), *Effective Public Relations*, and its subsequent editions. As she explained, the Cutlip and Center textbooks helped to "throw the field off the scent of the lost public, while turning attention to publics" (p. 322). Several decades and seven editions of the book later, Dewey's conceptualization of the public was gradually erased and replaced by a focus on *publics* (plural), defined as: "a group of individuals who together are affected by a particular action or idea. Thus, each issue or problem creates its own public" (Cutlip & Center, 1971, p. 128).

The contemporaneous development of the situational theory of publics by James Grunig (e.g., 1978, 1989) represents the most well-known connection within the field to Dewey's work. J. Grunig (1978) described a public as arising when a group of people: "1) face a similar indeterminant situation, 2) recognize what is indeterminant—problematic—in that situation, and 3) organize to do something about the problem" (p. 109). We see in this definition early glimpses of the situational theory's constitutive variables of *level of involvement, problem recognition*, and *constraint recognition*. J. Grunig drew from Dewey's writings on the public's propensity for information processing and problem solving and connected them to issues generated by an organization. As observed by Rakow (2018b), "[J. Grunig] concluded that organizations need public relations because they create problems that create publics, which begin as disconnected individuals but can evolve into organized, powerful groups" (p. 324). The development of the situational theory, coupled with the Cutlip and Center textbook, managed, as Rakow described: "to convert Dewey's original problem of the eclipse of the public to the problems that publics create for organizations" (p. 324). The public(s) went from being the solution to problems to becoming the problem.

Dewey, together with other writers such as Habermas (cf. Sommerfeldt, 2013), shape our conceptualization of publics (plural) as individuals centered around common problems and who organize to do something about them. With time, these concepts have trickled down into various theoretical and methodological approaches to understand public relations and its outcomes. Despite this intellectual heritage, there are dramatically different approaches to understanding the nature of publics in the broader public relations literature.

The Ontology of Publics in Public Relations

Goertz and Mahoney (2012) stated that "when scholars debate the meaning of a concept, they are arguing about the substance of the empirical world"

(p. 207). The central ontological questions about publics in public relations, therefore, might be: What is the nature or reality of publics? How can publics be best described or classified? As noted in the introduction of this chapter, most often publics are referred to casually, without any definition or clarification—making *publics* the primitive term it is today. However, when attempts have been made to explicate publics, scholars have roughly characterized publics—to borrow and adapt anthropological terms—emically or etically: as emerging through their own discourse, representation, and agency (emic) or through an imposed scheme of categorization based on shared attributes relevant to organizational needs or outcomes (etic). An emic approach pre-supposes that publics exist on their own merit, while an etic approach uses predefined variables to understand publics from unconnected individuals. A discussion of each general ontological approach follows.

Emic Publics

From the first general ontological perspective, publics are self-organized and become embodied through shared narratives and the circulation of texts, typically around shared problems or identity markers. Epistemologically, such approaches to understanding the nature of publics primarily inherit from rhetorical traditions in public relations research and are perhaps more closely related to Dewey's notion of the public. Yet, as has been embraced by most theorists, there are conceptual differences between treatments of *the* public and publics. As written by Pieczka (2019):

> The public appears to be something of an ideal-type rather than an empirical phenomenon. A public, on the other hand, is concrete and embodied; there are, in fact, multiple such publics in any society. Yet, even a public is hard to pin down due to the duality of its nature, oscil-lating between the individual and the collective, between "I" and "we."
> (p. 227)

Publics, from this view, are expressive of individuals' wishes and find com-monality in shared interest and issues (Warner, 2002). A recognition that multiple, discourse-based publics exist in society is reflected in public sphere literature that suggests multiple spheres of discussion are preferable to one overriding public sphere or arena (cf. Fraser, 1990; Sommerfeldt, 2013). As Fraser described it: "Arrangements that accommodate contestation among a plurality of competing publics better promote the ideal of participatory parity than does a single, overarching public" (p. 66). Indeed, subordinated social groups, also called *subaltern publics* or *counterpublics*, have often found it useful to form "parallel discursive arenas where members of subordinated social groups invent and circulate counter-discourses, which in turn permit them to formulate oppositional interpretations of their identities, interests, and needs" (Fraser, p. 67).

Public relations scholarship on publics from this approach concerns the ability of individuals to see connections among themselves—and focuses on the internal functioning of publics. A few published studies in the 1990s (i.e. Vasquez, 1993, 1994) advanced a *homonarrans* perspective, arguing that the existence of publics is the result of people sharing their interpretations of their environments in ways that lead to shared reality. In the *homonarrans* approach, humans are storytellers that share "fantasies" that build social consciousness (Vasquez, 1993). Fantasies are "creative and imaginative shared interpretations of events that fulfill a group's psychological or rhetorical need" (p. 202). Thus, from a *homonarrans* perspective, "a public represents individuals who have created, raised, and sustained a group consciousness around a problematic situation" (Vasquez, 1993, p. 209). Vasquez (1994) worked to connect a *homonarrans* perspective with J. Grunig's situational approach by suggesting that if organizations worked to share and understand a publics' symbolic reality, a more quality relationship would result.

Botan and Soto (1998) similarly described publics from the *semiotic* approach as "an ongoing process of agreement upon an interpretation" (p. 21). They argued that publics do not exist *a priori*. Unlike the *homonarrans* approach, which worked to conjoin itself with popular theories like STP, Botan and Soto's semiotic theory of publics advocated that publics cannot be understood before the creation and dissemination of a message—only after. The process of becoming a public is through the constant sharing of discourse upon the receipt of messages, resulting in more or fewer shared agreements. Botan and Soto argued this approach is inherently more ethical and humanistic than perspectives like STP, writing that "if publics only react to organizational behavior, no balance or participation in outcomes, is possible" (p. 27). They proposed a language-centered approach to understanding the internal functioning of publics, arguing that the interpretation of messages in a public relations campaign depends on the people who receive those messages: "Publics ought to be understood primarily as self-actuated and interactive social entities with values and internal dynamics at least as complex and important to communication campaigns as are message content or client/practitioner intentions" (p. 36).

Also essential to emic approaches to publics is a recognition of a publics' outward-facing communication style; to be a public means they must engage in public communication. In many cases, "to interact discursively as a member of a public—subaltern or otherwise—is to disseminate one's discourse into ever-widening arenas" (Fraser, 1990, p. 67). Warner (2005) argues that the discourse and texts circulated within a public have a performative dimension and work to characterize a public. As he wrote: "Public discourse says not only 'Let a public exist' but 'Let it have this character, speak this way, see the world in this way'" (p. 114). Individuals—as strangers—can organize as a collective around the creation and circulation of texts because an individual's subjectivity to the public communication at hand "is understood as having resonance with others" (Warner, 2002, p. 418). The stranger relationality that connects individuals engaging in discourse generates the interactive context and collective identity of the public, characterizing its public existence and communication (Warner, 2002).

Etic Publics

An etic ontology of publics typically presumes that publics exist only because scholars or practitioners use a particular approach or variable to describe them. Etic approaches describe subdivisions of publics, typically based on how important those publics might be to an organization. From this perspective, as Kim and Dutta (2009) wrote, "Publics are conceived as static entities to be measured through formative and evaluative research and to be targeted through messages" (p. 146). An etic ontology of publics further assumes that publics exist and have importance only in relation to an organization, and then mainly in relation to a problem. However, the problem's originating locus distinguishes the two general publics' ontologies, which is made clear in this quote by J. Grunig and Repper (1992): "Problems arise from the involvement of people in situations and their perceptions of situations and not from hidden internal needs" (p. 135). Whereas an emic approach assumes that internal hidden needs can stimulate the formation of publics—sustained by their own personal imperatives and agency—the preceding quote from Grunig and Repper illuminates a very different point of view in an etic ontology: one where publics only exist in relation to their perception and response to the problems caused by organizations.

Such approaches have been described as essential to effective public relations practice, as "practitioners need to identify and segment publics to increase the possibility of achieving communication goals with these publics" (Kim et al., 2008, p. 752). By this logic, one cannot effectively target or communicate with publics unless you have strategically segmented them by some communicatively meaningful dimension. The most prominent example of a top-down ontology of publics, and one tied to issues, is the situational theory of publics (STP). STP and its transition to the situational theory of problem solving (J.-N. Kim & Grunig, 2011) is well documented in the literature, including in this volume. As previously noted, J. Grunig built on Dewey's philosophy (albeit inaccurately) for his situational approach, arguing that "publics form around specific situations or issues produced by the consequences that organizations have on people outside the organization" (J. Grunig, 1989, p. 5). The constitutive variables of issue involvement, problem recognition, and constraint recognition generate three distinct types of publics: (1) *latent* publics may be involved with an issue but do not consider a situation to be a problem, (2) *aware* publics recognize the issue as a problem but do not participate in seeking a solution, and (3) *active* publics recognize a problem, seek out information, organize, and communicate with the organization to seek solutions to an issue. Publics might even be classified as *inactive* with minimal motivation to know or talk about issues related to organizations but who might eventually become latent or active (Hallahan, 2000). Later categorizations would differentiate active publics from more apathetic publics by suggesting some publics are organized around a *single issue*, whereas others might be active on many issues. J. Grunig (1997) also defined *hot-issue publics* as those who are "active only on a single problem that involves nearly everyone in the population and that has received extensive media coverage" (p. 13).

Each type of public in the situational perspective differs in regard to their relationship and communication style with an organization and an issue, with active or activist publics being the most important target of the public relations function (J. Grunig, 1978). Indeed, the theoretical impetus of STP was to detect and diffuse activist publics before they become serious problems for organizations (Sommerfeldt, 2012). Through STP, practitioners can segment publics that present either threats or opportunities as a means of identifying those individuals most likely to communicate about an issue and thereby determining with whom the organization should communicate (Grunig, 1989; Grunig & Repper, 1992).

Despite the situational theory's early misinterpretation of Dewey's public, STP regards publics as ideologically coherent entities that *organize to solve problems*. Publics' internal organizing activities may work to threaten an organization but may also improve the organization from the inside out through activist pressure (L.A. Grunig, 2013). However, other etic approaches to public segmentation stray far from an understanding of publics as a collective entity or disregard their intimate connection to an issue as an organizing principle. Indeed, public relations scholarship has also measured publics by simple categories or demographic/psychographic segmentation. For example, in their study examining the consequences of relationship management on the information behaviors of community members surrounding health issues, Ni et al. (2019) focused on individuals who identify as Asian American, a demographic they claimed is characterized by shared cultural identity and immigration history despite the diversity of backgrounds, languages, and socioeconomic status among this large population.

Scholars have also operationalized publics categorically, often by simply describing different stakeholders of organizations. For example, research on non-profit relationships has looked at donors or volunteers as categories of publics, such as donors at a large research university (Harrison, 2018). Similarly, studies on corporations have considered customers as publics, like Whole Foods customers (Ma, 2018), and government-public relationship research has examined voters or citizens as publics, such as examining first-time voters to understand relationships with political parties (Browning & Sweetser, 2020). These examples are a fundamental misrepresentation of the theoretical construct of publics and better exemplify market segments, categories of potential stakeholders, or even audiences. Significantly, operationalizing publics as presumed stakeholders of distinct institutions affirms an organization-centric approach that overlooks any real organizing principle of publics' internal coherence. Further, these approaches omit the factors that define a public and characterize their engagement by referring to pre-conceived notions of organizational involvement rather than reflecting on the context and nuances of a public as a collective.

Finally, etic conceptualizations of publics are often somewhat contrary as to describing a publics' agentic status. For example, in their explication of approaches to segmentation, Kim et al. (2008) stated: "In most cases, publics approach organizations hoping to gain organizational acknowledgement of their concerns and proactive corrections to the problem" (p. 753) only to later explain various top-down segmentation approaches—essentially ignor-ing that publics "approach organizations" of their own volition, suggesting that publics have internal functioning and agency independent of the organ-ization. As such, the top-down segmentation of publics can often ignore the identity, boundaries, and agency of publics by instead focusing on static, pre-given categories. The next section further critiques problems with how scholars have used the concept of publics through a brief discussion of the organization-public relationship (OPR) literature.

Publics in OPR

OPR research, which emerged around the turn of the century, is now an intensely popular line of inquiry in public relations. Conceptually, OPR research takes significant inspiration from relationship management theory (cf. Ledingham, 2006) by making the *relationship* between organizations and publics the focal point of investigation. Ledingham and Bruning (1998) defined OPR as "the state which exists between an organization and its key publics in which the actions of either entity impact the economic, social, political, and/or cultural well-being of the other entity" (p. 62). Scholars who approached OPR from the perspective of relational characteristics like trust, control mutuality, satisfaction—among other variables—expressed the duality of the concept's implications, noting its implications as a concept for both publics and organizations (Grunig & Huang, 2000).

However, in the two decades since the emergence of OPR scholarship, there is a concerning lack of definition of, or distinction among, publics in published OPR research. Publics remain an afterthought or even a non-entity in much of the OPR literature. Certainly, OPR's alleged shift in focus to the relationship was a step forward from past "functional" research that limited its aim to the analysis of one-way organizational communication practices (cf. Botan & Taylor, 2004). Nevertheless, OPR scholarship has proceeded in a manner that disregards a crucial dimension—the publics with whom a relationship is held. OPR scholarship is itself limited in what it can claim about relationships if research continually overlooks the details of precisely with whom organizational relationships are enacted. Relationships may be a concept in their own right, but they are foremost a connection implicated by the entities they exist between.

In many OPR studies—which are lately often set within the context of social media—publics are a vague entity, overlooked in favor of a laser focus on the analysis of the relationship. To be sure, this is a worthy endeavor, but what is the heuristic value of this research if no coherent public exists at one polar end of the relational tie? The history of OPR research has shown that scholars have provided minimal, if any, detail on just who the publics in their research are, or of how they are to be ontologically conceived. Frequently, there are no definitions or operationalizations of publics in the OPR literature. For example, Qin and Men (2019) stated that "social media have become an important platform for publics to share their attitudes toward brands, products, or companies . . . that could affect organization-public relationships (OPRs)" (p. 1). As seen here—and throughout the study—there is no definition or description of precisely who these publics are, nor of how they are to be conceived theoretically or in praxis.

The rampant ontological and definitional omission of publics in OPR research forces readers to accept an author's claim that publics are the concept being studied without even the most basic evidence. What factors make these populations a public besides the fact that they were included in a sample? The methods used to examine publics in OPR are even more troublesome. Studies that overlook distinctions of publics frequently utilize random participant samples—often recruited online or though panel generation platforms like MTurk—and are loosely defined to meet certain research questions within the limited paradigmatic scope of OPR scholarship (i.e., relationship indicators of trust, control mutuality, etc.). In such cases, there are no methodological strategies to assess whether the participants indeed represent publics in that they recognize shared problems and organize to do something about them. Our critique is not meant to renounce experimental research as a whole but instead to reaffirm the need for scholarship to be more specific in how publics are conceptualized and measured in future research engaging the concept. Are all the participants recruited and surveyed in an experiment a public of the organizations? Have criteria been clearly established to ascertain this?

The uncertainty as to whether recruited participants can truly be justified as publics of an organization is challenged by methodological trends that remove context, such as utilizing "any organization" for surveys. For example, participants may be asked whether they follow at least one public brand, company page, or company CEO on a social media platform as recruitment criteria (e.g., Chen, 2017; Men & Tsai, 2015, 2016; Tsai & Men, 2018). The conglomerate of recruited participants then answers survey questions in regard to their presumed relationship with a range of companies. Studies have additionally recruited participants based on whether they had recently engaged online with *any* government agency (Dong & Ji, 2018), whether they had volunteered with *any* organization (Harrison et al., 2017), and even whether they had discussed their interactions (specifically negative) with *any* organizations to their peers online (Qin & Men, 2019). Research has also asked participants to recall *any* organization with a recent crisis (Xu, 2018) and has provided hypothetical companies, relationships, and scenarios as the basis of their questionnaires (Kim, 2001).

The lack of attention to publics theory evidenced in the ontological and methodological choices of OPR research is deeply problematic. As already mentioned, it first raises the question of whether participants are truly publics in the context of the study. Second, can we say in these studies whether an organization-public relationship is actually being measured? When an individual participant within a study is reflecting on a distinct experience with a distinct organization, the emphasis is on the individual rather than the collective experience that most theories suggest is inherent to publics. Conducting OPR research with discrete individuals (re)enforces an assumption that all organizational relationships will be the same across their unique publics, purposes, and values in a given context or scenario.

Conclusion

As Warner (2002) eloquently wrote: "A public is never just congeries of people, never just a sum of persons who happen to exist" (p. 111). Ultimately, overlooking the ontology of publics, from their definition to measurement, will limit our understanding of public relations practices and outcomes. Our critique of OPR as a particularly egregious example of terminological misuse is merely to serve as an exemplar of what happens when terms are not defined or, worse, used without proper understanding. When the ontology of a thing is not examined, research findings may end up being incoherent—indeed, OPR scholarship seems to set out within one ontological position and ends up working within the logic of another. The point is that publics are actively communicating bodies of individuals with shared issue interpretations. If studies do not conceive of publics as such, or if they measure discrete individual attitudes with nameless, faceless organizations, what they are measuring is *not* relationships with publics—it is something else altogether with questionable implications for the development of theory and praxis.

Recipients of organizational messages are audiences. Stakeholders are categories of individuals who are impacted or may impact an organization. Audiences and stakeholders have fundamentally different consequences for organizations than publics and engage in fundamentally different kinds of communication behavior—if they engage at all. Winkler and Wehmeier (2018) argued that public relations research often treats organizations, stakeholders, and publics as defined by STP "as pre-given social identities with particular attributes and attitudes" (p. 146), which (in doing so) misses the performative dynamic of a public where identities and relationships arise out of internal deliberations. Publics engage in public communication. Future public relations scholarship must adhere to a standard of defining publics and presenting observable criteria of how research participants are indeed publics. We must pay attention to the very thing that makes them publics—their agency and capacity to organize in seeking redress of problems.

References

Botan, C. H., & Soto, F. (1998). A semiotic approach to the internal functioning of publics: Implications for strategic communication and public relations. *Public Relations Review*, 24(1), 21–44. https://doi.org/10.1016/S0363-8111(98)80018-0

Botan, C. H., & Taylor, M. (2004). Public relations: State of the field. *Journal of Communication*, 54(4), 645–661. https://doi.org/10.1111/j.1460-2466.2004.tb02649.x

Broom, G. M., Casey, S., & Ritchey, J. (1997). Toward a concept and theory of organization-public relationships. *Journal of Public Relations Research*, 9(2), 83–98. https://doi.org/10.1207/s1532754xjprr0902_01

Browning, N., & Sweetser, K. S. (2020). How media diet, partisan frames, candidate traits, and political organization-public relationship communication drive party reputation. *Public Relations Review*, 46(2). https://doi.org/10.1016/j.pubrev.2020.101884

Chaffee, S. H. (1991). *Explication*. Sage.

Chen, Y. R. (2017). Perceived values of branded mobile media, consumer engagement, business-consumer relationship quality and purchase intention: A study of WeChat in China. *Public Relations Review*, 43(5), 945–954. https://doi.org/10.1016/j.pubrev.2017.07.005

Cutlip, S. M., & Center, A. H. (1952). *Effective public relations: Pathways to public favor*. Prentice-Hall.

Cutlip, S. M., & Center, A. H. (1971). *Effective public relations* (4th ed.). Prentice Hall.

Dewey, J. (1927). *The public and its problems*. Holt.

Dong, C., & Ji, Y. (2018). Connecting young adults to democracy via government social network sites. *Public Relations Review*, 44(5), 762–775. https://doi.org/10.1016/j.pubrev.2018.05.004

Fraser, N. (1990). Rethinking the public sphere: A contribution to the critique of actually existing democracy. *Social Text*, 25–26, 56–80.

Goertz, G., & Mahoney, J. (2012). Concepts and measurement: Ontology and epistemology. *Social Science Information*, 51(2), 205–216. https://doi.org/10.1177/0539018412437108

Grunig, J. E. (1978). Defining publics in public relations: The case of a suburban hospital. *Journalism Quarterly*, 55(1), 109–124. https://doi.org/10.1177/107769907805500115

Grunig, J. E. (1989). Sierra club study shows who become activists. *Public Relations Review*, 15(3), 3–24. https://doi.org/10.1016/S0363-8111(89)80001-3

Grunig, J. E. (1997). A situational theory of publics: Conceptual history, recent challenges and new research. In D. Moss, T. MacManus, & D. Vercic (Eds.), *Public relations research: An international perspective* (pp. 3–48). International Thomson Business Press.

Grunig, J. E., & Huang, Y. H. (2000). From organizational effectiveness to relationship indicators: Antecedents of relationships, public relations strategies, and relationship outcomes. In J. A. Ledingham & S. D. Bruning (Eds.), *Public relations as relationship management* (pp. 23–53). Lawrence Erlbaum Associates.

Grunig, J. E., & Repper, F. C. (1992). Strategic management, publics, and issues. In J. E. Grunig (Ed.), *Excellence in public relations and communication management* (pp. 117–157). Routledge.

Grunig, L. A. (2013). Activism: How it limits the effectiveness of organizations and how excellent public relations departments respond. In J. E. Grunig (Ed.), *Excellence in public relations and communication management* (pp. 503–530). Routledge.

Habermas, J. (1989). *The structural transformation of the public sphere*. MIT Press.

Hallahan, K. (2000). Inactive publics: The forgotten publics in public relations. *Public Relations Review, 26*(4), 499–515. https://doi.org/10.1016/S0363-8111(00)00061-8

Harrison, V. S. (2018). Understanding the donor experience: Applying stewardship theory to higher education donors. *Public Relations Review, 44*(4), 533–548. https://doi.org/10.1016/j.pubrev.2018.07.001

Harrison, V. S., Xiao, A., Ott, H. K., & Bortree, D. (2017). Calling all volunteers: The role of stewardship and involvement in volunteer-organization relationships. *Public Relations Review, 43*(4), 872–881. https://doi.org/10.1016/j.pubrev.2017.06.006

Kent, M. L., & Theunissen, P. (2016). Elegy for mediated dialogue: Shiva the destroyer and reclaiming our first principles. *International Journal of Communication, 10*, 4040–4054. https://ijoc.org/index.php/ijoc/article/view/4571/1756

Kim, I., & Dutta, M. J. (2009). Studying crisis communication from the subaltern studies framework: Grassroots activism in the wake of Hurricane Katrina. *Journal of Public Relations Research, 21*(2), 142–164. https://doi-org.proxy-um.researchport.umd.edu/10.1080/10627260802557423

Kim, J.-N., & Grunig, J. E. (2011). Problem solving and communicative action: A situational theory of problem solving. *Journal of Communication, 61*(1), 120–149. https://doi.org/10.1111/2046147X19870269

Kim, J.-N., Ni, L., & Sha, B.-L. (2008). Breaking down the stakeholder environment: Explicating approaches to the segmentation of publics for public relations research. *Journalism & Mass Communication Quarterly, 85*(4), 751–768. https://doi.org/10.1177/107769900808500403

Kim, Y. (2001). Searching for the organization-public relationship: A valid and reliable instrument. *Journalism & Mass Communication, 78*(4), 799–815. https://doi.org/10.1177/107769900107800412

Ledingham, J. A. (2006). Relationship management: A general theory of public relations. In C. H. Botan & V. Hazelton (Eds.), *Public relations theory II* (pp. 465–483). Lawrence Erlbaum Associates.

Ledingham, J. A., & Bruning, S. D. (1998). Relationship management in public relations: Dimensions of an organization-public relationship. *Public Relations Review, 24*(1), 55–65. https://doi.org/10.1016/S0363-8111(98)80020-9

Lippmann, W. (1927). *The phantom public.* Palgrave Macmillan.

Ma, L. (2018). How to turn your friends into enemies: Causes and outcomes of customers' sense of betrayal in crisis communication. *Public Relations Review, 44*(3), 374–384. https://doi.org/10.1016/j.pubrev.2018.04.009

Men, R. L., & Tsai, W. S. (2015). Infusing social media with humanity: Corporate character, public engagement, and relational outcomes. *Public Relations Review, 41*(3), 395–403. https://doi.org/10.1016/j.pubrev.2015.02.005

Men, R. L., & Tsai, W. S. (2016). Public engagement with CEOs on social media: Motivations and relational outcomes. *Public Relations Review, 42*(5), 932–942. https://doi.org/10.1016/j.pubrev.2016.08.001

Ni, L., Xiao, Z., Liu, W., & Wang, Q. (2019). Relationship management as antecedents to public communication behaviors: Examining empowerment and public health among Asian Americans. *Public Relations Review, 45*(5). https://doi.org/10.1016/j.pubrev.2019.101835

Paquette, M., Sommerfeldt, E. J., & Kent, M. L. (2015). Do the ends justify the means? Dialogue, development communication, and deontological ethics. *Public Relations Review, 41*(1), 30–39. https://doi.org/10.1016/j.pubrev.2014.10.008

Pieczka, M. (2019). Looking back and going forward: The concept of the public in public relations theory. *Public Relations Inquiry*, 8(3), 225–244. https://doi.org/10.11 77/2046147X19870269

Qin, Y., & Men, L. R. (2019). Exploring negative peer communication of companies on social media and its impact on organization-public relationships. *Public Relations Review*, 45(4). https://doi.org/10.1016/j.pubrev.2019.05.016

Rakow, L. F. (2018a). Family feud: Who's still fighting about Dewey and Lippman? *Javnost: The Public*, 25(1–2), 75–82. https://doi.org/10.1080/13183222.2018.14239 45

Rakow, L. (2018b). On Dewey: Public relations and its eclipse of the Public. In Ø. Ihlen & F. Magnussen (Eds.), *Public relations and social theory: Key figures, concepts and developments* (pp. 315–334). Routledge.

Rawlins, B. L. (2006). *Prioritizing stakeholders for public relations*. Institute for Public Relations. www.instituteforpr.org/files/uploads/2006_Stakeholders.pdf

Sommerfeldt, E. J. (2012). The dynamics of activist power relationships: A structurationist exploration of the segmentation of activist publics. *International Journal of Strategic Communication*, 6(4), 269–286. https://doi.org/10.1080/1553118X.2012.686256

Sommerfeldt, E. J. (2013). The civility of social capital: Public relations in the public sphere, civil society, and democracy. *Public Relations Review*, 39(4), 280–289. https:// doi.org/10.1016/j.pubrev.2012.12.004

Tsai, W. S., & Men, R. L. (2018). Social messengers as the new frontier of organization-public engagement: A WeChat study. *Public Relations Review*, 44(3), 419–429. https:// doi.org/10.1016/j.pubrev.2018.04.004

Vasquez, G. M. (1993). A homo narrans paradigm for public relations: Combining Bormann's symbolic convergence theory and Grunig's situational theory of publics. *Journal of Public Relations Research*, 5(3), 201–216. https://doi.org/10.1207/ s1532754xjprr0503_03

Vasquez, G. M. (1994). Testing a communication theory-method-message-behavior complex for the investigation of publics. *Journal of Public Relations Research*, 6(4), 267–291. https://doi.org/10.1207/s1532754xjprr0604_04

Vasquez, G., & Taylor, M. (2001). Research perspectives on "the public". In R. L. Heath (Ed.), *Handbook of public relations* (pp. 139–154). Sage.

Warner, M. (2005). *Publics and counterpublics*. Zone Books.

Warner, M. (2002). Publics and counterpublics (abbreviated version). *Quarterly Journal of Speech*, 88(4), 413–425. https://doi.org/10.1080/00335630209384388

Winkler, P., & Wehmeier, S. (2018). On Harrison White: Rethinking relations in public relations. In Ø. Ihlen & M. Fredriksson (Eds.), *Public relations and social theory: Key figures, concepts and issues* (pp. 137–157). Routledge.

Xu, S. (2018). Discourse of renewal: Developing multiple-item measurement and analyzing effects on relationships. *Public Relations Review*, 44(1), 108–119. https://doi. org/10.1016/j.pubrev.2017.09.005

4 Theorizing Digital Engagement in Public Relations

Kim A. Johnston

Introduction

Over the last two decades, public relations scholarship has broadened its focus from traditional corporate-centered approaches (McKie & Munshi, 2005; Roper, 2005) to consider more community-centered approaches, where outcomes are valued by their contribution to organizations *and* society (Heath, 2006; Taylor, 2011, 2018). A sociocultural (Edwards & Hodges, 2011) and cocreational (Botan & Taylor, 2004) lens on theorizing public relations acknowledges the importance of facilitating and listening to diverse perspectives (Dutta-Bergman, 2004; Heath, 2014; Macnamara, 2016). Dutta and Elers (2020) contend that this paradigmatic shift is a rejoinder to "the harmful effects of public relations as propaganda" (p. 2), toward more authentic and *engagement*-centered approaches (see, Johnston & Lane, 2019; Johnston & Taylor, 2018; Stoker & Tusinski, 2006) with more emphasis on diverse voices, cultures, and perspectives (Dutta, 2013). Theories in public relations (for example, see Section 3 in this volume) elucidate this shift.

Public relations has always played a role in responding through communication and relationships to challenges and problems that are socially significant. Engagement is one such theory to respond to these types of problems, blending ideals of authenticity, agency, and affiliation as a theoretical scaffold. Some argue that engagement is "context specific" (Voorveld et al., 2018, p. 40) and the context therefore shapes the form, features, and nature of *engagement*. Given engagement is context-based, a digital environment presents a suite of unique influences on the state and the process of engagement.

Digital contexts and their use for engagement—including the opportunities to create, generate, and sustain meaningful interaction and outcomes—require particular attention. This chapter responds to that need.

The first section of this chapter situates engagement in public relations theory, specifically conceptualizing engagement, identifying tiers of engagement, and differentiating engagement at individual and at group levels. Digital engagement is then discussed, and a framework is introduced to further understand engagement as a state and a process within the platform and

DOI: 10.4324/9781003141396-5

system attributes of a digital setting. One of the contemporary challenges for both the academy and practice is knowing how to evaluate engagement. The chapter concludes with a discussion on methods and tools to measure and research digital engagement.

Engagement Theory

Engagement has emerged as a new paradigm for public relations. While engagement as a concept has experienced growth as a focal area of scholarship, Heath (2014) cautions that engagement is "more than two-way communication" and requires a commitment to developing community-building discourse and theoretical frameworks that support this momentum (cited in Johnston, 2014, p. 382).

Engagement was first recognized in the public relations literature in the 1990s discussed in the context of behavioral outcomes (Slater et al., 1992), capacity building (Heath & Abel, 1996; Heath et al., 2002; Woodward, 2000), and later in the context of organization-public relationships (Bortree, 2011; Johnston, 2010) and stakeholder participation (Heath, 2011). Taylor and Kent (2014) situate engagement as part of dialogue that "guides the process of interactions among groups" (p. 384). Interpretivist and constructionist approaches regard engagement as a socially situated process where meaning is created or cocreated through communication, or as Ledingham (2006) suggests, "social exchange" (p. 418).

Public relations scholars have lamented the lack of definitional clarity of engagement (Dhanesh, 2017; Jelen-Sanchez, 2017; Lane & Devin, 2018; Taylor & Kent, 2014; VanDyke & Lee, 2020). Contexts for engagement are many—including consumer, student, employee, stakeholder, organizational, community, civic, and digital (Taylor & Kent, 2014)—and each has specific features that influence the quality and the process of engagement. The paradigmatic nature of engagement and its broad contextual application challenge the notion of a singular, precise definition. As VanDyke and Lee (2020) conclude, rather than arguing for specific definitions, "careful work needs to be done to articulate various forms, components, and mechanisms" of engagement (p. 3). The next section aims to respond to this call.

Conceptualizing Engagement

Engagement is a psychological *state* achieved through a relational, interactive communication *process* with outcomes that are judged by their social value. Definitions of engagement in public relations describe a psychological concept that is multilevel (at individual, group/publics, and civic/social) and multidimensional (cognitive, affective, and behavioral), situated in communication-based, relational processes with outcomes that are valued (Heath, 2018; Jelen-Sanchez, 2017; Johnston, 2014; Johnston & Taylor,

2018; Lane & Devin, 2018; Morehouse & Saffer, 2019; Taylor & Kent, 2014). These conceptualizations traverse both individual and group levels.

Engagement has been described as a disposition (trait), a state, a behavior, and a process (see, for example, Macey & Schneider, 2008). A trait is an enduring disposition "to think, feel, or behave in a certain way" (Jeanes, 2019, p. 1) in response to a given situation (Colman, 2015). *Engagement as a trait* suggests that an individual would be predisposed to interact cognitively, affectively, and behaviorally for certain outcomes.

Engagement as a psychological state is operationalized through behavioral, cognitive, and affective dimensions—for example, knowledge, understanding, beliefs, attitude, motivation, connection, experience, involvement, interaction, action, and participation orientation—depending on the context. Calder et al. (2009) argue, however, that cognitive or affective dimensions need to be activated before behavioral engagement can be claimed, while others argue that more than one dimension needs to be activated (Brodie et al., 2011; Kang, 2014). Other scholars such as Kang (2014) regard engagement as an affective concept (motivation, commitment, positive affect) with empowerment (as power) dimensions and argue that engagement mediates relational variables and loyalty.

Individual-level engagement is primarily the focus of consumer, student, and employee engagement scholarship. Research suggests that individuals who are engaged are more likely to perform better in the workplace (Schaufeli, 2013), are more loyal as customers (Hollebeek, 2011, 2017) and exert more effort toward achieving an outcome (Linden et al., 2021). Public relations research in engagement at an individual level has focused on contexts and settings such as workplaces, communities, and in digital environments. Employee engagement links engagement states with quality of internal communication and messaging (see, for example, Dhanesh & Picherit-Duthler, 2021; Kang, 2014, Karanges et al., 2015; Lemon, 2019; Shen & Jiang, 2019).

Individual to Group-Level Engagement

At a social level, engagement is a *process* facilitated through communication participation, interaction, and involvement. Engagement is therefore situated within a social setting of relationships and is influenced by shared interests, collective meaning, and broader social benefits.

In public relations, social levels of engagement have predominantly been studied in contexts that facilitate engagement, such as community, civic, and stakeholder engagement. For example, Tsai and Men (2018) studied WeChat and found that social messengers play a vital role in online stakeholder engagement. Cho et al. (2014) examined Facebook message strategies and their influence on public engagement. While in a study of Instagram, Guidry et al. (2017) found that prior relationships were an indicator of engagement effectiveness. More broadly, studies have explored engagement's role in communicating legitimacy and corporate social responsibility.

For example, Devin and Lane (2014) examined engagement processes and found that organizations also communicated about engagement with stakeholders as part of the CSR communication.

The dichotomy of individual- and social-level engagement is currently treated in the literature separately with a few exceptions. Griffin (2015) explored aggregated individual level engagement to group level in the workplace and found that group-level engagement influenced individual-level engagement. Kilpatrick (2009) used a systems approach and argued for a multilevel approach to understand community engagement. Johnston (2018) modelled the interaction of individual- and social-level influences and further examined these in engagement contributing to disaster resilience (see Johnston et al., 2022; Ryan et al., 2022). Figure 4.1 illustrates the conceptual interaction of individual-level engagement and social-level engagement. The central core in Figure 4.1 represents individual-level engagement—with cognitive, affective, and behavioral dimensions—coupled with motivation and intention to engage. As noted earlier, engagement involves interaction and communication within a social setting. The form and nature of this interaction and communication is influenced by context as a social level of engagement (see Johnston, 2018). The outcome of the interaction is conceptualized as having value by the individual or groups.

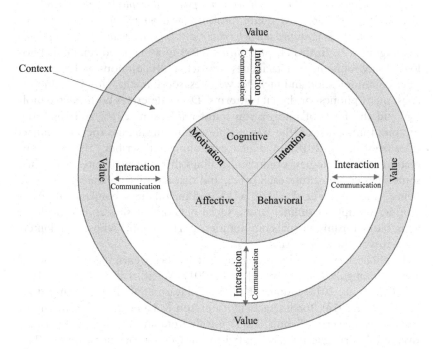

Figure 4.1 Relationship of Individual and Social Levels of Engagement

Source: Created by author

In summary, engagement theory recognizes:

- Engagement is a psychological multidimensional state (temporary) or disposition (enduring) that occurs through a relational process within a system of communication, participation, and interaction situated within a social setting and is influenced by shared interests, collective meaning, and (social) benefit.
- Engagement processes and outcomes are shaped and influenced by context.
- Engagement can span a continuum from high to low levels.
- Stakeholders, consumers, employees, community, and organizations, have agency, perspective, power, and voice within an engagement process.

However, what is less clear is what it means to be engaged in a digital environment, and there is little research to guide what digital engagement theory means for public relations. The next section addresses these questions. First, the digital environment will be discussed, followed by contemporary conceptualizations of digital engagement.

Digital Engagement

Digital engagement is *a four-dimensional process that involves user motivation and intention, platform and system capability for communicative interaction, and outcomes that can be measured through value cocreation, in digitally mediated settings* (see Figure 4.2). In this chapter, *digital* refers to a mediated online technological environment that facilitates interactive synchronous and asynchronous communication and includes websites, social media, cloud and mobile apps, smart phones, or digital platforms. *Digital* describes both the technology and the form of information transfer (Hanson, 2016) and has had a profound influence on the way people communicate and socially connect (Dezuanni et al., 2018). A digital environment describes "the conglomeration of technologies, events and realities that interpenetrate each other, sometimes co-constitute each other, and that have led to changed ways of being" (Frömming et al., 2017, p. 13) and include user-constructed virtual worlds, multiplayer online games, social networking sites and smartphone apps, blogs, forums, virtual communities, and the people who use and interact across all these platforms.

In public relations, digital engagement has been examined as an overall strategy (Yang, 2018), as a tool (Ji et al., 2017; Verčič et al., 2015), as a channel (Cho et al., 2014; Guidry et al., 2017; Hearn et al., 2018; Huang et al., 2021; Kent, 2013), for interactivity (Johnston & Lane, 2021), or to engage employees (Sievert & Scholz, 2017) usually from an organizational perspective. While dialogue remains central to engagement practice (Kent & Taylor, 2021; Lane & Kent, 2018; Sommerfeldt & Yang, 2018; Taylor & Kent, 2014), the operationalization of engagement in a digital environment remains

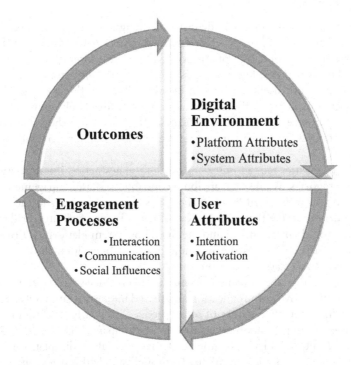

Figure 4.2 Digital Engagement Wheel—Four Dimensions of Digital Engagement

Source: Created by author

under-researched with a few exceptions. For example, Kent and Taylor (2021) outline four design frameworks that contribute to facilitating digital dialogic engagement—these include user expectations, engagement, content curation, and sustainment. Avidar et al. (2015), in a study of smartphone technology, recommend that more participatory approaches are used rather than pure advocacy or one way. Valentini (2015) cautions, however, that while the use of digital channels can support organization-public relationships, these channels "pose risks and contribute to failures in social relations" (p. 171). Synthesizing these and other studies on digital engagement point to the importance and interaction of the platform capabilities, the user capabilities, the processes of engagement, and outcomes, as these relate to digital engagement.

To operationalize the concept of digital engagement, Figure 4.2 (*The Digital Engagement Wheel*) illustrates four dimensions that comprise digital engagement: 1) the digital environment, specifically its *platform and system attributes*, 2) the *user attributes*, specifically intention and motivation to engage, 3) the *processes of engagement*, including interaction and communication with influence from the social environment, and 4) *outcomes* that are valued. Each of these is discussed in the following sections.

Platform and System Attributes

Platform and system attributes describe the design and system capabilities of a specific digital technology. O'Brien and McKay (2018) argue that digital engagement is an outcome of a process where users interact with technology and its attributes influenced by usability, functionality, and novelty. They suggest that both user- and system-based attributes influence engagement on a digital platform as the platform's design features "help users achieve a sense of presence" (O'Brien & McKay, 2018, p. 76), but they caution not to conflate design variables and argue user attributes in concert with system attributes.

Design qualities relate to user engagement in aesthetics, interactivity, and media categories. While each attribute contributes to user engagement, user experience is influenced by both the user's *own performance* and the *sharing of that experience* (O'Brien & McKay, 2018). These attributes bridge the user, the social environment, and the digital or system platform (O'Brien & McKay, 2018) as well as the psychological and behavioral dimensions of engagement as a state and as a process.

The use of digital platforms and systems can enhance social connectedness through interactive communication and shared interests (Campbell & Kwak, 2010). The interactive nature of social media particularly has "transformed consumers from passive observers to active participants" (Dolan et al., 2015, p. 261). Kent and Li (2020) note that many social media platforms have "institutionalized participation" (p. 3) through standardized responses using emojis and symbols such as likes and thumbs up, which constrain the potential for interaction and dialogue. They argue "genuine social media communication should be based on dialogic engagement rather than *faux engagement* or message reception" (Kent & Li, 2020, p. 6 [emphasis added]). The implications point to the potential for digital platforms to increase engagement through enhanced forms of interaction within a unique digital social setting.

Platform and system attributes relating to user engagement have been explored in contexts such as online shopping (O'Brien, 2010), government communications (Chan & Pan, 2008), and interactive media (Oh et al., 2018). Johnston and Taylor (2018) note the type of digital platform will determine the overall quality, strength, and duration of the engagement outcomes. Future research opportunities could examine the individual attributes of each type of platform and system, with consideration for its influence on engagement outcomes. The quality, capacity, and purpose of the interfaces within a digital environment can affect the type of engagement experienced by users and the value emerging from engagement processes.

User Attributes: Digital Engagement as a State

Individual-level engagement is commonly conceptualized as *user engagement* in a digital environment (Habibi & Salim, 2021; Lin, 2019; O'Brien,

2010; Oh et al., 2018; Seiffert-Brockmann et al., 2018; Weiger et al., 2019; Yarchi & Samuel-Azran, 2018), comprising cognitive, affective, and behavioral dimensions. These dimensions are activated through the interaction (engagement processes) with and within the platform that subsequently creates or cocreates value for the user.

Definitions of digital engagement highlight behavioral and psychological dimensions of engagement and the competencies needed to interact in digital ways. Brodie et al. (2011) define digital engagement as the interaction of the user with the platform that creates or potentiates engagement that "occurs by virtue of interactive, co-creative customer experiences with a brand" (Brodie et al., 2011, p. 260), while Rodgers and Thorson (2018) describes digital engagement as "consumers' interactions with a brand to strengthen emotional, psychological, or physical investments" (p. 1). Yoon et al. (2018) argues that digital engagement requires "active behavioral efforts that . . . ranges from actual transactional efforts (e.g., digital buying) to any behavioral efforts beyond transactions (e.g., commenting)" (p. 25). Others (see Eigenraam et al., 2018; Park, 2017; Suseno & Nguyen, 2021) relate engagement to obervable actions such as clicks or benefits beyond— for example, purchase.

Digital engagement broadly describes user motivations, interactions, intentions, and outcomes in settings such as social media, online, or any setting that is mediated by technology (Brodie et al., 2011, 2013; Eigenraam et al., 2018; Hollebeek & Chen, 2014; Hollebeek et al., 2014). O'Brien and McKay (2018) synthesized previous work in engagement and deconstructed *user attributes* that include attention, motivation, involvement, curiosity, and needs. Kahne and Bowyer (2019) note that a level of digital literacy is required to fully interact within a digital environment.

Motivation to Engage

Most human behavior is explained by *motivation* (Deci & Ryan, 1985). Kang (2014) conceptualized engagement as an affective motivator, while Jacques et al. (1995) argued that intrinsic and extrinsic motivation will determine the level of user engagement. Ryan and Deci (2000) distinguish between intrinsic and extrinsic motivation based on reasons for, or goals from, doing the action (see also Deci & Ryan, 1985)—self-determination theory (SDT). *Intrinsic* motivation refers to "doing something because it is inherently interesting or enjoyable, and extrinsic motivation . . . refers to doing something because it leads to a separable outcome" (Ryan & Deci, 2000, p. 55). For digital engagement, the role of intrinsic and extrinsic motivation at the individual level can be aligned with trait-based perspectives on engagement— that is, a disposition to engage.

User motivation is also closely aligned with user intention in an online environment. *User intention* can be broadly defined as a cognitive commitment that activates a behavior or series of actions to achieve an objective.

In digital environments, user intension is typically explored in the context of purchasing and repurchasing behaviors, recommendations, and reviews (Khattak et al., 2021; Kim, 2012). Kim (2012) found that user intention is enhanced by user satisfaction and perceived value. User satisfaction is an affective evaluative concept displayed as negative/neutral/positive feelings based on experience (Spreng et al., 1996). For users in a digital environment, perceived value is when users perceive something of worth to come from the interaction and the experience online reinforces that behavior to continue (Chen, 2017). At an individual or user level, user attributes, motivations, and intention contribute as antecedents to their state of engagement.

Levels of Engagement in Digital Contexts

Digital engagement has been used to describe everything from a "like" or a "share" to a comment, with varying levels of outcomes (Yoon et al., 2018). Smith and Gallicano (2015) differentiate digital engagement from engagement generally, noting that "social media interactivity may not be sufficient to render one engaged" (p. 82). A like or a comment, therefore, does not provide evidence that a user is engaged—more so, it shows a *potential* for engagement that can only be considered superficial, or what Johnston and Taylor (2018) call *low-level engagement*. Gavilanes et al. (2018) conceptualized digital engagement as four levels in a consumer context—consumption, filtering, processing, and advocacy, with measures reflecting clicks, likes, and shares. However, for individuals to be behaviorally engaged, interaction needs to move past this first superficial level (the act of a liking a page or a visit to a page) to interaction, collaboration, and participation—which can be viewed and conceptualized as a higher level of engagement. Interpersonal interactivity (Burton & Soboleva, 2011) is found on platforms where users respond to each other and extend or create meaning through the interaction. Digital interactivity has been found to positively influence organization-stakeholder relations (Saffer et al., 2013). The real value of this type of interactivity is found in tangible outcomes such as higher comprehension, more information processing, and more favorable experiences overall (Burton & Soboleva, 2011; Lee & Shin, 2012; Macias, 2003). The next section discusses digital engagement as a process.

Digital Engagement as a Process

Digital engagement *as a process* describes how the system and platform characteristics, or the use by a user, potentiate the interaction and relational engagement. Digital engagement has been conceived as primarily a *behavioral* concept—particularly in marketing and advertising, reflecting what people *do* in an online environment (see Yoon et al., 2018; Park, 2017; Eigenraam et al., 2018; Suseno & Nguyen, 2021). Helsper and Eynon (2013) characterize digital engagement as "the ways in which people use and participate in different Internet activities, contents, and platforms" (p. 698). Yoon et al. (2018) refer to the "active behavioral efforts" and transactions (such as buying or commenting) (p. 25), while Helsper and Eynon (2013), Park, (2017) and others refer to how people use the technology as digital engagement. There are also indications of different types or levels of user engagement, from simple clicks (Suseno & Nguyen, 2021) to something that is beyond (see, for example, Eigenraam et al., 2018, p. 102).

Communication facilitates the engagement process through interaction (Johnston & Lane, 2021) and is driven by the user attributes of motivation and intention. Interaction is "the formative iteration of communication acts over time—that lead to effects on two or more participants" (Johnston & Lane, 2021, p. 4). Digital interaction therefore involves "one-way, bilateral, and multilateral interactions and responses . . . the co-creation of new insights, information, attitudes, organizations, and relationships that stem from the use of digital resources" (Katz et al., 2013, p. 12). These outcomes are shaped by collective and social influences that are communicatively and culturally bound within a virtual community and feature the "attributes of connection, interaction, participation and involvement" (Johnston, 2018, p. 18). Chewning (2018) notes the relational and social influences of a digital environment that emerge from these interactions. The digital setting for such relationships "in which one connects with social, information, and resource networks in order to affect change, cocreation, and commitment toward a particular engagement object" (Chewning, 2018, p. 441) differentiates digital engagement from engagement generally. Overall, digital engagement manifests as communication engagement moderated by the contextual (platform/system) and user/s attributes. The digital platform in which engagement is being facilitated, therefore, influences how engagement is conceived, how it is enacted, and the outcomes that emerge. The next section looks at outcomes from digital engagement.

Digital Engagement Outcomes

Much of the focus in studies of digital engagement relate the outcomes to the creation or cocreation of value. The central premise of engagement and its outcomes in public relations is that they are *valued* according to their social consequence (Hurst & Johnston, 2021; Willis, 2012; Willis et al., 2018). The conceptualization of value as an outcome of digital engagement is therefore fundamental to understanding digital engagement processes and effectiveness. Higher-level outcomes from digital engagement are argued by scholars as an essential precondition of successful democratization. The notion of digital environments facilitating the public sphere emerges in ways that support voice and civil society (see Taylor, 2009; Taylor & Doerfel, 2005, 2011) and social capital. Social capital, Putnam (2001) argues, comes from the collective value from social connections "among individuals—social networks and the norms of reciprocity and trustworthiness that arise from them" (Putnam, 2001, p. 19). While Putnam was referring to social networks in a pure sense, in a digital setting strong social ties from digital networks generate social capital from the information seeking, bonding, bridging, and sharing behaviors (Hazleton & Tydings, 2021; You & Hon, 2019). Digital engagement establishes strong and weak ties to networks based on shared values (You & Hon, 2019) and offers opportunities to engage more fully, more widely, with more ease based on conceptualizing the value that the digitally generated and sustained network offers.

The varying conceptualizations of digital engagement as an interactive social process, and what it means, makes measuring and evaluating digital engagement challenging. There are opportunities to articulate both the influences on digital engagement and the potential for different levels of engagement that O'Brien and McKay (2018) previously recognized. Digital engagement consists of a framework of attributes that can be measured. The Digital Engagement Wheel as presented in Figure 4.2 identifies four dimensions and presents opportunities to further operationalize and investigate their influence within the framework. For example, does technological skill influence the potential for digital engagement at the individual level, or how does the strength or quality of a social network influence digital engagement? By further investigating each of the contributing dimensions, we can further understand the levels, states, and influences on digital engagement.

Measuring Digital Engagement

Industry and the academy have struggled to find ways to measure digital engagement, and this struggle reflects the various ways digital engagement is conceived and operationalized (see for example, You & Hon, 2022; Chewning, 2018). In digital and non-digital settings, there appears to be agreement that engagement occurs at different tiers from highly engaged to disengaged and negative engagement (Johnston, 2018; Kahn, 1990; Lievonen et al., 2018). Johnston and Taylor (2018) conceptualized three tiers of engagement—low-, mid-, and high-level engagement based on manifestation and outcomes. Tier 1 suggests individuals interacting with the content (such as likes or shares) and indicates a *potential* for engagement. Tier 2 suggests a mid-level of engagement with evidence of cognitive, affective, and behavioral outcomes such as network and relational interaction, understanding, trust, legitimacy, and satisfaction. Tier 3 suggests a higher level of engagement with evidence of social-level outcomes (action/change).

Methods and tools to research digital engagement have traditionally focused on the user or individual level (see O'Brien & Toms, 2010; O'Brien et al., 2018) as a unit of measurement, aligning with the behavioral approaches to digital engagement. These measure the platform or system attributes. For example, Vazquez (2020) conceptualized digital engagement as intention to recommend a brand online, while a scale created by Yang and Kang (2009) measured blog engagement based on cognitive, attitudinal, and behavioral dimensions.

Taylor et al. (2019, 2020) highlighted the importance of establishing benchmarks in measuring community engagement in community-based settings and developed a toolkit to measure community engagement for disaster resilience. A relational engagement perspective on digital engagement could benchmark and measure the quality of connection, interaction, and relationships. Measures of relational quality such as increased trust, satisfaction, new meaning, and value creation that emerge from the relationship can be indicators, for example, of the growth of relational capital (Johnston & Lane, 2018). Lombana-Bermudez et al. (2020) used a digital economy lens to measure digital engagement in youth. Their research encompassed all dimensions of a digital engagement framework, with indicators at the social level, linked to recognizing others, social capital, and social change.

Conclusion

The rapid adoption of digital tools provides a dynamic and enhanced environment for social connection and opportunities for engagement (Kim et al., 2016). As digital interfaces and technologies continue to advance, and the communication and relational opportunities offered by digital environments challenge how digital engagement is operationalized and measured, several research opportunities can be identified. Kent and Li (2020) offer principles to guide theorizing social media in public relations and the foundation of dialogic engagement in this mediated context. More specifically, they note the potential of social media "for rhetorical purposes such as persuasion, genuine relationships building via dialogue and engagement" (p. 7). Future research could investigate how digital engagement facilitates genuine relationships, particularly with the increasing adoption of artificial intelligence (AI), to facilitate customer and stakeholder engagement. For example, can you authentically engage with AI? Further research is also needed to understand motivations that influence organizational decisions to use a digital environment for relationship building and how stakeholders and publics conceive the use of digital tools to deliver on their needs and interactions. Finally, the dimensions of the measurement wheel of digital engagement (Figure 4.2) provide a framework to guide research to understand and test the relationship between each dimension individually and collectively with the outcomes of digital engagement in a digital environment and to understand episodic and relational digital engagement (see Johnston & Lane, 2018).

This chapter aimed to theorize digital engagement. It conceptualizes digital engagement as a four-dimensional process that involves platform and system features, user attributes, engagement processes, and outcomes that can be measured through value cocreation in digitally mediated settings such as social media, online, or any setting that is mediated by technology. This chapter offers a framework of digital engagement to guide theorizing and future research.

References

Avidar, R., Ariel, Y., Malka, V., & Levy, E. C. (2015). Smartphones, publics, and OPR: Do publics want to engage? *Public Relations Review*, *41*(2), 214–221. https://doi.org/10.1016/j.pubrev.2014.11.019

Bortree, D. S. (2011). Mediating the power of antecedents in public relationships: A pilot study. *Public Relations Review*, *37*(1), 44–49. https://doi.org/10.1016/j.pubrev.2010.11.002

Botan, C. H., & Taylor, M. (2004). Public relations: State of the field. *Journal of Communication*, *54*(4), 645–661.

Brodie, R. J., Hollebeek, L. D., Jurić, B., & Ilić, A. (2011). Customer engagement: Conceptual domain, fundamental propositions, and implications for research. *Journal of Service Research*, *14*(3), 252–271. https://doi.org/10.1177/1094670511411703

Brodie, R. J., Ilic, A., Juric, B., & Hollebeek, L. D. (2013). Consumer engagement in a virtual brand community: An exploratory analysis. *Journal of Business Research*, *66*(1), 105–114. https://doi.org/10.1016/j.jbusres.2011.07.029

Burton, S., & Soboleva, A. (2011). Interactive or reactive? Marketing with Twitter. *Journal of Consumer Marketing*, *28*(7), 491–499.

Calder, B. J., Malthouse, E. C., & Schaedel, U. (2009). An experimental study of the relationship between online engagement and advertising effectiveness. *Journal of Interactive Marketing*, *23*(4), 321–331.

Campbell, S. W., & Kwak, N. (2010). Mobile communication and civic life: Linking patterns of use to civic and political engagement. *Journal of Communication*, *60*(3), 536–555. https://doi.org/10.1111/j.1460-2466.2010.01496.x

Chan, C. M. L., & Pan, S. L. (2008). User engagement in e-government systems implementation: A comparative case study of two Singaporean e-government initiatives. *The Journal of Strategic Information Systems*, *17*(2), 124–139. https://doi.org/10.1016/j.jsis.2007.12.003

Chen, Y.-R. R. (2017). Perceived values of branded mobile media, consumer engagement, business-consumer relationship quality and purchase intention: A study of WeChat in China. *Public Relations Review*, *43*(5), 945–954. https://doi.org/10.1016/j.pubrev.2017.07.005

Chewning, L. V. (2018). Virtual engagement: A theoretical framework of affordances, networks, and communication. In K. A. Johnston & M. Taylor (Eds.), *The handbook of communication engagement* (pp. 439–451). Wiley Blackwell.

Cho, M., Schweickart, T., & Haase, A. (2014). Public engagement with nonprofit organizations on Facebook. *Public Relations Review*, *40*(3), 565–567. https://doi.org/10.1016/j.pubrev.2014.01.008

Colman, A. M. (2015). *Trait*. Oxford University Press.

Deci, E. L., & Ryan, R. M. (1985). *Intrinsic motivation and self-determination in human behavior*. Plenum Press.

Devin, B. L., & Lane, A. B. (2014). Communicating engagement in corporate social responsibility: A meta-level construal of engagement. *Journal of Public Relations Research*, *26*(5), 436–454.

Dezuanni, M., Foth, M., Mallan, K., Hughes, H., & Osborne, R. (2018). Social living labs for digital participation and connected learning. In M. Dezuanni, M. Foth, K. Mallan, & H. Hughes (Eds.), *Digital participation through social living labs: Valuing local knowledge, enhancing engagement*. Chandos Publishing.

Dhanesh, G. S. (2017). Putting engagement in its PRoper place: State of the field, definition and model of engagement in public relations. *Public Relation Review*. http://doi.org.ezp01.library.qut.edu.au/10.1016/j.pubrev.2017.04.001

Dhanesh, G. S., & Picherit-Duthler, G. (2021). Remote internal crisis communication (RICC)–role of internal communication in predicting employee engagement during remote work in a crisis. *Journal of Public Relations Research*, 1–22. https://doi.org/10.1 080/1062726X.2021.2011286

Dolan, R., Conduit, J., Fahy, J., & Goodman, S. (2015). Social media engagement behaviour: A uses and gratifications perspective. *Journal of Strategic Marketing*, *24*(3–4), 261–277. https://doi.org/10.1080/0965254x.2015.1095222

Dutta, M. J. (2013). Public relations in a global world: Culturally centering theory and Praxis. *Asia Pacific Public Relations Journal*, *14*(1–2), 21–31.

Dutta, M. J., & Elers, S. (2020). Public relations, indigeneity and colonization: Indigenous resistance as dialogic anchor. *Public Relations Review*, *46*(1), 101852. https://doi.org/10.1016/j.pubrev.2019.101852

Dutta-Bergman, M. J. (2004). The unheard voices of santalis: communicating about health from the margins of India. *Communication Theory*, *14*(3), 237–263. https://doi.org/10.1111/j.1468-2885.2004.tb00313.x

Edwards, L., & Hodges, C. E. M. (2011). *Public relations, society and culture: Theoretical and empirical explorations* (1st ed.). Routledge.

Eigenraam, A. W., Eelen, J., van Lin, A., & Verlegh, P. W. J. (2018). A consumer-based taxonomy of digital customer engagement practices. *Journal of Interactive Marketing*, *44*, 102–121. https://doi.org/10.1016/j.intmar.2018.07.002

Frömming, U. U., Köhn, S., Fox, S., & Terry, M. (2017). *Digital environments*. Transcript Verlag.

Gavilanes, J. M., Flatten, T. C., & Brettel, M. (2018). Content strategies for digital consumer engagement in social networks: Why advertising is an antecedent of engagement. *Journal of Advertising: Digital Engagement with Advertising*, *47*(1), 4–23. https://doi.org/10.1080/00913367.2017.1405751

Griffin, B. (2015). Collective norms of engagement link to individual engagement. *Journal of Managerial Psychology*, *30*(7), 847–860. https://doi.org/10.1108/JMP-12-2012-0393

Guidry, J. P. D., Jin, Y., Orr, C. A., Messner, M., & Meganck, S. (2017). Ebola on Instagram and Twitter: How health organizations address the health crisis in their social media engagement. *Public Relations Review*, *43*(3), 477–486. https://doi.org/10.1016/j.pubrev.2017.04.009

Habibi, S. A., & Salim, L. (2021). Static vs. dynamic methods of delivery for science communication: A critical analysis of user engagement with science on social media. *PLoS One*, *16*(3), e0248507–e0248507. https://doi.org/10.1371/journal.pone.0248507

Hanson, J. (2016). Digital. In J. Hanson (Ed.), *The social media revolution: An economic encyclopedia of friending, following, texting, and connecting* (pp. 126–128). Greenwood.

Hazleton, V., & Tydings, E. (2021). *The strategic application of social capital theory in public relations* (Vol. 27, pp. 489–508). De Gruyter.

Hearn, G., Wilson-Barnao, C., & Collie, N. (2018). New media challenges to the theory and practice of communication engagement. In K. A. Johnston & M. Taylor (Eds.), *The handbook of communication engagement* (pp. 515–527). Wiley Blackwell.

Heath, R. L. (2006). Onward into more fog: Thoughts on public relations' research directions. *Journal of Public Relations Research*, *18*(2), 93–114.

Heath, R. L. (2011). External organizational rhetoric: Bridging management and sociopolitical discourse. *Management Communication Quarterly*, *25*(3), 415–435. https://doi.org/10.1177/0893318911409532

Heath, R. L. (2014). *Public relations' role in engagement: functions, voices, and narratives.* Paper presented at the Engagement as Strategy, Theory and Practice, ICA Preconference.

Heath, R. L. (2018). How fully functioning is communication engagement if society does not benefit? In K. A. Johnston & M. Taylor (Eds.), *The handbook of communication engagement* (pp. 34–47). Wiley Blackwell.

Heath, R. L., & Abel, D. D. (1996). Proactive response to citizen risk concerns: Increasing citizens' knowledge of emergency response practices. *Journal of Public Relations Research, 8*(3), 151–171. Retrieved from http://gateway.library.qut.edu.au/login?url=http://search.ebscohost.com/login.aspx?direct=true&db=bsh&AN=6433397&site=ehost-live&scope=site

Heath, R. L., Bradshaw, J., & Lee, J. (2002). Community relationship building: Local leadership in the risk communication infrastructure. *Journal of Public Relations Research, 14*(4), 317–353. https://doi.org/10.1207/S1532754XJPRR1404_2

Helsper, E. J., & Eynon, R. (2013). Distinct skill pathways to digital engagement. *European Journal of Communication, 28*(6), 696–713. https://doi.org/10.1177/0267323113499113

Hollebeek, L. D. (2011). Demystifying customer brand engagement: Exploring the loyalty nexus. *Journal of Marketing Management, 27*(7–8), 785.

Hollebeek, L. D. (2017). Developing business customer engagement through social media engagement-platforms: An integrative S-D logic/RBV-informed model. *Industrial Marketing Management.* https://doi.org/10.1016/j.indmarman.2017.11.016

Hollebeek, L. D., & Chen, T. (2014). Exploring positively- versus negatively-valenced brand engagement: A conceptual model. *Journal of Product & Brand Management, 23*(1), 62–74. https://doi.org/10.1108/JPBM-06-2013-0332

Hollebeek, L. D., Glynn, M. S., & Brodie, R. J. (2014). Consumer brand engagement in social media: Conceptualization, scale development and validation. *Journal of Interactive Marketing, 28*(2), 149–165. http://dx.doi.org/10.1016/j.intmar.2013.12.002

Huang, Q., Jin, J., Lynn, B. J., & Men, L. R. (2021). Relationship cultivation and public engagement via social media during the covid-19 pandemic in China. *Public Relations Review, 47*(4), 102064. https://doi.org/10.1016/j.pubrev.2021.102064

Hurst, B., & Johnston, K. A. (2021). The social imperative in public relations: Utilities of social impact, social license and engagement. *Public Relations Review, 47*(2), 102039. https://doi.org/10.1016/j.pubrev.2021.102039

Jacques, R., Preece, J., & Carey, T. (1995). Engagement as a design concept for multimedia. *Canadian Journal of Learning and Technology, 24*(1), 49. https://doi.org/10.21432/T2VG77

Jeanes, E. (2019). Traits. In E. Jeanes (Ed.), *A dictionary of organizational behaviour* (1st ed.). Oxford University Press.

Jelen-Sanchez, A. (2017). Engagement in public relations discipline: Themes, theoretical perspectives and methodological approaches. *Public Relations Review, 43*(5), 934–944. https://doi.org/10.1016/j.pubrev.2017.04.002

Ji, Y. G., Li, C., North, M., & Liu, J. (2017). Staking reputation on stakeholders: How does stakeholders' Facebook engagement help or ruin a company's reputation? *Public Relations Review, 43*(1), 201–210. https://doi.org/10.1016/j.pubrev.2016.12.004

Johnston, K. A. (2010). Community engagement: Exploring a relational approach to consultation and collaborative practice in Australia. *Journal of Promotion Management, 16*(1), 217–234.

Johnston, K. A. (2014). Public relations and engagement: Theoretical imperatives of a multidimensional concept. *Journal of Public Relations Research, 26*(5), 1–3.

Johnston, K. A. (2018). Toward a theory of social engagement. In K. A. Johnston & M. Taylor (Eds.), *The handbook of communication engagement* (pp. 19–32). Wiley Blackwell.

Johnston, K. A., & Lane, A. B. (2018). Building relational capital: The contribution of episodic and relational community engagement. *Public Relation Review, 44*(5), 633–644. https://doi.org/10.1016/j.pubrev.2018.10.006

Johnston, K. A., & Lane, A. B. (2019). An authenticity matrix for community engagement. *Public Relations Review, 45*(4), 101811.

Johnston, K. A., & Lane, A. B. (2021). Communication with intent: A typology of communicative interaction in engagement. *Public Relations Review, 47*(1), 101925. https://doi.org/10.1016/j.pubrev.2020.101925

Johnston, K. A., & Taylor, M. (2018). Engagement as communication: Pathways, possibilities and future directions. In K. A. Johnston & M. Taylor (Eds.), *The handbook of communication engagement*. Wiley Blackwell.

Johnston, K. A., Taylor, M., & Ryan, B. (2022). Engaging communities to prepare for natural hazards: A conceptual model. *Natural Hazards (Dordrecht), 112*(3), 2831–2851. https://doi.org/10.1007/s11069-022-05290-2

Kahn, W. A. (1990). Psychological conditions of personal engagement and disengagement at work. *Academy of Management Journal, 33*(4), 692–724.

Kahne, J., & Bowyer, B. (2019). Can media literacy education increase digital engagement in politics? *Learning, Media and Technology, 44*(2), 211–224. https://doi.org/10.1080/17439884.2019.1601108

Kang, M. (2014). Understanding public engagement: Conceptualizing and measuring its influence on supportive behavioral intentions. *Journal of Public Relations Research, 26*(5), 399–416. https://doi.org/10.1080/1062726X.2014.956107

Karanges, E., Johnston, K. A., Beatson, A. T., & Lings, I. (2015). The influence of internal communication on employee engagement: A pilot study. *Public Relations Review, 41*(1), 129–131. https://doi.org/10.1016/j.pubrev.2014.12.003

Katz, J. E., Barris, M., & Jain, A. (2013). *The social media president Barack Obama and the politics of digital engagement*. Palgrave Macmillan US.

Kent, M. (2013). Using social media dialogically: Public relations role in reviving democracy. *Public Relations Review, 39*(4), 337–345. http://dx.doi.org/10.1016/j.pubrev.2013.07.024

Kent, M., & Li, C. (2020). Toward a normative social media theory for public relations. *Public Relations Review, 46*(1). https://doi.org/10.1016/j.pubrev.2019.101857

Kent, M., & Taylor, M. (2021). Fostering dialogic engagement: Toward an architecture of social media for social change. *Social Media + Society, 7*. https://doi.org/10.1177/2056305120984462

Khattak, A., Habib, A., Asghar, M. Z., Subhan, F., Razzak, I., & Habib, A. (2021). Applying deep neural networks for user intention identification. *Soft computing (Berlin, Germany), 25*(3), 2191–2220. https://doi.org/10.1007/s00500-020-05290-z

Kilpatrick, S. (2009). Multi-level rural community engagement in health. *The Australian Journal of Rural Health, 17*(1), 39–44. https://doi.org/10.1111/j.1440-1584.2008.01035.x

Kim, B. (2012). Understanding key factors of users' intentions to repurchase and recommend digital items in social virtual worlds. *Cyberpsychology, Behavior and Social Networking, 15*(10), 543–550. https://doi.org/10.1089/cyber.2012.0128

Kim, Y., Wang, Y., & Oh, J. (2016). Digital media use and social engagement: How social media and smartphone use influence social activities of college students. *Cyberpsychology, Behavior and Social Networking, 19*(4), 264–269. https://doi.org/10.1089/cyber.2015.0408

Lane, A. B., & Devin, B. (2018). Operationalizing stakeholder engagement in CSR: A process approach. *Corporate Social Responsibility and Environmental Management, 25*(3), 267–280. https://doi.org/10.1002/csr.1460

Lane, A. B., & Kent, M. (2018). Dialogic engagement. In K. A. Johnston & M. Taylor (Eds.), *The handbook of communication engagement* (pp. 61–72). Wiley Blackwell.

Ledingham, J. A. (2006). Relationship management: A general theory of public relations. In C. H. Botan & V. Hazleton (Eds.), *Public relations theory II* (1st ed.). Taylor and Francis.

Lee, E. J., & Shin, S. Y. (2012). When the medium is the message: How transportability moderates the effects of politicians' Twitter communication. *Communication Research.* https://doi.org/0093650212466407

Lemon, L. L. (2019). The employee experience: How employees make meaning of employee engagement. *Journal of Public Relations Research, 31*(5–6), 176–199. https://doi.org/10.1080/1062726X.2019.1704288

Lievonen, M., Luoma-aho, V., & Bowden, J. (2018). Negative engagement. In K. A. Johnston & M. Taylor (Eds.), *The handbook of communication engagement* (pp. 529–547). Wiley Blackwell.

Lin, T. T. C. (2019). Motivation and trust: How dual screening influences offline civic engagement among Taiwanese Internet users. *International Journal of Communication (Online), 4663.*

Linden, D., Tops, M., & Bakker, A. B. (2021). Go with the flow: A neuroscientific view on being fully engaged. *The European Journal of Neuroscience, 53*(4), 947–963. https://doi.org/10.1111/ejn.15014

Lombana-Bermudez, A., Cortesi, S., Fieseler, C., Gasser, U., Hasse, A., Newlands, G., & Wu, S. (2020). *Youth and the digital economy: Exploring youth practices, motivations, skills, pathways, and value creation.* Berkman Klein Center for Internet & Society. https://cyber.harvard.edu/publication/2020/youth-and-digital-economy

Macey, W. H., & Schneider, B. (2008). The meaning of employee engagement. *Industrial and Organizational Psychology, 1*(1), 3–30. https://doi.org/10.1111/j.1754-9434.2007.0002.x

Macias, W. (2003). A beginning look at the effects of interactivity, product involvement and web experience on comprehension: Brand web sites as interactive advertising. *Journal of Current Issues and Research in Advertising, 25*(2), 31–44.

Macnamara, J. (2016). Organizational listening: Addressing a major gap in public relations theory and practice. *Journal of Public Relations Research*, 1–24. https://doi.org/10.1080/1062726X.2016.1228064

McKie, D., & Munshi, D. (2005). Tracking trends: Peripheral visions and public relations. *Public Relations Review, 31*(4), 453–457. http://dx.doi.org/10.1016/j.pubrev.2005.08.001

Morehouse, J., & Saffer, A. J. (2019). Illuminating the invisible college: An analysis of foundational and prominent publications of engagement research in public relations. *Public Relations Review, 45*(5). https://doi.org/10.1016/j.pubrev.2019.101836

O'Brien, H. L. (2010). The influence of hedonic and utilitarian motivations on user engagement: The case of online shopping experiences. *Interacting with Computers, 22*(5), 344–352. http://dx.doi.org/10.1016/j.intcom.2010.04.001

O'Brien, H. L., Cairns, P., & Hall, M. (2018). A practical approach to measuring user engagement with the refined user engagement scale (UES) and new UES short form. *International Journal of Human-Computer Studies, 112*, 28–39. https://doi.org/10.1016/j.ijhcs.2018.01.004

O'Brien, H. L., & McKay, J. (2018). Modeling antecedents of user engagement. In K. A. Johnston & M. Taylor (Eds.), *The handbook of communication engagement* (pp. 73–88). Wiley Blackwell.

O'Brien, H. L., & Toms, E. G. (2010). The development and evaluation of a survey to measure user engagement. *Journal of the American Society for Information Science and Technology, 61*(1), 50–69. https://doi.org/10.1002/asi.21229

Oh, J., Bellur, S., & Sundar, S. S. (2018). Clicking, assessing, immersing, and sharing: An empirical model of user engagement with interactive media. *Communication Research, 45*(5), 737–763. https://doi.org/10.1177/0093650215600493

Park, S. (2017). Preconditions of digital engagement. In S. Park (Ed.), *Digital capital* (pp. 83–106). Palgrave Macmillan.

Putnam, R. D. (2001). *Social capital: Measurement and consequences.* Paper presented at the OECD/HRDC Conference, Quebec.

Rodgers, S., & Thorson, E. (2018). Special issue introduction: Digital engagement with advertising. *Journal of Advertising, 47*(1), 1–3. https://doi.org/10.1080/00913367.2017.1414003

Roper, J. (2005). Symmetrical communication: Excellent public relations or a strategy for hegemony? *Journal of Public Relations Research, 17*(1), 69.

Ryan, B., Johnston, K., & Taylor, M. (2022). Recognising and measuring competency in natural hazard preparation: A preparedness competency index. *International Journal of Disaster Risk Reduction, 73*, 102882. https://doi.org/10.1016/j.ijdrr.2022.102882

Ryan, R. M., & Deci, E. L. (2000). Intrinsic and extrinsic motivations: Classic definitions and new directions. *Contemporary Educational Psychology, 25*(1), 54–67. https://doi.org/10.1006/ceps.1999.1020

Saffer, A. J., Sommerfeldt, E. J., & Taylor, M. (2013). The effects of organizational Twitter interactivity on organization–public relationships. *Public Relations Review, 39*(3), 213. https://doi.org/10.1016/j.pubrev.2013.02.005

Schaufeli, W. B. (2013). What is engagement. In C. Truss, K. Alfes, R. Delbridge, A. Shantz, & E. Soane (Eds.), *Employee engagement in theory and practice* (pp. 15–35). Routledge.

Seiffert-Brockmann, J., Weitzl, W., & Henriks, M. (2018). Stakeholder engagement through gamification: Effects of user motivation on psychological and behavioral stakeholder reactions. *Journal of Communication Management (London, England), 22*(1), 67–78. https://doi.org/10.1108/JCOM-12-2016-0096

Shen, H., & Jiang, H. (2019). Engaged at work? An employee engagement model in public relations. *Journal of Public Relations Research, 31*(1–2), 32–49. https://doi.org/10.1080/1062726X.2019.1585855

Sievert, H., & Scholz, C. (2017). Engaging employees in (at least partly) disengaged companies. Results of an interview survey within about 500 German corporations on the growing importance of digital engagement via internal social media. *Public Relations Review, 43*(5). https://doi.org/10.1016/j.pubrev.2017.06.001

Slater, M. D., Chipman, H., Auld, G., Keefe, T., & Kendall, P. (1992). Information processing and situational theory: A cognitive response analysis. *Journal of Public Relations Research, 4*(4), 189–203. https://doi.org/10.1207/s1532754xjprr0404_1

Smith, B. G., & Gallicano, T. D. (2015). Terms of engagement: Analyzing public engagement with organizations through social media. *Computers in Human Behavior, 53*, 82–90.

Sommerfeldt, E. J., & Yang, A. (2018). Notes on a dialogue: Twenty years of digital dialogic communication research in public relations. *Journal of Public Relations Research, 30*(3), 59–64. https://doi.org/10.1080/1062726X.2018.1498248

Spreng, R. A., MacKenzie, S. B., & Olshavsky, R. W. (1996). A reexamination of the determinants of consumer satisfaction. *Journal of Marketing, 60*(3), 15–32. https://doi.org/10.2307/1251839

Stoker, K. L., & Tusinski, K. A. (2006). Reconsidering public relations' infatuation with dialogue: Why engagement and reconciliation can be more ethical than symmetry and reciprocity. *Journal of Mass Media Ethics, 21*(2–3), 156–176. https://doi.org/10.1080/08900523.2006.9679731

Suseno, Y., & Nguyen, D. T. (2021). Culture is in the eye of the beholder: Using metaphoric representations of cultural values to enhance consumer digital engagement. *Journal of Strategic Marketing*, 1–22. https://doi.org/10.1080/0965254X.2021.1902373

Taylor, M. (2011). Building social capital through rhetoric and public relations. *Management Communication Quarterly, 25*(3), 436–454. https://doi.org/10.1177/0893318911410286

Taylor, M. (2009). *Civil society as a rhetorical public relations process.* In R. L. Heath, E. Toth, & D. Waymer (Eds.), *Rhetorical and Critical Approaches to Public Relations II* (pp. 88-103). New York: Routledge.

Taylor, M. (2018). Reconceptualizing public relations in an engaged society. In K. A. Johnston & M. Taylor (Eds.), *The handbook of communication engagement* (pp. 103–114). Wiley Blackwell.

Taylor, M., & Doerfel, M. L. (2005). Another dimension to explicating relationships: Measuring inter-organizational linkages. *Public Relations Review, 31*(1), 121–129. https://doi.org/10.1016/j.pubrev.2004.11.013

Taylor, M., & Doerfel, M. L. (2011). Evolving network roles in international aid efforts: Evidence from Croatia's Post War Transition. *VOLUNTAS: International Journal of Voluntary and Nonprofit Organizations, 22*(2), 311–334. https://doi.org/10.1007/s11266-010-9155-3

Taylor, M., Johnston, K. A., & Ryan, B. (2019). *Monitoring, evaluation and learning toolkit: Mapping approaches to community engagement for preparedness in Australia.* www.bnhcrc.com.au/sites/default/files/managed/downloads/monitoring_evaluation_toolkit_3.pdf

Taylor, M., & Kent, M. (2014). Dialogic engagement: Clarifying foundational concepts. *Journal of Public Relations Research, 26*(5), 384–398.

Taylor, M., Ryan, B., & Johnston, K. A. (2020). The missing link in emergency management: Evaluating community engagement. *Australian Journal of Emergency Management, 35*(1), 45–52.

Tsai, W.-H. S., & Men, R. L. (2018). Social messengers as the new frontier of organization-public engagement: A WeChat study. *Public Relations Review, 44*(3), 419–429. https://doi.org/10.1016/j.pubrev.2018.04.004

Valentini, C. (2015). Is using social media "good" for the public relations profession? A critical reflection. *Public Relations Review, 41*(2), 170–177. https://doi.org/10.1016/j.pubrev.2014.11.009

VanDyke, M. S., & Lee, N. M. (2020). Science public relations: The parallel, interwoven, and contrasting trajectories of public relations and science communication theory and practice. *Public Relations Review, 46*(4), 101953. https://doi.org/10.1016/j.pubrev.2020.101953

Vazquez, E. E. (2020). Effects of enduring involvement and perceived content vividness on digital engagement. *Journal of Research in Interactive Marketing, 14*(1), 1–16. https://doi.org/10.1108/JRIM-05-2018-0071

Verčič, D., Verčič, A. T., & Sriramesh, K. (2015). Looking for digital in public relations. *Public Relations Review, 41*(2), 142–152. https://doi.org/10.1016/j.pubrev.2014.12.002

Voorveld, H. A. M., van Noort, G., Muntinga, D. G., & Bronner, F. (2018). Engagement with social media and social media advertising: The differentiating role of platform type. *Journal of Advertising: Digital Engagement with Advertising, 47*(1), 38–54. https://doi.org/10.1080/00913367.2017.1405754

Weiger, W. H., Wetzel, H. A., & Hammerschmidt, M. (2019). Who's pulling the strings?: The motivational paths from marketer actions to user engagement in social media. *European Journal of Marketing, 53*(9), 1808–1832. https://doi.org/10.1108/EJM-10-2017-0777

Willis, P. (2012). Engaging communities: Ostrom's economic commons, social capital and public relations. *Public Relations Review, 38*(1), 116–122. https://doi.org/10.1016/j.pubrev.2011.08.016

Willis, P., Tench, R., & Devins, D. (2018). Deliberative engagement and wicked problems: From good intentions to practical action. In K. A. Johnston & M. Taylor (Eds.), *The handbook of communication engagement* (pp. 383–396). Wiley Blackwell.

Woodward, W. D. (2000). Transactional philosophy as a basis for dialogue in public relations. *Journal of Public Relations Research, 12*(3), 255–275. https://doi.org/10.1207/S1532754XJPRR1203_3

Yang, A. (2018). Conceptualizing strategic engagement: A stakeholder perspective. In K. A. Johnston & M. Taylor (Eds.), *Handbook of communication engagement* (pp. 221–230). Wiley Blackwell.

Yang, S.-U., & Kang, M. (2009). Measuring blog engagement: Testing a four-dimensional scale. *Public Relations Review, 35*(3), 323–324. https://doi.org/10.1016/j.pubrev.2009.05.004

Yarchi, M., & Samuel-Azran, T. (2018). Women politicians are more engaging: Male versus female politicians' ability to generate users' engagement on social media during an election campaign. *Information, Communication & Society, 21*(7), 978–995. https://doi.org/10.1080/1369118X.2018.1439985

Yoon, G., Li, C., Ji, Y., North, M., Hong, C., & Liu, J. (2018). Attracting comments: Digital engagement metrics on Facebook and financial performance. *Journal of Advertising: Digital Engagement with Advertising, 47*(1), 24–37. https://doi.org/10.1080/00913367.2017.1405753

You, L., & Hon, L. (2019). How social ties contribute to collective actions on social media: A social capital approach. *Public Relations Review, 45*(4), 101771. https://doi.org/10.1016/j.pubrev.2019.04.005

You, L., & Hon, L. (2022). Measuring consumer digital engagement and political consumerism as outcomes of corporate political advocacy. *Public Relations Review, 48*(5). https://doi.org/10.1016/j.pubrev.2022.102233

5 Situational Theory of Problem Solving (STOPS)

A Foundational Theory of Publics and Its Behavioral Nature in Problem Solving

Myoung-Gi Chon, Lisa Tam, Hyelim Lee, and Jeong-Nam Kim

Introduction

The situational theory of problem solving (STOPS) was first published in 2011 as a generalized extension of the situational theory of publics (STP) (J.-N. Kim & Grunig, 2011). STP, which was first developed in the 1970s, explores how and why people do or do not use communication to cope with life situations (Grunig, 2003). Both theories were founded on the same assumptions: 1) communication is a purposive coping mechanism that individuals undertake when experiencing a problematic situation, 2) communicative action is epiphenomenal to decision-making or problem-solving actions, and 3) communicative action is a way to determine whether to act in indeterminate situations. STOPS also introduces the communicative action in problem solving (CAPS) framework, which examines publics' proactiveness and reactiveness in information acquisition, information selection, and information transmission (Ni & Kim, 2009). STOPS guides public relations practice to be more *strategic* by understanding what causes individuals to act communicatively for or against organizations.

Theoretical Origins and Conceptual Development of STOPS

STOPS was first published in the *Journal of Communication* in 2011 as an extension of STP (J.-N. Kim & Grunig, 2011). While both theories were founded on the concepts of *publics* and *public opinion*, STOPS reconceptualized STP by: 1) shifting the focus from decision making to problem solving, 2) re-explicating and reinstating *referent criterion* as an independent variable, 3) extending information acquisition to also include information selection and information transmission to form a comprehensive framework of communication action in problem solving (CAPS), and 4) re-explicating problem recognition, involvement recognition, constraint recognition, and situational motivation in problem solving in relation to CAPS.

DOI: 10.4324/9781003141396-6

Publics and Public Opinions

The concepts of publics and public opinion are fundamental to public relations theories and practice. Based on Blumler's (1966) and Dewey's (1927)
conceptualizations, STP was first developed to define and identify *publics* for
organizations (Grunig, 2003). *Publics* refers to groups of individuals who face
similar problems and are motivated for problem solving and who may arise
as situational collectives, organizing themselves to perform similar actions
to resolve their problems. Publics are tied to the concept of public opinion
because members of a public develop problem-specific ideas (referent criterion)—in other words, public opinions. Non-publics or passive publics (vs.
active publics) tend not to have elaborated and directed opinions, unless they
are improvised due to external pressure (e.g., polling). In contrast, (active)
publics are likely to have concrete, problem-specific ideas or opinions, such
as what caused problematic states and what should be done. However, publics who have opinions may differ in their expected solutions (e.g., pro-life
publics vs. pro-choice publics on the same issue).

Problems evolve into *issues* when active publics aim to mobilize social
attention and resources for their problem solving and attribute the problems
to an organization or a group (J.-N. Kim et al., 2008). Publics are *situational*, as they are not static and publics' motivations for resolving problems
can change over time (J.-N. Kim et al., 2008). Both STP and STOPS, as
the word *situational* in their titles suggests, acknowledge that problems arise
and fall and that issues may be created and dissolved over time. Because of
this, publics can be activated and de-activated by the problematic states they
experience, which organizations play a role in creating (J.-N. Kim et al.,
2008). In other cases, organizations cause no direct consequences, but a
group of people with common problems realize that some organizational or
social actors could help resolve the problems with their powers or resources.
In such a situation, publics approach or even pressure organizations to cooperate and lend their power and resources for their problem solving. Public
relations practitioners could act as boundary spanners to raise publics' concerns to the attention of organizations' decision makers.

Situational theories highlight that *publics* should be differentiated from
audiences, *stakeholders*, and *markets*. Publics are different from *audiences*
because publics are not passive recipients of information but active problem-
solvers in seeking, selecting, and sharing information. They are different
from *stakeholders* because publics are not just groups for which organizations
cause consequences or that hold resources crucial to organizations (J.-N.
Kim et al., 2008). Publics are groups of individuals who face similar problems, recognize the problems as affecting them, and organize themselves
to act on the problems (Grunig, 2003). Publics are also different from *markets*, which are created or anticipated by organizations. Organizations bring
markets into existence by generating interest in their products and services
(J.-N. Kim et al., 2008). On the other hand, publics can arise by themselves

(without being created by organizations), are organized around problems, and create issues to pressure organizations that cause those issues (J.-N. Kim et al., 2008).

Publics are central to situational theories, which particularly highlight that their active, purposive communicative behaviors require organizations to invest resources to identify them and prioritize strategic publics with whom organizations should build, cultivate, and maintain relationships (J.-N. Kim et al., 2008). The fundamental concept of publics also helps to differentiate public relations practice from marketing. While marketing creates markets to address an organization's economic or task environment (e.g., reducing the high costs of promoting products and services), public relations works with publics who arise themselves, and it deals with the social or institutional environment of organizations (e.g., reducing the high costs of problem solving and relationship building) (J.-N. Kim et al., 2008).

From STP to STOPS

STP and STOPS share similar theoretical roots. Both are critical frameworks for understanding publics and their behaviors in problematic situations, and both acknowledge communication as a purposive behavior to cope with those situations (J.-N. Kim & Grunig, 2011). Both represented a paradigm shift from dominant communication theories of the 1960s, which were developed based on media effects ("what communication does to people") and focused on the use of communication to change perceptions and attitudes through messaging strategies (i.e., "audience control paradigm") (Grunig, 2003; J.-N. Kim & Krishna, 2014).

STP and STOPS shifted focus to what people do, drawing attention to the behaviors of publics who are engaged in communication to resolve problematic life situations ("audience autonomy") (J.-N. Kim & Krishna, 2014). Rather than conceptualizing communication as an independent variable to cause changes in individuals' perceptions, attitudes, and behaviors, STP and STOPS conceptualize communication as a dependent variable that is initiated and influenced by individuals' subjective perceptions and cognitions (J.-N. Kim & Krishna, 2014). In other words, communication is a way for a person (problem solver) to understand, influence, and adapt to their social surroundings when they encounter problematic situations.

First, STOPS is a "generalized extension" of STP because of its generalized reconceptualization of dependent variables (i.e., CAPS) (J.-N. Kim & Grunig, 2011). STP adopted a narrower conceptualization of communicative behaviors, with information acquisition as the only dependent variable to describe communicative action (Grunig, 1997). On the other hand, STOPS proposed CAPS as a more comprehensive framework that captures the proactiveness (also known as activeness) and reactiveness (also known as passiveness) of three communicative behaviors: information acquisition (i.e., information seeking and information attending), information selection (i.e., information forefending and information permitting), and information transmission (i.e., information forwarding and information sharing) (J.-N. Kim & Grunig, 2011). As a result, CAPS, as a dependent variable, consists of a total of six communicative behaviors. According to J.-N. Kim and Grunig (2011), this extension reflects the idea that in problematic life situations, publics do not only engage in active information-seeking but in active information-sharing and selecting as well.

Second, STOPS reconceptualized and reintroduced the construct of referent criterion as an independent variable. *Referent criterion* is defined as "any knowledge or subjective judgmental system that influences the way in which one approaches problem solving" (J.-N. Kim & Grunig, 2011, p. 131). It was initially dropped from STP because it failed to predict information acquisition (Grunig, 1997). STOPS reinstated referent criterion in response to calls for attention to the variable's conceptual and practical utility in explaining and classifying publics' behaviors (J.-N. Kim & Grunig, 2011). Unlike the three situational/perceptual variables of STOPS that are tied to the problem at hand, referent criterion is a cognitive-perceptive variable that measures the available and applicable knowledge and experiences of a problem solver. The variable is important because it provides decisional guidelines to a problem solver, subsequently affecting their communicative behaviors regarding a given problem.

Third, situational motivation in problem solving was introduced in STOPS as a mediator between the three situational variables and CAPS. It represents a conceptual bridge between perceptions and behaviors, as a motivational variable that predicts communicative behaviors given individuals' situational perceptions.

Lastly, STP focuses on the role of *information* in decisional situations, whereas STOPS shifted focus from decisional situations (cf. a battle) to problematic situations (cf. a war) and the role of *information behavior* (e.g., selection, transmission) (J.-N. Kim & Krishna, 2014). Accordingly, it accentuates a conceptual shift from *decision making* to *problem solving*. In STP, information acquisition (seeing or paying attention to information) is the only communicative behavior. Thus, STP could be misconceived as endorsing, though not, the rational choice model with perfect knowledge: seeking information useful for making a decision and for dealing with one's decision situation[1] (Grunig, 1997). On the other hand, from a problem-solving perspective, STOPS explicitly outlines the nature of problem solving, often showing irrationality. A problem solver selects, creates, and circulates certain information over other information in order to increase and reproduce one's problem perceptions amongst others (J.-N. Kim & Grunig, 2011). Unlike STP, which treats *information as commodity* (to locate and accrue for decision making), STOPS shifts focus to *information behavior as instrumental process* for problem solving—information is fluid, constructed, and circulated for social influence to make problem solving feasible. This shift from decision making and information to problem solving and information behavior broadens the scope of public relations topics to which STOPS can be applied.

Independent Variables

Following its predecessor STP, STOPS includes three situational variables that measure individuals' perceptions of a given situation, namely: problem recognition, involvement recognition, and constraint recognition. As afore-mentioned, referent criterion is also reinstated as an independent variable.

Problem Recognition

Problem recognition is defined as "the extent of a perceived discrepancy between what one expects and what one experiences, or the indetermi-nacy that breaks into one's automaticity in routine perceptual and cognitive processes" (J.-N. Kim & Krishna, 2014, p. 77). As a result, communicative and behavioral efforts may be initiated to narrow this discrepancy. In STP, problem recognition included perception as well as motivation—"people detect that something should be done about a situation and stop to think about what to do" (Grunig, 1997, p. 10). However, in STOPS, problem rec-ognition is defined as the perceived state of discrepancy, while the epistemic motivation (i.e., "stop to think about what to do") is separated. This means that although one may have high discrepancy between what is expected and experienced, one would not engage in cognitive endeavors regarding the situation unless there are other situational triggers for cognitive efforts.

Involvement Recognition

While problem recognition is a "prime mover" of subsequent communica-tive and cognitive activities in a problematic situation, it is not the only one (J.-N. Kim & Grunig, 2011, p. 128). Involvement recognition is defined as people's perceived connection of themselves to the problematic situation (J.-N. Kim & Grunig, 2011). Individuals' perceived closeness to the situation can influence the likelihood and magnitude of their subsequent communi-cative behaviors (J.-N. Kim & Krishna, 2014). A low perceived connection is likely to trigger passive communicative behaviors.

Constraint Recognition

Constraint recognition is defined as people's perceptions of obstacles in a situation that limit their ability to take action in the situation (Grunig, 1997). When constraints prevent people from making actions or choices, communicative behaviors such as information acquisition are discouraged (even if problem recognition and involvement recognition are high) (J.-N. Kim & Grunig, 2011). If people do not believe that they have the personal capability to execute the behaviors, then they are also less likely to communicate about the problems or issues they experience.

Referent Criterion

Referent criterion was reconceptualized and reinstated as an independent variable, as people's recollections of success in dealing with similar problems in the past could become "a referent" to reduce their need to search for additional information (J.-N. Kim & Grunig, 2011, 130). A problem solver is likely to begin with an internal, cognitive search for prior experience (i.e., factual, experiential referent criterion). However, they could also improvise a new referent such as wishful or willful thinking toward an end state in problem solving (i.e., affective, expectational referent criterion). In other words, the construct of referent criterion has both objective and subjective aspects in which individuals could engage, potentially resulting in their search for self-fulfilling or self-complacent referents and eventually influencing their interpretations of information and communicative behaviors (J.-N. Kim & Grunig, 2011). An activated or improvised referent criterion leads to higher activeness in searching for, selecting, and giving information in problem solving.

Mediating Variable

Although STP used the three situational variables as perceptual variables to explain communicative behaviors, STOPS introduced situational motivation in problem solving as a mediating variable to examine the motivating effect between the situational variables and communicative behaviors.

Situational Motivation in Problem Solving

Situational motivation in problem solving is defined and measured as "the extent to which a person stops to think about, is curious about, or wants more understanding of the problem" (J.-N. Kim & Grunig, 2011, p. 132). J.-N. Kim and Grunig (2011) further explain it as "a state of situation-specific cognitive and epiestemic readiness to make problem-solving efforts" (J.-N. Kim & Grunig, 2011, p. 132). It represents the extent to which individuals are goal-oriented in addressing a situation-specific need in problematic situations.

Dependent Variables

STOPS introduced communicative action in problem solving (CAPS) as a new concept that explains a problem solver's activeness in information acquisition, information selection, and information transmission (J.-N. Kim & Grunig, 2011; Ni & Kim, 2009). The active and passive components of each of these communicative behaviors are measured. It should be noted that the active and passive components of each communicative behavior are not binary opposites. They can occur concurrently. Therefore, CAPS is a second-order variable consisting of six variables that share some common conceptual components, but it is not integrated by the same underlying variable. CAPS is developed based on the assumption that "communication is *epiphenomenal* to the human problem-solving process as a coping mechanism— that is, people communicate *instrumentally* and *purposefully* to solve their life problems" (J.-N. Kim & Grunig, 2011, p. 125). The six CAPS variables include information seeking, information attending, information forefending, information permitting, information forwarding, and information sharing.

Information Seeking

Information seeking represents the active (or proactive) communicative behavior of information acquisition, reflecting individuals' planned scanning of the environment for information about a specific topic (J.-N. Kim & Grunig, 2011). Information seeking is unique to active problem solvers, but active problem solvers may engage in *both* information seeking and information attending (J.-N. Kim & Krishna, 2014).

Information Attending

Information attending is defined as the unplanned discovery of information about a situation, such as discovering new information from news media (J.-N. Kim & Grunig, 2011). It reflects the passive dimension of information acquisition. A less-active problem solver may acquire information that simply comes their way without them making any efforts (J.-N. Kim & Krishna, 2014).

Information Forefending

Information forefending refers to the active dimension of information selection, reflecting a problem solver's "directedness in acquiring and sharing information either to *economize* his or her cognitive resources in problem solving or to *optimize* his or her preferred solution and end states" (J.-N. Kim & Grunig, 2011, p. 126). It reflects the extent to which a problem solver fends off certain information after judging its relevance and value in a problematic situation. He or she will become more specific and systematic in fending off and approaching certain information to reduce information overload or inconsistency between one's prior referent and new information in problem solving. Information forefending is driven by a "removing strategy" of information—i.e., an "only if" rule—as an active selection of information to effectuate problem solving (J.-N. Kim & Krishna, 2014).

Information Permitting

Information permitting takes place when a problem solver accepts any information *as long as it is related* to a current problematic situation (J.-N. Kim & Grunig, 2011). At times, active problem solvers remain open to accepting any information, especially at the inquiring phases of problem solving. Information permitting is described as driven by an "adding strategy" of information—i.e., an "anything if" rule—but should not be equated with communicative inaction, as it is still a type of selectivity at an early stage to facilitate cognitive problem solving (i.e., inquiring phrase, Figure 5.1) (J.-N. Kim & Krishna, 2014).

Information Forwarding

Information forwarding refers to an active problem solver's proactive transmission of information to others even if it is not solicited (J.-N. Kim & Grunig, 2011). It is characterized as "planned, self-propelled information giving to others" (J.-N. Kim & Grunig, 2011, p. 127). This is often the result of heighted problem perceptions as active problem solvers try to reproduce similar problem perceptions and promote preferred solutions (their referent criteria) in others. Such efforts decrease the costs and efficiency required for problem solving—the scale of economy in problem solving (J.-N. Kim & Gil de Zúñiga, 2021).

Information Sharing

Information sharing reflects passive, unplanned information transmission. It refers to "the sharing of information reactively only when someone requests one's opinion, idea, or expertise about the problem" (J.-N. Kim & Grunig, 2011, p. 127). Less-active problem solvers tend to share information only when they are asked to (J.-N. Kim & Krishna, 2014).

STOPS and Public Segmentation

Public segmentation is one of the key strategies for identifying publics in public relations and all other forms of strategic communication. STP and STOPS have contributed to the advanced development of public segmentation, particularly under the strategic behavioral paradigm (Grunig & Kim, 2017). In the strategic behavioral paradigm, publics are differentiated from stakeholders and audiences (Grunig & Repper, 1992). There is a variety of publics within issues and problems, as STP and STOPS constantly highlight. In this regard, J.-N. Kim (2011) introduced the summation method to implement public segmentation based on STOPS.

When a survey is conducted about a problem/issue adopting the STOPS frame, researchers can attain data about three major situational variables

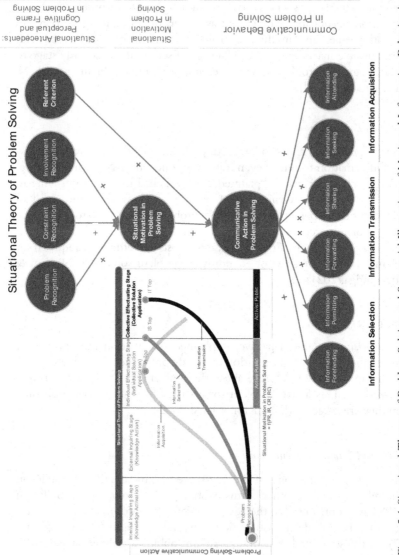

Figure 5.1 Situational Theory of Problem Solving and Sequential Illustration of Motivated Information Behavior in Problematic Situation

(problem recognition, constraint recognition, and involvement recognition). With this survey data, one can conduct the mid-point split of the three situational variables (for example, in the five-point Likert scale, the mid-point is three) to recode them as dummy variables (high =1 and low =0). Next, the recoded binary variables of the three situational constructs are combined (summed). With this method, four groups are created: Nonpublic (summation outcome = 0), Latent Public (1), Aware Public (2), Active Public (3), and Activist Public (4). For example, if problem recognition is 3 (higher than 3), constraint recognition (reversed) is 2 (lower than 3) and involvement recognition is 5 (higher than 3) on a five-point Likert scale, the total score is 2 (1 + 0+1). This simple method could identify active publics (vs. other passive publics) and provide a quick snapshot of the problem- and issue-specific distributions of publics.

Synthesizing STOPS in Public Relations Research

STOPS has been broadly applied to research in public relations and other disciplines. The following section explains how STOPS has been applied to public relations research. Scholars in public relations have extensively applied STOPS to solve their research problems since 2011.

To synthesize public relations studies using STOPS, we use a typology based on two types of public relations problems (i.e., organization-initiated public relations problems or OPR problem vs. public-initiated public relations problems or PPR problem) and two types of publics (i.e., external vs. internal publics) in this section. According to J.-N. Kim and Ni (2013), PPR problems occur when publics arise after sensing problems caused by organizational actions (e.g., organizational crises), while OPR problems occur when organizations sense potential problems, requiring them to increase awareness of publics (e.g., health information campaigns). In PPR problems, organizations should seek to work with active publics to reduce their problem perceptions. On the other hand, in OPR problems, organizations should seek to increase the problem perceptions of inactive publics (J.-N. Kim & Ni, 2013). Two types of publics including internal publics (e.g., employees) and external publics (e.g., consumers) have been examined in research related to OPR problems and PPR problems.

Using the typology (PPR vs. OPR, internal publics vs. external publics), thus, we classify STOPS studies in public relations research into four types of research areas. In the following sections, we explain four types of research (PE, OE, PI, and OI). *PE research* refers to PPR problems involving external publics. *OE research* refers to OPR problems involving external publics. *PI research* refers to PPR problems involving internal publics, and *OI research* refers to OPR problems involving internal publics.

PE Research

PE research (i.e., PPR and external publics) is defined as PPR problems that involve external publics. Current research has examined what organizations do to reduce external publics' problem perceptions. Major topics of PE research include crisis communication, rumor spread, and activism. PE research is the most popular in the application of STOPS.

STOPS has been used to investigate factors that motivate external publics to be active in their communicative behaviors. For instance, STOPS was applied to explore the effects of government decisions on U.S. beef import on the communicative actions of South Korean citizens (J.-N. Kim et al., 2012) and of Taiwanese citizens (Chen et al., 2017). Scholars have also integrated STOPS with other theories or variables to extend the application of STOPS in organizational crises. For example, J. Kim and Sung (2016) have examined whether communal and exchange relationships are associated with perceptions and communicative behaviors in the context of the university tuition issue in South Korea. The study found that the two types of relationships are differently related to the three perceptual variables of STOPS and communicative behaviors. Shin and Han (2016) tested the role of negative emotions (e.g., anger, sadness, and fear) in the framework of STOPS and revealed that negative emotions generated in response to a sex crime issue motivated publics to engage in communicative behaviors. Among the four types of publics (i.e., active, aware, latent, and non-publics), their study found that active and aware publics are more emotional than latent and non-publics on the issue. Scholars have also studied other types of issues. On the issue of food-related rumors spread on social media against McDonald's and genetically modified (GM) foods, the situational variables in STOPS were used to predict attitudes and the likelihood of rumor sharing (H. Lee et al., 2021).

STOPS has also been broadly explored to help derive crisis communication strategies. Grunig and Kim (2017) explained the concept of publics in detail and explained how publics can be segmented to solve crisis-related or risk-related communication problems. Chon (2019) tested how political dispositions, situational variables, and relationships can predict citizens' positive and negative megaphoning regarding government. Y. Kim et al. (2016) used CAPS as dependent variables to understand how differently framed messages were associated with publics' communicative actions, organizational reputation, and behavior intentions on an organizational crisis. On the issue of vaccinations, Krishna (2017) tested how cross-situational variables and situational factors, including knowledge deficiency and institutional trust, were associated with situational motivation and CAPS.

Scholars have also extended STOPS by integrating it with other theories. An integrative model of activism was tested with the incorporation of hostile media perception, affective injustice meaning negative emotion to perceive injustice, and social media efficacy (Chon & Park, 2020). The situational variables and situational motivation in problem solving were used to predict social media activism in the model. Using the spiral of silence theory and STOPS, Lee et al. (2014) investigated when publics wanted to express their opinions on gun possession and climate change. Chang and Kim (2019) also tested the spiral of silence theory to investigate the role of situational motivation of publics in the context of a genetically modified food controversy. In the context of COVID-19, Dam et al. (2021) integrated the spiral of silence theory and STOPS, and they identified that situational variables moderated the relationship between fear of isolation and opinion expression engagement.

OE Research

OE research refers to OPR problems that involve external publics. Unlike PE research aims to investigate how to decrease activeness of publics in the organizational crisis, OE research mostly attempts to enhance activeness of publics about an issue. An example is communication campaigns that are often recommended when organizations sense potential problems, causing the need to increase the problem perceptions of consumers. Some of the topics examined include fundraising events, corporate social responsibility (CSR) communication, health information, communication, and risk communication.

For fundraising campaigns and CSR communication, STOPS has been applied to understand the communicative behaviors of publics and to increase their participation in nonprofit fundraising events (e.g., Y. Lee & Tao, 2020; McKeever et al., 2016; Toledano et al., 2013). Using attitudes and subjective norms from the Theory of Reasoned Action and the three situational variables from STOPS, Toledano et al. (2013) sought to predict publics' supportive behaviors for the American Cancer Society. McKeever et al. (2016) proposed a model to explain information activity and behavioral intentions to support the fundraising events of nonprofit organizations. Using organization–public relationships in the framework of STOPS, Y. Lee and Tao (2020) explained communicative behaviors of publics and their participation behaviors in CSR campaigns. S. Lee and her colleagues (2020) examined how relationships of organizations with publics influence situational factors and their behaviors to participate in CSR activities.

In health communication, STOPS has been applied to examine organ donation issues. J.-N. Kim et al. (2011) developed the concept of *problem chain recognition* effect. For example, publics active in communicative actions on organ donation issues can also be active on blood donation issues. To understand the information seeking behaviors of publics interested in cancer-related information, Shen et al. (2019) applied STOPS to analyze secondary research data from the 2014 HINTS survey. Yoo et al. (2016) proposed an integrated health campaign model to test the effects of social media, health beliefs, and media perceptions on communicative behaviors and health behavioral intentions.

Furthermore, the information behaviors in STOPS have been used to build a theoretical model in health communication. J.-N. Kim and Lee (2014) derived the concept of *cybercoping*, examining the problem-solving efforts of individuals with health problems and the two information behaviors of STOPS (i.e., information seeking and information forwarding) and coping outcomes (i.e., affective and physical coping). The cybercoping model was also applied to dementia caregivers (J.-S. Jeong et al., 2018). In the context of medical talk shows, STOPS' information seeking and information sharing were used to test a theoretical model to predict unconditional acceptance based on the heuristic-systematic model (HSM) (J. S. Jeong & Lee, 2018). The information forefending behavior of STOPS was used to explain how publics actively select health information and reject information that is contradictory to their beliefs (J.-N. Kim et al., 2016).

In risk communication research related to public health issues and disasters, STOPS has been used to predict compliance behaviors for organizations in the public sector through communicative action of publics. Chon and Park (2021) proposed a theoretical model to predict publics' compliance behaviors for Centers for Disease Control and Prevention (CDC) guidance during infectious disease outbreaks. Incorporating organization-public relationships and fear into STOPS, the study predicted publics' behavioral intentions to follow the CDC's instructions. To understand the response behaviors of publics and their compliance behaviors when tornadoes occur, Liu et al. (2019) tested variables related to social mediated crisis communication (SMCC) by connecting the STOPS model.

PI Research

In the previous section, we explained how STOPS has been applied to explore external publics' communication behaviors and behaviors in PPR and OPR problems. In this section, we focus on internal publics in the two types of public relations problems. PI research refers PPR to problems targeting internal publics (e.g., employees). A few researchers have applied STOPS to internal problems. PI research attempts to understand and predict communication behaviors of active internal publics. For example, from the public segmentation approach, Y. Lee (2019) investigated the impact of cross-situational variables, pre-crisis relationship, and situational perceptions on the adversarial and advocatory communication of employees. Y. Lee (2022) also used CAPS to examine employees' active communicative behaviors during an organizational crisis. Chon et al. (2021) examined how previous organizational conflict history and employees' situational perceptions of COVID-19 were associated with employees' negative megaphoning and turnover intention. The findings of this study suggested the importance of managing organizational conflicts continually, as prior organizational conflict history negatively affected employees' megaphoning and turnover intentions during the COVID-19 pandemic.

OI Research

Few researchers have applied STOPS to this research area. OI research refers to OPR problems targeting internal publics. While previous research has paid attention to the role of public relations related to external publics, recently scholars have tried to incorporate internal publics in relation to strategic communication to bring the organizational effectiveness through employees. J.-N. Kim and Rhee (2011) proposed the concepts of megaphoning and scouting as an employee communication behavior (ECB) by adapting the communicative behaviors of STOPS.

Since then, other scholars in public relations have applied megaphoning and scouting to investigate the effects of ECB on organizational effectiveness. For example, Park and her colleagues (2014) investigated a theoretical model to predict employees' entrepreneurship and scouting behaviors. Y. Lee and Chon (2021) tested how transformational leadership and communal and exchange relationships were associated with positive and negative megaphoning effects. Y. Lee and Tao (2020) investigated employees as information influencers of an organization's CSR activities and found that employees' communicative actions affected external publics' perceptions on CSR activities and purchase intention. In addition, Y. Lee and Li (2021) applied STOPS to workplace racial discrimination issues, examining how diversity climate could moderate employees' situational perceptions and communicative action for employee engagement.

Future Directions

This chapter has explicated how STOPS has been developed and applied to public relations research. Although STOPS has been extensively applied in public relations research contexts, the theory still has yet-to-be explored areas and research problems to be advanced in many ways. Particularly, J.-N. Kim and Krishna (2014) suggested that further conceptual and empirical research be conducted to explore new research problems that explore the intertwined causal mechanisms between organizations and their publics. Of note, individuals' micro-information behaviors could result in macro-social and organizational consequences. As such, STOPS could be used to examine contemporary phenomena such as tracking *how* and *when* individuals engage in gossiping behaviors, how these behaviors result in differentiated patterns of information diffusion, and how individuals select information in accordance with their referent criteria to optimize communicative outcomes. In response to the rise of misinformation, J.-N. Kim and Grunig (2021) developed a conceptual framework based on STOPS to explain how individuals seek and share information that fits their expected conclusions (J.-N. Kim & Grunig, 2021). This phenomenon, known as cognitive retrogression, could lead to conspiratorial thinking and should be empirically explored in future research. Given the importance of organization-public relationships in mitigating the exacerbation of conspiratorial thinking in society, we believe STOPS could be used to explain people's inclination to seek and share conspiracy theories.

The use of STOPS in industry settings could also be further promoted. STOPS plays significant roles in explicating the importance of publics' segmentation and differentiating publics from stakeholders or markets in an organization's operating environment (J.-N. Kim, 2011; J.-N. Kim et al., 2008). Instructional papers could be published to guide industry professionals in identifying and segmenting publics, understanding their situational motivations, and tracking the development of an issue over time. For example, STOPS could guide industry professionals in conducting traditional and social media analyses (Tam & Kim, 2019). The content created and shared on traditional and social media is an example of communicative behaviors that reflect individuals' problem recognitions in dealing with issues they are confronted with. These problem recognitions are, in turn, issues for organizations. Individuals who produce and share content on online media are motivated problem solvers who acquire, select, and transmit information. While it is often assumed that "information is just out there," STOPS could be useful in explaining how and why information is created, modified, and shared across people's digital networks to explore the origins of information in the digital space. The use of STOPS could encourage industry practitioners to consider how organizational actions and decisions could motivate individuals to create and share content in favor of or against organizations, and to advocate for the voices of these motivated problem solvers in organizational decision-making processes.

A theoretical application of STOPS is also possible for future research in digital public relations. There have been some discussions surrounding the impact of digital shifts in public relations, but there has not yet been sufficient theoretical framework or understanding. When considering the importance of digital tools in public relations (Grunig, 2009), a recent article (Grunig et al., 2021) revived the digital public relations debate to discuss how the digital environment can increase the potential of public relations. Publics' empowered voices (via digital channels) can be utilized to affect organizational decisions. For organizations, it is possible to achieve a preemptive solution by using accessible data and knowledge about the relevant publics.

Lastly, STOPS can be utilized methodologically to understand digital publics' communication behaviors. For example, the STOPS measures can be redefined to detect publics' problem, constraint, and involvement recognition in digital platforms by creating a lexicon dictionary. The other network-related features in the platform (e.g., homophily, existence of counter-publics) can be introduced to STOPS as well for further understanding of digital publics' communication behaviors.

Notes

1   To be clear, STP never endorses the rational choice and perfect knowledge assumptions. When encountering problematic states, people also face decision situations. In decision making, people with problems tend to experience greater information need

for making a choice and taking action. Grunig and Hunt (1984) used behavioral molecules to explain that decision could be habitual or irrational if relevant information is not sought out. However, STP's narrow conceptualization of communicative action as only information acquisition limits the problem solver's other communicative actions: choosing, modifying, and giving information to influence others on ways of problem solving.

References

Blumler, H. (1966). The mass, the public, and public opinion. In B. Berelson & M. Janowitz (Eds.), *Reader in public opinion and communication* (2nd ed., pp. 43–50). Free Press.

Chang, B., & Kim, J. N. (2019). Silent minority? Willingness to express opinions of motivated public depending on the perceived group size in the context of GM food controversy. *Public Relations Review, 45*(5), 101786. https://doi.org/10.1016/j.pubrev.2019.05.007

Chen, Y.-R. R., Hung-Baesecke, C.-J. F., & Kim, J.-N. (2017). Identifying active hot-issue communicators and subgroup identifiers. *Journalism & Mass Communication Quarterly, 94*(1), 124–147. https://doi.org/10.1177/1077699016629371

Chon, M.-G. (2019). Government public relations when trouble hits: Exploring political dispositions, situational variables, and government–public relationships to predict communicative action of publics. *Asian Journal of Communication, 29*(5), 424–440. https://doi.org/10.1080/01292986.2019.1649438

Chon, M.-G., & Park, H. (2020). Social media activism in the digital age: Testing an integrative model of activism on contentious issues. *Journalism & Mass Communication Quarterly, 97*(1), 72–97. https://doi.org/10.1177/1077699019835896

Chon, M.-G., & Park, H. (2021). Predicting public support for government actions in a public health crisis: Testing fear, organization-public relationship, and behavioral intention in the framework of the situational theory of problem solving. *Health Communication, 36*(4), 476–486. https://doi.org/10.1080/10410236.2019.1700439

Chon, M.-G., Tam, L., & Kim, J.-N. (2021). Effects of organizational conflict history and employees' situational perceptions of COVID-19 on negative megaphoning and turnover intention. *Journal of Communication Management, 25*(3), 298–315. https://doi.org/10.1108/JCOM-10-2020-0114

Dam, L., Basaran, A. M. B., & Atkin, D. (2021). Fear of COVID-19 opinion expression: Digitally mediated spirals of silence and the situational theory of problem solving. *Journal of Broadcasting & Electronic Media*, 1–22. https://doi.org/10.1080/08838151.2021.2008937

Dewey, J. (1927). *The public and its problems*. Holt.

Grunig, J. E. (1997). A situational theory of publics: Conceptual history, recent challenges and new research. In D. Moss, T. MacManus, & D. Vercic (Eds.), *Public relations research: An international perspective* (pp. 3–48). International Thomson Business.

Grunig, J. E. (2003). Constructing public relations theory and practice. In B. Dervin, S. Chaffee, & L. Foreman-Wernet (Eds.), *Communication, another kind of horse race: Essays honoring Richard F. Carter* (pp. 85–115). Hampton Press.

Grunig, J. E. (2009). Paradigms of global public relations in an age of digitalisation. *Prism, 6*(2), 1–19. http://praxis.massey.ac.nz/prism_on-line_journ.html

Grunig, J. E., & Hunt, T. (1984). *Managing public relations*. CBS College Publishing.

Grunig, J. E., & Kim, J.-N. (2017). Publics approaches to health and risk message design and processing. In *Oxford research encyclopedia of communication* (Vol. 1). Oxford University Press. https://doi.org/10.1093/acrefore/9780190228613.013.322

Grunig, J. E., Kim, J.-N., & Lee, H. (2021). Paradigms of public relations in an age of digitalization. *Journal of Public Relations, 25*(1), 1–30.

Grunig, J. E., & Repper, F. C. (1992). Strategic management, publics, and issues. In J. E. Grunig (Ed.), *Excellence in public relations and communication management* (pp. 117–158). Lawrence Erlbaum Associates.

Jeong, J. S., Kim, Y., & Chon, M.-G. (2018). Who is caring for the caregiver? The role of cybercoping for dementia caregivers. *Health Communication, 33*(1), 5–13. https://doi.org/10.1080/10410236.2016.1242030

Jeong, J. S., & Lee, S. (2018). The influence of information appraisals and information behaviors on the acceptance of health information: A study of television medical talk shows in South Korea. *Health Communication, 33*(8), 972–979. https://doi.org/10.10 80/10410236.2017.1323365

Kim, J., & Sung, M. (2016). The value of public relations: Different impacts of communal and exchange relationships on perceptions and communicative behavior. *Journal of Public Relations Research, 28*(2), 87–101. https://doi.org/10.1080/1062726X.2016.1191014

Kim, J.-N. (2011). Public segmentation using situational theory of problem solving : Illustrating summation method and testing segmented public profiles. *Prism, 8.*

Kim, J.-N., & Gil de Zúñiga, H. (2021). Pseudo-information, media, publics, and the failing marketplace of ideas: Theory. *American Behavioral Scientist, 65*(2), 163–179. https://doi.org/10.1177/0002764220950606

Kim, J.-N., & Grunig, J. E. (2011). Problem solving and communicative action: A situational theory of problem solving. *Journal of Communication, 61*(1), 120–149. https://doi.org/10.1111/j.1460-2466.2010.01529.x

Kim, J.-N., & Grunig, J. E. (2021). Lost in informational paradise: Cognitive arrest to epistemic inertia in problem solving. *American Behavioral Scientist, 65*(2), 213–242. https://doi.org/10.1177/0002764219878237

Kim, J.-N., & Krishna, A. (2014). Publics and lay informatics: A review of the situational theory of problem solving. In E. L. Cohen (Ed.), *Communication yearbook* (Vol. 38, pp. 71–105). Routledge.

Kim, J.-N., & Lee, S. (2014). Communication and cybercoping: Coping with chronic illness through communicative action in online support networks. *Journal of Health Communication, 19*(7), 775–794. https://doi.org/10.1080/10810730.2013.864724

Kim, J.-N., & Ni, L. (2013). Two types of public relations problems and integrating formative and evaluative research: A review of research programs within the behavioral, strategic management paradigm. *Journal of Public Relations Research, 25*(1), 1–29. https://doi.org/10.1080/1062726X.2012.723276

Kim, J.-N., Ni, L., Kim, S.-H., & Kim, J. R. (2012). What makes people hot? Applying the situational theory of problem solving to hot-issue publics. *Journal of Public Relations Research, 24*(2), 144–164. https://doi.org/10.1080/1062726X.2012.626133

Kim, J.-N., Ni, L., & Sha, B.-L. (2008). Breaking down the stakeholder environment: Explicating approaches to the segmentation of publics for public relations research. *Journalism & Mass Communication Quarterly, 85*(4), 751–768. https://doi.org/10.1177/107769900808500403

Kim, J.-N., Oh, Y. W., & Krishna, A. (2016). Justificatory information forefending in digital age: Self-sealing informational donviction of risky health behavior. *Health Communication, 1*–9. https://doi.org/10.1080/10410236.2016.1242040

Kim, J.-N., & Rhee, Y. (2011). Strategic thinking about employee communication behavior (ECB) in public relations: Testing the models of megaphoning and scouting effects in Korea. *Journal of Public Relations Research, 23*(3), 243–268. https://doi.org/10.1080/1062726X.2011.582204

Kim, J.-N., Shen, H., & Morgan, S. E. (2011). Information behaviors and problem chain recognition effect: Applying situational theory of problem solving in organ donation issues. *Health Communication, 26*(2), 171–184. https://doi.org/10.1080/10410236.20 10.544282

Kim, Y., Miller, A., & Chon, M.-G. (2016). Communicating with key publics in crisis communication: The synthetic approach to the public segmentation in CAPS (communicative action in problem solving). *Journal of Contingencies and Crisis Management, 24*(2), 82–94. https://doi.org/10.1111/1468-5973.12104

Krishna, A. (2017). Motivation with misinformation: Conceptualizing lacuna individuals and publics as knowledge-deficient, issue-negative activists. *Journal of Public Relations Research, 29*(4), 176–193. https://doi.org/10.1080/1062726X.2017.1363047

Lee, H., Kim, J., & Kim, J. N. (2021). Mechanics of rumor mills and epistemic motivational processes of food-related rumor spread: Interplay between attitude and issue motivation. *Health Communication, 36*(6), 722–730. https://doi.org/10.1080/104102 36.2020.1712518

Lee, H., Oshita, T., Oh, H. J., & Hove, T. (2014). When do people speak out? Integrating the spiral of silence and the situational theory of problem solving. *Journal of Public Relations Research, 26*(3), 185–199. https://doi.org/10.1080/1062726X.2013.864243

Lee, S. Y., Kim, Y., & Kim, Y. (2020). The co-creation of social value: What matters for public participation in corporate social responsibility campaigns. *Journal of Public Relations Research, 32*(5–6), 198–221. https://doi.org/10.1080/1062726X.2021.1888734

Lee, Y. (2019). Crisis perceptions, relationship, and communicative behaviors of employees: Internal public segmentation approach. *Public Relations Review, 45*(4), 101832. https://doi.org/10.1016/j.pubrev.2019.101832

Lee, Y. (2022). The rise of internal activism: Motivations of employees' responses to organizational crisis. *Journal of Public Relations Research.* https://doi.org/10.1080/106 2726X.2022.2034630

Lee, Y., & Chon, M. G. (2021). Transformational leadership and employee communication behaviors: The role of communal and exchange relationship norms. *Leadership and Organization Development Journal, 42*(1), 61–82. https://doi.org/10.1108/ LODJ-02-2020-0060

Lee, Y., & Li, J.-Y. (2021). Discriminated against but engaged: The role of communicative actions of racial minority employees. *Communication Monographs.* https://doi.org/ 10.1080/03637751.2021.2021432

Lee, Y., & Tao, W. (2020). Employees as information influencers of organization's CSR practices : The impacts of employee words on public perceptions of CSR. *Public Relations Review.* https://doi.org/10.1016/j.pubrev.2020.101887

Liu, B. F., Xu, S., Rhys Lim, J. K., & Egnoto, M. (2019). How publics' active and passive communicative behaviors affect their tornado responses: An integration of STOPS and SMCC. *Public Relations Review, 45*(4), 101831. https://doi.org/10.1016/j. pubrev.2019.101831

McKeever, B. W., Pressgrove, G., McKeever, R., & Zheng, Y. (2016). Toward a theory of situational support: A model for exploring fundraising, advocacy and organizational support. *Public Relations Review, 42*(1), 219–222. https://doi.org/10.1016/j. pubrev.2015.09.009

Ni, L., & Kim, J.-N. (2009). Classifying publics: Communication behaviors and problem-solving characteristics in controversial issues. *International Journal of Strategic Communication, 3*(4), 217–241. https://doi.org/10.1080/15531180903221261

Park, S. H., Kim, J.-N., & Krishna, A. (2014). Bottom-up building of an innovative organization: Motivating employee intrapreneurship and scouting and their strategic value. *Management Communication Quarterly, 28*(4), 531–560. https://doi.org/10.1177/0893318914541667

Shen, H., Xu, J., & Wang, Y. (2019). Applying situational theory of problem solving in cancer information seeking: A cross-sectional analysis of 2014 HINTS survey. *Journal of Health Communication, 24*(2), 165–173. https://doi.org/10.1080/10810730.2019.1587111

Shin, K.-A., & Han, M. (2016). The role of negative emotions on motivation and communicative action: Testing the validity of situational theory of problem solving in the context of South Korea. *Asian Journal of Communication, 26*(1), 76–93. https://doi.org/10.1080/01292986.2015.1083597

Tam, L., & Kim, J.-N. (2019). Social media analytics: How they support company public relations. *Journal of Business Strategy, 40*(1), 28–34. https://doi.org/10.1108/JBS-06-2017-0078

Toledano, M., Riches, M., Waddingham, J., & McKeever, B. W. (2013). From awareness to advocacy: Understanding nonprofit communication, participation, and support. *Journal of Public Relations Research, 25*(4), 307–328. https://doi.org/10.1002/nvsm

Yoo, S.-W., Kim, J., & Lee, Y. (2018). The effect of health beliefs, media perceptions, and communicative behaviors on health behavioral intention: An integrated health campaign model on social media. *Health Communication, 33*(1), 32–40. https://doi.org/10.1080/10410236.2016.1242033

6 Applying the Network Perspective to Public Relations Theory and Practice

Adam J. Saffer and Aimei Yang

Networks are core to the human condition (Van Dijk, 2012). The connections among social entities and social artifacts create conduits for exchanging information and resources (Castells, 2009). For centuries, scholars like Plato wrestled with questions about connections such as: How can autonomous individuals connect to create enduring, functioning societies? (Borgatti et al., 2009). Today network theories and methods, which make up the network perspective, have enabled scholars to address some of the most complex questions in the social sciences at large (Borgatti et al., 2014) and within the discipline of public relations (Yang & Saffer, 2019).

Applied to public relations, the network perspective emphasizes the interdependencies and interactions among organizations, publics, issues, messages, and relationships (O'Connor & Shumate, 2018). Indeed, the field has long known of the significance of interactions among stakeholders and organizations but has been limited in analyzing these interactions. The network perspective broadens the scope from the interactions and interdependencies of an organization and its publics toward a view that accounts for how organizations, publics, issues, messages, and their relationships are embedded in webs of connections that enable and constrain opportunities.

Network theories, a critical portion of the network perspective, attempts to explain the antecedents and outcomes that come from the interactions and interdependencies among social entities and artifacts. Public relations scholars have leveraged network theory to consider how the structures of networks or one's network position associates with outcomes like engagement (Saffer, Yang, Morehouse, & Qu, 2019), relationship quality (Sommerfeldt, 2013), and social capital (Saffer, 2016; Sommerfeldt & Taylor, 2011). At the analytical level, network analysis is a unique set of analytic frameworks that account for the interdependencies of observations that inherently violate the assumption of independence required in more conventional methods. Network methods have addressed questions about the role of public relations in civil society (Taylor & Doerfel, 2005), the interactions between various voices that co-construct rhetorical crisis situations (Raupp, 2019), discussions on social media (Himelboim et al., 2014), the implications of everyday conversations (Saffer, Yang, & Qu, 2019), and other phenomena.

DOI: 10.4324/9781003141396-7

Despite these advances, a network perspective has the potential to provide even more powerful and pragmatic approaches for addressing some of the most pressing questions faced by the field of public relations.

This chapter attempts to equip public relations scholars and students with the capacity to use network theories more fully. We begin clarifying terms and differentiating between network perspective, network theory, and network analysis. Then we review the contributions of network research by focusing on one area where this most evident. Whereas public relations scholars have pondered "What comes of organization-public relationships (OPR)?," network researchers have asserted that social capital is one outcome (Saffer, 2016; Sommerfeldt, 2013). We conclude with considerations for how the perspective's tools can further advance public relations theory.

Emergence of the Network Perspective in Public Relations Research

The network perspective is a social scientific tradition characterized by its primary unit of analysis: relationships (Borgatti & Lopez-Kidwell, 2014). Other traditions see individuals, groups, organizations, and even artifacts as isolated entities. The network perspective sees each as embedded within webs of relationships (Wellman, 1988). Such a relational focus aligns well with public relations' emphases on relationship management and OPR (Sommerfeldt, 2013).

A decade before network analysis was first used in the field (cf. Jang, 1998), Ferguson (1984) sought to initiate public relations theory building by calling for a conceptual understanding of relationships between the dyad of an organization and a public. In part, this charge made relationships one of the field's main areas of conceptual development as evidenced by Broom et al.'s (1997) conceptualization of relationships, Ledingham and Bruning's (1998; Ledingham, 2003) operationalization, and numerous relationship management studies. Unfortunately, the dyadic assumptions embedded within this scholarship limited the theoretical development of relationship research.

In an early attempt to correct these dyadic assumptions, Taylor and Doerfel (2005) introduced network methods for studying how organizations and stakeholders are embedded in webs of relationships. Ensuing works studied interorganizational relationships by surveying organizations—known as *nodes* in network terms—to reveal the relationships among them, or what are referred to as *ties* or *edges*. This sociocentric or "whole network" approach takes all the nodes and ties into account to reveal network structure and nodes' positions. Network-level metrics like density assess the connectedness of entire networks or how efficiently organizations communicate (Saffer, 2019; Sommerfeldt, 2013). Node-level metrics identify those positioned as central in the network, which has been associated with organizations' importance, cooperativeness, and information exchange (Saffer et al.,

2021; Sommerfeldt, 2013; Sommerfeldt & Kent, 2015; Taylor & Doerfel, 2005). These studies establish that relationship quality is explained, in part, by structure and position rather than solely the attributes of an organization or publics' perceptions of the organization.

Network studies have emerged in other areas of public relations research. Take as evidence the topics of studies in a special issue of *Public Relations Review* (Yang & Saffer, 2019). Furthering interorganizational research, Fu and Li (2019) considered the determinants of firms' network ties with NGOs and public entities. Conversely, Zhou (2019) critiqued such studies and took a network ecology view of organization–public relationships to demonstrate how organizations and publics are connected by their overlapping ties. Others studied social artifacts like media coverage and social media content. Raupp (2019), for instance, used news articles to reveal the patterns of interactions among corporations and regulators in a rhetorical arena to raise questions about rhetorical power in discourses. Albishri and colleagues (2019), rooted in agenda-building theory, investigated the transfer of salience of objects like issues and stakeholders, and their attributes co-occurred in information subsidies, media coverage, and online discourses. Finally, in the area of activism, You and Hon (2019) investigated the impacts of individuals' social-tie activation on their intentions to participate in collective actions.

Indeed, many of the advances from *network analysis* in public relations scholarship have been methodological, but the *network perspective* is more than analyzing nodes and ties or visualizing networks. The network perspective provides an overhaul of research protocols that begins by seeing phenomena as occurring through and because of interactions and connections among social actors and artifacts. With an eye toward seeing public relations phenomena with a network perspective, we see three issues that must be addressed.

First, there is a myth that network research is solely a method. To dispel this, we clarify terms and highlight the core principle of interdependence in network research. Second, the scope of network studies has focused on organizations. To see public relations as more than the sum of its parts, researchers must account for the interdependence of organizations and all their stakeholders. Third, the theoretical benefits of network research have been murky. We offer some common findings among the extant literature before turning to the section on social capital.

Demystifying the Method Myth

Network research is unique in the social sciences because it bases the perspective, theorizing, and analyses on a fundamental construct: a network (Borgatti & Lopez-Kidwell, 2014). Many assume network researchers fall victim to the law of the hammer, where every problem is a network so the only tool is network analysis. Thus, the myth that network research is merely a method has taken hold (Borgatti et al., 2014), but it is much more. Differentiating the network perspective, network theory, and network analysis can help skeptics understand how network research is a distinct research orientation and set of theories, not just methods.

A network perspective is an orientation to seeing social phenomena where social actors and artifacts are *interdependent* (Carrington & Scott, 2014). Conventional research orientations assume social entities—people, organizations—are independent and emphasize their attributes, but network research recognizes that the patterns of interactions, whether direct or indirect, are consequential and create connections. The assumption of interdependence is core to unpacking the method myth.

For example, a conventional approach to stakeholder engagement focuses on individuals' attributes like social media dependency, which may be an engagement antecedent. The network perspective directs attention to stakeholders' interactions and their attributes. They may connect to others through everyday conversations or to organizations on social media (Saffer, Yang, & Qu, 2019). Network research accounts for such connections and assumes they are consequential for producing antecedents like the norms of engaging online. This is what Qu and colleagues (2021, in press) found: stakeholders' social media dependencies and their connections to others amplified online engagement behaviors.

Network theory further dispels the method myth. To clarify, network theory is a collection of ideas proposing the "processes and mechanisms that relate network properties to outcomes of interest" (Borgatti & Lopez-Kidwell, 2014, p. 40). Theories under the umbrella of "network theory" continue the focus on the interactions and interdependencies among social entities and artifacts to consider antecedents and outcomes of connections. These theories come in two forms: theory of networks and network theory.

A theory of networks puts a network property like the density of network or centralities of nodes as the dependent variable and the theorizing focuses on the antecedents to a network phenomenon (Borgatti & Halgin, 2011). A public relations theory of networks research would ask what organizational attributes or circumstances led those organizations to unique network positions. For instance, Sommerfeldt (2013) found that organizational importance was positively associated with an organization's centrality. As another example, Yang and Ji (2019) used legitimacy theory to predict cross-sector tie formation.

Network theory, on the other hand, puts a network property as the independent variable and theorizes an outcome (Borgatti & Lopez-Kidwell, 2014). Familiar examples include the strength of weak ties theory (Granovetter, 1973), which asserts that one's ties influence access to redundant or novel information, and structural holes theory (Burt, 1992), which suggests that bridging unconnected parts of networks yields influence. Public relations scholars have used Burt's theory to identify advantageously positioned organizations that reap some consequence (Kent et al., 2016; Saffer et al., 2013; Yang, 2013). Scholars have also used network theory to expand stakeholder influence theory like Yang et al. (2018), who found that stakeholder activists' network positions are a strong predictor of how companies responded to their demands.

By dispelling the method myth, readers can approach public relations problems with an eye toward the interdependencies among and between the parts of public relations. Seeing these interdependencies is the first step, and making sense of it with network theories is the second step. Yet, it should be made clearer how network researchers view the field.

Clarifying the Network View of the Field

When a research approach is introduced to a field—some might call it a new paradigm—scholars and students come to know it by how it is used and what questions it addresses. This is true for our field and the network perspective (Kent et al., 2016). Network researchers in public relations have drawn from adjacent fields, mostly organizational communication, to guide their research questions. Those less familiar with the perspective perceive that it is situated at the meso-level, given the unit of observation is often organizations. Understandably, then, the relevance of network research to the many parts of public relations is questioned.

As readers may know, public relations research tends to gravitate toward functional or cocreational approaches (Botan & Taylor, 2004). The functional approach "regards communication as mere information dissemination and considers publics as consumers of organizations' messages," while a cocreational approach sees it as the negotiation of relationships and meaning among communicators (Saffer, 2018, p. 285). Network researchers have gravitated toward the latter, given its ontological and axiological alignment (Yang & Saffer, 2019), and they have found civil society networks as appropriate sites for investigations (Saffer, 2016; Sommerfeldt, 2013; Yang & Taylor, 2010). Still, network research can inform the functional approach's focus on "techniques and production of strategic organizational messages" (Botan & Taylor, 2004, p. 651). Scholars have investigated techniques such as promoting messages on social media—like Himelboim et al. (2014), who showed that a network approach can identify "social mediators" on Twitter that are best positioned to help promote messages. Rim et al. (2020) turned attention to publics' responses to organizational messages to understand the ways they organize online. Others have looked at the connections in the production of communication content like Miño and Saffer's (2021) network analysis of public relations agencies and clients' connections.

Beyond these approaches, greater clarity of how network research views the field emerges when we consider the parts of public relations. As Zhou (2019) noted, when the organization is the primary unit of observation, the analysis often ignores publics' connections to organizations and other publics (Heath, 2013). Similarly, few studies have examined the interdependencies among and between issues, messages, and relationships. Public relations is best understood as more than the sum of its parts, and a network perspective can reveal this.

Public relations scholars have asserted that organizations are interdependent in their reliance on others for information and resources (Yang & Taylor, 2015), attention (Yang & Saffer, 2021), engagement (Saffer, Yang, Morehouse, & Qu, 2019), and amplification of messages (Himelboim et al., 2014). There are interdependencies between organizations and publics as well. Organizations rely on publics to consume products/services or perceive an image or relationship. Vice versa, publics rely on organizations to address economic, social, and political needs. Interdependencies exist among publics when they create coalitions or carry out collective actions (Rim et al., 2020). Issues are no exception either; they become connected via issue stakeholders such as organizations and publics (Saffer, 2019; Sommerfeldt & Yang, 2017). Even dimensions of relationships are interdependent or multiplexed. An affinity relation like cooperation or trust may affect or be affected by a flow relation such as information exchange (Saffer et al., 2021). Theorizing and analyzing the interdependence of the parts of public relations offers greater depth of knowledge about phenomena and explanatory power of factors influencing public relations outcomes.

Naming some of the interdependencies among and between the parts shows how network approaches can (and have) viewed the field. While past studies have focused on organizations, evidence is emerging about the interdependencies *among* publics, issues, and relationships. More investigations considering the connections *between* parts are needed. A study looking at how messages are interdependent between organizations and publics could produce a greater understanding of how advocacy organizations' issue promotions connect them to groups with similar messages or publics, how issues evolve, or even how a public engages with issues or organizations. Investigations that go across the micro, meso, and macro levels will move public relations scholarship closer to realizing the full potential from the network perspective. At the same time, it can balance the applied contribution of network research, which we discuss next.

Balancing the View of Applied Contributions

Applied contributions from network research have been lacking. In part, scholars' unclear orientations to the field have limited how findings can inform traditional public relations practice. That being recognized, the broadest—and possibly the most overlooked—contribution of network research is the overview effect. Much like the cognitive shift that astronauts have after viewing Earth from space, which invokes an "uncanny sense of understanding the "big picture," and of feeling connected to and yet bigger than the intricate processes bubbling on Earth" (De Luce, 2016, para 3), practitioners can see their organizations situated in webs of relationships with network graphs known formally as sociograms or colloquially as network maps. These are powerful heuristics for practitioners comprehending the ways their professional roles, functions, and abilities have impacts beyond day-to-day outputs or working with stakeholder groups.

Moving to the nuanced contributions of network research, it is first necessary to recognize that initial network studies in public relations extended OPR research and took interest in practitioners' boundary spanning roles, relationship building functions, and abilities to facilitate discourse among various types of actors, which are often outside mainstream public relations scholarship. Even the sites of these early studies—civil society networks—were uncommon. Nonetheless, they recommend how organizations can strategically position themselves in a network.

Using common research language, we can see the network and organizations' positions as dependent variables and the relationship-building strategies or other functions enacted as the independent variables (Yang & Taylor, 2015). And recognizing that practitioners have a host of relationship-building strategies they can enact depending on their objectives, the network literature suggests practitioners can improve an organization's relationship quality with certain partners by positioning the organization at a point of influence. Sommerfeldt and Taylor (2011) recommended that through boundary-spanning roles practitioners are best positioned to "facilitate the exchange of resources between the organization and the environment" (p. 199). Likewise, Sommerfeldt (2013) suggested that an awareness of one's network position can strengthen organizations' relationship qualities and increase their influence by brokering unconnected network regions. Yang and Taylor (2015) recommended practitioners focus on weak-tie strategies should an organization seek to have a greater reach across a network or diversity of ties or use strong-tie strategies if it needs greater network centrality and embeddedness. Other works position practitioners as facilitators of discourse, like Saffer (2016, 2019), who suggested they recognize partners on the network periphery and engage them should the social capital or sustainability of the network be a concern for core network members.

Other studies make recommendations more in line with traditional or mainstream functions like garnering media coverage or engagement online. Albishri and colleagues' (2019) study of a foreign government's public relations efforts to influence U.S. media coverage found that while the foreign government's information subsidies struggled to *independently* transfer the salience of objects and their attributes (first and second levels of agenda building), the co-occurrence of objects and their attributes (third or network level of agenda building) were influential. Their results direct practitioners to strategically situate objects and attributes to co-occur in information subsidies and evaluate the *interdependence* of elements.

In a series of our own studies, we demonstrated how network studies can inform media relations and social media functions. Our first study questioned whether organizations' network positions associated with their media coverage or public engagement (Yang & Saffer, 2018). We found that central organizations had more mentions online but had little impact on organizations' earned media. In our subsequent studies we classified organizations as having two types of network signatures: star or village (Saffer, Yang, Morehouse, & Qu, 2019). The results direct practitioners to enact strategies for building a star signature with a far-reaching network online if they seek to have their content amplified or be mentioned more by others. Or, if a practitioner's client has a limited network size, they can work strategically to build relationships with well-connected organizations and their partners to form a "village," which can help amplify content on social media. More recently, we found that network signatures interact with communication network structures (core-periphery), reiterating that practitioners must use network tools to reveal the structures they are communicating and engaging within to select appropriate relationship building or engagement strategies (Yang & Saffer, 2021).

Another contribution that emerged from the wedding of OPR and the network perspective attempted to answer, "What comes from networks?" Or, to put it more squarely with public relations research, "What comes from OPR?" Social capital is one such outcome. The research supporting this assertion captures the most significant conceptual advances of the network perspective to public relations theory, and it still holds much potential to advance endeavors within public relations research and practice to address the pressing issues societies face.

Social Capital

Social capital, in lay terms, describes the value of relationships. Or, as Coleman (1990) put it, social capital "is not a single entity, but a variety of different entities having two characteristics in common: they all consist of some aspect of a social structure and they facilitate certain actions of individuals who are within the structure" (p. 302). Sociologists and political scientists have used the concept to study implications of social relations at the micro level among individuals (Burt, 1992), the impacts of relations among organizations at the meso level (Nahapiet & Ghoshal, 1998), and how societal trends at the macro level can be explained by social capital or lack thereof (Fukuyama, 1995; Putnam, 1995). These works assert that social capital emerges from trust and shared norms, within dense networks of relationships, and through brokering information and resources.

Social capital has been situated as a "natural extension of public relations scholarship because of the theoretical emphasis practitioners and scholars have placed on measuring the value of intangible (e.g., relationships, reputation, trust) and tangible (e.g., financial profitability) outcomes of public relations activities" (Dodd et al., 2015, p. 473). Connecting to a specific line of research, Sommerfeldt (2013) contends that "the OPR and relationship management literature has recognized relationships as analogous to social capital in all but name" (p. 3). Others have used the concept, namely Bourdieu's (1986), to critique those afforded power from their resources, and subsequent social relations accrued (Ihlen, 2005). Despite the work to position social capital as a key concept in the field's lexicon, the notion of social capital remains murky.

To clarify, public relations scholars have proposed field-specific definitions. One early definition stated that social capital is "the ability that organizations have of creating, maintaining and using relationships to achieve desirable organizational goals" (Kennan & Hazleton, 2006, p. 322). Yet, social capital does not belong to a single entity, nor should it be regarded as a means to achieve organizational goals (Saffer, 2016). Social capital is "a relational resource that can emerge as communicators negotiate relationships and meanings that establishes norms, builds trust, and positions communicators to facilitate the exchange and mixing of resources and information within and across networks" (Saffer, 2019, p. 283). Such conceptualization remains methodologically agnostic yet applicable across levels of analysis and areas of research.

The three dimensions of social capital—structural, relational, and communication—further explicate the concept (cf. Kennan & Hazleton, 2006). The structural dimension captures the patterns of relationships that range from being dense to sparse (Saffer, 2019) and is rooted in Coleman's (1990) proposition that social capital emerges from well-connected networks where members hold others accountable. The relational dimension turns the attention toward the relationship quality, trust, and shared norms of social relations (Sommerfeldt, 2013; Saffer, 2016). Finally, the communication dimension considers the means through which social entities exchange information and resources and how they may produce shared meaning (Kennan & Hazleton, 2006; Saffer, 2016). Network researchers have used these dimensions to investigate the ways network structures (Saffer, 2019; Yang & Taylor, 2015), relational elements (Sommerfeldt, 2013), social actors' resources (Sommerfeldt & Taylor, 2011), and the symbolic mechanisms of communicative relations (Saffer, 2019; Taylor, 2011) affect social capital.

The advancements that social capital research has made in public relations scholarship are most pronounced when juxtaposed with OPR. As reviewed earlier, decades of scholarship theorized and empirically investigated the relationship between organizations and their publics. The ensuing knowledge "positioned relationships as a bellwether of organizational success or failure" (Sommerfeldt, 2013, p. 3). In essence, relationships were cast as means to organizational ends. Social capital theory does not dispute that those relationships are beneficial or detrimental; rather, it asserts that there are benefits and detriments to a collective that derive from networks. This moves public relations scholarship to put social capital as an outcome of relationships or even more as an end to public relations goals.

Moving forward, the social capital literature in the field needs to consider the ways social capital is an antecedent to key concepts. Take for instance

Heath's (2013) fully functioning society theory of public relations that asserts "for organizations to be successful they need to contribute to society, its dialogue quality, its sense of community, the quality of its structures and functions for collaborative decision making, the cocreation of meaning, and the alignment of interests" (2013, p. 368). For many of these elements to occur there must be social capital. Unfortunately, many researchers outside public relations have produced evidence suggesting that social capital is depleted in many countries after years of a global pandemic, political and social unrest, and overdue racial reckonings. If public relations researchers can begin to see social capital as an antecedent to crucial public relations functions in society, we can begin to understand how issues societies face like the erosion of trust in institutions, social isolation, disinformation, and systemic racism are topics public relations scholars must address and how they can do so in a comprehensive manner with network tools.

Advancing the Network Perspective

As much as network research has advanced over the past two decades, there are many more ways network approaches can contribute to our knowledge and theorizing about public relations processes, outputs, and outcomes. We identify two areas of research—issues management and OPR—that have important trends and budding lines of inquiry we believe are promising areas to further advance the network perspective. In addition, we review the gaps in the network perspective and offer insights for filling those gaps.

Promising Areas of Continued Advancement

Scholars have applied the network perspective to a wide range of topics like issues advocacy and management, CSR, crisis communication and management, public diplomacy, and public relations ethics, just to name a few. Among the areas of research, issues management and OPR are avenues for advancing the network perspective.

Issues Management

Issues management and advocacy is an important area of research into which the network perspective could provide valuable insights and methodological tools (Sommerfeldt & Yang, 2017). Issues evolve through various social networks both online and offline. The network perspective reveals the power of issue operatives' network and identifies important issue operatives. Sommerfeldt and Yang (2017), for instance, developed a theoretical model to explain the type of relationship-building strategies that social movement organizations need to adopt to successfully manage issues to achieve favorable policy outcomes. In another study, Rim et al. (2020) closely examined the network structures that emerged around boycotts of Starbucks and Budweiser when they responded to Trump's immigration ban. This study revealed strikingly different network structures among different issue operatives. More recently, Madden et al. (2021) used network analysis to identify key issue operatives in a university sexual assault prevention program and illustrated the issue-operatives' functions within social networks.

One common characteristic of contemporary issues-management studies guided by the network perspective is the shift away from organizations and toward issues and publics. Unlike early public relations research, when scholars examined issues management the focus was overwhelmingly centered on organizations and what strategies they could take to bend issues in their favor. Conversely, network studies ask what powers issue operatives have, what roles do they play in networks, and how can networks further empower them. Frameworks like the multi-stakeholder issue network perspective (cf. Saffer, 2019; Saffer et al., 2018; Sun et al., 2021) position organizations and publics as stakeholders to issues rather than each other. We argue that this change in research focus helps to diversify public relations research and move the field toward a more ethical direction that empowers publics and causes of social justice.

The emerging lines of inquiry within the issues-management literature about publics is ripe for continued advancement. As the studies mentioned earlier suggest, publics are now capable of publicly expressing their stances on issues in ways prior theorizing and research had not considered. At the same time, these publics have the means to connect with others who they may otherwise not have formed a relationship with. Many network researchers have correctly approached the phenomenon in ways that highlight the interdependencies and have conveniently accessed publics' communications and connections from Twitter and other platforms. The important theory questions now should center on the boundary of organizations and permeable public networks that are involved in issues, the mechanism of public networks in issue evolution, and how organizations could secure advantageous network positions in temporally changing issue networks. These theoretical questions could lead public relations scholars to redefine assumptions in issues management and open new frontiers of research.

Organization-Public Relationships

OPR is another area of research that still holds much promise for the advancement of network research. By this point, readers should hopefully be familiar with the lineage of network research and know that it was a natural extension of OPR approaches (Sommerfeldt, 2013; Yang & Taylor, 2015). But unpacking OPR research a bit further is warranted to show ways network research can continue improving our knowledge about relationships.

Traditional OPR research tends to focus on stakeholders' perceived relationship quality with an organization. Relationship qualities are difficult to assess through observational data and usually require the use of surveys, which often have a relatively small scope and may not actually gather insights from a specific organization's key publics (i.e., MTurk panels). More problematic than the data sources is the view that publics are isolated entities. We know very little about the connections among publics or with other organizations and how such interdependencies affect publics' relationships with organizations.

Recognizing these limitations, some have applied the network perspective to OPR research. Yang and Taylor (2015) proposed a theoretical model to systematically identify strategies for building relationships with publics depending on organizational goals and resources. Studies further applied the network perspective to examine organizations' relationships with strategic partners both online and offline. For example, Yang and Ji (2019) examined factors that drive the formation of cross-sector alliances on Facebook and revealed that social legitimacy and alliance legitimacy powerfully influence organizations' alliance choices.

Network studies could also reveal how elements of OPR shape network structures and how such relationships condition organizations' relationships with publics and vice versa. Those interested in investigating the elements of OPR could draw on work from organizational communication that differentiates between types of relations (affinity, flow, semantic, and representational) (Shumate & Contractor, 2013). Contemporary network research in public relations tends to assume relationships as the same type. And, where OPR research investigates perceptions of relationship qualities (e.g., trust or cooperation), network approaches transform these qualities from an attribute of a social actor into a relationship dimension. Network analysis treats multiple dimensions of relationships as unique relations. For instance, there can be trust relations, information exchange relations, or communication value relations. Investigating these dimensions or unique types of relations can offer a more nuanced understanding of what drives relationships formation among publics, groups, or organizations.

Gaps in the Network Perspective

The growing body of network research has gaps that could be closed through further work. More theoretical development around network concepts and public relations practice is needed. In the studies that we reviewed, the prominent approach merely applied social network methods or concepts to the field of public relations, rather than making substantial theoretical developments that extend or build new theoretical frameworks that draw from network and public relations research. We believe the lack of substantial theoretical development may limit the value of the network perspective in the field of public relations. We call on researchers to take up the conceptual labor of developing network theories like a network theory of situational crisis communication or a theory of civil society networks.

In fact, the network perspective provides many opportunities for theory development in the field of public relations. After all, public relations has a wealth of knowledge about relationship building and management, and it is consistent with the core of research in the field of network science. There is so much value that both fields could benefit from each other. Both public relations practice and social networks are complex and multifaceted. As Monge and Contractor (2003) have pointed out in their book on communication network theory, social networks are inherently multiplex and multi-level, and they could accommodate the research of communication processes that sprang a wide range.

Applying this idea to the field of public relations may offer us opportunities to remove the silos between subfields of public relations (e.g., CSR, crisis communication) and instead to develop theories and research designs that take a holistic approach to understanding the complex communication processes in public relations practice. For example, imagine there is a CSR campaign that has gone wrong and triggered both backlash and public support. What is involved in this process are companies' positions on CSR issues, broader social movement related to the issue, publics' previous relationships with this company, and questions about how this crisis influences different publics' positions. With so much complexity, any subfields of public relations—be that OPR, CSR, crisis, or social movement research—could not fully explain the case. Such relationships may have longitudinal dimensions and involve actors at different levels of analysis. A network perspective offers, in cases like this, the opportunity to consider multiplex relationships at multiple levels.

Armed with a network perspective, researchers can identify the ties among and between publics, organizations, issues, and messages. The network perspective thus provides researchers with the freedom to zoom in and out and look at many different aspects of the complex communication process without segmenting it into isolated components. This way of thinking allows us to develop research and theory that are no longer segmented into artificial subfield boundaries, but rather a more holistic approach that looks at the complexity facing public relations practitioners and offers solutions or suggestions that reflect such complexity.

Concluding Thoughts

Public relations scholarship, with the stated intention of informing the profession, often reflects the most pressing issues in the field. When the most central question was "What value does public relations provide to an organization's bottom line?", scholars responded with investigations about "excellent" public relations programs and frameworks for measuring organizations' relationships with publics. They used the tools available to them to address those issues. While some continue to use these tools and seem tethered to outdated questions and definitions of public relations, there are new tools, burning questions, and new ways of seeing public relations available with the network perspective. The network perspective offers our field the capacity to consider what value the profession can provide to publics and societies.

Scholars and practitioners need to see public relations through a lens that appreciates multiple parts of public relations and can capture the interdependence of those parts. The network perspective is the most robust and versatile approach available to scholars and students. We hope you will join us in taking up this way of conceptualizing public relations phenomena, theorizing about interdependencies, and analyzing connections among social actors and the artifacts they produce.

References

Albishri, O., Tarasevich, S., Proverbs, P., Kiousis, S. K., & Alahmari, A. (2019). Mediated public diplomacy in the digital age: Exploring the Saudi and the U.S. governments' agenda-building during Trump's visit to the Middle East. *Public Relations Review*, *45*(4), 101820. https://doi.org/10.1016/j.pubrev.2019.101820

Borgatti, S. P., & Halgin, D. S. (2011). On network theory. *Organization Science*, *22*(5), 1168–1181.

Borgatti, S. P., & Lopez-Kidwell, V. (2014). Network theory. In J. Scott & P. J. Carrington (Eds.), *The Sage handbook of social network analysis* (pp. 40–54). Sage. www.doi.org/10.4135/9781446294413.n4

Borgatti, S. P., Mehra, A., Brass, D. J., & Labianca, G. (2009). Network analysis in the social sciences. *Science*, *323*(5916), 892–895. https://doi.org/10.1126/science.1165821

Botan, C. H., & Taylor, M. (2004). Public relations: State of the field. *Journal of Communication*, *54*(4), 645–661. https://doi.org/10.1111/j.1460-2466.2004.tb02649.x

Bourdieu, P. (1986). The forms of capital. In J. Richardson (Ed.), *Handbook of theory and research for the sociology of education* (pp. 241–258). Greenwood.

Broom, G. M., Casey, S., & Ritchey, J. (1997). Toward a concept and theory of organization-public relationships. *Journal of Public Relations Research*, *9*(2), 83–98. https://doi.org/10.1207/s1532754xjprr0902_01

Burt, R. S. (1992). *Structural holes*. Harvard University Press.

Carrington, P., & Scott, J. (2014). Introduction. In J. Scott & P. J. Carrington (Eds.), *The Sage handbook of social network analysis* (pp. 1–8). Sage.

Castells, M. (2009). *Communication power*. Oxford University Press.

Coleman, J. S. (1990). *Foundations of social theory*. Harvard University Press.

De Luce, I. (2016). Profound things happen when astronauts first see earth from space. *Business Insider*. https://www.businessinsider.com/overview-effect-nasa-apollo8-perspective-awareness-space-2015-8

Dodd, M. D., Brummette, J., & Hazleton, V. (2015). A social capital approach: An examination of Putnam's civic engagement and public relations roles. *Public Relations Review*, *41*(4), 472–479. https://doi.org/10.1016/j.pubrev.2015.05.001

Ferguson, M. A. (1984, August). *Building theory in public relations: Interorganizational relationships as a public relations paradigm*. Paper presented to the annual conference of the Association for Education in Journalism and Mass Communication.

Fu, J. S., & Li, Y. (2019). The institutional antecedent to firms' interorganizational network portfolios: Evidence from China. *Public Relations Review*, *45*(4), 101776. https://doi.org/10.1016/j.pubrev.2019.04.009

Fukuyama, F. (1995). *Trust: The social virtues and the creation of prosperity*. Free Press.

Granovetter, M. S. (1973). The strength of weak ties. *American Journal of Sociology, 78*(6), 1360–1380.

Heath, R. L. (2013). Fully functioning society theory. In *Encyclopedia of public relations* (Vol. 1, pp. 369–371). Sage. www.doi.org/10.4135/9781452276236.n207

Himelboim, I., Golan, G. J., Moon, B. B., & Suto, R. J. (2014). A social networks approach to public relations on Twitter: Social mediators and mediated public relations. *Journal of Public Relations Research, 26*(4), 359–379. https://doi.org/10.1080/10 62726x.2014.908724

Ihlen, Ø. (2005). The power of social capital: Adapting Bourdieu to the study of public relations. *Public Relations Review, 31*(4), 492–496. https://doi.org/10.1016/j. pubrev.2005.08.007

Jang, H.-Y. (1998). Cultural differences in an interorganizational network: Shared public relations firms among Japanese and American companies. *Public Relations Review, 23*(4), 327–341. https://doi.org/10.1016/s0363-8111(97)90049-7

Kennan, W. R., & Hazleton, V. (2006). Internal public relations, social capital, and the role of effective organizational communication. In C. H. Botan & V. Hazleton (Eds.), *Public relations theory II* (pp. 311–338). Lawrence Erlbaum Associates.

Kent, M. L., Sommerfeldt, E. J., & Saffer, A. J. (2016). Social network analysis, power, and public relations: Tertius iungens as a cocreational approach to studying relationship networks. *Public Relations Review, 42*(1), 91–100. https://doi.org/10.1016/j. pubrev.2015.08.002

Ledingham, J. A. (2003). Explicating relationship management as a general theory of public relations. *Journal of Public Relations Research, 15*(2), 181–198.

Ledingham, J. A., & Bruning, S. D. (1998). Relationship management in public relations: Dimensions of an organization–public relationship. *Public Relations Review, 24*(1), 55–65.

Madden, S., Haught, M. J., & James, A. (2021). Key issue operatives in an issue-driven network: Public relations as a "pocket of strength" in campus sexual assault awareness and prevention. *Public Relations Review, 47*(5), 102114.

Miño, P., & Saffer, A. J. (2021). Networks of international public relations efforts: The case of Latin American organizations' connections to U.S. agents. *Public Relations Review, 47*(4), 102054. https://doi.org/10.1016/j.pubrev.2021.102054

Monge, P. R., & Contractor, N. (2003). *Theories of communication networks*. Oxford University Press.

Nahapiet, J., & Ghoshal, S. (1998). Social capital, intellectual capital, and the organizational advantage. *Academy of Management Review, 23*(2), 242–266.

O'Connor, A., & Shumate, M. (2018). A multidimensional network approach to strategic communication. *International Journal of Strategic Communication, 12*(4), 399–416.

Putnam, R. D. (1995). Bowling alone: America's declining social capital. *Journal of Democracy, 6*(1), 65–78.

Qu, Y., Saffer, A. J., & Riffe, D. (2021, in press). Revealing the social network influences on consumer engagement. *Corporate Communications: An International Journal*. https:// doi.org/10.1108/ccij-04-2021-0046

Raupp, J. (2019). Crisis communication in the rhetorical arena. *Public Relations Review, 45*(4), 101768. https://doi.org/10.1016/j.pubrev.2019.04.002

Rim, H., Lee, Y., & Yoo, S. (2020). Polarized public opinion responding to corporate social advocacy: Social network analysis of boycotters and advocators. *Public Relations Review, 46*(2), 101869.

Saffer, A. J. (2016). A message-focused measurement of the communication dimension of social capital: Revealing shared meaning in a network of relationships. *Journal of Public Relations Research*, *28*(3–4), 170–192. https://doi.org/10.1080/1062726X.2016.1228065

Saffer, A. J. (2018). The outcomes of engagement in activism networks: A co-creational approach. In K. Johnston & M. Taylor (Eds.), *The handbook of communication engagement* (pp. 285–300). John Wiley & Sons.

Saffer, A. J. (2019). Fostering social capital in an international multi-stakeholder issue network. *Public Relations Review*, *45*(2), 282–296. https://doi.org/10.1016/j.pubrev.2019.02.004

Saffer, A. J., Pilny, A., & Sommerfeldt, E. J. (2021). What influences relationship formation in a global civil society network? An examination of valued multiplex relations. *Communication Research*. https://doi.org/10.1177/00936502211016162

Saffer, A. J., Taylor, M., & Yang, A. (2013). Political public relations in advocacy: Building online influence and social capital. *Public Relations Journal*, *7*(4), 1–35.

Saffer, A. J., Yang, A., Morehouse, J., & Qu, Y. (2019). It takes a village: A social network approach to NGOs' international public engagement. *American Behavioral Scientist*, *63*(12), 1708–1727. https://doi.org/10.1177/0002764219835265

Saffer, A. J., Yang, A., & Qu, Y. (2019). Talking politics and engaging in activism: The influence of publics' social networks on corporations in the public sphere. *Journal of Broadcasting & Electronic Media*, *63*(3), 534–565. https://doi.org/10.1080/08838151.2019.1660130

Saffer, A. J., Yang, A., & Taylor, M. (2018). Reconsidering power in multistakeholder relationship management. *Management Communication Quarterly*, *32*(1), 121–139. https://doi.org/10.1177/0893318917700510

Shumate, M., & Contractor, N. (2013). Emergence of multidimensional social networks. In L. L. Putnam & D. K. Mumby (Eds.), *The Sage handbook of organizational communication* (pp. 449–474). Sage.

Sommerfeldt, E. J. (2013). Networks of social capital: Extending a public relations model of civil society in Peru. *Public Relations Review*, *39*(1), 1–12. https://doi.org/10.1016/j.pubrev.2012.08.005

Sommerfeldt, E. J., & Kent, M. L. (2015). Civil society, networks, and relationship management: Beyond the organization–public dyad. *International Journal of Strategic Communication*, *9*(3), 235–252. https://doi.org/10.1080/1553118x.2015.1025405

Sommerfeldt, E. J., & Taylor, M. (2011). A social capital approach to improving public relations' efficacy: Diagnosing internal constraints on external communication. *Public Relations Review*, *37*(3), 197–206. https://doi.org/10.1016/j.pubrev.2011.03.007

Sommerfeldt, E. J., & Yang, A. (2017). Relationship networks as strategic issues management: An issue-stage framework of social movement organization network strategies. *Public Relations Review*, *43*(4), 829–839. https://doi.org/10.1016/j.pubrev.2017.06.012

Sun, J., Yang, A., & Saffer, A. J. (2021). Evolving crisis and changing networks: NGOs' stakeholder engagement on the global refugee crisis. *Nonprofit and Voluntary Sector Quarterly*. https://doi.org/10.1177/08997640211057407

Taylor, M. (2011). Building social capital through rhetoric and public relations. *Management Communication Quarterly*, *25*(3), 436–454. https://doi.org/10.1177/0893318911410

Taylor, M., & Doerfel, M. L. (2005). Another dimension to explicating relationships: Measuring inter-organizational linkages. *Public Relations Review*, *31*(1), 121–129.

Van Dijk, J. (2012). *The network society*. Sage.

Wellman, B. (1988). Structural analysis: From method and metaphor to theory and substance. In B. Wellman, S. D. Berkowitz, & M. Granovetter (Eds.), *Social structures: A network approach* (pp. 19–61). Cambridge University Press.

Yang, A. (2013). When transnational civil network meets local context: An exploratory hyperlink network analysis of Northern/Southern NGOs' virtual network in China. *Journal of International and Intercultural Communication, 6*(1), 40–60. https://doi.org/10.1080/17513057.2012.719632

Yang, A., & Ji, Y. G. (2019). The quest for legitimacy and the communication of strategic cross-sectoral partnership on Facebook: A big data study. *Public Relations Review, 45*(5), 101839. https://doi.org/10.1016/j.pubrev.2019.101839

Yang, A., & Saffer, A. J. (2018). NGOs' advocacy in the 2015 refugee crisis: A study of agenda building in the digital age. *American Behavioral Scientist, 62*(4), 421–439. https://doi.org/10.1177/0002764218759578

Yang, A., & Saffer, A. J. (2019). Embracing a network perspective in the network society: The dawn of a new paradigm in strategic public relations. *Public Relations Review, 45*(4), 101843. https://doi.org/10.1016/j.pubrev.2019.101843

Yang, A., & Saffer, A. J. (2021). Standing out in a networked communication context: Toward a network contingency model of public attention. *New Media & Society, 23*(10), 2902–2925. https://doi.org/10.1177/1461444820939445

Yang, A., & Taylor, M. (2010). Relationship-building by Chinese ENGOs' websites: Education, not activation. *Public Relations Review, 36*(4), 342–351. https://doi.org/10.1016/j.pubrev.2010.07.001

Yang, A., Uysal, N., & Taylor, M. (2018). Unleashing the power of networks: Shareholder activism, sustainable development and corporate environmental policy. *Business Strategy and the Environment, 27*(6), 712–727. https://doi.org/10.1002/bse.2026

You, L., & Hon, L. (2019). How social ties contribute to collective actions on social media: A social capital approach. *Public Relations Review, 45*(4), 101771. https://doi.org/10.1016/j.pubrev.2019.04.005

Zhou, A. (2019). Bring publics back into networked public relations research: A dual-projection approach for network ecology. *Public Relations Review, 45*(4), 101772. https://doi.org/10.1016/j.pubrev.2019.03.004

7 Development of Intercultural Public Relations Theory

Lan Ni and Bey-Ling Sha

Introduction

Culture is intrinsic to human nature. Despite the presumed "objectivity" of most theories developed within any given culture, scholars of human behavior—including those of us in public relations—cannot continue to treat theory as culture-free or to develop theories with no self-awareness as to the cultures embedded in them. All theories of how humans behave are implicitly grounded in cultural understanding.

For this reason, intercultural public relations foregrounds the role of culture to offer a general theory at the intersection of culture and public relations while making explicitly visible the historically implicit and often invisible influences of culture on the management of relationships between organizations and publics. In sum, intercultural public relations theory explains and predicts the influence of culture, cultural identity, and cultural values on public relations, with particular focus on the segmentation of publics and the management of relationships and conflicts.

The chapter traces the original development of intercultural public relations theory, explains why it's needed, and articulates its foundational assumptions. Then the chapter outlines the scope of research in intercultural public relations theory, which to date has centered primarily on the identification of organizational publics, the management of intercultural organization-public relationships, and the management of organization-public conflicts, this latter largely by permitting the empowerment of the marginalized. The chapter concludes with research directions that the authors believe should be pursued in the furthering of theory in intercultural public relations.

Genesis and Assumptions of Intercultural Public Relations Theory

Just as considerations of the variable of national culture[1] by non-U.S. graduate students (e.g., Sriramesh, 1991) studying with professors in the United States led to increased scholarly examination of that variable in research on international or global public relations (e.g., Culbertson & Chen, 1996;

DOI: 10.4324/9781003141396-8

Grunig et al., 1995), graduate student interest in intercultural communication and cultural identity led to the development of a theory of intercultural public relations (cf. Ni, 2006; Sha, 1995; Wang, 2006).

Culture is generally defined as "the collective mental programming of the mind that distinguishes the members of one group or category of people from others" (Hofstede & Hofstede, 2005, p. 4). First articulated by Sha (1995), the then-emerging theory of intercultural public relations highlighted the importance of cultural identity. Specifically, Sha (1995) examined identity salience and identity avowal to define *intercultural public relations* as "a special case of public relations in which the salient cultural identity avowed by the organization differs from the salient cultural identity avowed by the public" (Sha, 2006, p. 54; cf. Sha, 1995). Broadly speaking, *identity* is defined as how we see ourselves (avowed identities) and how others see us (ascribed identities) (cf. Sha, 1995, 2006).

Originally developed as "an attempt to explain and account for the influence of cultural identity on the public relations behaviors of organizations and their publics" (Sha, 2006, p. 46), intercultural public relations theory was subsequently expanded to offer a general theory of culture and public relations, adopting an *intercultural* approach. This general theory focuses on "the actual process of interaction and communication among people from different cultural backgrounds both within a country and across borders" (Ni, Wang, & Sha, 2018, p. 4), with applications at the levels of individuals, organizations, and societies. In this theory, intercultural communication research, or the study of social interactions between culturally dissimilar people or groups (cf. Oetzel, 2009), has been incorporated through initial scholarship such as Ni and Wang (2011) and Wang et al. (2014).

Why Intercultural Public Relations Theory Is Needed

Today, intercultural public relations theory remains critically relevant for several reasons. First, the continued existence of many cultures and the increasing interactions among different cultural groups facilitated by digital technologies make intercultural communication an imperative quotidian practice in contemporary societies. Public relations researchers and practitioners must not only acknowledge cultural differences, but also develop effective and ethical processes of communicating with publics both internal and external to organizations and societies.

Second, as discussed in Ni, Wang, and Sha (2018), publics and public relations practices are different not just across countries but within countries as well, with the latter becoming increasingly important as more-frequent voluntary and involuntary migration across national boundaries has increased cultural diversity within nation-state borders. Terms for cultural groups within national boundaries commonly include "minority" cultures, "majority" cultures, or "dominant" cultures; however, intercultural communication scholars prefer the label "co-cultures" (cf. Samovar et al., 2016) because this term acknowledges the reality of simultaneous membership in more than one cultural group. Therefore, although country or nation-state undoubtedly constitutes an important aspect of cultural differences, the concept of culture entails much more than the one that spans national boundaries.

Third, traditional research on culture has focused on how organizations can best understand culture and cultural processes when interacting with culturally different publics. Thus, intercultural public relations theory has emphasized the need to enhance skills-based and behavior-based competencies of individuals and organizations in intercultural settings. This focus on how to enact what one knows about a certain culture serves to expand and supplement the knowledge-based competencies emphasized in previous research. For this reason, intercultural public relations theory is needed to further develop theory in multi-domain cultural competencies (Ni, Wang, & Sha, 2018).

Last and not least, intercultural interactions happen between two or more parties, all of which need to adapt and adjust to the intercultural setting or nature of the interaction. For these reasons, intercultural public relations theory has incorporated anxiety and uncertainty management theory (cf. Gudykunst, 2005) and cross-cultural adaptation theory (cf. Kim, 2005). The bottom line is that research needs to examine not only how organizations can best practice public relations in intercultural settings but also how publics (especially marginalized publics) can best adapt and empower themselves (cf. Ni, Wang, & Sha, 2018).

What Intercultural Public Relations Theory Assumes

This section articulates the conceptual assumptions undergirding intercultural public relations theory, as well as how some of these assumptions have been developed, challenged, or adapted. These assumptions pertain to the scope of public relations, the scope of culture, and the ways in which public relations and culture intersect.

Public Relations Can and Should Be Managed

First, our view of public relations builds upon the *behavioral, strategic management approach to public relations* (e.g., L. A. Grunig et al., 2002; Kim & Ni, 2013), which is grounded in the notion that relationships between organizations and publics should be strategically managed (see also Broom & Sha, 2013; Crable & Vibbert, 1986; Cutlip & Center, 1952; Grunig & Hunt, 1984). The basic premises of this approach are as follows: the public relations function should be structured and practiced to help achieve organizational effectiveness and contribute to societal interest. To do that, public relations needs to participate in the strategic management of an organization, as opposed to merely practicing at a technical level. Specifically, public relations practitioners should scan or monitor the organizational environment, analyze relevant trends and issues, identify important publics, and work with them in relationship building and, if needed, conflict management, to reach goals important to both the organization and its publics. Furthermore, public relations should provide counsel on internal organizational behaviors, not just organizational communications.

In developing intercultural public relations theory, Ni, Wang, and Sha (2018) modified some assumptions of the behavioral, strategic management approach to public relations. Specifically, while *organizations* tend to be the focal point in the management approach to public relations, intercultural public relations theory takes into account broad *issues* that may span different organizations, or that may not have any focal organization, and considers the development and well-being of the *community*. Thus, intercultural public relations theory pays greater attention to perspectives and interests of the public compared to traditional public relations taking the behavioral, strategic management approach.

Culture Is Multidimensional and Multilayered

The study of culture typically takes one of two approaches, emic or etic (Pike, 1967, as cited in Ni, Wang, & Sha, 2018). *Emic* research examines cultural phenomena from within, whereas *etic* research studies cultural phenomena from the outside. The problem with the imposed etic approach (cf. Berry, 1989) is that constructs and conceptual relations are identified and developed in one culture and then used in another culture directly, reflecting ethnocentric values and potentially invalidating the study due to a lack of equivalence. For this reason, the approach to culture in intercultural public relations theory is *emic*, emphasizing the importance of understanding complicated, multi-dimensional cultures *from within*. But what *is* culture?

Synthesizing the numerous definitions of culture, Ni, Wang, and Sha (2018) defined culture as follows:

> A culture is a system of meanings shared and continuously created among a specific group of people, whereby the meanings are created through symbolic social interactions and defined by an interface of dialectic symbolic elements: static and dynamic, explicit and implicit, creative and restrictive, and individual and collective.
>
> (p. 72)

Any specific group that shares and creates such a system of meanings or similar perceptions could be considered as a culture group; examples include groups based on gender, sexual orientation, religion, social economic status, country of origin, and more. Thus, culture is multi-dimensional or multi-faceted, and its influence is multi-layered.

THE MULTIPLE DIMENSIONS OF CULTURAL IDENTITY

Defined as "a person's concept of self in its entirety, which directs the person's cognitive, emotive, and behavioral manifestations" (Ni, Wang, & Sha, 2018, p. 75), identity—like culture itself—is multi-faceted. Individuals can perceive identity in multiple domains and with varying degrees of strength and salience.

First, identity involves different domains, where *personal identity* refers to one's self-perceived uniqueness and *social identity* refers to belonging to different social groups, also called *reference group orientation* (cf. Cross, 1987). This duality creates the delicate balance, and sometimes clashes, between individuals' desires to be different (from each other) and similar (with people in the same social group). In perceiving group connections, the ingroup vs. outgroup distinction is formed and negotiated, which has important implications for group dynamics and conflicts (e.g., Tajfel & Turner, 1979). Second, within the domain of social identity, people can perceive identity from different dimensions, e.g., age, gender, sexual orientation, religion, socioeconomic status, or country of origin. In short, just as culture itself involves multiple dimensions, identity (i.e., the self in relation to a cultural group) is likewise multidimensional.

Third, these dimensions of identities are dynamic cross-sectionally and longitudinally. At a given time, these dimensions may intersect with one another, forming multiple layers of identity. They can also show different levels of strength (or the "degree of importance of a particular identity" over time across situations [Oetzel, 2009, p. 59]). Across time, certain aspects of identity may be stable (core identity) or fluid (flexible and adaptive); and different aspects of identity can be salient or have varying degrees of relative importance (or different identities standing out in different situations). Finally, identity can show differences between internal avowal and external ascription. Avowed identity refers to the self-perceived identity from an individual themselves, whereas ascribed identity refers to the other-perceived identity that others assign or impose on an individual (Collier, 2003; Sha, 2006).

THE MULTIPLE LAYERS OF CULTURAL INFLUENCE

Some scholars have used an iceberg (cf. Oetzel, 2009) to illustrate the multiple layers at which cultural dimensions impact human knowledge, attitudes, and behaviors. The explicit (visible or surface) layers include various artifacts, symbols, language, and overt behaviors; less-explicit layers include meanings, beliefs, and norms; and the implicit (least-visible) layers include fundamental assumptions about the world, existence, or core values (Trompenaars & Hampden-Turner, 1998). Intercultural public relations theory is particularly concerned with this deepest layer of culture: the orientation of core cultural values.

Value orientations affect how people perceive and assign values to various aspects of existence and living (Kluckhohn & Strodtbeck, 1961). When examining fundamental cultural value orientations, some important assumptions are to be noted (e.g., Hofstede, 2001). They are summarized as follows (cf. Ni, Wang, & Sha, 2018, p. 80):

1. Cultural universals exist.
2. People's scores vary in magnitude along a value dimension.
3. Cultures can be located along a value dimension based on the group's average score.
4. Ecological fallacy should be avoided (i.e., a cultural group's average score on a dimension does not represent a cultural member's individual score).

Culture and Public Relations Are Inextricably Intertwined

Because it foregrounds the significance and relevance of culture, intercultural public relations theory assumes that culture must be an embedded component of every aspect of public relations: not only specific public relations programs, but also the overall strategic management of the public relations function. Culture cannot be treated as a separate component added to public relations programming after the fact.

Theoretically, culture variables can be important antecedents to enacting and prioritizing environmental influences in the public relations *function*. How the dominant coalition and public relations practitioners make sense of the organizational environment is heavily influenced by the wide range of social and cultural issues and trends, as well as the multi-faceted manifestations of culture as discussed earlier (i.e., identity, values, and deep-rooted assumptions) in various cultural groups. This then influences prioritizing and strategy development for the public relations function. As organizations scan the environment to identify strategic stakeholders and publics, as well as to monitor for potential conflicts, these cultural issues and groups are deeply embedded.

Furthermore, cultural influences can play a role in the strategic management of public relations *programs* themselves. This includes determining the types of public relations programs and the ultimate goals, as well as the specific objectives for each cultural public, as well as strategies and tactics to reach these publics.

Table 7.1 offers a high-level depiction of such multi-layered intersections, taken together at different levels, and the next section on research scope and theory development provides more detailed explanations.

Development and Research Scope of Intercultural Public Relations Theory

This section discusses the theory's development through the various lenses of its research scope. Recognizing that systematic theorizing was still

Table 7.1 Intercultural Public Relations: Intersecting Public Relations and Culture

Scope of Public Relations		Scope of Culture		
		Explicit	Middle	Implicit
Strategic management of public relations	Identifying/segmenting publics	Language barriers in cultural publics	Identity, lived experiences affecting situational perceptions	Core values affecting situational perceptions
	Relationship management	Translation and use of symbols	Using relationship strategies that adhere to cultural norms (e.g., family tradition)	Cultural value orientations affecting the management of relationships
	Conflict management	Inappropriate use of language or symbols as source of conflict	Identifying conflict strategies that fit cultural norms such as "face" concerns	Identifying value clashes in conflicts
Managing public relations programs	Messaging strategy/tactic	Translation; use of cultural symbols	Messaging that makes meaning to cultural groups	Messaging that appeals to core values
	Messenger choice	Speaks the same language	Shares the same identity/experiences	Shares the same values
	Communication channels	Multi-lingual channels	Channels trusted by cultural groups	Core assumptions in human relations behind the use of channels
Practitioner perspective	Intercultural competency and training	Culture-specific competency: language, traditions of diverse publics	Respecting cultural norms and beliefs	Understanding core values and assumptions of diverse publics
(Marginalized) Publics perspective	Intercultural competency, cultural adaptation, identity management	Learning new language, adapting to new communication styles	Adapting to new cultural norms and reshaping beliefs	Renegotiating core values and assumptions

Source: Ni (2022). Reproduced with permission of Routledge, New York.

lacking, Ni, Wang, and Sha (2018) developed a holistic theoretical framework and offered the following key questions as being worthy of scholarly investigation:

1. How do organizations better identify and segment publics[2] that are from different cultural backgrounds, with different identities and different values?
2. How do organizations build relationships with publics who are so culturally diverse amongst themselves and culturally different from organizations?
3. How do organizations manage conflicts interculturally?
4. How do individuals, both public relations practitioners and in publics, build and develop intercultural competency in their communication approaches and activities?
5. How do marginalized publics engage with and empower each other for social change?
6. How does society recognize and embrace cultural differences to contribute to societal cohesiveness and individual well-being?

Integrating the multi-domain and multi-level manifestations of culture with the different areas in public relations, the following key research areas are examined.

Organizational Level: Understanding Cultural Publics

Understanding and segmenting publics has long been an important function of public relations theory and practice (cf. Broom & Sha, 2013; Grunig & Hunt, 1984). Intercultural public relations examines how and to what extent our understanding of publics, their perceptions, and their communication behaviors is inherently influenced by and therefore benefits from an in-depth understanding of culture, cultural identity, and cultural values.

In developing an integrated, theory-driven framework of public segmentation, Kim, Ni, and Sha (2008) identified two main categories of approaches: situational (which focuses on dynamic or non-enduring characteristics) and cross-situational (which focuses on concepts based on more stable characteristics such as demographics). Both situational and cross-situational factors are perceived and driven by the publics themselves. In the context of intercultural public relations, cultural factors can play an important role as the cross-situational approach in affecting situational perceptions (e.g., problem recognition, involvement recognition, and constraint recognition), thereby acting as antecedents to the formation of publics (e.g., Ni et al., 2019). At the same time, cultural factors can simultaneously affect information behaviors (e.g., information acquisition, transmission, and selection) together with situational perceptions.

Earlier examinations that connected culture to public segmentation focused on how different types of cultural identities, i.e., gender (e.g., Aldoory, 2001) and racial identity (e.g., Sha, 2006), were related to the situational perceptions and communication behaviors of publics. As indicated in the theoretical assumptions earlier, understanding culturally different publics should be an integral part of identifying publics and needs to go beyond any single dimension to involve multiple levels of cultural manifestations; different types, strength, and salience of identity; and different value orientations (Ni, 2022).

Cultural Manifestations

First, our view of culture and identity needs to be expanded to include multiple levels of cultural manifestation, as discussed earlier. The *explicit* level of culture examines differences in publics based on external and easily observable attributes. These correspond to the objective variables for identifying publics (Grunig & Repper, 1992). Such demographic categories reflect *surface-level diversity* based on "recognizable characteristics" (Oetzel et al., 2012, p. 145) and align with ascribed identities (cf., Sha, 2006). Individuals are only recognized through their appearances and characteristics as observed by others; they are not asked or involved in any way but are automatically assigned group labels and stereotypes associated with those labels.

On the contrary, the *middle* level of culture examines meanings and beliefs. This level corresponds to the inferred variables (Grunig & Repper, 1992) that are not directly observable, such as individuals' perceptions, cognitions, and attitudes. It also relates to avowed identities and the intersectionality of multiple identities (cf., Sha, 2006; Vardeman et al., 2013).

The *implicit* level of culture, which is the most-rarely examined in current public relations literature, involves more-fundamental assumptions about human existence and values. Both the middle and implicit levels of culture address *deep-level diversity* because such diversity is based on people's own self-concepts and value systems (cf. Oetzel et al., 2012).

Identity

In the current public relations literature, certain dimensions/types of identities and their interaction have been examined most often (e.g., Aldoory, 2001; Sha, 2006; Vardeman et al., 2013). The types of identities need to be expanded to include both inherited identities or primary markers (i.e., things we cannot typically change, like demographic markers) and achieved identities or secondary markers (e.g., things that can be changed through actions such as migration, education level, or socioeconomic status; see Kulich et al., 2017; Sha & Ford, 2007). More research on the latter needs to be developed (e.g., immigrant identity; see Jang & Kim, 2013; Ni, Wang, & Gogate, 2018).

At the same time, the aspects of identity that change across time and situations are seldom examined. Individuals can perceive different *strengths* of their identities, where some may perceive a stronger identity than others in the same area. Further, the *relative importance* of the strength of a particular identity, called the *salience* of identity, is also critical to consider.

Cultural Value Orientations

Publics' situational perceptions and communication behaviors are also likely to be influenced by their value orientations, as noted previously. Some overarching categories of individuals' value orientations can indicate sharp differences in cultural groups that may go beyond demographic diversity. Integrating the various approaches to cultural value orientations, Ni, Wang, and Sha (2018) identified five major value orientation questions (p. 79). Some useful implications can be drawn. See Table 7.2 for how value orientation includes different value dimensions and how these have implications for public perceptions about issues.

When examining different social, cultural, and political issues, these value orientations can be used in conjunction with other cultural aspects, such as personal identity and lived experiences, to examine how different publics are formed and communicate. For a theoretical framework for understanding multi-level antecedents to publics in intercultural settings, see Ni, Wang, and Sha (2018, p. 204).

Organizational Level: Management of Intercultural Relationships and Conflicts

Managing intercultural relationships and conflicts involves examining culture at multiple levels and at different stages of these practices, based on an in-depth understanding of culturally different publics. Relationship management is a main focus of public relations research (Ferguson, 1984, 2018). Following the general model of antecedents, cultivation strategies, and consequences (cf. Ki et al., 2015), research in this area typically has been interested in how organizations cultivate relationships with their strategic publics, measure the quality of relationships, and what these relationships bring to the organizations in the forms of perceptual, attitudinal, communicative, and behavioral outcomes. Such research has examined culture, if at all, primarily from the angle of national cultures, especially through cross-cultural or cross-national differences.

Intercultural relationship management, as Ni, Wang, and Sha (2018) advocated, should examine the antecedents, process, quality, and consequences of relationship management from diverse publics' perspectives (e.g., Ni et al., 2019). Some examples of potential research questions include: What cultural identities and values motivate a group of individuals to enter or not enter a relationship with an organization or with each other (i.e.,

Table 7.2 Value Orientations and Implications

Value Orientation	Questions	Value Dimensions	Examples of Cultural Implications
Human nature	What is human nature?	• Good, evil, or a mixture	Attitude toward criminal justice
Relationships between humans and nature, the natural environment, the supernatural	Could we control our fate and environment?	• Domination, submission, or stewardship • Internal or external control • Mastery vs. harmony	Attitude toward environment and technology Attitude toward emergency/disaster management
Time orientation	What is the concept of time?	• Long- vs. short-term orientation • Sequential or synchronous (linear or repetitive and cyclical) • Focus on past, present, or future	Attitude toward financial planning and disaster management (immediate results vs. future rewards)
Motivation for human behaviors	What motivates human behavior, being (expressing internal self), being-in-becoming (personal growth), or achieving (obtaining external materials and power)?	• Conservatism vs. Intellectual autonomy and affective autonomy • Uncertainty avoidance • High- vs. low-context	Attitude toward social change
Human relations	What is the nature of human relations: lineal (hierarchical), collateral (equal), or varied based on individual merits (equity-driven)?	• Power distance • Hierarchy vs. egalitarianism • Universalism vs. particularism • Individualism vs. collectivism • Neutral vs. emotional • Diffuse vs. specific • Achievement vs. ascription	Attitude toward employee relations; social mobility

Source: Ni (2022). Reproduced with permission of Routledge, New York.

become a public)? What relationship management strategies take into consideration multiple levels of cultural identity (e.g., Ni, Dai, & Liu, 2022) and are most effective for empowering organizational publics, especially marginalized ones, to gain voice? What consequences of relationships may be compatible with the publics' cultural values and achieve the goals that are important to the publics themselves (e.g., Ni et al., 2021)?

At the same time, conflict management needs to embrace culture, cultural identity, and cultural values at a deeper level. Conflict is defined as "perceived incompatible verbal or nonverbal activities between interdependent parties in achieving salient goals; it is prone to arouse emotional responses" (Ni, Wang, & Sha, 2018, p. 120).

Drawing primarily from the dual-concern model (concern for self and concern for others; cf. Carnevale & Pruitt, 1992; Pruitt & Rubin, 1987), conflict management research in public relations has involved the two-way and symmetrical practices of public relations (e.g., L. A. Grunig et al., 2002), relationship management (e.g., Huang, 2001), conflict resolution theory (e.g., Plowman, 2005), and the contingency theory (Cancel et al., 1997). Studies have not always explicitly examined the role of culture, and those that have done so have focused almost exclusively on the conflict stage, with special attention on conflict stance and conflict strategies (e.g., Huang, 2008), and very little on the pre-conflict and post-conflict stages.

The importance of intercultural conflict management is becoming increasingly obvious, as conflicts nowadays, especially social conflicts, are often value- and identity-based; cultural considerations involving different groups have become critical. Ni, Wang, and Sha (2018) developed a model of intercultural conflict management, adapting the pre-conflict, conflict, and post-conflict stages.[3] The process starts with the pre-conflict stage, where identifying and understanding cultural groups and managing relationships with them are important. When it comes to the conflict stage, multiple steps in conflict assessment (including goal assessment) influence the adoption of different conflict management strategies and tactics. Finally, the post-conflict stage assesses the conflict management and its outcomes; identifies any changes in identity, positions, and relationships; and sets goals for the next stage.

Focusing on the conflict stage, within this general framework of a goal-driven conflict management process, all the components are heavily influenced by culture, cultural identity, and cultural values. First, in determining the *goals* of managing a conflict, the identity goal (which is a secondary goal to maintain personal moral standards; cf. Dillard et al., 1989) is increasingly more important to consider aside from the primary goal dimensions of socioemotional, instrumental, competitive, and cooperative (Wang et al., 2012).

Second, when analyzing the conflict situation, it is critical to distinguish between explicit position and the actual, and sometimes hidden, rationale and interests. The position tends to be singular and thus seems impossible to change; sticking to positions may lead to an impasse. Yet if the deeper-level rationale is unpacked to reveal the underlying rationale, values, and/ or interests, it is more likely to yield multiple aspects of the conflict goal, which may provide more room for negotiation between parties in conflict. Finally, various strategies and tactics are developed based on these cultural understandings.

Personal Level: Intercultural Competence and Empowerment of Publics

Increasingly, the need for cultural diversity, equity, and inclusion not only has pushed more public relations practitioners to seek to gain intercultural competency as they interact with various publics, but it also has encouraged more members of previously marginalized groups to empower themselves. Theoretical development has been made in this area, but more needs to be done.

Intercultural Competency

Extending previous research on multicultural competence (e.g., Sha & Ford, 2007) and various conceptualizations of cultural competence (e.g., Gudykunst, 2005; Kim, 2005; Lustig & Koester, 2009, van der Zee & van Oudenhoven, 2000), a multi-domain, multi-level framework of intercultural communication competence and training has been developed (cf. Ni, Wang, & Sha, 2018) and extended (cf. Schlupp, 2022). The three main categories of competencies are culture-general (or the ability to behave both effectively and appropriately across different cultural contexts), culture-specific (or the ability to adapt to a specific new cultural environment), and enactment competencies (or the actual capacity of engaging in effective and appropriate communication in intercultural settings). These competencies can be developed and enhanced through both informational and experiential training.

Empowerment of Publics

Individuals who are from marginalized or traditionally less-powerful groups, broadly defined (e.g., female in predominantly male or patriarchal cultures, non-White members in predominantly White cultures, immigrants in predominantly native-born cultures), are facing challenges of crossing cultural boundaries and negotiating and reshaping their identities. As indicated in Ni, Wang, and Sha (2018), various theoretical models can be used to examine this process of identity negotiation, not only in terms of how "minority" public relations practitioners interact with dominant cultural group members within an organization, but also how marginalized publics such as immigrants grow by coping with and adapting to crossing boundaries, both external and internal to the self (e.g., Ni, Wang, & Gogate, 2018).

Applications of Intercultural Public Relations Theory

The general theory of intercultural public relations—in examining the role of culture, cultural identity, and cultural values in identifying publics, managing relationships and conflicts, building cultural competencies, and empowering the traditionally marginalized—can be applied at multiple levels and in different contexts (e.g., Ni, Schlupp, & Sha, 2022).

First, the importance and challenges of identifying intercultural publics have been examined. In the corporate setting, Fitzsimmons et al. (2022) highlighted the importance of identifying and harmonizing the divergent interests of all stakeholders in the context of planning and implementing corporate purpose. Smith and Ni (2022) brought cultural identity to the forefront in activist organizations and examined how identity at both personal and organizational levels was embraced and negotiated as the organization communicated with various publics to achieve its purpose.

At the same time, building and managing relationships with culturally diverse publics are important at all levels of intercultural public relations practices, from the high-level corporate purpose (Fitzsimmons et al., 2022), culturally relevant social media strategies (Hu et al., 2022), to more specific messaging strategies that reflect in-depth cultural values (Alkazemi et al., 2022).

The role of cultural identity has also been examined at different stages of conflict management. Theye and Amundson (2022) examined the cultural implications of the sources of conflict—how fundamental organizational identity and identification in the meat industry impacted its marginalized employee publics (typically immigrants and those with low socioeconomic status). Daniels and Coleman (2022) examined a crisis of presidents of historically Black colleges and universities (HBCUs) visiting the White House during the Trump administration, where racial identities were juxtaposed. Summerall-Jabro (2022) applied the theory in intercultural conflict resolution and negotiation to a conflict between the faculty union and university administration in the context of COVID-19.

In various contexts, the importance of intercultural competency has been found to be critical, either in terms of contributing to the effective resolution of conflicts (Summerall-Jabro, 2022) and a global mindset in military public affairs to navigate through complex cultural contexts (Naumann & Jefferson, 2022), or negatively influencing relationship management due to the lack of intercultural competency (e.g., Theye & Amundson, 2022).

Research Directions and the Future of Intercultural Public Relations Theory

Research in intercultural public relations can be further developed through adopting a more holistic view of culture, cultural identity, and cultural values; integrating more intercultural communication theories; and expanding to more domains of practice.

First, more holistic examinations of culture, cultural identity, and cultural values orientations are needed. Researchers can take a more-comprehensive view of self-concept along with identity and further examine the process of cultural and/or intercultural identity development (e.g., Ni, Wang, & Gogate, 2018). More research should examine not only additional types of identity, but also the strengths and salience of such identities.

In addition, research needs to examine the role of culture-level value orientations that may transcend different demographics. One starting point for this work may lie in the area of Moral Foundations Theory, which suggests five dimensions comprising the main moral foundations of all humans: care/harm, fairness/cheating, loyalty/betrayal, authority/subversion, and sanctity/degradation (cf. Graham et al., 2013).

Second, to date, public relations scholarship has not fully examined or used many well-conceptualized and consistently validated intercultural communication theories, and—as with the application to public relations of other theories of interpersonal communication—the conflating levels of analysis between the interpersonal and the intergroup remains a vexing challenge for researchers. For example, the use of cross-cultural adaptation theories (cf. Kim, 2005) can help cultural groups in a more general sense to adapt and thrive.

Third, such a holistic examination of culture can be expanded to more areas of research in organizational and professional settings. In addition to identifying cultural publics, more research is needed to examine relationship and conflict management with organizational publics. More work also is necessary on the identities of public relations practitioners themselves—beyond extant research on minority practitioners (e.g., Tindall, 2009), roles (e.g., Dozier & Broom, 2006), or competency and professionalization (e.g., Freitag, 2009; Sha, 2011)—to consider the ways in which practitioners personally adapt to their organizational contexts and nurture their own well-being and identities. Relatedly, practitioner-competency training based on theoretically derived frameworks would do much to enhance scholarly work on the professionalization of practitioners.

Further, extending the research to the community level holds much promise. More studies on community engagement and important outcomes such as community empowerment, disaster and emergency communication, and public health have implications for public relations management and effectiveness. Future scholars might consider how engaging with culturally diverse communities helps build resilience, increase efficacy, and contribute to community well-being.

Finally, intercultural public relations research should also extend beyond organizations and tackle societal-level challenges. For example, how enriched cultural understanding can have implications for the management and resolution of social conflicts, especially in the context of polarized public opinions. Incorporating core values across different social groups may potentially serve as a healing mechanism and thus enable more readily a fully functioning society (cf. Heath, 2006) or more-functional democracies (cf. Sha, 2022).

In short, we believe that intercultural public relations theory offers strong potential for rich streams of future scholarship. This work will be not only intellectually rewarding for researchers and strategically helpful to organizations and to publics, but it will also be critically important for societies to rebuild civic discourse and to repair the social fabric that has frayed dangerously in these pandemic times.

Notes

1   Early research on public relations and culture defined "culture" using national boundaries and centered on Hofstede's (1980, 2001) dimensions of culture: power distance, individualism-collectivism, uncertainty avoidance, masculinity-femininity, and long- vs. short-term orientation (cf. Sriramesh & Vercic, 2003). For example, researchers examined if and how the "generic principles of public relations Excellence" (cf. L. Grunig et al., 2002) could be applied to different countries, with those national cultures operationalized using Hofstede's dimensions (e.g., Rhee, 2002; Sriramesh & Vercic, 2003).

2   Because intercultural public relations theory assumes that public relations can and should be managed, Ni, Wang, and Sha (2018) treated the identification and segmentation of publics as being done by and from the perspective of organizations. For a discussion of the distinction between "publics as collectives" identified and predicted by organizations versus "publics as constituents" self-motivated toward collective action, see Sha (2022).

3   See Ni, Wang, and Sha (2018) for an overview of the model.

References

Aldoory, L. (2001). Making health communications meaningful for women: Factors that influence involvement. *Journal of Public Relations Research*, *13*, 163–185. https://doi.org/10.1207/S1532754XJPRR1302_3

Alkazemi, M. F., Alkhubaizi, N. B., & Smith, J. J. (2022). The implications of public health messaging strategies: How branding disease may improve public health awareness in the Gulf cooperation council (GCC). In L. Ni, Q. W. Schlupp, & B.-L. Sha (Eds.), *Intercultural public relations: Realities and reflections in practical contexts* (pp. 149–172). Routledge.

Berry, J. W. (1989). Imposed etics-emics-derived etics: The operationalization of compelling idea. *International Journal of Psychology*, *24*, 721–735. https://doi.org/10.1080/00207598908247841

Broom, G., & Sha, B.-L. (2013). *Cutlip and Center's effective public relations* (11th ed.). Upper Pearson.

Cancel, A. E., Cameron, G. T., Sallot, L. M., & Mitrook, M. A. (1997). It depends: A contingency theory of accommodation in public relations. *Journal of Public Relations Research*, *9*, 31–63.

Carnevale, P. J., & Pruitt, D. G. (1992). Negotiation and mediation. *Annual Review of Psychology*, *43*, 531–582.

Collier, M. J. (2003). Understanding cultural identities in intercultural communication: A ten-step inventory. In L. A. Samovar & R. E. Porter (Eds.), *Intercultural communication: A reader* (10th ed., pp. 412–429). Wadsworth Publishing.

Crable, R. E., & Vibbert, S. L. (1986). *Public relations as communication management*. Bell-wether Press.

Cross, W. (1987). A two-factor theory of Black identity: Implications for the study of identity development in minority children. In J. Phinney & M. Rotheram (Eds.), *Children's ethnic socialization: Pluralism and development*. Sage.

Culbertson, H. M., & Chen, N. (1996). *International public relations: A comparative analysis*. Routledge.

Cutlip, S. M., & Center, A. H. (1952). *Effective public relations: Pathways to public favor*. Prentice-Hall.

Daniels, G., & Coleman, K. (2022). When Black college presidents visit the White House: The case of a culture clash in crisis management. In L. Ni, Q. W. Schlupp, & B.-L. Sha (Eds.), *Intercultural public relations: Realities and reflections in practical contexts* (pp. 107–127). Routledge.

Dillard, J. P., Segrin, C., & Harden, J. M. (1989). Primary and secondary goals in the production of interpersonal influence messages. *Communications Monographs, 56*, 19–38. https://doi.org/10.1080/03637758909390247

Dozier, D. M., & Broom, G. M. (2006). The centrality of practitioner roles to public relations theory. In C. H. Botan & V. Hazelton (Eds.), *Public relations theory II* (pp. 120–148). Sage.

Ferguson, M. A. (1984, August). *Building theory in public relations: Interorganizational relationships as a public relations paradigm*. Paper presented at the meeting of the Association for Education in Journalism and Mass Communication.

Ferguson, M. (2018). Building theory in public relations: Interorganizational relationships as a public relations paradigm. *Journal of Public Relations Research, 30*(4), 164–178. https://doi.org/10.1080/1062726X.2018.1514810

Fitzsimmons, A., Heffron, E., Qin, Y. S., & DiStaso, M. W. (2022). Pinpointing, prioritizing, and practicing purpose. In L. Ni, Q. W. Schlupp, & B.-L. Sha (Eds.), *Intercultural public relations: Realities and reflections in practical contexts* (pp. 41–61). Routledge.

Freitag, A. (2009). Ascending cultural competence potential: An assessment and profile of U.S. public relations practitioners' preparation for international assignments. *Journal of Public Relations Research, 14*, 207–277. https://doi.org/10.1207/S1532754XJPRR1403_3

Graham, J., Haidt, J., Koleva, S., Motyl, M., Iyer, R., Wojcik, S. P., & Ditto, P. H. (2013). Moral foundations theory. In P. Devine & A. Plant (Eds.), *Advances in experimental social psychology* (Vol. 47, pp. 55–130). Elsevier.

Grunig, J. E., Grunig, L. A., Sriramesh, K., Huang, Y. H., & Lyra, A. (1995). Models of public relations in an international setting. *Journal of Public Relations Research, 7*(3), 163–187.

Grunig, J. E., & Hunt, T. T. (1984). *Managing public relations*. Holt, Rinehart and Winston.

Grunig, J. E., & Repper, F. C. (1992). Strategic management, publics, and issues. In J. E. Grunig (Ed.), *Excellence in public relations and communication management* (pp. 31–64). Lawrence Erlbaum Associates.

Grunig, L. A., Grunig, J. E., & Dozier, D. M. (2002). *Excellent public relations and effective organizations: A study of communication management in three countries* (pp. 306–382). Lawrence Erlbaum Associates.

Gudykunst, W. B. (2005). An anxiety/uncertainty management (AUM) theory of strangers' intercultural adjustment. In W. B. Gudykunst (Ed.), *Theorizing about intercultural communication* (pp. 419–457). Sage.

Heath, R. L. (2006). Onward into more fog: Thoughts on public relations' research directions. *Journal of Public Relations Research, 18*, 93–114. https://doi.org/10.1207/s1532754xjprr1802_2

Hofstede, G. (1980). *Culture's consequences: International differences in work-related values.* Sage.

Hofstede, G. (2001). *Culture's consequences: Comparing values, behaviors, institutions and organizations across nations* (2nd ed.). Sage.

Hofstede, G., & Hofstede, G. J. (2005). *Cultures and organizations: Software of the mind* (2nd ed.). McGraw-Hill.

Hu, Y., Lu, W., & Ngai, C. S. B. (2022). Building relationship with the public from different cultural backgrounds on social media: A case study on Estée Lauder's social media communication strategies in the United States and China. In L. Ni, Q. W. Schlupp, & B.-L. Sha (Eds.), *Intercultural public relations: Realities and reflections in practical contexts* (pp. 84–105). Routledge.

Huang, Y. (2001). Values of public relations: Effects on organization-public relationships mediating conflict resolution. *Journal of Public Relations Research, 13*(4), 265–301.

Huang, Y. (2008). The role of third-party mediation and face and favor in executive-legislative relations and conflict. *Asian Journal of Communication, 18*(3), 239–263. https://doi.org/10.1080/01292980802207249

Jang, A., & Kim, H. (2013). Cultural identity, social capital, and social control of young Korean Americans: Extending the theory of intercultural public relations. *Journal of Public Relations Research, 25*, 225–245. https://doi.org/10.1080/1062726X.2013.788444

Ki, E.-J., Kim, J.-N., & Ledingham, J. A. (Eds.). (2015). *Public relations as relationship management: A relational approach to the study and practice of public relations* (2nd ed.). Routledge.

Kim, J.-N., & Ni, L. (2013). Two types of public relations problems and integrating formative and evaluative research: A review of research programs within the behavioral, strategic management paradigm. *Journal of Public Relations Research, 25*, 1–29. https://doi.org/10.1080/1062726X.2012.723276

Kim, J.-N., Ni, L., & Sha, B.-L. (2008). Breaking down the stakeholder environment: Explicating approaches to the segmentation of publics for public relations research. *Journalism and Mass Communication Quarterly, 85*, 751–768.

Kim, Y. Y. (2005). Adapting to a new culture: An integrative communication theory. In W. B. Gudykunst (Ed.), *Theorizing about intercultural communication* (pp. 375–400). Sage.

Kluckhohn, F. R., & Strodtbeck, F. L. (1961). *Variations in value orientations.* Row, Peterson.

Kulich, C., de Lemus, S., Kosakowska-Berezecka, N., & Lorenzi-Cioldi, F. (2017). Multiple identities management: Effects on (of) identification, attitudes, behavior and well-being. *Frontiers in Psychology, 8*, 1–4. https://doi.org/10.3389/fpsyg.2017.02258

Lustig, M. W., & Koester, J. (2009). *Intercultural competence: Interpersonal communication across cultures.* Pearson.

Naumann, K., & Jefferson, O. (2022). Enhancing the global mindset in military public affairs. In L. Ni, Q. W. Schlupp, & B.-L. Sha (Eds.), *Intercultural public relations: Realities and reflections in practical contexts* (pp. 128–147). Routledge.

Ni, L. (2006). *Exploring the value of public relations in strategy implementation—employee relations in the globalization process* [Unpublished doctoral dissertation, University of Maryland].

Ni, L. (2022). A theoretical framework of intercultural public relations. In L. Ni, Q. W. Schlupp, & B.-L. Sha (Eds.), *Intercultural public relations: Realities and reflections in practical contexts* (pp. 10–38). Routledge.

Ni, L., Dai, Y., & Liu, W. (2022). Dynamics between fragmentation and unity: Identity and nonprofit relationship management in the Asian American community. *Public Relations Review, 48*(2), 102157, https://doi.org/10.1016/j.pubrev.2022.102157

Ni, L., De la Flor, M., Wang, Q., & Romero, V. (2021). Engagement in context: Making meaning of the Latino community health engagement process. *Public Relations Review*, 47(2), 102036. https://doi.org/10.1016/j.pubrev.2021.102036

Ni, L., Schlupp, Q. W., & Sha, B.-L. (Eds.). (2022). *Intercultural public relations: Realities and reflections in practical contexts*. Routledge.

Ni, L., & Wang, Q. (2011). Anxiety and uncertainty management in an intercultural Setting: The impact on organization-public relationships. *Journal of Public Relations Research*, 23, 269–301. https://doi.org/10.1080/1062726X.2011.582205

Ni, L., Wang, Q., & Gogate, A. (2018). Understanding immigrant internal publics of organizations: Immigrant professionals' adaptation and identity development. *Journal of Public Relations Research*, 30, 146–163. https://doi.org/10.1080/10627 26X.2018.1490289

Ni, L., Wang, Q., & Sha, B.-L. (2018). *Intercultural public relations: Theories for managing relationships and conflicts with strategic publics*. Routledge.

Ni, L., Xiao, Z., Liu, W., & Wang, Q. (2019). Relationship management as antecedents to public communication behaviors: Examining community empowerment and public health in Asian community. *Public Relations Review*, 45(5), 101835. https://doi.org/10.1016/j.pubrev.2019.101835

Oetzel, J. G. (2009). *Intercultural communication: A layered approach*. Vango Books.

Oetzel, J. G., McDermott, V. M., Torres, A., & Sanchez, C. (2012). The impact of individual differences and group diversity on group interaction climate and satisfaction: A test of the effective intercultural workgroup communication theory. *Journal of International and Intercultural Communication*, 5, 144–167. https://doi.org/10.1080/17 513057.2011.640754

Pike, K. L. (Ed.) (1967). *Language in relation to a unified theory of structure of human behavior* (2nd ed.). Mouton.

Plowman, K. D. (2005). Conflict, strategic management, and public relations. *Public Relations Review*, 31(1), 131–138. https://doi.org/10.1016/j.pubrev.2004.10.003

Pruitt, D. G., & Rubin, J. Z. (1987). *Social conflict: Escalation, stalemate, and settlement*. Random House.

Rhee, Y. (2002). Global public relations: A cross-cultural study of the excellence theory in South Korea. *Journal of Public Relations Research*, 14(3), 159–184. https://doi.org/10.1207/S1532754XJPRR1403_1

Samovar, L. A., Porter, R. E., McDaniel, E. R., & Roy, C. S. (2016). *Communication between cultures* (9th ed.). Cengage Learning.

Schlupp, Q. W. (2022). Intercultural communication competence in the moral circle: Learning from research and practice. In In L. Ni, Q. W. Schlupp, & B.-L. Sha (Eds.), *Intercultural public relations: Realities and reflections in practical contexts* (pp. 225–261). Routledge.

Sha, B.-L. (1995). *Intercultural public relations: Exploring cultural identity as a means of segmenting publics* [Unpublished master's thesis, University of Maryland].

Sha, B.-L. (2006). Cultural identity in the segmentation of publics: An emerging theory of intercultural public relations. *Journal of Public Relations Research*, 18, 45–65. https://doi.org/10.1207/s1532754xjprr1801_3

Sha, B.-L. (2011). 2010 practice analysis: Professional competencies and work categories in public relations today. *Public Relations Review*, 37(3), 187–196. https://doi.org/10.1016/j.pubrev.2011.04.005

Sha, B.-L. (2022). Evolving our conceptualizations of "publics" and "the public" to reimagine public relations and sustain democratic society. In D. Pompper, K. R. Place, & C. K. Weaver (Eds.), *The Routledge companion to public relations*. Routledge.

Sha, B.-L., & Ford, R. L. (2007). Redefining "requisite variety": The challenge of multiple diversities for the future of public relations excellence. In E. L. Toth (Ed.), *The future of excellence in public relations and communication management: Challenges for the next generation* (pp. 381–398). Lawrence Erlbaum Associates.

Smith, L., & Ni, L. (2022). Exploring an integrated approach to understanding and communicating with publics for activist organizations: Black liberation movement. In L. Ni, Q. W. Schlupp, & B.-L. Sha (Eds.), *Intercultural public relations: Realities and reflections in practical contexts* (pp. 200–222). Routledge.

Sriramesh, K. (1991). *The impact of societal culture on public relations: An ethnographic study of South Indian organizations* [Unpublished doctoral dissertation, University of Maryland].

Sriramesh, K., & Vercic, D. (2003). *The global public relations handbook: Theory, research, and practice* (1st ed.). Routledge.

Summerall-Jabro, A. D. (2022). Managing a relational triad during COVID-19: Strategic management, intercultural competency, and negotiation savvy. In L. Ni, Q. W. Schlupp, & B.-L. Sha (Eds.), *Intercultural public relations: Realities and reflections in practical contexts* (pp. 174–198). Routledge.

Tajfel, H., & Turner, J. C. (1979). An integrative theory of intergroup conflict. In W. G. Austin & S. Worchel (Eds.), *The social psychology of intergroup relations* (pp. 33–37). Brooks, Cole.

Theye, K., & Amundson, N. G. (2022). Unpacking the meat industry's COVID-19 response. In L. Ni, Q. W. Schlupp, & B.-L. Sha (Eds.), *Intercultural public relations: Realities and reflections in practical contexts* (pp. 62–83). Routledge.

Tindall, N. J. (2009). In search of career satisfaction: African-American public relations practitioners, pigeonholing, and the workplace. *Public Relations Review, 35*, 443–445.

Trompenaars, F., & Hampden-Turner, C. (1998). *Riding the waves of culture: Understanding cultural diversity in global business* (2nd ed.). McGraw-Hill.

Vardeman-Winter, J., Jiang, H., & Tindall, N. T. (2013). Information-seeking outcomes of representational, structural, and political intersectionality among health media consumers. *Journal of Applied Communication Research, 41*(4), 389–411. https://doi.org/10.1080/00909882.2013.828360

Van der Zee, K. I., & Van Oudenhoven, J. P. (2000). The multicultural personality questionnaire: A multidimensional instrument of multicultural effectiveness. *European Journal of Personality, 14*, 291–309.

Wang, Q. (2006). *Linking goals to avoidance in interpersonal conflict situations: A cognitive approach* [Unpublished doctoral dissertation, University of Maryland].

Wang, Q., Fink, E. L., & Cai, D. A. (2012). The effect of conflict goals on avoidance strategies: What does not communicating communicate? *Human Communication Research, 38*, 222–252. https://doi.org/10.1111/j.1468-2958.2011.01421.x

Wang, Q., Ni, L., & De la Flor, M. (2014). An intercultural competence model of strategic public relations management in the Peru mining industry context. *Journal of Public Relations Research, 26*, 1–22. https://doi.org/10.1080/1062726X.2013.795864

8 Agenda Building Through Community Building

Theorizing Place and Digital Space in Grassroots Activist Public Relations

Stephanie Madden and Mikayla Pevac

Within past public relations theorizing, activists have traditionally been viewed as external threats to an organization rather than practitioners unto themselves (Ciszek, 2015). However, the increasing corpus of public relations research focused on digital activism is demonstrating shifting power dynamics and the sophistication of activists as public relations practitioners (e.g., Smith et al., 2019; Stokes & Atkins-Sayre, 2018). Yet, theorizing about digital activism within public relations has focused to a great extent on how activists have responded to actions by large corporations such as Chick-Fil-A (Ciszek, 2016) or participated in large-scale movements such as the Women's March on Washington (Vardeman & Sebesta, 2020). This affords opportunities to better understand what digital activism looks like in a local context. Specifically, how might interrogating national social media efforts in local settings expand our theoretical considerations of digital activism, particularly when considering community (Hallahan, 2004) as foundational to public relations theory and practice?

To better understand digital activism in a local or community context within public relations, we believe that considering the importance of place will inspire new theoretical opportunities at the intersections between online and offline activism. To date, there has been little theorizing in public relations about the intersection between local activism rooted in place and digital activism. One notable exception comes from Xu and Luttman (2020) and their work on activist publics and the influence of locality and proximity on socially mediated networks. As these authors argued, "Research on networked publics [has not paid] enough attention to the role of physical space and issue proximity in affecting online interactions" (Xu & Luttman, 2020, p. 2). The study of place is essential to the future of public relations theory because with the new digital tools melting away geographic boundaries, it is necessary to not overlook the ways in which place can shape and ground digital activism within local communities.

Activism and Community in Public Relations

We begin this chapter by overviewing key literature in the areas of grassroots activism, digital activism, and place-based communities that lay the foundation for our later theoretical arguments.

DOI: 10.4324/9781003141396-9

Grassroots Activism

Smith (2005) defined activism as "the process by which groups of people exert pressure on organizations or other institutions to change policies, practices, or conditions that the activists find problematic" (p. 5). Historically, public relations has been corporate-centric, viewing activist efforts in relation to how they could negatively impact a company (Coombs & Holladay, 2012). However, this is rapidly changing "due to the fact that activist communication and the evolution of the field of public relations are inherently intertwined" (Wolf, 2018, p. 308). This chapter contributes to the growing body of research within public relations that argues that "[a]ctivists are not just publics of an organization; they are frequently organizations themselves who often know sophisticated public relations strategies and theory" (Aldoory & Sha, 2007, p. 352). As acknowledgement of activism as a public relations practice grows, though, conceptual differences between types of activist groups remain muddied (Weaver, 2018). Therefore, public relations theory must be adapted to better understand how different types of activist groups are using communication tools in complex, understudied ways.

Wolf (2018) argued that the implied monolithic concept of activism within public relations "fails to recognize the variety in structures, activities, communication styles and sources of capital" (p. 309). Within public relations, we see few authors specifically interrogating the messier local context of grassroots activism (e.g., Kim & Dutta, 2009; Stokes & Rubin, 2010; Demetrious, 2013). In fact, Demetrious (2001) called for greater attention to be paid to how grassroots activists use public communication. Distinguishing it from other forms of activism, Sommerfeldt (2013a) defined grassroots activism as "a form of spontaneous activism with a bottom-up system of organization without high levels of professionalization" (p. 351), with some grassroots groups built on personal relationships and others built on more impersonal relationships facilitated by digital technologies.

One reason, among others, for the dearth of public relations research specifically related to local grassroots activism may be that digital technologies have contributed to an illusion of an absence of place in this digitally mediated world as geographical boundaries can be easily overcome. This process of "disembedding" can be understood as "the 'lifting out' of social relations from local contexts of interaction and their restructuring across indefinite spans of time-space" (Giddens, 1990, p. 21). Furthermore, the Internet has been viewed as a panacea for grassroots activism to have unprecedented access to audiences that may not have been available due to limited economic resources (Weaver, 2018). In the next section, we discuss current theorizing related to digital activism and public relations.

Digital Activism

Digital technologies can both accelerate and amplify traditional activist activities such as resource mobilization, legitimacy building, culture jamming, and cause promotion (Hon, 2015; Sommerfeldt, 2011; Madden et al., 2018; Mundy, 2013). Not only can digital technologies provide a boost to traditional activities, but in many ways digital technologies change the process of activism, such as removing media gatekeepers and creating opportunities for individuals outside of activist organizations to create successful campaigns (Hon, 2015; Guo & Saxton, 2014). Vardeman and Sebesta (2020) even noted how online discourse can evolve into activist organizations—for example, the Black Lives Matter organization that was formed from the #BlackLivesMatter online social movement.

Using the Justice for Trayvon campaign, Hon (2015) proposed the model of public relations and digital social advocacy. Specifically, Hon was interested in looking at "how the digital media ecosystem allows publics to mobilize in unprecedented ways" (p. 299), particularly related to grassroots activism. Hon's model includes antecedents (social, political, economic), processes (strategy, tactics), digital media ecosystem (supersizing and leveraged affordances), and consequences (outputs and outcomes) to understand digital social advocacy. While potentially understood as part of the antecedents, we argue that more attention can be paid to place—particularly in the context of grassroots activism—as a key context for activism as it is tied to digital media ecosystems.

More recently, Chon and Park (2020) proposed an integrative model of activism rooted in the Situational Theory of Problem Solving (STOPS) to explain and predict how individuals engage with contentious issues through both social media and offline activism. Chon and Park found that "social media activism is a positive and critical mediator through which situational motivation increases offline activism" (p. 90). Because of the focus on three specific contentious issues (gun ownership, immigration, and police use of power), Chon and Park also introduced the concept of affective injustice into public relations literature related to activism. Affective injustice was defined as negative emotions related to contentious issues stemming from perceptions of unfairness (Zomeren et al., 2008), whether experienced directly or indirectly (Chon & Park, 2020). One limitation of this study is that personal involvement is conceptualized only at the individual level rather than within the wider local community in which the precipitating cause for activism took place. In the next section, we further explore the connection between place-based community and local activism in public relations.

Place-Based Community

Community of place is foundational when considering local activism. Several scholars have also noted how community-building is a way that public relations can serve society (e.g., Fitzpatrick & Gauthier, 2001; Holtzhausen, 2000; Holtzhausen & Voto, 2002; Starck & Kruckeberg, 2001), including civil society (e.g., Sommerfeldt, 2013b; Taylor, 2010). Hallahan (2004) argued for community as a foundational concept for both public relations theory and practice. Community can be defined many ways (see Hallahan). Dunham et al. (2006) argued that communities can be determined by geography (physical location), interaction (face-to-face or electronic), and identity (proactive/agenda-driven or oppositional).

Place can also be thought of as a lens through which people see and understand the world (Cresswell, 2008), which can work to foster a common identity. While place is often considered "concrete, local and territorialised" (Pierce et al., 2010, p. 57), other scholars have viewed place at a multi-scalar level not contingent on a particular locale (e.g., Bosco, 2001; Massey, 1994; Nicholls, 2009). For this chapter, we ground our understanding of place in its local and territorialized conceptualization.

Place-frames offer a conceptual framework for understanding how place-based identity is discursively constituted as part of collective action (Martin, 2003). Martin's conceptualization of place-frames is drawn from Snow and Benford's (1992) collective action frames in social movement literature, which focus on how shared understandings of a situation can motivate and enable a collective response. The local particularities of place can inform and motivate activism (Elwood, 2006; Martin, 2003). Rhetorical scholars such as Endres and Senda-Cook (2011) have long argued for the symbolic importance attached to physical location and protest, although the interplay with digital activism provides new and unique considerations for public relations scholars.

New Directions for Theorizing Place and Digital Activism in Public Relations

Based on this brief review of existing literature, we argue for three key areas of theoretical expansion in public relations related to place-based communities and digital activism. These areas are: 1) agenda building, 2) connection with local government, and 3) community care.

Agenda Building

Agenda building theory has been applied less to activist public relations (e.g., Benecke & Oksiutycz, 2015), especially for local grassroots organizations and their use of digital strategy. Developed from agenda setting theory, agenda building helps us understand the process of salience formation for policymakers, media, and the public (Lang & Lang, 1981). Various scholars (e.g., Lang & Lang, 1981; Walters & Gray, 1996; Johnson et al., 1996; Corbett & Mori, 1999) have modeled the process of agenda building. With its focus on interest groups, Corbett and Mori's (1999) circular relationship model provides a relevant entry point for theorizing agenda building and activist communication for public relations. Essentially, Corbett and Mori argue that: 1) issues arise in society, 2) interest groups get involved and take positions on those issues, 3) interest groups then influence the news media and public, and 4) news media coverage then influences the public, interest groups, and politicians. Because of its origins in agenda setting, agenda building has been primarily conceptualized at two levels: object level (transfer of object salience to relevant stakeholders) and attribute level (salience of attributes—substantive and affective—being emphasized about the object) (Kiousis et al., 1999; Kim & Kiousis, 2012). While Carroll (2015) theorized a third level of agenda building that explores how the co-occurrence of objects and attributes impacts the process of salience formation and transfer, we focus specifically on the object level and attribute level for our specific theoretical advancement.

As Hon (2015) and others have argued, one of the benefits of digital activism is the ability to remove media gatekeepers. As such, an opportunity is presented to more fully consider how agenda building functions for activist public relations in this digital context. This is also in alignment with Zoch and Molleda's (2006) call to develop public relations knowledge on agenda building from the standpoint of the source of information, in this case, local activist groups. We argue that the intersection between place and digital activism has a significant agenda building function for activist communication. As such, we offer suggestions for how considerations of place can advance agenda building theories at all three levels for digital activism.

Geography and First-Level Agenda Building

Geography and community of place create significant opportunities for developing issue salience as part of the first-level agenda building function. When local activist groups are addressing issues within a geographic community, the local connection for media coverage is clear. Decades of research has shown that public relations materials and practices (i.e., press releases, newsletters, speeches) play an important role in first-level agenda building by providing information subsidies (e.g., Curtin, 1999; Kiousis et al., 2006, 2015). Considering geography as part of digital activism at the local level opens further opportunities for the type of information subsidies that may be most effective for developing issue salience. For example, how might local activists strategically leverage local symbols or places as part of a visual rhetorical strategy on social media (Endres & Senda-Cook, 2011)? Local symbols enforce that the issues activists are fighting for are not abstract or distant—they very tangibly affect the community in which people live. This can create a more personal connection to the issue. Furthermore, image events such as die-ins and occupations of physical spaces can be powerful for attracting media attention (DeLuca, 2009). With the prominence of digital activism, these events can also be live streamed and reported by the activist groups on their own social media channels. The geographic proximity of the protest may also encourage community members who see the event on social media to go in-person to observe or participate in the event as well.

Place-Identity and Second-Level Agenda Building

Each local community has its own identity, which we argue is important for attribute level of agenda building for local activists. Zenker (2011) defined place identity as "the visual, verbal and behavioural [sic] expressions of a place, which are embodied in the aims, communication, values and general culture of the place's stakeholders and overall place design" (p. 42). One way a place-based identity is constituted is through place-frames, which "describe common experiences among people in a place, as well as imagining an ideal of how the [place] *ought* to be" (Martin, 2003, p. 733). Substantive and emotional attributes of place, and how they are framed by local activists, are worth further consideration in activist public relations agenda building.

There is an opportunity within public relations research to further explore the degree to which place can foster a common identity on issues and how local activist groups may or may not be leveraging this identity as part of agenda building. Research on place has shown positive emotional connections with familiar locations (Jorgensen & Stedman, 2006) and that both "physical and symbolic attributes of a place contribute to an individual's sense of self" (Devine-Wright, 2009, p. 428). Yet, what if something negative happens in a familiar place, and how might activists use this as part of their messaging? As a starting point, we believe that the solidarity-discord identity paradox in social justice communication theorized by Vardeman and Sebesta (2020) was a useful heuristic for understanding tensions that may exist between place-identity and activist place-frames. In their study on intersectionality and digital activism in the context of the Women's March on Washington, Vardeman and Sebesta argued that "while discord can be fruitful, messages of cooperation and solidarity still seem to be prioritized" (p. 18). Though Vardeman and Sebesta were looking at identities related to race, gender, class, etc., how might the solidarity-discord identity paradox found in digital activist communication translate to place-identity related to larger social justice issues? And importantly, how does this potentially serve the second-level agenda building functioning for activist public relations?

Connection With Local Government

We also believe that there are opportunities to expand public relations theory on place-based communities and digital activism to a connection with local government. This can both complement and expand the existing work of scholars like Hon (2015), who have noted the importance of recognizing the antecedents of digital activism, such as political conditions, that provide opportunities and constraints for communicators. While federal and state governments have an impact on the local level, we focus specifically on theorizing opportunities to explore local government connections to digital activism within public relations. Kim and Cho (2019) found that an individual's sense of community is vital to local government relationships and community-building. Yet, a limitation to the existing work in public relations and local government is that it has largely been limited to only considering government public relations practitioners. For activists, working through local government to create change can be a very embodied experience as it is possible to attend city council meetings, know local politicians personally, and create direct action opportunities at local government buildings. How are grassroots activists using digital activism at the local level to potentially build relationships with local government officials or even mobilize others in the community to participate? Has digital activism opened new spaces for community members not previously involved in local issues to pay more attention to policy discussions and elections at the local level? These, and other questions, are worth exploring within public relations.

One area of great opportunity in public relations is exploring local grassroots activists who choose to run for local government offices. Research by Madden and Levenshus (2021) argued for expanding considerations of public relations leadership to those running for and holding public office. This ethnographic research project followed a cohort of women being trained to run for public office, most of whom were participating in some form of activism within their local communities. One reason these women were choosing to run for office is because of the limitations of advocating for new laws and policies from the outside and instead wanting a seat at the decision-making channel. What does it look like when local community activists hold local government positions? Is there a difference in how community-building proceeds? For those who spearheaded digital activism efforts in their communities, does this then translate to their elected official positions? There are robust opportunities to expand research and theory in public relations related to civil society and community building at this intersection of activists running for and winning local government seats.

Community Care

As mentioned previously, one limitation of current work in public relations exploring issue involvement both online and offline is that it is only considered at an individual level (Chon & Park, 2020). There is an opportunity to theorize issue involvement at a community level, not only in discussions of getting people to care about or being involved in issues, but what it means to develop a community of care and that cares. The concept of "community care" is a budding area of discussion that prioritizes fostering compassion amongst the members of a community by sharing resources for the betterment of all (Dockray, 2019). Much like ethics of care scholarship, research on community care has traditionally been focused within health-related and social work fields (e.g., Burrows et al., 2000; Thiam et al., 2021). For example, community care can manifest as a specific model for caring for the elderly, disabled, and mentally ill within a community. Yet, as with work on ethics of care—which is becoming more prominent in public relations theorizing (e.g., Fraustino & Kennedy, 2018; Madden & Alt, 2021; Formentin & Bortree, 2019)—we believe the concept of community care has potential for public relations theorizing as well.

The concept of care must also be further unpacked in public relations, especially as the risk of "carewashing" is salient in terms of materials that use the language of care without tangible actions, particularly by large corporations and organizations (e.g., Chatzidakis & Littler, 2021). The hyperlocal context of community, and demonstrating and organizing care, offers an interesting avenue of future research for activist public relations theorizing, particularly how digital activism is used in this context. Ethics of care offers an entry point to this discussion. Ideally, care focuses on relationship-based ethics based on mutually beneficial relationships that are developed and governed by responsibilities to others (Held, 2006). Caring is both a practice (actions taken to support others in relationships) and values (desires to do good). This combination of caring practices and values leads to relationships based on "care and concern and mutual responsiveness to need on both the personal and wider social levels" (Held, p. 43). We argue that place-based communities offer an opportunity to explore the intersection of both the personal and wider social levels of mutual responsiveness as enacted through digital activism.

In their article on digital activism and trade unionism, Dencik and Wilkin (2020) articulated that "digital activism expands repertoires of resistance to groups who might otherwise lack resources" (p. 1734). Dencik and Wilkin were exploring horizontal organizing amongst workers facilitated through digital activism, but we also believe there is an opportunity to look at this type of horizontal organizing in the context of local communities. In particular, the concept of mutual aid as a tangible form of caring may offer a theoretical entry point that has been nascently explored in public relations. Marsh (2013) wrote about the metatheory of mutual aid and its direct connections to the communitarianism paradigm (Starck & Kruckeberg, 2001) in public relations. While Marsh (2013) takes an evolutionary perspective on social harmony and mutual aid by drawing on Darwin and Kropotkin, the concept of mutual aid is one used prominently in social justice circles for liberation movements to "establish community connections and put in place structures for meeting needs" (Spade, 2020, p. 135). Importantly, "mutual aid is not charity," but it is instead about self-organization and self-determination (Spade, p. 140). At its core, mutual aid focuses on ensuring vulnerable populations are supported and people's immediate needs are met, while working to address the root cause of issues and develop alternative structures that do not reproduce the harms of existing systems (Spade). Because such systems exist outside of traditional organizational and capitalist logics, there is a great opportunity to consider how digital activism is contributing to mutual aid work and alternatively, how an organization might support mutual aid work as part of community care. What role, if any, does public relations play for mutual aid work in local communities? How does such an approach change the very logics under which public relations scholarship and practice operate? In the next section, we offer an example of a local organization doing this type of community work through digital activism.

Case of the 3/20 Coalition

To offer context to our ideas for the theoretical expansion of place and digital space in public relations, we offer an illustrative case of an activist organization, the 3/20 Coalition, established in our local community of State College, PA. The 3/20 Coalition is named for the month and date (March 20) of the murder of Osaze Osagie, a 29-year-old Black man shot by a police officer during a mental health wellness check. While briefly receiving national attention, this specific case, like so many others, has faded from national conversation although the online discourse around hashtags like #BlackLivesMatter and #DefundThePolice continue. However, local activism efforts continue to try and create dialogue around race relations and mental health access within the community of State College, specifically calling for the police officers who killed Osagie to be held responsible.

In the aftermath of the death of Osagie, members of the local State College community rallied and created the 3/20 Coalition. The 3/20 Coalition's mission was to not only mourn the loss of Osagie, but to "make sure that justice is served and that people are held accountable for their actions" (3/20 Coalition, n.d., Facebook bio statement). The 3/20 Coalition has since held a variety of events in honor of seeking justice for Osagie, as well as events targeted toward participating in the national dialogue on issues of race, like the celebration of Black History Month and a "Justice for Breonna Taylor" protest. Ranging from educational community events to protests calling for change within the local police force, the 3/20 Coalition held over 20 local events in its first two years that aimed to inform the State College public about the reality of race relations within the State College borough and surrounding townships. Without a website, the 3/20 Coalition utilized the power of social media, specifically Facebook, Twitter, and Instagram, to get the word out about their events, as well as to provide information for the community about race-related issues. With their Facebook page boasting over 1,600 followers, over 200 followers on Twitter, and over 1,000 followers on Instagram, the 3/20 Coalition successfully established ties with the greater local community of State College.

Agenda-Building in Real Time

The organization used its social media platforms as a key information subsidy, from posting traditional press releases and letters to elected officials on the social media platforms to using specific affordances of the platforms (such as live streaming events). Although unaffiliated with the university, the

3/20 Coalition activists reappropriated Penn State symbols and slogans to highlight the difference between community ideals and reality for marginalized groups. For example, State College resides in Happy Valley and the Penn State slogan of #WeAre connotes a collective orientation. However, the original name of the 3/20 Coalition in the immediate aftermath of the shooting was #WeAreNot, reframing place-identity as not a happy or welcoming place for all people. Activists were able to use geography and a pre-existing place identity to very specifically tailor digital messages to a hyperlocal context. In a smaller community, this may function practically as there are fewer sites for groups to meet to protest. In the State College community, the Allen Street Gates serve as a prominent symbolic focus in connecting Penn State University with the local community and were a frequently site of in-person protest. In addition to the Allen Street Gates, local government sites and offices were also used as places for image events such as die-ins and 24-hour occupations. Thus, the physicality of the Gates' geographical location simultaneously alerts the community to where the Coalition operates, as well as highlights the organization's local attachment to a space used by generations of social movements.

The local community context also offers an illumination of Vardeman and Sebesta's (2020) solidarity-discord identity paradox in social justice communication. While there was clear discord in messaging toward calling for change from local government institutions and specific local government officials, there was also a heavy focus on celebrating community. The celebration came not only in the form of honoring Osagie's life, but also in the way that the Coalition highlighted the fundamental principle of care as part of community. The Coalition made it clear that even if one person does not feel safe in the State College community or have adequate access to medical or mental health resources, then a place-identity that claims to be "Happy Valley" is essentially disingenuous.

The Role of Local Government

The 3/20 Coalition communication also focused heavily on how national discourse (such as #DefundThePolice and #AbolishThePolice) translated to the local level in terms of policy and budgeting decisions. Rather than abstract statements, the 3/20 Coalition created digital education events to define these terms. For example, on August 26, 2020, a Zoom teach-in and discussion was held during the 3/20 Coalition's Black August Week of Action to "define 'defund' and 'abolish' the police and how this fits in with the 3/20 Coalition's demands for justice for Osaze Osagie." The 3/20 Coalition also used social media to make public responses sent to the State College Borough Council regarding budget voting decisions. Furthermore, one of the co-chairs of the 3/20 Coalition, Tierra Williams, ran for and was elected to the Board of Supervisors in Ferguson Township (located within State College). She is the first Black woman to serve in this position. Her activism with the 3/20 Coalition and community involvement were key aspects of her campaign for local office in order "to fight for, uplift, and inspire people of color within her local community 'by any means necessary'" (The Future of Ferguson, n.d.).

Community Care for All

In addition to the calls for accountability, there is joy behind some of the Coalition's messaging that calls for the building of a better community, or "beloved community." It is important to note that the phrasing of "beloved community" comes from Martin Luther King Jr.'s vision for a nonracist, embracing, and inclusive society (Herstein, 2009). One way that the Coalition extends their mission to the betterment of the wider community is exemplified by their event held on the two-year anniversary of Osagie's shooting that included 10 days of action, culminating in an event called "Honoring Osaze's Legacy Community Day." This event was a fundraiser for a scholarship endowment set by the Osaze family, which raised more than $5,000 and focused on "Osaze's Beloved Community." The 3/20 Coalition went live on Facebook for this community event, which included local speakers and a call for celebration of community. People were then encouraged to write messages in chalk. Interestingly, many of these chalk messages and pieces of community art included three specific hashtags "#blacklivesmatter, #mentalhealthmatters, and #communitycarematters." One of the primary tactics that the 3/20 Coalition discusses to advance this idea of community is through supporting and creating mutual aid in the community to support programs that address the root causes of suffering and violence instead of further funding the police.

Conclusion

The illustrative case of the 3/20 Coalition exemplifies how the three research gaps we identified in digital activism and place-based community—agenda-building, connections to the local community, and community care—have application to public relations theorizing in this area. Although further empirical work must be done, this case presents evidence that these concepts do manifest in local activism in ways that can help add nuance to current public relations theorizing on digital activism often focused on a broader national level. Throughout our section on new directions for theorizing digital activism and place and public relations we offer potential research questions and ideas that public relations scholars could explore. To reiterate, some ideas include: How might the solidarity-discord identity paradox found in digital activist communication translate to place-identity related to larger social justice issues? How are grassroots activists using digital activism at the local level to potentially build relationships with local government officials or even mobilize others in the community to participate? What role, if any, does public relations play for mutual aid work in local communities? There are ample and relevant opportunities for public relations scholars to advance theory at the intersections of place and digital space in grassroots activist public relations.

References

3/20 Coalition. (n.d.). Retrieved February 9, 2021, from www.facebook.com/pages/category/Community-Organization/320-Coalition-2244750575843126/

Aldoory, L., & Sha, B. L. (2007). The situational theory of publics: Practical applications, methodological challenges and theoretical horizons. In E. L. Toth (Ed.), *The future of excellence in public relations and communications management: Challenges for the next generation* (pp. 339–356). Lawrence Erlbaum Associates.

Benecke, D. R., & Oksiutycz, A. (2015). Changing conversation and dialogue through LeadSA: An example of public relations activism in South Africa. *Public Relations Review, 41*(5), 816–824. https://doi.org/10.1016/j.pubrev.2015.06.003

Bosco, F. J. (2001). Place, space, networks, and the sustainability of collective action: The Madres de Plaza de Mayo. *Global Networks, 1*(4), 307–329. https://doi.org/10.1111/1471-0374.00018

Burrows, R., Nettleton, S., Pleace, N., Loader, B., & Muncer, S. (2000). Virtual community care? Social policy and the emergence of computer mediated social support. *Information, Communication & Society, 3*(1), 95–121. https://doi.org/10.1080/136911800359446

Carroll, C. E. (2015). Mapping the contours of the third level of agenda setting: Uniplex, duplex and multiplex associations. In L. Guo & M. McCombs (Eds.), *The power of information networks* (pp. 34–52). Routledge.

Chatzidakis, A., & Littler, J. (2021). An anatomy of carewashing: Corporate branding and the commodification of care during Covid-19. *International Journal of Cultural Studies.* https://openaccess.city.ac.uk/id/eprint/27134/3/An%20anatomy%20of%20carewashing%20resubmission%20accepted%2019%20No.pdf

Chon, M.-G., & Park, H. (2020). Social media activism in the digital age: Testing an integrative model of activism on contentious issues. *Journalism & Mass Communication Quarterly, 97*(1), 72–97. https://doi.org/10.1177/1077699019835896

Ciszek, E. L. (2015). Bridging the gap: Mapping the relationship between activism and public relations. *Public Relations Review, 41*(4), 447–455. https://doi.org/10.1016/j.pubrev.2015.05.016

Ciszek, E. L. (2016). Digital activism: How social media and dissensus inform theory and practice. *Public Relations Review, 42*(2), 314–321. https://doi.org/10.1016/j.pubrev.2016.02.002s

Coombs, W. T., & Holladay, S. J. (2012). Privileging an activist vs. a corporate view of public relations history in the U. S. *Public Relations Review, 38,* 347–353. https://doi.org/10.1016/j.pubrev.2011.11.010

Corbett, J. B., & Mori, M. (1999). Medicine, media, and celebrities: News coverage of breast cancer, 1960–1995. *Journalism and Mass Communication Quarterly, 76,* 229–249.

Cresswell, T. (2008). Place: Encountering geography as philosophy. *Geography, 93*(3), 132–139. https://doi.org/10.1080/00167487.2008.12094234

Curtin, P. A. (1999). Reevaluating public relations information subsidies: Market-driven journalism and agenda-building theory and practice. *Journal of Public Relations Research, 11*(1), 53–90. https://doi.org/10.1207/s1532754xjprr1101_03

DeLuca, K. M. (2009). *Image politics: The new rhetoric of environmental activism.* Lawrence Erlbaum Associates.

Demetrious, K. (2001). People, power and public relations. *Asia Pacific Public Relations Journal, 3*(2), 109–120. http://hdl.handle.net/10536/DRO/DU:30012645

Demetrious, K. (2013). *Public relations, activism, and social change: Speaking up.* Routledge.

Dencik, L., & Wilkin, P. (2020). Digital activism and the political culture of trade unionism. *Information, Communication & Society, 23*(12), 1728–1737. https://doi.org/10.10 80/1369118X.2019.1631371

Devine-Wright, P. (2009). Rethinking NIMBYism: The role of place attachment and place identity in explaining place-protective action. *Journal of Community & Applied Social Psychology, 19*(6), 426–441. https://doi.org/10.1002/casp.1004

Dockray, H. (2019, May 24). *Self-care isn't enough: We need community care to thrive.* Mashable. https://mashable.com/article/community-care-versus-self-care/

Dunham, L., Freeman, R. E., & Liedtka, J. (2006). Enhancing stakeholder practice: A particularized exploration of community. *Business Ethics Quarterly, 16*(1), 23–42. www.jstor.org/stable/3857725

Elwood, S. (2006). Beyond cooptation or resistance: Urban spatial politics, community organizations, and GIS-based spatial narratives. *Annals of the Association of American Geographers, 96*(2), 323–341. https://doi.org/10.1111/j.1467-8306.2006.00480.x

Endres, D., & Senda-Cook, S. (2011). Location matters: The rhetoric of place in protest. *Quarterly Journal of Speech, 97*(3), 257–282. https://doi.org/10.1080/00335630.2011 .585167

Fitzpatrick, K., & Gauthier, C. (2001). Toward a professional responsibility theory of public relations ethics. *Journal of Mass Media Ethics, 16*(2–3), 193–212. https://doi.org /10.1080/08900523.2001.9679612

Formentin, M., & Bortree, D. (2019). Giving from the heart: Exploring how ethics of care emerges in corporate social responsibility. *Journal of Communication Management, 23*(1), 2–17. https://doi.org/10.1108/JCOM-09-2018-0083

Fraustino, J. D., & Kennedy, A. K. (2018). Care in crisis: An applied model of care considerations for ethical strategic communication. *Journal of Public Interest Communications, 2*(1), 18–40. https://doi.org/10.32473/jpic.v2.i1.p18

Giddens, A. (1990). *The consequences of modernity.* Polity Press.

Guo, C., & Saxton, G. D. (2014). Tweeting social change: How social media are changing nonprofit advocacy. *Nonprofit and Voluntary Sector Quarterly, 43*(1), 57–79. https://doi.org/10.1177/0899764012471585

Hallahan, K. (2004). "Community" as a foundational for public relations theory and practice. *Annals of the International Communication Association, 28*(1), 233–279. https://doi.org/10.1080/23808985.2004.11679037

Held, V. (2006). *The ethics of care: Personal, political, and global.* Oxford University Press.

Herstein, G. (2009). The Roycean roots of the beloved community. *The Pluralist, 4*(2), 91–107. www.jstor.org/stable/20708980

Holtzhausen, D. R. (2000). Postmodern values in public relations. *Journal of Public Relations Research, 12*(1), 93–114. https://doi.org/10.1207/S1532754XJPRR1201_6

Holtzhausen, D. R., & Voto, R. (2002). Resistance from the margins: The postmodern public relations practitioner as organizational activist. *Journal of Public Relations Research, 14*(1), 57–84. https://doi.org/10.1207/S1532754XJPRR1401_3

Hon, L. (2015). Digital social advocacy in the Justice for Trayvon campaign. *Journal of Public Relations Research, 27*(4), 299–321. https://doi.org/10.1080/10627 26X.2015.1027771

Johnson, T. J., Wanta, W., Boudreau, T., Blank-Libra, J., Schaffer, K., & Turner, S. (1996). Influence dealers: A path analysis model of agenda building during Richard Nixon's war on drugs. *Journalism, and Mass Communication Quarterly, 73*, 181–194.

Jorgensen, B. S., & Stedman, R. C. (2006). A comparative analysis of predictors of sense of place dimensions: Attachment to, dependence on, and identification with lakeshore properties. *Journal of Environmental Management, 79*(3), 316–327. https://doi.org/10.1016/j.jenvman.2005.08.003

Kim, I., & Dutta, M. J. (2009). Studying crisis communication from the subaltern studies framework: Grassroots activism in the wake of Hurricane Katrina. *Journal of Public Relations Research, 21*(2), 142–164. https://doi.org/10.1080/10627260802557423

Kim, J. Y., & Kiousis, S. (2012). The role of affect in agenda building for public relations: Implications for public relations outcomes. *Journalism & Mass Communication Quarterly, 89*(4), 657–676. https://doi.org/10.1177/1077699012455387

Kim, M., & Cho, M. (2019). Examining the role of sense of community: Linking local government public relationships and community-building. *Public Relations Review, 45*(2), 297–306. https://doi.org/10.1016/j.pubrev.2019.02.002

Kiousis, S., Bantimaroudis, P., & Ban, H. (1999). Candidate image attributes: Experiments on the substantive dimension of second level agenda setting. *Communication Research, 26*(4), 414–428. https://doi.org/10.1177/009365099026004003

Kiousis, S., Kim, J. Y., Ragas, M., Wheat, G., Kochhar, S., Svensson, E., & Miles, M. (2015). Exploring new frontiers of agenda building during the 2012 US presidential election pre-convention period: Examining linkages across three levels. *Journalism Studies, 16*(3), 363–382. https://doi.org/10.1080/1461670X.2014.906930

Kiousis, S., Mitrook, M., Wu, X., & Seltzer, T. (2006). First- and second-level agenda building and agenda setting effects: Exploring the linkages among candidate news releases, media coverage, and public opinion during the 2002 Florida gubernatorial election. *Journal of Public Relations Research, 18*(3), 265–285. https://doi.org/10.1207/s1532754xjprr1803_4

Lang, G. E., & Lang, K. (1981). Watergate: An exploration of the agenda building process. *Mass Communication Review, 2*, 447–468.

Madden, S., & Alt, R. A. (2021). More than a "bad apple": Applying an ethics of care perspective to a collective crisis. *Journal of Public Interest Communication, 5*(1), 24–44. https://doi.org/10.32473/jpic.v5.i1.p24

Madden, S., Janoske, M., Winkler, R. B., & Harpole, Z. (2018). Who loves consent?: Social media and the culture jamming of Victoria's secret. *Public Relations Inquiry, 7*(2), 171–186. https://doi.org/10.1177/2046147X18764216

Madden, S., & Levenshus, A. (2021). Broadening the umbrella of women's leadership and public relations: An ethnographic case study of a women's political leadership development program. *Journal of Public Relations Research, 33*(3), 168–184. https://doi.org/10.1080/1062726X.2021.2015354

Marsh, C. (2013). Social harmony paradigms and natural selection: Darwin, Kropotkin, and the metatheory of mutual aid. *Journal of Public Relations Research, 25*(5), 426–441. https://doi.org/10.1080/1062726X.2013.795861

Martin, D. G. (2003). "Place-framing" as place-making: Constituting a neighborhood for organizing and activism. *Annals of the Association of American Geographers, 93*(3), 730–750. https://doi.org/10.1111/1467-8306.9303011

Massey, D. (1994). *Space, place, and gender*. University of Minnesota Press.

Mundy, D. E. (2013). The spiral of advocacy: How state-based LGBT advocacy organizations use ground-up public communication strategies in their campaigns for the "equality agenda". *Public Relations Review, 39*(4), 387–390. https://doi.org/10.1016/j.pubrev.2013.07.021

Nicholls, W. (2009). Place, networks, space: Theorising the geographies of social movements. *Transactions of the Institute of British Geographers, 34*(1), 78–93. https://doi.org/10.1111/j.1475-5661.2009.00331.x

Pierce, J., Martin, D. G., Murphy, J. T. (2010). Relational place-making: The networked politics of place. *Transactions of the Institute of British Geographers, 36*(1), 54–70. https://doi.org/10.1111/j.1475-5661.2010.00411.x

Smith, B. G., Krishna, A., & Al-Sinan, R. (2019). Beyond slacktivism: Examining the entanglement between social media engagement, empowerment, and participation in activism. *International Journal of Strategic Communication, 13*(3), 182–196. https://doi.org/10.1080/1553118X.2019.1621870

Smith, M. (2005). Activism. In R. L. Heath (Ed.), *Encyclopedia of public relations* (pp. 5–9) Sage.

Snow, D., & Benford, R. (1992). Master frames and cycles of protest. In A. Morris & C. M. Mueller (Eds.), *Frontiers in social movement theory*. Yale University Press.

Sommerfeldt, E. (2011). Activist online resource mobilization: Relationship building features that fulfill resource dependencies. *Public Relations Review, 37*(4), 429–431. https://doi.org/10.1016/j.pubrev.2011.03.003

Sommerfeldt, E. (2013a). Online power resource management: Activist resource mobilization, communication strategy, and organizational structure. *Journal of Public Relations Research, 25*(4), 347–367. https://doi.org/10.1080/1062726X.2013.806871

Sommerfeldt, E. (2013b). The civility of social capital: Public relations in the public sphere, civil society, and democracy. *Public Relations Review, 39*(4), 280–289. https://doi.org/10.1016/j.pubrev.2012.12.004

Spade, D. (2020). Solidarity not charity: Mutual aid for mobilization and survival. *Social Text, 38*(1), 131–151. https://doi.org/10.1215/01642472-7971139

Starck, K., & Kruckeberg, D. (2001). Public relations and community: A reconstructed theory revisited. In R. L. Heath (Ed.), *Handbook of public relations* (pp. 51–60). Sage.

Stokes, A. Q., & Atkins-Sayre, W. (2018). PETA, rhetorical fracture, and the power of digital activism. *Public Relations Inquiry, 7*(2), 149–170. https://doi.org/10.1177/2046147X18770216

Stokes, A. Q., & Rubin, D. (2010). Activism and the limits of symmetry: The public relations battle between Colorado GASP and Philip Morris. *Journal of Public Relations Research, 22*(1), 26–48. https://doi.org/10.1080/10627260903150268

Taylor, M. (2010). Public relations in the enactment of civil society. In R. L. Heath (Ed.), *The Sage handbook of public relations* (pp. 5–16). Sage.

The Future of Ferguson. (n.d.). *Tierra4ferguson*. Retrieved February 14, 2022, from https://tierra4ferguson.com

Thiam, Y., Allaire, J. F., Morin, P., Hyppolite, S. R., Doré, C., Zomahoun, H., & Garon, S. (2021). A conceptual framework for integrated community care. *International Journal of Integrated Care, 21*(1), 1–13. https://doi.org/10.5334/ijic.5555

Vardeman, J., & Sebesta, A. (2020). The problem of intersectionality as an approach to digital activism: The women's March on Washington's attempt to unite all women. *Journal of Public Relations Research, 32*(1–2), 7–29. https://doi.org/10.1080/1062726X.2020.1716769

Walters, L. M., & Gray, R. (1996). Agenda building in the 1992 presidential campaign. *Public Relations Review, 22*(1), 9–24.

Weaver, C. K. (2018). The slow conflation of public relations and activism: Understanding trajectories in public relations theorising. In A. Adi (Ed.), *Protest public relations: Communicating dissent and activism* (pp. 12–28). Routledge.

Wolf, K. (2018). Power struggles: A sociological approach to activist communication. *Public Relations Review, 44*, 308–316. https://doi.org/10.1016/j.pubrev.2018.03.004

Xu, S., & Luttman, S. (2020). Networked publics in #NoDAPL protests: Interactions among activist publics and influence of locality and proximity on socially mediated networks. *New Media & Society.* https://doi.org/10.1177/1461444820954200

Zenker, S. (2011). How to catch a city? The concept and measurement of place brands. *Journal of Place Management and Development, 4*(1), 40–52. https://doi.org/10.1108/17538331111117151

Zoch, L. M., & Molleda, J.-C. (2006). Building a theoretical model of media relations using framing, information subsidies, and agenda-building. In C. H. Botan & V. Hazleton (Eds.), *Public relations theory II* (pp. 279–309). Routledge.

Zomeren, M., Postmes, T., & Spears, R. (2008). Toward an integrative social identity model of collective action: A quantitative research synthesis of three sociopsychological perspectives. *Psychological Bulletin, 134*(4), 504–535. https://doi.org/10.1037/0033-2909.134.4.504

Section 2

New and Revised Theories

9 Dialogic Theory in Public Relations

Michael L. Kent

The exploration of dialogic theory as a public relations concept goes back more than 30 years. Over the last decade, dialogue has played an increasingly important role in research and practice, with dozens of scholars drawing upon dialogic theory in their research, and thousands of professionals aware of the importance of dialogue in relationship building.

The academic or philosophical concept of dialogue is not the same as the everyday meaning of dialogue. In common parlance, dialogue means simply talk or conversation, a communicative interaction between two or more people. However, from an academic or professional standpoint, dialogue means much more than just two-way communication or talk. When a public relations professional uses dialogic theory as a strategy for communicative interaction, s/he is making a commitment to be honest, take a risk, be respectful, and be willing to let others speak.

Dialogue is considered an important model for thinking about communication in public relations because dialogue seems ethical and "natural," despite its technical nature. People talk with one another, we hold conversations, we tell stories, we share information. Although many theories of public relations are focused on strategic communication outcomes and achieving organizational goals, dialogue is focused on relationship building and understanding. Dialogue is used to understand others, not to get people to act. Dialogue, perhaps more than any other theory, is the closest theory to an interpersonal communication ideal. Dialogic exchanges are enacted as private conversations, not undertaken to persuade someone to do something for someone else or the organization.

To understand dialogue more fully, this chapter will focus on three areas: (1) a review of the key features of dialogic theory, (2) a summary of the various approaches to studying dialogic public relations, and (3) a review of the practical approaches to understanding dialogue. The first section will begin with an overview of the key features of dialogue, as well as reviewing the fundamental "ologies:" ontology, epistemology, axiology.

DOI: 10.4324/9781003141396-11

Literature and Key Issues of Dialogic Theory

Dialogue has become an increasingly important theory in public relations over the last three decades (cf., Botan, 1997; Kent & Taylor, 1998, 2002; Pearson, 1989a, 1989b), having spawned thousands of articles, book chapters, and theses, and having influenced four generations of public relations scholars: Pearson (1989b), in the 1980s; Kent and Taylor (1998, 2002), and others, in the 1990s onward; doctoral students and younger scholars of those second-generation scholars such as Sommerfeldt and Yang (2018), Saffer (Kent et al., 2016), Uysal (2018); and now, students of those students such as Capizzo (2018) and Morehouse (Morehouse & Saffer, 2018).

Dialogue refers to an interactive conversation between *two people* (sometimes more) taking place in real time, but there are other features of dialogue that should be explained first. *First,* there is the dictionary definition sense of dialogue as a conversation or interaction between two people. This sense of dialogue as a conversation includes everyday conversations that can take place anywhere, as well as politicians "having a dialogue with the voters," scripted or textual conversations such as characters in literature, theatre, cinema, and television, and in public spaces referred to as "the public sphere" (Habermas, 1984). This first sense of dialogue as a conversation also includes organizations talking about dialogue (or "two-way communication") in social media, "having a dialogue with customers," as well as instances of "mandated dialogue," where governments mandate that stakeholders be consulted on projects (Lane, 2018; Russmann & Lane, 2020).

A *second* sense of dialogue is the sense written about by modern philosophers such as Bakhtin (1981), Gadamer (1991), and others, where dialogue is a textual "conversation" that takes place between an author and reader. As Capizzo (2018) notes, "Bakhtin's dialogism . . . uses a unit of meaning at the sentence or paragraph level (the utterance)" (p. 525). Dialogue in this sense has to do with our encounter with texts. Philosophical texts such as the Platonic dialogues are an example of this second type of dialogue (Plato, 1999a, 1999b), where Plato created fictitious conversations with Socrates, who would then question the beliefs of the other conversational participants and attempt to lead people to the "truth." Some movies have effectively illustrated aspects of type two dialogue such as the "Pulp Fiction" (Tarantino, 1994) "foot massage" discussion (Marshall, 2022) and the "My Dinner with Andre" (1981) discussion, which features a lengthy dialogue between two friends (Linton, 2016).

The *third* sense of dialogue, and the focus of this chapter, is often referred to as "genuine dialogue" by many because unscripted and substantive conversations can take place between two or more people. A genuine dialogue is characterized by an assortment of conversational and ethical principles that include face-to-face interactions, two-way communication, honesty, risk, trust, fairness, etc.

Features of Dialogue

To understand dialogue fully, one must first understand that dialogue is a conversational ideal, not just a process or knack. Most conversations that people have in any circumstance are not dialogic. Dialogue is an uncommon and experiential activity. Not every conversation leads to dialogue, even if we want them to. Dialogue is both a process (a set of steps, guidelines, or rules) and a product (a relationship of trust and positive regard that emerges over time) (Kent & Taylor, 1998).

Additionally, one cannot have a dialogue with someone who is not trusted. Many people have employers, colleagues, fellow students, and even friends or family members whom they do not trust. Obviously, we have "conversations" with those people, but for a "dialogue" to emerge, there must be trust that the other individual(s) will not use what we say against us or to harm us. There must also be a reciprocal exchange of information. Dialogue is a two-way street. For a dialogue to emerge, there are several prerequisites. A brief summary of the primary features of dialogue include the following (cf. Kent & Taylor, 2002, 2018, 2021):

Propinquity

Nearness, closeness. Typically enacted as face-to-face communication. However, psychological propinquity, or a sense of closeness or nearness, can be achieved in many ways, such as the many software applications (Blackboard, Facetime, Skype, Teams, WeChat, WhatsApp, Zoom) that allow people to come together in a virtual face-to-face space. Thus, physical proximity is the dialogic ideal but is not required. However, some sense of psychological propinquity is necessary when physical proximity is not possible.

Risk

Where an individual self-discloses personal information to another. A dialogic encounter is not a superficial exchange of trivialities about the weather or sports. In genuine dialogue, the interlocutors take relational risks by sharing important, personal, and non-trivial information with their conversational partner. Taking informational risks and sharing personal or private information is part of how all interpersonal relationships are formed. Self-disclosure and reciprocation are part of the formation of relational bonds (Watzlawick et al., 1967).

Trust

Refers to the closeness that comes from knowing, or believing, that a partner, family member, friend, colleague, associate, or even a stranger will not share your personal or private information and will not use what they know or learn against us. Thus, trust and risk go hand-in-hand as part of dialogue.

Positive Regard

Refers to respect for others; involves a conversational tone of politeness, respect, and cultural sensitivity. Positive regard is demonstrated by learning people's names, referring to individuals by their preferred gender pronouns, titles, etc., as well as keeping one's nonverbal communication in check, appearing attentive and respectful of what others are saying. Displaying positive regard can be difficult when one's interlocutor represents an organization, cause, group, etc. that someone does not like or trust. For example, one of the most common examples of a lack of positive regard for others has been the notion that "activists" are the enemy of organizations. How can you treat someone with positive regard who wants to destroy you? In reality, of course, activists have been responsible for acting as ethical checks on organizations for decades, forcing organizations to "do the right thing." To activists, the organization is the enemy. Maintaining positive regard is one of the most difficult aspects of dialogue.

Vulnerability

Vulnerability happens when participants are honest, self-disclose personal information, answer questions, and thereby open themselves up to potential harm. Being vulnerable is a prerequisite to trust. A person who is not vulnerable and will not reciprocate in a communication exchange will not engender any trust. Vulnerability may take the form of sharing information about an individual's own beliefs, values, or attitudes, or many take the form of an organization being willing to share plans and past actions as a way of building trust with others.

Unanticipated Consequences or Strange Otherness

Occurs when interlocutors enter conversation without knowing where the conversation might go—not trying to control what happens. The purpose or goal of dialogue is not agreement but understanding. Thus, the idea of being spontaneous, of not trying to persuade, but being open to the encounter with others, with "strange otherness" (Cissna & Anderson, 1994, p. 14), necessarily leads to unanticipated consequences or "the feeling of surprise that comes when humans encounter the unfamiliar" (Cypher & Kent, 2018, p. 6), leading people to think about issues, problems, and the world in new ways.

Mutuality

The process of treating participants in a dialogue as colleagues rather than enemies or opponents. In relationships characterized by mutuality, participants do not walk away feeling manipulated, slighted, or disrespected. Mutuality is not about giving in to the other side or telling someone what s/he wants to hear, but of working to understand a problem, issue, or person more fully. Indeed, in a relationship characterized by mutuality, the participants may engage in what an outsider might deem a "heated" discussion, only to come away from the exchange invigorated at having arrived at new insight or understanding, even if the topic of discussion was not resolved.

Fairness

In any system, particular players often have more power than others. Organizational communicators, for example, have access to more knowledge, resources, and network partners than the average person, so organizations need to be honest and tell the truth. In a conversational exchange, being fair means having rules that apply to everyone and constructing a conversational system whereby the party with more power (usually the organization) is not taking advantage of the party with less power or resources. Creating "rules" (Pearson, 1989a; Taylor & Kent, 2014) that all interlocutors must follow is a way to make an interaction fair.

Collaboration

About helping others to achieve as well as working to achieve our own goals. Collaboration is not about winning or competition, but about fostering cooperation and intersubjectivity, about cocreating and negotiating a shared "reality." When people collaborate, they come to know each other better, they learn about what people think and believe, and they often begin to question their own long-held beliefs.

Empathy

A communal orientation that includes acknowledgement and confirmation of others, and sympathetic treatment of others. Empathy also involves compassion or caring about others, accepting people on their own terms, and understanding that all people face personal, relational, economic, health, and other hardships and are worthy of our support. *Empathy* is often used interchangeably with *sympathy*. Both concepts are relevant in dialogic research. However, empathy is an internal activity—an effort to understand what someone else is experiencing—while sympathy is an outward expression of kindness and support.

Confirmation

A powerful psychological concept involving acknowledgment of others. On the most basic level, eye contact or a head nod when passing someone in a hallway is an example of confirmation, while showing genuine interest in another person, acknowledging their successes, and being sympathetic in their failures are also examples of confirmation. Confirmation may seem trivial; however, disconfirmation and isolation can do great harm to people. As Sommerfeldt and Kent (2020) note: "Words hurt a great deal and can do tremendous psychological harm to people's relational skills, self-images, and sense of self and identity" (p. 2.; see also Rogers, 1992; Watzlawick et al., 1967).

Commitment and Commitment to the Conversation

Being committed, caring, promising, obligation, all are synonyms for the willingness to work hard to understand the beliefs, values, and attitude of others, as well as the willingness to continue talking about difficult topics, rather than simply giving up and moving on.

The dialogic conversation is an ongoing activity where the partners should be willing to be changed, and where all parties should work and struggle to make their views clear and understand the other. Very often we hear the phrase "Let's just agree to disagree" used as a way of ending a discussion, of basically saying "I don't want to talk to you about this anymore." The assumption of this termination move is that both sides are unwilling to change their views, so why continue "arguing." However, genuine dialogue is a non-competitive interaction focused on understanding the other, not on *convincing* them of your own views, nor of maintaining one's own views at all costs. Dialogic interlocutors must be willing to admit when they are wrong. Interlocutors in a dialogue do not just change their views to suit the other party, but neither do they give up on understanding the other out of convenience.

Genuineness

Honest and truthful communication, free of any effort to deceive or manipulate others. For some communicators, immersed in a defensive mindset of "protecting" their clients and organizations, the concept pf genuineness is difficult. Genuineness requires risk and trust. However, genuineness also represents an expression of an individual's personality and mindset: what someone believes in; what someone values; what someone desires.

Commitment to Interpretation and Authenticity

As Watzlawick et al. (1967) noted half a century ago, relationships are defined by time and interaction. Authenticity, or being upfront about our intent and goals, recognizing when what we want is not in the best interest of others, and working to understand the position of others are central concepts in dialogue.

Psychological Readiness

Refers to the constant struggle to enact dialogic principles and behave ethically. As the lengthy list of dialogic concepts should make clear, dialogue is hard. Imagine the one person you have the most difficulty communicating with—a parent, sibling, partner, colleague, friend, etc.—and imagine that your life depended on your having a positive conversation with that person. What would you do to prepare? That "openness to new information, openness to the dialogic process, and openness to persuasion" (Cypher & Kent, 2018; p. 2; see also, Theunissen, 2015) is what psychological readiness is about.

Overview of Dialogic Assumptions

To help understand the value and process of dialogue, a brief examination of the assumptions of dialogue are in order. Managers and professional communicators are often only vaguely aware of epistemology (knowledge) vs. ontology (experience) or axiology (values), so understanding the assumptions of a theory can provide more insight into how to use the theory effectively and the kinds of questions that can be asked or answered. All theories can be reduced to their basic assumptions/practices, what we refer to as the "ologies:" axiology, epistemology, ontology. As Littlejohn et al. (2017) suggest, "Every theory, explicitly or implicitly, includes assumptions about these areas—about the nature of knowledge and how it is obtained, about what constitutes existence, and about what is valuable" (p. 8).

Axiology refers to the values or assumptions inherent in a theory. For example, profit over people. Many articles have been written in public relations describing *normative theory* (an axiological theory that assumes that people have social and moral obligations to behave ethically and do what is right), vs. *positive theories* (another axiological theory that attempt to describe the world as it is, placing no moral judgement on the behavior of communication professionals) (Kent & Lane, 2021; Kent & Li, 2020; Li & Kent, 2021).

Axiologically, dialogue is considered a normative theory that instructs others about ethical practices and how to treat other people. Additionally, dialogue assumes that we cannot know what is inside someone's head simply by observing them. Dialogue assumes that some form of communicative interaction needs to take place between two people for them to truly understand each other. Moreover, dialogue assumes that the communicative interactions need to be "meaningful"—more than a conversation about the weather or television—if we are to understand other people.

Epistemology tries to explain knowledge, or how people come to know what we know. There are many sources of knowledge, including: empiricism (science), cognition (reasoning, intellect), logic (induction and deduction), unconscious insights (dreams, imagination, visions), social interactions (interpersonal, group, public, cultural beliefs), spiritual/cosmological (altered mental states, drugs, religious beliefs), aesthetic (art, music, nature, transportation/immersion of books), sensorial (sight, smell, hearing, touch, taste), and extra-sensorial (deja vu, satori, unexplained insights).

As Littlejohn et al. (2017) note, "Any good discussion of theory will inevitably come back to epistemological issues" (p. 8). Epistemology asks five questions: "To what extent can knowledge exist before experience? To what extent can knowledge be certain (absolute or contingent)? By what process does knowledge arise? Is knowledge best understood in parts or as a whole? To what extent is knowledge explicit?" (pp. 8–9).

In dialogic theory, the assumption is that knowledge and experience are intertwined. An individual can read a book about a person, group, culture, etc., but to truly understand something, time must be spent interacting with him/her/it. In terms of the certainty of what we know, dialogue assumes that what we know is relative and changing. Human beings typically change their view over the course of their lifetimes. Although some views are relatively unchanging, what people think about specific events, issues, and people change. Thus, knowledge of other people is a contingent thing that can only be fully realized through interaction. To the third question, the process through which knowledge arises, there are many types of knowledge, but in dialogue we assume that knowledge of other people arises through human contact and respectful interaction. In terms of the fourth question, whether knowledge is best understood in parts or as a whole, as in systems theory (equifinality, non-summativity, wholeness) (cf. Watzlawick et al., 1967), dialogue in public relations sees knowledge as both part of a wider social whole—the parts of a system influence the wider system, so we need to understand what individual people think—and part of an interpersonal interaction. The system itself influences how people think and experience the world, but everyone is different, and individuals also influence the system. Finally, ontology helps to explain the assumptions of dialogic theory more fully.

Ontology refers to the study of the nature of being or existence. Ontology questions what is real; the difference between appearance and reality; the relation between mind and body. Are numbers and "facts" real or are only physical objects?

Four issues are important to ontology: "1. To what extent do humans make real choices? 2. Is human behavior best understood in terms of states or traits? 3. Is human experience primarily individual or social? 4. To what extent is communication contextual?" (Littlejohn et al., p. 10).

For dialogue, the questions are straightforward. "Do humans make real choices?" Yes. Dialogue assumes that our actions are influenced by our personal experiences and our interactions with those around us. Knowing what another person has experienced, thinks, or believes, necessarily will, and should, influence the choices that we make.

To the second question, "Is human behavior best understood in terms of *states* (situational conditions, a common public relations assumption) or *traits* (stable, relatively inflexible beliefs and values)?," dialogue lands near the middle of this continuum. In dialogue we generally assume that individuals have stable beliefs (traits, or how someone experiences the world, based on their past experiences, etc.), but dialogue also assumes that our own views and those of others can be influenced, something at the heart of public relations practice. Thus, dialogue is deeply rooted in ontological experience.

The third question, "Is human experience primarily individual or social?" From what has already been said, the assumption of dialogic theory is that individuals are social beings, and that organizations exist in social systems and are understood as part of their social system. Decisions are not made in isolation, and our experiences with others necessarily shape how each person sees the world.

The final question, "To what extent is communication contextual?" has already been answered. For decades, public relations professionals have described themselves as situationalists, believing that situation and audience adaptation was necessary to be effective communicators. At the same time, communication and public relations professionals believe that communication skills can be learned, and networks of weak ties allow someone to be a more effective communicator (Granovetter, 1973). The notion that knowing more about an individual or group will necessarily lead to communication success has been well entrenched in communication for decades. Thus, dialogue assumes that understanding others, knowing their beliefs, values, and appreciating their views, necessarily leads to better communication.

What Led to the Development of the Dialogic Assumptions

Like all theories, the development of the assumptions of dialogue is based on the concepts and ideals of the theory itself. Some theories place priority on observation, some on objectivity, some on persuasion, etc. In public relations, many of the earliest theories were managerial theories that were focused on serving the needs of managers and organizations; activists were seen as enemies of organizations (primarily corporations) (cf., Kent & Taylor, 2007). Because of the managerial focus, many theories were more about control than understanding.

Dialogue assumes that what people have to say matters, because of where the theory first emerged: Ancient Greece. The assumption in Ancient Greece 2,600 years ago among philosophers and educators was that "humans are the measure of all things" (Kennedy, 1987). Truth, knowledge, and understanding were believed to come from personal experience and collective cultural experiences. Thus, the emphasis on an ontology grounded in lived experience, an epistemology grounded in interpersonal interactions, and a normative axiology based on truth and ethical personal behavior naturally emerged.

As we look to the work of the dialogic scholars, philosophers, and theorists in the 20th century, we see a continuation of the study of dialogue to access personal experience, understanding of others, etc. Dialogue has been used to help groups with intractable differences communicate (Toledano, 2017), as well as by psychologists to help people understand human differences. Dialogue evolved as a theory about how to communicate ethically with others, how to avoid oppression and exploitation, how to minimize the power of those with more power (Freire, 1970) and maximize the power of those with less power to create an environment of trust, honesty, and "truth" (cf. Laing, 1961; Noddings, 1984; Pearson, 1989a, 1989b; Rogers, 1992; Taylor & Kent, 2014).

Historical Treatments and Relevant Literature

In the field of public relations, there have been three influential treatments of dialogue: Ron Pearson, who centered his dialogic theory on the work of Jürgen Habermas; Michael Kent and Maureen Taylor, who centered their work on Martin Buber's (1970) scholarship; and, most recently, Luke Capizzo, who has explored dialogue from the standpoint of Mikhail Bakhtin. Each scholar's contributions have moved the field further and expanded and solidified the place of dialogic theory in public relations.

The first treatment of dialogic theory in public relations (beyond use of the word to describe conversations, etc.) is attributed to Ron Pearson, a prolific scholar who first introduced dialogue to public relations in his dissertation (1989a) and a series of articles and book chapters. Pearson published before his untimely death (1989b, 1989c). Pearson's work drew heavily on the work of Habermas and the notion of ideal speech situations. However, Pearson was quite critical of the management-centric approaches of the day and sought to create a practical or pragmatic approach to dialogue that integrated it into the practice of corporate communication and public relations.

Around the same time as Pearson, Botan (1997) wrote an excellent essay on "ethics in strategic communication," arguing for a dialogic ethic in business. As Botan explained, the monologic approach has been "the dominant model behind current public relations campaigns . . . [however] the dialogic model is a more ethically sound alternative" (p. 190).

Starting in the late 1990s, Kent and Taylor (1998), wrote an article exploring whether dialogue might be useful in social media contexts, an area that was new to the field at the time, and following up with articles examining activism, responsiveness, and dialogic use of the world wide web (Kent et al., 2003; Taylor et al., 2001). A few years after the original article, Kent and Taylor (2002) wrote an article summarizing five key features (and other sub-features) of dialogue, framing them within a Buberian/hybrid model that drew upon features of dialogue from various sources and provided a framework for studying dialogue that has since been used by hundreds of scholars in articles, books, and theses.

Other notable dialogic scholars include Theunissen, who has published several theoretical articles on dialogue including an article examining the place of dialogue in persuasion (2015), as well as her work in earlier articles arguing that dialogue is more than a two-way communication tool (Theunissen & Wan Noordin, 2012), and arguing for a more sophisticated treatment of dialogue (Kent & Theunissen, 2016). Lane has also contributed to expanding the role of dialogue in public relations by examining how dialogue is often misused by organizations to take advantage of stakeholder/publics (Lane, 2018; Lane & Bartlett, 2016), combining theoretical discussions of dialogue and engagement (Lane & Kent, 2018), and describing how dialogue can be used as an ongoing communication tool (Kent & Lane, 2017; Lane, 2020).

Finally, as noted earlier, Capizzo (2018) represents what might be thought of as a fourth-generation dialogic public relations scholar. Capizzo introduces a new twist to public relations dialogue by examining Bakhtin's text-based sense of dialogue as an interpretive tool, akin to the work of Gadamer (1991) and other scholars who see dialogue as an interpretive activity—shifting the focus from ontology to epistemology.

Scholars such as Cypher and Kent (2018) have also started to push dialogue further, exploring the dialogic principles in more depth and trying to explore what it means to have "unconditional positive regard" for another, or what the concept of "strange otherness" means in practice. Other dialogic essays worth mentioning include Pieczka's (2011) critical essay on dialogic expertise, examining "dialogue in public relations theory, pedagogy, and practice" (p. 108), as well as Toledano's excellent work exploring the application of dialogue (2017), and the life and work of Martin Buber (2018).

The last issue in this section is to briefly describe the ways that dialogue has been used ineffectively in public relations. To fully understand any theory, scholars should also look at what a theory is *not*.

What Dialogue Is Not, and Where Dialogue Cannot Happen

As already noted, dialogue is more than just a conversation. Genuine dialogue involves interaction among two or more individuals who know what dialogue is or how it works. They know the "rules" of the conversation or interaction, what to do to change or question the rules, etc. Dialogue cannot take place between individuals or groups when only one of the participants in the conversation understands what dialogue is.

Thus scholars who look to social media posts as sources of data are rarely examining dialogue, and many studies of dialogue simply assume that two-way communication equates to dialogue (Kent & Lane, 2021). Indeed, the concept of "dialogic potential" (Kent & Taylor, 1998) is often invoked to talk about social media contexts that have the "potential" to be dialogic because of their structure and design (Kent & Lane, 2021; Kent & Taylor, 2021), but because the social media participants have no training or understanding of dialogue, calling social media posts dialogic is problematic.

Kent and Lane (2021) note a number of other contexts where dialogue either is not taking place or is not possible. *First is a concept called "ticking the box"* (Lane, 2018), where organizations are mandated (often by the government) to hold public meetings/dialogues, or where organizations claim to have dialogued with members of their publics about upcoming decisions, when in fact all they did was look at social media posts or ask people for their opinions on a proposed action.

A second setting where dialogue is not possible is where the goal of an interaction is persuasion. In practice, a dialogue should not be based on persuasion—although Theunissen (2015) acknowledges that there is necessarily some overlap that may take place in dialogic conversations. In a genuine dialogue, sharing, empathizing, being open to change, etc., necessarily lead people to let others talk and tell their stories, rather than trying to persuade them. When organizations are hosting a "public dialogue" to "share their side," etc., there is no dialogue.

A third non-dialogic context has to do with issues of fact. Attempts to change people's views about "facts" are not dialogic. Facts are verifiable things. Arguing about fact is usually nothing more than an attempt to persuade someone that you are right, and they are wrong.

A fourth area of dialogic concern is where there is no trust, respect, or where power is being exerted over others. A dialogue without trust, respect, or one influenced by fear is not a dialogue. Forcing individuals to participate in a conversation that they do not believe to be risk-free or safe is also not an example of dialogue.

Finally, a fifth area where dialogue is not possible is when one or more of the parties involved in the interaction are unwilling to be changed. Recalcitrant or intractable participants who are not open to the encounter with "strange otherness" are not useful dialogic partners.

Approaches to Studying Dialogue

As noted many times, dialogue is an experiential activity, an interpersonal exchange between two or more people where each shares information in an atmosphere of trust and goodwill. But studying or describing an ontic experience is not an easy thing. The next subsections briefly take up some of the issues to consider when studying dialogue.

Qualitative vs. Quantitative

In theory, anything can be studied either qualitatively or quantitively, if the right variables are examined or the correct questions are asked. However, in the case of dialogue, many scholars over the years have sought to quantify the practice of dialogue, reducing the study of dialogue to a stimulus-response measurement activity of variables or behaviors, rather than considering the whole (cf., Lee, 2022; McAlister-Spooner, 2008). The move to quantify dialogue, however, is inconsistent with dialogic practice. In general, qualitative research looks at things that need to be described (experiential, interpretive, opinions, etc.), while quantitative research looks at things that can be counted.

Although arguments have been made that qualitative research is a precursor or handmaiden to "real science," which is quantifiable (Bowers, 1972), most scholars reject that notion as an attempt to diminish the role, value, importance, or purpose of qualitative research. A few extreme examples should illustrate what qualitative experiences are about.

Many life events are essentially one-off experiences that only someone who has lived through them can fully understand: near death experiences; surviving a suicide attempt; the loss of a child, pet, or loved one; drug addiction; traumatic injuries; and thousands of other things. Although we can count the number of suicides or attempted suicides, or survey survivors about their experiences, genuinely understanding what a person has experienced, why someone tried to take their life, etc. cannot be done via quantification. Thus, the experience of dialogue is ontological.

Additionally, in the humanities, theories are not built numerically, and quantification is just a *tool* to test theories. Even number theory and mathematical theories require words to explain. Perhaps the most famous example in the world of the qualitative/quantitative relationship is Einstein's $E=mc^2$, often mistaken for the actual theory, rather than an equation used to describe *part* of Einstein's Theory of Special Relativity. The study of dialogue has also been reduced to numbers and quantification, counting responses to tweets, etc., but whether genuine dialogue is being studied is another issue. Many studies simply assume the presence of dialogue whenever there is two-way communication (Kent & Lane, 2021), but dialogue is more than just messages and feedback.

Direct the Focus to Ontology and Experience

Dialogue is an experiential phenomenon. Often the desire of quantitative researchers is to *reduce* the number of variables of study, as in a factor analysis, down to the bare minimum to represent the area of study, or sometimes to *increase* the data being studied, as in big data and network theory. However, both approaches necessarily reduce experience (the qualitative) to numerical data, or categories, rather than making the data more rich and vivid. As noted earlier, knowing the factors that lead to suicide is not the same as having had a close friend or family member try to kill themselves.

Obviously, both quantitative and qualitative theories can be used to inform communication in several ways, however, the experience of an interpersonal relationship cannot be reduced to descriptive "variables" concerning what a relationship is about. Why a person likes another person cannot be reduced to a few variables. Sometimes we are attracted to others because of their intelligence; their outward appearance; their political, social, or economic power; their confidence; their age (younger/older/the same age); their career stage; their personal interests, etc.; other times we are attracted to people because they seem friendly, kind, honest, funny, trustworthy, etc. Additionally, what a person sees in a prospective life partner is often different than what they want in a friend or mentor. Friends, and partners, can be of the same gender, another gender, more intelligent, less intelligent, introverted, extroverted, culturally or socially similar/different, etc.

Thus, ontological theories call on researchers to understand that what they explain is the nature or quality of the shared experience, rather than specific variables. The focus of dialogic research should be on the relationship, the communication, the nature of the environment, and not "how many messages are exchanged," whether the interaction is two-way, etc.

The final section of the chapter describes the process of dialogue. Dialogue does not just happen randomly. Dialogue involves various steps before a dialogic encounter (the predialogic) as well as steps after the dialogue (the postdialogic) (cf., Kent & Lane, 2017).

The Predialogic and Postdialogic

As noted earlier, dialogic theory is a normative theory about how people should, or could, communicate for the betterment of individuals, organizations, and society. Thus, that a theory such as dialogue has found a place in public relations is not surprising. Most people probably want to do the right thing, and using a tool like dialogue to facilitate effective and ethical communication is desirable. Fortunately, the practice of dialogue is not particularly difficult once the process is understood.

Dialogue is often mistakenly thought of as simply an event or occurrence that happens whenever people of goodwill get together, rather than as a product of an assortment of preparations. As Kent and Taylor (1998) argued, "Dialogue is product rather than process" (p. 323). Although dialogue involves various processes and preparations, having a successful dialogue involves both work up front, as well as work at the back end. The process can be thought of as the predialogic, dialogic, and postdialogic, with no guarantee that a dialogic interaction actually happens.

Dialogic theory includes a process of preparation, communication, and continued communication (Kent & Lane, 2017). The theory of dialogue describes more than an event or a happening, more than a set of steps or approaches, and more than just a description of what is happening. Dialogue is a multilayer process that requires thought/preparation, skillful conversation, rhetorical skill and sensitivity, and a genuine empathetic understanding of others.

Dialogue, as a tool of organizational success, works to emphasize the interconnectedness of individuals and organizations in society, to understand other people, groups, and organizations, and to benefit all parties involved. Dialogue is a tool of cocreation, or the process of creating the reality of ourselves and others. Cocreation is an important concept in public relations and an important part of dialogue, because at the heart of "unconditional positive regard" and "the encounter with strange otherness" is the idea of humility: that we need others to make sense of the world; no one knows everything.

Conclusion

As should be clear, the theory of dialogue is an exciting communicative theory because of the important role that interpersonal communication plays in our lives and profession. Dialogue, as a theory firmly rooted in interpersonal interaction and discussion, is about how communication professionals can use communication to make the world better, not just achieve success. Public relations is often thought of as an unethical activity, on par with deceptive marketing and advertising practices, unethical politicians, or even a used car salesman trying to make a buck by selling someone a lemon (Sommerfeldt & Kent, 2020). In truth, public relations is both about helping organizations manage their communication, as well as helping publics to manage their communication with organizations and negotiate their success in an increasingly complex and fragmented communication milieu.

Dialogue is one of a handful of theories that does not simply describe reality, but helps people manage it. Public relations professionals would do well to learn from dialogic theory and become more aware of their own limitations, biases, and unquestioned assumptions. The principles that make up dialogic theory constitute powerful concepts that have each been studied on their own, and each is about contributing to a more ethical public relations practice.

Bibliography

Bakhtin, M. M. (1981). *The dialogic imagination: Four essays* (C. Emerson & M. Holquist, Trans.). University of Texas Press.

Botan, C. (1997). Ethics in strategic communication campaigns: The case for a new approach to public relations. *The Journal of Business Communication, 34*(2), 188–202.

Bowers, J. W. (1972). The pre-scientific function of rhetorical criticism. In D. Ehninger (Ed.), *Contemporary rhetoric* (pp. 163–173). Random House.

Buber, M. (1970/1923). *I and thou* (W. Kaufmann, Trans.). Charles Scribner's Sons.

Capizzo, L. (2018). Reimagining dialogue in public relations: Bakhtin and open dialogue in the public sphere. *Public Relations Review, 44*(4), 523–532.

Cissna, K. N., & Anderson, R. (1994). Communication and the ground of dialogue. In R. Anderson, K. N. Cissna, & R. C. Arnett (Eds.), *The reach of dialogue: Confirmation, voice, and community* (pp. 9–30). Hampton Press.

Cypher, J. M., & Kent, M. L. (2018, April). *Authenticity in the dialogic encounter.* Competitive panel delivered to the Central States Communication Association (CSCA), The Difficulties [or Paradoxes] of Identity and Difference in Everyday Life and mass

Communication. Co-Sponsors, Media Studies Interest Group, and Interpersonal and Small Group Communication Interest Group.

Freire, P. (1970/1968). *Pedagogy of the oppressed* (M. B. Ramos, Trans.). Continuum Publishing Company.

Gadamer, H.-G. (1991/1960). *Truth and method*. Crossroad Publishing.

Granovetter, M. S. (1973). The strength of weak ties. *American Journal of Sociology, 78*(6), 1360–1380.

Habermas, J. (1984). *The theory of communicative action* (McCarthy, Trans., Vol. 1). Beacon Press.

Kennedy, G. A. (1987). *Classical rhetoric and its christian and secular tradition from ancient to modern times*. Longman Press.

Kent, M. L., & Lane, A. (2017, September). A rhizomatous metaphor for dialogic theory. *Public Relations Review, 43*(3), 568–578.

Kent, M. L., & Lane, A. (2021). Two-way communication, symmetry, negative spaces, and dialogue. *Public Relations Review, 47*(2), 1–9.

Kent, M. L., & Li, C. (2020). Toward a normative social media theory of public relations. *Public Relations Review, 46*(1), 1–10.

Kent, M. L., Saffer, A. J., & Sommerfeldt, E. J. (2016, May–August). From communitarianism to dialogue: Building better relationships. *NIDA Journal of Language and Communication, 21*(28), 1–15.

Kent, M. L., & Taylor, M. (1998). Building dialogic relationships through the World Wide Web. *Public Relations Review, 24*(3), 321–334.

Kent, M. L., & Taylor, M. (2002). Toward a dialogic theory of public relations. *Public Relations Review, 28*(1), 21–37.

Kent, M. L., & Taylor, M. (2007). Beyond "excellence" in international public relations research: An examination of generic theory in Bosnian public relations. *Public Relations Review, 33*(1), 10–20.

Kent, M. L., & Taylor, M. (2018). Chapter 22: Understanding the rhetoric of dialogue and the dialogue of rhetoric. In Ø. Ihlen & R. L. Heath (Eds.), *Handbook of organizational rhetoric and communication: Foundations of dialogue, discourse, narrative, and engagement* (pp. 315–327). Wiley-Blackwell.

Kent, M. L., & Taylor, M. (2021, January–March). Fostering dialogic engagement: Toward an architecture of social media. *Social Media + Society, 7*(1), 1–10.

Kent, M. L., Taylor, M., & White, W. (2003). The relationship between Web site design and organizational responsiveness to stakeholders. *Public Relations Review, 29*(1), 63–77.

Kent, M. L., & Theunissen, P. (2016). Elegy for mediated dialogue: Shiva the destroyer and reclaiming our first principles. *International Journal of Communication, 10*, 4040–4054.

Laing, R. D. (1961/1969). *Self and others*. Pantheon Books.

Lane, A. B. (2018). If it's so good, why not make them do it? Why true dialogue cannot be mandated. *Public Relations Review, 44*(5), 656–666.

Lane, A. B. (2020). The dialogic ladder: Toward a framework of dialogue. *Public Relations Review, 46*(1), 1–8.

Lane, A. B., & Bartlett, J. (2016). Why dialogic principles don't make it in practice—and what we can do about it. *International Journal of Communication, 10*, 4074–4094.

Lane, A. B., & Kent, M. L. (2018). Chapter 5: Dialogic engagement. In K. Johnston & M. Taylor (Eds.), *Handbook of engagement* (pp. 61–72). Wiley-Blackwell.

Lee, Y. (2022). How dialogic internal communication fosters employees' safety behavior during the COVID-19 pandemic. *Public Relations Review, 48*(1), 1–10.

Li, C., & Kent, M. L. (2021). Explorations on mediated communication and beyond: Toward a theory of social media. *Public Relations Review, 47*(5), 1–9.

Linton, P. (2016, April 2). Movies make me a better man: "My Dinner with Andre". *A&E: The Good Men Project.* https://goodmenproject.com/arts/movies-make-better-man-dinner-andre-knts

Littlejohn, S. W., Foss, K. A., Oetzel, J. G. (2017). *Theories of human communication* (11th ed.). Waveland Press.

Marshall, C. (2022, January 14). How pulp fiction uses the socratic method, the philosophical method from ancient Greece. *Open Culture: Film Philosophy.* www.openculture.com/2022/01/how-pulp-fiction-uses-the-socratic-method-the-philosophical-method-from-ancient-greece.html

McAlister-Spooner, S. (2008). User perceptions of dialogic public relations tactics via the Internet. *Public Relations Journal, 2*(1), 1–18.

Morehouse, J., & Saffer, A. J. (2018). A bibliometric analysis of dialogue and digital dialogic research: Mapping the knowledge construction and invisible colleges in public relations research. *Journal of Public Relations Research, 30*(3), 65–82.

Noddings, N. (1984). *Caring: A feminine approach to ethics and moral education.* University of California Press.

Pearson, R. (1989a). *A theory of public relations ethics* [Unpublished doctoral dissertation, Ohio University].

Pearson, R. (1989b). Chapter 7: Business ethics as communication ethics: Public relations practice and the idea of dialogue. In C. H. Botan & V. Hazleton (Eds.), *Public relations theory* (pp. 111–131). Lawrence Erlbaum Associates.

Pearson, R. (1989c). Chapter 3: Beyond ethical relativism in public relations: Coorientation, rules, and the idea of communication symmetry. In J. E. Grunig & L. A. Grunig (Eds.), *Public relations research annual* (Vol. 1, pp. 67–86). Lawrence Erlbaum Associates.

Pieczka, M. (2011). Public relations as dialogic expertise? *Journal of Communication Management, 15*(2), 108–124.

Plato. (1999a) *Gorgias* (B. Jowett, Trans.). Project Guttenberg. Etext #1672. www.gutenberg.org/files/1636/1636-h/1636-h.htm

Plato. (1999b). *Phaedrus* (B. Jowett, Trans.). Project Guttenberg. Etext #1636. www.gutenberg.org/files/1636/1636-h/1636-h.htm

Rogers, C. R. (1992/1956). The necessary and sufficient conditions of therapeutic personality change. *Journal of Consulting and Clinical Psychology, 60*(6), 827–832.

Russmann, U., & Lane, A. B. (2020). Mandating dialogue? International perspectives on differences between theory and practice. *Public Relations Review, 46*(1), 1–11.

Sommerfeldt, E. J., & Kent, M. L. (2020). Public relations as "dirty work": Disconfirmation, cognitive dissonance, and emotional labor among public relations professors. *Public Relations Review, 46*(4), 1–9.

Sommerfeldt, E. J., & Yang, A. (2018). Notes on a dialogue: Twenty years of digital dialogic communication research in public relations. *Journal of Public Relations Research, 30*(3), 59–64.

Tarantino, Q. (Director) (1994). *Pulp fiction. A band apart.* Jersey Films.

Taylor, M., & Kent, M. L. (2014). Dialogic engagement: Clarifying foundational concepts. *Journal of Public Relations Research, 26*(5), 384–398.

Taylor, M., Kent, M., & White, W. (2001). How activist organizations are using the Internet to build relationships. *Public Relations Review, 27*(3), 263–284.

Theunissen, P. (2015). The quantum entanglement of dialogue and persuasion in social media: Introducing the per–di principle. *Atlantic Journal of Communication, 23*(1), 31–45.

Theunissen, P., & Wan Noordin, W. N. (2012). Revisiting the concept "dialogue" in public relations. *Public Relations Review, 38*(1), 5–13.

Toledano, M. (2017). Dialogue with the enemy: Lessons for public relations on dialogue facilitation drawn from the Israeli-Palestinian conflict. In I. Somerville, O. Hargie, M. Taylor, & M. Toledano (Eds.), *International public relations: Perspectives from deeply divided societies* (pp. 9–26). Routledge.

Toledano, M. (2018). Dialogue, strategic communication, and ethical public relations: Lessons from Martin Buber's political activism. *Public Relations Review, 44*(1), 131–141.

Uysal, N. (2018). On the relationship between dialogic communication and corporate social performance: Advancing dialogic theory and research. *Journal of Public Relations Research, 30*(3), 100–114.

Watzlawick, P., Beavin, J. H., & Jackson, D. D. (1967). *Pragmatics of human communication: A study of interactional patterns, pathologies, and paradoxes.* W.W. Norton.

10 Capturing the Complexity and Dynamism of Decision Making in PR

The Contingency Theory of Strategic Conflict Management

Augustine Pang, Yan Jin, and Glen T. Cameron

Introduction

In the high plains of Montana at the turn of the 21st century, 14-year-old Ernie became a rancher after he was chased out of school. By the 1930s, he owned almost 10,000 acres of land. His dream was for his children and their children to live as ranchers.

Trouble came when the US Forest Service wanted Ernie to fence up parcels of his land from those owned by the federal government. Ernie was adamant: "If anyone crosses my land . . . I'll shoot 'em!" When his son Turk took over the running of the land, he was faced with a new set of problems. To demands from the Forest Service officers and other congressional aides, Turk was willing to listen and cooperate, in part because he wanted to be a good corporate citizen—give in and accommodate to some of their requests. However, when dealing with a group of environmentalists whose aim was to rid the land of ranchers and free Montana of cattle rearing, Turk became defensive. He promised to do everything within his powers to stop them.

This narrative is instructive for the science of communication. As communication scientists, even as we grapple continually with how to refine a structure to help us order, explain, predict, and control the world around us (Chaffee & Berger, 1987) by building theories, and even as we build theories through research (Heath & Coombs, 2006) and through observations of best practices (Seeger, 2006), the challenge remains for us to relate theories to the real world, one that is grounded in the practitioners' world (Pang et al., 2006).

The story of the rancher was narrated by Professor Glen T. Cameron (now emeritus at the University of Missouri School of Journalism), one of the prime movers of the contingency theory at a conference in Norway in 1997 (Cameron, 1997). Ernie was Glen's uncle, and Turk his cousin. Their experiences were used to illustrate the inspiration behind the conceptualization of the theory. Ernie's stance toward the federal government when it asked him to fence up his land, just like Turk's stance toward the environmentalists, could be described as advocacy, arguing one's position. Turk's

DOI: 10.4324/9781003141396-12

stance toward the Forest Service and congressional aides could be described as accommodation, or giving in. These two concepts were to form the central tenets of the contingency theory: How public relations could be practiced through the enactment of stances. At that time, the predominant thought was symmetrical communication, described in the excellence theory as the model by which the most ethical and excellent public relations was practiced. Through Ernie and Turk, Glen saw a different reality.

The contingency theory of strategic conflict management (hereafter "the contingency theory"), which originated as the contingency theory of accommodation in public relations (Cameron, 1997; Cancel et al., 1999), began questioning the excellence theory's positioning of symmetrical communication as normative theory on how organizations should be practicing public relations that was regarded as the most ethical and effective (L. A. Grunig, 1996). It might have had its humble beginnings as an elaboration, qualification, and extension of the value of symmetry (Cameron, 1997; Cameron et al., 2001). Since the 1990s, it has emerged as an empirically tested perspective, grounded on how intuitive, nuanced, and textured public relations have been practiced (Cancel et al., 1999; Jin et al., 2021; Pang et al., 2020, 2010a, 2010b).

Coombs (2010) described the contingency theory as a "grand theory of public relations" (p. 41). A "grand theory" is one that "seeks to explain how public relations as a whole operates" (p. 41). Citing Botan (2006), Coombs (2010) argued that a grand theory "helps us to understand what guides policy-level decisions an organization makes about goals, alignments, ethics, and relationships with publics and other forces in its environment" (p. 41). Grand theories, argued Coombs (2010), began by seeking to explain an entire discipline and "can be adapted to specific areas of the discipline" (p. 41). Contingency theory began essentially as a public relations theory in the 1990s but has since been adapted and applied to crisis situations. Frandsen and Johansen (2020) described it as a first-generation theory. In another study, Frandsen and Johansen (2017) wrote, "It was not until the mid-2000s that Cameron's contingency theory of accommodation became a genuine theory of crisis communication. It was in particular Augustine Pang and Yan Jin who contributed to this development" (p. 116). Today it is regarded more as a conflict management theory and one of the key theories applied in crisis communication research (An & Cheng, 2010; Jin et al., 2021; Liu & Fraustino, 2014; Pang et al., 2020, 2021, 2010a, 2010b).

This chapter has the following sections. The first chronicles the contingency theory's origins, its theoretical platform, and the nascent testing and expounding of the theory in the field of public relations. The second seeks to consolidate the theoretical development by mapping out the predisposing, situational, and proscriptive contingency variables along the life cycle of complex and challenging public relations issues (e.g., conflicts and crises). The third assesses the application of the theory in various scenarios and contexts. The last section contemplates new directions of research as the theory develops.

It is hoped that this chapter can spur further examination of how the contingency theory can provide a framework to capture the complexity and dynamism of public relations decision making, especially when organizations are confronted by challenging issues (e.g., conflicts and crises) and to provide the impetus for practitioners to view communication as opportunities to engage in strategic management. Strategic management is defined as "the set of decisions and actions that results in the formulation and implementation of plans designed to achieve a company's objectives" (Pearce & Robinson, 2015). Kim and Ni (2010) argued for public relations to be part of the strategic management function. Besides strategic communication, key contributions can include working with stakeholders and reputation management.

The Evolution of the Contingency Theory

How the Contingency Theory Evolved Since the 1990s

The theory has evolved since its beginnings in the 1990s. More recently, it was identified and recommended by the Crisis Communication Think Tank (CCTT) at the University of Georgia as one of the four leading crisis communication theories that are most applicable to advancing crisis communication practice, especially in tackling complex and challenging issues that threaten the industry as a whole (Jin et al., 2021), highlighted in the book *Advancing Crisis Communication Effectiveness: Integrating Public Relations Scholarship and Practice* (2021).

Central Concepts of the Contingency Theory: Stance and Factors

The overarching approach of the contingency theory is: "It depends." In the context of public relations practice, "it" refers to *stance* (i.e., an organization's position), which changes through a continuum from pure advocacy to pure accommodation. To describe, explain, and predict how the *stance* of an organization in dealing with changes (with a given public at a given time in a given situation), not the changes in communication outcomes, is the focus of the contingency theory.

Stance. As a core construct of the contingency theory, *stance* is proposed to be measured through a continuum that has, at one end of the continuum, advocacy (which meant arguing for one's own) and at the other end, accommodation (which meant accepting the other party's proposal). These two ends represent an organization's willingness to make concessions or give or offer trade-offs: at one end the organization pleads its case and at the other makes overtures toward a trade-off or toward concessions.

Advocacy   Accommodation

I———————————————————————————————————————I

Between the two ends is a wide range of operational stances, and these entailed "different degrees of advocacy and accommodation" (Cancel et al., 1997, p. 37) as stance moves along the continuum of accommodation. Organizations practice a variety of stances with their publics at any given point, and these stances change, depending on the circumstances. Stance is operationalized as the position an organization takes in decision making, which is supposed to determine which strategies and subsequently tactics to employ.

To further explicate the concept of stance, Jin and Cameron (2006) developed a multiple-item scale for measuring public relations stance, conceptualizing stance into the sub-levels of advocacy and accommodation, with the concept of accommodation as the focus of this scale development. Specifically, stance is operationalized as degrees of accommodation or willingness of taking accommodations toward a given public in a given situation (i.e., "Given the situation, [a practitioner] will be (1, completely unwilling; 7, completely willing)" to take different stances, Jin & Cameron; p. 425). Based on survey data collected from public relations practitioners and vetted through a systematic scale development and psychometric assessment procedure including exploratory factor analysis (EFA) and confirmatory factor analysis (CFA), stance was found to be represented by two distinguishable but related clusters of enactments as action-based accommodations (AA) and qualified-rhetoric-mixed accommodations (QRA).

AA refers to stances enacted, for instance, by agreeing to the other party's proposal, acceptance of the public's suggestions, composed by five items (i.e., to yield to the public's demands; to agree to follow what the public proposed; to accept the public's propositions; to agree with the public on future action or procedure; to agree to try the solutions suggested by the public) (coefficient alpha = .89, Jin & Cameron, 2006). QRA is weighted more toward expressing regrets and qualifying the organization's tendency of collaboration and so forth without explicitly taking concrete actions, contributed by five items (i.e., to express regret or apologize to the public; to collaborate with the public in order to solve the problem at hand; to change one's own position toward that of the public; to make concessions with the public; to admit wrongdoing) (coefficient alpha = .79, Jin & Cameron, 2006). Both stance enactments, though each captures different aspects of stance, are consistently measuring the degrees of accommodation toward the public as the contingency theory proposed.

Contingency factors. According to the contingency theory, the stance an organization takes is driven by circumstances, which are shaped by different factors. There are 87 contingent factors (see Pang et al., 2021, 2010a, 2010b) (see Table 10.1).

The contingency theory argues that any of the 87 factors can affect the location of an organization's stance on that continuum "*at a given time regarding a given public*" (Cancel et al., 1999 p. 172; Yarbrough et al., 1998, p. 40). Three ways of organizing and understanding the contingency factors have been developed:

Table 10.1 Variables that Affect an Organization's Response

1. Organization characteristics
   A. Open or closed culture
   B. Dispersed widely geographically or centralized
   C. Level of technology the organization uses to produce its product or service
   D. Homogeneity or heterogeneity of officials involved
   E. Age of the organization/value placed on tradition
   F. Speed of growth in the knowledge level the organization uses
   G. Economic stability of the organization
   H. Existence or non-existence of issues management officials or program
   I. Organization's past experiences with the public
   J. Distribution of decision-making power
   K. Formalization: number of roles or codes defining and limiting the job
   L. Stratification/Hierarchy of positions
   M. Existence or influence of legal department
   N. Business exposure
   O. Corporate culture
2. Public Relations department characteristics
   A. Number of practitioners total and number of college degrees
   B. Type of past training: Trained in PR or ex-journalists, marketing, etc.
   C. Location of PR department in hierarchy: Independent or under marketing umbrella/experiencing encroachment of marketing/persuasive mentality
   D. Representation in the Dominant Coalition
   E. Experience level of PR practitioners in dealing with crisis
   F. General communication competency of department
   G. Autonomy of department
   H. Physical placement of department in building (near CEO and other decision makers or not)
   I. Staff trained in research methods
   J. Amount of funding available for dealing with external publics
   K. Amount of time allowed to use dealing with external publics
   L. Gender: percentage of female upper-level staff/managers
   M. Potential of department to practice various models of public relations
3. Characteristics of Dominant Coalition (top management)
   A. Political values: Conservative or liberal/open or closed to change
   B. Management style: Domineering or laid-back
   C. General altruism level
   D. Support and understanding of PR
   E. Frequency of external contact with publics
   F. Departmental perception of the organization's external environment
   G. Calculation of potential rewards or losses using different strategies with external publics
   H. Degree of line manager involvement in external affairs
4. Internal threats (How much is at stake in the situation)
   A. Economic loss or gain from implementing various stances
   B. Marring of employees' or stockholders' perception of the company
   C. Marring of the personal reputations of the company decision makers
5. Individual characteristics (public relations practitioners, domestic coalition, and line managers)
   A. Training in diplomacy, marketing, journalism, engineering, etc.
   B. Personal ethics
   C. Tolerance or ability to deal with uncertainty
   D. Comfort level with conflict or dissonance

(Continued)

Table 10.1 (Continued)

E. Comfort level with change
F. Ability to recognize potential and existing problems
G. Extent to openness to innovation
H. Extent to which individual can grasp other's worldview
I. Personality: Dogmatic, authoritarian
J. Communication competency
K. Cognitive complexity: Ability to handle complex problems
L. Predisposition toward negotiations
M. Predisposition toward altruism
N. How individuals receive, process, and use information and influence
O. Familiarity with external public or its representative
P. Like external public or its representative
Q. Gender: Female versus male
6. Relationship characteristics
   A. Level of trust between organization and external public
   B. Dependency of parties involved
   C. Ideological barriers between organization and public
7. External threats
   A. Litigation
   B. Government regulation
   C. Potentially damaging publicity
   D. Scarring of company's reputation in business community and in the public
   E. Legitimizing activists' claims
8. Industry environment
   A. Changing (dynamic) or static
   B. Number of competitors/level of competition
   C. Richness or leanness of resources in the environment
9. General political/social environment/external culture
   A. Degree of political support of business
   B. Degree of social support of business
10. The external public (e.g., group, individual)
   • Size and/or number of members
   • Degree of source credibility/powerful members or connections
   • Past successes or failures of groups to evoke change
   • Amount of advocacy practiced by the organization
   • Level of commitment/involvement of members
   • Whether the group has public relations counselors or not
   • Public's perception of group: reasonable or radical
   • Level of media coverage the public has received in the past
   • Whether representatives of the public know or like representatives of the organization
   • Whether representatives of the organization know or like representatives from the public
   • Public's willingness to dilute its cause/request/claim
   • Moves and countermoves
   • Relative power of organization
   • Relative power of public
11. Issue under question
   A. Size
   B. Stake
   C. Complexity

Internal vs. external variables. These factors were initially grouped into *internal variables* related to the characteristics of the organization and *external variables* regarding the environment and publics' characteristics.

Predisposing vs. situational factors. Predisposing factors include the characteristics of dominant coalition, public relations' access to top management, organizational size and culture, and so forth. *Situational factors* include the characteristics of the external public, perceived urgency and threat, and the feasibility of accommodation. Predisposing variables determine the stance of an organization before it enters a situation dealing with a given public while the combination and variability of situational factors might shift the stance of the organization over time, depending on whether the situational factors are powerful enough to change the predisposing positioned stance on the continuum of accommodation.

Proscriptive factors. To understand why accommodating stances cannot be taken in some situations, Cameron et al. (2001) studied the following key *proscriptive factors*: 1) the morality of top management, 2) the position caught in-between two contending publics at the same time, and 3) restriction from regulation, and regulation and jurisdictions, which were found to preclude an organization from accommodating or even communicating with a public. It is concluded that for those situations, an organization's stance can swiftly change and move on the continuum of accommodation, based on the influence of those proscriptive factors.

Of the list of factors, Pang (2006) found the key roles five factors play. They are: the influence of the dominant coalition, influence of PR in the crisis, influence of legal, importance of the primary publics to the organization, and the organization's perception of threat to its reputation. These factors have been validated in studies (Hwang & Cameron, 2008, 2009).

As a Strategic Conflict Management Theory: Dynamics of the Contingency Theory Developing a New Cluster of Variables: Ethical Variables

As practitioners face ethical dilemmas and there is interest in understanding the dilemmas relative to the profession (Hove & Paek, 2017), contingency theorists have called for identifying ethical variables and adding them to the contingency factor matrix. Pang et al. (2010c) posited a set of ethical variables that influence an organization's stance before it engages in any communication with affected publics: 1) the role of public relations practitioners, 2) the role of top management, 3) exposure of organizational business and cultural diversity, 4) government influence and intervention, 5) nature of the crisis, and 6) stakeholder activism. These proposed ethical factors are likely to influence the organization's adoption of an ethical stance toward a given public at a given time from pure advocacy to pure accommodation.

The new ethical factors have been explored with practitioners in Singapore (Pang et al., 2016) and the United States (Jin et al., 2018). Through their lens and practices, an organization's ethical communication in times of escalated conflicts (e.g., a crisis) is evidenced in communicating with publics with accurate and timely information, through the crisis cycle, transparently, responsibly, and honestly; it is also essential to integrate ethical considerations in overall business strategy and the long-term reputational well-being plan for the organization (Pang et al., 2020).

To sum up, the role of the four clusters of factors in determining what stance an organization takes in a public relations issue can be depicted in Figure 10.1.

While not exhaustive, this represents an important first step in the synthesis of theoretical insights and analyzing which factors play more critical roles.

Further Elaborations of the Theory

The two central concepts of the contingency theory, factors and stance, have been further elaborated systematically across different generations of contingency theorists.

Examining contingency factors. The approaches to further elaborating the contingency factors take two main routes: 1) *categorizing* contingency factors as groups according to the way the factors exert influences on public relations practice, primarily for the theory parsimony's purpose, and 2) further *explicating* specific factors.

As examples of attempting to categorize contingency factors, Shin et al. (2002) conducted a national survey of practitioners on the perceived importance of contingent factors and the influence in their daily public relations practice. Practitioners identified organization-related characteristics as most influential. Further, through a survey of top public relations practitioners, Reber and Cameron (2003) quantified contingency theory by constructing scales of five theoretical constructs: *external threats, external public characteristics, organizational characteristics, public relations department characteristics,* and *dominant collation characteristics.* Practitioners cited fear of legitimizing activist

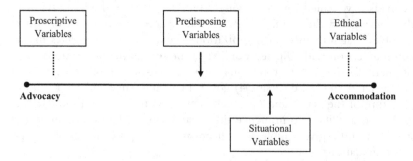

Figure 10.1 Contingency Variables at a Glance

claims, credibility and commitment of an external public, and the place of public relations in the dominant collation as contingencies impacting the dialogue with contending publics.

One example of deepening the understanding of individual contingency factors is in the explication of *threat*. Threats—both internal and external as identified in the original contingency factor matrix—have been identified as among the most important but yet-to-be-explicated contingency factors, Jin and Cameron (2007) and Jin et al. (2012) conceptually differentiated threats from "risk," "fear," and "conflict," which are the cause and the effect of crisis. Jin and Cameron (2007) proposed a threat appraisal model, based on the assessments of situational demands and organizational resources, and found that external and long-term threat combination led to higher situational demands appraisal and more intensive emotional arousal. Jin et al. (2012) further proposed the explication of the concept of "threat" by expanding, cross-fertilizing, and integrating ideas from an inter-disciplinary review of literature and enumerated the dimensionality of threats such as duration, severity, and type. Most recently, Kim et al. (2020) further examined the multidimensionality of crisis distance (i.e., temporal, social, and hypothetical), perceived distance of a threat as appraised by publics in a given conflict or crisis situation, taking a systematic approach to understanding publics' crisis responses (e.g., reputation, supportive behavioral intention, crisis attitudes).

Stance from the publics' perspective. As Jin et al. (2021) pointed out, one area of exploration for the contingency theory development is geared toward the publics' minds and perspectives. In terms of adopting publics' perspectives in the contingency theory's framework, scholars suggested that developing and testing a new publics-centered continuum would be an essential starting point (Kim et al., 2017). The proposed continuum has two ends—total confidence and total doubt as represented here:

Total Confidence   Total Doubt

I————————————————————————————————————I

Between the two ends of the publics' continuum, how the publics perceive organizations as capable of handling a crisis or conflict is manifested (Kim et al., 2017). Confidence is originally a concept that is based on "the belief, based on experience or evidence that certain future events will occur as expected" (Earle et al., 2007, p. 4). In this regard, organizational confidence from publics' view should examine whether they would believe the crisis or conflict is managed well or stopped by the organization confronted by the situation. Previous literature about confidence suggests that knowledge and information about past performance determine one's confidence level (Siegrist et al., 2007). Those who are confident of the organization's ability are likely to have prior experience to observe that it performs well, which applies to the publics' perception toward an organization in the context of crises (Jin et al., 2021).

According to Jin et al. (2021), on the confidence-doubt continuum, when one is closer to the end of total doubt, it indicates one's awareness of the past similar crises with which the organization was involved. This publics-driven stance approach, adopting publics' viewpoints, sheds light on integrating stances from both organizational positioning and the publics' perception of both the crisis/conflict and the organization.

Contingency Theory Across Conflict Life Cycle

Scholars agree that strategic crisis management is a dynamic, ongoing process through a life cycle. For instance, Coombs (2019) argued for a three-staged approach—pre-, during, and post-crisis. Others like Fearn-Banks (2017) and James et al. (2013) argued for a five-staged approach—detection, prevention/ preparation, containment, recovery, and learning. George (2012) argued for a three-phase strategy, similar to Coombs' (2010) approach. At each step of the life cycle, key tasks are recommended for organizations to engage in.

Siah et al. (2010) mapped out the key elements of the contingency theory in their New Media Crisis Communication model, which provided an illustration of how the contingency theory could be applied across the life cycle of a conflict event in an increasingly complex digital environment (see Figure 10.2).

In the issues management stage (first stage) of the life cycle, organizations are encouraged to engage in active online news monitoring and environmental scanning. Here, the predisposing variables are at work. The variables include the size of the organization—where a larger organization is assumed to have more resources than a smaller organization; the corporate culture of the organization— where an organization with an open culture would be receptive to adopting new practices; the business exposure the organization has; the corporate communications practitioner's access to the leadership; and the enlightenment of the leadership on the importance of corporate communications. These all play their parts in encouraging the organization toward planning for crisis. These translate into organizational actions. At this stage, the focus is to identify, track, and manage potentially conflicting issues online—a crucial part of corporate communications in the Internet age (Gonzalez-Herrero & Smith, 2008). Such activities include the development of the company's website, the updating of important emailing lists and contact databases, a vigilant online media monitoring service, the registering of all possible domain names, and getting the corporate communications team to gain familiarity with the virtual world.

In the planning and prevention stage (second stage) of the life cycle, the organization engages the online world more actively, identifying and responding to potential threats. Prominent online influencers/opinion leaders are identified, and new media technologies such as RSS feeds and Twitter are utilized to establish an online monitoring alert system, while a hidden or "dark" website—a site that could be used externally in the event of a crisis to update all constituencies about the issue (Gonzalez-Herrero & Smith, 2008, p. 149)—is created. A global mindset is adopted, with the tone and

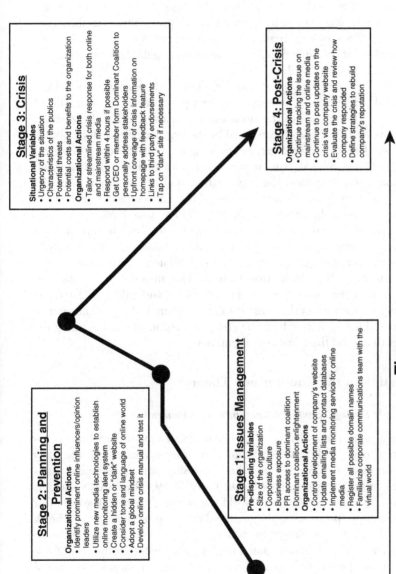

Stage 2: Planning and Prevention

Organizational Actions
• Identify prominent online influencers/opinion leaders
• Utilize new media technologies to establish online monitoring alert system
• Create a hidden or "dark" website
• Consider tone and language of online world
• Adopt a global mindset
• Develop online crisis manual and test it

Stage 3: Crisis

Situational Variables
• Urgency of the situation
• Characteristics of the publics
• Potential threats
• Potential costs and benefits to the organization

Organizational Actions
• Tailor streamlined crisis response for both online and mainstream media
• Respond within 4 hours if possible
• Get CEO or member form Dominant Coalition to personally address stakeholders
• Upfront coverage of crisis information on homepage with feedback feature
• Links to third party endorsements
• Tap on "dark' site if necessary

Stage 1: Issues Management

Pre-disposing Variables
• Size of the organization
• Corporate culture
• Business exposure
• PR access to dominant coalition
• Dominant coalition enlightenment

Organizational Actions
• Control development of company's website
• Update emailing lists and contact databases
• Implement media monitoring service for online media
• Register all possible domain names
• Familiarize corporate communications team with the virtual world

Stage 4: Post-Crisis

Organizational Actions
• Continue tracking the issue on mainstream and online media
• Continue to post updates on the crisis via company website
• Evaluate the crisis and review how company responded
• Define strategies to rebuild company's reputation

Time

Figure 10.2 The New Media Crisis Communication Model

Source: Siah et al. (2010)

language of the online world taken into consideration; at the same time an online crisis manual is developed and tested. We argue that the predisposing factors continue to be considered as part of organizational decision making. Even as the predisposing variables are considered, the deliberation process would include under what circumstances the organization does not accommodate. This is when the contingency theory's proscriptive variables (i.e., the morality of top management, the position caught in-between two contending publics at the same time, restriction from regulation, regulation and jurisdictions) are considered.

At the crisis stage (third stage), the contingency theory's situational variables would influence how organizations react to the crisis. These situational variables are the urgency of the situation, the characteristics of the stakeholders involved, potential threats faced by the organization, and the potential costs and benefits to the organization. Organizational actions at the crisis stage include streamlined crisis response for both online and mainstream media and a response from the organization within four hours after the crisis erupts. Also needed is involvement of the CEO or a member of the leadership to personally address stakeholders. There should also be transparent coverage of the crisis on the homepage with a feedback feature, links to third-party endorsements, and the tapping on the "dark" site if necessary.

In the post-crisis stage (last stage), the organization embarks on several measures to help the organization recover. This includes the continuous tracking of how the issue is portrayed in traditional and online media, regular posting of updates on the crisis via the company website, evaluation of the crisis and the review of how the company responded, and defining the strategies to rebuild the company's reputation.

Application of the Contingency Theory

Exemplar 1: Strategic Conflict Management of a Pandemic

The contingency theory has been applied to understanding pandemic communication (e.g., SARS [severe acute respiratory syndrome] in the early 2000s). Jin et al. (2006) examined how the Singapore government managed the crisis at the national level. Like COVID-19, when SARS made its appearance in China in 2003, the world was not ready for it. However, fear of the contagion spread across the world when it appeared that the outbreak was fast claiming lives. Singapore was one of the earlier countries to be infected. Faced with a health epidemic, the government set up a task force to combat the spread of the virus (Jin et al., 2006). Communication was at red-alert level.

The Singapore government had to work with several publics including its own agencies to contain the outbreak. Jin et al. (2006) identified the strategic and contingent factors that the government adopted at the time to combat the situation. The authors noted that, over time, external contingent factors affected the government's posture toward its publics. It was observed that while the government accommodated some publics, there were those that it had advocated. For example, the government dealt a firm hand with the general public and those who were under quarantine. On occasions, it used the law to affirm its advocative stance with those who had endangered the lives of others with non-compliance of the measures put in place. At the other end of the continuum, the government showed that it was accommodative toward healthcare workers and service staff, especially those who had been adversely affected by the outbreak.

The study also identified the communication strategies that the government had adopted at the time. For all five publics, while attack was adopted when dealing with service professionals, neighboring countries, quarantined public, and general public, ingratiation was used on service professionals in recognition of their work and sacrifice.

The government also adopted a corrective stance with the World Health Organization (WHO), while with its neighboring countries, it additionally assumed the justification stance. Along with these strategies, the factors that strongly impacted the government's stance included threats, external public and issue under question, industry environment, and general culture.

From the study, it emerged that there were more occasions of accommodation than advocacy in the communication process. Those who required more advocacy were publics that needed a stronger hand and control in dealing with the epidemic, and in this case, it was the quarantined public.

Jin et al. (2007) extended their research to draw comparison between Singapore and China, from where SARS was first reported. Results from this study showed the different stances between the two countries. In dealing with WHO, foreign countries, and the general public, China exhibited a more accommodative approach than did Singapore. Under contingent factors, threat was top concern for both countries, and under external publics, Singapore appeared more concerned than China did. Similarly, the publics for both countries perceived threat to be most critical. The authors also noted that given the dynamic nature of an epidemic that crossed borders, a similarly dynamic approach was required to manage it. In which case, marrying the contingency theory with management theory allowed better understanding of crisis management.

Exemplar 2: Strategic Conflict Management of Online Disruption

Until recently, satire was in the confines of art, entertainment, and literature. LeBoeuf (2007) identified satire as "a very powerful artistic form used to critique specific human behaviors" through the use of irony in speech or in visual forms. Satire works to censure bad behaviors by ridiculing them, presenting them out of context, or exaggerating them (LeBoeuf, 2007). However, a recent study argued that satire can also affect an individual or an organization's reputation (Lee et al., 2019). The authors suggested that those under attack should employ contingency theory to manage the situation. With the continuum in mind, the authors proposed any of these four actions: *Join in, Do nothing, Clarify,* or *Refute.* Figure 10.3 is adapted from Lee et al.'s (2019) study.

Should the situation meet at least any two criteria under a strategy, a suitable action may be taken. Table 10.2 offers a continuum of responses organizations can consider.

Before adopting the right posture, organizations should be aware of predisposing, situational, and proscriptive variables (Lee et al., 2019). The four actions to adopt:

Join in. Organizations under attack should engage in affiliative humor such as poking fun at oneself. By accepting the satire and joining in the fun, it helps them to bond with others (Martin et al., 2003). Their ability to laugh at themselves will endear them to their publics and increase their likeability (Ziv, 1984). When the satire has gone viral, its impact is blunted if organizations are able to laugh at themselves, resulting in minimal damage to their reputation.

Do nothing. When a satire has little to no bite, with no resulting harm or confusion, it augurs well for organizations to not overreact or simply do nothing about it. It is a matter of time before the satire dies a quiet death.

Clarify. Clarification is required when a satirical article goes viral both off and online, causing harm to organizations' reputation. The need to clarify is also critical if the article causes mass confusion that could possibly affect jobs and the prospects of the public.

Refute. While satire and satirical news sites are protected by law, it does not mean organizations cannot refute them, especially if the satire has called into question the integrity of the organization and has created confusion among the publics. However, if it has done nothing of such magnitude, it is in the interest of the organization not to refute it.

The contingency theory, according to Pang et al. (2020), is applicable for organizations when handling disruptions (Pang et al., 2010a). Instead of just relying on strategic communication, organizations should identify the stances on the continuum—whether to accommodate or advocate its publics. Models like the two-way symmetrical restricts the organization from thinking out of the box—crisis and conflicts are dynamic situations (Seeger, 2006, p. 241) and require equally dynamic communication solutions. Assuming certain stances on the continuum allows practitioners to effect a targeted communication approach to the situation.

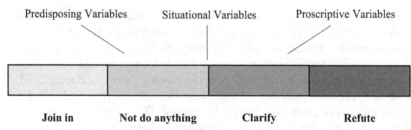

Figure 10.3 The Continuum of Organizational Response to Manage Satire

Table 10.2 Criteria for Continuum of Organizational Response for Satire News

Factors	Join In	Do Nothing	Clarify	Refute
Predisposing Variables Culture, values, reputation, size of the organization, corporate culture, business exposure, public relations	Affiliative humor	Benign humor	Does confusion ensue? (Online/mainstream media)	Concerns the ethics of the individual/company or company values
to dominant coalition, dominant coalition enlightenment, and individual characteristics of key individuals (e.g., CEO)	Virality of satire article	Doesn't help to do anything; doing something will exacerbate the situation	Does it affect tangible aspects of reputation? (e.g., political voting)	Causes turmoil/chaos
Situational Variables Urgency of the situation, potential cost and benefits, characteristics	Minimal to acceptable extent of reputational damage		Virality of the confusion	Concerns the company's dealings with the law
of other publics, and potential or obvious threats	Potential benefits of joining in		Affects livelihood of people	
Proscriptive Variables Moral conviction, moral neutrality in the face of contending publics, legal constraints, regulatory restraints, senior management prohibition of response strategy, and jurisdictional concerns				

Putting theory into practice allows organizations to better understand predisposing, situational, and proscriptive variables and the part they play in crisis and conflict situations. Seeger (2006) stated that strategic communication is "most effective when it is part of the decision process itself"

(p. 236), and awareness of these variables will help organizations make better decisions. These variables are predisposing factors—organizational traits, intentions, and motivations—and situational factors, i.e., variables outside the organization and the crisis itself.

Evaluation of the publics and multi-faceted threats outside of the organization—requirements in contingency theory—will be analyzed together with internal factors to manage both the demands of the publics and the crises. Seeger (2006) has contended that publics play a critical role during a crisis, as such knowing factors that impact the crisis, and the publics must be identified before the start of a crisis communication plan.

Conflicts and crises are unpredictable events (Seeger, 2006), whereby organizations attempt to make sense of them while considering the options available in managing them. Choosing appropriate stances along the continuum will enable them to assess the possible outcomes and make informed decisions. The choice of stances to adopt is flexible depending on situations. It is a dynamic undertaking that allows both the organization and the publics to negotiate for the best outcome in a bad situation.

Conclusion

The contingency theory has been evolved, modified, tested, and improved consistently over the last two decades. J. E. Grunig (2006) argued that when assessing a theory, one way is to examine whether "it makes sense of reality (in the case of a positive, or explanatory, theory)" (p. 152). The contingency theory has thus far offered a perspective supported by empirical foundations. Moving forward, there are areas into which the theory can expand.

Moving From Testing Individual Factors to a Conjoint Approach

As more measurement and scale development research projects are going on, each identified contingent factor or the clusters of those factors have been and will be examined systematically. Multiple methods are employed to ensure the validity and reliability of those measurements. The interrelationship between contingency factors also needs to be tapped in a deeper sense. Thus far, the contingency factors have either been introduced and examined individually, contributing to the factor matrix, or jointly examined in a pair or so in an experimental setting. However, the challenge remains for us to examine how the different contingency variables interact with each other to influence the decision making process.

To tackle this complex task of mapping, dissecting, and decision choice-making among the clusters of 87 contingency factors along with different conflict management stages, types of publics, types of industry, organizational types and histories, perceived threats, and other internal and external realities an organization is facing in daily public relations practice, the authors started to apply more advanced analytical frameworks and techniques that will have the capacity to capture the complexity of decision making that involves evaluating, weighing, and mapping a large cluster of factors at one time. The conjoint model—a theoretical foundation that will then allow conjoint analysis, a statistical technique mostly used in market research, product design research, and operations research in analyzing rated/ranked choices and decisions—is identified.

In the current body of public relations research, the only publication that has employed conjoint analysis is Brønn and Olson's (1999) study. Brønn and Olson's research and their application of conjoint analysis in the crisis communication decision making process can be applied to strategic conflict management and provide unique opportunities, from the contingency theory's perspective, to determine how practitioners value different contingency variables that strategically position an organization's stance (in a given situation, at a given time, toward a given public) along the continuum from pure advocacy to pure accommodation. Emerging research should further examine the interactions between contingency factors, taking a conjoint analysis approach (Voges et al., 2022) to gauge what combination of different clusters of factors, in what situation, is most influential on practitioners' decision making when it comes to recommending conflict positioning, organizational stance, and eventually effective and ethical strategies in managing competition and/or conflict faced by any organization.

Testing the Contingency Theory in Different Cultures

Pang et al. (2021) contended that contingency theory could be applied in practice beyond the United States. Studies in South Korea (Shin et al., 2006) and in China (Li et al., 2010)—territories with different cultures—have validated the effectiveness of contingency theory of strategic conflict management in application.

Shin et al. (2006) surveyed Korean public relations practitioners to identify contingent factors they viewed as critical in their work. Practitioner's individual ability to navigate complicated issues, communicate and use information, along with ethical standards were seen as most impactful. Strong support from C-suite was also a factor. The study found that practitioners at different levels viewed the variable factors differently. At staff level, practitioners saw factors within the PR department as having an impact on them, whereas factors at the organizational level affected practitioners at the upper management more. A key factor that affects public relations work is bad publicity.

Li et al. (2010) studied Chinese practitioners and their perceptions of the contingency variables. Personal traits regarding managing conflicts and political-social variables were deemed the most important. The study also looked at how gender and types of organization influenced the Chinese practitioners' practice in public relations.

These two studies informed both practitioners and researchers on contingency factors that were most impactful and ethical in the management of conflict management outside of the United States. As conflicts and crises become increasingly complicated, organizations must be apprised of internal and external factors that could impact them. Their communication responses and their approach must be dynamic and strategic to reflect the organization's purpose and values.

While challenges facing public relations and conflict management are ever evolving, they allow for contingency theory to be rigorously tested and fine-tuned in the management of crisis (Jin et al., 2021) and in the uncovering of new factors and new connections that could possibly lead to better resolution of crisis, conflicts, and public relations issues. These challenges could also bring about better knowledge of existing factors and the role they play in decision making. Practitioners can put the enhanced knowledge to use in further development and refinement in the stances of their organizations and the publics with a deepened understanding of ethical factors and expectations in conflict with values between publics and organizations.

Broom (2006) stated that building theory is laborious, starting from the conceptualization stage. The process is particularly onerous where public relations is concerned as it must make sense to practitioners. As the theory of continency continues to grow and scholars uncover new findings, it behooves them to ensure the theory mirrors practice.

Acknowledgements

- Figure 10.3 and Table 10.2 were first published in Vol. 2, No. 2 (July–December) of the 2019 edition of *Communication and Media in Asia-Pacific*. They are used with permission from the journal.
- Figure 10.2 was first published in Vol. 15, No. 2 of the 2010 edition of *Corporate Communications: An International Journal*. The authors thank the journal for the use of the figure as well as the co-authors of the article, Joanna Siah Ann Mei and Namrata Bansal.

References

An, S., & Cheng, I. (2010). Crisis communication research in public relations journals: Tracking research trends over thirty years. In W. T. Coombs & S. J. Holladay (Eds.), *Handbook of crisis communication* (pp. 65–90). Wiley-Blackwell.

Botan, C. (2006). Grand strategy, strategy, and tactics in public relations. In C. Botan & V. Hazelton (Eds.), *Public relations theory II* (pp. 223–248). Lawrence Erlbaum Associates.

Brønn, P. S., & Olson, E. L. (1999). Mapping the strategic thinking of public relations managers in crisis situation: An illustrative example using conjoint analysis. *Public Relations Review, 25*(3), 351–368. https://doi.org/10.1016/s0363-8111(99)00023-5

Broom, G. M. (2006). An open system approach to building theory in public relations. *Journal of Public Relations Research, 18*(2), 141–150. https://doi.org/10.1207/s1532754xjprr1802_4

Cameron, G. T. (1997). *The contingency theory of conflict management in public relations.* Proceedings of the Norwegian Information Service.

Cameron, G. T., Cropp, F., & Reber, B. H. (2001). Getting past platitudes: Factors limiting accommodation in public relations. *Journal of Communication Management, 5*(3), 242–261. https://doi.org/10.1108/13632540110806802

Cancel, A. E., Cameron, G. T., Sallot, L. M., & Mitrook, M. A. (1997). It depends: A contingency theory of accommodation in public relations. *Journal of Public Relations Research, 9*(1), 31–63. https://doi.org/10.1207/s1532754xjprr0901_02

Cancel, A. E., Mitrook, M. A., & Cameron, G. T. (1999). Testing the contingency theory of accommodation in public relations. *Public Relations Review, 25*(2), 171–197. https://doi.org/10.1016/S0363-8111(99)80161-1

Chaffee, S. H., & Berger, C, R. (1987). What communication scientists do. In C. R. Berger & S. H. Chaffee (Eds.), *Handbook of communication science* (pp. 99–122). Sage.

Coombs, W. T. (2010). Parameters for crisis communication. In W. T. Coombs & S. J. Holladay (Eds.), *Handbook of crisis communication* (pp. 17–53). Wiley-Blackwell.

Coombs, W. T. (2019). *Ongoing crisis communication* (5th ed.). Sage.

Fearn-Banks, K. (2017). *Crisis communications* (5th ed.). Routledge.

Earle, T. C., Siegrist, M., & Gutscher, H. (2007). Trust, risk perception and the TCC model of cooperation. In M. Siegrist, T. C. Earle, & H. Gutscher (Eds.), *Trust in cooperative risk management: Uncertainty and scepticism in the public mind* (pp. 1–50). Earthscan.

Frandsen, F., & Johansen, W. (2017). *Organizational crisis communication.* Sage.

Frandsen, F., & Johansen, W. (2020). A brief history of crisis management and crisis communication: From organizational practice to academic discipline. In F. Frandsen & W. Johansen (Eds.), *Crisis communication* (pp. 17–58). De Gruyter Mouton.

George, A. M. (2012). The phases of crisis communication. In A. M. George & C. B. Pratt (Eds.), *Case studies in crisis communication: International perspectives on hits and misses* (pp. 31–50). Routledge.

Gonzalez-Herrero, A., & Smith, S. (2008). Crisis communications management on the Web: How Internet-based technologies are changing the way public relations professionals handle business crises. *Journal of Contingencies and Crisis Management, 16*(3), 143–153. https://doi.org/10.1111/j.1468-5973.2008.00543.x

Grunig, L. A. (1996). Public relations. In M. D. Salwen & D. W. Stacks (Eds.), *An integrated approach to communication theory and research* (pp. 459–477). Lawrence Erlbaum Associates.

Grunig, J. E. (2006). Furnishing the edifice: Ongoing research on public relations as strategic management function. *Journal of Public Relations Research, 18*(2), 151–176. https://doi.org/10.1207/s1532754xjprr1802_5

Heath, R. L., & Coombs, W. T. (2006). *Today's public relations: An introduction.* Sage.

Hove, T., & Paek, H.-J. (2017). The personal dimensions of public relations ethical dilemmas. *Journal of Media Ethics, 32*(2), 86–98. https://doi.org/10.1080/23736992.2017.1294018

Hwang, S. W., & Cameron, G. T. (2008). Public's expectation about an organization's stance in crisis communication based on perceived leadership and perceived severity of threats. *Public Relations Review, 34*(1), 70–73. https://doi.org/10.1016/j.pubrev.2007.11.008

Hwang, S. W., & Cameron, G. T. (2009). The estimation of a corporate crisis communication. *Public Relations Review, 35*(2), 136–138. https://doi.org/10.1016/j.pubrev.2009.01.005

James, E. H., Crane, B., & Wooten, L. P. (2013). Managing the crisis lifecycle in the information age. In A. J. DuBrin (Ed.), *Handbook of research on crisis leadership in organizations* (pp. 177–192). Edward Elgar Publishing.

Jin, Y., & Cameron, G. T. (2006). Scale development for measuring stance as degree of accommodation. *Public Relations Review, 32*, 423–425. https://doi.org/10.1016/j.pubrev.2006.09.012

Jin, Y., & Cameron, G. T. (2007). The effects of threat type and duration on public relations practitioner's cognitive, affective, and conative responses in crisis situations. *Journal of Public Relations Research, 19*(3), 255–281. https://doi.org/10.1080/10627260701331762

Jin, Y., Pang, A., & Cameron, G. T. (2006). Strategic communication in crisis governance: Singapore's management of the SARS crisis. *Copenhagen Journal of Asian Studies, 23*, 81–104. https://doi.org/10.22439/cjas.v23i1.693

Jin, Y., Pang, A., & Cameron, G. T. (2007). Different means to the same end: A comparative contingency analyses of Singapore and China's management of the severe acute respiratory syndrome (SARS) crisis. *Journal of International Communication, 13*(1), 39–70. https://doi.org/10.1080/13216597.2007.9674707

Jin, Y., Pang, A., & Cameron, G. T. (2012). Pre-crisis threat assessment: A cognitive appraisal approach to understanding of the faces and fabric of threats faced by organizations. In B. Olaniran, D. Williams, & W. T. Coombs (Eds.), *Pre crisis management: Preparing for the inevitable* (pp. 125–143). Peter Lang.

Jin, Y., Pang, A., Cameron, G. T., Kim, S., & Pagano, L. A. (2021). Managing complexity: Insights from the contingency theory of strategic conflict management. In Y. Jin, B. H. Reber, & G. J. Nowak (Eds.), *Advancing crisis communication effectiveness: Integration of public relations scholarship and practice* (pp. 181–197). Routledge.

Jin, Y., Pang, A., & Smith, J. (2018). Crisis communication and ethics: The role public relations. *Journal of Business Strategy, 39*(1), 43–52. https://doi.org/10.1108/JBS-09-2016-0095

Jin, Y., Reber, B. H., & Nowak, G. J. (Eds.). (2021). *Advancing crisis communication effectiveness: Integration of public relations scholarship and practice.* Routledge.

Kim, J., & Ni, L. (2010). Seeing the forest through the trees. In R. L. Heath (Ed.), *Sage handbook of public relations* (pp. 35–57). Sage.

Kim, S., Jin, Y., & Reber, B. H. (2020). Assessing an organizational crisis at the construal level: How psychological distance impacts publics' crisis responses. *Journal of Communication Management, 24*(4), 319–337. https://doi.org/10.1108/JCOM-11-2019-0148

Kim, S., Jin, Y., Reber, B. H., Pang, A., & Cameron, G. T. (2017, October). *The publics' response continuum in crisis communication: Extending the contingency theory of strategic conflict management.* 5th International Crisis Communication Conference (Crisis5).

LeBoeuf, M. (2007). *The power of ridicule: An analysis of satire* (Paper 63). University of Rhode IslandDigitalCommons@URI.

Lee, L., Chia, J., & Pang, A. (2019). Mocked and shamed: Satirical news and its effects on organizational reputation. *Communication and Media in Asia Pacific, 2*(2), 1–26.

Li, C., Cropp, F., & Jin, Y. (2010). Identifying key influencers of Chinese PR professionals' strategic conflict management practice: A national survey on 86 Contingent factors in Chinese context. *Public Relations Review, 36*(3), 249–255. https://doi.org/10.1016/j.pubrev.2010.05.006

Liu, B. F., & Fraustino, J. D. (2014). Beyond image repair: Suggestions for crisis communication theory development. *Public Relations Review, 40*, 543–546. https://doi.org/10.1016/j.pubrev.2014.04.004

Martin, R., Puhlik-Doris, P., Larsen, G., Gray, J., & Weir, K. (2003). Individual differences in uses of humor and their relation to psychological well-being: Development of the humor styles questionnaire. *Journal of Research in Personality, 37*(1), 48–75. http://dx.doi.org/10.1016/s0092-6566(02)00534-2

Pang, A. (2006). *Conflict positioning in crisis communication: Integrating contingency stance with image repair strategies* [Doctoral dissertation, University of Missouri].

Pang, A., Cropp, F., & Cameron, G. T. (2006). Corporate crisis planning: Tensions, issues, and contradictions. *Journal of Communication Management, 10*(4), 371–389. https://doi.org/10.1108/13632540610714818

Pang, A., Jin, Y., & Cameron, G. T. (2010a). Contingency theory of strategic conflict management: Directions for the practice of crisis communication from a decade of theory development, discovery and dialogue. In W. T. Coombs & S. J. Holladay (Eds.), *Handbook of crisis communication* (pp. 527–549). Wiley-Blackwell.

Pang, A., Jin, Y., & Cameron, G. T. (2010b). Strategic management of communication: Insights from the contingency theory of strategic conflict management. In R. L. Heath (Ed.), *Sage handbook of public relations* (pp. 17–34). Sage.

Pang, A., Jin, Y., & Cameron, G. T. (2010c, March). *Contingency theory of strategic conflict management: Unearthing factors that influence ethical elocution in crisis communication.* 13th Annual International Public Relations Research Conference.

Pang, A., Jin, Y., & Cameron, G. T. (2021). Contingency theory of strategic conflict management: Explicating a "grand" theory of public relations. In C. Valentini (Ed.), *Public relations* (pp. 381–398). De Gruyter Mouton.

Pang, A., Jin, Y., & Ho, B. (2016). How crisis managers define ethical crisis communication in Singapore: Identifying organizational factors that influence adoption of ethical stances. *Media Asia, 43*(3–4), 191–207. https://doi.org/10.1080/01296612.2016.1276316

Pang, A., Jin, Y., Kim, S., & Cameron, G. T. (2020). Contingency theory: Evolution from a public relations theory to a theory of strategic conflict management. In F. Frandsen & W. Johansen (Eds.), *Crisis communication* (pp. 141–164). De Gruyter Mouton.

Pearce, J. A., & Robinson, R. B. (2015). *Strategic management.* McGraw-Hill.

Reber, B., & Cameron, G. T. (2003). Measuring contingencies: Using scales to measure public relations practitioner limits to accommodation. *Journalism and Mass Communication Quarterly, 80*(2), 431–446. https://doi.org/10.1177/107769900308000212

Seeger, M. W. (2006). Best practices in crisis communications. *Journal of Applied Communication Research, 34*(3), 232–244. https://doi.org/10.1080/00909880600769944

Siah, J., Bansal, N., & Pang, A. (2010). New media: A new medium in escalating crises? *Corporate Communications: An International Journal, 15*(2), 143–155. https://doi.org/10.1108/13563281011037919

Siegrist, M., Gutscher, H., & Keller, C. (2007). Trust and confidence in crisis communication: Three case studies. In M. Siegrist, T. C. Earle, & H. Gutscher (Eds.), *Trust in cooperative risk management: Uncertainty and scepticism in the public mind* (pp. 267–286). Earthscan.

Shin, J. H., Cameron, G. T., & Cropp, F. (2002, August). *Asking what matters most: A national survey of PR professional response to the contingency model.* Association for Education in Journalism and Mass Communication (AEJMC) Annual Conference.

Shin, J. H., Park, J., & Cameron, G. T. (2006). Contingent factors: Modeling generic public relations practice in South Korea. *Public Relations Review, 32,* 184–185. https://doi.org/10.1016/j.pubrev.2006.02.015

Voges, T. S., Jin, Y., Chen, X., & Reber, B. H. (2022). What drives a tough call: Determining the importance of contingency factors and individual characteristics in communication executives' stance decision-making through a conjoint analysis. *Public Relations Review, 48*(1), 102141. https://doi.org/10.1016/j.pubrev.2021.102141

Yarbrough, C. R., Cameron, G. T., Sallot, L. M., & McWilliams, A. (1998). Tough calls to make: Contingency theory and the Centennial Olympic Games. *Journal of Communication Management, 3*(1), 39–56. https://doi.org/10.1108/eb023483

Ziv, A. (1984). *Personality and sense of humor.* Springer.

11 Crisis Communication Theory

Emergence of a Vibrant Subfield of Public Relations Theory

W. Timothy Coombs and Elina R. Tachkova

Crisis communication has transformed from a small, niche area of public relations research to one of the dominant research areas in public relations in about two decades. This chapter focuses on the development and future of crisis communication theory. Its rapid growth has even caused some to question whether crisis communication fits within public relations. The question of fit can be due in part to the interdisciplinary nature of crisis communication (Bundy et al., 2017). We begin the chapter by documenting how crisis communication is indeed public relations, followed by defining the key terms that guide the chapter. The focus then shifts to the development of crisis communication theory. Three foundational theories in crisis communication are presented, followed by a presentation of the key trends in crisis communication theory. We then consider the contributions of crisis communication research to the practice of crisis communication and the development of public relations theory. We conclude with a discussion of future directions for crisis communication research and theory.

Crisis Communication as Public Relations

Since the first edition of this book, a central tenet has been that public relations is a form of applied communication rooted in social science that seeks to solve problems through communication. Public relations theory can explain and predict the practice, while the practice can trigger theory development (Botan & Hazleton, 1989). Crisis communication fits within these initial parameters for public relations. Crisis communication theory helps managers to leverage communication to reduce the negative effects of a crisis on stakeholders and the organization in crisis (Coombs, 2019). Crisis communication is a relatively new area of public relations. Crisis communication theory began as descriptive research written primarily by practitioners who intended to explain how it worked and was followed by more predictive theories of crisis communication (Coombs, 2020). Hence, crisis communication is a specialty within the public relations practice and part of the public relations theory body of knowledge. Crisis communication is a thriving and rapidly growing facet of public relations research and theory.

DOI: 10.4324/9781003141396-13

If we consider the stimulation of research as an important quality of theory, crisis communication theory is doing well within public relations research.

Defining the Key Terms

In research, it is important to define terms to increase precision. Thus far, we have used the terms *crisis* and *crisis communication* without clear definitions. A crisis is generally taken as a disruption to the organization and to some stakeholders. In terms of research, the topic of crisis has generated distinctive lines of research including disaster communication, political crises, public health crises, and organizational crises. While these lines of research overlap due to their focus on crisis, the dynamics underlying the various lines of research have distinct differences that make applying research from one line to another problematic. In this chapter we focus on organizational crises.

We can define an organizational crisis as "the perceived violation of salient stakeholder expectations that can create negative outcomes for stakeholders and/or the organization" (Coombs, 2019, p. 3). This definition captures how a crisis is perceptual (socially constructed) and driven by stakeholders. Crisis managers reserve the term *crisis* for serious matters that will demand time and attention because the situations either disrupt or have the potential to disrupt operations (Barton, 2001). We view crisis communication as the enactment of crisis management. It is through communication that people engage in crisis management. For instance, a crisis management plan (CMP) is just a document; it is through communication that the CMP becomes a resource that informs crisis management processes.

Initial Crisis Communication Theory Development Within PR

This section reviews the three foundational theories in crisis communication. The term *foundational* is used because these are the first theories to be applied widely and consistently to the study of crisis communication within public relations.

Corporate Apologia

How do corporations react to situations in which their character is under attack? This was the initial question that drove the corporate apologia research. Apologia is a rhetorical concept that examines how communication could be used for self-defense when someone's character is being attacked. Dionisopolous and Vibbert (1988) were the first to adapt and to apply the concept of apologia to corporate communication. They argued that perceptions of corporate wrongdoing could be perceived as an attack on the character of an organization and thus create the need for corporate apologia. Hearit (1995), however, was the first to apply the concept of apologia to crisis communication research. He integrated ideas from social legitimacy and rhetorical theory to develop a framework for crisis management.

Hearit viewed crises as a threat to corporate social legitimacy, "the congruence between the values of a corporations and those of a larger social system in which it operates" (Hearit, 1995, p. 2). Corporate social legitimacy centers on the relationship between organizational and stakeholder values. Organizations earn legitimacy by meeting stakeholder expectations for shared social values. A crisis is a threat to the social legitimacy of an organization because it exposes value incongruencies, thereby violating expectations (Hearit, 1995). For example, food contamination could make a company appear incompetent because certain rules and procedures have not been implemented and can thus violate people's trust in the organization and its products. Moreover, social legitimacy violations are a form of character attack which in turn prompts the need for self-defense through apologia (Hearit, 1995).

The line of research that Hearit (1994) developed established the first inventory of crisis-response strategies available to crisis practitioners. The five strategies are *denial* (the organization denies committing any wrongdoing), *counterattack* (the organization not only denies responsibility for the crisis but claims the accuser is responsible), *differentiation* (the organization identifies factors that limit its responsibility but still accepts some), *apology* (the organization accepts responsibility), and *legal* (the organization does not make any public statements and the crisis is handled by the legal team).

Important contributions from the corporate apologia research include the identification of dissociation strategies and evidence for the importance of stakeholder perceptions in defining crises. Hearit's (1994) application of the dissociation concept to crisis communication highlighted the potential complexity of crisis responses. Dissociations attempt to separate the organization from the crisis, thereby reducing the negative effects of the crisis upon the organization. Hearit (1994) identified three different dissociations crisis managers might use to distance an organization from a crisis: opinion/ knowledge, in which the manager denies a crisis by claiming that only opinions say a crisis exists but knowledge (facts) show there is no crisis; individual/group, which claims that only a few individuals and not the organization as a whole were responsible for the crisis; and act/essence, which admits the organization engaged in wrongdoing but that does not represent the true essence of the organization. Hearit's (1999) analysis of the Pentium chip flaw case illustrated how customers forced Intel to recognize that the minor mathematical calculation flaw was a product harm crisis that warranted corrective action. A small segment of vocal customers defined the chip flaw as a crisis, and Intel eventually had to accept that the organization was in crisis.

Image Repair/Restoration Theory (IRT)

Benoit felt apologia offered too few response options and sought to expand the repertoire by integrating literatures from rhetoric and account giving (sociology). This integration resulted in the creation of image repair/restoration theory (IRT), initially developed from political communication. Benoit's (1995) IRT is one of the primary frameworks utilized in crisis communication research. IRT holds that when an organization is accused of bad behavior (a crisis), its image (reputation) is threatened. Communication is then used to protect the image, a primary goal for IRT. The theory has been applied to a variety of crisis types, with the research relying heavily upon the case study method.

The theory proposes five major categories of strategies that organizations can employ as part of their image restoration efforts. The *denial* strategies claim the organization has no responsibility for a crisis. The *evading responsibility* strategies seek to reduce perceived organizational responsibility for a crisis. The *reducing offensiveness* image repair strategies seek to improve stakeholder perceptions of the organization. *Corrective action* strategies seek to prevent the repeat of the crisis. The *mortification strategy* accepts responsibility for the crisis and asks for forgiveness.

Brinson and Benoit (1996) examined Dow Corning's efforts to respond to criticism about the safety of its silicone breast implants. The study examines the discourse used by the company over an extended period of 9 months. As one of the first works applying IRT to study crisis responses, the paper contributes to our understanding of crisis complexity. The authors note that image repair efforts go through different stages as part of the crisis life cycle and, in order to respond to situational demands, companies should understand how crises evolve over time. Falkheimer and Heide (2015) used IRT to explore a transboundary crisis, one that spreads across functional, geographical, and time boundaries. Transboundary crises pose challenges for organizations because they involve multiple stakeholders from different arenas. The study combines IRT with the concept of the rhetorical arena (Frandsen & Johansen, 2017). Developed as a critique to IRT and other crisis communication theories, the study illustrated how the rhetorical arena aims to understand crisis communication as a multivocal process.

Situational Crisis Communication Theory (SCCT)

SCCT is a cognitive-based framework that examines how to protect organizational reputation and other crisis outcomes following a crisis based on the responsibility attributed to the organization (Coombs, 1995). The roots of SCCT lie in attribution theory, a social-psychological theory that explains how people make sense of negative events (Weiner, 1995). Applied to crisis events, attribution theory suggests that stakeholders will create an explanation for the occurrence of a negative event (i.e., a crisis) and will attribute responsibility for it. SCCT classifies crises into three main clusters, namely *victim* (the organization is a victim of the crisis itself), *accidental* (the cause of the crisis is due to a technical error/accident), and *preventable* (the organization knowingly put stakeholders at risk).

SCCT matches these crisis types with the most appropriate crisis response based on how much responsibility is attributed to an organization. Coombs (1995) combined work in corporate apologia, corporate impression management, and IRT to develop the SCCT crisis response typology. Following Sturges (1994), SCCT divides crisis responses into three categories: 1) *instructing information*, which helps to protect people physically from a crisis; 2) *adjusting information*, which helps people to cope psychologically with a crisis; and 3) *reputation management*, which helps to repair reputation damage from the crisis. The crisis response strategies are arranged on a continuum from defensive (denying responsibility for the crisis) to accommodative (accepting responsibility). The responses of instructing and adjusting information are combined to form the ethical base response (Coombs & Holladay, 2007). The ethical base response is a required response for any crisis. The reputation management crisis responses can be added once the ethical base response is provided. The more severe the crisis, the more accommodative the response an organization should adopt.

Unlike IRT and corporate apologia, SCCT utilizes experimental research to test the effectiveness of the crisis responses and is therefore prescriptive in its recommendations. Coombs and Holladay used experiment studies to demonstrate that apology was not more effective at reducing negative crisis outcomes than compensation or sympathy (Coombs & Holladay, 2008) and that anger moderated the relationship between crisis responsibility and purchase intention reinforcing the importance of affect in crisis communication (Coombs & Holladay, 2007). Park's (2017) experimental research documented how the ethical base response did mitigate reputational damage and how bolstering provided very little benefit to organizations during a crisis. Coombs et al. (2016) used experiments to debunk the benefits of denial by establishing the negative reactions to denial when there is any evidence that the organization has some responsibility for a crisis.

Trends in the Development of Crisis Communication Theory

As we view the development of crisis communication theory emerging from and including these three foundational theories, there are three trends worth discussing. The first is movement from descriptive to prescriptive theory.

Descriptive to Prescriptive Theory

Descriptive theories seek to explain the crisis communication process and can include attempts to model the process. As noted earlier, crisis communication research began as a set of ideas about what practitioners found did and did not work when they managed a crisis—a set of accepted practices. Descriptive theories tried to capture what was happening in the crisis communication process. A better understanding of the crisis communication process could result in improvements to practice. Corporate apologia was the first descriptive theory of crisis communication, but IRT set the standard for descriptive crisis communication theories. While similar in origins and assumptions, IRT became the more popular theory in published research. IRT, like corporate apologia, posits that crisis communication is a result of some entity being perceived as connected to a negative event. Furthermore, IRT holds that crisis communication is goal-directed, with the primary goal being to protect the entity's image (Benoit, 1995). IRT articulated a detailed list of image repair strategies that a crisis manager might utilize to achieve the goal of protecting an image.

Research applying IRT focuses on a case study approach. The researcher analyzes a crisis communication event by identifying the image repair strategies utilized by the crisis manager. The researcher also looks for evidence to help interpret whether the use of the strategy or strategies was a success or failure. IRT is descriptive because of its focus on identifying the image repair strategies used during a crisis event. Research applying corporate apologia follows an analogous process of describing the crisis response and interpreting the effects of that response on the crisis outcomes.

Prescriptive theory, in contrast, generates guidelines for action to achieve specific outcomes. Prescriptive crisis communication theories move from describing crisis events, and interpreting the outcomes, to specifying causal relationships between specific crisis response strategies and specific crisis outcomes. SCCT is the primary prescriptive crisis communication theory. SCCT used experimental methods to establish cause-and-effect relationships between crisis response strategies and a set of crisis outcomes that include post-crisis reputation, purchase intention, negative word-of-mouth intentions, and anger. SCCT is a contingent approach, meaning the optimal crisis response is largely a function of the crisis type. Various experimental studies were conducted to determine which crisis response strategies had the greatest positive effect on the crisis outcomes for particular crisis types including the pioneering work of Coombs and Holladay (1996) and later works such as Park (2017). The SCCT guidance is derived from the experimental results documenting the effect of crisis response strategies on various crisis outcomes across a range of crisis types (Coombs, 2007, 2020). In SCCT, the prescriptions were built using the crisis response strategies developed using the descriptive crisis communication theories.

Stealing thunder is another notable prescriptive crisis communication theory. Stealing thunder is a very robust finding documented through several experimental studies focused on the timing of an organization's disclosure of a crisis. The experiments have demonstrated a cause-and-effect relationship between an organization being the first to disclose a crisis and the crisis inflicting less damage on the organization (Arpan & Pompper, 2003; Claeys, 2017; Claeys & Cauberghe, 2014). Stealing thunder prescribes being the first source to disclose a crisis, when the option exists for managers, to reduce the damage a crisis inflicts upon the organization.

Rhetorical to Cognitive

Crisis communication theory began primarily from a rhetorical perspective. A rhetorical perspective focuses on messages and how meaning is created in a communicative situation and reflects the humanistic aspect of social science (Hazleton & Botan, 1989). As noted in the previous section, both corporate apologia and IRT drew heavily from the rhetorical study of political communication. Following a rhetorical approach, the method for corporate apologia and IRT studies is predominantly case studies.

One problem with case studies is the variability in how they are conducted as well as what outcomes (if any) have been used to evaluate the effectiveness of the crisis response. Outcomes are variable and have included polls and surveys (Wen et al., 2012), attendance at sports games (Compton & Compton, 2014), university admission applications rates (Len-Ríos, 2010), and the role of third parties for establishing credibility and improving perceptions of an organization following a crisis (Lancaster & Boyd, 2015).

Although these studies discuss the effectiveness of different image repair responses, clear evaluation criteria are missing. Context-specific crisis outcomes are useful but: 1) they do not allow for comparison among different crisis types, and 2) there might be factors other than crisis communication solely that affect these outcomes. For instance, although polls might be useful in measuring public opinions, it should be considered that other situational factors besides the crisis response might influence responses. Ideally multiple case study designs follow similar procedures to identify patterns in their results. Because of a lack of consistency in how various researchers evaluate the effectiveness of image repair strategies, comparing or compiling results between the IRT case studies is not possible. Thus, the case study results using the rhetorical approach tend to generate idiosyncratic rather than cumulative knowledge about crisis communication.

The cognitive approach to crisis communication theory focuses on people's perceptions—cognitions—and reflects the empirical side of social science (Hazleton & Botan, 1989). Cognitive crisis communication theory seeks to understand how people perceive crisis situations, how people perceive crisis response strategies, and the interplay between the two. SCCT was the first cognitive crisis communication theory. SCCT's concept of crisis responsibility is derived from attribution theory's premise that people make mental attributions for the causes of events, especially negative events. Crises are negative events and should trigger causal attributions among stakeholders. Early research in marketing established how product harm situations led to attributions and the way increases in attributions of crisis responsibility negatively affected social assessments and purchase intentions (e.g., Stockmyer, 1996). SCCT built upon the negative effects of crisis responsibility by documenting the perceptual effects of various crisis types and by connecting responsibility with the perceptions created by crisis response strategies. SCCT used crisis responsibility to map different crisis types. Coombs and Holladay (2002) documented that different crisis types consistently generate predictable levels of crisis responsibility. Those differences have been confirmed in later studies that assessed the levels of crisis responsibility associated with various crisis types (e.g., Tachkova, 2021). The crisis response strategies could affect perceptions of the crisis situation and perception-related outcomes such as post-crisis reputations and emotions (Coombs, 2007).

Essentially, different crisis response strategies can change post-crisis cognitions, resulting in different perception-based crisis outcomes than would have emerged if there had been no crisis communication. In other words, crisis communication altered how people reacted to a crisis by changing cognitions related to the crisis. The communicative effect could be positive or negative. *Suboptimal responses*, especially denial, tend to increase negative perception-based crisis outcomes such as reputation, purchase intention, and anger (Coombs et al., 2016). *Optimal response strategies* are victim-centered and seek to be accommodative. The ethical base response and compensation are both optimal responses. Optimal responses, such as apologies, can result in less negative perception-based crisis outcomes (Coombs & Tachkova, 2019).

The social-mediated crisis communication model (SMCC) (see Liu, Jin & Austin's chapter in this book) and the contingency theory-related crisis communication research also use a cognitive perspective (Austin et al., 2012). The contingency theory-based crisis research has explored practitioner perceptions of crisis threats and the emotions a crisis evokes from stakeholders. This line of research advocates an emotion-based approach to crisis communication (Jin et al., 2012). Emotions in crisis communication research draw heavily from emotional appraisal theory, which also is cognitive-based. Emotional appraisal theory is collection of theories arguing that people react to a situation based upon cues. Different cues will evoke different emotions in a situation. The contingency theory-based crisis communication research tends to be quantitative, including the use of experimental methods (e.g., Jin & Cameron, 2007). The cognitive perspective focuses on the processes behind crisis communication to illuminate why crisis communication has certain effects upon people.

Single Voice to Multivocal

Crisis communication research began with a focus on the organization-in-crisis communicating about the crisis. Early writings focused on the crisis spokesperson (e.g., Barton, 2001). Corporate apologia, IRT, and SCCT all emphasized the organization-in-crisis being the crisis voice. This early research has been characterized as "single voice" because the emphasis was on one voice—the organization's crisis management effort (Frandsen & Johansen, 2017). This does not mean other voices were not considered, but they were a minor concern or background element at best. For instance, Holladay (2009) found that first responders and government officials often were used as sources in news accounts about crises. Their voices were included along with the organization's voice.

The rhetorical arena theory (RAT) introduced the idea of a "multivocal" approach to crisis communication. RAT holds when a crisis occurs, a social space opens around the crisis where various multiple voices talk about the crisis (Frandsen & Johansen, 2017). RAT is even referred to by many as the multivocal approach (Frandsen & Johansen, 2020). The multivocal perspective is central to the macro component of RAT that "describes and explains the interaction between the multiple voices that communicate to, with, against, past or about each other in the arena of an organizational crisis" (Frandsen & Johansen, 2020, p. 198). The micro component of RAT explores the communication process of individuals within the arena. The multivocal approach does not necessarily mean there are multiple crisis managers; rather there are multiple crisis voices—those talking about the crisis. Moreover, the importance of the various voices is variable as voices vary in their ability to affect the crisis communication process. Some voices may be important, while others can be irrelevant.

The ripple effect from the multivocal approach has been felt throughout a range of crisis communication theories. SMCC, for example, is multivocal given its focus on voices emerging from social media platforms (Austin et al., 2012). Drawing from SMCC, Zhao et al. (2018) sought to develop a system for identifying social media influencers in a crisis. Their identification system offers a way to identify the salient crisis voices and thus addresses a key concern in RAT—which voices matter. SCCT has moved to recognize other crisis voices as contextual factors that influence how stakeholders perceive the crisis situation (Coombs, 2020). Crisis communication theories must find a way to account for multiple crisis voices if even one of those other voices is shaping the crisis communication process.

Implications for the Practice of Crisis Communication

The results generated by the crisis communication research provide a foundation for an evidence-based approach to the topic. The evidence-based approach gained traction in medicine over 20 years ago. The idea is that current research findings (evidence) should be used to inform the practice of interventions such as medicine and management—research results should be translated into practice (Rousseau, 2006). We would include crisis communication in the list. The evidence-based approach is a fusion of research results and practitioner experience. Practitioners learn the latest developments from research—evidence—and interpret it through their own experience. Practitioners need to decide whether the evidence will be applicable in their circumstances (Briner, 2019; Briner et al., 2009). It is egocentric to think academic research has all the answers for practitioners, thereby negating the value of their experience. Crisis communication theory has been generating research that forms evidence for those practicing crisis communication (Coombs, 2020).

Theoretical Trends and an Evidence-Based Approach to Crisis Communication

Many fields that rely upon interventions, including medicine and social work, believe in the value of an evidence-based approach (Latham, 2011). Research provides evidence for how different interventions might work or not work in the field. Practitioners then interpret that evidence through the lens of their experiences when deciding how to use that evidence. The quality of evidence varies, with cause-and-effect evidence being the most valued because it provides specific evidence about the effects of the intervention (Latham, 2011). Crisis communication is an intervention; hence, the crisis communication research generated by crisis communication theory can be assessed in terms of the quality of the evidence it creates for crisis managers.

Generally, the descriptive-rhetorical crisis communication theories proffer less compelling evidence than the evidence produced by the prescriptive-cognitive crisis communication theories. The descriptive-rhetorical crisis communication theories tend to describe and interpret a mix of evidence when judging the effectiveness of a crisis intervention. The lack of methodological consistency between various case study-based articles limits the ability to develop and to test theory (Cutler, 2004). Moreover, the research provides interpretive evidence that is suggestive rather than cause-and-effect. Consider how the communicative recommendations emerging from a descriptive-rhetorical analysis of Texaco's racism crisis (Brinson & Benoit, 1999) failed to be validated when examined from a prescriptive-cognitive analysis (Coombs & Schmidt, 2000). It is risky to accept advice derived only from descriptive-rhetorical case studies because the evidence it generates cannot be used to support causal claims.

The value in the descriptive-rhetorical crisis communication theories resides in their ability to stimulate new ideas and to understand processes, including how experiences and contexts interact to impact outcomes. Rhetorical analyses of crises cases can, in the words of rhetorical analysis expert Hart (1990), tell a story larger than itself. The case analyses can illuminate a problem or explore unique circumstances. Moreover, these observations can serve as a foundation for further study, including application of prescriptive-cognitive crisis communication theory. Consider how SCCT integrated elements of corporate apologia and IRT along with attribution theory for its development (Coombs, 2020).

The prescriptive-cognitive crisis communication theories produce stronger evidence by explaining why crisis interventions have particular effects and establishing cause-and-effect relationships between specific crisis interventions and crisis outcomes. The "why" behind the interventions is drawn from several prescriptive-cognitive crisis communication theories that provide explanations for why the concepts are related to one another. Furthermore, experimental designs typically used in cognitive crisis communication theories can demonstrate how specific crisis response strategies result in predictable crisis outcomes. For instance, the use of denial crisis response strategies when an organization is responsible for a crisis intensifies negative reactions to the crisis, while action to prevent a repeat of the crisis coupled with expression of concern lessens negative reactions, within limits. Or the use of stealing thunder reduces the reputational damage inflicted by a crisis. However, there are limits to the evidence generated by research using the prescriptive-cognitive theories because all theories have boundaries beyond which their applications are no longer valid

Both the single voice and the multivocal approaches have and continue to contribute to an evidence-based approach to crisis communication. There are times when insights from a single-voice approach are applicable in crisis communication and other times when a multivocal approach insights are applicable. Not all crises will have other strong crisis voices that influence the crisis communication process, making a polyvocal approach relevant. Multivocal is more appropriate when other strong crisis voices do emerge in a crisis.

Timing Evidence

One of the earliest pieces of crisis communication advice is that it should be quick (Caruba, 1994). That advice means crisis managers should be communicating as soon as possible during a crisis. The stealing thunder research is related to "be quick." In stealing thunder, the organization is the first to announce the crisis. In a way, the organizational announcement creates the crisis. Stealing thunder research consistently produces the same evidence—an organization harms the organization less when the organization is first to disclose the existence of the crisis (e.g., Claeys, 2017). Stealing thunder seems to be the most robust and reliable piece of crisis communication evidence. In fact, when an organization steals thunder, the benefit typically gained from crisis response strategies is lost (Claeys & Cauberghe, 2014).

Crisis Response Strategies

When crisis managers cannot steal thunder, the crisis response strategies can affect a variety of crisis outcomes. Ideally, optimal crisis response strategies lessen the negative effects of the crisis. However, suboptimal crisis response strategies can intensify the negative effects of a crisis. Crisis managers cannot simply say anything and expect the situation to improve. Frandsen and Johansen (2017) refer to the problems a crisis response can create as a double crisis. In a double crisis, the crisis response is so bad, it becomes its own crisis. Research exploring the effects of crisis response strategies on crisis outcomes have documented both the positives and negatives of crisis communication.

Victim-Centered Crisis Response Strategies

From the early days of practitioner writings (e.g., Jackson & Peters, n.d.), crisis research has recognized the value of addressing the needs of crisis victims (actual and potential victims). SCCT highlights that need by arguing that an *ethical-based response* must be the first crisis message and responses need to become more accommodative as perceptions of crisis responsibility increase. The ethical-based response addresses the physical safety (instructing information) and psychological coping (adjusting information) of crisis victims. Accommodative crisis response strategies focus more on the needs of victims than the needs of the organization in crisis (Coombs, 2007; Coombs & Holladay, 2007; Holladay, 2009). Generally, the research data concludes that focusing on victim concerns results in better crisis outcomes than more defensive strategies. The research includes documenting the value of adjusting information (e.g., Zhang & Zhou, 2020), the positive effects of accommodative strategies within the boundaries of SCCT (Coombs & Holladay, 2002; Wu & Xu, 2020), and the positive effects of accommodative strategies on share prices (Racine et al., 2020).

Conclusion: Future Directions for Crisis Communication Theory Research

Crisis communication theory witnessed its "big bang moment" in the 1990s. Corporate apologia, IRT, and SCCT all emerged in the 1990s giving researchers theoretical options for exploring crisis communication. Since the 1990s, there has been an acceleration in crisis communication research and theory development. Important theoretical developments include stealing thunder, RAT, and SMCC. From this research we know how various crisis response strategies will affect how people react to organizations in crisis across an array of crisis types. We also have a solid understanding of how crises affect people cognitively and emotionally along with a growing understanding of the role of emotions in crisis communications.

The growth of crisis communication research should include the advancement of crisis communication theory. Future research should continue to refine the existing theories because each is still contributing to our understanding of crisis communication. SCCT and stealing thunder have provided strong crisis communication evidence, while RAT and SMCC show promise as those theories are refined. We can now argue for an evidence-based approach to crisis communication predicated upon the research results generated by existing crisis communication theory. However, there is always a need for additional evidence to aid crisis managers. In this section we will focus on identifying salient useful future directions for crisis communication research and theory development.

Operationalization of Crisis Response Strategies

The various crisis response strategies emerging in crisis communication theory are defined, but how those strategies become operationalized by crisis researchers naturally can vary (Fediuk et al., 2010). The examination of various ways to operationalize crisis response strategies is a promising area of continued crisis communication research that can advance theory. Researchers have begun to explore tone of voice, emotionality in messages, and symbolic versus substantial actions in messages (Wu & Xu, 2020) as ways to operationalize crisis response strategies. The operationalization of crisis response strategies helps to refine theory by improving our understanding of the various effects crisis response strategies can have upon stakeholders and the organization in crisis. Additional research is needed to explore the operationalization of crisis response strategies and to use that knowledge to refine existing crisis communication theory and to develop new crisis communication theory.

Behavioral Crisis Communication Theory

Crisis communication research has documented how crisis managers often ignore the research evidence that could help them to respond more effectively to a crisis. We see that in case studies of failed crisis communication efforts and data showing crisis managers often do not follow the advice offered by crisis communication theory (e.g., Claeys & Opgenhaffen, 2016; Holladay, 2009). Too often these results are dismissed as practitioners not knowing the research. Claeys and Coombs (2020) argue that such a simple dismissal is insulting to crisis managers and misses an opportunity to explore why crisis evidence is ignored. They turn to behavioral economics (BE) to understand decision-making processes that can explain why crisis managers often choose to ignore the crisis evidence.

Crises create time pressures for managers to act. Because of these time pressures, crisis managers rely heavily upon intuitive decision making rather than analytic decision making (van der Meer et al., 2017). Intuitive decision making, when guided by experience, can produce decision quality equivalent to analytic decisions. However, intuitive decision making becomes problematic when it is based upon heuristic biases. BE has explored heuristic biases in great detail. BE seeks a more realistic explanation of people's economic behavior. BE felt that ignoring anomalies, when people acted in ways that did not fit rational economic models, was a mistake. Instead, researchers studied the patterns in the anomalous behaviors giving rise to BE (Thaler, 2015). The crisis communication evidence from stealing thunder and SCCT has a rational base akin to the rational models of economics. The failures to follow the crisis advice are anomalies that require analysis instead of dismissal. Claeys and Coombs (2020) articulated how the heuristic biases of myopic loss aversion (people fear loss) and hyperbolic discounting (people value current rewards more than future rewards) provide explanations of why crisis manager often avoid the evidence suggesting optimal crisis responses and choose suboptimal crisis responses. Pursuing the anomalies of crisis communication creates a behavioral approach. Further research is needed to expand the behavior approach to crisis communication to develop it into a complete theory.

Affect in Crisis Communication Theory

Affect has long been part of the cognitive approaches to crisis communication (e.g., Coombs & Holladay, 2007). However, affect has been in the background and theorists have argued that it needs to be more in the foreground (e.g., Jin & Pang, 2010). Crisis communication theory has contributed to our understanding of anger and anxiety during crises. Yet how crisis communication affects these two emotions is more speculation than evidence-based at this point. More crisis research and theorizing must untangle the relationships between crisis types, crisis response strategies, and the emotions of anger and anxiety.

The early interest in sympathy during crisis has been subsumed by the research on empathy in crisis. We are just beginning to understand the effects of stakeholder empathy for organizations (De Waele et al., 2020; Schoofs et al., 2019). We know that expressing sympathy by organizations (part of the ethical base response in SCCT) is important to stakeholder crisis perceptions, but the dynamics and details of that effect are limited (Coombs, 1999; Coombs & Holladay, 2002, 2007; Zhang & Zhou, 2020). Crisis communication theory must refine the role of empathy and enhance our understanding of this critical emotion in crisis communication.

Moral outrage is another emotion that requires further research. Moral outrage is a powerful negative emotion formed by cues of injustice and exploitation (Antonetti & Maklan, 2016). Scandals provide a means of integrating moral outrage into crisis communication. Scandals are characterized by moral violations (Nichols, 1997). Researchers mistakenly have equated scandal and crisis. Not all crises are scandals, and not all scandals are crises. Situations do emerge when a crisis is also a scandal, producing what is called a scansis (Coombs et al., 2018). A scansis is one form of crisis that evokes moral outrage. Scansis research demonstrated that moral outrage is a boundary condition for SCCT. In other words, the crisis communication recommendations from SCCT do not hold when the crisis evokes moral outrage (Coombs & Tachkova, 2019). Moreover, outrage leads us to explore sticky crises. "Sticky crises" are particularly complex and/or challenging crises (Reber et al., 2020). A scansis is a sticky crisis, but so are crises that extend over a long period time, crises that are related to social issues, and crises that have a strong racial component. Researchers have just begun to examine sticky crises. More work is needed to understand how sticky crises relate to existing crisis communication theory (Coombs et al., 2020) and drive the need to create new crisis communication theories.

Final Thoughts

Crisis communication reflects the applied nature of public relations whereby theory and practice inform one another. Research reviews in this chapter provide the raw materials necessary for creating an evidence-based approach to crisis communication. Along the way, crisis communication theory has contributed to public relations theory by providing a rich source of theory-oriented research that has enhanced our understanding of public relations. Early crisis communication theories have provided a solid foundation for theoretical expansion, the creation of new theories, and the ability of crisis communication research to improve an evidence-based approach to crisis communication.

References

Antonetti, P., & Maklan, S. (2016). An extended model of moral outrage at corporate social irresponsibility. *Journal of Business Ethics, 135*(3), 429–444.

Arpan, L. M., & Pompper, D. (2003). Stormy weather: Testing "stealing thunder" as a crisis communication strategy to improve communication flow between organizations and journalists. *Public Relations Review, 29*(3), 291–308.

Austin, L., Liu, B. F., & Jin, Y. (2012). How audiences seek out crisis information: Exploring the social-mediated crisis communication model. *Journal of Applied Communication Research, 40*(2), 188–207.

Barton, L. (2001). *Crisis in organizations II* (2nd ed.). College Divisions South-Western.

Benoit, W. L. (1995). *Accounts, excuses, and apologies: A theory of image restoration*. State University of New York Press.

Botan, C. H., & Hazleton, V. (1989). Preface. In C. H. Botan & V. Hazleton (Eds.), *Public relations theory* (p. xiii). Lawrence Erlbaum Associates.

Briner, R. B. (2019). The Basics of evidence-based practice. *People + Strategy Journal*. www.shrm.org/executive/resources/people-strategy-journal/winter2019/pages/ebp-briner.aspx

Briner, R. B., Denyer, D., & Rousseau, D. M. (2009). Evidence-based management: Concept cleanup time? *Academy of Management Perspectives, 23*(4), 19–32.

Brinson, S. L., & Benoit, W. L. (1996). Dow corning's image repair strategies in the breast implant crisis. *Communication Quarterly, 44*(1), 29–41.

Brinson, S. L., & Benoit, W. L. (1999). The tarnished star: Restoring Texaco's damaged public image. *Management Communication Quarterly, 12*(4), 483–510.

Bundy, J., Pfarrer, M. D., Short, C. E., & Coombs, W. T. (2017). Crises and crisis management: Integration, interpretation, and research development. *Journal of Management, 43*(6), 1661–1692.

Caruba, A. (1994). Crisis PR: Most are unprepared. *Occupational Hazards, 56*(9), 85.

Claeys, A. S. (2017). Better safe than sorry: Why organizations in crisis should never hesitate to steal thunder. *Business Horizons, 60*(3), 305–311.

Claeys, A. S., & Cauberghe, V. (2014). What makes crisis response strategies work? The impact of crisis involvement and message framing. *Journal of Business Research, 67*(2), 182–189.

Claeys, A. S., & Coombs, W. T. (2020). Organizational crisis communication: Suboptimal crisis response selection decisions and behavioral economics. *Communication Theory, 30*(3), 290–309.

Claeys, A.-S., & Opgenhaffen, M. (2016). Why practitioners do (not) apply crisis communication theory in practice. *Journal of Public Relations Research, 28*(5–6), 232–247.

Compton, J., & Compton, J. L. (2014). College sports, losing seasons, and image repair through open letters to fans. *Communication & Sport, 2*(4), 345–362.

Coombs, W. T. (1995). Choosing the right words: The development of guidelines for the selection of the "Appropriate" crisis-response strategies. *Management Communication Quarterly, 8*(4), 447–476. https://doi.org/10.1177/0893318995008004003

Coombs, W. T. (1999). Information and compassion in crisis responses: A test of their effects. *Journal of Public Relations Research, 11*(2), 125–142.

Coombs, W. T. (2007). Protecting organization reputations during a crisis: The development and application of a situational crisis communication theory. *Corporate Reputation Review, 10*(3), 163–176. http://dx.doi.org/10.1057/palgrave.crr.1550049

Coombs, W. T. (2019). *Ongoing crisis communication: Planning, managing, and responding* (5th ed.). Sage.

Coombs, W. T. (2020). Situational crisis communication theory: Influence, provenance, evolution, and prospects. In F. Frandsen & W. Johansen (Eds.), *Crisis communication* (pp. 121–140). Walter de Gruyter.

Coombs, W. T., & Holladay, S. J. (2002). Helping crisis managers protect reputational assets initial tests of the situational crisis communication theory. *Management Communication Quarterly, 16*(2), 165–186. https://doi.org/10.1177/089331802237233

Coombs, W. T., & Holladay, S. J. (1996). Communication and attributions in a crisis: An experimental study in crisis communication. *Journal of Public Relations Research, 8*(4), 279–295.

Coombs, W. T., & Holladay, S. J. (2007). The negative communication dynamic: Exploring the impact of stakeholder affect on behavioral intentions. *Journal of Communication Management, 11*(4), 300–312. https://doi.org/10.1108/13632540710843913

Coombs, W. T., & Holladay, S. J. (2008). Comparing apology to equivalent crisis response strategies: Clarifying apology's role and value in crisis communication. *Public Relations Review, 34*(3), 252–257.

Coombs, W. T., Holladay, S. J., & Claeys, A. S. (2016). Debunking the myth of denial's effectiveness in crisis communication: Context matters. *Journal of Communication Management, 20*(4), 381–395.

Coombs, W. T., Holladay, S. J., & Tachkova, E. R. (2018). When a scandal and crisis fuse: Exploring the communicative implications of scansis. In A. Haller, H. Michael, & M. Kraus (Eds.), *Scandalogy* (pp. 172–190). Herbet Von Halem Verlag.

Coombs, W. T., Holladay, S. J., & White, R. (2020). Corporate crises: Sticky crises and corporations. In Y. Jin, B. H. Reber & G. J. Nowak (Eds.), *Advancing crisis communication effectiveness: Integrating public relations scholarship with practice* (pp. 35–51). Routledge.

Coombs, T., & Schmidt, L. (2000). An empirical analysis of image restoration: Texaco's racism crisis. *Journal of Public Relations Research, 12*(2), 163–178.

Coombs, W. T., & Tachkova, E. R. (2019). Scansis as a unique crisis type: Theoretical and practical implications. *Journal of Communication Management, 23*(1), 72–88.

Cutler, A. (2004). Methodical failure: The use of case study method in public relations research. *Public Relations Review, 30*(3), 365–375.

De Waele, A., Schoofs, L., & Claeys, A. S. (2020). The power of empathy: The dual impacts of an emotional voice in organizational crisis communication. *Journal of Applied Communication Research, 48*(3), 350–371.

Dionisopolous, G. N., & Vibbert, S. L. (1988). CBS vs Mobil oil: Charges of creative bookkeeping. In H. R. Ryan (Ed.), *Oratorical encounters: Selected studies and sources of 20th century political accusations and apologies* (pp. 214–252). Greenwood Press.

Falkheimer, & Heide, M. (2015). Trust and brand recovery campaigns in crisis: Findus Nordic and the horsemeat scandal. *International Journal of Strategic Communication, 9*(2), 134–147.

Fediuk, T., Pace, K. M., & Botero, I. C. (2010). Crisis-response effectiveness: Methodological considerations for advancement in empirical investigation into response impact. In W. T. Coombs & S. J. Holladay (Eds.), *Handbook of crisis communication* (pp. 221–242). Wiley-Blackwell Publishing.

Frandsen, F., & Johansen, W. (2017). *Organizational crisis communication*. Sage.

Frandsen, F., & Johansen, W. (2020). Arenas and voices in organizational communication: How far have we come? In F. Frandsen & W. Johansen (Eds.), *Crisis communication* (pp. 195–212). Walter de Gruyter.

Hart, R. P. (1990). *Modern rhetorical criticism*. Scott Foresman, Little, Brown Higher Education.

Hazleton, V., & Botan, C. H. (1989). The role of theory in public relations. In C. H. Botan & V. Hazleton (Eds.), *Public relations theory* (pp. 3–16). Lawrence Erlbaum Associates.

Hearit, K. M. (1994). Apologies and public relations crises at Chrysler, Toshiba, and Volvo. *Public Relations Review, 20*(2), 113–125.

Hearit, K. M. (1995). "Mistakes were made": Organizations, apologia, and crises of social legitimacy. *Communication Studies, 46*(1–2), 1–17.

Hearit, K. M. (1999). Newsgroups, activist publics, and corporate apologia: The case of Intel and its Pentium chip. *Public Relations Review, 25*(3), 291–308.

Holladay, S. J. (2009). Crisis communication strategies in the media coverage of chemical accidents. *Journal of Public Relations Research, 21*(2), 208–217.

Jackson, P., & Peters, R. (n.d.). *Issue anticipation/crisis management for beginning professionals.* http://patrickjacksonpr.com/Theories%20&%20Models/Issues%20Anticipation-Crisis%20Management%20For%20Beginning%20Professionals%20for%20PRSSA.pdf

Jin, Y., & Cameron, G. T. (2007). The effects of threat type and duration on public relations practitioner's cognitive, affective, and conative responses in crisis situations. *Journal of Public Relations Research, 19*(3), 255–281.

Jin, Y., & Pang, A. (2010). Future directions of crisis communication research: Emotions in crisis—the next frontier. In W. T. Coombs & S. J. Holladay (Eds.), *Handbook of crisis communication* (pp. 677–682). Blackwell.

Jin, Y., Pang, A., & Cameron, G. T. (2012). Toward a publics-driven, emotion-based conceptualization in crisis communication: Unearthing dominant emotions in multi-staged testing of the integrated crisis mapping (ICM) model. *Journal of Public Relations Research, 24*(3), 266–298.

Lancaster, K., & Boyd, J. (2015). Redefinition, differentiation, and the farm animal welfare debate. *Journal of Applied Communication Research, 43*(2), 185–202.

Latham, G. P. (2011). *Becoming the evidence-based manager: Making the science of management work for you.* Davis-Black.

Len-Ríos, M. E. (2010). Image repair strategies, local news portrayals and crisis stage: A case study of Duke University's lacrosse team crisis. *International Journal of Strategic Communication, 4*(4), 267–287.

Nichols, L. T. (1997). Social problems as landmark narratives: Bank of Boston, mass media and "money laundering". *Social Problems, 44*(3), 324–341.

Park, H. (2017). Exploring effective crisis response strategies. *Public Relations Review, 43*(1), 190–192.

Racine, M., Wilson, C., & Wynes, M. (2020). The value of apology: How do corporate apologies moderate the stock market reaction to non-financial corporate crises? *Journal of Business Ethics, 163*(3), 485–505.

Reber, B. H., Yarbough, R. C., Nowak, G., & Jin, Y. (2020). Complex and challenging crises: A call for solutions. In Y. Jin, B. H. Reber, & G. J. Nowak (Eds.), *Advancing crisis communication effectiveness: Integrating public relations scholarship with practice* (pp. 3–16). Routledge.

Rousseau, D. M. (2006). Is there such a thing as "evidence-based management"? *Academy of Management Review, 31*(2), 256–269.

Schoofs, L., Claeys, A. S., De Waele, A., & Cauberghe, V. (2019). The role of empathy in crisis communication: Providing a deeper understanding of how organizational crises and crisis communication affect reputation. *Public Relations Review, 45*(5), 101851.

Stockmyer, J. (1996). Brands in crisis: Consumer help for deserving victims. *ACR North American Advances in Consumer Research, 23*(1), 429–435.

Sturges, D. L. (1994). Communicating through crisis: A strategy for organizational survival. *Management Communication Quarterly, 7,* 297–316.

Tachkova, E. R. (2021). *Parameters of scansis: Exploring the interconnectedness of crises and scandal* [Doctoral dissertation, Texas A&M University, TAMU Campus].

Thaler, R. H. (2015). *The making of behavioral economics: Misbehaving.* W.W. Norton & Company.

van der Meer, T. G., Verhoeven, P., Beentjes, H. W., & Vliegenthart, R. (2017). Communication in times of crisis: The stakeholder relationship under pressure. *Public Relations Review, 43*(2), 426–440.

Weiner, B. (1995). *Judgments of responsibility: A foundation for a theory of social conduct.* Guilford Press.

Wen, W., Yu, T., & Benoit, W. L. (2012). The failure of 'scientific' evidence in Taiwan: A case study of international image repair for American beef. *Asian Journal of Communication, 22*(2), 121–139.

Wu, F., & Xu, D. (2020). Making the most effective strategy more effective: Examining the situational and interaction effects of accommodative CCSs in corporate crises. *International Journal of Business Communication.* https://doi.org/10.1177/2329488420929748

Zhang, X., & Zhou, Z. (2020). Do instructing and adjusting information make a difference in crisis responsibility attribution? Merging fear appeal studies with the defensive attribution hypothesis. *Public Relations Review, 46*(5), 101979.

Zhao, X., Zhan, M., & Liu, B. F. (2018). Disentangling social media influence in crises: Testing a four-factor model of social media influence with large data. *Public Relations Review, 44*(4), 549–561.

12 Digital Crisis Communication Theory

Current Landscape and Future Trajectories

Brooke Fisher Liu, Yan Jin, and Lucinda Austin

In the past two decades, there has been rapid growth in public relations scholarship on crises as evidenced by the heavy increase of publications and their quantifiable impact (Coombs, 2010; Manias-Muñoz et al., 2019). Crisis communication was ranked third among emerging research areas in public relations according to trend and bibliometric analyses (Ki et al., 2019; Pasadeos et al., 2010). Much of this rapid growth can be attributed to the expansion in digital media as it intersects with crises. Accordingly, Jin and Liu (2010) proposed the first public relations model to explain and predict the impact of digital media on crisis communication management: the social-mediated crisis communication (SMCC) model. At the time there was not any theory specifically about digital crisis communication.

More than a decade later, the SMCC model remains a dominant theory in digital crisis communication research. Yet, much has changed over the past decade in the digital media landscape. In this chapter, we first define crisis, crisis communication, and digital public relations. We then trace the development and evolution of the SMCC model along with other digital crisis communication theories. Next, we propose the first significant revision of the SMCC model since 2012. We conclude with a research roadmap for the next decade of digital crisis communication scholarship.

Defining Crisis and Crisis Communication

A crisis is "a major occurrence with a potentially negative outcome affecting an organization, company or industry as well as its publics, products or good name" (Fearn-Banks, 2017, p. 1). Crises can lead to physical, emotional, and financial harm to a wide range of publics and cause harm that disrupts lives and organizational operations (Sellnow & Seeger, 2020). Coombs (2010) defined crisis communication as "the collection, processing, and dissemination of information required to address a crisis situation" (p. 20). Crisis communication plays a critical role in constructing the meaning of a crisis, ranging from event uncertainty, crisis responsibility, to emotional connectedness among affected organizations, communities, and individuals (Sellnow & Seeger, 2020).

DOI: 10.4324/9781003141396-14

Crisis communication theory is deeply rooted in organizational communication and business management. The two seminal crisis chapters in *Public Relations Theory II*, contributed by Coombs (2006) ("Crisis Management: A Communicative Approach") and Gilpin and Murphy (2006) ("Reframing Crisis Management through Complexity"), signaled the establishment of crisis communication in the domain of public relations theory. We next discuss the intersection of crisis communication and digital public relations theory.

Digital Crisis Communication

Historically speaking, there are several interesting observations when it comes to the key words *crisis communication, digital,* and associated concepts such as *technology*. First, neither *digital* nor *crisis communication* was included as an issue of theory or application in *Public Relations Theory* (Botan & Hazleton, 1989), the first comprehensive theory book for our discipline. In *Public Relations Theory II* there were two chapters on crisis management (Coombs, 2006; Gilpin & Murphy, 2006) and one on technology (Kazoleas & Teigen, 2006). About half a decade later, the first public relations theory focusing on social media and crisis communication, the SMCC model, was published (Jin & Liu, 2010). The SMCC model has been heralded as a dominant theory for understanding how organizations and publics communicate in a changing media landscape (Balog-Way et al., 2020; Sellnow & Seeger, 2020).

From the 2000s and onward, public relations scholarship has increasingly examined digital crisis communication to explicate and predict the increasingly complex information environment. However, the potential of utilizing digital communication content and forms in crisis communication is not yet fully realized, including the capacity for organizations to listen to publics' crisis needs and co-create responses with publics (Jin & Austin, 2021). Therefore, based on this "digital" umbrella specified in public relations (Verčič et al., 2015) and Coombs' (2010) definition of crisis communication, we define *digital crisis communication* as the collection, processing, and dissemination of information required to address a crisis situation triggered, mediated, and/or aggravated by digital social media.

Digital crisis communication has emerged and further matured as an important converging point of digital public relations and crisis communication theories. As Coombs (2014) emphasized, the effects of the online world on crisis communication and management has brought forward unprecedented challenges to crisis communication practice. Accordingly, there is an urgent need to advance digital crisis communication theory.

Brief Overview of the Landscape of Digital Crisis Communication Theories

As previously noted, digital media has permeated all areas of public relations research, but scholars have been slow to shift from description to theorizing

(Huang et al., 2017) in order to make predictions about the likely effectiveness of public relations strategies. Within the crisis communication scholarship, situational crisis communication theory and dialogic theory have dominated research (Huang et al., 2017; Liu & Fraustino, 2014). These theories are not reviewed in this chapter because other chapters of this book focus on them.

Three theories have emerged that were specifically developed for communication in the digital realm: the SMCC model, message convergence theory, and the media affordances framework. These three perspectives are reviewed in the following sections. Additionally, a rapidly expanding area of theorizing addresses combating misinformation and disinformation, which we also review in the next section.

Dominant Digital Crisis Communication Theories

The SMCC Model

The SMCC model (Liu et al., 2012), which extended from the blog-mediated crisis communication (BMCC) model (Jin & Liu, 2010), examines information flow and adoption in crises among media, publics, and organizations. The model has been applied to a wide variety of crises including terrorism (e.g., Zhao et al., 2019), natural disasters (e.g., Liu et al., 2019), and organizational misdeeds (e.g., Mak & Song, 2019). Recent updates to the model include further exploration of misinformation and information vetting, pressing problems in today's media environment. Other recent additions include combining the SMCC model with other theories. We further discuss the history and recent trends in SMCC model research in the next section. The BMCC model focused on guidance for identifying and responding to influential blogs at different stages of rumor transmission—corresponding to crisis phases, helping crisis communicators with limited resources to better focus their monitoring and response capabilities. In this model, influential blogs were identified through issue- and self-involvement, and the bloggers' authority and credibility with respect to the given issue. Influential bloggers exerted unique issue-fit opinion leadership and influence, filling informational and emotional needs for followers during crises. A checklist matrix helped to identify the potential influence for blogs and provided organizations with recommended crisis communication strategies. Communication strategies were informed by rumor psychology theory, as well as the stage of rumor transmission (Jin & Liu, 2010).

In 2012, scholars enhanced and renamed the BMCC model the SMCC model due to the emerging influence of social networks and social media as tools for crisis management (Liu et al., 2012). The SMCC model highlights the influence of varying social media platforms, key publics including influential content creators, news media (traditional media), organizations, and offline, word-of-mouth communication (Jin et al., 2014) (see Figure 12.1).

Social-Mediated Crisis Communication Model

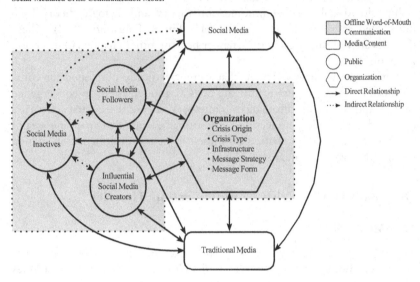

Figure 12.1 The Social-Mediated Crisis Communication Model

Source: Jin et al. (2014)

Key Publics

The SMCC model identifies three key publics who contribute to information production, seeking, and sharing at different crisis stages: influential social media creators, social media followers, and social media inactives (Jin et al., 2014). Influential creators produce and distribute crisis messages. Followers consume and share this crisis information on and offline. Inactives receive crisis information from channels other than social media including news media and word-of mouth communication with those in their social networks.

Information Flow

Also represented in the model is information flow, including direct relationships, as shown by solid arrows, and indirect relationships, as shown by dotted arrows.

For example, influential creators may still share crisis information with social media inactives through an indirect relationship with social media, via other channels. All arrows are bi-directional, indicating the flow of information may move both ways. For example, crisis coverage from news media (labeled here as traditional media) is often linked with social media coverage, utilizing sources and information or even linking directly to these sources on their platforms (Austin & Jin, 2017).

Information Form

Highlighted in the model are three forms of crisis communication: social media, traditional media, and offline word-of-mouth communication. Offline communication is represented by a gray box, given the pervasive nature of offline word-of-mouth communication among key publics during many crises.

Organizational Considerations

The model includes five criteria for organizations to consider: 1) crisis origin, 2) crisis type, 3) organizational infrastructure, 4) message strategy, and 5) message form. *Origin* refers to where the crisis emanates from (i.e., internally or externally). Origin can in turn affect how publics attribute responsibility for crises (Coombs, 2007). Attribution of responsibility, or blame, affects which message strategies are recommended for responses (Jin & Liu, 2010). Next, *type* suggests that crises may be perceived in three clusters: victim-based (i.e., organizations as victims), accidental (i.e., organizational actions were unintentional), or intentional (i.e., organization willfully took risks) (Coombs, 2007; Jin & Liu, 2010). Given potential links to attribution of responsibility, crisis types and clusters should also be considered for how publics are impacted, and message responses should be adjusted accordingly. Infrastructure highlights whether an organization is centralized or localized in its operations and crisis communication, illuminating whether responses would be best through tailored, localized messages or through unified organizational messages (Jin et al., 2014). Message strategy describes the recommended organizational crisis response options. To inform impacted publics of crises in early stages, content must include instructing, which orients affected publics to the crisis and helps them understand any protective actions they may take; content must also include adjusting information, which provides emotional support (Coombs, 2007). Beyond this stage, message strategies may shift to reputation management for the organizations in crisis.

Finally, form describes how the message is distributed through social media, news media, and/or word-of mouth communication. Form has been shown to sometimes impact publics' acceptance of crisis messages (Xu, 2020).

Emerging Research

Some of the newest SMCC model research has examined social media frames, influencer types, shifts in the media environment, non-Western contexts, employee communication, information vetting, social networks, and image repair.

For example, Zhao et al. (2019) examined social media functions, as well as differing frames and styles for a variety of publics—including social media influencers and followers, as conceptualized by the original model. Zhao et al. proposed an integrated model, which combined a uses and gratifications perspective with the SMCC model to understand communication functions, content frames, and communication styles in a disaster context.

Mak and Song (2019) further identified four sub-categories for social media influencers (i.e., people involved in crises, news media accounts, key opinion leaders, and self-involved social media influencers). Self-involved influencers were usually celebrities, politicians, or news media trying to advance an interest. Mak and Song (2019) also called for subcategories of other publics to be identified, including active publics (e.g., social media followers).

Eriksson (2018) called for more SMCC research from non-Western contexts, with Cheng (2020) specifically calling out the need for more work in China. Cheng identified, through a review of Chinese SMCC research, three major types of organizations: government, corporate, and non-profit. Additionally, in a Chinese context, Zhu et al. (2017) found that the importance of influential social media creators may be magnified due to the collectivist nature of the culture; these findings might also apply to other collectivistic cultures.

Opitz et al. (2018) expanded the SMCC model to employee communication and found that the impact of employee communication is dependent on the medium and message frame employed. In their study, employees were not effective advocates for their employers in social media spaces, but when employees become adversaries, their messages are much more impactful.

Additionally, as discussed later in this chapter, information vetting (Lu & Jin, 2020) has recently been incorporated into SMCC model research. Lastly, using a social network approach, Jin (2020) examined connections and betweenness centrality based on publics' account metrics (e.g., follows, likes, etc.) and demonstrated how this approach could be used to better understand connections during crises.

Message Convergence Theory

Message convergence is the first framework to theorize that crisis communication is most persuasive when publics receive multiple, congruent messages from diverse credible sources (Anthony et al., 2013). Congruence is facilitated by the plethora of digital communication channels. The framework posits that "simple exposure to information does not translate to understanding" (p. 115), but convergent messages help publics understand what information is credible (Sellnow & Sellnow, 2010). The framework further posits that in order for message convergence to occur, organizations must collaborate to disseminate similar, though not identical, crisis information (Herovic et al., 2014; Sellnow et al., 2018). Publics actively seek and recognize points of convergence, and their conclusions about message convergence can change as more crisis information becomes available

(Sellnow & Seeger, 2020). Ultimately, the framework advocates for organizations to strategically collaborate in emphasizing points of convergence (Sellnow & Seeger, 2020) while considering their publics' crisis information needs (Woods, 2018).

Research applying the framework finds that when publics perceive that messages converge, they are more likely to take actions recommended by authorities to keep themselves and others safe (Anthony et al., 2013; Sellnow et al., 2018). Convergent messages also help publics understand who is responsible for causing and solving a crisis (Ye & Ki, 2018). Conversely, when publics perceive that messages do not converge (i.e., message divergence), they wait for more information before deciding how to respond (Anthony et al., 2013; Herovic et al., 2014). Divergent messages also increase publics' likelihood of negatively assessing organizations' crisis responses (Ye & Ki, 2018).

However, questions remain about the framework in large part due to its nascent development. For example, the "perfect" amount of message convergence is unknown. Also unknown is the role of publics' trust in organizations that communicate about crises, which no doubt affects publics' perceptions of source credibility (Liu & Mehta, 2020). Additionally, publics are diverse groups of people, but the message convergence framework does not consider individual or group-level differences. Furthermore, the framework has not been tested in experimental contexts. Accordingly, we do not yet have solid evidence that convergent messages do indeed increase publics' trust in organizations and the likelihood of following crisis guidance. Finally, questions remain about "the threshold between transparency and manipulation for organizations promoting convergence" (Seeger & Sellnow, 2020, p. 237).

Media Affordances Framework

In recent years, scholars have pointed to media affordances as a promising approach for understanding how people engage with social media over time (Evans et al., 2017; Zhou & Xu, 2019). Affordances are multidimensional relationships that offer possible outcomes when people interact with technology (Evans et al., 2017; Gibson, 1979).

Public relations scholars have heralded media affordances as an ideal lens for examining fundamental differences among social media platforms and how these differences may generate varied crisis communication outcomes for publics and organizations (Zhou & Xu, 2019). Indeed, research finds that the affordances of some social media platforms can help authorities build their credibility during crises. For example, organizational affiliations (Lin et al., 2016) and the number of followers on a given social media account can serve as credibility cues (Westerman et al., 2012). Some affordances can contribute to organizational-public dialog during crises. For instance, most social media platforms allow for mechanical affordances such as openness, reach, networking capabilities, immediacy, back-and-forth communication, and affordability (Bruns, 2017; Ostertag & Ortiz, 2017).

The primary contribution of the affordances framework is that it overcomes a major limitation in prior research. Social media platforms are not homogenous, but most research does not distinguish between the affordances of different platforms (Eriksson, 2018). Additionally, the framework allows for understanding how different publics use social media for different crisis outcomes.

The framework has multiple weaknesses. First, the framework neglects publics who are not active social media users during crises. Second, there is not a single affordances approach (Zhou & Xu, 2019), which means that researchers employ different affordances without consistent terminology. Third, much of the research focuses on positive affordances, which neglects the possibility for negative affordances. Perhaps most significantly, much of the research focuses on technology attributes rather than linking affordances to specific crisis outcomes (Evans et al., 2017; Zhou & Xu, 2019). Fourth, the impact of affordances is likely to vary according to the speed and magnitude of crisis information spread. We posit that affordances tend to have higher impact when crisis information spread increases than when crisis information spread is minimal or receding.

Emerging Digital Crisis Communication Theories

In this section we review emerging digital crisis communication theories, which focus on crisis misinformation. While not as well-tested as the theories reviewed in the prior section, these approaches show promise for significantly advancing understanding of the digital crisis communication landscape.

Crisis Misinformation

The digital crisis communication landscape is flooded with misinformation, and the fight against misinformation is critical for safeguarding organizational reputation and publics' wellbeing (Coombs, 2014). *Crisis misinformation* is "false information about any aspect of an ongoing crisis or any incorrect information that can lead to a crisis according to factual evidence from credible source(s) (e.g., the organization, news media, third-party experts, government agencies, and internal/external witnesses)" (Jin et al., 2020b). So far, crisis scholars have identified two approaches for misinformation management, which are discussed next.

Organizational Corrective Communication

Correction attempts can help debunk misinformation and correct misperceptions (van der Meer & Jin, 2020). Scholars found that debunking strategies are effective irrespective of the strength of publics' preexisting beliefs in correcting misinformation when debunking occurs via automated and social mechanisms (Bode & Vraga, 2018). Digital media have presented unprecedented opportunities for organizations to intercept misinformation spread and engage publics with corrective information (Jin et al., 2020b; Vijaykumar et al., 2021).

Denial has been recommended as a best practice for combating misinformation attacks (e.g., Coombs, 2014), which reflects the essence of refutation as a viable approach for misinformation responses (Lewandowsky et al., 2012). However, only recently have scholars systematically defined organizational correction attempts as a unique crisis communication strategy. Focusing on an ongoing crisis, Jin et al. (2020b) presented the concept of *organizational corrective communication*, defining it as an organizational crisis response that establishes a prior message as misinformation.

Thus far, organizational corrective communication has focused primarily on identifying message strategies and examining correction effectiveness as a function of message characteristics (e.g., debunking strategies and sources). Similar to what van der Meer and Jin (2020) found in the public health crisis context, Jin and colleagues (2020) reported that, compared to simple rebuttal, the use of factual elaboration lessened organizational reputational damage and lowered publics' organizational crisis responsibility attribution.

In terms of organizational corrective information sources, scholars have further explored correction-amplifying sources (i.e., sources joining the organization-led correction attempts). Specifically, supportive supplemental information from a third actor was found to boost an organization's attempt to debunk misinformation and correct misbeliefs about an organizational crisis (Jin et al., 2020b). Employee's supportive messages on social media, when carried by an authentic voice with first-hand experience, was found to add credibility to organizational corrective crisis messages. As public relations scholars continue identifying effective approaches to debunking misinformation, the optimal timing and proper dosage of organizational correction needs to be further assessed. In addition, publics' information vetting behaviors need to be further understood.

Publics' Crisis Information Vetting

As the SMCC model outlines, crisis information can influence publics' comprehension of the situation and their potential information seeking and/or sharing behaviors. However, little research has examined whether and how publics validate or vet the crisis information they are exposed to. Due to this research gap, Lu and Jin (2020) adapted the concept of vetting from computer science to the communication literature.

Vetting is a careful and critical examination for faults and errors (Hawkins & Le Roux, 1986). To addresses the rise of misinformation online during crises, Lu and Jin (2020) developed a framework of publics' crisis information vetting. This framework aims to: a) identify a proactive approach that can enable publics to validate crisis information, and b) explore how and why publics may choose to vet crisis information.

Furthermore, Lu and Jin (2020) developed a two-step information vetting model grounded in the elaboration likelihood model and the mega-cognition theory. In the initial step (primary vetting), publics may access initial crisis information based on: a) how consistent the crisis information is with their memories and common sense, b) how certain publics feel after consuming crisis information, and c) how publics feel about themselves when consuming crisis information. From there, some publics will further assess their feelings, have second thoughts about their initial reactions and judgment, thus activating the second step of crisis information vetting. Secondary vetting includes assessing: a) whether the crisis information appears objective and makes publics feel satisfied and confident, and b) how strongly publics feel the urge to counter-argue against initial crisis information when source bias cues are detected.

As Lu and Jin (2020) further noted, not all publics will vet initial crisis information. Some publics may not feel motivated to vet at all, thus either taking no further action or proceeding toward crisis (mis)information transmission to others. For publics who are motivated to vet crisis information, they may enter the primary vetting process, during which some of them may stop further vetting and accept the initial crisis information as is, while others may proceed toward the secondary vetting process until they obtain satisfying vetting results. As an emerging concept, additional research is needed to understand how some publics initiate vetting while others do not before sharing crisis (mis)information and take other potentially damaging actions.

Current Gaps and New Needs: Introducing the Updated SMCC Model

In this final section, we propose an updated SMCC model based on the literature previously reviewed in this chapter. This model integrates new theoretical developments since the model was first proposed (Jin & Liu, 2010). This new model also integrates changes in the digital media landscape such as the rise of online misinformation and the plethora of new channels. See Figure 12.2 for the new model (SMCC 2.0). Table 12.1 accompanies the model and is explained at the end of this section.

Reconceptualizing Organizational Sources

In the new model, we reconceptualize organizational sources of crisis information. The original SMCC model focused on one organization as the primary source of crisis information (Liu et al., 2012). In the new model (SMCC 2.0), we recognize that there are multiple sources of crisis

Social-Mediated Crisis Communication Model 2.0

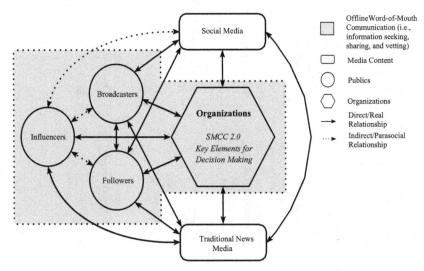

Figure 12.2 The Revised Social-Mediated Crisis Communication Model: SMCC 2.0

information. In line with the message convergence framework, we propose that when multiple sources provide complementary crisis information, publics are more likely to trust this information and take appropriate protective actions (Anthony et al., 2013). Furthermore, different types of organizational sources (e.g., news media, government agencies, corporations, and nonprofits) will be viewed with varying degrees of trust; likewise, some publics will bring to crises pre-existing relationships with these organizations (Liu & Mehta, 2020). Future SMCC model research should test how different crisis information sources, including when messages converge and diverge, affect publics' responses to crises. Equally important to consider is when information comes from crisis information sources not directly charged with responding to the crisis, such as employers.

Recategorizing Publics

In the new SMCC model we recategorize publics as influencers, broadcasters, and followers (Zhao et al., 2018). Influencers can include scientific experts and other credible sources such as doctors or celebrities—all of which may not be directly associated with organizations responding to crises. While news, government, and expert sources have been identified as information providers, celebrities have been identified as attention keepers who highlight pertinent aspects of crisis information on which to focus

Table 12.1 Table of Key SMCC 2.0 Elements for Crisis Response Decision Making

Crisis Issue Status	Dormant	Amplified	Full-Blown	Neutralized
Crisis Information Spread	None/Minimal	Increased	Peak	Receding
Crisis Communicative Behaviors Among Publics	Influencers are active in online crisis issue communication: Active/High in —Information vetting —Information seeking —Information sharing	Influencers and broadcasters are active in online crisis issue communication: Active/High in —Information vetting —Information seeking —Information sharing	Influencers, broadcasters, and followers are active in online crisis issue communication: Active/High in —Information vetting —Information seeking —Information sharing	Influencers, broadcasters, and followers are active in online crisis issue communication: Passive/Low in —Information vetting —Information seeking —Information sharing
Driving Forces/ Voices	—Issue-based groups —News media —Employer	—News media —Influencers (e.g., experts/celebrity) —Employer	—News media —Internal and external publics —Social peers —Influencers —Organizations in crisis —Employer	—News media —Organizations in crisis —Employer —Other organizations —Social Peers
Impact of Media Affordances	Low	High	High	Low
Message Convergence vs. Divergence	—Convergence: High —Divergence: Low	—Convergence: Low —Divergence: High	—Convergence: Low —Divergence: High	—Convergence: High —Divergence: Low
Misinformation Threat	Low	High	High	Low

	Prevention	Preparedness	Response	Recovery
Organizational Crisis Management Stages and Considerations	—Questions to ask: Characteristics of industry sector and organizational type? Crisis history and existing reputation? Trust level between organization and internal and external publics? —Engage in social listening	—Engage in misinformation correction; monitor conflicting information and opposing opinions —Identify and engage (if proper) with influencers —Manage uncertainty; maintain message consistency —Engage in social dialogue on issues	—Respond on relevant digital and social media platforms —If needed, issue corrective communication; enable publics' information vetting —Align issue stance and all messages with organizational purpose and solicit employees' support	—Engage in social listening; engage in social dialogue —Use crisis recovery narratives for storytelling to news media and influencers —Rebuild/strengthen trust —Manage ongoing and upcoming conflict and competition
Publics' Responses to Crisis Management (Crisis Outcomes)	**Intended:** —Questions to ask: Trust in credible sources? —Sensemaking via information from credible sources? —Preventive action taking	**Intended:** —Trust in credible sources? —Sensemaking via information from credible sources? —Preparedness action taking?	**Intended:** —Cognitive coping via information seeking from credible sources —Cognitive coping via sharing credible information to others and following recommended actions	**Intended:** —Cognitive coping via information seeking from credible sources —Cognitive coping via sharing credible information to others and following recommended actions

(Continued)

Table 12.1 (Continued)

Crisis Issue Status	Dormant	Amplified	Full-Blown	Neutralized
	Unintended: —Distrust incredible sources? —Mistrust in sources that are not credible or intend to mislead? —Message and channel fatigue? —Risk tolerance?	—Encouraging others to take actions to prepare? **Unintended:** —Distrust in credible sources —Mistrust in sources that are not credible or intend to mislead? —Message and channel fatigue? —Risk tolerance? —Unintentional spread of misinformation?	—Vetting information from questionable sources? —Supportive behaviors? **Unintended:** —Doubting information from credible sources? —Reactance against recommendations from by credible sources? —Unintentional spread of misinformation? —Organizational reputation damage?	—Vetting information from questionable sources? —Supportive behaviors? **Unintended:** —Message and channel fatigue? —Risk tolerance? —Disengagement or breaking up organization–public relationships?

(Stieglitz, 2017). Influential publics also can be powerful peers such as friends, family members, neighbors, or colleagues. Broadcasters share influentials' crisis information, and followers consume crisis information provided by influentials and broadcasters.

It is critical for future research to consider how a variety of publics interact on and offline during crises. For instance, strong vs. weak ties predict how publics communicate online and the subsequent communicative and non-communicative actions they may take (Ostertag & Ortiz, 2017; Spottswood & Wohn, 2019). Another promising avenue for future research is how publics' real offline relationships compared to their online parasocial relationships affect crisis responses (Coombs & Holladay, 2015).

Reconsidering the Information Environment

Since we first proposed the SMCC model and its predecessor, the digital media landscape has exponentially transformed. For example, when we proposed the first model (Jin & Liu, 2010), Facebook and Twitter had only been available to the public for a few years. WhatsApp, Instagram, and Pinterest had just been launched. Many of today's popular social media channels such as TikTok had not yet been imagined. The popular digital social media channels will continue to evolve, but what will remain the same is the importance of these channels on how organizations and publics communicate about crises.

In the revised SMCC model, we argue that several revisions are critical considering the evolution of digital media over the past decade. Attention is clearly needed to consider how media affordances affect publics' consumption and production of crisis information. To date, crisis communication researchers largely ignore these affordances (Eriksson, 2018). As previously explained, affordances are the unique features of different digital platforms and how these features affect crisis outcomes. Furthermore, communication research in general neglects to link media affordances to specific outcomes (Evans et al., 2017; Zhou & Xu, 2019), including positive outcomes like protective action taking and negative outcomes like organizational distrust.

Relatedly, the affordances literature calls for more attention to how publics consume crisis information. Limited research has examined how publics interact with the unique features of different digital platforms and how these features affect crisis outcomes. For instance, Spottswood and Wohn (2019) found that individuals tend to use reaction buttons (e.g., likes, angry emoji, support emoji, etc.) only for loose ties in their social networks when communicating about traumatic life events including crises. It may be that using certain reaction buttons compared to free-form comments have different impacts on how publics respond to crisis information. In the context of infectious diseases, Jin et al. (2020a) distinguished between passive behavioral intentions (e.g., see how friends respond before following government guidance) and active behavioral intentions (e.g., follow health organizations' instructions step by step). We argue that future SMCC model research should investigate such active and passive communicative and non-communicative behaviors. Another promising area for future research is examining publics' behaviors when platforms are open vs. closed and when platforms offer the possibility of anonymous posting and sharing (Scott & Rains, 2020).

Re-evaluating Crisis Communication Outcomes

We argue that crisis communication outcomes need to be further developed including intended vs. unintended organizational crisis communication consequences and active vs. passive engagement among publics. The original SMCC model focused on organizational outcomes such as reputation repair (Jin & Liu, 2010). Only recently has SMCC model scholarship considered other outcomes like publics' protective action taking (e.g., Liu et al., 2019). As scholars have argued, there should be an ethical imperative in all crisis communication to protect publics first (Coombs, 1999; Liu et al., 2021).

Health scholars have long warned about the unintended effects of communication (e.g., Wurz et al., 2013). Yet, crisis communication research has examined unintended consequences of information dissemination in a competitive and conflicting digital environment. For example, message fatigue can trigger publics' message resistance (Dillard & Shen, 2005; Niederdeppe et al., 2012) and negative online word-of-mouth communication (Verhagen et al., 2013).

Furthermore, publics differ by their influence on and engagement with crisis information (Zhao et al., 2019). In addition to receiving and consuming crisis information, some publics actively participate in creating content and/or supplying new crisis information. Publics in digital crisis communication contribute to both the generation and regeneration of crisis information (Mak & Song, 2019). Accordingly, publics' digital crisis communication engagement level (i.e., active vs. passive) needs to be further operationalized. A recent public health crisis study (Jin et al., 2020a) identified publics' passive (e.g., one would see how friends are responding before deciding how to respond) vs. active (e.g., one takes initiative to take actions) crisis coping behaviors as outcome measures, which need to be further incorporated into digital crisis communication frameworks across crisis types.

Crisis Communication Decision Making in the SMCC Model 2.0

Along with the revised SMCC model, we propose a table of the key elements of the SMCC Model 2.0 for crisis response decision making, based on the literature reviewed in this chapter. Table 12.1 is organized by the crisis issue status: whether the issue is dormant, amplified, full-blown, or neutralized. Adapting public relations scholars' previous work on the issue life cycle (e.g., Botan & Taylor, 2004; Coombs & Holladay, 2012; Crable & Vibbert, 1985; Hallahan, 2001; Sommerfeldt & Yang, 2017), we posit four issue types in a social-mediated crisis situation. First, in the *dormant status* a crisis issue is at the potential stage when concerns emerge among key publics, but those concerns remain largely unrecognized by most publics. Second, in the *amplified status* a crisis issue is at the imminent stage when concerns are widely spread online, and those concerns obtain attention from traditional media. Third, in the *full-blown status* an issue reaches the peak of information dissemination and public engagement, demanding crisis management and issue resolution. Fifth, in the *neutralized status* an issue fades out of public discourse online and offline, signaling that the issue resolution is accepted by key publics and crisis recovery is on the horizon.

Depending upon the issue status, the table theorizes how crisis information spreads and the communicative behaviors among influencers, broadcasters, and followers. The table further theorizes the driving forces in crisis issue spread along with the following considerations: media affordances, publics' relationships with crisis information sources, and the extent of message convergence. Finally, the table theorizes organizational crisis management stages and decision making considerations along with potential crisis outcomes for publics.

Conclusion

Theories should be dynamic so that they can "accommodate new understandings and insights" (Sellnow & Seeger, 2020, p. 32). Ultimately, the goal of crisis communication theory should be "to make the world safer for those impacted by crises" (Sellnow & Seeger, 2020, p. 304). Our hope is that the SMCC 2.0 model inspires the next generation of scholars to investigate the roles of digital crisis communication in facilitating and inhibiting crisis coping.

References

Anthony, K. E., Sellnow, T. L., & Millner, A. G. (2013). Message convergence as a message- centered approach to analyzing and improving risk communication. *Journal of Applied Communication Research, 41*(4), 346–364. https://doi.org/10.1080/00909882.2013.844346

Austin, L., & Jin, Y. (2017). *Social media and crisis communication.* Routledge.

Balog-Way, D., McComas, K., & Besley, J. (2020). The evolving field of risk communication. *Risk Analysis, 40*(S1), 2240–2262. https://doi.org/10.1111/risa.13615

Bode, L., & Vraga, E. K. (2018). See something, say something: Correction of global health misinformation on social media. *Health Communication, 33*(9), 1131–1140. https://doi.org/10.1080/10410236.2017.1331312

Botan, C. H., & Hazleton, V. (Eds.). (1989). *Public relations theory.* Lawrence Erlbaum Associates.

Botan, C. H., & Taylor, M. (2004). Public relations: State of the field. *Journal of Communication, 54*(4), 645–661. https://doi.org/10.1111/j.1460-2466.2004.tb02649.x

Bruns, A. (2017). Conflict imagery in a connective environment: Audiovisual content on Twitter following the 2015/2016 terror attacks in Paris and Brussels. *Media, Culture & Society, 39*(8), 1122–1141. https://doi.org/10.1177%2F0163443717725574

Cheng, Y. (2020). The social-mediated crisis communication research: Revisiting dialogue between organizations and publics in crises of China. *Public Relations Review, 46*(1), 101769. https://doi.org/10.1016/j.pubrev.2019.04.003

Coombs, W. T. (1999). Information and compassion in crisis responses: A test of their effects. *Journal of Public Relations Research, 11*(2), 125–142. https://doi.org/10.1207/s1532754xjprr1102_02

Coombs, W. T. (2006). Crisis management: A communicative approach. In C. H. Botan & V. Hazleton (Eds.), *Public relations theory II* (pp. 171–197). Lawrence Erlbaum Associates.

Coombs, W. T. (2007). Protecting organization reputations during a crisis: The development and application of situational crisis communication theory. *Corporate Reputation Review, 10*, 163–176. https://doi.org/10.1057/palgrave.crr.1550049

Coombs, W. T. (2010). Parameters for crisis communication. In W. T. Coombs & S. J. Holladay (Eds.), *The handbook of crisis communication* (pp. 17–53). Blackwell Publishing Ltd.

Coombs, W. T. (2014). State of crisis communication: Evidence and the bleeding edge. *Research Journal of Institute of Public Relations, 1*(1), 1–12.

Coombs, W. T., & Holladay, S. J. (2012). Privileging an activist vs. a corporate view of public relations history in the US. *Public Relations Review, 38*(3), 347–353. https://doi.org/10.1016/j.pubrev.2011.11.010

Coombs, W. T., & Holladay, S. J. (2015). Public relations' "relationship identity" in research: Enlightenment or illusion. *Public Relations Review, 41*(5), 689–695. https://doi.org/10.1016/j.pubrev.2013.12.008

Crable, R. E., & Vibbert, S. L. (1985). Managing issues and influencing public policy. *Public Relations Review, 11*(2), 3–16. https://doi.org/10.1016/S0363-8111(82)80114-8

Dillard, J. P., & Shen, L. (2005). On the nature of reactance and its role in persuasive health communication. *Communication Monographs, 72*(2), 144–168. https://doi.org/10.1080/03637750500111815

Eriksson, M. (2018). Lessons for crisis communication on social media: A systematic review of what research tells the practice. *International Journal of Strategic Communication, 12*(5), 526–551. https://doi.org/10.1080/1553118X.2018.1510405

Evans, S. K., Pearce, K. E., Vitak, J., & Treem, J. W. (2017). Explicating affordances: A conceptual framework for understanding affordances in communication research. *Journal of Computer-Mediated Communication, 22*(1), 35–52. https://doi.org/10.1111/jcc4.12180

Fearn-Banks, K. (2017). *Crisis communications: A casebook approach.* Lawrence Erlbaum Associates.

Gibson, J. J. (1979). *The ecological approach to visual perception.* Houghton Mifflin.

Gilpin, D., & Murphy, P. (2006). Reframing crisis management through complexity. In C. H. Botan & V. Hazleton (Eds.), *Public relations theory II* (375–392). Lawrence Erlbaum Associates.

Hallahan, K. (2001). The dynamics of issues activation and response: An issues processes model. *Journal of Public Relations Research, 13*(1), 27–59. https://doi.org/10.1207/S1532754XJPRR1301_3

Hawkins, J., & Le Roux, S. (Eds.). (1986). *The Oxford reference dictionary*. Clarendon Press.

Herovic, E., Sellnow, T. L., & Anthony, K. E. (2014). Risk communication as interacting arguments: Viewing the L'Aquila earthquake disaster through the message convergence framework. *Argumentation and Advocacy, 51*(2), 73–86. https://doi.org/10.1080/00028533.2014.11821840

Huang, Y.-H. C., Wu, F., & Huang, Q. (2017). Does research on digital public relations indicate a paradigm shift? An analysis and critique of recent trends. *Telmatics and Informatics, 34*(7), 1364–1376. https://doi.org/10.1016/j.tele.2016.08.012

Jin, X. (2020). Exploring crisis communication and information dissemination on social media: Social network analysis of Hurricane Irma tweets. *Journal of International Crisis and Risk Communication Research, 3*(2), 179–210. https://doi.org/10.30658/jicrcr.3.2.3

Jin, Y., & Austin, L. (2021). A cocreational approach to social mediated crisis communication: Communicating health crises strategically on social media. In C. H. Botan (Ed.), *The handbook of strategic communication*. Wiley-Blackwell.

Jin, Y., Iles, I. A., Austin, Liu, B. F., & Hancock, G. R. (2020a). The infectious disease threat (IDT) appraisal model: How perceptions of IDT predictability and controllability predict individuals' responses to risks. *International Journal of Strategic Communication, 14*(4), 246–271. https://doi.org/10.1080/1553118X.2020.1801691

Jin, Y., & Liu, B. F. (2010). The blog-mediated crisis communication model: Recommendations for responding to influential external blogs. *Journal of Public Relations Research, 22*, 429–455. https://doi.org/10.1080/10627261003801420.

Jin, Y., Liu, B. F., Anagondahalli, D., & Austin, L. (2014). Scale development for measuring publics' emotions in organizational crises. *Public Relations Review, 40*, 509–518. https://doi.org/10.1016/j.pubrev.2014.04.007

Jin, Y., van der Meer, T. G. L. A., Lee, Y.-I., & Lu, X. (2020b). The effect of corrective communication and employee backup on the effectiveness of fighting crisis misinformation. *Public Relations Review, 46*(3), 101910. http://doi.org/101910.10.1016/j.pubrev.2020.101910

Kazoleas, D., & Teigen, L. G. (2006). The technology-image expectancy gap: A new theory of public relations. In C. H. Botan & V. Hazleton (Eds.), *Public relations theory II* (pp. 415–433). Lawrence Erlbaum Associates.

Ki, E.-J., Pasadeos, Y., & Ertem-Eray, T. (2019). Growth of public relations research networks: A bibliometric analysis. *Journal of Public Relations Research, 31*(1–2), 5–31. https://doi.org/10.1080/1062726X.2019.1577739

Lewandowsky, S., Ecker, U. K. H., Seifert, C. M., Schwarz, N., & Cook, J. (2012). Misinformation and its correction: Continued influence and successful debiasing. *Psychological Science in the Public Interest, 13*(3), 106–131. https://doi.org/10.1177/1529100612451018

Lin, X., Spence, P. R., Sellnow, T. L., & Lachlan, K. A. (2016). Crisis communication, learning and responding: Best practices in social media. *Computers in Human Behavior, 65*, 601–605. https://doi.org/10.1016/j.chb.2016.05.080

Liu, B. F., & Fraustino, J. D. (2014). Beyond image repair: Suggestions for crisis communication theory development. *Public Relations Review, 40*(3), 543–546. https://doi.org/10.1016/j.pubrev.2014.04.004

Liu, B. F., Jin, Y., Briones, R., & Kuch, B. (2012). Managing turbulence in the blogosphere: Evaluating the blog-mediated crisis communication model with the American red cross. *Journal of Public Relations Research, 24*, 353–370. https://doi.org/10.1080/1062726X.2012.689901

Liu, B. F., Lim, J. R., Shi, D., Edwards, A. L., Islam, K., Sheppard, R., & Seeger, M. (2021). Evolving best practices in crisis communication: Examining U.S. higher education's response to the COVID-19 pandemic. *Journal of International Crisis and Risk Communication Research.* https://doi.org/10.30658/jicrcr.4.3.1

Liu, B. F., & Mehta, A. (2020). From the periphery and towards a centralized model for trust in government risk and disaster communication. *Journal of Risk Research.* Advance online publication. https://doi.org/10.1080/13669877.2020.1773516

Liu, B. F., Xu, S., Lim, J. R., & Egnoto, M. (2019). How publics' active and passive communicative behaviors affect their tornado responses: An integration of STOPS and SMCC. *Public Relations Review, 45,* 1–13. https://doi.org/10.1016/j.pubrev.2019.101831

Lu, X., & Jin, Y. (2020). Information vetting as a key component in social-mediated crisis communication: An exploratory study to examine the initial conceptualization. *Public Relations Review, 46*(2), 101891. https://doi.org/10.1016/j.pubrev.2020.101891

Manias-Muñoz, I., Jin, Y., & Reber, B. H. (2019). The state of crisis communication research and education through the lens of crisis scholars: An international Delphi study. *Public Relations Review, 45*(4), 101797. https://doi.org/10.1016/j.pubrev.2019.101797

Mak, A. K. Y., & Song, A. (2019). Revisiting social-mediated crisis communication model: The Lancôme regenerative crisis after the Hong Kong umbrella movement. *Public Relations Review, 45*(4), Article 101812. https://doi.org/10.1016/j.pubrev.2019.101812

Niederdeppe, J., Kim, H. K., Lundell, H., Fazili, F., & Frazier, B. (2012). Beyond counterarguing: Simple elaboration, complex integration, and counter-elaboration in response to variations in narrative focus and sidedness. *Journal of Communication, 62*(5), 758–777. https://doi.org/10.1111/j.1460-2466.2012.01671.x

Opitz, M., Chaudhri, V., & Wang, Y. (2018). Employee social-mediated crisis communication as opportunity or threat? *Corporate Communications: An International Journal, 23*(1), 66–83. https://doi.org/10.1108/CCIJ-07-2017-0069

Ostertag, S. F., & Ortiz, D. G. (2017). Can social media use produce enduring social ties? Affordances and the case of Katrina bloggers. *Qualitative Sociology, 40*(1), 59–82. https://doi.org/10.1007/s11133-016-9346-3

Pasadeos, Y., Berger, B., & Renfro, R. B. (2010). Public relations as a maturing discipline: An update on research networks. *Journal of Public Relations Research, 22*(2), 136–158. https://doi.org/10.1080/10627261003601390

Scott, C. R., & Rains, S. A. (2020). (Dis)connections in anonymous communication theory: Exploring conceptualizations of anonymity in communication research. *Annals of the International Communication Association, 44*(4), 385–400. https://doi.org/10.1080/23808985.2020.1843367

Sellnow, D. D., Johansson, B., Sellnow, T. L., & Land, D. R. (2018). Toward a global understanding of the effects of the IDEA model for designing instructional risk and crisis messages: A food contamination experiment in Sweden. *Journal of Contingencies and Crisis Management, 27*(2), 102–115. https://doi.org/10.1111/1468-5973.12234

Sellnow, T. L., & Seeger, M. W. (2020). *Theorizing crisis communication* (2nd ed.). Wiley-Blackwell.

Sellnow, T. L., & Sellnow, D. (2010). The instructional dynamic of risk and crisis communication: Distinguishing instructional messages from dialogue. *The Review of Communication, 10*(2), 112–126. https://doi.org/10.1080/15358590903402200

Sommerfeldt, E., & Yang, A. (2017). Relationship networks as strategic issues management: An issue stage framework of social movement organization network strategies. *Public Relations Review*, *43*(4), 829–839. https://doi.org/10.1016/j.pubrev.2017.06.012

Spottswood, E., & Wohn, D. Y. (2019). Beyond the "like": How people respond to n egative posts on Facebook. *Journal of Broadcasting and Electronic Media*, *63*(2), 250–267. https://doi.org/10.1080/08838151.2019.1622936

Stieglitz, S., Mirbabaie, M., Schwenner, L., Marx, J., Lehr, J., & Brünker, F. (2017). *Sensemaking and communication roles in social media crisis communication*. Wirtschaftsinformatik 2017 Proceedings. https://aisel.aisnet.org/wi2017/track14/paper/1

van der Meer, T. G. L. A., & Jin, Y. (2020). Seeking formula for misinformation treatment in public health crises: The effects of corrective information type and source. *Health Communication*, *35*(5), 560–575. https://doi.org/10.1080/10410236.2019.1573295

Verčič, D., Verčič, A. T., & Sriramesh, K. (2015). Looking for digital in public relations. *Public Relations Review*, *41*(2), 142–152. https://doi.org/10.1016/j.pubrev.2014.12.002

Verhagen, T., Nauta, A., & Feldberg, F. (2013). Negative online word-of-mouth: Behavioral indicator or emotional release? *Computers in Human Behavior*, *29*(4), 1430–1440. https://doi.org/10.1016/j.chb.2013.01.043

Vijaykumar, S., Jin, Y., Rogerson, D., Lu, X., Sharma, S., Maughan, A., Fadel, B., Costa, M. S. O., Pagliari, C., & Morris, D. (2021). How shades of truth and age affect responses to COVID-19 (mis)information: Randomized survey experiment among WhatsApp users in UK and Brazil. *Humanities and Social Sciences Communications*, *8*, Article 88. https://doi.org/10.1057/s41599-021-00752-7

Westerman, D., Spence, P. R., & Van Der Heide, B. (2012). A social network as information: The effect of system generated reports of connectedness on credibility on Twitter. *Computers in Human Behavior*, *28*(1), 199e206. http://dx.doi.org/10.1016/j.chb.2011.09.001

Woods, C. L. (2018). "Are your tanks filled with orca tears?" Crisis frames and message convergence in SeaWorld's tanked Twitter campaign. *Corporate Reputation Review*, *21*(1), 9–21. https://doi.org/10.1057/s41299-017-0039-y

Wurz, A., Nurm, U., & Ekdahl, K. (2013). Enhancing the role of health communication in the prevention of infectious diseases. *Journal of Health Communication*, *18*(12), 1566–1571. http://doi.org/10.1080/10810730.2013.840698

Xu, J. (2020). Does the medium matter? A meta-analysis of using social media vs. traditional media in crisis communication. *Public Relations Review*, *46*(4), 101947. https://doi.org/10.1016/j.pubrev.2020.101947

Ye, L., & Ki, E. J. (2018). Impact of message convergence on organizational Reputation: An examination of organizational crisis communication on Facebook. *Corporate Reputation Review*, *21*(4), 1–8. https://doi.org/10.1057/s41299-017-0040-5

Zhao, X., Zhan, M., & Liu, B. F. (2019). Understanding motivated publics during disasters: Examining message functions, frames, and styles of social media influentials and followers. *Journal of Contingencies and Crisis Management*, *27*(4), 387–399. https://doi.org/10.1111/1468-5973.12279

Zhao, X., & Zhan, M., & Wong, C.-W. (2018). Segmenting and understanding publics in a social media information sharing network: An interactional and dynamic approach. *International Journal of Strategic Communication*, *12*(1), 25–25. https://doi.org/10.1080/1553118X.2017.1379013

Zhou, X., & Xu, S. (2019). *Remaking dialogic principles for the digital age: The role of affordances in dialogue and engagement.* Paper presented at the International Communication Association Conference.

Zhu, L., Anagondahalli, D., & Zhang, A. (2017). Social media and culture in crisis communication: McDonald's and KFC crises management in China. *Public Relations Review, 43*(3), 487–492. https://doi.org/10.1016/j.pubrev.2017.03.006

13 Social Theory in Public Relations

Insights and Directions

Lee Edwards and Øyvind Ihlen

Introduction

Social theory can be thought of as a broad term, encompassing many academic disciplines including sociology and political theory. Social theory is basically intended to make sense of society—that is, the structured social relations and institutions that make up a large community (Giddens & Sutton, 2017). The ambition of social theory is often to explain and/or address some imperfection or social ill—a social problem that should be rectified. Issues of social inequality loom large in this regard, explained by social hierarchies structured by class, gender, race, dis/ability, sexuality and other identities. In the last few years such issues have received renewed attention, as witnessed by the rise to global prominence of the Black Lives Matter and #MeToo movements. While such movements are politically oriented and argue for fundamental changes in the power structures of society, they also prompt debates about broader forms of gender and racial (in)equality across society—for example, in housing, equal pay, and access to healthcare (see e.g., Elliott, 2014). The COVID-19 pandemic has laid these inequalities bare, prompting important conversations among global leaders about how to create a recovery that mitigates, rather than exacerbates, already existing inequity (e.g., Stiglitz, 2020).

Social theory frequently aims to contribute insight that can potentially alter policies, ideas, and behaviors to address inequalities, thus constituting a two-way exchange between researchers and society (Giddens & Sutton, 2017). The ability to suggest a "cure," however, is dependent on the ability to provide a good diagnosis. In other words, social theory must offer concepts and approaches that are suitable to understand what is going on in society. The challenge to understand what is going on in society is of course extremely broad, but it nonetheless lies at the heart of all social theorists' endeavors. Correspondingly, social theory ranges over a remarkably diverse set of social phenomena, from our relationships with each other, to our communicative habits and norms, our political arrangements and hierarchies, and the ways in which we interact with the various structures, institutions, and material realities that shape our lives.

DOI: 10.4324/9781003141396-15

Transferred to public relations, approaches drawing on social theory aim to provide insight into what is going on when public relations is practiced. A pertinent question is: What does public relations do in, to, and for society (Ihlen & van Ruler, 2007)? How does it affect the relationships, communicative interactions, and social hierarchies that we encounter daily? For example, some social theories enable scholars to challenge "the hegemonic assumptions in public relations" around gender, race, and other inequalities in contexts where public relations practices and professional norms play a role (Ciszek, 2018; Daymon & Demetrious, 2013, p. 3; Logan, 2018; Waymer & Heath, 2015). Other theories facilitate investigations into how public relations practices are reshaping relationships between individuals and groups, through the digital and analogue interventions that public relations campaigns initiate.

In general, there has been an increase in the use of social theory in public relations, as, for instance, detailed in a study of the application of the German scholar Jürgen Habermas to public relations research (Buhmann et al., 2019). A whole range of other theorists have also been applied, something that is showcased in the volume *Public Relations and Social Theory*, now in its second edition (Ihlen & Fredriksson, 2018; Ihlen et al., 2009). The latter volume draws on the work on both classical and modern sociologists and political theorists such as Marx (Weaver, 2018), Weber (Wæraas, 2018), Spivak (Dutta, 2018), Latour (Somerville, 2021; Verhoeven, 2018), Mouffe (Davidson & Motion, 2018), and Bauman (Bachmann, 2019; Pieczka, 2018). Following the ground-breaking work of L'Etang and Pieczka (1996) applying critical perspectives to public relations (see also L'Etang et al., 2015), which drew on the Frankfurt School of critical theory (L'Etang, 2005), a growing number of publications and scholars have also applied culture-centered analytical frameworks to public relations, adopting a critical approach in their analyses (Bardhan & Weaver, 2011; Curtin & Gaither, 2005; Daymon & Demetrious, 2013; Dutta & Elers, 2020; Edwards & Hodges, 2011; Fitch, 2016).

If there is an analytical idea that unites this output, it is arguably that public relations is diverse and multifaceted in its practices and effects. In such a field, critical perspectives of the public relations industry co-exist with more positive interpretations of its role. One such stance is rooted in the conception of the public relations practitioner being an activist in his or her organization (Holtzhausen, 2012). Practitioners should "always question the nature of their own institutions and strive to improve them and make them more just" (Holtzhausen, 2012, p. 234). Sharing power between organizations and their stakeholders is an important goal for practitioners embracing this activist role (Berger, 2005). Public relations should contribute to "the democratic, deliberative and decision-making roles of civil society" by opening up organizations to genuine dialogue and engagement with stakeholders (Motion & Leitch, 2015, p. 148). As for scholars, the basic question concerns whether we can "retain our desire to change the way the world is" (Edwards, 2015, p. 24).

While there have been extensive explorations of social theory in public relations scholarship, applications of social theory to *empirical* sites, where its value as a means of understanding, challenging, and changing practice can be explained and illustrated more fully, remain scarce. Some theorists and theories are used more regularly than others in public relations scholarship (e.g., Habermas, various feminist theories), some are used only by one or very few scholars (e.g., queer theory, critical race theory, actor-network theory, postcolonial theory), and some have not been used at all in empirical work (e.g., Mouffe, Baumann, Castells). This chapter issues a call for more empirical research in this vein. We consider how the application of social theory to empirical sites is crucial to understand and challenge contemporary public relations practices and power. The two driving questions for the chapter are: What do public relations practitioners do, and with what effect on society? How does public relations uphold or disrupt social inequality? In the following, we first lay out some of the insights that social theory has contributed to public relations to answer these two questions. In the final part of the chapter, we consider potential research avenues for future public relations scholarship drawing on social theory.

What Do Practitioners Do?

A recurring theme in social theory is the relationship between individuals as agents and social structures. At one end of the continuum, "structuralists" tend to locate power in, for instance, economic structures or social hierarchies (e.g., gender or class). At the other end, you find the perspective of the free agent in control of his or her destiny, often referred to as having *agency*. Here, structures are always vulnerable to challenge by individuals who resist their imposition, and power is located in agency as a locus of change. In this vein, "the systematic study of the reasons, motives, beliefs, emotions and desires of people is regarded as the most appropriate way in which to develop critical social analysis" (Elliott & Lemert, 2022, p. 11). Both structuralist and agentic approaches are found in public relations research. For example, applications of critical race theory to public relations are situated at structuralist end of the continuum because they emphasize the structural embedding of racial discrimination in the field (Edwards, 2013). In contrast, studies of ethics in public relations, of dialogical principles, proposals for feminist ethics of care, and applications of queer theory can all be placed toward the agentic end of the continuum because they make space for practitioners and audiences to shape and change the norms and values associated with public relations and its practices. Other theoretical approaches call attention to culture, norms, and social orders, seeing organizations and their communication as embedded in their social context where practices are created, altered, maintained, and contested in the wake of organization-environment relations (Fredriksson et al., 2013). Applying dialogic principles, this kind of approach asks challenging questions that consider the structural *and* agentic power of organizations and practition-ers. For example, is it possible for corporations to engage in dialogue in a manner that satisfies the ideals of dialogic theory? Can corporations avoid reducing dialogue to an instrument to create a profit (Ihlen & Levenshus, 2017)? Since the corporate institution is founded on a fundamental motive of providing profit, the only check on its action is either through rules and regulations or reputation damage that can hurt profit. Obviously, the "evangelical" activist practitioner can alert the organization to the impor-tance of reputation and engage in issues management (Heath & Palenchar, 2008). The remaining question, however, is what a corporation does in a situation where it must choose between ethics and profit. One argument is that there are systemic limits in such situations whereby good intentions will take second place (Logan, 2018).

Structure and Agency: A Balancing Act

Most of today's social theorists are likely to argue for a mixed perspective on this question, "allowing" agents some rein within a system, while simul-taneously recognizing that the agent is embedded in a social structure that exerts influence on what he or she can do (Elliott & Lemert, 2014). Two major sociologists who have furthered such a perspective are Bourdieu and Giddens. The former writes about the structuring mechanism of *habitus* that holds a key role as a form of internalized mental or cognitive structure, functioning both consciously and unconsciously to constrain what people should and should not do. Habitus, however, can be shaped and resisted through reflection—for example, based on new information that individu-als encounter in other fields. Thus, "[w]hile a practitioner could have a preconceived conception of what a dialogue is and how it works, he or she could alter this perspective and thus the strategies for conducting dialogue" (Ihlen & Levenshus, 2017, p. 226).

The theory of structuration proposed by Giddens (1984/1995), sees structure as both a medium and an outcome of reproductive individual prac-tices. We interact with structures in a conscious way, and as we do so, our reflective practices may prompt both their replication and their evolution. In other words, social structures are human-made and can change and even be replaced. Falkheimer (2018) has used this theory to write about what he calls a "third way public relations perspective" (p. 190) that lies between managerial, functionalistic, and prescriptive traditions and between critical and interpretative approaches. In essence, it could be argued that public rela-tions functions as a reflexive social expert system, as it assists organizations in maneuvering their position in societies that are changing and changing fast (Ihlen et al., 2018).

As shown earlier, public relations theory drawing on social theory offers several different ways to understand what influences practitioners. Just like in sociology in general, disputes about the balance and interactions between structure and agency are ongoing. Today, however, the most pressing debates are tied to issues of power and inequality.

What Power Do Practitioners Have?

All social theory addresses power, whether implicitly or explicitly, because it deals with the ways we relate to each other and to the institutions and organizations around us. Consequently, the question of what power public relations practitioners have can be answered in as many ways as there are theories. In this section, we point to three areas of power that social theory has addressed: power and social hierarchies; power on a global scale; and discursive/networked power.

Power and Social Hierarchies

Most traditionally, one might explore social hierarchies based around identities that we know subordinate some groups in relation to others. Gender, sexuality, and race are three obvious candidates that have been extensively researched in public relations, albeit by a minority of scholars. Perhaps the most extensive work here has been conducted by feminist theorists, extending back to the Velvet Ghetto report that highlighted and critiqued the patriarchal nature of the profession nearly 40 years ago, through to the application of more radical feminist approaches to explain the gendered experiences of women in 21st-century public relations (Cline et al., 1986; Daymon & Demetrious, 2013; Place, 2015; Yeomans, 2019). Rakow and Nastasia (2018) have for instance drawn on the writing of Dorothy E. Smith (1974, 1987), pointing out that power is typically held by "the circle of men." Smith has pointed out, "Women have not participated [in] the construction of knowledge in the social sciences, and . . . women's ways of constructing knowledge about the social world [are] different from those described and canonized by sociologists" (Rakow & Nastasia, 2009, p. 264). Similarly, there is a growing scholarly output "challenging the heterosexist foundations and presumptions that constitute theory in public relations" (Ciszek, 2018, p. 134) and seeking to secure a place for LGBT issues in public relations (Tindall & Waters, 2014; Vardeman-Winter & Tindall, 2010).

The feminist and queer bodies of work have revealed gendered ways of thinking about, and being, public relations practitioners and audience members. Practices that devalue women's contribution to the field—paying them less, imposing emotional labor, stereotyping their identities and minimizing their representation as leaders—are all common, and they illustrate the power that many practitioners do *not* have (Yeomans, 2019). When it comes to audiences, feminist research has deconstructed the ways in which campaigns can ignore the realities of women's lives and perpetuate gendered stereotypes rather than support women to resist the inequalities they face (Hutchins & Tindall, 2021; Vardeman-Winter, 2016). While there is more to do, including integrating a wider range of feminist theories into the field (Golombisky, 2015), there is no doubt that this research strand has been particularly productive.

Like feminist research, research on racial inequalities has been present in the field since the 1980s (Kern-Foxworth, 1989), persistently pursued by a small number of scholars over time. Their findings constitute clear evidence of a profession and practices that are racialized just as they are gendered. Scholars have applied a racial lens to reveal the voices of practitioners of color, and the myriad ways in which their working lives are permeated by assumptions and practices associated with whiteness, repeatedly marginalizing their identities (Clark et al., 2019; Edwards, 2014; Logan, 2021; Pompper, 2005). Communications practices have also been shown to both support racialized hierarchies in the ways they privilege the pursuit of capital and ignore its racialized effects. On the other hand, some scholars have re-written histories of public relations to reveal the prolific use of public relations strategies by anti-racist individuals and movements for well over a century, and to consider how the field might change if race were a central, rather than a marginalized topic (Heath & Waymer, 2009; Straughan, 2004; Waymer & Heath, 2015). Research has shown how racialized hierarchies can be countered when deployed by powerful social movements such as Black Lives Matter (Ciszek & Logan, 2018; Edrington & Lee, 2018). Resistance that draws on the power of communication also emerges in national and localized territories—for example, among subaltern populations and indigenous communities (Duarte, 2017; Dutta & Elers, 2020; Munshi & Kurian, 2007).

Power at a Global Scale

One important expansion of the landscape for public relations scholarship has been to reflect on the profession's global footprint. Global public relations has been a focus for several decades, led by the groundbreaking work of Sriramesh and Verčič, who insistently argued for analyses of public relations beyond the Western context. While initial studies tended to focus on the characteristics of public relations in different countries (e.g. Sriramesh & Vercic, 1995, 2009, 2012), the advent of more critically oriented social theories has led to an explicit engagement with the ways that public relations is enmeshed with global power structures through its deployment by corporations and governments (Dutta & Pal, 2020). Here, postcolonial theory has offered crucial avenues for revealing the voices and experiences of the most marginalized populations of the world, who are subjected to the communicative violence that public relations can exert but frequently use those same public relations tactics to resist the impositions of global capital (Dutta, 2015, 2016; Munshi & Kurian, 2005; Pal, 2016). Dutta has spearheaded studies drawing on postcolonial theory, also criticizing public relations scholarship for serving "the goals of the transnational elite" and actively participating "in the marginalization of the Third World participant" through the trope of civil society (Dutta-Bergman, 2005, p. 267). Using a Marxist-feminist-deconstructivist perspective, Spivak (as cited in, Dutta, 2009) points to how neo-liberal transnational capitalism breeds fundamental inequities. Dutta has also extended this work to health communication (Dutta, 2007). Within nation states, indigenous communities have been subjected to the same processes of expropriation of their land, water, and cultures (Munshi & Kurian, 2021). While only a handful of scholars have used indigenous theories in their work, the numbers of studies are likely to grow as climate change raises the profile of indigenous rights and knowledge, leading to more communication in this space (Munshi & Kurian, 2021, 2015).

Discursive and Networked Power

A final but critical set of theories that address the power of public relations are those that move away from the traditional structure-agency divide and instead engage with the complexity of discursive and relational power. Foucauldian approaches to discourse, first introduced to the field by Motion and, have been fundamental in shifting the understanding of public relations as a neutral pipeline for messages to a more holistic analysis of its role as a central actor in the constitution and circulation of discursive power across society. Foucauldian discourse theory differs from other social theories in that it situates power in the discursive fabric of our lives. Public relations practitioners exercise this power as "discourse technologists" (Motion & Leitch, 1996), crafting communication in ways that normalize certain types of subjectivity and worldview, presenting them as rational and reasonable while alternative perspectives are marginalized (Motion & Leitch, 2018). Work drawing on Foucauldian discourse theory has revealed how campaigns of all kinds govern our sense of self and "other," our perception of the powerful and our dismissal of those whose voices are not heard, and how the profession's self-narration privileges certain identities, backgrounds, and types of practice and "others" those who do not fit the mold.

Discursive analyses of public relations reflect a conception of power as a multidirectional, distributed force that is always in flux and never completely secure. When power is in relations, rather than structures or individual agency, the same principles apply. Actor-network theory, which extends the idea of networks to incorporate non-human actors, has been used to explain public relations practices that go beyond human practitioners to leverage algorithmic techniques, platform infrastructures, and data capture (Somerville, 2021; Verhoeven, 2018). These technological actors are as fundamental to any contemporary campaign as any verbal or visual messages that practitioners craft, and they can act autonomously to change the way a campaign evolves (Collister, 2019; Schölzel & Nothhaft, 2016). Such analyses pull scholarship into the realm of rapidly evolving practice and enable a better understanding of how the communication networks that

Castells (2009) argues are so powerful shape our lives in their most intimate and most public spaces.

Interrogating the practices and power of public relations through social theory opens different ways to understand the multiple channels through which the practice has an impact on society. Communication practices are only one place where power circulates. It is also inherent in the way the professional field operates, in the audiences and communities that are both targeted by campaigns and use them agentically, and in the institutions and organizations that use public relations to change the way society operates. Asking about power invites us to follow the threads of domination and resistance, and to see where they flex and change. This complicates the public relations landscape, drawing our gaze beyond the immediate and the local to incorporate wider temporal and geographical boundaries. It also promotes perspectives that go beyond discourse to incorporate the material realities affected by public relations—whether that be the desire to overcome individual suffering and choose to live, sacrificing the health of subaltern communities, depriving oppressed people of a voice or facilitating resistance to all these forms of domination (Ciszek, 2014; Dutta, 2015; Logan, 2018; Sejrup, 2014).

The multiplicity of research about practices and power that draws on social theory is clearly productive and has enhanced the depth and breadth of the field. However, if we look to the future, there is scope for an even stronger extension of such work. In the final section of this chapter, we reflect on some of these issues as potential directions for future research.

The Next Decade? Public Relations and Social Theory in the Future

Understanding public relations' position in society through the lenses offered by social theory expands the analytical capacity of the field by providing a route out of the tight and long-established scholarly territory of public relations in/and organizations. In a digitized, globalized era, it makes little sense to limit our analyses in this way. All public relations work is implicated in wider social, political, and economic arrangements, and those arrangements in turn underpin its function as a location of dominance or resistance, or where power is in flux. Understanding how public relations works within these broader contexts is an essential aspect of our advancing knowledge. In the next section, we sketch out a few areas where we argue that perspectives drawing on social theory would be particularly helpful.

Incorporating Networks, the Digital, and AI

One major priority for public relations research is to use social theory to help us understand the rapidly moving world of practice. Here, it is essential to integrate theories that address the ways in which practice is underpinned by complex technologies and how voice and diversity are deeply affected by the (increasingly) digital and networked fabrics of campaigning (Bourne & Edwards, 2021). In this regard, future research could for instance draw on the work of Castells (2000) and the theory of the "Network Society." This work, which has not been put to much use in public relations so far, begins with the assumption that in a digitizing world, static notions of structure and agency fail to reflect the importance of network dynamics to the circulation and exercise of power. In a network society, positions of power relate to the influence an actor has over the constitution, content, and orientation of networks. Two key roles that public relations practitioners execute are those of programmers and switchers (Castells, 2009). Programmers define the content and direction of a network, and this kind of activity is reflected in practitioners' efforts to set agendas for public discussion by crafting campaign messages and enabling them to circulate, as well as constructing types of network membership that will deliver particular outcomes. Switchers define the interfaces and interactions between networks and practitioners to this kind of work when they engage in stakeholder relations, set up collaborative networks, or build alliances that bring together groups and individuals working in different industries or spheres of society (e.g., NGOs, corporations, and policymakers). Understood in these terms, public relations work can occur in the wider relational, material, and discursive landscapes that provide the context for its influence.

In network societies power also comes from the position occupied in a network, because it helps to determine relationships that can provide access to resources (in public relations, examples include the ability to use a celebrity to influence a target audience, access to financial resources via sponsorship, or reputational benefits through association with a non-profit organization). Public relations work often focuses on fostering relationships, but in a network context this means considering the position one holds in relation to the desired stakeholders. Network position—or networked power, as Castells (2009) calls it—is therefore a central objective of public relations practice.

While networks emerge based on pre-existing power hierarchies (so that, for example, the pre-existing status and resources of traditional media organizations generally help to secure a strong network position), they continually evolve as the actions of programmers, switchers, and other network participants alter the network landscape. This means that public relations plays a critical role in the evolution of power, not only because it works on behalf of organizations and individuals engaged in struggles over discursive and material resources, but also because the core practices of public relations work are implicated in the ways relationships and resources move across networks.

Political-Economic Analyses

While analyses that take seriously the networked, digitized nature of practice may have an eye to understanding the futures of practice, revealing and analyzing the continued impact of traditional power structures remains essential. Here, we suggest that taking public relations seriously as a mechanism for the pursuit of capital is an important task, critical to our understanding of how the manifestations of racial, gendered, and other forms of discrimination in the profession and its practices are linked to this pursuit. Moreover, a better understanding of public relations as capital can explain its increasing imbrication in the political sphere and in our civic lives (Cronin, 2018). Yet detailed political economic analyses of the profession and its activities are still needed. While some UK scholars have undertaken such work (Dinan & Miller, 2007; Miller & Dinan, 2000, 2008), these studies are in dire need of being updated to the present-day situation and should be extended to include other geographical settings. In other words, more economic analyses of the profession and its activities are needed, as many empirical studies remain focused on specific cases, and we fail to "connect the dots" between them to reveal the systemic nature of power and resistance in the field.

Extending Existing Theoretical Arenas

As we have attempted to illustrate in this chapter, public relations scholars have offered several different theoretical arenas that are fruitful to analyze the practice as well as the theorizing about the practice. We do, however, want to argue that this theorizing can be extended and brought into conversation with both established and newer approaches to public relations. Here we are thinking about usage of, for instance, different types of discourse theory, as well as different types of feminist theory. Combining different theoretical approaches is also productive. For example, bringing Foucauldian discourse theory into conversation with indigenous worldviews and political economic analyses of climate change campaigns could generate important insights into the discursive processes that marginalize indigenous voices in the context of climate campaigns. In other words, we could do a better job of integrating insights from social theory by facilitating cross-theoretical conversations to address the complex present-day issues that practitioners and audiences must grapple with.

In conclusion, it is worth noting Castells' (2009) argument about the importance of communication in society. He argues that networks can emerge around any kind of activity (e.g., finance, higher education, extraction industries), but communication networks play a particularly important role because they underpin all other networks, acting as the mechanism through which ideas and imaginaries hold those networks together. If we take this as the case, then the public relations profession, its practices, practitioners, and audiences are all truly powerful social actors. Reiterating our earlier call, we argue that using social theory to explore the empirical realities of public relations in their complex contexts is an essential task. The list of possible research avenues given here is necessarily brief and obviously not exhaustive. The toolbox of social theory is vast and the number of social issues extensive. Engaging with its breadth and depth can help public relations scholars to provide numerous answers to the crucial question: What is going on when public relations is practiced in society?

References

Bachmann, P. (2019). Public relations in liquid modernity: How big data and automation cause moral blindness. *Public Relations Inquiry, 8*(3), 319–331. https://doi.org/10.1177/2046147X19863833

Bardhan, N., & Weaver, C. K. (Eds.). (2011). *Public relations in global cultural contexts: Multi-paradigmatic perspectives.* Routledge.

Berger, B. K. (2005). Power over, power with, and power to relations: Critical reflections on public relations, the dominant coalition, and activism. *Journal of Public Relations Research, 17*(1), 5–28.

Bourne, C., & Edwards, L. (2021). Critical reflections on the field. In C. Valentini (Ed.), *Handbook of public relations* (pp. 601–614). De Gruyter Mouton.

Buhmann, A., Ihlen, Ø., & Aaen-Stockdale, C. (2019). Connecting the dots: A bibliometric review of Habermasian theory in public relations research. *Journal of Communication Management, 23*(4), 444–467. https://doi.org/10.1108/JCOM-12-2018-0127

Castells, M. (2000). *The rise of the networked society.* Blackwell.

Castells, M. (2009). *Communication power.* Oxford University Press.

Ciszek, E. (2014). Cracks in the glass slipper: Does it really "get better" for LGBTQ youth, or is it just another Cinderella story? *Journal of Communication Inquiry, 38*(4), 325–340.

Ciszek, E. (2018). Queering PR: Directions in theory and research for public relations scholarship. *Journal of Public Relations Research, 30*(4), 134–145. https://doi.org/10.1080/1062726X.2018.1440354

Ciszek, E., & Logan, N. (2018). Challenging the dialogic promise: How Ben & Jerry's support for Black lives matter fosters dissensus on social media. *Journal of Public Relations Research, 30*(3), 115–127. https://doi.org/10.1080/1062726X.2018.1498342

Clark, T., Guivarra, N., Dodson, S., & Widders Hunt, Y. (2019). Asserting an indigenous theoretical framework in Australian public relations. *Prism, 15*(1). www.prismjournal.org

Cline, C. G., Toth, E. L., Turk, J. V., Walters, L. M., Johnson, N., & Smith, H. (1986). *The velvet ghetto: The impact of the increasing percentage of women in public relations and business communication.* IABC Foundation.

Collister, S. (2019). *Towards a theory of media power in a networked communication environment: Case studies of #Demo2012, Adidas, and #AskSnowden* [PhD, Royal Holloway, University of London].

Cronin, A. (2018). *Public relations capitalism: Promotional culture, publics and commercial democracy.* Palgrave Macmillan.

Curtin, P. A., & Gaither, T. K. (2005). Privileging identity, difference, and power: The circuit of culture as a basis for public relations theory. *Journal of Public Relations Research, 17*(2), 91–115. www.informaworld.com/10.1207/s1532754xjprr1702_3

Davidson, S., & Motion, J. (2018). On Mouffe: Radical pluralism and public relations. In Ø. Ihlen & M. Fredriksson (Eds.), *Public relations and social theory: Key figures, concepts and developments* (2nd ed., pp. 394–413). Routledge.

Daymon, C., & Demetrious, K. (Eds.). (2013). *Gender and public relations: Critical perspectives on voice, image and identity*. Routledge.

Dinan, W., & Miller, D. (Eds.). (2007). *Thinker, faker, spinner, spy: Corporate PR and the assault on democracy*. Pluto.

Duarte, M. E. (2017). Connected activism: Indigenous uses of social media for shaping political change. *Australasian Journal of Information Systems, 21*. https://doi.org/10.3127/ajis.v21i0.1525

Dutta, M. J. (2007). Communicating about culture and health: Theorizing culture-centered and cultural sensitivity approaches. *Communication Theory, 17*(3), 304–328. https://doi.org/10.1111/j.1468-2885.2007.00297.x

Dutta, M. J. (2009). On Spivak: Theorizing resistance: Applying Gayatri Chakravorty Spivak in public relations. In Ø. Ihlen, B. van Ruler, & M. Fredriksson (Eds.), *Public relations and social theory: Key figures and concepts* (pp. 278–300). Routledge.

Dutta, M. J. (2015). Decolonizing communication for social change: A culture-centered approach. *Communication Theory, 25*(2), 123–143. https://doi.org/10.1111/comt.12067

Dutta, M. J. (2016). A postcolonial critique of public relations. In J. L'Etang, D. McKie, N. Snow, & J. Xifra (Eds.), *The Routledge handbook of critical public relations* (pp. 248–260). Routledge.

Dutta, M. J. (2018). On Spivak: Theorizing resistance in public relations. In Ø. Ihlen & M. Fredriksson (Eds.), *Public relations and social theory: Key figures, concepts and developments* (2nd ed., pp. 374–393). Routledge.

Dutta, M. J., & Elers, S. (2020). Public relations, indigeneity and colonization: Indigenous resistance as dialogic anchor. *Public Relations Review, 46*(1), 1–9. https://doi.org/10.1016/j.pubrev.2019.101852

Dutta, M. J., & Pal, M. (2020). Theorizing from the global south: Dismantling, resisting, and transforming communication theory. *Communication Theory, 30*(4), 349–369.

Dutta-Bergman, M. J. (2005). Civil society and public relations: Not so civil after all. *Journal of Public Relations Research, 17*(3), 267–289.

Edrington, C., & Lee, N. (2018). Tweeting a social movement: Black lives matter and its use of Twitter to share information, build community, and promote action. *Journal of Public Interest Communications, 2*(2). https://doi.org/10.32473/jpic.v2.i2.p289

Edwards, L. (2013). Institutional racism in cultural production: The case of public relations. *Popular Communication: The International Journal of Media and Culture, 11*(3), 242–256.

Edwards, L. (2014). *Power, diversity and public relations*. Routledge.

Edwards, L. (2015). An historical overview of the emergence of critical thinking in PR. In J. L'Etang, D. McKie, N. Snow, & J. Xifra (Eds.), *Routledge handbook of critical public relations* (pp. 16–27). Routledge.

Edwards, L., & Hodges, C. E. M. (Eds.). (2011). *Public relations, society & culture: Theoretical and empirical explorations*. Routledge.

Elliott, A. (2014). *Contemporary social theory: An introduction*. Routledge.

Falkheimer, J. (2018). On Giddens: Interpreting public relations through Anthony Giddens's structuration and late modernity theories. In Ø. Ihlen & M. Fredriksson (Eds.), *Public relations and social theory: Key figures, concepts and developments* (pp. 177–192). Routledge.

Fitch, K. (2016). *Professionalizing public relations: History, gender and education*. Palgrave Macmillan.

Fredriksson, M., Pallas, J., & Wehmeier, S. (2013). Public relations and neo-institutional theory. *Public Relations Inquiry, 2*(2), 183–203. https://doi.org/10.1177/2046147x13485956

Giddens, A. (1984/1995). *The constitution of society: Outline of the theory of structuration.* Polity Press.

Giddens, A., & Sutton, P. W. (2017). *Essential concepts in sociology* (2nd ed.). Polity.

Golombisky, K. (2015). Renewing the commitments of feminist public relations theory: From velvet ghetto to social justice. *Journal of Public Relations Research, 27*(5), 389–415. https://doi.org/10.1080/1062726X.2015.1086653

Heath, R. L., & Palenchar, M. (2008). *Strategic issues management: Organizations and public policy challenges* (2nd ed.). Sage.

Heath, R. L., & Waymer, D. (2009). Activist public relations and the paradox of the positive. In R. Heath, E. Toth, & D. Waymer (Eds.), *Rhetorical and critical approaches to public relations II* (pp. 194–215). Routledge.

Holtzhausen, D. R. (2012). *Public relations as activism: Postmodern approaches to theory & practice.* Routledge.

Hutchins, A., & Tindall, N. (2021). *Public relations and online engagement: Audiences, fandom and influencers.* Routledge.

Ihlen, Ø., & Fredriksson, M. (Eds.). (2018). *Public relations and social theory: Key figures, concepts and developments* (2nd ed.). Routledge.

Ihlen, Ø., & Levenshus, A. (2017). Panacea, placebo or prudence: Perspectives and constraints for corporate dialogue. *Public Relations Inquiry, 6*(3), 219–232. https://doi.org/10.1177/2046147X17708815

Ihlen, Ø., & van Ruler, B. (2007). How public relations works: Theoretical roots and public relations perspectives. *Public Relations Review, 33*(3), 243–248.

Ihlen, Ø., van Ruler, B., & Fredriksson, M. (Eds.). (2009). *Public relations and social theory: Key figures and concepts.* Routledge.

Ihlen, Ø., Verhoeven, P., & Fredriksson, M. (2018). Conclusions on the compass, context, concepts, concerns and empirical avenues for public relations. In Ø. Ihlen & M. Fredriksson (Eds.), *Public relations and social theory: Key figures, concepts and developments* (2nd ed., pp. 414–431). Routledge.

Kern-Foxworth, M. (1989). Status and roles of minority PR practitioners. *Public Relations Review, 15*(3), 39–47.

L'Etang, J. (2005). Critical public relations: Some reflections. *Public Relations Review, 31*, 521–526.

L'Etang, J., McKie, D., Snow, N., & Xifra, J. (Eds.). (2015). *Routledge handbook of critical public relations.* Routledge.

L'Etang, J., & Pieczka, M. (Eds.). (1996). *Critical perspectives in public relations.* International Thomson Business Press.

Logan, N. (2018). The flint water crisis: An analysis of public relations as a mediator between human and corporate persons. *Public Relations Review, 44*(1), 47–55.

Logan, N. (2021). A theory of corporate responsibility to race (CRR): Communication and racial justice in public relations. *Journal of Public Relations Research.* https://doi.org/10.1080/1062726X.2021.1881898

Miller, D., & Dinan, W. (2000). The rise of the PR industry in Britain, 1979–98. *European Journal of Communication, 15*(1), 5–35.

Miller, D., & Dinan, W. (2008). *A century of spin: How public relations became the cutting edge of corporate power.* Pluto Press.

Motion, J., & Leitch, S. (1996). A discursive perspective from New Zealand: Another world view. *Public Relations Review, 22*(3), 297–310.

Motion, J., & Leitch, S. (2015). Critical discourse analysis: A search for meaning and power. In J. L'Etang, D. McKie, N. Snow, & J. Xifra (Eds.), *Routledge handbook of critical public relations* (pp. 142–150). Routledge.

Motion, J., & Leitch, S. (2018). On Foucault: Engaging with Foucault's critical theory and methods. In Ø. Ihlen & M. Fredriksson (Eds.), *Public relations and social theory* (pp. 334–353). Routledge.

Munshi, D., & Kurian, P. (2005). Imperializing spin cycles: A postcolonial look at public relations, greenwashing, and the separation of publics. *Public Relations Review, 31*.

Munshi, D., & Kurian, P. (2007). The case of the subaltern public: A postcolonial investigation of corporate responsibility's (o)missions. In S. K. May, G. Cheney, & J. Roper (Eds.), *The debate over corporate social responsibility* (pp. 438–447). Oxford University Press.

Munshi, D., & Kurian, P. (2015). Public relations and sustainable citizenship: Towards the goal of representing the unrepresented. In J. L'Etang, D. McKie, N. Snow, & J. Xifra (Eds.), *Routledge handbook of critical public relations* (pp. 405–414). Routledge.

Munshi, D., & Kurian, P. (2021). *Public relations and sustainable citizenship: Representing the unrepresented.* Routledge.

Pal, M. (2016). Organization at the margins: Subaltern resistance of Singur. *Human Relations, 69*(2), 419–438. https://doi.org/10.1177/0018726715589797

Pieczka, M. (2018). On Bauman: Power, ethics and social hermeneutics. In Ø. Ihlen & M. Fredriksson (Eds.), *Public relations and social theory: Key figures, concepts and developments* (2nd ed., pp. 61–79). Routledge.

Place, K. R. (2015). Binaries, continuums, and intersections: Women public relations professionals' understandings of gender. *Public Relations Inquiry, 4*(1), 61–78. https://doi.org/10.1177/2046147X14563430

Pompper, D. (2005). "Difference" in public relations research: A case for introducing critical race theory. *Journal of Public Relations Research, 17*(2), 139–169.

Rakow, L. F., & Nastasia, D. I. (2009). On feminist theory of public relations: An example from Dorothy E. Smith. In Ø. Ihlen, B. van Ruler, & M. Fredriksson (Eds.), *Public relations and social theory: Key figures and concepts* (pp. 252–277). Routledge.

Rakow, L. F., & Nastasia, D. I. (2018). On Dorothy E. Smith: Public relations and feminist theory at the crossroads. In Ø. Ihlen & M. Fredriksson (Eds.), *Public relations and social theory: Key figures, concepts and developments* (2nd ed., pp. 354–373). Routledge.

Schölzel, H., & Nothhaft, H. (2016). The establishment of facts in public discourse: Actor-network-theory as a methodological approach in PR-research. *Public Relations Inquiry, 5*(1), 53–69. https://doi.org/10.1177/2046147X15625711

Sejrup, J. (2014). Awakening the sufferers: Reflections on public relations, activism, and subalternity in postcolonial controversies between Taiwan and Japan. *Public Relations Inquiry, 3*(1), 51–68. https://doi.org/10.1177/2046147X13519637

Smith, D. E. (1974). Women's perspective as a radical critique of sociology. *Sociological Inquiry, 44*(1), 7–13.

Smith, D. E. (1987). *The everyday world as problematic: A feminist sociology.* University of Toronto Press.

Somerville, I. (2021). Public relations and actor-network theory. In C. Valentini (Ed.), *Handbook of public relations* (pp. 525–540). De Gruyter Mouton.

Sriramesh, K., & Vercic, D. (1995). International public relations: A framework for future research. *Journal of Communication Management, 6*(2), 103–117.

Sriramesh, K., & Verčič, D. (2009). *The global public relations handbook: Theory, research and practice.* Routledge.

Sriramesh, K., & Verčič, D. (Eds.). (2012). *Culture and public relations: Links and implications.* Routledge.

Stiglitz, J. (2020). Conquering the great divide. *Finance & Development,* 17–19.

Straughan, D. M. (2004). "Lift every voice and sing": The public relations efforts of the NAACP, 1960–1965. *Public Relations Review, 30,* 49–60.

Tindall, N. T. J., & Waters, R. D. (Eds.). (2014). *Coming out of the closet: Exploring LGBT issues in strategic communication with theory and research.* Peter Lang.

Vardeman-Winter, J. (2016). The framing of women and health disparities: A critical look at race, gender, and class from the perspectives of grassroots health communicators. *Health Communication, 32*(5), 1–10. https://doi.org/10.1080/10410236.2016.1 160318

Vardeman-Winter, J., & Tindall, N. T. J. (2010). Toward an intersectionality theory of public relations. In R. L. Heath (Ed.), *The Sage handbook of public relations* (pp. 223–236). Sage.

Verhoeven, P. (2018). On latour: Actor-networks, modes of existence and public relations. In Ø. Ihlen & M. Fredriksson (Eds.), *Public relations and social theory: Key figures and concepts* (2nd ed., pp. 99–116). Routledge.

Wæraas, A. (2018). On Weber: Legitimacy and legitimation in public relations. In Ø. Ihlen & M. Fredriksson (Eds.), *Public relations and social theory: Key figures, concepts and developments* (2nd ed., pp. 19–38). Routledge.

Waymer, D., & Heath, R. (2015). Critical race and public relations: The case of environmental racism and risk bearer agency. In J. L'Etang, D. McKie, N. Snow, & J. Xifra (Eds.), *The Routledge handbook of critical public relations* (pp. 289–302). Routledge.

Weaver, C. K. (2018). On Marx: Capitalism and public relations. In Ø. Ihlen & M. Fredriksson (Eds.), *Public relations and social theory: Key figures, concepts and developments* (2nd ed., pp. 295–314). Routledge.

Yeomans, L. (2019). *Public relations as emotional labour.* Routledge.

14 The IDEA Model Theoretical Framework

An Explication of Risk Communication as Engaged Public Relations

Timothy L. Sellnow, Deanna D. Sellnow,
Bengt Johansson, Derek R. Lane,
and Matthew W. Seeger

At the core, risk is threat combined with uncertainty (Sellnow et al., 2009). To clarify, although we can identify looming threats through experience, technology, and intuition, we cannot know with certainty when and to what extent they will manifest harm. Since threats are typically experienced by multiple publics, decisions about how to manage and reduce risk are a highly social and communicative endeavor. Moreover, organizations and industries often bring both financial security and some degree of environmental threat to communities. Risk communication is the means through which communities and organizations can mutually reconcile these threats and opportunities. Thus, public relations and risk communication at the community level are inescapably entwined in the case of organizations and their publics (e.g., Heath & Able, 1996; Heath & Nathan, 1990; Palenchar & Heath, 2002). Public relations scholars argue further that emphasizing the relational aspects of risk communication requires engagement among publics, organizations, industries, agencies, and governments. Ultimately, engagement among multiple stakeholders leads to the cocreation of strategies to mitigate harm.

This chapter presents the IDEA model as a comprehensive and relationship-centered framework for understanding the dynamic interaction between risk communication and public relations. Although the link between public relations and risk communication for communities is well-established, the IDEA model provides strategies, well-grounded in instructional communication, for effective message design. The IDEA model clarifies how audiences engage in dialogue to generate mutually acceptable and efficacious instructive messages for self-protection. The model's components (internalization, distribution, explanation, and action) align to fulfill both the relational and pragmatic demands of risk communication. Our chapter begins with an explanation of the synergistic relationship between risk communication and public relations and the role of engagement in maximizing the relational aspects of risk communication. We then detail the IDEA model's

DOI: 10.4324/9781003141396-16

components and previous applications. We end with examples of how the IDEA model has been applied in various public relations settings and provide recommendations for future use.

Risk Communication and Public Relations

Effective risk communication engages subject matter experts and disparate publics strategically in dialogue about how to minimize potential threats to life, health, and safety. Ineffective risk communication occurs when subject matter experts identified by organizations and government agencies engage in linear one-way information-sharing and wrongly assume that publics will use that information to make the best decisions (Irwin, 2008). Seeking to correct this pervasive misunderstanding, the National Research Council (NRC) (1989) made a formal proclamation that risk communication must be a "democratic dialogue" (p. 21). By advocating that risk communication be an "interactive process of exchange of information and opinion among individuals, groups, and institutions" (p. 21), the NRC introduced a relational aspect into risk communication. Despite these efforts, however, public relations scholars continue to face resistance to their contention that effective risk communication is enacted as "a dialogue instead of a monologue" (Williams & Olaniran, 1998, p. 393). Heath and Abel (1996) explain more specifically this dialogue must "address the frustration, lack of trust, rage, politics, and conflicting zones of meaning that make risk communication so frustrating to people who represent the sources of risk and to people who believe they incur risks that may be intolerable" (p. 53).

As a profession, public relations remains committed to moving beyond the simplistic knowledge deficit perspective (Irwin, 2008) where publics are seen as passively absorbing information and toward applying "risk communication to serve many public and private interests" (Heath & Nathan, 1990). To clarify, the role of risk communication in public relations serves two primary purposes. First, risk communication helps publics recognize risks and action step options for reducing such risks (e.g., not drinking alcohol or getting vaccinated). Second, risk communication can help publics set thresholds for the risks they are willing to tolerate using the best information available. Providing either service is successful only when all affected publics are both adequately informed and empowered to make informed decisions about their safety without pressure to acquiesce to potentially dangerous risks that benefit an organization's cost-effectiveness. To achieve these standards, Heath and Nathan argue that practitioners must account for the potential politicization or manipulation of risk information. In other words, knowledge, or information about a risk, without consideration of context and influence, is insufficient for meeting essential standards for ethical and effective public relations.

Considerable research has explored the dialogic approach to risk through public relations. Much of this effort has focused on what Palenchar and

Heath (2002) establish as the goal of risk communication: to "increase the quality of risk decisions through better communications" (p. 129). The standards for dialogue are clearly established by public relations scholars investigating risk and crisis communication (Taylor & Kent, 2007; Lane & Kent, 2018). These standards are evident in a variety of risk contexts. For example, warning messages during natural disasters such as tornados have been evaluated and recommendations generated using a public relations approach to risk communication (Liu et al., 2019). Similarly, public relations scholars have provided recommendations for risk communication during public health crises (Avery et al., 2011; Jin et al., 2019). Public relations scholars have also taken a lead in assessing the viability and function of new media in risk communication (Austin et al., 2012; Cheng, 2020).

A common theme running throughout the body of work studying risk as a public relations endeavor is the emphasis on tailoring specialized and often complex information for disparate publics. As such, risk communication in public relations is essentially an "inextricable part of scientific communication" (Borchelt & Nielsen, 2008, p. 58). By *scientific information*, we mean the detailed research findings used by subject matter experts. Such information is difficult to comprehend for those who do not have expertise in a specific area of research. Embracing the relational aspect of sharing scientific information requires specialists to engage publics in both negotiating meaning and building relationships (Taylor, 2018). For example, agencies such as the National Weather Service regularly work with communication experts to translate their findings into terms that are comprehendible for residents of communities at risk (Anthony et al., 2014). Next, we detail the relevance of engagement to relationship-driven risk communication.

Engaged Public Relations as Risk Communication

Heath (2018) describes engagement as a way to "enlighten choices" through "collective meaning making" or "sensemaking" about matters of importance (p. 40). Information is exchanged via dialogue among organizations and those impacted by the issue under consideration. Thus, risk solutions are co-created by organizations and publics. In this way, engagement can enhance an organization's legitimacy with publics because it signals support for "collaborative decision-making; being proactive in response to others' communication and opinion needs; and working to meet or exceed the requirements of relationship management, including being a good corporate citizen" (p. 40). Through engaged risk communication, organizations help to coordinate the exchange of information among publics as gains and losses that are "perceived, weighed, and managed" (Heath, 2018, p. 41).

Lane and Kent (2018) agree with Heath's (2018) observation that engagement can lay the foundation for corporate social responsibility. They explicate the function and influence of dialogue in assuring engagement meets the potential of empowering publics to make informed decisions. Rather than simple two-way communication where information is exchanged between a communication manager and a "random customer," dialogue emphasizes "person to person" communication in a "genuine" relationship. From this perspective, risk messages are created and adapted through dialogue that considers the personal gains and losses for all stakeholders. The goal of such engaged dialogue is "not only to reach but also to interest its recipients" in mitigating potential risks (Lane & Kent, 2018, pp. 69–70). The extended relationships formed as a result of engaged dialogue are particularly pertinent in cases of prolonged risk or during post-crisis recovery where the goal is to reduce the risk of similar calamities occurring in the future (Ulmer et al., 2019).

Instructional Risk Communication as Engaged Public Relations

Previous research has established instructional communication as an inherent element of crisis communication (Coombs, 2009), risk communication (Sellnow & Sellnow, 2010; Sellnow et al., 2019), and dialogue (Freire, 1996; Greene, 1988). Instructional risk communication is the process of transforming knowledge into actionable warnings and advice, sharing those recommendations with at-risk publics through engaged dialogue, and adapting the actionable messages based on feedback from continuous interaction. Thus, instructional risk communication defies the pitfalls of a one-way, knowledge deficit view of risk communication (Heath & Abel, 1996; Irwin, 2008) by establishing an ongoing relational commitment to learning and responding with actions that lower the threat of harm or loss (Frisby et al., 2014).

In essence, effective instructional risk communication is measured according to learner achievement of three measurable outcomes: cognitive, affective, and behavioral (Sellnow, Lane et al., 2017). Cognitive learning focuses on comprehension. Simply sharing information does not ensure a level of comprehension where publics are able to make informed or enlightened choices about the actions they take in response to risk. Rather, cognitive learning is measured based on the degree to which learners (a.k.a. target audiences) accurately understand that information as it occurs in relevant contexts. Comprehension cannot be assessed without ongoing interaction allowing for questions, reflections, and applications of information (Sellnow-Richmond et al., 2018). Affective learning addresses the perceived value or relevance of the information. From a risk communication perspective, affective learning is achieved when learners (a.k.a. individuals, groups, communities, industries) are motivated to attend due to the potential threat imposed (Edwards et al., 2021). Behavioral learning is measured by the degree to which target audiences engage in desired actions for risk reduction (Sellnow, Lane et al., 2017).

Cognitive, affective, and behavioral learning are also central to engagement in public relations. To clarify, instructional communication principles provide a framework for building relationships, as well as collaboratively developing and enacting action steps for reducing risks. Similarly, Johnston (2018) establishes affective, cognitive, and behavioral learning as the key elements needed for engagement in public relations. Employing a highly pragmatic view, Johnston (2018) defines engagement as "a dynamic multidimensional relational concept featuring psychological and behavioral attributes of connecting, interaction, participation, and involvement, designed to achieve or elicit an outcome at individual, organizational, or social levels" (p. 19). Johnston's illustrations of affective, cognitive, and behavioral engagement converge noticeably with the explanation of instructional risk communication provided earlier. Johnston sees affective engagement as a source of emotions such as "enjoyment, fear, anger, support, and belonging;" cognitive engagement as "a willingness to exert the effort necessary to comprehend complex ideas;" and behavioral engagement as "participation, collaboration, action, and involvement" (p. 22). Engagement, like instructional risk communication, advances beyond an individual to a social state. At the social level, engagement fosters a collective orientation to problems that can influence shared experiences. These perceptions and experiences inspire participation in the negotiation of solutions that result in collective action through "a shared consensus or agreed definition or salience of the topic" (p. 24). The outcome is an intention or "readiness to perform behaviour" (p. 24). Thus, instructional risk communication and engagement share the same relational approach to informing and guiding audiences toward behavioral outcomes that are beneficial to them. Absent from both instructional risk communication and engagement are the one-sided manipulations deemed unworthy of public relations as risk communication (Heath & Abel, 1996; Heath &Nathan, 1990; Williams & Olaniran, 1998). Instead, instructional risk communication adheres to the expectation for ongoing dialogue as is endorsed in the view of engaged public relations. With these principles established, we turn next to an explanation of the IDEA model and its utility in designing and adapting risk messages.

The IDEA Model

The IDEA model has been established as a best practice for risk and crisis communication (Sellnow, Lane et al., 2017). The model's emphasis on interaction, rhetorical sensitivity, message tailoring, and audience efficacy is fitting with the view of risk communication as public relations established by Heath and Abel (1996), Heath and Nathan (1990), Palenchar and Heath (2002), and others. The model is a succinct encapsulation, adaptation, and extension of previous foundational research conducted in the emergency management communication context (Mileti & Sorenson, 1990; Mileti & Peek, 2000). Each element of the model requires detailed consideration of audience needs. Particularly in risk communication, ongoing relationships emphasizing consistent dialogue are essential for the model to reach its full potential of protecting stakeholders (Sellnow & Sellnow, 2010).

The IDEA model includes four elements that comprise an ideal risk message: internalization, distribution, explanation, and action (see Figure 14.1). As already described, internalization accentuates affective learning,

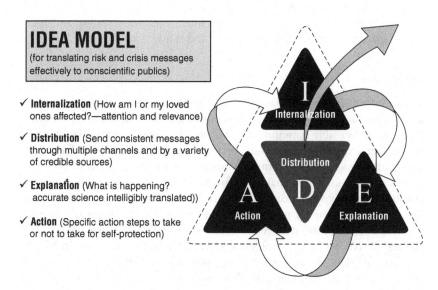

IDEA MODEL
(for translating risk and crisis messages
effectively to nonscientific publics)

✓ **Internalization** (How am I or my loved
ones affected?—attention and relevance)

✓ **Distribution** (Send consistent messages
through multiple channels and by a variety
of credible sources)

✓ **Explanation** (What is happening?
accurate science intelligibly translated))

✓ **Action** (Specific action steps to take
or not to take for self-protection)

Figure 14.1 The IDEA Model for Effective Risk Communication

explanation aligns with cognitive learning, and action manifests in behavioral learning. As we detail later in this chapter, the model has been applied consistently in a variety of risk communication contexts such as earthquake early warning, epidemic and pandemic communication, food safety, emergency planning, and others.

Internalization

Internalization focuses on recognition of risk relevance. This component of a risk message provides audiences with answers to the question, "How am I and those I care about affected (or potentially affected) by the risk and to what extent?" Aspects such as nearness of the risk's source or the expected timing of the risk's intensification are also part of the internalization process. The objective for message content focused on internalization is to generate a clear understanding of who is at greatest immediate risk and who is at a lesser or delayed risk, as well as potential impact of harms. The hope is that risk messages with internalization as a component will inspire those at risk to attend to the message. Thus, the degree and success of internalization is assessed through affective learning. Consistent with affective engagement where audiences experience "positive and negative emotional reactions" that create "conditions for motivation, interest, or concern" (Johnston, 2018, p. 22), affective learning is the recognition of susceptibility and the emotional responses related to that susceptibility. Internalizations should not, however, be considered only as a source of fear. Rather internalization of risk, from an engaged dialogue perspective, is the expression of "ideas

234 Timothy L. Sellnow et al.

that are sensitive and tailored to the needs and preferences of participants" (Lane & Kent, 2018, p. 69). Accordingly, internalization reveals to audiences which groups are at greatest risk, when, and why.

Distribution

While internalization, explanation, and action focus on message content, distribution accounts for the channels through which risk communication takes place. Available communication channels range from traditional media to the ever-expanding options of social media. Similarly, face-to-face communication might range from personal contacts to town halls to door-to-door campaigns. Simply making information available does not, however, constitute effective risk communication. Rather, an ongoing assessment of the intended audience's access to and preference for the potential communication channels is needed. As Lane and Kent (2018) explain, "Respect for, and responsiveness to, stakeholders' communication preferences is an important part of dialogic engagement" (p. 68). They admonish organizations and agencies that conforming to these preferences is essential, even though doing so "might seem inefficient" (p. 68). For example, providing the same message through multiple channels, all of which the intended audience sees, may seem repetitive and ineffective. Previous research, however, indicates that convergence of similar messages through multiple channels can increase confidence in the message (Sellnow & Sellnow, 2019). In fact, audiences regularly engage in confirmation of risk communication messages by viewing multiple sources and milling with others to discuss the threat (Wood et al., 2018).

Explanation

In the most basic sense, explanation answers questions about both what is happening and why. Effective explanations identify both what is known and unknown, as well as what is being done to reduce uncertainty. The expectation is that organizations and agencies remain transparent in sharing what they know, admitting what they do not know about a given risk with all vulnerable publics and their advocates (Seeger & Sellnow, 2019). The explanation process is ongoing, open to tailoring based on audience needs, and welcoming of feedback (Sellnow & Sellnow, 2019). The success or failure of explanation in risk messages is determined by the cognitive learning of intended audiences. Cognitive learning cannot occur, however, unless the audience is engaged. As Johnston (2018) explains, cognitive engagement requires "an individual's attention and processing to develop understanding or knowledge about a topic or an idea" (p. 22). Thus, explanation requires the level of interest Lane and Kent (2018) establish as an essential criterion for engaged dialogue. Maintaining such interest in the explanation process requires constant audience analysis and openness to message tailoring (Sellnow et al., 2012). Many risks are complex and difficult to explain to audiences whose science or health literacy may be low. As we mentioned earlier, the National Weather Service provides an example of an agency that cannot rely solely on communicating risk in scientific terms. Instead, the agency must work with publics to develop, test, and revise risk messages so that publics are enlightened rather than confused or bewildered by esoteric language. Thus, risk communicators can find a common level of understanding when translating science or health communication to levels comprehendible by their audiences. Without such translation and adaptation, risk communication cannot satisfy the expectation for dialogue set forth by the National Research Council (1989).

Although explanation is an essential component, it should not dwarf the other elements of the IDEA model message. Previous research has shown a tendency by those with expertise on a risk issue to explain risk at great length without focusing on internalization or action (Sellnow-Richmond, 2018). This overemphasis on explanation can diminish audience interest or create a sense of helplessness (Frisby et al., 2014).

Action

The action component of risk messages is intended to guide the behavior of those at risk. Action messages may recommend protective actions to take as well as actions to avoid. Simply put, the action element of the IDEA model answers the question, what should I do or avoid doing to protect myself and those I care about? For the action component or risk messages to succeed, audiences must experience behavioral learning. As such, audiences must comprehend what they are asked to do, possess the wherewithal to complete the actions recommended, and perceive the benefits of doing so. For the action element to succeed, therefore, an ongoing and engaged dialogue with close attention to audience feedback is essential. Johnston (2018) explains that behavioral engagement "embodies concepts of participation, collaboration, action, and involvement" (p. 22). Thus, at no point in the risk communication process is engaged dialogue more important than in the formation, explanation, and evaluation of protective actions. Lane and Kent (2018) see engaged dialogue in the realm of action as a means for collaboratively "identifying new perspectives, innovative approaches, and potential solutions to problems" (Lane & Kent, p. 67). The action element of the IDEA model has little chance of success, however, if recommendations provided in a linear or even two-way exchange that fails to prioritize the needs and preferences of at-risk populations. Determining appropriate protective actions, then, is a "deliberative" process of collective sensemaking where stakeholders are involved in discussion intended to enact solutions and strategies to create the "greatest good with the least cost" (Johnston, 2018, p. 39).

IDEA Model Theoretical Framework of Instructional Risk and Crisis Communication

Propositions of the IDEA Theoretical Framework

The previous section described the IDEA model for effective risk communication as a conceptual model that was originally created to identify the four elements that comprise an ideal risk message: internalization, distribution, explanation, and action. At first glance, the original IDEA model might be dismissed as a simple conceptual framework for informing message design. Over the past decade, however, the original conceptual framework (presented in Figure 14.1) has been revised and expanded into a more detailed theoretical framework that not only explains the relationships among the four elements but also predicts specific actions (e.g., affective engagement, cognitive engagement, behavioral engagement). As such, the relationships and predictive nature of the theoretical framework has resulted in formal propositions and testable hypotheses.

Although there are a multitude of explanations that can be used to delineate the characteristics of theory (or theoretical framework), we prefer Kerlinger and Lee's (2000) elucidation, "A theory is a set of interrelated constructs (concepts), definitions, and propositions that present a systematic view of phenomena by specifying relations among variables, with the purpose of explaining or predicting the phenomena" (p. 11).

Thus, the more contemporary IDEA Model Theoretical Framework of Instructional Risk and Crisis Communication (see Figure 14.2) provides a graphical representation of a tightly integrated theoretical framework that can ultimately be used to explain and predict public action. The more recent theoretical framework includes: 1) the risk and crisis context (dotted line), 2) audience and situational considerations (including audience characteristics, needs, preferences, and susceptibility, and any situational challenges inherent in the situation), 3) risk message content (where the elements of internalization, explanation, and action from the conceptual model are critical), and finally, 4) channels to access, exchange, and share risk messages with the intended public (expanding on the earlier conceptualization of the distribution element by highlighting the importance of access, interaction, dialogue, and the appropriate sharing of the risk message content).

Inherent in the more contemporary representation of the theoretical framework of instructional risk and crisis communication as public relations is: 1) an emphasis on interaction, 2) rhetorical sensitivity, 3) message tailoring, and 4) audience efficacy. The IDEA Model Theoretical Framework can be used to explore risk communication as public relations with respect to any of the risk and crisis communication best practices as outlined by Seeger (2006). For example, the model can be used to inform risk reduction and crisis avoidance, improve coordination with community partners and first responders, and illuminate message characteristics to increase self-efficacy and the likelihood that intended audiences will engage in life-saving strategic responses.

As described in the previous section of this chapter, the most common characteristic of risk messages is explanation—an attempt to describe what is

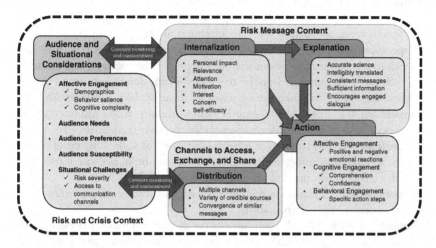

Figure 14.2 IDEA Model Theoretical Framework of Instructional Risk and Crisis Communication

happening and why. Explanation typically includes a discussion of blame—that is, who (or what) is responsible for the crisis. Furthermore, to reduce uncertainty, many risk messages contain only tentative details about facts that have not yet been verified. While explanation is the most common characteristic of risk messages, action is arguably the most critical component of the IDEA Model. As such, action (e.g., affective engagement, cognitive engagement, and behavioral engagement) is the behavior that functions as a criterion variable within the theoretical framework that is predicted by explanation, internalization, and distribution—the other primary features of the IDEA Model theoretical framework.

Here, we describe the primary propositions of the IDEA Model Theoretical Framework of Instructional Risk and Crisis Communication as public relations to predict actions of intended at-risk audiences.

Proposition #1: Internalization, explanation, and action focus on risk message content.

Proposition #2: Actions (affective, cognitive, and behavioral engagement) of those at risk are optimized when the intended audience is attentive to the risk messages, that is, when the messages are perceived as relevant and framed using strategies that increase internalization. (Internalization)

Proposition #3: The degree and success of internalization is assessed through actions (especially those related to affective engagement) and is positively correlated with self-efficacy. (Internalization)

Proposition #4: The distribution of risk messages should be based on an ongoing assessment of the intended audience's access to and preference for potential communication distribution channels. (Distribution)

Proposition #5: Rather than focus on risk message content, distribution focuses on the channels through which risk messages are accessed, exchanged, and shared with the intended public. (Distribution)

Proposition #6: The convergence of similar messages through multiple channels can increase both the confidence in the message and the self-efficacy of an intended public to engage in the action promoted by the message (e.g., to guide the behavior of those at risk). (Distribution)

Proposition #7: Engaged dialogue is most authentic when intended audiences have sufficient information about the risk. (Explanation)

Proposition #8: Explanation is a necessary (but not sufficient) component of all risk communication as public relations content because it provides the information needed for engaged dialogue. (Explanation)

Proposition #9: Explanation mediates the relationship between internalization and action. (Explanation)

Proposition #10: All risk communication as public relations messages are designed to guide the actions (affective, cognitive, and behavioral engagement) of those at risk. (Action)

Proposition #11: The success or failure of explanation in risk messages is ultimately determined by actions (affective, cognitive, and behavioral engagement) of the intended audience. (Action)

To date, the propositions related to the IDEA Model and its components have been tested using two primary statistical strategies: 1) experimental designs that involve comparisons of existing (status quo) risk messages to treatment messages with similar content that have been designed using the elements of the IDEA model theoretical framework (see Sellnow et al. (2015) for a side-by-side comparison of message transcripts), and 2) regression analyses that include action as the primary criterion variable and internalization, distribution, and explanation as the critical predictor variables (e.g., predicting mask-wearing and physical-distancing compliance during the global coronavirus pandemic). Before moving to a discussion of the published research describing the various applications of the IDEA Model, Table 14.1 identifies typical exemplar research questions and hypotheses that have been used to test the theoretical framework.

Applications of the IDEA Model Theoretical Framework

The IDEA model has been applied in several studies, including both short- and long-term hazards. Focus has been on a variety of issues, such as food-borne illness (Frisby et al., 2014; Littlefield et al., 2014; Sellnow et al., 2015, 2018), disease outbreaks (Sellnow, Parker et al., 2017; Sellnow-Richmond et al., 2018), and crisis preparedness (Johansson et al., 2021). Most studies have been carried out in the United States, although some have shown the applicability of the IDEA model in other cultural contexts as well (Sellnow

Table 14.1 IDEA Model Exemplar Research Questions and Hypotheses

---

Experimental Design Research Questions

Does self-reported **attention to message characteristics** vary as a function of message type (**condition**)?

What relationships exist among **sex, race,** and **message type** relative to **behavioral intentions to engage in the actions promoted in the message**?

To what degree will . . .
a) cultural groups' **behavioral intentions** reflect the **effectiveness** of instructional crisis communication messages?
b) instructional crisis messages that address all elements of the IDEA model be **perceived as similar** to a typical food outbreak news story message?

Regression Analysis Research Questions

How do participants in Canada and the United States differ in their self-reported compliance (action) related to staying safe during the global coronavirus pandemic?

How do the components of the IDEA Model (internalization, distribution, and explanation) vary in their ability to predict compliance in the early stages of the coronavirus global pandemic when comparing participants living in Canada to participants living in the United States?

Experimental Design Hypotheses

An instructional crisis message that addresses all elements of the IDEA model will:
a) **be perceived as more useful to prepare for a crisis** than the status quo message.
b) have an increased impact on the **perceived importance of effective crisis knowledge** than the status quo message.
c) result in greater **perceived crisis response efficacy** than the status quo message.
d) have an increased impact on **cognitive crisis knowledge** than the status quo message.
e) have an increased impact on **self-reported behavioral intentions** than the status quo message.
f) be perceived as more **effective** than the status quo message.
g) have a more **positive impact** on cultural groups' self-reported **behavioral intentions** than status quo messages.

---

et al., 2018; Johansson et al., 2021). The dominant methodological approach to applying the IDEA framework has been experiments, however, content analyses (Sellnow-Richmond et al., 2018) and interviews with experts (Sellnow, Parker et al., 2017) have also been utilized.

Sellnow Parker et al. (2017) used the IDEA model to investigate the rapid response to the outbreak of the devastating Porcine Epidemic Diarrhea virus

(PEDv) in the US. PEDv caused major economic damage to the industry with its high morbidity and mortality among piglets, and effective risk communication was needed to help farmers stop the spread of the virus. The researchers interviewed representatives from different agencies (state veterinarians and other experts) responsible for translating research about an unknown virus into practical guidelines, which could be understood and followed by producers. The authors found that the measures taken were effective, and that agencies were able to help producers to internalize the risk of the spread of the disease, but also how it affected animals and how the virus was spreading. One important application of the IDEA model was connected to the distribution element. During the crisis, industry leaders used well-developed networks that were in place before the outbreak to rapidly disseminate updates and recommendations. Recommended actions focused on the importance of following biosecurity protocols and stressed why breaches of these protocols could rapidly escalate the spread of the virus. Participants described the breaches that occurred during the PEDv crisis as largely due to bad habits and a failure to comprehend the potential consequences of these breaches. The authors emphasize the need to tailor messages so that receivers understand not only what to do (action), but also why these recommended actions are essential (internalization and explanation).

Sellnow et al. (2018) applied the IDEA model in the context of foodborne illness using a survey experiment (posttest) about a fictive outbreak of E. coli tainted ground beef in Sweden (Sellnow et al., 2018). For this study, two mock newspaper stories were developed based on an actual story reporting an E. coli outbreak. To ensure both accuracy and ecological validity of the news stories, the stimulus materials were constructed and evaluated by risk and crisis communication experts, journalists, and food scientists. One of the stories was modified to meet the demands of the IDEA model in terms of internalization, action, and explanation, and the outcome variables tested focused on behavioral learning, in terms of self-protection (e.g., discarding and not eating potentially tainted meat). The study found general support for increased learning in the condition with the news story containing the elements of the IDEA model. The authors also found that proximity was important in understanding the acceptance of risk messages, where audiences at greatest risk based on proximity to the outbreak were more likely to follow the recommended actions.

In relation to the Ebola outbreak 2014, Sellnow-Richmond et al. (2018) conducted a content analysis to evaluate crisis communication from an IDEA perspective. The authors collected and analyzed a large dataset comprised of local news from Dallas, Texas, where Ebola spread locally, the CDC Twitter Live Chat on the national level, and website content about the disease from international health organizations (WHO, UNICEF, and Doctors Without Borders). In contrast to the IDEA model recommendations, the authors found that most messages focused on explanation with little or no mention of internalization and action. Consequently, the explanation-centered messages (promoting cognitive learning) failed to include aspects of affective and behavioral learning. Another shortcoming of existing messages was the limited inclusion of who was at risk and which actions could help to limit the spread the Ebola. Sellnow-Richmond et al. emphasize how alarm creates a learning opportunity where audiences are receptive to risk messages and actively seek to learn from new information. However, when instructional risk messages offer explanation without internalization, they often fail to achieve compliance, and even when specific action steps are offered, they are typically ignored or not sustained when internalization is not also integrated.

Another study using the IDEA framework in a risk context outside the US focused on winter storm preparedness and the effectiveness of designing risk preparedness messages with IDEA elements (Johansson et al., 2021, in press). The original campaign in the city of Gothenburg in Sweden was designed to enhance citizens' preparedness in case of a crisis where the supply of heat, water, and electricity would be out for 72 hours. An original campaign video was used as the control message in a post-test quasi-experiment, and the authors created a treatment message using images and text from the original video, but with a new voiceover adding IDEA elements. The results showed significant effect on both affective and cognitive learning, although behavioral intentions (obtain sufficient food, water, flashlight, and radio with batteries, etc.) was not increased by the IDEA message. The lack of behavioral intention was interpreted by authors in the light of the general difficulty associated with motivating people to act during quiet times, when no threat is imminent. Even so, they conclude that the findings of affective and cognitive learning might help risk communication efforts, so that only a brief reminder is needed rather than an entire message about what being prepared means in times of crisis.

Future Research

There are at least three promising opportunities for future research, each dealing with a unique area of theory construction for the IDEA Model. The first opportunity relates to exploring varying crisis types. The second opportunity relates to incorporating additional constructs within each of the four components of the IDEA Model to clarify which specific variables are important to intended audiences in any given risk or crisis event. The third opportunity deals with methodological triangulation using both quantitative and qualitative research methods data and improves our understanding of risk communication as engaged public relations.

Exploring Crisis Type and Timing

There are three types of crises that are worthy of our attention: crises originating from *natural disasters* (e.g., hurricanes, earthquakes, tornados), crises originating from *accidents* (e.g., especially events caused by human error such as unintentional fires or those caused by equipment malfunction that result in oil spills, etc.), and *terrorist events* (e.g., intentional sabotage of food or water supply; bombings, arson, etc.). The first type is natural disasters. When the IDEA Model is used to study natural disasters, messages can be tested to improve risk reduction or crisis avoidance by focusing on emergency preparedness. The second crisis type, accidents, has received the most attention from risk and crisis researchers using the IDEA Model to study risk communication as engaged public relations. As discussed earlier in this chapter, previous research involving the IDEA Model theoretical framework has focused primarily on accidents (e.g., foodborne illness, Porcine Epidemic Diarrhea (PEDv)), where the focus is testing message characteristics to increase self-efficacy and the likelihood that intended audiences will engage in life-saving strategic responses. However, there are ample opportunities to test the IDEA model as it relates to natural disasters—where the focus could be on emergency preparedness actions or on improving coordination with community partners. There are also opportunities to explore how the tenets and propositions of the model are different when they are used to examine risk communication as engaged public relations as it relates to intentional terrorist events. How do the predictive components of the IDEA Model change when terrorist events occur and as public relations professionals attempt to manage public outrage as well as public behavior that is primarily aimed at keeping the public safe?

There are also important factors associated with the timing of crisis events that are worthy of future research. The first few hours of a crisis can be critical to public safety. How do the behavioral recommendations coming from public relations professionals change as more information becomes available? Is the public more (or less) likely to engage in the behavior over the life cycle of the event? How does the IDEA Model help clarify (and shape) our understanding of the public relations recommendations about preparedness immediately preceding a crisis event, the recommendations during the first few hours of the event, and those messages that occur during other critical milestones in determining the overall impact on whether (or not) the intended public will take the appropriate recommended actions? The coronavirus pandemic provides an interesting case study to explore how physical distancing recommendations, limited group interactions, and face covering mandates were adhered to over the life cycle of the global pandemic.

Clarifying Components With Additional Constructs

The second opportunity for future research involves incorporating additional constructs within each of the four components of the IDEA Model to clarify which specific variables are predictive of the recommended behavior in any given risk or crisis event. For example, in a recent analysis of survey data collected in Canada and the United States, we were able to identify and test several constructs related to the global coronavirus pandemic that mapped nicely onto the four components of the IDEA Model.

The internalization component was measured using constructs such as "level of trust in public health experts," "level of trust in government messages," "perceptions that the coronavirus in no more dangerous than the seasonal flu," and "agreement with government sanctions." The distribution component was measured with constructs that included, "information seeking channel sources," "social network preferences," and "messages about the coronavirus from family and friends." The explanation component included constructs such as "current information about the coronavirus" and "information needed to fully understand the coronavirus." Finally, we measured *compliance with sanctions* as the single criterion variable within the ACTION component.

A separate regression analysis of the Canadian and US samples revealed two consistent—but very different—models to explain compliance with government sanctions. The Canadian data revealed a model that accounted for 43.9% of the variance in compliance (R^2_{adj}=.439; $F(7, 689)$=78.093, p=.001), whereas the US data revealed a model that accounted for 55.3% of the variance in compliance (R^2_{adj}=.553; $F(11,423)$=48.551, p=.001). Canadian participants reported significantly more trust in government and agreement with public health sanctions, whereas the US participants reported significantly greater information comprehension and a more substantial social threat associated with COVID-19. These types of data, when analyzed within the theoretical framework of the IDEA model can assist scholars and practitioners in framing messages to engage intended audiences. From this perspective, the IDEA model offers a form of audience analysis that translates directly into message design and response to valuable audience feedback.

Methodological Triangulation Using Sophisticated Analyses

The third opportunity related to future research involving the IDEA Model deals with methodological triangulation and using sophisticated quantitative and qualitative methods to test the propositions of the model. For example, proposition #7 involves a mediation analysis to explore the relationship between the internalization, explanation, and action components. Quantitative analyses should continue to rely on customary methods such as multiple regression and factorial analyses of variance but should be expanded to include Structural Equation Modeling (to test model fit) and Hierarchical Linear Modeling (to test whether any of the components are nested). In addition, sophisticated network analyses can be conducted to determine how influencers within certain populations of intended audiences could be leveraged to improve the distribution of messages to increase their impact on public safety behaviors. Such research potentially improves not only the predictive quality of the IDEA Model but also our understanding of risk communication as engaged public relations.

Qualitative analyses are equally important to triangulate data and improve the explanatory power of the IDEA Model. How do public relations risk messages improve the interaction and behaviors of intended influencer and stakeholders? How does rhetorical sensitivity influence compliance with recommended behaviors? How does message tailoring impact intended audience efficacy? Qualitative interviews, focus groups, and naturalistic inquiry can all be used (along with quantitative research methods), with the IDEA Model as a lens, to answer these and other important questions related to improving risk communication as engaged public relations.

Conclusion

Throughout his chapter, we explored the IDEA Model as a theoretical framework for explaining, predicting, and understanding risk communication as engaged public relations. We began with an explanation of the synergistic relationship between risk communication and public relations and the role of engagement in maximizing the relational aspects of risk communication. We then detailed the four major components of the model and explained the major propositions associated with each component before describing how the IDEA model has been applied in various public relations settings. We concluded by providing specific recommendations for future use that included various applications of crisis type and timing, additional clarification of constructs related to the four components, and the importance of methodological triangulation.

The IDEA model is a comprehensive and relationship-centered framework for understanding the dynamic interaction between risk communication and public relations. To date, the IDEA model clarifies how audiences engage in dialogue to generate mutually acceptable and efficacious instructive messages for self-protection. The model's components (internalization, distribution, explanation, and action) align to fulfill both the relational and pragmatic demands of risk communication as engaged public relations.

References

Anthony, K. E., Cowden-Hodgson, K. R., Dan O'Hair, H., Heath, R. L., & Eosco, G. M. (2014). Complexities in communication and collaboration in the hurricane warning system. *Communication Studies, 65*(5), 468–483.

Austin, L., Fisher Liu, B., & Jin, Y. (2012). How audiences seek out crisis information: Exploring the social-mediated crisis communication model. *Journal of Applied Communication Research, 40*(2), 188–207.

Avery, E. J., & Lariscy, R. W. (2011). Public information officers' perceived control in building local public health agendas and the impact of community size. *Health Communication, 26*(8), 691–700.

Borchelt, R. E., & Nielsen, K. H. (2008). Public relations in science: Managing the trust portfolio. In M. Bucchi & B. Trench (Eds.), *Routledge handbook of public communication of science and technology* (2nd ed., pp. 58–69). Routledge.

Cheng, Y. (2020). The social-mediated crisis communication research: Revisiting dialogue between organizations and publics in crises of China. *Public Relations Review, 46*(1). Advanced online publication.

Coombs, T. W. (2009) Conceptualizing crisis communication. In R. L. Heath & H. D. O'Hair (Eds.), *Handbook of risk and crisis communication* (pp. 99–118). Routledge.

Edwards, A. L., Sellnow, T. L., Sellnow, D. D., Iverson, J., Parrish, A., & Dritz, S. (2021). Communities of practice as purveyors of instructional communication during crises. *Communication Education*, 70(1), 49–70.

Freire, P. (1996). *Pedagogy of the oppressed* (revised ed.). Continuum.

Frisby, B. N., Veil, S. R., & Sellnow, T. L. (2014). Instructional messages during health-related crises: Essential content for self-protection. *Health Communication*, 4, 347–354. https://doi.org/10.1080/10410236.2012.755604

Greene, M. (1988). *The dialectic of freedom*. Teachers College Press.

Heath, R. L. (2018). How fully functioning is communication engagement if society does not benefit? In K. A. Johnston & M. Taylor (Eds.), *The handbook of communication engagement* (pp. 31–47). Wiley-Blackwell.

Heath, R. L., & Abel, D. D. (1996). Types of knowledge as predictors of company support: The role of information in risk communication. *Journal of Public Relations Research*, 8(1), 35–55.

Heath, R. L., & Nathan, K. (1990). Public relations' role in risk communication: Information, rhetoric and power. *Public Relations Quarterly*, 35(4), 15–22.

Irwin, A. (2008). Risk, science, and public communication: Third-order thinking about scientific culture. In M. Bucchi & B. Trench (Eds.), *Routledge handbook of public communication of science and technology* (2nd ed., pp. 160–172). Routledge.

Jin, Y., Austin, L., Vijaykumar, S., Jun, H., & Nowak, G. (2019). Communicating about infectious disease threats: Insights from public health information officers. *Public Relations Review*, 45(1), 167–177.

Johansson, B., Lane, D. R., Sellnow, D. D., & Sellnow, T. L. (2021, in press). No heat, no electricity, no water, oh no! An IDEA model experiment in instructional risk communication. *Journal of Risk Research*, 24.

Johnston, K. A. (2018). Toward a theory of social engagement. In K. A. Johnston & M. Taylor (Eds.), *The handbook of communication engagement* (pp. 19–32). Wiley Blackwell.

Kerlinger, F. N., & Lee, H. B. (2000). *Foundations of behavioral research* (4th ed.). Cengage Learning.

Lane, A., & Kent, M. L. (2018). Dialogic engagement. In K. A. Johnston & M. Taylor (Eds.), *The handbook of communication engagement* (pp. 61–72). Wiley Blackwell.

Littlefield, R. S., Beuchamp, K., Lane, D. R., Sellnow, D. D., Sellnow, T. L., Venette, S., & Wilson, B. (2014). Instructional crisis communication: Connecting ethnicity and sex in the assessment of receiver-oriented message effectiveness. *Journal of Management and Strategy*, 5, 16–23. https://doi.org/10.5430/jms.v5n3p16

Liu, B. F., Xu, S., Lim, J. R., & Egnoto, M. (2019). How publics' active and passive communicative behaviors affect their tornado responses: An integration of STOPS and SMCC. *Public Relations Review*, 45(4), Advance online publication.

Mileti, D. S., & Peek, L. (2000). The social psychology of public response to warnings of a nuclear power plant accident. *Journal of Hazardous Materials*, 75, 181–194. https://doi.org/10.1016/S0304-3894 (00)00179-5

Mileti, D. S., & Sorenson, J. H. (1990). *Communication of emergency public warnings: A social science perspective and state-of-the-art assessment*. Oak Ridge National Laboratory.

National Research Council. (1989). *Improving risk communication*. National Academy Press.

Palenchar, M. J., & Heath, R. L. (2002). Another part of the risk communication model: Analysis of communication processes and message content. *Journal of Public Relations Research*, 14(2), 127–158.

Seeger, M. W. (2006). Best practices in crisis communication: An expert panel process. *Journal of Applied Communicaton Research*, 34, 232–244. https://doi.org/10.1080/00909880600769944

Seeger, M. W., & Sellnow, T. L. (2019). *Communication in times of trouble: Best practices of crisis communication and emergency risk communication.* Wiley-Blackwell.

Sellnow, D. D., Johansson, B., Sellnow, T. L., & Lane, D. R. (2018). Toward a global understanding of the effects of the IDEA model for designing instructional risk and crisis messages: A food contamination experiment in Sweden. *Journal Contingencies and Crisis Management,* 1–14. https://doi.org/10.1111/1468-5973.12234

Sellnow, D. D., Jones, L. M., Sellnow, T. L., Spence, P., Lane, D. R., & Haarstad, N. (2019). The IDEA model as a conceptual framework for designing earthquake early warning (EEW) messages distributed via mobile phone apps. *Earthquakes: Impact, Community Vulnerability and Resilience, IntechOpen,* 11–20.

Sellnow, D. D., Lane, D. R., Littlefield, R. S., Sellnow, T. L., Wilson, B., Beauchamp, K., & Venette, S. (2015). A receiver-based approach to effective instructional crisis communication. *Journal of Contingencies and Crisis Management, 23,* 149–158. https://doi.org/10.1111/1468-5973.12066

Sellnow, D. D., Lane, D. R., Sellnow, T. L., & Littlefield, R. S. (2017). The IDEA model as a best practice for effective instructional risk and crisis communication. *Communication Studies, 68,* 552–567.

Sellnow, D. D., & Sellnow, T. L. (2019). The IDEA model for effective instructional risk and crisis communication by emergency managers and other key spokespersons. *Journal of Emergency Management, 17,* 67–78.

Sellnow, T. L., Parker, J. S., Sellnow, D. D., Littlefield, R. R., Helsel, E. M., Getchell, M. C., Smith, J. M., & Merrill, S. C. (2017). Improving biosecurity through instructional crisis communication: Lessons learned from the PEDv outbreak. *Journal of Applied Communications, 101*(4). Advanced online publication. https://doi.org/10.4148/1051-0834.1298

Sellnow, T. L., & Sellnow, D. D. (2010). The instructional dynamic of risk and crisis communication: Distinguishing instructional messages from dialogue. *The Review of Communication, 10*(2), 112–126.

Sellnow, T. L., Sellnow, D. D., Lane, D. R., Littlefield, R. S. (2012). The value of instructional communication in crisis situations: Restoring order to chaos. *Risk Analysis, 32*(4), 633–643.

Sellnow, T. L., Ulmer, R. R., Seeger, M. W., & Littlefield, R. S. (2009). *Effective risk Communication: A message-centered approach.* Springer Science+Business Media, LLC.

Sellnow-Richmond, D., George, A., & Sellnow, D. (2018). An IDEA model analysis of instructional risk communication messages in the time of Ebola. *Journal of International Crisis and Risk Communication Research. 1,* 135–165.

Taylor, M. (2018). Reconceptualizing public relations in an engaged society. In K. A. Johnston & M. Taylor (Eds.), *The handbook of communication engagement* (pp. 103–114). Wiley Blackwell.

Taylor, M., & Kent, M. L. (2007). Taxonomy of mediated crisis responses. *Public Relations Review, 33*(2), 140–146.

Ulmer, R. R., Sellnow, T. L., & Seeger, M. W. (2019). *Effective crisis communication: Moving from crisis to opportunity* (4th ed.). Sage.

Williams, D. E., & Olaniran, B. A. (1998). Expanding the crisis planning function: Introducing elements of risk communication to crisis communication practice. *Public Relations Review, 24,* 387–400.

Wood, M. M., Mileti, D. S., Bean, H., Liu, B. F., Sutton, J., & Madden, S. (2018). Milling and public warnings. *Environment and Behavior, 50,* 535–566.

15 Public Relations in a Postdisciplinary World

On the Impossibility of Establishing a Constitutive PR Theory Within the Tribal Struggles of Applied Communication Disciplines

Howard Nothhaft and Ansgar Zerfass

Introduction

This chapter contributes to the debate about public relations' disciplinary status, its inner center and outer boundaries as an intellectual endeavor in an increasingly postdisciplinary world. We argue that attempts to arrive at a constitutive theory of public relations—i.e., a theory that *precisely defines* what public relations *is* as a subject of inquiry or object of research—have always been doomed to failure. The reason is that clear-cut distinctions—historically correct, and compatible with every other author's position—presume the inherent logic of a coherent academic enterprise. That logic does not exist, we suggest, because neither public relations nor other applied communication disciplines—such as integrated marketing communication, corporate communication, strategic communication, organizational communication, digital communication—originated as intellectually coherent projects. They also never made discoveries that would give coherence, like cell theory in biology, for example. Drawing on Silvio Waisbord's (2019) *tour de force* of communication as an academic endeavor, we argue that the applied communication disciplines evolved as "de facto disciplines," i.e., disciplines that are not materially defined by a common subject or object but by administrative institutionalization. Currently, public relations research's intellectual center lies in its mixed community of scholars, practitioners, and scholar-practitioners, as well as in its ability to serve as a feeder for attractive job markets.

Despite the inherent impossibility of a universally satisfactory constitutive theory, the chapter aims to contribute to public relations theory in an alternative, non-definitional way. Recognizing the centrality of public relations education's applied role as a job market feeder, we argue that the differences between public relations and the other applied communication disciplines

DOI: 10.4324/9781003141396-17

are not logical but *tribal* (or neo-tribal) in nature. While there is no clear-cut *logical* difference between e.g., marketing communication and public relations, there are marked and systematic differences in habits of thought.

The chapter concludes by acknowledging that scholars have worked diligently to transform the practically oriented de facto discipline of public relations into an academically respectable discipline. But we see only limited success here. Given the current academic trend toward postdisciplinary views, one must ask whether public relations should continue the project of becoming what it is not. In a postdisciplinary world, the acceptance of public relations may not depend on achieving an impressive complexity that gives the appearance of academic dignity. It may depend, quite simply, on giving the right answers to seemingly mundane but enormously complex *practical* questions.

Public Relations' Disciplinary Troubles

What is the problem with public relations as an academic discipline? Why does it appear so difficult to arrive at a clear and focused theoretical self-understanding and gain recognition in the eyes of other disciplines? And in what ways is public relations ready for a postdisciplinary academic world?

Public Relations Becoming Itself: Transient Tribes and Ugly Ducklings

Two decades ago, George Cheney and Lars Thøger Christensen criticized that many formulations of public relations, i.e., theories about what public relations essentially *is*, were "parochial, utilitarian, and insufficiently self-reflective" (Cheney & Christensen, 2001, p. 179). At the same time, the discipline was harboring "imperialistic pretensions" (Cheney & Christensen, 2001, p. 180). Along this line, Lisa Dühring formulated an indictment of the academic discipline's internal incoherence:

> Situated in the no-man's land between different disciplinary fields and scholarly traditions, PR shows, on the one hand, clear imperialistic tendencies toward all of these fields, but is, on the other hand, rather isolated and struggles for academic recognition. Its bad reputation, affiliated with its roots in propaganda, lobbying, and media manipulation, and also its excessive pluralism, eclecticism, and failure to accomplish a unique body of knowledge, acknowledged beyond its own boundaries, have prevented PR research from gaining true acceptance from any of its feeder disciplines (Toth, 2010, pp. 712–714). This leaves the discipline in a vicious circle of self-assertion and self-defence.
>
> (Dühring, 2015, p. 6)

Dühring portrays the academic discipline as a kind of transient tribe. Haunted by its past, unable to settle on its own turf but adept at raiding others, public relations—parochial *and* imperialistic—lives by feeding off others. Yet, despite achieving very little of its own, the tribe craves nothing more than recognition as a civilized people.

The motif of the misunderstood outsider craving recognition appears elsewhere. In 2006, Robert L. Heath wrote that public relations was "at best, an ugly duckling with prospects for a better future or, at worst, an irredeemable bête noir" (2006, p. 93). The reference presumably suggests that public relations, like the swan in H. C. Andersen's fairy tale, is a misunderstood creature. Hopefully, one day the discipline will become beautiful and find its true home. Where the home lies is not entirely clear, but one may assume that public relations' modest wish boils down to acceptance as a proper academic discipline by insiders and outsiders alike. Fulfilment still seems far off, however. Mary Ann Ferguson (2018) stated that there is a goodly number of success-oriented, critical students in every class who dismiss public relation's academic offerings as unconvincing and self-serving. And public relations scholars, Ferguson suggests, openly admit that a similar dismissal, in politer terms, awaits in the faculty boardroom: "Public relations theory, what a quaint notion" (Ferguson, 2018, p. 165).

References to self-critical remarks about public relations, although often more nuanced in tone, could be multiplied at will. At least to some inside observers, then, not everything is well with the academic project. What is perhaps more important, however, are outside observers. Sociological heavyweights like Jürgen Habermas have singled out public relations as a catalyst for all the evils the cultural industry inflicts. Admittedly, in *The Structural Transformation of the Public Sphere*, Jürgen Habermas (1991) condemns public relations *practice* first and foremost. But one can easily imagine what Habermas would make of Heath's attempt to place public relations center-stage in a theory of the fully functioning society. Recently, anthropologist David Graeber, in a popular book titled *Bullshit Jobs*, classified public relations practitioners as "goons," i.e., those who are aggressive on behalf of their employers, while contributing very little of value to society: "The same can be said of most lobbyists, PR specialists, telemarketers, and corporate lawyers" (Graeber, 2018, p. 36). As for public relations research, Graeber mentions it as one of the inspirations for the very concept of bullshit jobs: "Everyone is familiar with those sort of jobs that don't seem, to the outsider, to really do much of anything: HR consultants, communications coordinators, PR researchers, financial strategists, corporate lawyers" (Graeber, 2018, p. 69). On the less polemic, more serious side, Erich Sommerfeldt and Michael Kent (2020) argue that public relations is viewed as "dirty work," with the academic discipline's status tainted by the profession's bad reputation.

Communication's Legacy: A Muddle of a Field and a Vast Scholarly Territory

It seems, then, that public relations research aspires to recognition as a "proper" academic discipline but remains frustrated. However, before one searches for defects specific to public relations, one must ask whether public relations is alone in its confusion.

In a grand tour surveying the state of the field, Silvio Waisbord, former editor-in-chief of the *Journal of Communication*, took stock of "communication" as an academic endeavor. After tracing the discipline's emergence and subsequent fragmentation, he describes the field, on the positive side, as an "intellectually omnivorous, porous, multifaceted, protean, academic enterprise" (2019, p. 623). On the negative side, he admits: "It is a muddle of a field, with no theoretical or analytical center that could give intellectual coherence to a vast scholarly territory" (2019, p. 121). Waisbord's account is fascinating not only because of the admission of constitutional "muddledness" but because it explains communication's coherence despite incoherence: "What keeps this unwieldy area of scholarship loosely together are not the intellectual bonds found in disciplines and fields—shared epistemologies, theories, objects of study, methodologies." On the contrary, Waisbord argues: "Communication studies is held together by an institutional architecture of professional organizations, academic units, and journals" (2019, p. 123). At the end of the day, "institutional scaffolding" (2019, p. 125), not grand theories, holds communication together: "Identity-building efforts driven by administrative and institutional urgencies and incentives were better at stitching together different ontological fabrics than intellectual bridging" (2019, p. 124).

Public relations is one stop on Waisbord's grand tour. The argument is that the applied communication disciplines (he does not use the term) emerged because of the growing demand in fast-rising, ever-changing media industries. "Academic units responded by creating technology-centered departments and programs such as print journalism, broadcasting, mass communication, and media studies" (2019, p. 76). These new and applied disciplines, he points out, were never meant to be intellectually coherent agendas. Marketability was the name of the game: "These became a mix of liberal arts and social science programs with clear career orientation toward specific 'media industries' for educating increasing numbers of students interested in working in mass media—from journalism to public relations" (Waisbord, 2019, pp. 76–77).

Waisbord is not the first or only one to note that administrative realities, not intellectual coherence, keep the field together. In his investigation of "institutional sources of intellectual poverty," John D. Peters pointed out long ago that communication became "administratively defined" (Peters, 1986, p. 528). We, the authors, only recently argued that the "business model" of applied communication disciplines does not lie in securing public or industry funding but in positioning themselves as "the premier entry ticket to a lucrative career" (Nothhaft et al., 2018, p. 362). Whether academics like it or not, applied disciplines are commercial services to a degree. Their academic development is largely resourced by the faculty's leftover energy after a day of teaching. "The discipline must secure a constant stream of students who can be educated to their satisfaction at a reasonable cost because it is by and large the surplus, in the form of academic staff's remains of the day, that finances the discipline's development" (Nothhaft et al., 2018, p. 362). Jefferson Pooley argues along the same line, maintaining that communication scholarship is in a "vocational bind" (Pooley, 2016). Although the applied disciplines work as a marketable package, they are ill-conceived as intellectual endeavors: "A mere classroom wall, in other words, separates the lesson on how to write a press-release lead from a lecture on the damage to democracy wrought by public relations" (Pooley, 2016). Student numbers, not society's expectation of beneficial breakthroughs, sustain communication as an academic discipline: "Bankrolled by the throngs of undergraduates who fill our lecture halls, we enjoy relative plenitude in faculty-size and funding terms" (Pooley, 2016, p. 623).

Disciplines and the Idea of Critical Mass

Even if one accepts that the academic discipline of public relations, like the rest of communication studies, is a "muddle of a field," one might ask, why does it matter? In what way, exactly, is "muddledness" a problem? Why should the impossibility of developing an identity-constituting public relations theory be a dealbreaker? What is wrong with universities and colleges simply training and educating for jobs that actually exist? In practice, very few worry about the boundaries and center of "pure" public relations.

Despite close ties, it is important here not to conflate the academic discipline with the public relations industry. The most straightforward reason disciplinary borders are under scrutiny remains the *convergence* of media usage. Admittedly, the way audiences interact with media across platforms and genres does not always map onto boundaries, academic or departmental. It makes no difference whether a company succeeds because of "influencer marketing" or "public relations." Consequently, corporate leaders tell communication practitioners that departmental silos—marketing not talking to public relations and so on—will not be tolerated. If the educational system maintains silos discouraged in practice, it will sooner or later become out of sync.

But even in practice, there is the danger of throwing out the baby with the bathwater. Silos are not only a device to irritate progressive, laterally minded managers. Departmental boundaries, defined responsibilities, and professional cultures reduce coordination requirements and stress. Co-workers pay the price if boundaries are eliminated to serve the *Zeitgeist* of flexibility and agility (Dühring & Zerfass, 2021). Furthermore, it is by no means guaranteed that a campaign run jointly by marketers and public relations people generates better results than one run by either alone, as matters of *internal coherence* come into play. Many questions will be asked when a consummate public relations professional fails in overseeing the world's slickest marketing campaign, or when a thoroughbred marketeer upsets journalists.

Similarly, if an academic discipline is constantly aspiring yet failing—as public relations seem to be, at least according to the colleagues cited earlier— scholars should engage in some self-reflection. *Results* and *internal coherence* are the keywords to reflect on. It might be that internal coherence is far more critical for an academic discipline than for a corporate department. The corporate department has a natural focus point: the company. The institutionalization of disciplines, on the other hand, is based on the idea of a critical mass of scholars who apply themselves to the same questions in similar (but not identical) ways. The question, the subject of inquiry or object of research, is the focal point.

Doing the Right Thing Among Cannibals

One could say, then: When public relations scholars engaged in the struggle to clearly define public relations, they tried to honor the obligations that come with disciplinarity. It would have been intellectually dishonest to enjoy the autonomy of a discipline without living up to the ensuing duty, i.e., at least to work toward that critical mass. Public relations' problem is that this did not work out. As in many other applied communication disciplines, attempts to reverse-engineer internal coherence into what came together opportunistically did not play out very well. Although public relations did develop a limited number of candidates for focal points—Excellence Theory (Grunig, 2006) was perhaps the strongest candidate—these remained projects with very little impact outside. Perhaps Cheney and Christensen's (2001) indictment was too harsh. But the ugly duckling certainly did not transform into a swan. There are several reasons why.

Why Is Public Relations Scholarship Dismissed So Easily?

Presumably, the ugly duckling image resonates because public relations scholars experience that their research is dismissed elsewhere, not because it lacks merit but prestige. Waisbord diagnoses "chronic difficulties for communication studies in getting much-deserved recognition from other fields and disciplines" (p. 88). But why is that so? For communication scholarship, Pooley argued that the "vocational bind" condemns scholarship: "The reputational hit from all that advertising and journalism instruction means that our colleagues across campus have license to look the other way" (Pooley, 2016, p. 623). Yet Pooley is not entirely clear why "all that journalism and marketing instruction" has a negative reputational impact. Quality is not the issue, as he asserts that the quality gap between communication and established social sciences has been overcome. But if the quality is high and the recognition much-deserved, how can educational activities be the problem? Surely, "all that instruction" does not marginalize the law faculty?

The Quest for Impressive Scientific Dignity

For public relations, the missing link lies in a mismatch compounded by a marked bias in academia that puts the discipline at a severe disadvantage—although it is in illustrious company. Nearly two hundred years ago, Carl von Clausewitz pointed out that in military affairs, complexity resulted mainly from the clash with reality, something that Clausewitz terms "friction" (1989, p. 119). On a sheet of paper, even high-level strategies looked mundane: "Everything looks simple; the knowledge required does not look remarkable, the strategic options are so obvious that by comparison the simplest problem of higher mathematics has an impressive scientific dignity" (Clausewitz, 1989, p. 119). Public relations, we suggest, is similarly configured. Like grand strategy ("Defend in the east, attack in the west"), its *topic* does not lend itself to sophisticated theorization. By no means trivial in practice, public relations problems look simple on paper.

The problem is not triviality per se. As Kevin Moloney (2006) very rightly pointed out, it cannot be that public relations is dangerous to democracy *and* trivial. The problem particularly pronounced in public relations, and not pronounced in law schools, is that many communication issues are essentially matters of good judgment (or *phronesis*) and are thus easily expressed in everyday language. Ordinary language is incredibly nuanced, to be sure, but contrary to differential equations or the technical jargon of engineering, it is *common*, i.e., accessible to everyone.

The complexity of public relations problems is not located in the mastery of the discipline, thus, but in the application of simple concepts in the complexity of the real world. But academic respectability, for good or for worse, derives from *intra-disciplinary complexity*. That is the reason, we believe, why public relations as an academic discipline relies almost entirely on theory imports from "respected" disciplines like sociology, philosophy, economics, ethnography, and anthropology.

The primary flaw of public relations in its current configuration as an academic discipline, one could say, is a *mismatch* between its intra-disciplinary complexity on one side and the complexity of its reality on the other. From experience, we know that the mismatch shows very concretely in the everyday work of many of our colleagues: After judging 50 campaign papers on a largely a-theoretical, experiential basis, the public relations scholar routinely returns to her desk to write something theoretically sophisticated and empirically elaborated—and often something that has very little to do with what can be applied in practice.

The problem goes far beyond the rigor-relevance gap well known in management studies. As Ferguson (2018) suggests, the theoretical ambitions entertained by scholars and the bread-and-butter of instruction expected by students are often at odds. On the one side, practically oriented students raise their eyebrows at the ivory tower renderings. Theoretically oriented students, on the other hand, perceive public relations as "communication sociology light" and would rather engage in the real thing—in any case, not dirty their hands (Sommerfeldt & Kent, 2020) with something as mundane or unsavory as "mere" public relations theory.

But why is it so difficult to tackle this? One reason lies in a disciplinary mindset bred by decades of chasing after practice and ruthless cross-cannibalization. Oriented toward student attractiveness and practical resonance, the applied communication disciplines have been raiding and plundering each other ever since their inception. If a concept was successful in one academic discipline, the others integrated it. Nowadays, *all* applied communication disciplines claim the key concepts that give organizational prestige: strategic outlook, value creation and accountability, ethical high ground, co-creation, dialogue, relationships, and authenticity. The result is not only a bewildering disciplinary landscape. The result is a belief that any commitment to public relation's *own agenda* might mean a lost opportunity, a potential loss of territory.

Real and Artificial Complexity

The real struggle of public relations research is the one for academic recognition, of course. Our suspicion here is that many public relations scholars shy away from tackling the real complexities of their topic because the result, they fear, would not conform to expectations of academic respectability. What many public relations scholars find hard to understand, it seems, is that building up intra-disciplinary complexity by importing theory from other "respected" disciplines is not the real thing. The shortcut may *kickstart* a discipline's own development, but ultimately, we would suggest the aim is a match between the discipline's own questions and its own answers. The ability to reformulate a public relations problem in terms of Bourdieu, Habermas, Luhmann or any other luminary may be enlightening for internal consumption (Ihlen & Fredriksson, 2019). What draws the ridicule of outside observers is when theory import exhausts itself, when nothing new, nothing genuinely original is added. Schulz (2001) observed long ago that public relations research offers very little explanatory power, as it is mainly concerned with *artificially* raising the complexity of its area of study.

Postdisciplinarity to the Rescue?

Our argument so far has been predicated on the assumption that disciplines stand and fall as such. The disciplinary game, in other words, is the most important battle for academics, as everything hinges on autonomy, institutionalization, critical mass, intra-disciplinary complexity, and genuine disciplinary achievement.

However, with the postdisciplinary rearrangement of the academic world, many hitherto unquestioned disciplinary pretensions appear more and more unnecessary. Waisbord asserts, for example, that communication's robust pragmatism may turn out to be its greatest strength: "As a whole, communication studies has [sic] not waited for the arrival of the theoretical cavalry, armed with grand arguments and methodologies, to qualify it as a field or a discipline" (2019, p. 133). As for the future, communication scholarship should "embrace its postdisciplinary status." In Waisbord's words, it should "draw various threads of research around the study of theoretical questions and social problems that cross multiple communication perspectives" (Waisbord, 2019, p. 127).

Waisbord's pamphlet concludes with a positive postdisciplinary vision, then. It is perhaps inevitable that it will be read, by some, as the permission to bury awkward disciplinary debates once and for all. There is very little triumphant gloating over dead disciplines, however. More thoughtful and farsighted, Waisbord makes clear that "postdisciplinary was not an act of abandoning or betraying disciplinary roots" (Waisbord, 2019, p. 129). By no means new, postdisciplinarity is driven by the insight that "[c]ertain themes and questions are deemed to be too complex to be approached successfully by one discipline or field" (Waisbord, 2019, p. 129).

In its best sense, then, postdisciplinarity means a coming together of well-conceived academic endeavors that have established a solid methodology of their own and are now ready to apply themselves, in concert with others, to issues that exceed their intra-disciplinary complexity. In the worst sense, it should be admitted, postdisciplinarity gives sterile and obscure dead-end disciplines another lease on life. Thus, in order not to belong to the second category, public relations should not abandon the project of becoming clearer and more focused.

An Alternative to Definitions: A Tribal View of the Applied Communication Disciplines

If postdisciplinary perspectives make us aware that disciplines are perhaps fuzzier than they pretend to be for academic respectability's sake, what are alternatives to the classic definition?

We, the authors, started as public relations and communication management scholars (Nothhaft, 2010; Zerfass, 2008). During the last two decades, we have moved to the strategic communication discipline (Nothhaft et al., 2019; Zerfass et al., 2018). In the course of our transformation, we learned a lot about disciplinary debates. One insight was that academic projects, over time, pick up a lot of historical baggage. Historical baggage often comes in the form of foundational myths, like, e.g., that public relations is essentially about dialogue.

We believe that the holding on to foundational myths, not necessarily intrinsic complexity, makes the disciplinary landscape appear bewildering. With due respect to real historical injustices, one could say the current map is populated by academic tribes that successfully conquered some administrative piece of turf by making big claims: strategic, inherently ethical, and socially functional. The tribes believe they conquered their plot because of their foundational myth, some ancestral right. But the land was never conquered. Instead, it was granted, and the grant had little to do with big claims. Waisbord's grand tour suggests that far more important was the realization, by some faculty or university officials, that the tribe's offerings might be attractive to a goodly number of students. Where the shamans refuse to acknowledge that mundane reality, the tribe remains captive to its own story, stuck in a vicious cycle of self-assertion and self-defense.

What does one see when one takes the liberty to strip away the tribes' own stories? In our view, one can currently identify *six applied communication disciplines, or tribal territories,* that are comprehensive in their ambition but with a different look and feel from what is most evident in textbooks or overview articles:

- public relations (Valentini, 2021; Tench & Waddington, 2021; Broom & Sha, 2013);
- (integrated) marketing communication (see e.g., Pelsmacker et al., 2021; Percy, 2018; Ju, 2018; Balmer & Greyser, 2006);
- corporate communication (Doorley & Garcia, 2021; Cornelissen, 2020; Argenti, 2016; Riel & Fombrun, 2007);
- strategic communication (Nothhaft et al., 2019; Falkheimer & Heide, 2023; Botan, 2018; Holtzhausen & Zerfass, 2015);
- organizational communication (see e.g., Feldner & Fyke, 2018; Putnam et al., 2017; Cheney et al., 2010);
- digital communication and social media culture (see e.g., Fuchs, 2021; Luttrell & Wallace, 2021; Delfanti & Arvidsson, 2019; Georgakopoulou & Spilioti, 2016).

Other subdisciplines might also qualify as applied communication disciplines, but they are not comprehensive. One cannot run a company's communication department solely from a public speaking or business communication perspective. *Applied* means that the disciplines have a marked career orientation: they dangle the carrot of a career in the communication industry. *Look and feel* covers that authors share characteristics but that there is not necessarily one criterion, subject to one coherent logic, that unites authors A and B, while C is different. Perhaps the strongest determinant is terminology and vocabulary. Marketing communication authors are not limited to talking about sales and customer loyalty, but they employ other concepts than authors in organizational communication. As public relations scholars, we remember distinctly the feeling that there are things that marketing scholars "don't get"—presumably, it is the same the other way round.

Habits of Thought, Comfort Zones, and Affinities

The reason why marketing communication and public relations scholars mutually suspect each other of not getting it, we believe, lies not so much in clear-cut disciplinary assumptions but in cultural differences—in *habits of thought, comfort zones,* or simply *affinities*. A view of affinities, rather than borders, allows us to look at the applied communication landscape without making retrospective sense of divisions that are essentially not intellectual but institutional-historical.

In what way can cultures be different? The most popular analytical view of cultures was developed by Dutch social psychologist Geert Hofstede (Hofstede et al., 2010). In its current version, Hofstede's system differentiates six dimensions: *power distance, collectivism vs. individualism, uncertainty avoidance, femininity vs. masculinity, short-term vs. long-term, restraint vs. indulgence.* To understand the applied communication disciplines, we suggest seven logically similar dimensions:

- complexity vs. simplification;
- truth vs. attraction;
- direct vs. indirect;
- immersion vs. control;
- holistic vs. focused;
- conflict vs. cooperation;
- empathic vs. systemic.

Like Hofstede, our cultural view uses bipolar dichotomies: working holistically is good, yet focus is also good. Our cultural view avoids contested qualities or definitional criteria furthermore. It might or might not be so that corporate communication is more strategic than marketing, but any such claim will not be accepted by marketing. Perhaps dialogue and relationship building are strong suits for public relations, but they are not exclusive definitional criteria since they are also claimed by relationship marketing.

Complexity vs. Simplification

This dimension asks to what degree the discipline demands and encourages the breaking down of real-world complexity, i.e., to what degree is it comfortable with simplification. Some believe that the minimal requirement for art that seeks to capture the complexity of life is the 1,000 pages of Tolstoy's *War and Peace*; others are more impressed with a three-line *haiku*. The marketing communication mindset gravitates toward simplification. Marketers are used to encapsulate the heart of the matter in a slogan. That does not mean that they are simple-minded and incapable of dealing with complex questions: the market-analyses that drive simplification are highly complex. It means that successful marketing communication must simplify the matter at hand, sometimes radically: nuance is sacrificed for distinction. Digital communication and organizational communication are perhaps the disciplines with the greatest affinity to complexity: here, distinction is sacrificed for nuance. Public relations and strategic communication are in between, on the higher side. The level on which public relations operates in terms of complexity is the journalistic story. In the case of strategic communication, it is a limited number of viable scenarios. Corporate communication, we would argue, is on the lower side, not as radical as marketing, but still more concerned with distinction than nuance.

Truth vs. Attraction

Put simply, truth vs. attraction asks to what degree the discipline is more concerned with truth or beauty, whether it favors the philosopher or the poet. Culturally closest to journalism, we would suggest public relations is the highest on truth, while marketing communication is highest on attraction. With many marketing campaigns, the question of whether claims are true or not does not arise. Whether a product is "light yet filling" is hard to ascertain. Corporate communication and strategic communication are once again in between, we propose, with corporate communication tending toward the attraction side, and strategic communication toward the truth side. The same tendency applies to digital and organizational communication, with digital tending toward attraction, and organizational communication toward truth. There are substantial differences as to the reasons why, however. Strategic communication shuns the glamor that corporate communication brought in from marketing. Influenced by strategic management, it places a premium on stone-cold analysis: "hard truths" not "creative solutions" are the currency. Because strategic communication puts a premium on decision making at risk, it is highly sensitive to the question of who will be right in the end. Organizational communication's tendency toward truth derives from its academic anchoring, which results in a more text-based, more epistemically accessible culture. Yet organizational communication places a greater emphasis on writing style and originality of thought. Digital communication's tendency toward attraction, in contrast, derives from the visual culture of social media; whether a meme is true is not as relevant as whether it is shareable.

Direct vs. Indirect

This distinction captures whether a discipline favors straightforward approaches that pitch strength against strength or roundabout ways where strengths are applied against weaknesses. We would argue that public relations is highest in indirectness, marketing communication in directness. The Torches of Freedom campaign by Edward Bernays (Murphree, 2015) fascinates public relations theorists because Bernays's campaign illustrates a roundabout approach: marketing cigarettes via the detour of women's liberation is the epitome of indirectness. In contrast, today's energy drinks Monster and Red Bull use nearly identical, high-profile marketing communications and pitch strength against strength—both sponsor high-octane extreme sports. If corporate communication constitutes a "best of" of the two disciplines, it tries to blend public relations' indirect emphasis on earned media with marketing's directness. Strategic communication is, in principle, agnostic but tilts toward indirect. The tilt derives from a concern about competitors' actions. If a course of action is obvious, it will be obvious to competitors as well. This can result in a duopolistic structure like Monster and Red Bull, but too often it results in ruinous attrition that consumes resources without a winner. Organizational communication has a similar tilt, which results from its emphasis on originality. As for digital communication, it is too early to tell.

Immersion vs. Control

This dimension reflects the distinction between etic and emic research paradigms. Immersion-oriented disciplinary cultures, like organizational communication, place a premium on understanding stakeholder collectives "from the inside," whereas control-oriented cultures emphasize distance. With (n)ethnographic roots, digital communication is high on immersion, while strategic communication, with its strong emphasis on reflection, is low. "Going native" is familiar among social media practitioners who take the sides of the stakeholders against the company. It is rare among high-level strategists. What is common among strategists, in contrast, are control fantasies, which have no basis other than ignorance of what is going on at the sharp end. At the risk of complicating matters, we would argue that marketing communication and public relations embrace immersion-oriented as well as control-oriented styles. The default is perhaps a tilt toward control. However, in some areas of public relations work, intimate familiarity with the players in the game is far more critical than strategizing. Lobbyists dealing with the European Union or the United States need to know Brussels or Washington, D.C. Similarly, marketing streetwear with creative campaigns is easier when one is a true believer. Corporate communication is agnostic.

Holistic vs. Focused

This distinction captures whether a discipline tends to narrow or widen the practitioner's view. Although we see nothing wrong with focus, this dimension is perhaps the most contested—every discipline claims to be holistic. Nevertheless, we would argue that strategic communication (see, e.g.,

Zerfass et al., 2018) offers the most holistic mindset, marketing communication the most focused. Digital communication and social media culture are similarly focused but on audiences, not organizational goals or products. If a company needs to raise sales figures in the next six months, they'd better hire a marketing person. If you need to understand what is going on in the minds of a very peculiar subculture, digital communication offers the best approach. Corporate communication started as the attempt to overcome respective narrowness in marketing communication and public relations, but whether the reshuffle led to a more holistic view varies from author to author. Organizational communication is quite holistic, as its academic orientation comes with an inherent societal perspective. Then again, individual projects often display a strong theoretical focus. If an author chooses a neo-institutionalist view, for example, the theoretical perspective leads to focus in the double sense, i.e., sharpening and narrowing.

Conflict vs. Cooperation

The theoretical distinction of conflict vs. cooperation is old. In political philosophy, it is often portrayed as the juxtaposition of Hobbes vs. Rousseau. The distinction captures whether the discipline ultimately views the world as a zero-sum or a win-win game. Strategic communication leans most toward the zero sum–perspective, while public relations, organizational communication, as well as digital communication and social media culture tend toward win-win—with "communication" as the magic ingredient. Even in Grunig's (2006) highly strategic theoretical rendering, public relations is focused on mutual benefit. To be sure, strategic communication does pay attention to alliances and coalitions and encourages actors to develop win-win solutions. It just does not make the assumption that the world always yields a win-win scenario, but adopts a more down-to-earth view of business (Ragas & Culp, 2021). Inspired more by Hobbes than Rousseau, strategic communication tends to view cooperation as a way of prevailing in a fundamentally conflicted world of limited resources. It is not a coincidence that strategic communication is most closely associated with the military, i.e., organizations that conduct violent conflict when other options have failed. While marketing communication in its classic forms used to fall on the conflict side, one could argue that recent developments, emphasizing co-creation, have mellowed the marketing outlook. With newer marketing renderings, the difference to public relations is not always easy to see (Düh-ring, 2017). Corporate communication, understood as a "best of" of public relations and marketing, is the disciplinary expression of this tendency.

Empathic vs. Systemic

The distinction between emphatic and systemic goes back to a suggestion developed by Baron-Cohen and colleagues, who differentiated five different brain types according to the capability to empathize (E) and systemize (S) (Baren-Cohen et al., 2005). They state that "'[e]mpathizing' is the capacity to predict and to respond to the behavior of agents (usually people) by inferring their mental states and responding to these with an appropriate emotion" (Baron-Cohen et al., 2005, p. 819). Systemizing, on the other hand, "is the capacity to predict and to respond to the behavior of non-agentive, deterministic systems, by analyzing input-operation-output relations and inferring the rules that govern such systems" (Baron-Cohen et al., 2005, p. 819). In this nomenclature, Type E persons are markedly better at empathizing than systemizing, while Type S persons are the other way around. We suggest the idea as a valuable way of reconceptualizing the old distinction between nomothetic and idiographic approaches or *Verstehen* and *Erklären* (Apel, 1982). Against that backdrop, strategic communication, marketing communication, corporate communication, and functional public relations tribes with their emphasis on "best practices" tend toward the S-side. Digital communication and social media culture as well as organizational communication and critical or rhetorical public relations, with a stronger emphasis on idiosyncrasy and "human factors," tend toward the E-side.

Clarifications of the Cultural Perspective

The cultural or "tribal" view explains the co-existence of a variety of applied communication disciplines. On a collective level, the cultural view explains, to a degree, why organizations may wish to entertain several applied communication cultures in co-existence. The view also shows why marketing culture does not fit with crisis communication, for example. Marketing communication prefers to operate in attraction categories rather than truth and does not cope well with complexity. Journalistic interest, which is high in a crisis, can only be satisfied with high truth value.

Of course, our suggestions are presently just that: suggestions. Empirical research, perhaps exploring practitioner preferences employing surveys, must show whether our dimensions hold up to scrutiny. Maybe we are wrong, and our cultural view is misguided. Maybe the cultural perspective is valuable, but disciplinary differences lie in other yet unfound dimensions. Presumably, critics will point out that intra-disciplinary differences are more pronounced than inter-disciplinary ones. There is no theoretical argument against that. Maybe meaningful clusters *within* the discipline are more important than boundaries. Perhaps every cluster is inherently conflicted so that there is always a mainstream, which is always challenged by alternative paradigms. We predict, then, that the opposition to the mainstream runs along the lines suggested: critical public relations scholars protest the functional paradigm, in other words, because they prefer immersion over control. In the end, empirical research must ascertain whether the dimensions hold up to scrutiny.

Outlook: A Place for Public Relations in the Postdisciplinary World?

Can public relations as an academic discipline overcome the dynamics that hold the discipline back, benefit from postdisciplinarity, and find new ways of establishing an identity without limiting itself? Perhaps, if it plays its cards right. To be sure, we do not suggest that public relations is a dead-end discipline and should seek a new lease on life in union with "proper" disciplines. Public relations has more to offer. But to become an attractive partner, it must resolve its identity issues. The fierce, nomadic tribe that wants so much to become part of the civilized world must take a hard look at itself.

Our hope for the academic tribe of public relations scholars, then, is three-fold. Public relations scholarship, first, should accept its applied nature. Second, it should abandon the quest for imitative academic respectability for the real thing. Third, it should relinquish its imperialistic pretensions in exchange for a research agenda focusing on what its scholars are best at.

As for the first suggestion, frankly, we do not see what is wrong or undignified with an applied discipline. Applied status does not mean that scholars should resign to being pawns in the PR for PR game. Instead, it means that education and practice are "field laboratories," where theories must prove their utility or, at least, their resonance. Relevance and attractiveness—not as chasing after practice, but as a commitment to a generation of young adults—are important. We believe that professional ties are a healthy corrective if they keep public relations from building up *artificial* intra-disciplinary complexity. In Pooley's (2016) critical account, the "vocational bind" drags the field back. It prevents the applied disciplines from achieving the intra-disciplinary complexity that lends impressive academic dignity. Our account emphasizes not only the negative but also the positive consequences. The applied nature of the discipline, its commitment to education, and its vibrant interaction with practice not only holds public relations back - it also holds it on course.

As for the second suggestion, we argue that public relations wastes energy chasing the *appearance* of academic respectability. The chase diverts attention from the real thing and embroils the discipline in unresolvable internal identity debates. On the positive side, we believe that a postdisciplinary shake-up would impact respectability criteria: intra-disciplinary sophistication will count less, utility more. Our experience from inter-disciplinary projects, admittedly subjective, is that our peers in highly respected disciplines dismiss academic pretensions not out of arrogance, but because of respect for the real thing. In inter-disciplinary research projects, the benchmark is not whether the public relations scholar can out-sociologize the sociologist, out-economize the economist, or out-psychologize the psychologist. It is, conversely, that our peers expect to be "out-communicated" by the communication researcher. Thus, their questions are more straightforward but much harder to answer: *What is it that you have found out in your discipline that* explains real-life communication by organizations? What methods and tools have you developed? What do your theories and frameworks predict? In other words, how can you contribute to understanding and solving challenges in the real world? As for the third suggestion, a *cultural view* should hint at where public relations research's strengths and weaknesses lie. If our cultural dimensions hold up to scrutiny, public relations scholarship should focus on the *epistemic* or *truth dimension* in matters of *medium-to-high complexity*, especially when organizations pursue their aims in *indirect*, roundabout, covert ways. The juxtaposition of immersion vs. control—co-creation and management, in other words—has fueled disciplinary debates for years. But we expect a more sophisticated engagement with public relations' fundamentally cooperative worldview and its peculiar brand of *focused holism*, in which every stakeholder is accounted for, yet the future and technological development are strangely absent. Finally, many ideological debates can be conducted more productively if reframed as a clash of empathic and systemic worldviews.

References

Apel, K.-O. (1982). The Erklären-Verstehen controversy in the philosophy of the natural and human sciences. In G. Fløistad (Ed.), *La philosophie contemporaine/contemporary philosophy* (Vol. 2, pp. 19–49). Springer.

Argenti, P. A. (2016). *Corporate communication* (7th ed.). McGraw Hill.

Balmer, J. M. T., & Greyser, S. A. (2006). Corporate marketing—integrating corporate identity, corporate branding, corporate communications, corporate image and corporate reputation. *European Journal of Marketing, 40*(7–8), 730–741.

Baron-Cohen, S., Knickmeyer, R. C., & Belmonte, M. K. (2005). Sex differences in the brain: Implications for explaining autism. *Science, 310*(5749), 819–823.

Botan, C. H. (2018). *Strategic communication in theory and practice: The co-creational model.* Wiley-Blackwell.

Broom, G. M., & Sha, B.-L. (2013). *Cutlip and Center's effective public relations— international edition* (11th ed.). Pearson.

Cheney, G., & Christensen, L. T. (2001). Public relations as contested terrain: A critical response. In R. L. Heath (Ed.), *Handbook of public relations* (pp. 167–182). Sage.

Cheney, G., Christensen, L. T., Zorn, T. E., & Ganesh, S. (2010). *Organizational communication in an age of globalization* (2nd ed.). Waveland Press.

Clausewitz, C. (1989). *On war.* Princeton University Press.

Cornelissen, J. (2020). *Corporate communication* (6th ed.). Sage.

Delfanti, A., & Arvidsson, A. (2019). *Introduction to digital media.* Wiley-Blackwell.

Doorley, J., & Garcia, H. F. (2021). *Reputation management* (4th ed.). Routledge.

Dühring, L. (2015). Lost in translation? On the disciplinary status of public relations. *Public Relations Inquiry, 4*(1), 5–23.

Dühring, L. (2017). *Reassessing the relationship between marketing and public relations.* Springer.

Dühring, L., & Zerfass, A. (2021). The triple role of communications in agile organizations. *International Journal of Strategic Communication, 15*(2), 93–112.

Falkheimer, J., & Heide, M. (2023). *Strategic communication* (2nd ed.). Routledge.

Feldner, S. B., & Fyke, J. P. (2018). Organizational communication. In R. L. Heath & W. Johansen (Eds.), *The international encyclopedia of strategic communication* (Vol. 3, pp. 1048–1061). Wiley-Blackwell.

Ferguson, M. A. (2018). Building theory in public relations: Interorganizational relationships as a public relations paradigm. *Journal of Public Relations Research, 30*(4), 164–178.

Fuchs, C. (2021). *Social media: A critical introduction*. Routledge.

Georgakopoulou, A., & Spilioti, T. (Eds.). (2016). *The Routledge handbook of language and digital communication*. Routledge.

Graeber, D. (2018). *Bullshit jobs: A theory*. Simon & Schuster.

Grunig, J. E. (2006). Furnishing the edifice: Ongoing research on public relations as a strategic management function. *Journal of Public Relations Research, 18*(2), 151–176.

Habermas, J. (1991). *The structural transformation of the public sphere*. MIT Press.

Heath, R. (2006). Onward into more fog: Thoughts on public relations' research directions. *Journal of Public Relations Research, 18*(2), 93–114.

Hofstede, G., Hofstede, G. J., & Minkov, M. (2010). *Cultures and organizations* (3rd ed.). McGraw Hill.

Holtzhausen, D., & Zerfass, A. (Eds.). (2015). *The Routledge handbook of strategic communication*. Routledge.

Ihlen, O., & Fredriksson, M. (2019). *Public relations and social theory* (2nd ed.). Routledge.

Ju, I. (2018). Marketing communication. In R. L. Heath & W. Johansen (Eds.), *The international encyclopedia of strategic communication* (Vol. 2, pp. 895–908). Wiley-Blackwell.

Luttrell, R., & Wallace, A. A. (2021). *Social media and society*. Rowman & Littlefield.

Moloney, K. (2006). *Rethinking public relations: PR propaganda and democracy* (2nd ed.). Routledge.

Murphree, V. (2015). Edward Bernays's 1929 "torches of freedom" march: Myths and historical significance. *American Journalism, 32*(3), 258–281.

Nothhaft, H. (2010). Communication management as a second-order management function: Roles and functions of the communication executive—results from a shadowing study. *Journal of Communication Management, 14*(2), 127–140.

Nothhaft, H., Verčič, D., Werder, K. P., & Zerfass, A. (Eds.). (2019). *Future directions of strategic communication*. Routledge.

Nothhaft, H., Werder, K. P., Verčič, D., & Zerfass, A. (2018). Strategic communication: Reflections on an elusive concept. *International Journal of Strategic Communication, 12*(4), 352–366.

Pelsmacker, P. de, Geuens, M., & Berg, J. van den (2021). *Marketing communications: A European perspective* (7th ed.). Pearson.

Percy, L. (2018). *Strategic integrated marketing communications* (3rd ed.). Routledge.

Peters, J. D. (1986). Institutional sources of intellectual poverty in communication research. *Communication Research, 13*(4), 527–559.

Pooley, J. D. (2016). The field, fermented: Prestige and the vocational bind in communication research. *International Communication Gazette, 78*(7), 621–626.

Putnam, L., Woo, D., & Banghart, S. (2017). Organizational communication. In *Oxford bibliographies on communication*. Oxford University Press. https://doi.org/10.1093/obo/9780199756841-0137

Ragas, M. W., & Culp, R. (2021). *Business acumen for strategic communicators*. Emerald.

Riel, C. B. M. van, & Fombrun, C. J. (2007). *Essentials of corporate communication*. Routledge.

Schulz, W. (2001). Public relations/Öffentlichkeitsarbeit. In E. Noelle-Neumann, W. Schulz, & J. Wilke (Eds.), *Fischer Lexikon Publizistik/Massenkommunikation* (pp. 517–545). Fischer.

Sommerfeldt, E. J., & Kent, M. L. (2020). Public relations as dirty work: Disconfirmation, cognitive dissonance, and emotional labor among public relations professors. *Public Relations Review, 46,* 101933.

Tench, R., & Waddington, S. (Eds.). (2021). *Exploring public relations and communication management* (5th ed.). Pearson.

Toth, E. L. (2010). Reflections on the field. In R. L. Heath (Ed.), *The Sage handbook of public relations* (2nd ed., pp. 711–722). Sage.

Valentini, C. (Ed.). (2021). *Public relations.* DeGruyter Mouton.

Waisbord, S. (2019). *Communication: A post-discipline.* Polity.

Zerfass, A. (2008). Corporate communication revisited: Integrating business strategy and strategic communication. In A. Zerfass, B. van Ruler, & K. Sriramesh (Eds.), *Public relations research* (pp. 65–96). VS Verlag für Sozialwissenschaften.

Zerfass, A., Verčič, D., Nothhaft, H., & Werder, K. P. (2018). Strategic communication: Defining the field and its contribution to research and practice. *International Journal of Strategic Communication, 12*(4), 487–505.

Section 3

Race, Gender, and Culture Interact With Theories

16 Introduction to and Advances in Feminist Theory for Public Relations

Elizabeth L. Toth

Women make up 71.4% of those who practice public relations (Meng & Neill, 2021, p. 4). However, 70% of executive public relations positions are held by men (Arthur W. Page Center, 2021). These ratios of women to men in public relations and in executive positions have held steady since the mid-1980s (Cline et al., 1986; Toth & Cline, 1989; L. Grunig, 1988; Wright et al., 1991; Dozier et al., 2019; Place & Vardeman-Winter, 2015; Vardeman-Winter & Place, 2017; Strong, 2019).

Public relations practitioners' perceptions persist that the gender inequities in the field are "just a woman's issue" (Aldoory et al., 2008; Dubrowski et al., 2019). However, feminist theories of public relations regard every person as gendered; that is, their actions are influenced by social expectations and constraints based on sex and sexuality identities. In public relations scholarship, feminist theory seeks to expose gendered beliefs, expectations, and actions that hinder the practice of public relations (Aldoory, 2001, 2003; Aldoory & Toth, 2002; L. A. Grunig et al., 2001). Indeed, feminist theories of public relations are contributing a paradigmatic body of knowledge that can strengthen mainstream theoretical areas of public relations (Aldoory, 2005).

There are myriad definitions of what is meant by "feminist theory." While Aldoory and Toth (2021) chose to define feminist theory as about gender and power, Golombisky (2015) argued for a moral imperative for feminist theory "to examine interlocking systems of oppression based on race, ethnicity, class, age, ability, sexuality, nationality, and religion among others" (p. 391). This chapter acknowledges the diverse ways that feminist scholars define feminism. It starts by introducing the development of feminist theory from the early descriptive research on women practitioners' inequitable careers to the deeper explanations of gender influences on and about public relations provided by feminist scholars. It explains what feminist theories do and theoretical influences on feminist theory from discourse theory, critical race theory, intersectionality and standpoint theories, and queer theories. The chapter ends by proposing a socio-ecological model for advancing feminist theory for public relations.

DOI: 10.4324/9781003141396-19

History Feminist Research in Public Relations

This brief history of feminist research presented is United States-based but acknowledges that feminist scholars from all over the world have helped advance knowledge about the various ways that power, social norms, and unwritten institutional gendered and raced oppressions are part of public relations (Daymon & Demetrious, 2014; Edwards, 2013, 2014; Fitch, 2016; Fitch et al., 2016; Fitch & Third, 2010; L'Etang, 2015; Topic et al., 2020).

Prior to the 1980s, men made up approximately 70% of public relations practitioners (Reskin & Roos, 1990). Early scholarship documented salary and advancement inequities faced by typically White women practitioners who were increasingly entering the public relations field (Cline et al., 1986; Toth & Cline, 1989; L. Grunig, 1988; Wright et al., 1991). Feminist theories applied to identify the root causes of gender disparities and appropriate solutions to the complex issues of gender and public relations were little seen until 1995 (Hon, 1995) culminating in a first book, *Women in public relations: How gender influences practice* (L. Grunig et al., 2001).

Three contributions by feminist scholars Hon (1995), Aldoory (2005), and Rakow and Nastasia (2009) provided significant breakthroughs for feminist understandings of gender and race discrimination in public relations. Hon (1995) made several contributions to a feminist theory of public relations. Among them, she highlighted the practical activist goal of raising consciousness about gender issues germane to public relations. She urged that study be of the experiences of female communicators from their points of view to establish constructs in public relations from women's and men's perspectives. Hon's feminist theory proposed new methodologies that employed subject participation and collaboration. Hon argued against research implying that women must strive for a White male managerial standard, as women were effective communicators and managers in their own right.

Aldoory (2005) advanced a feminist paradigm for public relations scholarship by (re)conceptualizing the concepts of gender, power, and diversity as discursive practices that led to invalid constructed meanings of public relations. Aldoory urged getting beyond conceptualizations of gender as "women or female" to study all humans affected by gender constructions, stereotypes, and gender socialization (p. 675). Her reconceptualization of power began with a critique of the unconscious assumptions that power was a property to be given away, as for example through an act of empowerment (L. A. Grunig et al., 2002). She acknowledged feminist scholars' definitions of power; including: 1) power as the control and fixing of meanings to the advantage of specific groups, or 2) power as capacity, energy, ability, strength, and action to "counter means of power as coercive and patriarchal" (p. 676). However, Aldoory argued for an understanding of power in public relations "as a discursive construction, in order to open up new theories about gender, race, management, and leadership because these factors are imbedded within traditional languages of power" (p. 676).

Third, Aldoory (2005) challenged feminist public relations theorists to study how diverse practitioners making meaning of difference in their practice of public relations, calling out the over-study of White women's salaries, roles, and other job factors. She defined diversity, as she had gender and power, as discursive practices that led to biased individual practitioner and organizational actions. She argued that the pervasiveness of diversity must be acknowledged in public relations research.

> Diversity should be conceived and studied as situated knowledge, including interrogating Whiteness, which influences the research participant, his/her performance and communication, the researcher, and his/her data collection and interpretation.
>
> (p. 676)

In sum, Aldoory challenged a first wave of public relations feminist scholarship to go beyond residual androcentrism: "Modern, Western, and often elitist thought has implicitly and perhaps unconsciously undergirded many gender studies in public relations" (p. 672).

Rakow and Nastasia (2009) introduced a critical feminist theory focused on the consequences to women because of public relations discourses reflecting the structures of institutional power that reinforced patriarchy. They contributed a classification of feminist theoretical positions that conceptualize feminist theory based on gender systems, women's identities, power relations, social justice, and social change. They called for a feminist theory of public relations that moved beyond the man/woman dichotomy, that recognized that women practitioners learn a "fathertongue," a patriarchal way of speaking that results in forms of patriarchal organizing and ruling. In sum, Rakow and Nastasia's work called attention to the impact of institutions on women's lives and for realizing the responsibilities of public relations practice to society.

Feminist theory and public relations became richer and more complex because of these three scholarly contributions. Hon (1995) provided the introductory parameters for a feminist theory of public relations. Aldoory (2005) widened a view of feminism as gender, power, and diversity; and Rakow and Nastasia (2009), summarizing a comprehensive categorization of feminist theories, argued for a feminist theory for public relations that considered the impact of institutional discourses on the lives of women.

Feminism's Intellectual Domain

Feminist theory belongs in an intellectual domain that has widening study beyond what public relations practitioners do in and for organizations to the study of intended and unintended consequences of public relationships on individuals and society (see the work of Dozier and Lauzen (2000). Feminist theory has sought to widen the intellectual domain of public relations beyond how it functions to maintain power and constructs identities that lead to oppression and marginalization of specific groups. Stated another way, Daymon and Demetrious (2014) called out an anti-intellectualism to academic inquiry in public relations because it was overly concerned with vocational outcomes. Daymon and Demetrious argued for examining public relations' implications and works using the sociological, the cultural, and the political rather than a positivist knowledge bias. In contrast to the definition of public relations as a management function (Grunig & Hunt, 1984), Daymon and Demetrious defined public relations as a "communicative activity used by organizations to intervene socially in and between competing discourses in order to facilitate a favorable position within a globalized context" (p. 3).

Feminism and Capitalism

Feminist scholarship needs better recognition of how capitalism, based in patriarchy, influences public relations (Rakow & Nastasia, 2009). Feminist scholars have identified salary disparities, glass ceilings, work-life conflicts, and even devaluing women's work without recognizing that they are the outcomes of a capitalistic economic system. As Caldera argued (2020) in her Black feminist/womanist commentary, capitalism needs more study in its role of "dehumanizing women and people of color. It forces us to neglect our personal and communal well-being for the sake of thriving industries and robust economies" (p. 711).

One variant of capitalism, the human capital model, was addressed by Aldoory and Toth (2002). They debunked claims that public relations women's lesser investments in education, years of experience, and professional advancement explained inequities in their productivity and earnings. Aldoory and Toth found that when holding these variables constant, women practitioners still significantly earned lower salaries when compared to the male practitioners in their sample. However, despite their research exposing gender bias as a better explanation of gender inequities and debunked beliefs about individualistic claims of equal opportunities, human capital theory still persists in public relations research (Jin et al., 2014).

Lawniczak (2009) called attention to the role of public relations in promoting economic theories and the "neo-liberal ideology that encouraged deregulation, discouraged oversights, and created an environment conducive to greed focused management practices" (p. 346). Lawniczak identified a "critical school" in public relations research that has acknowledged power, economic corporate power, the impact of media ownership on media content, postcolonialism, and public relations promotion of economic systems that should encourage feminist theory to challenge capitalistic principles' effects on human rights.

Tenets of Gender and Feminism

Gender

Much of public relations scholarship on gender and public relations uses a definition of gender based on the ascribed-at-birth biological differences between males and females. In both quantitative and qualitative studies, this binary has proven parsimonious but oversimplifies and homogenizes a more valid understanding of gender based on social constructions. Gender is neither binary nor stationary. Feminist scholars argue that gender should reflect a meaning system for such concepts as womanhood, femininity, manhood, and masculinity (Aldoory & Toth, 2021). Rakow and Wackwitz (2004) explain: "Gender (and race) are meaning systems arising from the cultural activity of creating similarities and differences rather than as biological or metaphysical givens that culture modifies" (p. 13).

Gender in feminist public relations research should be understood as constantly enacted and reinforced through language, communication, and action. Rakow (1989) defined gender as "a way of organizing and making sense of the world in which we live—gender is not something that we are but something we do and believe, it is performative" (p. 289). As such, understanding the influence of gender on public relations and of public relations on gender requires more participatory and collaborative observations to reveal individuals' gendered perceptions of themselves as well as others. According to Van Zoonen (1994), "Gender is not constructed in human relations alone but intersects with ethnicity, sexuality, class and a range of other discourses, often in contradictory ways" (p. 3). Aldoory and Toth (2021) called for theorizing the social meaning of gender reinforced through communication and intersecting with race, ethnicity, sexual orientation, and class that create understandings of its influences.

Feminist Theoretical Positions and Waves

Feminist scholarship is guided by different theoretical positions: liberal, socialist, radical, postmodern, multicultural, and postcolonial (Rakow & Nastasia, 2009). Three written about by public relations feminist scholars have been the liberal, radical, and socialist positions (Hon, 1995; Rakow & Nastasia, 2009; Toth & Aldoory, 2021). Public relations feminist scholarship illustrative of *liberal feminism* in public relations research examined "disparities in work practices, salaries, and promotions for purposes of equality between the sexes" (Aldoory, 2005, p. 670). Liberal feminism was critiqued by Steeves (1987) as speaking "only to White heterosexual middle and upper-class women" (p. 95).

The *radical feminist position* represents attempts to reverse masculine systems governing society, media, and organizations (Nachescu, 2009). Its goal is to analyze the structures of power that oppress women and create female spaces that value women. Radical public relations feminist research has critiqued gendered systems, such as in Creedon's (1993) case study of the NCAA's takeover of the AIAW, resulting in the powerful structure that advanced "competitive exclusionary sports for the elite athlete" (p. 163) rather than equal opportunities for women to play sports, and in O'Neil's (2003) finding of gendered organizational structures that gave greater organizational power access to male practitioners. The radical feminist position is seen in the arguments of Grunig et al. (2000) to change the profession of public relations from one with embedded masculine values to a field that represents feminist values.

The third perspective, *socialist feminism*, with ties to Marxism and feminism, Steeves believed, offered the "greatest potential for a comprehensive framework in addressing women's devaluation in communication" (1987, p. 97). Socialist feminism considered the racial, class, sexual orientation, and cultural background that cause women's oppression (Steeves, p. 106). Rakow and Nastasia (2009) posited that socialist feminism could better show the "complex connection between gender and class for public relations and questioning the work of capitalistic enterprises which employ public relations to carry out exploitive social relations" (p. 257). Aldoory (2005) and Rakow and Nastasia (2009) concluded that public relations feminist scholarship reflects liberal and radical positions rather than a socialist feminist position.

Discussions of feminism have offered different assumptions and theoretical developments across generations or waves. The first wave of feminism, considered to be between 1840 and 1920 focused on equality of citizenry; the second wave between 1960 and 1988 focused on equal rights, workplace equality, and reproductive freedom; the third wave between 1988 and 2010 represented activists against a singular goal for feminism; and a fourth wave looked to find common ground between groups linked to feminism (Looft, 2017, p. 984). Feminist thought and theories of public relations continue to be enriched by these perspectives and waves.

Post-Feminism

Post-feminism is the belief that public relations no longer needs feminism. "Post-feminism is a step backwards from the arguments for systemic change to the celebration of personal responsibility, individualism, and autonomy" (Fitch, 2016). Fitch and Third (2010) argue that we've entered an era of post-feminism, a period of assumed equality and backlash. The post-feminist position "assumes that explicit consideration of 'the gender question' is no longer necessary" (Fitch & Third, 2010, np).

In some ways, post-feminism represents the exhaustion to the strictures of the public relations profession and a resignation to the spaces women have been given to practice public relations. Yet, if the practice of public relations seeks a professional status, it cannot ignore institutional processes and issues of power evident in public relations (Fitch & Third, 2010). Public relations practitioners continue to be marginalized by gender's association with "women's work" or "emotional labor" (Bridgen, 2011; Sommerfeldt & Kent, 2020). Men, women, and practitioners of color work in a public relations field that expects them to adopt professional values reinforcing gendered stereotypes rather than having the power to influence and break down patriarchal norms embedded in public relations practice (Rakow & Nastasia, 2009).

Theoretical Influences of Feminist Theory

Feminist Public Relations Theory Focused on Discourses

Aldoory (2005) and Rakow and Nastasia (2009) argued for a discourse view of how public relations language creates gender bias. The discourses themselves are persuasive interpretations of messages between actors that create organizational structures and gendered expectations. Discourses carry gendered ideologies that propelled women and men to enact certain performances that are gendered. Aldoory et al. (2021) defined discourses as master narratives that provide a "seemingly real story to tell," thus producing identities for individuals in that story (Trethewey, 2001, p. 187) One master narrative, the individualism and autonomy narrative (Aldoory et al., 2021, p. 294) told repeatedly, is that individuals alone have the power or agency and autonomy to make change in and define public relations. This master narrative is exemplified in *PR News'* headline featuring top women practitioners: "Onus on us and industry to close leadership gap" (Arenstein, 2019, np). A second master narrative, the diversity and equality narrative (Aldoory et al., 2021, p. 294), provides cover for "talking the talk" without acknowledging the complexities of how racial identities are negotiated. Parker's research (2002) makes the point that African American women executives have succeeded in their roles because they have created communication strategies that made co-workers aware of their normative, dominant culture, discriminatory behavior. A third master narrative playing out in crisis communication research is found in the term *reputation repair* (Ferguson et al., 2018). This narrative focuses on a "fix-it" meaning with one-way communication stereotypically associated with the masculine traits of strength and power without interrogating whether masculine expectations of success in overcoming an organizational crisis run counter to community concerns (Aldoory et al., p. 295). Feminist theory deepens an understanding of how unconscious and/or dominant cultural language choices, the discourses themselves, reinforce discriminatory beliefs.

Critical Race Theory

Race, defined as the social categories constructed based on physical appearance, particularly skin color (Center for the Study of Social Policy, 2019), has received attention by several feminist scholars (Aldoory, 2005; Pompper, 2005; Sha, 2006; Vardeman-Winter, 2011). Pompper introduced critical race theory (CRT) to public relations research to reveal discrimination. Based on the work of Delgado and Stefancic (2001), Pompper argued that CRT examines economics, history, context, group-and self-interest, feelings, and the unconscious (p. 145) and that CRT revealed "masked institutions' subversion of race equality ensuring White privilege, and normalizing or naturalizing racism in American society" (p. 144).

CRT calls feminist public relations scholars to make visible the different experiences of practitioners of color (Edwards & Munshi, 2011; Applebaum et al., 2015; Ford & Brown, 2015). Implications of CRT from feminist scholarship for public relations have recognized the overstudy of White heterosexual American women practitioners' perceptions of gender issues (Vardeman-Winter & Place, 2017), the White privilege of societal and organizational norms within which public relations practitioners work and reinforce (Logan, 2011, 2021), and the institutionalized racism embedded in campaigns and research about women (Vardeman-Winter, 2011).

Intersectionality and Standpoint Theory

Golombisky (2015) advanced feminist theory in public relations through intersectionality theory and standpoint theory "to get beyond the paradoxes of binary difference" (p. 388). Emerging from critical race theory and the work of Dill and Kohlman (2012) and Crenshaw (1989), intersectionality recognized individuals' many interlocking identifications, such as "gender identity, race, ethnicity, economic and social class, sexuality, ability, nationality, religion, etc." (Golombisky, p. 403). Noting public relations feminist scholars who have developed intersectionality and standpoint theories through their work (Pompper, 2007; Vardeman-Winter & Tindall, 2010; Tindall & Waters, 2012; Waymer & Dyson, 2011), key dimensions of intersectionality theory got at individuals' identifications based on privilege and oppression, took in avowed and ascribed identifications, and "by virtue of definition engages in the work of social justice" (Golombisky, p. 403).

Intersectionality theory referenced social relations, while standpoint theory considered one's awareness of positionality (Golombisky, 2015, p. 404). Standpoint theory has explained how those positioned in oppressed groups had the advantage of learning to understand the dominant group as well as their own, called "double-consciousness" (Dubois, 1903). Standpoint theory also reminds producers of knowledge to reflexively consider theirs and their participants' positionality when producing new knowledge (Golombisky, 2015, p. 404).

From their focus group research, Vardeman-Winter et al. (2013) illustrated how intersectionality and standpoint theories work together to explain how interlocking political, structural, and representational identities such as gender, race, class, and age led to different consumption of health campaign messages. From one African American female participant's standpoint: "I think [the messages talk to] mainly Caucasian women. That's all I really saw in the [video] except for the ultrasound technician. I think most women in my community see breast cancer as a Caucasian women's disease" (p. 402–403).

Multiple Genders and the Individual Practitioner: Queer Theory

Rarely have practitioners been asked to discuss their own sexuality with the notable exception of Tindall and Water's 2013 edited volume, *Coming out of the closet: Exploring LGBT issues in strategic communication with theory and research.* Public relations research has assumed invisible heterosexual norms and expectations around gender, marriage, and sexuality. Heterosexual expectations in gender research on public relations are "taken for granted," so that those who construct their sexual identities differently are marginalized into the categories of LGBT, lesbian, gay, bi-sexual, and transgender (McDonald, 2015).

Queer theory is contributing to an understanding of the normative expectation of heterosexuality as natural, given, and taken for granted (Yep et al., 2003, p. 3). Queer theorists focus on institutional critiques and practices that oppress LGBTQ people and examine "how those categories as defined, by whom and through what processes, what boundaries they set on what we know, and how and whom we desire and so on" (Gamson, 2003, p. 386). Queer theory approaches sexual identities as multiple, unstable, fluid social constructions (Gamson, 2003; Yep et al., 2003). Ciszek (2018) adds that "queer analysis is a critique of practices and discourses that produce sexual knowledge and how these discourses structure social life, focusing on how such knowledge and practices repress differences" (p. 135). Ciszek argued that queer theory answers Golombisky's (2015) call to strengthen feminist public relations theory with contributions to theory-building focused on performativity, queer of color critique, and multiplicity.

Advancing Feminist Theory for Public Relations: A Socio-Ecological Model

To advance feminist theory for public relations, Aldoory and Toth (2021) proposed a socio-ecological model by which to depict layers of discriminatory influences throughout public relations. "Socio- defines the model as interactive and relational, as opposed to psychological or individual; and ecological describes the process by which influences move and interact with their environment, the individual, and each other" (Aldoory & Toth, 2021, p. 8). The model's purpose is to overcome critiques of feminist scholarship as too centered on the psychological experiences of White heterosexual women practitioners and to draw more attention to the missing work on race and LGBTQ issues and to encourage more examination of the processes of oppression by capitalism, societal norms, organizational structures, and professional values.

The model consists of five levels or layers: the ideological, media, professional, organizational, and practitioner (see Figure 16.1). The outermost level of the model addresses ideology and its overarching power through hegemony. The ideological level includes capitalism, Marxism and classism, patriarchy, critical race theory, and racism. Dutta (2009) illustrates the ideological level in his discussion of the hegemonies inherent in neocolonial structures that maintain division of labor and disparities in access to resources. Dutta urges public relations scholars to resist the taken-for-granted capitalistic basis of dominant public relations scholarship. He encourages a more reflexive role for public relations scholars who are interested in the emancipatory goals of activist politics.

The next inner *media* or mediated level recognizes the codependency of public relations and media. Media constitutes and is constituted by an ideology powerful enough to merit its own layer of analysis, particularly social media that are dominating social discourses. Public relations has long been associated with media because of its outsized role in distributing public

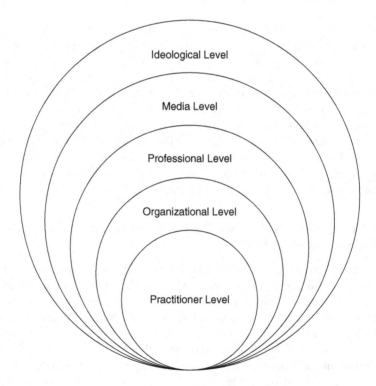

Figure 16.1 A Socio-Ecological Model for Feminist Research in Public Relations

Source: Aldoory & Toth (2021, p. 192)

relations messages. The ownership structures, routines, and practices of media industries result in privileging certain story frames that reinforce social beliefs and values and in ways that stereotype and marginalize groups such as women and people of color. Feminist understandings of the media level are enhanced with framing theory and information subsidies theory, political economy theory, and the power of the digital mediascape (Pal & Dutta, 2008).

The third interior *professional* level seeks to considers how and in what ways the aspirations of public relations to be considered a profession influence actions to achieve diversity, equity, and inclusion (DEI) on the practice of public relations. Professional aspirations of public relations continue to be challenged by encroachment by other communication disciplines, stereotyping, and the limited value of public relations education on who enters and succeeds in public relations. Despite the longevity of professional public relations associations, their interest in DEI has been lacking enough that practitioners have founded associations advancing diversity such as the Association for Women in Communication, the National Black Public Relations Society, and the Hispanic Public Relations Association to better represent their gender, race, and ethnic interests.

The fourth, the organizational level of the socio-ecological model, represents the influences of organizational culture, the dominant coalition, the glass and lavender ceilings, and other gendered structures that reinforce sexism, racism, homophobia, and classism in public relations. Feminist scholars have contributed to the understanding of how organizations use systems theory, excellence theory, and strategic communication theory to reinforce dominant beliefs. Organizational gendered structures ignore differences as revealed in critical race, intersectionality, and standpoint theories. Feminist approaches have sought to expose how organizational discourses reinforce gendered and raced norms. Their research points to how organizational socialization creates cultural barriers that discourage entry into and advancement in the practice of public relations by marginalized groups.

The fifth individual and inner-most level of the socio-ecological model represents the lived experiences of public relations practitioners; that is, the perceptions of oppressions by women and men, LGBTQ practitioners, practitioners of color, and international practitioners.

Feminist public relations scholars have identified as belonging to the individual level research on practitioner role disparities and the challenges to attain leadership influence because of gender, race, ethnicity, age, sexual orientation, and class identities. The individual level of analysis includes research on micro-aggressions and sexual harassment.

The socio-ecological model of influences seeks to advance a more comprehensive view of feminist research for public relations. This categorization has the potential advantage of identifying gaps in theory and research and encourages studies of interactivity and relationships between theories. The model urges the consideration of one topic from multiple angles and iterative properties. Any model faces the criticism of implying a functionalist worldview. However, the socio-ecological model of influences intends to provide a multiplicative, paradigmatic approach to revealing a broader understanding of ideological discriminatory influence on the multiple, interconnected, two-way actions of society, media, professional associations, organizations, and individuals that make up the field of public relations.

Conclusion

Feminist scholarship contributes to public relations theory as part of the intellectual movement to theorize beyond what practitioners do to the consequences to society of public relations as an organizational function. Feminist scholarship has made known that public relations practitioners reinforce societal biases and oppressions based on gender, race, ethnicity, age, and sexual orientation. Feminism scholars have opened up theories to transform public relations practitioners and practice. They argue for change in the communicated discourses that assume and privileges masculine, beliefs, and expectations. Feminism argues for equity for all human affected by gender constructions, stereotypes, and gender socialization (Aldoory, 2005). Feminist theories have embraced and have been enriched by interconnections to critical race theory, intersectionality theory, standpoint theory, and queer theory. Its future work is challenged to find the influences of the several levels of research and analysis proposed by a socio-ecological model. Despite the post-feminist exhaustion seen in some quarters, the impact of patriarchy on the field of public relations means that there is still much to be done to achieve the professional reputation that the public relations industry seeks as a contributor to public and societal interests.

References

Aldoory, L. (2001). The standard white woman in public relations. In E. L. Toth & L. Aldoory (Eds.), *The gender challenge to media: Diverse voices from the field* (pp. 105–149). Hampton Press.

Aldoory, L. (2003). The empowerment of feminist scholarship and the building of a feminist paradigm in public relations. *Communication Yearbook, 27*, 221–255.

Aldoory, L. (2005). A (re)conceived feminist paradigm for public relations: A case for substantial improvement. *Journal of Communication, 55*, 668–684.

Aldoory, L., Jiang, H., Toth, E. L., & Sha, B.-L. (2008). Is it still just a women's issue? A study of work-life balance among men and women in public relations. *Public Relations Journal, 2*(4), 1–20.

Aldoory, L., & Toth, E. L. (2002). Gendered discrepancies in a gendered profession: A developing theory for public relations. *Journal of Public Relations Research, 14*, 103–126.

Aldoory, L., & Toth, E. L. (2021). *The future of feminism in public relations and strategic communication: A socio-ecological model of influences*. Rowman & Littlefield.

Aldoory, L., Toth, E. L., & Ma, L. (2021). Gender in US strategic communication research and practice: Confronting master narratives. In E. H. Botan (Ed.), *The handbook of strategic communication* (pp. 292–305). John Wiley & Sons, Inc.

Applebaum, L., Walton, E., & Southerland, E. (2015). *An examination of factors affecting the success of underrepresented groups in the public relations profession.* The City College of New York.

Arenstein, S. (2019, January 16). PR News' top women in PR speak: Onus on us and industry to close leadership gap. *PR News.* Retrieved July 3, 2020, from www. prnewsonline.com/women-Top+Women+in+PR-leadership

Arthur W. Page Center. (2021). *Public relations ethics.* Retrieved February 18, 2021, from www.pagecentertraining.psu.edu/public-relations-ethics/introduction-to-diversity-and-public-relations/lesson-2-how-to-reach-diverse-stakeholders/social-interpretive-approach/

Bridgen, L. (2011). Emotional labour and the pursuit of the personal brand: Public relations Practitioners' use of social media. *Journal of Media Practice, 12,* 61–76.

Caldera, A. (2020). Challenging capitalistic exploitation: A Black feminist/womanist commentary on work and self-care. *Feminist Studies, 46,* 707–716.

Center for the Study of Social Policy. (2019, September). *Key equity terms & concepts: A glossary for shared understanding.* Center for Study of Social Policy. https://cssp.org/wp-content/uploads/2019/09/Key-Equity-Terms-and-Concepts-vol1.pdf

Ciszek, E. (2018). Queering PR: Directions in theory and research for public relations scholarship. *Journal of Public Relations Research, 30,* 134–145.

Cline, C. G., Toth, E. L., Turk, J. V., Walters, L. M., Johnson, N., & Smith, H. (1986). *The velvet ghetto: The impact of the increasing percentage of women in public relations and business communication.* IABC Foundation.

Creedon, P. J. (1993). Acknowledging the infrasystem: A critical feminist analysis of systems theory. *Public Relations Review, 19,* 157–166.

Crenshaw, K. (1989). Demarginalizing the intersection of race and sex: A Black feminist critique of antidiscrimination doctrine, feminist theory and antiracist politics. *University of Chicago Legal Forum, 1989*(1), Article 8. https://chicagounbound.uchicago.edu/uclf/vol1989/iss1/8/

Daymon, C., & Demetrious, K. (2014). Introduction. Gender and public relations: Making meaning, challenging assumptions. In C. Daymon & K. Demetrious (Eds.), *Gender and public relations: Critical perspectives on voice, image and identity* (p. 3). Routledge.

Delgado, R., & Stefancic, J. (2001). *Critical race theory: An introduction.* New York University Press.

Dill, B. T., & Kohlman, M. H. (2012). Intersectionality: A transformative paradigm in feminist theory and social justice. In *Handbook of feminist research: Theory and praxis* (2nd ed., pp. 154–174). Sage.

Dozier, D. M., & Lauzen, M. M. (2000). Liberating the intellectual domain from the practice: Public relations, activism, and the role of the scholar. *Journal of Public Relations Research, 12*(1), 3–22.

Dozier, D. M., Place, K., Vardeman, J., Sisco, H. F., & Sha, B.-L. (2019, Winter). A longitudinal analysis of the gender income gap in public relations in the U.S. 1979–2014. *Media Report to Women, 47*(1), 12–19.

DuBois, W. E. B. (1903). *The soul of Black folk: Essays and sketches.* A. C. McClug & Co.

Dubrowski, M., McCorkindale, T., & Rickert, R. (2019). *Mind the gap: Women's leadership in public relations.* https://instituteforpr.org/mind-the-gap-womens-leadership-in-public-relations/

Dutta, M. J. (2009). On Spivak: Theorizing resistance—applying Gaytri Chakravorty Spivak in public relations. In Ø. Ihlen, B. van Ruler, & M. Fredriksson (Eds.), *Public relations and social theory* (pp. 278–300). Routledge.

Edwards, L. (2013). Institutional racism in culture production: The case of public relations. *Popular Communication, 11,* 242–256.

Edwards, L. (2014). Discourse, credentialism and occupational closure in the communication industries: The case of public relations in the UK. *European Journal of Communication, 29*, 319–334.

Edwards, L., & Munshi, D. (Eds.). (2011). Race in/and public relations [Special issue]. *Journal of Public Relations Research, 23*(4).

Ferguson, D. P., Wallace, J. D., & Chandler, R. C. (2018). Hierarchical consistency of strategies in image repair theory: PR practitioners' perceptions of the effective and preferred crisis communication strategies. *Journal of Public Relations Research, 30*(5–6), 251–272.

Fitch, K. (2016). Feminism and public relations. In J. L'Etang, D. McKie, N. Snow, & J. Xifra (Eds.), *The Routledge handbook of critical public relations* (pp. 54–63). New York University Press.

Fitch, K., James, M., & Motion, J. (2016). Talking back: Reflecting on feminism, public relations and research. *Public Relations Review, 42*, 279–287.

Fitch, K., & Third, A. (2010). Working girls: Revisiting the gendering of public relations. *Prism, 7*(4), 1–13.

Ford, R., & Brown, C. (2015). *State of the PR industry: Defining and delivering on the promise of diversity*. White paper of the National Black Public Relations Society, Inc. http://nbprs.org/wp-content/uploads/2017/11/NBPRS-State-of-the-PR-Industry-White-Paper-FINAL.pdf

Gamson, J. (2003). Reflections on queer theory and communication. *Journal of Homosexuality, 45*, 385–389.

Golombisky, K. (2015). Renewing the commitments of feminist public relations theory from Velvet Ghetto to social justice. *Journal of Public Relations Research, 27*, 389–415.

Grunig, J. E., & Hunt, T. (1984). *Managing public relations* (p. 6). Holt.

Grunig, L. A. (Ed.).(1988). Women in public relations (Special issue). *Public Relations Review, 14*(3).

Grunig, L. A., Grunig, J. E., & Dozier, D. M. (2002). *Excellent public relations and effective organizations: A study of communication management in three countries*. Lawrence Erlbaum Associates.

Grunig, L. A., Toth, E. L., & Hon, L. (2000). Feminist values in public relations. *Journal of Public Relations Research, 12*(1), 49–681.

Grunig, L. A., Toth, E. L., & Hon, L. (2001). *Women in public relations: How gender influences practice*. Guilford Press.

Hon, L. C. (1995). Toward a feminist theory of public relations. *Journal of Public Relations Research, 7*, 27–88.

Jin, Y., Sha, B.-L., Shen, H., & Jiang, H. (2014). Tuning in to the rhythm: The role of coping in strategic management of work-life conflicts in the public relations profession. *Public Relations Review, 40*, 69–78.

Lawniczak, R. (2009). Re-examining the economic roots of public relations. *Public Relations Review, 35*, 346–352.

L'Etang, J. (2015). "It's always been a sexless trade"; "It's clean work", "There's very little velvet curtain". *Journal of Communication Management, 19*, 354–370.

Logan, N. (2011). The white leader prototype: A critical analysis of race in public relations. *Journal of Public Relations Research, 23*(4), 442–457.

Logan, N. (2021). A theory of corporate responsibility to race (CRR): Communication and racial justice in public relations. *Journal of Public Relations Research, 33*(1), 6–22.

Looft, R. (2017). #girlgaze: Photography, fourth wave feminism, and social media advocacy. *Journal of Media and Cultural Studies, 31*, 892–902.

McDonald, J. (2015). Organizational communication meets queer theory: Theorizing relations of "difference" differently. *Communication Theory, 25*, 310–329.

Meng, J., & Neill, M. S. (2021). *PR women with influence: Breaking the ethical and leadership challenges.* Peter Lang.

Nachescu, V. (2009). Radical feminism and the nation. *Journal of the Study of Radicalism, 3*, 29–59.

O'Neil, J. (2003). An analysis of the relationships among structure, influence, and gender: Helping to build a feminist theory of public relations. *Journal of Public Relations Research, 15*, 151–179.

Pal, M., & Dutta, M. J. (2008). Public relations in a global context: The relevance of critical modernism as a theoretical lens. *Journal of Public Relations Research, 20*(2), 159–179.

Parker, P. S. (2002). Negotiating identity in raced and gendered workplace interactions: The use of strategic communication by African American women senior executives within dominant culture organizations. *Communication Quarterly, 50*, 251–268.

Place, K., & Vardeman-Winter, J. (2015). *Status report: Public relations research 2005–2015.* Lillian Lodge Kopenhaver Center for the Advancement of Women in Communication, Florida International University.

Pompper, D. (2005). "Difference" in public relations research: A case for introducing critical race theory. *Journal of Public Relations Research, 17*, 139–169.

Pompper, D. (2007). The gender-ethnicity construct in public relations organizations: Using feminist standpoint theory to discover Latinas' realities. *Howard Journal of Communication, 18*, 291–311.

Rakow, L. F. (1989). From the feminization of public relations to the promise of feminism. In E. L. Toth & C. G. Cline (Eds.), *Beyond the velvet ghetto* (pp. 298–298). IABC Foundation.

Rakow, L. F., & Nastasia, D. I. (2009). On Dorothy E. Smith: Public relations and feminist theory at the crossroads. In O. Ihlen & M. Fredriksson (Eds.), *Public relations and social theory* (pp. 252–277). Routledge.

Rakow, L. F., & Wackwitz, L. A. (Eds.). (2004). *Feminist communication theory: Selections in context.* Sage.

Reskin, B. F., & Roos, P. A. (1990). *Job queues, gender queues.* Temple University Press.

Sha, B.-L. (2006). Cultural identity in the segmentation of publics: An emerging theory of intercultural public relations. *Journal of Public Relations Research, 18*, 45–65.

Sommerfeldt, E. J., & Kent, M. L. (2020). Public relations as "dirty work": Disconfirmation, cognitive dissonance, and emotional labor among public relations professors. *Public Relations Review, 46*, 1–9.

Steeves, L. H. (1987). Feminist theories and media studies. *Critical Studies in Mass Communication, 4*, 95–135.

Strong, F. (2019). PR salary 2019: What do public relations salary ranges look like? *Sword and the Script.* Retrieved February 18, 2021, from www.swordandthescript.com/2019/04/public-relations-salary-2019/

Tindall, N. T. J., & Waters, R. D. (2012). Coming out to tell out stories: Using queer theory to understand the career experiences of gay men in public relations. *Journal of Public Relations Research, 24*, 451–475.

Tindall, N. T. J., & Waters, R. D. (Eds.). (2013). *Coming out of the closet: Exploring LGBT Issues in strategic communication with theory and research.* Peter Lang.

Topic, M., Cunha, J. M., Reigstad, A., Jelen-Sanchez, A., & Moreno, A. (2020). Women in public relations (1982–2019). *Journal of Communication Management, 24*, 391–407.

Toth, E. L., & Aldoory, L. (2021). Women in public relations: A feminist perspective. In C. Valentini (Ed.), *Public relations: Handbooks of communication science* (pp. 46–60). De Gruyer Mouton.

Toth, E. L., & Cline, C. G. (Eds.). (1989). *Beyond the velvet ghetto*. IABC Research Foundation.

Trethewey, A. (2001). Reproducing and resisting the master narrative of decline: Midlife professional women's experiences of aging. *Management Communication Quarterly, 15*, 183–226.

Van Zoonen, L. (1994). *Feminist media studies*. Sage.

Vardeman-Winter, J. (2011). Confronting whiteness in public relations campaigns and research with women. *Journal of Public Relations Research, 23*, 412–441.

Vardeman-Winter, J., Jiang, H., & Tindall, N. T. J. (2013). Information-seeking outcomes of representational, structural, and political intersectionality among health media consumers. *Journal of Applied Communication Research, 41*, 389–411.

Vardeman-Winter, J., & Place, K. R. (2017). Still a lily-white field of women: The state of workforce diversity in public relations practice and research. *Public Relations Review, 43*, 326–336.

Vardeman-Winter, J., & Tindall, N. (2010). Toward an intersectional theory of public relations. In R. L. Heath (Ed.), *Handbook of public relations* (2nd ed., pp. 223–235). Sage.

Waymer, D., & Dyson, O. (2011). The journey into an unfamiliar and uncomfortable territory: Exploring the role and approaches of race in PR education. *Journal of Public Relations Research, 23*, 458–477.

Wright, D. K., Grunig, L. A., Springston, J. K., & Toth, E. L. (1991). *Under the glass ceiling: An analysis of gender issues in American public relations* (PRSA Foundation Monographs Series, Vol. 1, No. 2). PRSA Foundation.

Yep, G. A., Lovass, K. E., & Elia, J. P. (2003). Introduction: Queering communication: Starting the conversation. In G. A. Yet, K. E. Lovaas, & J. P. Elia (Eds.), *Queer theory and communication: From disciplining queers to queering the discipline(s)* (pp. 1–10). Routledge.

17 Critical Race Theory, Identity, and Public Relations

Nneka Logan

Introduction

In 1903, preeminent African American sociologist W.E.B. Du Bois urged people to take seriously the proposition that "the problem of the twentieth century is the problem of the color-line—the relation of the darker to the lighter races of men in Asia and Africa, in America and in the islands of the sea" (1995, p. 54). Almost a hundred years later, renowned Jamaican-British sociologist Stuart Hall (1993) advised, "The capacity to *live with difference* is, in my view, the coming question of the twenty-first century" (p. 361). This chapter begins with these observations because both are still problematically relevant in society and hold significant implications for public relations theory and practice.

To remain relevant in an ever-changing society marked by increasing diversity and struggles over inclusion and exclusion, equity and inequity, public relations needs to engage with the complexities of race and identity that shape the experiences of stakeholders, publics, and organizations. Developing, contextualizing, and analyzing theory for its explanatory and practical value presents a productive avenue to achieve that goal. Theory helps people to see, interpret, and make sense of phenomena in their environment (Littlejohn et al., 2017). This chapter employs critical race theory (CRT) as a guiding framework to examine and expand theoretical connections between race and identity as well as their implications for public relations theory. CRT is an important theoretical consideration for public relations because it encourages a raw and lucid assessment of the symbolic and material realities that are associated with racial identities and that constitute race relations.

Race and identity are central to the human experience, which makes them central to public relations although the field has not always fully valued

Author Note

Nneka Logan https://orcid.org/0000-0001-6648-1925

Correspondence concerning this chapter should be addressed to Nneka Logan, Virginia Tech, Shanks Hall (0311), Blacksburg, VA 24060. Email: nlogan@vt.edu

DOI: 10.4324/9781003141396-20

their importance (see Curtin & Gaither, 2005; Munshi & Edwards, 2011). For example, several volumes dedicated to public relations theory did not feature a single chapter that explicitly focused on race or identity (Botan & Hazleton, 1989, 2006; Brunner, 2019), though these subjects may have been tangentially addressed. Formally including race and identity in *Public Relations Theory III* represents an important shift in the way the discipline recognizes the significance of race and identity to public relations, to society, and to the everyday, lived experience of human beings. The inclusion of this chapter in this volume testifies to the extent that critical cultural scholarship has raised the prominence of race and identity as key public relations concerns.

The purpose of this chapter is to illustrate how CRT can encourage theoretical development in public relations within the contexts of race and identity. The first section of the chapter discusses race in terms of the color line and describes race research in public relations. The second section focuses on identity research in public relations, describing its connections to race and exploring how public relations scholars have addressed racial and ethnic identity. The first two sections lay the foundation for the third section, which explicates CRT and its application in public relations. Future directions for public relations research are offered in the fourth section. The chapter concludes by suggesting that public relations has a role to play in eradicating the color line and helping society to live successfully with its differences.

Race and Rendering the Color Line

Historically, the color line has defined how society deals with difference, demarcating racial and ethnic identity as well as designating the power, privilege, and oppression associated with individual and collective identities. Even today, it remains a formidable hurdle to overcome. One reason the color line has endured is the lasting influence of those who helped to establish it.

As one example, for leading Enlightenment thinker Immanuel Kant, skin color was among the most conspicuous forms of human difference; he used it to define race and linked it to intellectual capacity, moral aptitude, and other attributes (Bernasconi, 2001). Kant categorized human beings by skin color, ranking those who looked like him—meaning white—as superior to others, particularly those with darker skin. He once assessed, "This fellow was quite black from head to foot, a clear proof that what he said was stupid" (as cited in West, 1999, p. 84). Such an assessment was not an anomaly for Kant, who also explained:

> The Negroes of Africa have by nature no feeling that rises above the trifling. Mr. Hume challenges anyone to cite a single example in which a Negro has shown talents, and assert that among the hundreds of thousands of blacks who are transported elsewhere from their countries,

although many of them have been set free, still not a single one was ever found who presented anything great in art or science or any other praise-worthy quality, even though among the whites some continually rise aloft from the lowest rabble, and through superior gifts earn respect in the world. So fundamental is the difference between these two races of man, and it appears to be as great in regard to mental capacities as in color.

(as cited in Farr, 2004, p. 147)

Kant, Hume, and other Enlightenment philosophers propagated racist beliefs as scientific fact (Farr, 2004) and influenced the beliefs of countless others—scholars and laypersons alike—for generations to follow. This history is not offered to blame the Enlightenment for racism. It is intended to illustrate how ideologies of race were historically established, helped to create the color line, and functioned to inculcate a racial hierarchy of humanity that situated white people at the top.

The color line served several ideological functions. It suggested that people who were on the wrong side of it (e.g. *Plessy v. Ferguson*, 1896) did not deserve the protections or promises of America's foundational principles (cf. Morey, 2021; Myrdal, 1944) such as liberty, equality, freedom, and justice for all (Library of Congress, n.d.). In doing so, the color line helped to normalize and justify America's betrayal of those principles, enabling the nation to preach a rhetoric of equal opportunity while practicing inequality based on race. As a conduit of racism, and particularly anti-black racism, the color line served as a primary basis for white identity formation by providing an "illusion of unity" (Crenshaw, 1995, p. 113) against a darker "other" that served as inspiration for the social construction of a white ideal image.

Kimberlé Crenshaw (1995) invoked Derrida's (1978) notion of *différance*, which theorized identity in terms of oppositions, to explicate white racial identity formation. From a Derridean perspective, identity has no inherent essence. Rather, it is structured by and emerges from an economy of differences whereby a subject identifies itself not primarily through the expression of any natural or core essence but by how it differs from others that the subject encounters (Derrida, 1978). Applying Derrida's framework, Crenshaw (1995) described the process of white identity formation, writing:

> The establishment of an Other creates a bond, a burgeoning common identity of all non-stigmatized parties—whose identity and interests are defined in opposition to the other. . . . Racist ideology replicates this pattern of arranging oppositional categories in a hierarchical order; historically, whites have represented the dominant element in the antinomy, while blacks came to be seen as separate and subordinate.
>
> (p. 113)

To illustrate her point that racial identities were socially constructed in oppositional terms, Crenshaw (1995) juxtaposed popular beliefs about white people against those of black people. She illustrated how white people were considered industrious, intelligent, moral, and knowledgeable, while black people were believed to be lazy, unintelligent, immoral, and ignorant.

Within this context, white identity has no intrinsic characteristics other than its opposition to a socially constructed negative black image. These dynamics are at play in the social and legal construction of Asian Americans as perpetual foreigners (Chang, 1993; Gee, 1998). The racialized oppositions laid out by Crenshaw (1995) can be understood as extensions of Enlightenment racism that reproduce the color line in various contexts.

In public relations, for example, the overwhelming majority of the field—more than 80%—identified as white in 2020; approximately 14% as Hispanic or Latino; approximately 11% as black; and approximately 3% as Asian (United States Bureau of Labor Statistics, n.d.). Scholarship about race and ethnicity in public relations has made several key contributions. It has heightened awareness of the connection between race, ethnicity, and identity, outlined differences in the experiences of white and non-white members of the field and demonstrated the persistence of the color line. For example, scholars have described public relations as a "lily white field of women" (Vardeman-Winter & Place, 2017). Scholars have also explored the lack of racial diversity among public relations practitioners as well as the perceptions of minority practitioners (Abeyta & Hackett, 2002; Kern-Foxworth, 1989; Kern-Foxworth et al., 1994; Lee et al., 2021; Len-Ríos, 1998; Pompper, 2004, 2007; Qiu & Muturi, 2016; Tindall, 2009a; Wallington, 2020; Zerbinos & Clanton, 1993). Research has also shown that practitioners who do not embody the white ideal image or conform to heteronormativity are often marginalized (Logan & Ciszek, 2022). Research has also explored how race effects perceived credibility (Hong & Len Ríos, 2015). Additionally, race-related public relations scholarship has addressed the perspectives of educators and students of color as well (Brown et al., 2011; Tindall, 2009b; Waymer & Dyson, 2011) and noted the fluidity of racial identity (Xifra & McKie, 2011), with fluidity serving as an indication of how arbitrarily yet persistently the color line marginalizes racial identities at different periods in history and across contexts.

Considering Identity

As the public relations field has increasingly recognized the need to become more racially and ethnically diverse, equitable, and inclusive, research concerning identity has grown in importance. Racial identity is defined as "the sense of a group or collective identity based on one's *perception* that he or she shares a common racial heritage with a particular racial group" (Helms, 1990, p. 3). Ethnic identity has been organized around resistance to oppression but is commonly defined through origin or nationality, shared history, language, values, and beliefs (cf. Hall, 2005, 2019). Personal or individual identities are conceptualized as individualized attributes or personal traits

(Turner, 1982), while social identity describes how ingroups and outgroups form in terms of racial, ethnic, gender, sexual orientation, or ability characteristics (e.g. Pompper, 2014b). Although identities are described in terms of particular characteristics, they are never fixed, meaning permanent or stable. They are always in the process of becoming, and they remain open to contestation and constitution, which is why identities are often the site of ideological, social, and political struggle over who gets to create and define them (Hall, 2005, 2019).

In capitalist societies, it is common for identity to be constituted through culture and consumption (Deleuze & Guattari, 1983). As Borchers and Hundley (2018) have explained,

> Cultural texts encourage identification on the part of the audience member. If we look at advertisements for expensive cars, elegant homes, and designer clothing, these advertisements encourage us to identify with the people pictured in the ads. In doing so, we construct an identity for ourselves based on these images. Our feelings of who we are become deeply influenced by how we identify with images or symbols in our culture.
>
> (p. 300)

The ways that identity forms through cultural texts (e.g., media representations) are connected to processes of capitalism and consumerism and have been explored by public relations scholars.

For example, Marilyn Kern-Foxworth's (1994) important early work on the role of racial identity in advertising examined racially coded turn-of-the-century product advertisements such as Aunt Jemima, Rastus, and Uncle Ben's. She showed how these forms of corporate discourse ideologically functioned to return black people to a slave-like, subservient status—an image that is familiar and comforting to some people but disconcerting and demeaning to others.

Lambert (2017) also explored the relationship between media texts and racial identity. Her study of *Scandal*—one of a few network television shows to feature a black woman as the lead character—used representational intersectionality (Crenshaw, 1991) to reveal how the show attempted to promote positive images of black women but ultimately deprioritized racial identity and drew upon fantasies of a post-racial society. The disempowering racial tropes and unrealistic portrayals of the public relations practice exposed through Lambert's analysis demonstrated how representations of race and identity—both of individuals and of the public relations profession—continue to be problematic and ripe for ongoing scholarly inquiry.

Logan and Ciszek's (2022) study of transgender communicators of color found that queer people of color engaged in public relations practices to counter negative, stereotypical media and cultural representations that stigmatized their identities, threatening their safety and survival. In sum, public relations studies that have addressed the ways in which identity and race are represented have revealed that cultural texts such as campaigns, advertisements, television shows, and other forms of corporate discourse produce racial identities that often reproduce a racial status quo that alienates many people. Several studies show how the intersection of race, identity, and media representation have come together to find expression in public relations.

How individuals and groups are portrayed in media and cultural texts can influence the development and expression of their avowed identities, which describes how individuals are self-directed in defining and actualizing themselves (Sha & Ford, 2007). In addition to affecting an individual's avowed identity, media and cultural texts can influence ascribed identities, that is, identity characteristics that some people assign to others based on their perception of the others' appearance, character, and similar personal expressions (Sha & Ford, 2007). Thus, media and cultural texts can be harmful when they support the ascription of identities that counter an individual's avowed identity and reinforce offensive or negative stereotypes. On the other hand, cultural representations articulated through media texts can be affirming when their ascriptions align with and uplift avowed identities. When providing counsel, strategy, or messaging, public relations scholars and practitioners should be aware of the potential impact of media and cultural texts, as well as various forms of corporate discourse, on stakeholders and publics.

Public relations scholars have also advanced identity research by theorizing the relationship between communication, culture, and identity. For example, Curtin and Gaither (2005) wrote, "Communication is the means by which individuals and groups negotiate, co-create, reinforce, and challenge cultural identity" (p. 69) as they also navigate culture, power, and difference in identity contexts. Sha (2006) extended the theorization of cultural identity, defining it in terms of race and ethnicity, further exploring how cultural identities emerge in and through communication contexts, and arguing that identity is produced through the "enactment of cultural communications" (Sha et al., 2012, p. 68). More recently, Ni et al. (2018) explored the significance of racio-ethnic identity on Indian immigrant professionals in the United States, finding that the intersection of race, ethnicity, and immigrant status can significantly impact how these professionals experience and express a sense of belonging within American organizations. Using the concept of intercultural identity, in which "identity spans at least two countries as cultural groups" (Ni et al., 2018, p. 148), their study elucidated the complexity associated with operating in the postmodern world of work, where people may perform their professions across countries and cultures and encounter various identities as they also are subjected to various perceptions of their own identities.

The dynamics of inclusion and exclusion based on differences of race and identity are addressed in CRT. The theory directs sharp attention to the historical constitution of race and racism and connects history to contemporary race relations to show how racial inequity is reproduced structurally and systematically over time through society's institutions, organizations, policies, and processes. As a theoretical framework, CRT moves race from the periphery to center, rendering it a vital analytical lens for understanding society and its inner workings.

Critical Race Theory in Public Relations

Public relations can benefit from the generation and application of theory that confronts the persistence of the color line and facilitates its demise in all its various forms. Learning to live with difference is imperative for public relations if the field is to counsel as well as lead others to do so. A particularly important moment of theoretical development in public relations race research was the introduction of CRT by Donnalyn Pompper in 2005. Her article challenged dominant assumptions of public relations as a colorblind, race-neutral field merely focused on building mutually beneficial relationships between organizations and publics. It expanded thinking about race in public relations to focus on the ways in which the field contributed to the social construction of race and reproduced a racial status quo that tended to privilege whites over non-whites. Calling attention to racial inequality within the field, Pompper (2005) urged public relations to take a more well-rounded, introspective appraisal of itself and make changes. Ultimately, Pompper's introduction of CRT led to several significant theoretical developments in public relations.

Edwards (2010), for example, critiqued the lack of racial minorities practicing public relations and explained how the profession became marked by its whiteness. Relating the contemporary state of the field to its historical evolution and drawing connections between the theoretical concept of habitus (Bourdieu, 1990) and CRT (Crenshaw et al., 1995), Edwards argued that public relations emerged at a time when—by law or custom—blacks and other people of color were denied entry into certain occupations such as public relations. She also explained that in active sites of early public relations practice—namely, the United States and the United Kingdom—practitioners primarily focused on serving the needs of political and economic elites such as government and industry—the same institutions that often fostered and benefitted from racial discrimination. Collectively, these circumstances laid the foundation for whiteness to become a public relations norm for generations to come. Edwards (2012) used CRT to expand theoretical development of public relations by posing several CRT-inspired questions directed at imagining what the field might look like if race was the central focus. Consistent with a CRT approach, Edwards' work acknowledged the significance of history as it also centered race through its examinations of how slavery, imperialism, and conquest influenced the evolution of public relations.

To help explain the lack of racial minorities at leadership levels in public relations, Logan (2011) introduced the concept of the White Leader Prototype, which also connected current patterns to the impact of historical, systemic racial oppression as articulated through chattel slavery, Jim Crow, and widespread, ongoing racial discrimination. Continuing an earlier push for equitable change, Pompper (2014a) united CRT with intersectionality to demonstrate how power imbalances shaped the experiences of African American, Asian American, Caucasian/white, and Latino/a practitioners as well as fueled workplace inequality.

Helping to expand CRT public relations research beyond the scope of professional experiences, Logan (2016) offered a theoretical contribution by showing how CRT could be used to analyze public relations campaigns though her analysis of the Starbucks Race Together campaign. Although the campaign's efficacy has been debated (Novak & Richmond, 2019), Logan found that the campaign displayed fundamental CRT principles by acknowledging systemic and structural racism in the U.S., amplifying the voices and experiences of racial minorities and making race the central focus of the campaign.

Expanding CRT into several public relations directions, Waymer and Heath (2016) used CRT to analyze organizational messages from the National Football League during a racism crisis; to assess messages from a major corporation that downplayed the moral imperative of diversity, equity, and inclusion (DEI) in favor of upholding the business case rationale (that primarily values DEI as a conduit to advance organizational goals); and to describe how black neighborhoods are victimized by environmental racism. Their work highlighted the theoretical dexterity of CRT and the breadth of public relations situations to which it can be applied.

Most recently, CRT has been employed to develop a public relations theory of race, the Corporate Responsibility to Race (CRR) (Logan, 2021a). CRR emanated from empirical observations of how some corporations were communicating about race. It holds that:

- Corporations are organizational forms that have emerged through processes of racism and racialization.
- Corporations have directly and indirectly perpetuated—and benefited from—racial discrimination and oppression, which has contributed to racial strife and social instability.
- Corporations have a responsibility to support racial justice by communicating in ways that improve race relations (Logan, 2021a, p. 8).

Ultimately, CRR "contributes to theory building in public relations by providing a new theoretical perspective that enables us to more readily identify, understand, contextualize, and analyze corporate communications that address race relations" (Logan, 2021a, p. 1). By incorporating CRT, CRR also outlines a pathway for public relations to participate in the project of achieving racial justice.

CRT emerged during the 1970s and 1980s among legal scholars who began to question how and why the law—though framed as colorblind and objective—functioned in ways that reproduced white racial power while disempowering and discriminating against black people. Since its emergence, CRT has been used to analyze a variety of racialized dynamics adversely affecting people of many different racial and ethnic identities. It has also been applied in several other disciplines such as education (Ladson-Billings & Tate, 1995), psychology (Yoo et al., 2021), business (Parker & Grimes, 2009), rhetorical studies (Martinez, 2020; Olmsted, 1998), marketing (Poole et al., 2021), and public relations to critique "how the social construction of race and institutionalized racism perpetuate a racial caste system that relegates people of color to the bottom tiers" (George, 2021, para. 2).

CRT Principles

CRT has several core principles that guide its application as a theoretical framework or analytical lens. Some of these are provided here and can be explored in more comprehensive CRT works (see Crenshaw et al., 1995; Delgado & Stefancic, 2012, 2013; Harris, 1995).

- Racism is an everyday part of life in America.
- Although overt, individual acts of racism (e.g., hanging a noose in the workplace) are harmful, the ways that racism is systematically and structurally embedded into society's institutions and organizations (e.g., redlining in real estate) is especially harmful. Systematic and structural racism are particularly harmful because they tend to operate invisibly as the taken-for-granted norm, stealthily sustaining racial inequity and injustice.
- The epistemic violence done to communities of color by official discourses such as philosophy, history, law, and education should be countered with the experiences, voices, and knowledges of people of color because their perspectives help to provide a fuller, fairer account of life in the United States.
- CRT acknowledges that the past lives in the present and shapes the future. This means that the racial problems of today cannot be solved without first acknowledging how the present state came to be. Similarly, appraisals of the past should be honest so that they can appropriately inform the solutions pursued to address today's problems.
- Whiteness, as both property and privilege, accrues a plethora of advantages for those who can fit within that racial category. CRT reveals those racialized advantages and shows how they can constitute disadvantage for those who are non-white. In other words, CRT makes the normally hidden manifestations of whiteness visible.
- Although CRT centers race, it also acknowledges the multifaceted and complex nature of human identity through its attention to intersectionality and the ways in which race, class, gender, ability, and so on collectively influence individual and group identities.

These points broadly describe the fundamental assumptions of CRT.

CRT and Society

In 2020, backlash against CRT led to the theory being banned in some states (Ray & Gibbons, 2021). Most criticisms of CRT are based on three broad assertions: that CRT teaches that white people are racist, that the theory is divisive, and that it undermines traditional American values (Asare, 2021; Baragona, 2021; Heritage Foundation, n.d.). CRT scholars reject such assertions. CRT does not teach hate. Similarly, CRT does not undermine traditional American values. It asks America to live up to those values and apply them equally to its populace regardless of race. While critics favor a colorblind approach that downplays the importance of race in America's past and present, CRT points out that race has played—and continues to play—a fundamental organizing role in American society.

One way to understand CRT is as a response to the observations by W.E.B. Du Bois and Stuart Hall that began this chapter. CRT is a reaction to the persistence and prevalence of the color line and to society's difficulties in dealing with its differences. CRT acknowledges both that progress has been made and that the instruments of racial progress have faced significant and consistent resistance. CRT refuses to ignore that since chattel slavery was abolished, almost every single effort toward racial equality in America has been met with staunch opposition—from reconstruction (Du Bois, 1995), to desegregation (Bell, 1995b), to the Civil Rights Movement (Bell, 1995a), to affirmative action (Freeman, 1995), to DEI (Logan, 2021b; Mac Donald, 2018), and to today's Black Lives Matter movement (Ciszek & Logan, 2018).

CRT acknowledges that everyone wants to be valued and included. However, it illuminates the importance of valuing, including, and amplifying the voices, experiences, and knowledges of those who have been historically excluded. CRT presents an opportunity to have important conversations about race and identity. The theory is like a mirror with magnification power held up to society's face. CRT exposes what is hidden from plain view, forcing us to see our blemished record on race and challenging us to improve for the future. Incorporating the theoretical tenants of CRT has allowed public relations scholars to direct necessary attention to both the shortcomings and the promise of the field; that is, how public relations has both contributed to racial inequity as well as to how it can contribute to a more racially equitable and just society.

This overview of CRT in public relations illustrates a variety of ways that CRT can be employed to theoretically invigorate the field. CRT allows scholars to better understand and explicate how the history of race relations affects the present state of public relations. CRT encourages scholars to take seriously the inclusion of marginalized voices to continually analyze, evaluate, and challenge the ontological and epistemological assumptions of the field. CRT also functions heuristically, expanding the field's perspectives on race and identity while it also elucidates relevant axiological perspectives and their implications for race in public relations and in society. Ultimately, CRT helps to push the theoretical boundaries of public relations thought in provocative and innovative directions by posing new questions and introducing new ideas and approaches to solving some of the age-old problems associated with race, identity, and difference.

Future Directions

As extant research shows, CRT has inspired substantive theory building in public relations, yet other promising avenues for theory development at the nexus of public relations, race, and identity await exploration. Three directions will be addressed in this section: corporate social responsibility (CSR), intersectionality, and race and identity.

CRT and Corporate Social Responsibility

Ron Pearson's (1989) account of the importance of business ethics and social responsibility in communication appeared in *Public Relations Theory I* and helped to open the door for ongoing CSR and public relations scholarship. This line of thinking continued in *Public Relations II* with Pratt's (2006) exploration of CSR in Africa, and it gained strength from Waymer's (2010) research that connected CSR to race as a means to avoid crises and to illuminate the social significance of race to public relations. Building on previous CSR and public relations research, Logan's (2021a) CRR theory incorporated CRT to situate race as a corporate responsibility, with implications for public relations theory and practice. In doing so, CRR suggested a new direction for future theory development: addressing how and why organizations have a responsibility to support healthy race relations and what they can do to fulfill that responsibility. Theoretical frameworks that situate race as a corporate responsibility present a promising way to help dismantle the color line that makes it so challenging to live with differences of race, ethnicity, and other identity-related characteristics.

CRT and Intersectionality

Though not thoroughly explained in this chapter, intersectionality (Logan & Ciszek, 2022; Place, 2022; Pompper, 2014a; Vardeman & Sebesta, 2020; Vardeman-Winter & Tindall, 2010) is a fruitful avenue for theory-building in public relations. While CRT places race at the center, intersectionality recognizes that racial identity intersects with gender, sexuality, class, ability, and so on, creating an array of power dynamics that multiply the marginalization of individuals who belong to more than one oppressed group. In more concrete terms, for example, the discrimination and resulting harms faced by black women may be greater than those faced by either white women or black men because of the historical privileges granted to white women and black men. While white women can rely on the historical privilege of whiteness and black men can rely on the gender privilege historically bestowed upon men, black women and other women of color have comparatively little historical privilege, leaving them particularly vulnerable (Crenshaw, 1989) in a society still largely defined by racial and gender advantages as well as heteronormativity. Uniting CRT with intersectionality positions scholars to better see the nuances associated with race and identity, allowing them to expand their theorization of stakeholders, publics, and organizations as they also work to dismantle structures and systems of oppression that continue to disadvantage those who have not fit public relations' traditional norms (e.g., Edwards, 2010).

CRT, Race, and Identity

There are many avenues available to pursue ongoing theoretical development at the nexus of CRT, race, and identity. Scholars can build on extant identity research (e.g., Curtin & Gaither, 2005; Pompper, 2014b; Sha, 2006) to chart new directions. For example, Xu (2020) found that personal identities affect individuals' feelings of connection or disconnection to an organization; when organizations affirm stakeholder identities, those stakeholders are likely to view the organization as an ally and feel a deeper sense of belonging to the organization. Given the level and prevalence of alienation that some individuals and groups experience in the workplace (e.g., Edwards, 2015), identity research attuned to the lessons of CRT could help communication leaders and management position their organizations as authentic allies to vulnerable internal and external stakeholders and publics, which could be invaluable in times of political polarization and social strife.

In addition, not enough public relations research addresses indigenous groups (cf. Clark et al., 2021; Curtin, 2011; Schoenberger-Orgad & Toledano, 2011). Thus, there are opportunities to apply CRT to explore how public relations activities impact indigenous identities, how native people employ public relations strategies and tactics to advocate for, and empower, their communities, and to analyze the workplace experiences of indigenous practitioners as a means to build public relations identity theory. Ongoing theorization from the perspectives of Asian American and Pacific Islander, Hispanic and Latinx, African American, and other people marginalized by race and/or ethnicity with CRT is also a public relations imperative. This work may take the form of renewing the field's commitment to publics (Mundy, 2022) or tapping into its critical humanist theoretical dimensions (Ciszek et al., 2022).

It is also important to further theorize whiteness and white identity within public relations. As Hall (2005, 2019) pointed out, identity is not stable; it is always in flux. The historical constitution and conceptualization of white identity, dating back to the Enlightenment, is being questioned and challenged in unprecedented ways today. The tension between rein-forcing the status quo and leaving it behind to embrace a more inclusive future characterized by increasing diversity and equity seem more acute than ever before. Critical theories of race provide a pathway to understanding and to healing. Public relations scholarship in this vein (e.g., Edwards, 2010; Pompper, 2014a; Vardeman-Winter, 2011) can inspire future theoretical work that reveals how the social construction of whiteness plays out in myriad public relations contexts.

Conclusion

This chapter began with a discussion of how the color line has prevented society from effectively dealing with its differences. It suggested that a fundamental responsibility for public relations, grounded in critical race theory, is to dismantle the color line so that human difference no longer denotes or connotes human value. Through attention to the areas discussed in this chapter—such as acknowledging the significance of history, understanding identity formation processes, and comprehending CRT—public relations can participate in healthier social constructions of racial identities by building and applying theories that value human difference.

References

Abeyta, N., & Hackett, M. (2002). Perspectives of Hispanic PR practitioners. *Public Relations Quarterly*, 47(1), 27–30.

Asare, J. G. (2021, May 9). The war on critical race theory continues as some call it anti-white. *Forbes*. www.forbes.com/sites/janicegassam/2021/05/09/the-war-on-critical-race-theory-continues-as-some-call-it-anti-white/?sh=2aed873a73a7

Baragona, J. (2021, June 24). Newsmax host claims critical race theory will cause kids to "marry their mother". *The Daily Beast*. www.thedailybeast.com/newsmax-host-dick-morris-claims-critical-race-theory-will-cause-kids-to-marry-their-mother

Bell, D. (1995a). Racial realism. In K. Crenshaw, N. Gotanda, G. Peller, & K. Thomas (Eds.), *Critical race theory: The key writings that formed the movement* (pp. 302–312). The New Press.

Bell, D. (1995b). *Brown v. board of education* and the interest convergence dilemma. In K. Crenshaw, N. Gotanda, G. Peller, & K. Thomas (Eds.), *Critical race theory: The key writings that formed the movement* (pp. 20–28). The New Press.

Bernasconi, R. (2001). *Race*. Routledge Philosophy Companions.

Borchers, T., & Hundley, H. (2018). *Rhetorical theory: An introduction*. Waveland Press.

Botan, C., & Hazleton, V. (Eds.). (1989). *Public relations theory*. Lawrence Erlbaum Associates.

Botan, C., & Hazleton, V. (Eds.). (2006). *Public relations theory II*. Lawrence Erlbaum Associates.

Bourdieu, P. (1990). *The logic of practice*. Stanford University Press.

Brown, K. A., White, C., & Waymer, D. (2011). African-American students' perceptions of public relations education and practice: Implications for minority recruitment. *Public Relations Review*, 37(5), 522–529. https://doi.org/10.1016/j.pubrev.2011.09.017

Brunner, B. R. (Ed.). (2019). *Public relations theory: Application and understanding*. John Wiley & Sons.

Chang, R. S. (1993). Toward an Asian American legal scholarship: Critical race theory, post structuralism, and narrative space. *California Law Review, 81,* 1241.

Ciszek, E., & Logan, N. (2018). Challenging the dialogic promise: How Ben & Jerry's support for Black lives matter fosters dissensus on social media. *Journal of Public Relations Research, 30*(3), 115–127. https://doi.org/10.1080/1062726X.2018.1498342

Ciszek, E., Place, K. R., & Logan, N. (2022). Critical humanism for public relations: Harnessing the synergy of gender, race and sexuality research. *Public Relations Review, 48*(1), 102151.

Clark, T., Dodson, S., Guivarra, N., & Widders Hunt, Y. (2021). "We're not treated equally as Indigenous people or as women": The perspectives and experiences of Indigenous women in Australian public relations. *Public Relations Inquiry, 10*(2), 163–183.

Crenshaw, K. (1989). Demarginalizing the intersection of race and sex: A Black feminist critique of antidiscrimination doctrine, feminist theory, and antiracist politics. *University of Chicago Legal Forum, 1989*(8).

Crenshaw, K. (1991). Mapping the margins: Intersectionality, identity politics, and violence against women of color. *Stanford Law Review, 43*(6), 1241–1299.

Crenshaw, K. (1995). Race, reform, and retrenchment: Transformation and legitimation in antidiscrimination law. In K. Crenshaw, N. Gotanda, G. Peller, & K. Thomas (Eds.), *Critical race theory: The key writings that formed the movement* (pp. 103–122). The New Press.

Crenshaw, K., Gotanda, N., Peller, G., & Thomas, K. (Eds.). (1995). *Critical race theory: The key writings that formed the movement*. The New Press.

Curtin, P. A. (2011). Discourses of American Indian racial identity in the public relations materials of the Fred Harvey Company: 1902–1936. *Journal of Public Relations Research, 23*(4), 368–396. https://doi.org/10.1080/1062726X.2011.605972

Curtin, P. A., & Gaither, T. K. (2005). Privileging identity, difference, and power: The circuit of culture as a basis for public relations theory. *Journal of Public Relations Research, 17*(2), 91–115.

Deleuze, G., & Guattari, F. (1983). *Anti-Oedipus: Capitalism and schizophrenia* (R. Hurley, M. Seem, & H. R. Lane, Trans.). University of Minnesota Press (Original work published 1972).

Delgado, R., & Stefancic, J. (2012). *Critical race theory: An introduction*. New York University Press.

Delgado, R., & Stefancic, J. (Eds.). (2013). *Critical race theory: The cutting edge* (3rd ed.). Temple University Press.

Derrida, J. (1978). *Writing and difference*. The University of Chicago Press.

Du Bois, W. E. B. (1995). *The souls of Black folk*. Signet Classic.

Edwards, L. (2010). "Race" in public relations. In R. Heath (Ed.), *The Sage handbook of public relations* (pp. 205–221). Sage.

Edwards, L. (2012). Critical race theory and public relations. In D. Waymer (Ed.), *Culture, social class and race in public relations: Perspectives and applications* (pp. 57–78). Lexington Books.

Edwards, L. (2015). *Power, diversity and public relations*. Routledge.

Farr, A. (2004). Whiteness visible: Enlightenment racism and the structure of racialized consciousness. In G. Yancy (Ed.), *What White looks like: African-American philosophers on the whiteness question* (pp. 143–158). Routledge.

Freeman, D. A. (1995). Legitimizing racial discrimination through anti-discrimination law: A critical review of supreme court doctrine. In K. Crenshaw, N. Gotanda, G. Peller, & K. Thomas (Eds.), *Critical race theory: The key writings that formed the movement* (pp. 29–46). The New Press.

Gee, H. (1998). Beyond Black and White: Selected writings by Asian Americans within the critical race theory movement. *Mary's Law Journal, 30*, 759–783.

George, J. (2021, January 21). A lesson on critical race theory. *American Bar Association.* www.americanbar.org/groups/crsj/publications/human_rights_magazine_home/ civil-rights-reimagining-policing/a-lesson-on-critical-race-theory/

Hall, S. (1993). Culture, community, nation. *Cultural Studies, 7*(3), 349–363.

Hall, S. (2005). New ethnicities. In D. Morley & K. Chen (Eds.), *Critical dialogues in cultural studies* (pp. 442–451). Routledge.

Hall, S. (2019). What is this "black" in black popular culture? In D. Morley (Ed.), *Essential essays* (Vol. 2, pp. 479–489). Duke University Press.

Harris, C. (1995). Whiteness as property. In K. Crenshaw, N. Gotanda, G. Peller, & K. Thomas (Eds.), *Critical race theory: The key writings that formed the movement* (pp. 276–291). The New Press.

Helms, J. E. (1990). *Black and White racial identity: Theory, research, and practice.* Praeger.

Heritage Foundation. (n.d.). *Critical race theory.* www.heritage.org/crt

Hong, S., & Len-Riós, M. E. (2015). Does race matter? Implicit and explicit measures of the effect of the PR spokesman's race on evaluations of spokesman source credibility and perceptions of a PR crisis' severity. *Journal of Public Relations Research, 27*(1), 63–80. https://doi.org/10.1080/1062726X.2014.929502

Kern-Foxworth, M. (1989). Status and roles of minority public relations practitioners. *Public Relations Review, 15*(3), 39–47.

Kern-Foxworth, M. (1994). *Aunt Jemima, Uncle Ben and Rastus: Blacks in advertising, yesterday, today, and tomorrow.* Praeger.

Kern-Foxworth, M., Gandy, O., Hines, B., & Miller, D. A. (1994). Assessing the managerial roles of black female public relations practitioners using individual and organizational discriminants. *Journal of Black Studies, 24*(4), 416–434. https://doi. org/10.1177/002193479402400404

Ladson-Billings, G., & Tate, W. F. (1995). Toward a critical race theory of education. *Teachers College Record, 97*(1), 47–68.

Lambert, C. A. (2017). Post-racial public relations on primetime television: How *Scandal* represents Olivia Pope. *Public Relations Review, 43*(4), 750–754. https://doi. org/10.1016/j.pubrev.2017.07.004

Lee, Y., Li, J. Y., & Sunny Tsai, W. H. (2021). Diversity-oriented leadership, internal communication, and employee outcomes: A perspective of racial minority employees. *Journal of Public Relations Research*, 1–21. https://doi.org/10.1080/10627 26X.2021.2007388

Len-Riós, M. E. (1998). Minority public relations practitioner perceptions. *Public Relations Review, 24*(4), 535–555. https://doi.org/10.1016/S0363-8111(99)80116-7

Library of Congress. (n.d.). *Creating the United States.* www.loc.gov/exhibits/creating-the-united-states/founded-on-a-set-of-beliefs.html

Littlejohn, S. W., Foss, K. A., & Oetzel, J. G. (2017). *Theories of human communication* (11th ed.). Waveland Press.

Logan, N. (2011). The White leader prototype: A critical analysis of race in public relations. *Journal of Public Relations Research, 23*(4), 442–457. https://doi.org/10.1080/10 62726X.2011.605974

Logan, N. (2016). The Starbucks race together initiative: Analyzing a public relations campaign with critical race theory. *Public Relations Inquiry*, *5*(1), 93–113. https://doi.org/10.1177/2046147X15626969

Logan, N. (2021a). A theory of corporate responsibility to race (CRR): Communication and racial justice in public relations. *Journal of Public Relations Research*, 1–17. https://doi.org/10.1080/1062726X.2021.1881898

Logan, N. (2021b). Breaking down barriers of the past and moving toward authentic DEI adoption. In D. Pompper (Ed.), *Public relations for social responsibility: Affirming DEI commitment with action* (pp. 3–17). Emerald Publishing.

Logan, N., & Ciszek, E. (2022). At the intersection of race, gender and sexuality: A queer of color critique of public relations habitus. *Journal of Public Relations Research*, *33*(6), 487–503.

Mac Donald, H. (2018). *The diversity delusion: How race and gender pandering corrupt the university and undermine our culture*. St. Martin's Press.

Martinez, A. Y. (2020). *The rhetoric and writing of critical race theory*. National Council of Teachers of English.

Morey, M. (2021). *White philanthropy: Carnegie corporation's an American dilemma and the making of a white world order*. The University of North Carolina Press.

Mundy, D. (2022). From relationship management to change empowerment: Shifting public relations theory to prioritize publics. *Journal of Public Relations Research*. https://doi.org/10.1080/1062726X.2022.2053856

Munshi, D., & Edwards, L. (2011). Understanding "race" in/and public relations: Where do we start and where should we go? *Journal of Public Relations Research*, *23*(4), 349–367. https://doi.org/10.1080/1062726X.2011.605976

Myrdal, G. (1944). *An American dilemma: The Negro problem and modern democracy*. Harper and Brothers Publishers.

Ni, L., Wang, Q., & Gogate, A. (2018). Understanding immigrant internal publics of organizations: Immigrant professionals' adaptation and identity development. *Journal of Public Relations Research*, *30*(4), 146–163. https://doi.org/10.1080/1062726X.2018.1490289

Novak, A. N., & Richmond, J. C. (2019). E-racing together: How Starbucks reshaped and deflected racial conversations on social media. *Public Relations Review*, *45*(3). https://doi.org/10.1016/j.pubrev.2019.04.006

Olmsted, A. P. (1998). Words are acts: Critical race theory as a rhetorical construct. *Howard Journal of Communications*, *9*(4), 323–331.

Parker, P. S., & Grimes, D. S. (2009). "Race" and management communication. In F. Bargiela-Chiappini (Ed.), *The handbook of business discourse* (pp. 292–304). Edinburgh University Press.

Pearson, R. (1989). Business ethics as communication ethics: Public relations practice and the idea of dialogue. *Public Relations Theory*, *27*(2), 111–131.

Place, K. R. (2022). Toward a framework for listening with consideration for intersectionality: Insights from public relations professionals in borderland spaces. *Journal of Public Relations Research*. https://doi.org/10.1080/1062726X.2022.2057502

Plessy v. Ferguson, 163 U.S. 537. (1896).

Pompper, D. (2004). Linking ethnic diversity & two-way symmetry: Modeling female African American practitioners' roles. *Journal of Public Relations Research*, *16*(3), 269–299. https://doi.org/10.1080/1532-754X.2004.11925130

Pompper, D. (2005). "Difference" in public relations research: A case for introducing critical race theory. *Journal of Public Relations Research*, *17*(2), 139–169. https://doi.org/10.1207/s1532754xjprr1702_5

Pompper, D. (2007). The gender-ethnicity construct in public relations organizations: Using feminist standpoint theory to discover Latinas' realities. *The Howard Journal of Communications*, *18*(4), 291–311. https://doi.org/10.1080/10646170701653669

Pompper, D. (2014a). Interrogating inequalities perpetuated in a feminized field: Using critical race theory and the intersectionality lens to render visible that which should not be disaggregated. In C. Damon & K. Demetrious (Eds.), *Gender and public relations: Critical perspectives on voice, image and identity* (pp. 67–86). Routledge.

Pompper, D. (2014b). *Practical and theoretical implications of successfully doing difference in organizations*. Emerald Group Publishing.

Poole, S. M., Grier, S. A., Thomas, K. D., Sobande, F., Ekpo, A. E., Torres, L. T., Addington, L. A., Weekes-Laidlow, M., & Henderson, G. R. (2021). Operationalizing critical race theory in the marketplace. *Journal of Public Policy & Marketing*, *40*(2), 126–142. https://doi.org/10.1177/0743915620964114

Pratt, C. B. (2006). Reformulating the emerging theory of corporate social responsibility as good governance. In C. H. Botan & V. Hazelton (Eds.), *Public relations theory II* (pp. 249–277). Lawrence Erlbaum Associates.

Qiu, J., & Muturi, N. (2016). Asian American public relations practitioners' perspectives on diversity. *Howard Journal of Communications*, *27*(3), 236–249. https://doi.org/10.10 80/10646175.2016.1172527

Ray, R., & Gibbons, A. (2021). Why are states banning critical race theory? *Brookings*. www.brookings.edu/blog/fixgov/2021/07/02/why-are-states-banning-critical-race-theory/

Schoenberger-Orgad, M., & Toledano, M. (2011). Strategic framing: Indigenous culture, identity, and politics. *Journal of Public Affairs*, *11*(4), 325–333.

Sha, B. L. (2006). Cultural identity in the segmentation of publics: An emerging theory of intercultural public relations. *Journal of Public Relations Research*, *18*(1), 45–65. https://doi.org/10.1207/s1532754xjprr1801_3

Sha, B. L., & Ford, R. L. (2007). Redefining "requisite variety": The challenge of multiple diversities for the future of public relations excellence. In E. L. Toth (Ed.), *The future of excellence in public relations and communication management: Challenges for the next generation* (pp. 381–398). Routledge.

Sha, B. L., Tindall, N. T., & Sha, T. L. (2012). Identity and culture: Implications for public relations. In K. Sriramesh & D. Verčič (Eds.), *Culture and public relations* (pp. 73–96). Routledge.

Tindall, N. T. (2009a). In search of career satisfaction: African-American public relations practitioners, pigeonholing, and the workplace. *Public Relations Review*, *35*(4), 443–445. https://doi.org/10.1016/j.pubrev.2009.06.007

Tindall, N. T. (2009b). The double bind of race and gender: Understanding the roles and perceptions of Black female public relations faculty. *Southwestern Mass Communication Journal*, *25*(1), 1–16.

Turner, J. C. (1982). Towards a cognitive redefinition of the social group. In H. Tajfel (Ed.), *Social identity and intergroup relations*. Cambridge University Press.

United States Bureau of Labor Statistics. (n.d.). www.bls.gov/cps/aa2020/cpsaat11. htm

Vardeman, J., & Sebesta, A. (2020). The problem of intersectionality as an approach to digital activism: The women's march on Washington's attempt to unite all women. *Journal of Public Relations Research*, *32*(1–2), 7–29.

Vardeman-Winter, J. (2011). Confronting whiteness in public relations campaigns and research with women. *Journal of Public Relations Research*, *23*(4), 412–441. https://doi. org/10.1080/1062726X.2011.605973

Vardeman-Winter, J., & Place, K. R. (2017). Still a lily-white field of women: The state of workforce diversity in public relations practice and research. *Public Relations Review*, *43*(2), 326–336. https://doi.org/10.1016/j.pubrev.2017.01.004

Vardeman-Winter, J., & Tindall, N. T. (2010). Toward an intersectionality theory of public relations. In R. L. Heath (Ed.), *The Sage handbook of public relations* (pp. 223–235). Sage.

Wallington, C. (2020). Barriers, borders, and boundaries: Exploring why there are so few African-American males in the public relations profession. *Public Relations Journal*, *12*(3), 1–17.

Waymer, D. (2010). Does public relations scholarship have a place in race? In R. L. Heath (Ed.), *The Sage handbook of public relations* (pp. 237–260). Sage.

Waymer, D., & Dyson, O. (2011). The journey into an unfamiliar and uncomfortable territory: Exploring the role and approaches of race in PR education. *Journal of Public Relations Research*, *23*(4), 458–477. https://doi.org/10.1080/1062726X.2011.605971

Waymer, D., & Heath, R. L. (2016). Critical race and public relations: The case of environmental racism and risk bearer agency. In J. L'Etang, D. McKie, & N. Snow (Eds.), *The Routledge handbook of critical public relations* (pp. 313–326). Routledge.

West, C. (1999). *The Cornel West reader*. Basic Civitas Books.

Xifra, J., & McKie, D. (2011). Desolidifying culture: Bauman, liquid theory, and race concerns in public relations. *Journal of Public Relations Research*, *23*(4), 397–411. https://doi.org/10.1080/1062726X.2011.605975

Xu, S. (2020). Issues, identity salience, and individual sense of connection to organizations: An identity-based approach. *Journal of Public Relations Research*, *32*(3–4), 120–139.

Yoo, H. C., Gabriel, A. K., & Okazaki, S. (2021). Advancing research within Asian American psychology using Asian critical race theory and an Asian Americanist perspective. *Journal of Humanistic Psychology*. https://doi.org/10.1177/00221678211062721.

Zerbinos, E., & Clanton, G. A. (1993). Minority practitioners: Career influences, job satisfaction, and discrimination. *Public Relations Review*, *19*(1), 75–91.

18 Public Relations Theory Development in China

In the Areas of Dialogic Communication, Crisis Communication, and CSR Communication

Yi-Ru Regina Chen, Chun-Ju Flora, Hung-Baesecke, and Yang Cheng

Introduction

The practice of public relations in a country and its impact on the country are significantly shaped by the country's social context—a combination of its political, economic, media, and cultural systems—and vice versa (Grunig et al., 2002; A. Yang & Taylor, 2013). If we take a close look at the multiplicity of examples of national development in the contemporary world, mainland China (hereinafter "China") certainly represents one of the fastest-growing nations with distinctive political, economic, and media systems as well as cultural orientations. Because China is rising as a global superpower politically and economically, it is imperative to examine its public relations practice and theory, shaped by its social context, for advancing the theory of public relations.

We see that the development of public relations theory in China centers on three areas: dialogic communication, crisis communication, and corporate social responsibility (CSR) communication. First, as the dominant approach to public relations in social media (Kent & Li, 2020), the theory of dialogic communication for public relations is affected by the country's burgeoning adoption of media digitalization, high levels of political censorship, a booming economy and e-commerce market (the largest globally; International Trade Administration, 2021), and social media culture. Second, crisis communication in China has long been examined by public relations scholars. Modifications and directions in theories of crisis communication in China are driven by its political (powerful government authorities), economic (e.g., rapid economic growth), cultural (e.g., collectivism and national pride), and media (e.g., capitalization of digital platforms) factors. Finally, CSR practices and communication have rapidly gained in importance in the country. The development of public relations theory in this area is most affected by its political and economic factors, followed by cultural factors.

DOI: 10.4324/9781003141396-21

To explicate the development of public relations in China in the three areas, this chapter first examines its social context, to introduce the salient political, economic, media, and cultural factors that have shaped the development of public relations theory in the country. It then discusses the theoretical developments in the areas by explaining how the contextual factors contribute to these developments.

China's Social Context

Political Factors

China has an authoritarian, one-party regime governed by the Chinese Communist Party (CCP). Under Xi's leadership, the CCP's authority has been further centralized and bolstered by its deepened control over the state's institutions (Congressional Research Service, 2021) and media. Consequently, the government has a greater influence in shaping the theory and practice of public relations in China than ever before.

Economic Factors

China has employed a socialist market economy, a system that seeks to strike a balance between pure capitalism and social welfare by means of the government controlling the overall direction of economic development (Deng, 1993). This pragmatic approach resulted in a tenfold GDP growth from that of 1978 (*The World Factbook*, 2021), booming private firms that generate 60% of Chinese GDP (Guluzade, 2020), and advanced digital networks and technologies (Zhu & Keane, 2021). However, the rapid economic development has also produced risks (e.g., food safety, pollution, product quality) and social issues (e.g., income inequality; Yan, 2012).

Media Factors

When discussing media as a contextual factor affecting public relations theory and practice, scholars should go beyond the information transparency aspect of media systems (i.e., controlled versus free media) by examining the system's technological and operational aspects. Indeed, how people use media technologies and consume the information produced by the media system significantly determine their social patterns (e.g., communication with others and organizations) and consequently, their cognitions, attitudes, behaviors, and relationship networks (Sodré et al., 2021). We see that China has a controlled media system with a high level of media digitalization and capitalization.

Media Digitalization and Convergence

China has the world's largest Internet population—1.11 billion as of June 2021—who depend on the Internet in every aspect of their lives, mostly (99.6%) through mobile devices (CNNIC, 2021). The Internet reinforces the infrastructure of China's economy and society (Thussu, 2019). China's high level of media digitalization allows the CCP to merge different types of mass media (i.e., media convergence) through vertical media integration, mobile-first technology, artificial intelligence, and the collaboration between different media and organizations in different sectors (e.g., between media and tourism organizations) (Z. Hu et al., 2021, p. 129). Z. Hu et al. (2021) argued that by using media convergence (a pragmatic approach to media reforms), the legacy media are empowered by digitalization and the CCP regains control in a fast-changing information environment by modernizing its national governance system and reconfiguring its power with media elites (i.e., the leading media platform companies). China's convergent media organizations are able to increase their international communication capacity to reach global audiences by innovative digital means (e.g., TikTok) (Thussu, 2019). Media digitalization and convergence also enable Chinese citizens to express themselves in cyberspace and thus, facilitate the segmentation (e.g., urban middle class or migrant workers) of publics.

Capitalization of Digital Platforms

The capitalization of digital media has greatly influenced how social media platforms obtain funding. The popularity of a social media account, which is measured by user engagement metrics (e.g., hits, followers, retweets/shares, and comments), determines the amount of funding that one particular piece of content can get (Tong, 2019). Additionally, the paying function (i.e., "rewards/donations" (dashang)) on Chinese social media platforms, such as WeChat, Weibo, and Douyu TV, allows the audience to easily pay for the content they like. Popular types of content in China's social media are commonly apolitical and entertainment-oriented rather than serious reports on social and political issues (Tong, 2019). Coupled with the tightening of media control under Xi's administration (Tong, 2019), Chinese social media users have developed a taste for sensationalism and engage most with emotionally loaded content, even when related to public issues or corporate crises (e.g., food safety) (Song et al., 2016). Lei and Liang (2017) argued that this phenomenon fosters a social media culture of amorality and lacking in deep thinking.

Cultural Factors

Collectivism, individualism, and pragmatism are cultural orientations of Chinese people to be considered when analyzing the development of public relations theory in China. While collectivism and individualism have been much examined in the public relations literature (Rhee, 2002), pragmatism deserves a discussion as a salient cultural value in China's modernization.

Collectivism

Numerous studies (e.g., L. Chen, 2016) have concluded that the Chinese are collectivists in general. Collectivism means that individuals from their birth and throughout their lifetime are blended into strong ingroups, and they are protected by the groups in exchange for absolute loyalty (Hofstede, 2001). This leads the Chinese to subscribe to the ingroup-outgroup dynamic and use face and favor to gain social capital (Hwang, 1987). For example, L. Chen (2016) attributed the behavior of Chinese consumers, in frequently sharing negative product reviews online, to their ingroup-outgroup heuristic. That is, Chinese consumers perceive the brand or product as an outgroup member.

Worth noting is the nationalist orientation among Chinese youth resulting from their ingroup identity. The "little pink" group, which comprises a sizable number of Chinese netizens who show a strong sense of nationalism and defense of China's political system online, first emerged on the Internet in 2016 (Capelli, 2021). In commerce, young Chinese shoppers are increasingly showing a domestic brand bias amid growing national pride (J. Li, 2018). The nation's recent trade war with the United States and geopolitical squabbles with neighboring countries have stoked nationalist enthusiasm among millennial consumers who splurge on domestic goods at the expense of foreign brands, according to Liu and Ding (2020), or boycott foreign brands originating from countries in conflict with China (H. Zhao, 2021). Nationalist enthusiasm becomes a sociopolitical factor to consider when foreign organizations are communicating with their Chinese stakeholders in general and managing issues and crises.

Individualism

Individualism refers to a society in which "the ties between individuals are loose: everyone is expected to look after her/his immediate family only" (Hofstede, 2001, p. 225). Chinese people apply different levels of collectivism to different social relations (Brewer & Chen, 2007) because they adopt a collectivist orientation while maintaining strong individuality (Dien, 1999). Indeed, overtly individualistic behaviors are exhibited in Chinese workplaces (Mo & Berrell, 2004) in highly practical ways that simultaneously foster harmony and balance in the given environment. As a result, the idea of practicality is a distinct feature of the Chinese way of thinking (Malhotra & McCort, 2001). In addition, Chinese youth have a more individualist notion of the self than their senior counterparts. For example, they crave authenticity at work by taking on what they feel passionate about or what they are good at to gain personal worth, rather than achieving personal worth through their contribution to the communal interests of the group (Long et al., 2018).

Pragmatism

Pragmatism can be understood as "instrumentalism taking effectiveness" (T. Li & Wu, 2016, p. 40). The pragmatic approach employed by the CCP, which encourages a pursuit of capitalism while maintaining the CCP's leadership by innovative methods, has resulted in the success of China's economic and media reforms and subsequently, its rapid development (B. Zhao, 1997). Experiencing the benefits (i.e., a large increase in personal incomes) achieved by pragmatism at the national level, Chinese citizens, especially the young generation, adopt the pragmatic approach in their lives (Long et al., 2018); that is, to quickly obtain tangible results through feasible or innovative operations (T. Li & Wu, 2016). For example, pragmatism is frequently observed as a salient cultural value in the workplace, such as tactically seeking opportunities and politics (e.g., China's push for entrepreneurship and technological innovation) for personal gains (Long et al., 2018). In addition, Chinese citizens prefer companies to resolve environmental or social issues in society while making profits via innovations rather than cutting profits to resolve the issues (Y. R. Chen et al., 2020a). Pragmatism, therefore, has become a new cultural value in contemporary China that guides people's behaviors.

Having delineated the social context of China, we next detail the theoretical development of public relations in China in the areas of dialogic communication, crisis communication, and CSR communication, as influenced by the context.

Public Relations Theory Development in China

This chapter centers public relations theory development in China on dialogic communication, crisis communication, and CSR communication for two reasons. First, public relations significantly contributes to the three crucial functions of organizations in China. Second, China's unique social context modifies the practice of public relations in the three areas and provides great potential for the development of theory. Through the lens of China's social context, the dialogic communication section theorizes the premises of dialogic communication in China's social media, the crisis communication section discusses the theoretical modifications in China, and the CSR communication section proposes effective CSR practices and communication strategies targeting Chinese publics.

Dialogic Communication in China's Social Media

Dialogic communication in China as a public relations concept should focus on mediated dialogic communication, even though offline dialogic communication is possible. Based on the previously discussed contextual factors, we propose the following development of the theory of dialogic communication in social media for public relations in China.

Conceptualization and Purposes

Kent and Taylor (1998) first proposed dialogic principles to model an Internet-mediated organizational communication for public relations by tapping into the features of the Internet, such as availability, interactivity, and multimediality (Treem & Leonardi, 2012). They (2002) further developed the dialogic theory of public relations, by which *dialogue* is a pivotal concept of organizational communication in new media (see Kent (this volume) for more details on dialogic theory). Conceptualized by Kent and his colleagues, dialogue is "the form of communication that displays a *high* level of ethical, honest, empathetic, inclusive, and trustworthy communication" (Kent & Lane, 2021, p. 1) and has five tenets: mutuality (equality), propinquity, empathy, risk, and commitment (Kent & Taylor, 2002). However, the scholarship of dialogic public relations in social media provides few real-life examples because dialogue is an effort-taking process that has multiple prerequisites (Kent & Theunissen, 2016). Later, Kent and Lane (2021) acknowledged the limited dialogic potential of digital media platforms (e.g., WeChat) and pinpointed eight situations (the negative space) where dialogue is not possible or appropriate. That is, where there is no trust, no respect, no *power equality*, and no ability to change, as well as where communication is instrumental, persuasive, informational, and fact-focused.

We agree with Kent and Lane and argue that China's social context particularly restricts organization-public dialogue in most social media platforms. Affected by government censorship and collectivism, there is a high–power distance resulting from hierarchy (L. Chen, 2016) between the content initiator (i.e., the organization or the social media influencer) and the content receiver (i.e., the stakeholder and public or the social media user) in China's social media (Shao & Wang, 2017). Conversations in social media are conducted by people who have various interests (e.g., loyal consumers or the "Internet water army" who are paid ghostwriters to post comments in social media with particular content), ideologies (e.g., the "little pink" group), and positions; a desire for sensationalism; or are eager to engage with emotional or amusing content without deep thought (Shao & Wang, 2017). Achieving organization-public dialogue in China's social media at large is not practical nor desirable (too much risk and too much effort involved).

However, it is evident that organizations in China increasingly adopt a dialogic approach to communicate with their publics in social media (e.g., Gao, 2016; Cheng & Lee, 2019). Socially mediated dialogic communication in China is interactive, timely, informative, empathetic, mutual, authentic, and with a human voice (Z. F. Chen et al., 2021; Gao, 2016). Such communication aims to achieve *engagement*, rather than dialogue, with publics. *Engagement* refers to "a dynamic multidimensional relational concept featuring psychological and behavioral attributes of connection, interaction, participation, and involvement designed to achieve or elicit an outcome at individual, organizational, or social levels" (Johnston, 2018, p. 19). As social media become a primary source of information for people in China and their platforms are used for follow-up actions (e.g., purchases, filling out forms, and donations via WeChat mini programs), organizations must employ the media to reach their publics to attain their goals and thus, their survival. Indeed, the literature has suggested that when organizations practice effective dialogic communication in social media, they elicit engagement with publics and among them (Y. R. Chen & Zhao, 2021). Organization-public and public-public engagement can contribute to purchase intention (Y. R. Chen, 2017) and mutual benefits (e.g., brand co-creation; Tajvidi et al., 2020) to the organization and its publics.

We, therefore, define dialogic communication in China's social media as *the form of organizational communication that is audience-centered, interactive, open, and timely and creates engagement with publics and among publics by tapping into the affordances of the social media in which the communication takes place, to deliver mutual gains (e.g., mutual understanding, co-creation, high-quality organization-public relationships, or mutually beneficial outcomes).* We also propose the development of engagement measurements targeting various stakeholders in China as a key direction for future research.

Being Strategic and Rule-Based

Social media form a fragmented Chinese cyberspace involving multiple communicators, such as the government authority, the capital market, news media, the intellectual elite, and stakeholders (Shao & Wang, 2017). Practicing effective communication with a dialogic orientation in social media in China poses a challenge, not only because all organizations are competing fiercely with many others for a user's attention but also because they need to communicate with publics with different subcultures, inconsistent interests and demands, and even emotions, interferences (e.g., rumors), and resistances (Shao & Wang, 2017). Therefore, constructive dialogic communication in social media in China must be strategic and goal-oriented; that is, what and to whose benefit(s) the organization's dialogic communication aims to produce, through which strategy.

For example, the Chinese government's dialogic communication about COVID-19 with citizens in social media was for pandemic-related information provision, dissemination, verification, and adoption of the actions required/recommended by the government (W. X. Zhang & Yang, 2020; Y. R. Chen et al., 2020b). Non-governmental organizations (NGOs) perform dialogic communication on Weibo for issue advocacy or stakeholder relationship building (Gao, 2016). Brand-consumer dialogic communication on Weibo and WeChat aims at superior consumer services that respond to their needs by apprehending their reality and building online brand community. This brand community is where consumers can gain utilitarian benefits (e.g., seeking and giving information or obtaining exclusive offers) and psychological benefits (e.g., para-social relationship with the brand and hedonic gratification through interacting with other brand fans) through experimental engagement (Tsai & Men, 2017). Extant literature has suggested several strategies to drive dialogic communication in Chinese social media in addition to Kent and Taylor's (1998) dialogic principles: social presence (Z. F. Chen et al., 2021), conversational human voice (Z. F. Chen et al., 2021), and WeChat's affordances of character input, conversational abridgement, mixing of language, and changes in footing (Ju et al., 2019).

With the large number of active Chinese netizens participating in public discourses (Y. Xu, 2012) and a social media culture of amorality, rules are needed to conduct socially mediated dialogic communication that drives experiential engagement. Additionally, in China's high power-distance culture that embraces a pragmatic approach (obtaining outcomes through feasible operations), rulemaking is likely to be accepted by Chinese social media users for fairness, efficiency, and intended outcomes. In practice, some corporations use Artificial Intelligence-based tools to remove any comments on their social media platforms that come from members of an Internet water army (Y. Yang, 2018). Clear rule-setting for organization–public communication on an organization's social media platforms and managing the communication by closely following the rules can be an effective dialogic communication strategy in the context of China.

Incorporating Affordances to Theorize Socially Mediated Dialogic Communication Outcomes

When Chinese social media become more interactive through the technological affordances enabled by the nation's information infrastructure, organization–public communication experiences and outcomes are increasingly shaped by the media; that is, by how the communicators interact with one another *via* the media. Thus, we argue that affordances should be used to advance our theorization of how publics in a particular medium react to organizations' dialogic communication in social media. This also echoes Kent and Li's (2020) call to apply mediated theory in public relations.

Affordances are possibilities for action suggested visually by the environment (i.e., socially mediated dialogic communication) (Gibson, 1979). Dialogical communication affordances on social media platforms vary, depending on which actions of the dialogical communication are enabled by the features of the platform wherein the communication occurs. Adapting from the Theory of Interactive Media Effects (Sundar et al., 2015), Y. R. Chen (2021) proposed a dual-route framework for analyzing the outcomes of dialogic communication in social media. Her framework suggests that affordances rendered by the organization's dialogic communication in social media can trigger the public's perception (the *cue route*) and participation (the *action route*), thereby shaping the communication's effect on the public.

On the one hand, affordances form perceptions by serving as cues that activate the public's cognitive heuristics about social media-mediated dialogic communication, and then heuristics further shape their evaluated perceptions (Sundar et al., 2015). For example, a brand's dialogic communication with its consumers on WeChat that utilizes the platform's interactivity, connectivity, accessibility, and voice message-to-text conversion (a fast messaging function without using the keyboard) could trigger the helper heuristic (i.e., the communication helps solve my problem by giving me the information I need in a timely fashion or letting other consumers on the account provide me with the information), the mutual heuristic (it's asking about my input, so the brand cares about me), or the social/relational heuristic (it's trying to engage with me, so the brand wants to connect with me). Therefore, the consumers would perceive the brand's dialogic communication on WeChat as helpful, communal, and relational and directly form engagement or relationships or do business with the brand or indirectly engage with it through participating in the dialogic communication.

On the other hand, affordances can drive gratifications for the publics who participate in the organization's dialogic communication. The literature has suggested several affordance-driven gratifications gained by participating in dialogical communication on Facebook and WeChat, such as information exchange through modality (i.e., the affordance to present content using different methods), agency (i.e., the affordance to be the source of content), interactivity, navigability (i.e., the affordance to move through the medium), and quick texting methods and entertainment through agency and interactivity (Ju et al., 2019; Sundar, 2008). The gratifications not only reinforce the participation but also lead to positive outcomes of the dialogic commutation in social media among the public participants.

Examining socially mediated dialogic communication outcomes in China from an affordance approach can further develop public relations theory in two ways. First, to conceptualize affordances' crucial role in the outcomes of dialogic communication because they can generate positive responses from the public with or without the participation of dialogic communication in social media. Second, the dialogic communication affordances in each social medium may differ. Thus, public relations scholars should advance their understanding of affordances and explore new heuristics and gratifications triggered by the affordances of new or evolving social media platforms in China.

Crisis Communication Theories in China

Crisis communication is a major research area of public relations in China starting from 2008. China has experienced an increasing number of corporate crises resulting from rapid economic growth. The national orientation among consumers and media digitalization and capitalization let the crises spread fast. Crises are further amplified by the public's engagement with emotional and amoral content in social media. A variety of public relations theories have been applied in crisis communication research in China. Among them, image repair theory (Benoit, 1995) and the situational crisis communication theory (SCCT; Coombs, 2007) are the most dominant, followed by relationship management theories (e.g., Hon & Grunig, 1999) and the contingency theory of accommodation (Cancel et al., 1997) (cf. Cheng & Lee, 2019). In the following text, we discuss these theories' modifications in China's social context.

Image Repair Theory and SCCT

The development of Benoit's (1995) image repair theory and Coombs' (2007) SCCT primarily lies in the crisis communication strategies used in China's social context. China's face-saving culture facilitates not only the frequent use of denial, modification, scapegoating, and reduction of offensiveness but also the avoidance of accommodative strategies such as apology (Cheng, 2018). Triggered by political authority and collectivism, covering up and manipulation strategies are employed by deception, risk communication avoidance, lying, bribing, and forging social media content by hiring Internet users to conceal crises, work to lessen negative media exposure, and mold public opinion about the crises (Cheng, 2018; King et al., 2013). Because of China's controlled media, Veil and Yang (2012) found a company leveraged relationships with the government and media to reduce any negative media exposure during its crisis. Future theoretical development in China might focus on these crisis communication strategies, evaluate their effectiveness, and develop useful theoretical frameworks for crisis management.

Integrated Crisis Mapping

Emotions, highly contagious online, significantly divide Chinese netizens participating in online discourses into groups (Song et al., 2016). When the Chinese discuss public issues online, they are not only susceptible to emotions (G. Yang, 2018) and social influence (e.g., a posting's status) instead of judgment (Song et al., 2016) but are also constantly under the pressure of receiving angry or disparaging comment exchanges (W. Zhang, 2005). The negative emotions generated or amplified in online discourses further trigger Chinese netizens' uncivil behaviors, such as using swear words (Song & Wu, 2018). Guided by integrated crisis mapping (ICM; Jin et al., 2007), Chinese communication researchers have increasingly examined the role of emotion among stakeholders and publics in strategizing crisis communication in cyberspace. The findings of this research differ from that conducted in the Western context; disgust and anger are the salient emotions expressed by Chinese netizens during preventable crises (Liu & Ding, 2020). Chinese people do not demonstrate the high level of anxiety that ICM predicts.

It might be a result of their confidence in the government in maintaining social order. It is noteworthy that, with China's increasing political and economic power, Chinese netizens show a high emotional level of pride in crisis situations that involve a foreign country (Wan, 2019). We argue that modifications of the ICM framework are necessary when applying it to China. Further examination of how emotions function during crises in China is crucial for crisis communication theory building.

Relationship Management Theory

Regarding relationship management in crises, the relationship management theory from Ledingham (2003) and Hon and Grunig's (1999) scale of organization–public relationships have been frequently applied in China. For instance, Cheng et al. (2019) studied relationship management in China after typhoon (hurricane) disasters and found that strategically driven motives were the only CSR motives that did not have any impact on perceived relational outcomes between the organization and its publics. A possible reason is that Chinese citizens who hold a cultural tradition in collectivism and pragmatism are neutral to strategic-driven CSR (Hung-Baesecke et al., 2018).

Meanwhile, as social media has been increasingly applied in crisis communication, its empowering functions on relationship management have also been emphasized. Scholars found that the online public began to dominate their relationships with the organization and led the agenda during crises. As a result of the rising economic and political power of China and problems in China–U.S. relations, the young generation in China especially has become more susceptible to nationalism and emotion amplification (Cheng & Chan, 2015). Future scholars may further advance relationship management theory in China by exploring the effects of relationships between organizations and their publics in social media on the role and behavior of the public in crisis management.

Contingency Theory of Accommodation

A growing number of studies have tested and extended the contingency theory of accommodation from the U.S. to the Chinese context. For instance, Cheng (2016) discovered six contingency factors in the Chinese context: three main short-term factors (i.e., the powerful public-led agenda, negative media publicity, and the low-trust society) and three long-term factors (i.e., China's central political control, media censorship, and the closed culture of NGOs in China). These unique factors effectively determined the stances of organizations in strategic crisis communication and enhanced the theory building. Additionally, the contingent organization–public relationships (COPR) model has been an applicable framework to examine dynamic relational changes between a non-profit organization and its Chinese publics

(Cheng & Cameron, 2019) and can be used to explore the role of OPRs in crisis communication in China.

Theorizing CSR Practices and Communication in China

CSR in China

China's economic growth has resulted in increasing CSR practices because of emergent social issues that required the government and companies to work together to overcome (L. Hu, 2020) and greater demands for CSR from stakeholders in society (Tang et al., 2015). Overall, CSR in China has been pushed by the government's mandate or incentives. As China develops in a more globalized way economically, Chinese CSR practices and communication become similar to those in Western countries (Tang et al., 2015).

CSR is culturally contextualized. We contend collectivism and pragmatism to be salient cultural factors in CSR theory development in China. The collectivist orientation enhances CSR efforts in China (Tang et al., 2015). For example, Chinese managers are committed to CSR because they see it as a means toward "social stability and progress," for which individuals in society are responsible (S. Xu & Yang, 2010). In addition, the ingroup versus outgroup concept derived from collectivism also explains why multinational corporations utilize CSR initiatives in order to be accepted and trusted by Chinese consumers (Hung, 2004).

The influence of pragmatism on CSR practices and communication can be illustrated by Porter and Kramer's (2011) concept of creating shared value (CSV). CSV refers to "policies or practices that enhance the business competitiveness of a company while simultaneously advancing social and economic conditions in a community where it operates" (p. 66). They argued that CSV allows corporations to *consistently* address *any* societal issues and create *scalable* social impact due to business returns generated. In practice, an increasing number of leading Chinese enterprises are practicing CSV, such as Tencent (Tencent, 2021). Previous literature has concluded that people in China very much welcome such initiatives, so long as they truly benefit the community and/or the society (Chen et al., 2020a). Furthermore, Chinese people report a higher level of trust in corporations practicing CSV than those conducting traditional CSR activities (e.g., donations to NGOs and community services; Hung-Baesecke et al., 2018). They are more willing to recommend (positive word-of-mouth) CSV-performing corporations and purchase their products than those of traditional CSR-performing ones (Hung-Baesecke et al., 2018). In addition to the CSV preference, the pragmatism orientation also explains why corporate self-promotion of their CSR efforts and results is readily accepted by the public in China (Kim, 2022) and why Chinese consumers are willing to reward corporations' CSR efforts (Contini et al., 2020).

Effective CSR Practices and Communication in China

Guided by the earlier discussion, we argue that CSV is particularly suitable in China's social context. CSV can be more effective than CSR in engaging with publics and creating mutual benefits to corporations and society. Indeed, it is not easy to practice CSV that requires corporations to improve their status quo or address their critical issues by a systematic examination and a new or reinvented business model. In addition to their CSR activities, corporations should aim to practice CSV to produce scalable social impact and competitive advantages in China. As a result, public relations scholars should pay attention to CSV in developing CSR (communication) theory for public relations. For example, what role public relations plays in implementing successful CSV is a key question to be answered.

We theorize effective CSR communication in China as CSR communication that: 1) highlights government involvement in or endorsement for the CSR initiative, 2) triggers the public's pragmatic heuristic (i.e., mutual gains to the market and the society) and the innovation heuristic to the CSR initiative, 3) uses a self-promotion tone, and 4) is primarily in social media. With a limited knowledge of CSR as a concept, most Chinese people understand the concept as making donations or volunteering work (e.g., educating children in rural areas or helping victims in a disaster). Their skepticism toward CSR activity is often aroused by their negative experiences with donations or volunteer activities that have resulted in unfulfilled promises by corporations (i.e., those in need are not being helped). Therefore, CSR messages that trigger their pragmatic heuristic and innovation heuristic can prime and shape Chinese stakeholders' judgment of the CSR *outcome*, thereby leading to an increasing sense of the impact of the CSR initiative. In addition, employing innovation and pragmatic frames in the CSR communication can generate public interest and media attention.

Last but not least, we propose that organizations can optimize their CSR outcomes by forming online or offline dialogic communication with their Chinese publics that allows the organizations and publics to engage in co-learning (through information, knowledge, experience, explanations, and transparency), co-innovating (for initiatives), and co-decision making (on CSR involvement and initiative options through reconsidering agenda and doubts) (Illia et al., 2017).

Conclusion

China, as a global leader politically and economically, provides abundant opportunities for theory building in public relations. This chapter has outlined the theoretical development of public relations in China regarding dialogic communication in social media, crisis communication, and CSR communication as influenced by its social context. Further empirical explorations are necessary for the "China" theory to form. Possible research areas include developing and validating the instruments of dialogic engagement for different Chinese publics (e.g., consumers, government officials, and NGO leaders); exploring new gratifications derived from the affordances of dialogic communication on a particular social media platform and examining the effect of gratifications on such mediated dialogic communication; investigating the social and psychological consequences of emotions aroused organically or intentionally by social media influencers during a crisis, using mixed or new methods; and to test the effect of CSV communication on Chinese publics by exploring its boundary conditions.

References

Benoit, W. L. (1995). *Accounts, excuses, and apologies: A theory of image restoration strategies.* State University of New York Press.

Brewer, M. B., & Chen, Y.-R. (2007). Where (Who) are collectives in collectivism? Toward conceptual clarification of individualism and collectivism. *Psychological Review, 114*(1), 133–151. https://doi.org/10.1037/0033-295X.114.1.133

Cancel, A. E., Cameron, G. T., Sallot, L. M., & Mitrook, M. A. (1997). It depends: A contingency theory of accommodation in public relations. *Journal of Public Relations Research, 9*(1), 31–63. https://doi.org/10.1207/s1532754xjprr0901_02

Capelli, N. (2021). *Little pink, the new shade of Chinese cyber-nationalism.* www.european guanxi.com/post/little-pink-the-new-shade-of-chinese-cyber-nationalism

Chen, L. (2016). Learning the culture of a people: Chinese communication as an example. *Intercultural Communication Studies, 25*(1), 53–65.

Chen, Y. R. (2017). Perceived values of branded mobile media, consumer engagement, business-consumer relationship quality and purchase intention. *Public Relations Review, 43*(5), 945–954. https://doi.org/10.1016/j.pubrev.2017.07.005

Chen, Y. R. (2021). *Conceptualizing the effect of affordances on mediated dialogic communication using TIME: A dual framework.* Unpublished manuscript.

Chen, Y. R., Hung-Baesecke, C. J. F., Bowen, S. A., Zerfass, A., Stacks, D., & Boyd, B. (2020a). The role of leadership in shared value creation from the public's perspective: A multi-continental study. *Public Relations Review, 46*(1), Article e101749. https://doi.org/10.1016/j.pubrev.2018.12.006

Chen, Y. R., Hung-Baesecke, C. J. F., & Chen, X. H. (2020b). Moving forward the dialogic theory of public relations: Concepts, methods and applications of organization-public dialogue. *Public Relations Review, 46*(1), Article e101878. https://doi.org/10.1016/j.pubrev.2019.101878

Chen, Y. R., & Zhao, X. (2021). Digital dialogue in online brand communities: Examining the social network outcomes of brands' dialogue with Facebook users. *Telematics and Informatics, 57*, Article e101507. https://doi.org/10.1016/j.tele.2020.101507

Chen, Z. F., Ji, Y. G., & Men, L. R. (2021). Effective social media communication for startups in China: Antecedents and outcomes of organization–public dialogic communication. *New Media & Society.* Advance online publication. https://doi.org/10.1177/14614448211051984

Cheng, Y. (2016). Social media keep buzzing! A test of contingency theory in China's red cross credibility crisis. *International Journal of Communication, 10*, 1–20. http://dx.doi.org/1932-8036/20160005

Cheng, Y. (2018). Online social media and crisis communication in China: A review and critique. In J. Servaes (Ed.), *Handbook of communication for development and social change.* Springer Nature. http://doi.org/10.1007/978-981-10-7035-8_5-1

Cheng, Y., & Cameron, T. G. (2019). Examining six modes of relationships in a social-mediated crisis in China: An exploratory study of contingent organization-public relationship (COPR). *Journal of Applied Communication Research, 47*(6), 689–705. http://doi.org/10.1080/00909882.2019.1695874

Cheng, Y., & Chan, C. M. (2015). The third level of agenda setting in contemporary China: Tracking descriptions of moral and national education in media coverage and people's minds. *International Journal of Communication, 9.* 1090–1107. http://dx.doi.org/1932-8036/20150005

Cheng, Y., Chen, Y. R., Hung-Baesecke, R., & Jin, Y. (2019). When CSR meets mobile SNA users in mainland China: An examination of gratifications sought, CSR motives, and relational outcomes in natural disasters. *International Journal of Communication, 13,* 319–341. https://ijoc.org/index.php/ijoc/article/view/10169

Cheng, Y., & Lee, C., J. (2019). Online crisis communication in a post-truth Chinese society: Evidence from interdisciplinary literature. *Public Relations Review, 45*(4), Article e101826. https://doi.org/10.1016/j.pubrev.2019.101826

CNNIC. (2021). *The 48th statistical report on China's Internet development.* www.cnnic.com.cn/IDR/ReportDownloads/202111/P020211119394556095096.pdf

Congressional Research Service. (2021). *China's political system in charts: A snapshot before the 20th party congress.* https://crsreports.congress.gov/product/pdf/R/R46977

Contini, M., Annunziata, E., Rizzi, F., & Frey, M. (2020). Exploring the influence of corporate social responsibility (CSR) domains on consumers' loyalty: An experiment in BRICS countries. *Journal of Cleaner Production, 247.* https://doi.org/10.1016/j.jclepro.2019.119158

Coombs, W. T. (2007). Protecting organization reputations during a crisis: The development and application of situational crisis communication theory. *Corporate Reputation Review, 10*(3), 163–176.

Deng, X. P. (1993). *Selected works of Deng Xiaoping* (Vol. III). People's Publishing House.

Dien, D. S. (1999). Chinese authority-directed orientation and Japanese peer-group orientation: Questioning the notion of collectivism. *Review of General Psychology, 3*(4), 372–385. https://doi.org/10.1037/1089-2680.3.4.372

Gao, F. (2016). Social media as a communication strategy: Content analysis of top non-profit foundations' micro-blogs in China. *International Journal of Strategic Communication, 10*(4), 255–271.

Gibson, J. J. (1979). *The ecological approach to visual perception.* Houghton Mifflin.

Grunig, L. A., Grunig, J. E., & Dozier, D. M. (2002). *Excellent public relations and effective organizations: A study of communication management in three countries.* Lawrence Erlbaum Associates.

Guluzade, A. (2020, May 21). *How reform has made China's state-owned enterprises stronger.* www.weforum.org/agenda/2020/05/how-reform-has-made-chinas-state-owned-enterprises-stronger/

Hofstede, G. (2001). *Culture's consequences: Comparing values, behaviors, institutions, and organizations across nations.* Sage.

Hon, L. C., & Grunig, J. E. (1999). *Guidelines for measuring relationships in public relations: A report for the commission on public relations measurement and evaluation.* Institute for Public Relations.

Hu, L. (2020). The integration between and common prosperity of government and market: China's experience of common prosperity of government and market economic development. *China Political Economy, 3*(2), 289–302.

Hu, Z., Ji, D., Xu, P., & Bhuju, K. (2021). Beyond convergence: Rethinking China's media system in a global context. In D. K. Thussa & K. Nordenstreng (Eds.), *BRICS media: Reshaping global communication order?* (pp. 127–137). Routledge.

Hung, C. F. (2004). Cultural influence on relationship cultivation strategies: Multinational companies in China. *Journal of Communication Management, 8*(3), 264–281. https://doi.org/10.1108/13632540410807682

Hung-Baesecke, C. J. F., Stacks, D. W., Coombs, W. T., Chen, Y. R., & Boyd, B. (2018). Creating shared value, public trust, supportive behavior, and communication preferences: A comparison study in the United States and China. *Public Relations Journal, 11*(4). https://prjournal.instituteforpr.org/wp-content/uploads/Flora-Final.pdf

Hwang, K.-K. (1987). Face and favor: The Chinese power game. *The American Journal of Sociology, 92,* 944–974.

Illia, L., Romenti, S., Rodríguez-Cánovas, B., Murtarlli, G., & Carroll, C. E. (2017). Exploring corporations dialogue about CSR in the digital era. *Journal of Business Ethics, 146,* 39–58.

International Trade Administration. (2021, February 3). *China – eCommerce.* https://www.trade.gov/country-commercial-guides/china-ecommerce

Jin, Y., Pang, A., & Cameron, G. T. (2007). Integrated crisis mapping: Towards a publics-based, emotion-driven conceptualization in crisis communication. *Corporate Communications: An International Journal, 15*(4), 428–452.

Johnston, K. (2018). Toward a theory of social engagement. In *The handbook of communication engagement* (pp. 17–32). John Wiley & Sons, Inc. https://doi.org/10.1002/9781119167600.ch2

Ju, B., Sandel, T. L., & Fitzgerald, R. (2019). Understanding Chinese Internet and social media: The innovative and creative affordances of technology, language and culture. *Se Mettre en Scène en Ligne: La Communication Digitale, 2,* 161–177.

Kent, M. L., & Lane, A. (2021). Two-way communication, symmetry negative spaces, and dialogue. *Public Relations Review, 47*(1), Article e102014. https://doi.org/10.1016/j.pubrev.2021.102014

Kent, M. L., & Li, C. (2020). Toward a normative social media theory for public relations. *Public Relations Review, 46*(1), Article e101857. https://doi.org/10.1016/j.pubrev.2019.101857

Kent, M. L., & Taylor, M. (1998). Building dialogic relationships through the World Wide Web. *Public Relations Review, 24*(3), 321–334.

Kent, M. L., & Taylor, M. (2002). Toward a dialogic theory of public relations. *Public Relations Review, 28,* 21–37.

Kent, M. L., & Theunissen, P. (2016). Elegy for mediated dialogue: Shiva the destroyer and reclaiming our first principles. *International Journal of Communication, 10*(2016), 4040–4054.

Kim, S. (2022). The process of CSR communication—culture-specific or universal? Focusing on mainland China and Hong Kong consumers. *International Journal of Business Communication, 59*(1), 56–82. https://doi.org/10.1177/2329488418805523

King, G., Pan, J., & Margaret, R. (2013). How censorship in China allows government criticism but silences collective expression. *The American Political Science Review, 107*(2), 1–18.

Ledingham, J. A. (2003). Explicating relationship management as a general theory of public relations. *Journal of Public Relations Research, 15*(2), 181–198. http://doi.org/10.1016/S0363-8111(98)80020-9

Lei, Q., & Liang, C. (2017). The new media and social culture demoralized and demoralizing in China. *Cultural Studies, 31*(6), 877–893. https://doi.org/10.1080/09502386.2017.1374430

Li, J. (2018, March 22). China's young consumers are snubbing foreign brands amid growing national pride, says credit suisse. *South China Morning Post.* http://consumers-are-snubbing-foreign-brands-amid

Li, T., & Wu, Y. (2016). Pragmatism in China—Chinese pragmatism. *Proceedings of the 2016 International Conference on Humanity, Education and Social Science*, 40–43. https://doi.org/10.2991/ichess-16.2016.9

Liu, N., & Ding, H. (2020). From anger to disgust: The picture of public's emotions in crisis event. *Journalism Research*, *12*(176), 35–48 (in Chinese).

Long, Z., Buzzanell, P. M., & Kuang, K. (2018). Chinese post80s generational resilience: Chengyu (成语) as communicative resources for adaptation and change. *International Journal of Business Communication*. Advance online publication https://doi.org/10.1177/2329488417747598

Malhotra, N. K., & McCort, J. D. (2001). A cross-cultural comparison of behavioral intention models: Theoretical consideration and an empirical investigation. *International Marketing Review*, *18*(3), 235–269. https://doi.org/10.1108/02651330110396505

Mo, H., & Berrell, M. (2004, July 19–20). Chinese cultural values and workplace behaviour: Implications for continued economic growth. In J. Laurenceson, K. Tang, & S. Waldron (Eds.), *Proceedings of the 16th annual conference of the association for Chinese economics studies, Australia*. ACESA.

Porter, M. E., & Kramer, M. R. (2011). The big idea: Creating shared value. How to reinvent capitalism—and unleash a wave of innovation and growth. *Harvard Business Review*, *89*, 62–77.

Rhee, Y. (2002). Global public relations: A cross-cultural study of the excellence theory in South Korea. *Journal of Public Relations Research*, *14*(3), 159–184.

Shao, P., & Wang, Y. (2017). How does social media change Chinese political culture? The formation of fragmentized public sphere. *Telematics and Informatics*, *34*(3), 694–704. https://doi.org/10.1016/j.tele.2016.05.018

Sodré, M., Paiva, R., Nordenstreng, K., & Custódio, L. (2021). Shifting paradigms in communication research. In D. K. Thussa & K. Nordenstreng (Eds.), *BRICS media: Reshaping global communication order?* (pp. 39–52). Routledge.

Song, Y., Dai, X., & Wang, J. (2016). Not all emotions are created equal: Expressive behavior of the networked public on China's social media site. *Computers in Human Behavior*, *60*, 525–533.

Song, Y., & Wu, Y. (2018). Tracking the viral spread of incivility on social networking sites: The case of cursing in online discussions of Hong Kong–Mainland China conflict. *Communication and Public*, *3*(1), 46–61.

Sundar, S. S. (2008). The MAIN model: A heuristic approach to understanding technology effects on credibility. In M. J. Metzger & A. J. Flanagin (Eds.), *Digital media, youth, and credibility* (pp. 72–100). The MIT Press.

Sundar, S. S., Jia, H., Waddell, T. F., & Huang, Y. (2015). Toward a theory of interactive media effects (TIME). In S. S. Sundar (Ed.), *The handbook of the psychology of communication technology* (pp. 47–86). Wiley Blackwell.

Tajvidi, M., Marie-Odile, R., Wang, Y., & Hajli, N. (2020). Brand co-creation through social commerce information sharing. *Journal of Business Research*, *121*, 476–486. https://doi.org/10.1016/j.jbusres.2018.06.008

Tang, L., Gallagher, C. C., & Bie, B. (2015). Corporate social responsibility communication through corporate websites. *International Journal of Business Communication*, *52*(2), 205–227. https://doi.org/10.1177/2329488414525443

Tencent. (2021, April 19). Tencent unveils blueprint of sustainable innovations for social value as core development strategy: Initial investment of RMB 50 billion for the new initiative. *Tencent*. https://static.www.tencent.com/uploads/2021/05/27/c947815a6b7558d6843b24741ffac5e9.pdf

Thussu, D. K. (2019). *International communication: Continuity and change* (3rd ed.). Bloomsbury Academic.

Tong, J. (2019). The taming of critical journalism in China. *Journalism Studies, 20*(1), 79–96. https://doi.org/10.1080/1461670X.2017.1375386

Treem, J. W., & Leonardi, P. M. (2012). Social media use in organizations: Exploring the affordances of visibility, editability, persistence, and association. *Communication Yearbook, 36*, 143–189.

Tsai, W. S., & Men, L. R. (2017). Consumer engagement with brands on social network sites: A cross-cultural comparison of China and the USA. *Journal of Marketing Communications, 23*(1), 2–21. https://doi.org/10.1080/13527266.2014.942678

Veil, S. R., & Yang, A. (2012). Media manipulation in the Sanlu milk contamination crisis. *Public Relations Review, 38*(5), 935–937.

Wan, N. (2019, January 10). *Shejiao meiti huanjing xia minzhong canyu yulun de qinggan tezheng fenxi* [Analysis of the emotional characteristics of public participation in public opinion under the social media environment]. http://media.people.com.cn/n1/2019/0110/c424557-30515543.html

The world factbook. (2021). Central Intelligence Agency. www.cia.gov/the-world-factbook/countries/china/#economy

Xu, S., & Yang, R. (2010). Indigenous characteristics of Chinese corporate social responsibility conceptual paradigm. *Journal of Business Ethics, 93*, 321–333.

Xu, Y. (2012). Understanding netizen discourse in China: Formation, genres, and values. *China Media Research, 8*(1), 15–24.

Yan, Y. (2012). Food safety and social risk in contemporary China. *The Journal of Asian Studies, 71*(3), 705–729. https://doi.org/10.1017/S0021911812000678

Yang, A., & Taylor, M. (2013). The relationship between the professionalization of public relations, societal social capital and democracy: Evidence from a cross-national study. *Public Relations Review, 39*(5), 257–270.

Yang, G. (2018). Demobilizing the emotions of online activism in China: A civilizing process. *International Journal of Communication, 12*, 1945–1965.

Yang, Y. (2018, August 1). China's battle with the "internet water army". *FT Magazine.* www.ft.com/content/b4f27934-944a-11e8-b67b-b8205561c3fe

Zhang, W. X. (2005). *Are online discussions deliberate? A case study of Chinese online discussion board.* III International conference on communication and reality. Digital Utopia in the media: From discourses to facts. A balance. http://cicr.blanquerna.url.edu/2005/Abstracts/PDFsComunicacions/vol1/02/ZHANG_Weiyu.pdf

Zhang, W. X., & Yang, L. (2020). Duoyuan duihua: Tufa gonggong weisheng shijian de xinxi chuanbo zhili [Multiple dialogues: Information dissemination and governance of public health emergencies]. *Journal of Shandong University (Philosophy and Social Sciences), 2020*(5), 24–30.

Zhao, B. (1997). Consumerism, Confucianism, communism: Making sense of China today. *New Left Review*, 43–59.

Zhao, H. (2021). Beyond culture: Advancing the understanding of political and technological contexts in crisis communication. *The International Communication Gazette, 83*(5), 517–537. https://doi.org/10.1177/17480485211029066

Zhu, Y., & Keane, M. (2021). China's cultural power reconnects with the world. In D. K. Thussa & K. Nordenstreng (Eds.), *BRICS media: Reshaping global communication order?* (pp. 209–222). Routledge.

19 Culture and Dialogic Theory in Public Relations

The Middle Eastern Context

Ganga S. Dhanesh and Ruth Avidar

Introduction

The Public Relations Society of America has defined public relations as "a strategic communication process that builds mutually beneficial relationships between organizations and their publics" (www.prsa.org). While various models of communication can engender relationships, the dialogic theory of public relations foregrounds the use of dialogue that is premised on ideas of open and transparent communication that celebrates the respectful voicing of differences, focused on experiencing and understanding, and potentially developing mutual satisfaction and commitment among organizations and their publics (Kent & Taylor, 2002; Kent & Lane, 2021). However, most theorizing and empirical work on dialogue within public relations scholarship has been centered in Euro-American worldviews and organization-centered approaches, ignoring the critical influence of cultures as environments, which restricts the global applicability of dialogic theory. While the body of work on dialogic theory is robust, it can be enriched by a more holistic approach to dialogic communication by acknowledging the impact and importance of a broader set of cultural variables and their influence on dialogue.

Accordingly, the purpose of this chapter is to broaden the scope of dialogic theory by examining the diverse cultural environments in the Middle East in which organizations engage in dialogue, thus foregrounding the importance of cultures in dialogic theory. Our work situates the study of global public relations in between ethnocentric and ethnorelativist approaches supporting the argument that effective public relations includes generic principles that hold across cultures, while specific applications can differ according to variables such as the political system and societal culture (Vercic et al., 1996; Sriramesh & Vercic, 2009, 2019). Although the Euro-centric dialogic theory may not always fit the Middle East, we embrace the dialogic theory as part of a deductive approach aimed at contrasting Middle Eastern reality with Western idealistic dialogical conduct that promotes openness, transparency, and respect of different voices. We believe that in this way the differences between the Western ideal of dialogical communication and the Middle East context can be more easily highlighted and emphasized.

DOI: 10.4324/9781003141396-22

We examine the Middle East for multiple reasons. In addition to deep historical significance, the region continues to play a pivotal role in modern times producing a substantial share of the world's oil, creating transformative economic growth, especially in the countries of the Gulf Cooperation Council (GCC), while also dealing with deep divisions, conflict, and humanitarian crises in some countries. These widely divergent situations that reflect assorted political, economic, and cultural milieus offer a rich test case to examine contextual factors that could inform and challenge widely accepted notions of dialogic theory and generate new pathways for theorizing that reflect the nuances of varied cultural contexts. This chapter will also answer the call for more culturally grounded scholarship on public relations in the Middle East (Dhanesh & Duthler, 2019a).

First, this chapter briefly reviews the basic tenets of the dialogic theory, which has been elaborated in another chapter of this book. Second, it explores the Middle Eastern cultural environments using the Global Public Relations framework (GPRF) (Sriramesh & Vercic, 2009, 2019), which defines culture broadly to include political, economic, media, societal, and activist cultures. The GPRF discusses societal culture using various cultural frameworks including Hofstede, which has been criticized for assuming cultural homogeneity although most nations are groups of ethnic units, for ignoring the importance of community and its influences on the individual, and for using national divisions as units of analysis although cultures are not necessarily bounded by borders (Jones, 2007; McSweeney, 2000; Smith, 1998). However, we decided to adopt the GPRF as it is one of the most comprehensive and holistic frameworks to study public relations globally. Third, we discuss the implications of these cultural contexts on dialogic theory, how they can affect positive and negative spaces of dialogue, and how the theory can be adapted to suit divergent cultural contexts.

The Dialogic Theory

The dialogic theory is one of the most popular theoretical perspectives in public relations research (Morehouse & Saffer, 2018). Despite the ongoing interest in dialogue and dialogic communication, the term *dialogue* still does not have a definition that is satisfactory for all (Lane & Kent, 2018), and public relations scholars strive to define this elusive concept.

Overall, the dialogic communication approach suggests that in order to create effective communication channels, organizations must be willing to communicate with publics in honest and ethical ways (Taylor et al., 2001). Unlike the symmetrical approach, the dialogic communication approach does not focus on conflict-solving; rather, it encourages participants to speak their voices, air different opinions, and exchange ideas. Dialogic communication looks at the presentation of differences, with struggle and conflict being perceived as natural states (Deetz, 2001). Therefore, the aim of dialogic communication is to reveal existing problems, conflicts, and disagreements and to address them without the compulsion to reach an agreement. Pearson (1989) considered dialogue to be the most ethical form for conducting public relations.

In 1998, Kent and Taylor presented five dialogic principles for guiding organizations in incorporating dialogic public relations into their websites: dialogic loop, usefulness of information, generation of return visits, ease of the interface, and conservation of visitors. In 2002, Kent and Taylor revised and expanded their research, proposing five principles of dialogic public relations theory: mutuality, propinquity, empathy, risk, and commitment. These principles suggest that a true dialogue involves open, accessible, respectful, trustworthy, and transparent dialogic communication between participants.

Scholarly work related to dialogue in public relations research mainly focuses on how the dialogic principles of Kent and Taylor (1998, 2002) are implemented on websites and social media platforms (i.e., Gálvez-Rodríguez et al., 2018; Linvill et al., 2012; Watkins & Lewis, 2014) without exploring deeper layers of the concept (Magen & Avidar, 2019). As noted by Taylor and Kent (2014), "The biggest flaw in how dialogue has been examined in web-based public relations has involved treating features of dialogue as a series of categories that had to be present for the potential for dialogue" (p. 388). Furthermore, most theorizing and empirical work in public relations scholarship has been centered in Euro-American worldviews and elides nuances of concepts such as dialogue that are deeply embedded in cultural, political, economic, and social contexts of practice (Sriramesh & Vercic, 2009, 2019).

Exploring misperceptions of dialogue in public relations research, Kent and Lane (2021) challenged the assumption that dialogue is the right answer to any troubled communication situation, arguing that there are "negative spaces," or contexts, where dialogue is not possible or appropriate. They refer to situations where two-way communication is used instrumentally as a means to achieve organizational goals, where persuasive communication occurs, where there is no trust between the parties, where one party believes in their superiority over the others, where there is fear or when power is disproportionate, where there is no ability and/or willingness to change or to admit a change, when there is no openness to new ideas and worldviews, where there is no respect, and where there is a focus on information rather than experiencing and understanding. Kent and Lane (2021) further argued that dialogue as a normative paradigm should not be perceived as an "all or nothing" challenge, but practitioners might create and structure rules and guidelines to set participant expectations appropriately, thus encouraging a dialogue-like communication with the intention that "eventually, through practice and familiarity, dialogic communication could become the real thing" (p. 7).

Looking at the dialogic approach from a cultural perspective, we argue that various cultural, economic, political, and societal contexts might challenge the normative notion of dialogue as an open, honest, and transparent two-way communication that engenders understanding and relationships between organizations and their publics. Instead, we argue that myriad cultural factors could affect the enactment of dialogue, offering a complex mosaic of negative spaces where dialogue is not possible or appropriate (Kent & Lane, 2021), and positive spaces where they can promote dialogic communication. Using the Middle East as a case study, we would like to further elaborate on this argument using the GPRF (Sriramesh & Vercic, 2009; 2019).

Culture and Diversity in the Middle East Using the Global Public Relations Framework

According to the GPRF (Sriramesh & Vercic, 2009, 2019), it is critical to simultaneously examine the influence of political, economic, media, societal, and activist cultures on public relations practice and theorizing because focusing on only one of these variables would run the risk of ignoring interconnectivities among them. Examining cultural variables concurrently to understand environments in which organizations operate will help to expand our understanding of the nuances and complexities of enacting concepts such as dialogue in myriad contexts.

Political System

According to Freedom House (www.freedomhouse.org), a US-based NGO that issues the Freedom in the World report, which assesses the level of freedom in countries across the world, each of the seven categories of political systems—democracies, restricted democratic practices, monarchies, authoritarian regimes, totalitarian regimes, colonial and imperial dependencies, and protectorates—is associated with varying degrees of tolerance for open discussion and dissent. Strategic public relations thrives in pluralistic societies typically associated with democracies wherein public opinion is shaped through the wrangle of open discussion and debate (Sriramesh & Vercic, 2009, 2019).

The Middle East has a wide range of political systems ranging from traditional monarchies in Saudi Arabia and Oman to parliamentary democracy in Israel and a parliamentary republic in Lebanon. According to Freedom House, which ranks countries as free, partly free, and not free based on an assessment of factors such as the electoral process, political pluralism and participation, the functioning of the government, and freedom of expression and belief, only Tunisia and Israel are classified as Free countries in the region and Kuwait, Lebanon, and Morocco as Partly Free. In the Freedom House Report (2020), Qatar has a low political rights rating, while Saudi Arabia has one of the lowest scores.

The region has also been marked by vast swathes of war and conflict and pockets of peace and stability. This includes a civil war in Syria, labeled as the world's least free country for the last seven years; a continuing war in Yemen; and mass protests against corruption and sectarian politics in Lebanon, Iraq, and Iran (Freedom House, 2020). It also includes the relatively stable and peaceful countries of the GCC, consisting of Bahrain, Kuwait, Oman, Qatar, Saudi Arabia, and United Arab Emirates.

The myriad political systems and diverse political stability in the region often leads to shifting political relationships. For instance, Saudi Arabia, Bahrain, the United Arab Emirates, and Egypt imposed an embargo on Qatar in 2017, and individuals and organizations in these countries were barred from engaging with Qatari individuals, groups, and organizations (Kabbani, 2021). However, relationships were restored in 2021 and restrictions lifted. Similarly, in 2020, UAE and Bahrain normalized diplomatic relations with Israel.

How does this varied and dynamically shifting political environment marked as mostly partly free affect organizations and their practice of public relations in the Middle East? Public relations in the Middle East, strongly connected to government institutions and public affairs has been a publicity tool for governments (Kirat, 2005; Toledano & McKie, 2013). Subsequently, research on public relations in the region has mostly examined the effectiveness of political public relations messages on media coverage (Albishri et al., 2019) and the use of propaganda and military public diplomacy in countries such as Iran, Iraq, and Israel (e.g., Jo et al., 2008; Magen, 2013; Magen & Lapid, 2016, 2018; Sweetser & Brown, 2010). Most studies seem to concur that propaganda can thrive and affect public opinion in the absence of pluralistic opinions that are openly expressed and debated. However, research is yet to empirically examine how the political environment can affect how organizations practice concepts such as dialogue.

Economic System

A country's economic system, often intertwined with its political system, tends to reflect the characteristics of the political system, hence the term *political economy*. For instance, political pluralism tends to drive greater economic freedom and private entrepreneurship and thus foster greater competition among economic players, which in turn implies a greater need for strategic public relations to garner public support (Sriramesh & Vercic, 2009, 2019). However, in centrally regulated economies built around monopolistic public sector enterprises, with blurred boundaries between *government* and *corporation*, the government becomes the main public for public relations practitioners. In the Middle East, there is wide variation in economic growth and outlook reflecting diverse conditions of political stability, war and conflict, access to natural resources, diversification of economies, and differing fiscal policies. Despite these wide-ranging differences, growth in regional economic cooperation and trade and investment exchanges could push for increased strategic public relations.

Although the state plays a major role in the economy of the leading oil producers, since the 1990s, there have been attempts to diversify, reduce the economic role of the state, and encourage private sector investment in infrastructure (www.eiu.com), which has implications for both public-private sector partnership and employment of nationals. In the Middle East, public-private sector partnership dominates, often blurring the boundaries between governments and corporations. Although there is limited research on the impact of economic systems on public relations practice, sectoral differences have been found to affect professionalism in public relations in Kuwait (Almutairi & Dashti, 2019) and the adoption of the Internet by public relations professionals in Saudi Arabia (Al-Shohaib et al., 2009).

Another pertinent issue is the composition of the labor force. While several countries have a majority of nationals in the labor force, in GCC countries expatriates comprise a large portion of the private sector workforce. This diverse mix of nationals and expatriates, who represent over 200 nationalities, has posed challenges for the practice of public relations, particularly in addressing the needs of diverse publics. For instance, in Saudi Arabia domestic practitioners were employed when addressing Saudi audiences, while expatriates were chosen to deal with non-national audiences (Alanazi, 1996). The deeply uneven mix of locals and expatriates with differential rights also has complex implications for the creation of the public sphere and the constitution of public opinion (Vora & Koch, 2015) that could affect the practice of public relations. It is important to examine how such contextual factors can impact the building of dialogic relationships between organizations and their publics.

Culture

The GPRF stresses the important linkages between culture and communication, arguing that they affect and are affected by each other. The framework distinguishes between societal culture and organizational culture and argues that both play important roles in organizations. To understand societal culture, the framework draws on Hofstede's (2001) six *dimensions* of culture that are common across many countries. The framework highlights that while classifications across countries based on global cultural dimensions are useful, societies also have unique cultural characteristics that could affect the practice of public relations. Research on public relations in the Middle East has examined unique societal features such as Islamic value orientations, and more universal dimensions such as collectivism, and organizational culture variables such as management styles to explain the effect of culture on public relations practice.

Some of these societal cultural variables include Israeli's high solidarity that is reflected in the high level of directness in Israeli discourse and the lack of importance that Israelis attach to social distance (Blum-Kulka et al., 1985; Katriel, 1986); Arab cultural value orientations such as commitment to religion, devotion to the group, resistance to change/attachment to history, and recognition of hierarchal order (Al-Kandari & Gaither, 2011); and Islamic values and ethics such as building relationships with others, serving society, working for the community, and respect for religious authority (Al-Saqer & Al-Hashimi, 2019; Gaither & Al-Kandari, 2014). Societal features such as recognition of hierarchy and group affiliation are also reflected in universal dimensions of culture, particularly Hofstede's cultural dimensions of power distance and collectivism.

Due to high-power distance, vertical hierarchies dictate communication channels and decision-making processes making Arab managerial and organizational styles authoritative and centralized (Bashir & Aldaihani, 2017; Kirat, 2005), which in turn explains the prevalence of one-way and asymmetrical models of public relations across countries such as Saudi Arabia, Kuwait, and the UAE (Al-Shohaib et al., 2009; Almutairi & Dashti, 2019; Kirat, 2006). Collectivism, social bonding, and group attachment could set the base for relationship building between various entities such as the private and public sectors (Al-Kandari & Gaither, 2011; Al-Saqer & Al Hashimi, 2019). A combination of variables such as loyalty to the group and relationship building suggest that public relations in Middle Eastern nations will be successful if they adopt the personal influence model of public relations, premised on the use of social connections or *wasta* (Almutairi & Dashti, 2019; Badran, 2019; Gaither & Al-Kandari, 2014). *Wasta* is a common practice and a social norm in many Arab countries. It means that people use their family or social contacts to receive various benefits, such as quicker and better access to institutions, jobs, and governmental services (Transparency International, 2019).

Finally, varying levels of cultural diversity in the Middle East further complicate the practice of public relations. For instance, there are high levels of ethnic (Arabs, Kurds, Jews, etc.), religious (Sunnis, Shiites, Yazidis, Jews, Christians, Druze, etc.), and linguistic (i.e., Arabic dialects, from Egyptian Arabic to Khaleeji Arabic, and Hebrew) diversity among local populations. In addition, countries such as the UAE, Kuwait, and Qatar have large resident expatriate populations from Asia, Europe, Australia, and North America. This multicultural environment has strong implications for how dialogic communication can be practiced.

Media System

Different societies have different perceptions of the role of media in society based on various social, political, and philosophical principles. The GPRF refers to the normative media theory first proposed by Siebert et al. (1956) that offered various theoretical approaches to understanding diverse media environments around the world. Although political and social systems across the world have changed since the 1950s, basic principles of the media-society nexus persist due to the continued power of media and society to reciprocally influence media and public agendas. Close relationships between public relations and media call for a deeper understanding of the effect of media systems on the practice of public relations. The rise of social media has also impacted ways in which public relations builds and maintains relationships with multiple publics and needs to be studied in conjunction with mainstream media.

Research on the intersections of public relations and media in the Middle East has focused on a few key themes such as the models of public relations (Al-Kindi, 2019; Kirat, 2015), leveraging affordances of the Internet and social media such as avoiding traditional media gatekeepers (Curtin & Gaither, 2004), fostering dialogue, two-way models of public relations, engagement with stakeholders online (Avidar, 2015, 2017; Avidar et al., 2013; Storie, 2015), and ethical practices and influencer relations on social media (Dhanesh & Duthler, 2019b; Lahav, 2016; Toledano & Avidar, 2016).

Models of public relations used in the Middle East reflect various aspects of political, economic, and cultural environments discussed earlier. For instance, public relations in the Middle East is strongly connected with government institutions and public affairs. Subsequently, some of the most commonly used public relations models include press agentry and one-way, asymmetrical, public information models that foreground the role of media relations in public relations practice (AlKindi, 2019; Kirat, 2015). In addition, culture-centered models of two-way interaction could include the *majlis* in the UAE, an informal public forum for men (Badran, 2019); the *Wali* office in Oman, led by a *Wali* or a local governor who is the boundary spanner between the government and local communities; and the *Sablah*, a meeting point for members of local communities (AlKindi, 2019).

Another key strand of research in public relations in the Middle East has examined the changes wrought by the Internet and social media. For instance, Curtin and Gaither (2004) examined the dialogue building capabilities of 10 official English-language Middle East government and presidential web sites and found that Middle Eastern practitioners employed a personal relations model that leverages the lack of media gatekeepers on the web. However, reflecting much of global public relations scholarship, studies in Kuwait have found that organizations do not leverage the potential of social media to use two-way models to build relationships. They continue to use Twitter and Instagram mostly for promotion and one-way information dissemination (Al-Kandari et al., 2019; Bashir & Aldaihani, 2017).

Similarly, Avidar et al. (2013) found that neither do organizations utilize smartphones to build relationships with young publics in Israel (Avidar et al., 2013), nor do smartphone users in Israel perceive engagement as beneficial primarily for themselves compared to organizations (Avidar, 2015). Adding more nuance to factors that drive social media engagement from the perspective of publics, Storie (2015) found that young publics' preferences for online engagement are influenced by cultural factors, such as cultural and linguistic proximity, and political factors, such as perceived risks of online engagement driven by laws and internal political climate.

Finally, researchers have questioned issues of disclosure of paid content in Israel and the UAE (Dhanesh & Duthler, 2019b; Lahav, 2016). To summarize, due to a confluence of political, economic, and cultural factors, despite the widespread adoption of social media, traditional media relations and one-way models of communication continue to dominate with strong implications for dialogic communication.

Activism

According to GPRF, nations with pluralistic, democratic systems, high economic development, and cultures that encourage debate and discussion not only tolerate but also foster activism. Although early theorizing in public relations considered activists as a threat to be managed, later theorizing has discussed notions of public relations practitioners not only as boundary spanners but also as activists within organizations advocating for stakeholder perspectives.

Stakeholder groups such as trade unions and lobbyists are limited in many Arab states (Ararat, 2006). This could be one of the reasons that public relations scholarship has limited research on activism and NGOs in the Middle East (Duthler et al., 2015; Magen & Avidar, 2019). This was also reflected in research on the Arab Spring, the string of protests across the Middle East and North Africa in 2010 and 2011, except for a rare study in public relations on the Syrian Electronic Army that questioned its hacktivist credentials and argued that it was intended to promote the Syrian government narrative (Al-Rawi, 2014) and others that identified political and economic causes of the rebellion and the role played by social networks, both online and offline (Al-Jenaibi, 2014; Allagui & Kuebler, 2011). Allagui (2017) also analyzed award-winning communication campaigns in the UAE and argued that corporate public relations activism can advocate for minority groups within a monarchy.

To summarize, this discussion has shown that the Middle East is marked by varied political and economic systems, a wide range of political stability, diversified economies, and dynamically shifting relationships among countries. The practice of public relations has been strongly connected with government institutions and is often seen as a publicity tool in contexts that are devoid of pluralistic opinions, where propaganda can thrive. The deeply diverse mix of locals and expatriates also complicates the practice of public relations. Further, universal cultural dimensions such as power distance and collectivism map well with Arab and Islamic value orientations such as respect for authority and hierarchical order and devotion to the group, manifested in authoritative and centralized Arab management styles and the prevalence of the personal influence model built on social connections and relationships. In addition, traditional media relations thrives with the dominance of press agentry and one-way, asymmetrical, public information models of public relations. The difficult political, socio-economic conditions and social repression in some countries have fanned flames of protest and activism, and public relations practitioners have been seen as social activists promoting social causes through campaigns. What does this smorgasbord of macro environmental variables mean for dialogic theory? How do these variables challenge and/or inform dialogic theory?

Dialogue in the Middle Eastern Context

As previously explained, a true dialogue involves open, accessible, respectful, trustworthy, and transparent two-way communication between participants who display positive attitudes toward each other and toward the process of communication in which they are involved (Lane & Kent, 2018). Nevertheless, as a normative paradigm, the dialogic communication approach embraces a Euro-American worldview and doesn't consider various cultural, political, and societal factors that might affect the form of dialogue evolved. Given the lack of theory development in the region and contributing to examining how the generic notion of dialogue might be applied to the specificities of the Middle East, this section will combine the GPRF with the dialogic communication approach to elaborate on how culture might affect dialogue and its practice.

As previously explained, research on the cultural aspects that drive public relations practice in the Middle East has examined the impact of societal and organizational cultures. Concepts of societal culture such as *wasta* and social connections are encapsulated in the tenets of the personal influence model. Orientations of collectivism and group affiliation contribute to building of relationships between organizations and society. Concepts of organizational culture such as the prevalence of an authoritarian Arab managerial style characterized by one-way, asymmetrical models of communication predominate. Power is respected and high-power distance tends to be the norm. Traditional models of public relations such as press agentry, one-way public information, and one-way asymmetrical tend to dominate, with public relations often equated with media relations, as a publicity tool for governments. This role is further accentuated using propaganda and military public diplomacy in a region plagued with war and conflict.

Embracing the GPRF, this chapter argues that various cultural factors can affect dialogue both positively and negatively, through simultaneously creating a complex set of enabling and limiting conditions. Although we focus only on the Middle East here, we argue that cultural factors worldwide can challenge or promote the classical idea of dialogue.

Positive Spaces

Perhaps the strongest enabler that contributes to relationship building through dialogue in the Middle East is the Arab social norm of *wasta*, characterized by close social ties and small groups of connected people who can offer great conditions for a true dialogue. As argued by Kent and Lane (2021), "Interpersonal, face-to-face, situations are of course the dialogic ideal . . . small group contexts are often, but not always, face to face, so some group contexts have great dialogic potential" (p. 5). Similarly, the culture-centered models of face-to-face, two-way interaction such as those offered by the *majlis* (Badran, 2019), the *wali* office, or the *sablah* (Al-Kindi, 2019) could create positive contexts and opportunities for dialogue to occur for those publics and individuals who can access these spaces. In other words, the personal influence model, based on a quid pro quo relationship between public relations practitioners and strategically placed individuals such as those in the government and media (Sriramesh et al., 1999), built on *wasta* enables small-group interaction through mostly face-to-face communication and can create conducive conditions for dialogue to occur. Further, publics from diverse nationalities that live and work together could contribute to a more pluralistic and diverse society, which in turn might foster understanding of the other and promote *mutuality* and *empathy*, bolstering the creation of positive spaces for dialogue to thrive (Kent & Lane, 2021).

Negative Spaces

On the other hand, another strong mix of societal cultural variables negatively influence the chance for dialogue. For instance, due to the prevalence of respect for hierarchy, reflected in the universal cultural dimension of Hofstede (2001) as high-power distance, vertical hierarchies dictate communication channels and decision-making processes, making Arab managerial and organizational styles authoritative and centralized (Bashir & Aldaihani, 2017). This in turn helps explain the prevalence of one-way and asymmetrical models of public relations across countries such as Saudi Arabia, Kuwait, and the UAE (Al-Shohaib et al., 2009; Almutairi & Dashti, 2019; Kirat, 2006) that challenge the occurrence of a true dialogue. As argued by Kent and Lane (2021), "Where power is disproportionate, dialogue is not possible" (p. 6).

To further complicate the influence of culture on dialogue, rather paradoxically, while ethnic, religious, and linguistic diversity can create opportunities to be aware and open to differences and understanding the other, thus creating positive spaces for dialogue, extreme levels of diversity can also create barriers to dialogue due to ethnocentrism, wherein people tend to evaluate other cultures negatively based on the norms of their own cultures (Levine & Campbell, 1972).

In addition to these societal and organizational cultural variables, a mix of political, economic, media, and activist cultures also creates negative spaces for dialogue. For instance, in the mostly centralized and undemocratic regimes, public relations is strongly connected to government institutions, public affairs, and propaganda without enabling pluralistic expression of opinions and debate (Jo et al., 2008; Magen, 2013; Magen & Lapid, 2016,

2018; Sweetser & Brown, 2010). The use of public relations as publicity and propaganda tools for governments poses challenges to foster dialogue as it is currently theorized. Centralized and undemocratic regimes, in addition to shifting political relationships, place further stress on publics and organizations, often preventing them from conducting open and visible engagement with other publics, organizations, and countries, thus creating negative spaces for dialogue to occur.

Further, existing hierarchical power structures and the strong emphasis on media relations manifested in the prevalence of mediated press agentry, and one-way, asymmetrical, public information models reduce the possibility of a dialogue to materialize. In addition, despite the widespread adoption of social media in the region, it is not utilized for two-way communication and relationship-building partly due to factors such as publics' perceived risks of online engagement driven by laws and internal political climate. In centralized and undemocratic societies, where hierarchical order and power distance are very important, it is difficult and risky to express opposing beliefs or perceptions, thus visible activism (either organizational or political) is not common, which means that dialogue between organizations and activist groups is mostly not on the agenda. This climate of perceived risk, which is also reflected in the low levels of activism, offers yet another negative space where dialogue cannot thrive.

Paradoxically, the myriad cultural environments simultaneously offer positive and negative spaces for dialogue to occur and thrive. This could be a perfect example of the co-existence of multiple approaches to building relationships between organizations and publics. In some cases, due to cultural variables such as power differentials and hierarchical structures, public relations practitioners will need to use one-way, asymmetrical, informational models, thus dampening the creation of spaces for dialogue, while within the smaller socially connected groups closely knit through *wasta* dialogue could be sustained, premised on the personal influence model.

Overall, this chapter argues that to understand the chances for a true dialogue to occur, various cultural, political, societal, and other factors that are usually ignored when analyzing dialogic communication must be considered. Combining these factors with the dialogic theory we reach a better understanding of the dialogic perspective. As we can see, in the Middle East, various factors affect dialogue positively and negatively.

Conclusion

This analysis highlights the importance of studying the impact of *culture*—as broadly defined here—to dialogic theory. As argued by Kent and Lane (2021) there are factors that constitute negative spaces, or contexts, where dialogue is not possible or appropriate. These include situations where persuasive communication occurs, where there is no trust between the parties, where one party believes in his superiority over the others, where there is fear or when power is disproportionate, where there is no ability and/or willingness to change or to admit a change, when there is no openness to new ideas and worldviews, where there is no respect, and where there is a focus on information rather than experiencing and understanding. Referring to the five dialogic principles of Kent and Taylor (2002), we argue that the centralized and undemocratic Middle Eastern regimes that mostly control the economy and the media systems do not encourage dialogue or even two-way communication. Thus, when exploring the dialogic principles of Kent and Taylor (2002) as operationalized by Magen and Avidar (2019) in the Middle East, we usually will not expect to find *mutuality*, or the acceptance of other opinion as worthy of consideration, acknowledgement of the views and desires of others, and a free flow of conversation. Similarly, we will not expect to find *propinquity*, or publics who are being consulted about matters that influence their lives, while organizations strive to engage with them online. We also will not expect to find *empathy*, or governments and organizations encouraging or facilitating the participation of publics or expressing empathy or understanding to other perspectives; or *risk*, when organizations and governments interact with individuals and publics on their terms, accepting the uniqueness and individuality of others; or finally *commitment*, when organizations and governments try to understand opinions of others or work toward a common understanding.

On the other hand, various economic, cultural, and media-related factors might serve as positive spaces, contributing to the potential of a true dialogue to occur. These include employees and publics from diverse nationalities who live and work together, contributing to a more pluralistic and diverse society, thus fostering *mutuality* and *empathy*; cultural attributes of collectivism, *wasta*, social bonding, group attachment, and the adoption of the personal influence model of public relations that set perfect conditions for dialogue to occur through face-to-face, small-group, two-way interactions; and the existence of social media that can be leveraged to promote organization-public relationship building as a first step toward dialogue to occur in later phases.

The main argument in this chapter is that the global applicability of dialogic communication scholarship in public relations would be significantly enhanced by integrating varied forms of culture as organizational environments— political, economic, societal and organizational, media, and activist— into nuanced understandings of dialogic communication. It may also serve as a first step in developing a ground-up new theory that better reflects and represents public relations in the Middle East. Indeed, existing work on dialogue within public relations scholarship reflects predominantly Euro-American worldviews and organization-centered approaches, undervaluing the critical influence of cultures as environments. By analyzing the impact and importance of a broader set of cultural variables on dialogic communication, we have demonstrated how cultural factors can affect dialogic communication through the simultaneous creation of positive and negative spaces for dialogue. Future research can extend this argument to other cultural contexts of practice, thus expanding the global applicability of dialogic theory.

References

Alanazi, A. (1996). Public relations in the Middle East: The case of Saudi Arabia. In H. M. Culbertson & N. Chen (Eds.), *International public relations: A comparative analysis* (pp. 239–256). Lawrence Erlbaum Associates.

Albishri, O., Tarasevich, S., Proverbs, P., Kiousis, S. K., & Alahmari, A. (2019). Mediated public diplomacy in the digital age: Exploring the Saudi and the U.S. governments' agenda-building during Trump's visit to the Middle East. *Public Relations Review, 45*(4), 101820. https://doi.org/10.1016/j.pubrev.2019.101820

Al-Jenaibi, B. (2014). The nature of Arab public discourse: Social media and the "Arab Spring". *Journal of Applied Journalism & Media Studies, 3*(2), 241–260. https://doi.org/10.1386/ajms.3.2.241_1

Al-Kandari, A., & Gaither, T. K. (2011). Arabs, the west and public relations: A critical/cultural study of Arab cultural values. *Public Relations Review, 37*(3), 266–273. https://doi.org/10.1016/j.pubrev.2011.04.002

Al-Kandari, A. A., Gaither, T. K., Alfanad, M. M., Dashti, A. A., & Alsaber, A. R. (2019). An Arab perspective on social media: How banks in Kuwait use Instagram for public relations. *Public Relations Review, 45*(3), 101774. https://doi.org/10.1016/j.pubrev.2019.04.007

Al-Kindi, A. K. (2019). Public relations units in the Omani civil service sector: Historical background and current characteristics. In T. M. Almutairi & D. Kruckeberg (Eds.), *Public relations in the Gulf cooperation countries: An Arab perspective* (pp. 53–73). Routledge.

Allagui, I. (2017). Towards organizational activism in the UAE: A case study approach. *Public Relations Review, 43*, 258–266. https://doi.org/10.1016/j.pubrev.2016.12.007

Allagui, I., & Kuebler, J. (2011). The Arab Spring and the role of ICTs: Editorial introduction. *International Journal of Communication, 5*, 1435–1442.

Almutairi, T. M., & Dashti, A. A. (2019). Public relations in Kuwait: A historical, practical, and theoretical perspective. In T. M. Almutairi & D. Kruckeberg (Eds.), *Public relations in the Gulf cooperation countries: An Arab perspective* (pp. 31–52). Routledge.

Al-Rawi, A. K. (2014). Cyber warriors in the Middle East: The case of the Syrian electronic army. *Public Relations Review, 40*(3), 420–428. https://doi.org/10.1016/j.pubrev.2014.04.005

Al-Saqer, L., & Al-Hashimi, S. (2019). The status and new directions of public relations practice in Bahrain. In T. M. Almutairi & D. Kruckeberg (Eds.), *Public relations in the Gulf cooperation countries: An Arab perspective* (pp. 5–30). Routledge.

Al-Shohaib, K., Frederick, E., Al-Kandari, A. A. J., & Dorsher, M. D. (2009). Factors influencing the adoption of the internet by public relations professionals in the private and public sectors of Saudi Arabia. *Management Communication Quarterly, 24*(1), 104–121. https://doi.org/10.1177/0893318909351433

Ararat, M. (2006, April 1). *Corporate social responsibility across Middle East and North Africa*. SSRN. http://ssrn.com/abstract=1015925

Avidar, R. (2015). Smartphones, publics, and OPR: Do publics want to engage? *Public Relations Review, 41*(2), 214–221. https://doi.org/10.1016/j.pubrev.2014.11.019

Avidar, R. (2017). Public relations and social businesses: The importance of enhancing engagement. *Public Relations Review, 43*(5), 955–962. https://doi.org/10.1016/j.pubrev.2017.03.015

Avidar, R., Ariel, Y., Malka, V., & Levy, E. C. (2013). Smartphones and young publics: A new challenge for public relations practice and relationship building. *Public Relations Review, 39*(5), 603–605. https://doi.org/10.1016/j.pubrev.2013.09.010

Badran, B. A. (2019). A critical snapshot of the practice of public relations in the United Arab Emirates. In T. M. Almutairi & D. Kruckeberg (Eds.), *Public relations in the Gulf cooperation countries: An Arab perspective* (pp. 118–144). Routledge.

Bashir, M., & Aldaihani, A. (2017). Public relations in an online environment: Discourse description of social media in Kuwaiti organizations. *Public Relations Review, 43*(4), 777–787. https://doi.org/10.1016/j.pubrev.2017.05.004

Blum-Kulka, S., Danet, B., & Gerson, R. (1985). The language of requesting in Israeli society. In J. Forgas (Ed.), *Language and social situation* (pp. 113–141). Springer Verlag.

Curtin, P. A., & Gaither, T. K. (2004). International agenda-building in cyberspace: A study of Middle East government English-language websites. *Public Relations Review, 30*(1), 25–36. https://doi.org/10.1016/j.pubrev.2003.11.003

Deetz, S. (2001). Conceptual foundations. In F. M. Jablin & L. L. Putnam (Eds.), *The new handbook of organizational communication: Advances in theory, research and methods* (pp. 3–46). Sage.

Dhanesh, G. S., & Duthler, G. P. (2019a). Public relations in the Middle East: An editorial introduction. *Journal of Public Relations Research, 31*(3–4), 71–83. https://doi.org/10.1080/1062726X.2019.1679436

Dhanesh, G. S., & Duthler, G. P. (2019b). Relationship management through social media influencers: Effects of followers' awareness of paid endorsement. *Public Relations Review, 45*(3), 101765. https://doi.org/10.1016/j.pubrev.2019.03.002

Duthler, G., Watson, T., Theofilou, T., & Sthapitanonda, P. (2015). CSR and stakeholder engagement perspectives from the United Arab Emirates. *Journal of Communication Arts, 33*(2), 48–56.

Freedom House. (2020). *Freedom in the world: A leaderless struggle for democracy*. https://freedomhouse.org/sites/default/files/2020-02/FIW_2020_REPORT_BOOKLET_Final.pdf

Gaither, T. K., & Al-Kandari, A. J. (2014). The cultural-economic model and public relations in the Middle East: An examination of the Islamic banking system in Kuwait. *Public Relations Review, 40*(1), 33–41. https://doi.org/10.1016/j.pubrev.2013.11.003

Gálvez-Rodríguez, M. D. M., Sáez-Martín, A., García-Tabuyo, M., & Caba-Pérez, C. (2018). Exploring dialogic strategies in social media for fostering citizens' interactions with Latin American local governments. *Public Relations Review, 44*(2), 265–276.

Hofstede, G. (2001). *Culture's consequences: Comparing values, behaviors, institutions and organizations across nations.* Sage.

Jo, S., Shim, S. W., & Jung, J. (2008). Propaganda or public relations campaign? International communication on the war against Iraq. *Public Relations Review, 29*(3), 243–255.

Jones, M. L (2007, June 24–26). *Hofstede—culturally questionable?* Oxford Business & Economics Conference. https://ro.uow.edu.au/commpapers/370

Kabbani, N. (2021). *The blockade on Qatar helped strengthen its economy, paving the way to stronger regional integration.* www.brookings.edu/blog/order-from-chaos/2021/01/19/the-blockade-on-qatar-helped-strengthen-its-economy-paving-the-way-to-stronger-regional-integration/

Katriel, T. (1986). *Talking straight: Dugri speech in Israeli Sabra culture.* Cambridge University Press.

Kent, M. L., & Taylor, M. (1998). Building dialogic relationships through the world wide web. *Public Relations Review, 24*(3), 321–334. https://doi.org/10.1016/S0363-8111(99)80143-X

Kent, M. L., & Taylor, M. (2002). Toward a dialogic theory of public relations. *Public Relations Review, 28*(1), 21–37. https://doi.org/10.1016/S0363-8111(02)00108-X

Kent, M. L., & Lane, A. (2021). Two-way communication, symmetry, negative spaces, and dialogue. *Public Relations Review, 47*(2), 102014. https://doi.org/10.1016/j.pubrev.2021.102014

Kirat, M. (2005). Public relations practice in the Arab World: A critical assessment. *Public Relations Review, 31*(3), 323–332. https://doi.org/10.1016/j.pubrev.2005.05.016

Kirat, M. (2006). Public relations in the United Arab Emirates: The emergence of a profession. *Public Relations Review, 32*(3), 254–260. https://doi.org/10.1016/j.pubrev.2006.05.006

Kirat, M. (2015). Corporate social responsibility in the oil and gas industry in Qatar: Perceptions and practices. *Public Relations Review, 41*(4), 48. https://doi.org/10.1016/j.pubrev.2015.07.001

Lahav, T. (2016). The changing blogosphere and its impact on public relations practice and professional ethics: The Israeli case. *Public Relations Review, 42*(5), 929–931. https://doi.org/10.1016/j.pubrev.2016.08.006

Lane, A., & Kent, M. L. (2018). Dialogic engagement. In K. Johnston, & M. Taylor (Eds.), *Handbook of engagement* (pp. 61–72). Wiley-Blackwell.

Levine, R. A., & Campbell, D. T. (1972). *Ethnocentrism: Theories of conflict, ethnic attitudes, and group behavior.* Wiley.

Linvill, D. L., McGee, S. E., & Hicks, K. (2012). Colleges' and universities' use of Twitter: A content analysis. *Public Relations Review, 38*(4), 636–638.

Magen, C. (2013). The Israeli Mossad and the media: Historical and theoretical perspectives. *Public Relations Review, 39*(2), 111–123. https://doi.org/10.1016/j.pubrev.2013.01.005

Magen, C., & Avidar, R. (2019). Introducing the strata approach to dialogue analysis (SADA): The case of political NGOs in Israel. *Journal of Public Relations Research, 31*(3–4), 97–117.

Magen, C., & Lapid, E. (2016). Facing peace and war: Israel's government press office, 1948–2014. *Public Relations Review, 42*(5), 776–786. https://doi.org/10.1016/j.pubrev.2016.08.004

Magen, C., & Lapid, E. (2018). Israel's military public diplomacy evolution: Historical and conceptual dimensions. *Public Relations Review, 44*(2), 287–298. https://doi.org/10.1016/j.pubrev.2017.11.003

McSweeney, B. (2000). *The fallacy of national culture identification.* 6th Interdisciplinary Perspectives on Accounting Conference.

Morehouse, J., & Saffer, A. J. (2018). A bibliometric analysis of dialogue and digital dialogic research: Mapping the knowledge construction and invisible colleges in public relations research. *Journal of Public Relations Research, 30*(3), 65–82. https://doi.org/10.1080/1062726X.2018.1498343

Pearson, R. (1989). Business ethics as communication ethics: Public relations practice and the idea of dialogue. In C. H. Botan & J. V. Hazelton (Eds.), *Public relations theory* (pp. 111–134). Lawrence Erlbaum Associates.

Siebert, F. S., Peterson, T., & Schramm, W. (1956). *Four theories of the press.* University of Illinois Press.

Smith, M. (1998). Culture and organisational change. *Management Accounting, 76*(7), 60.

Sriramesh, K., Kim, Y., & Takasaki, M. (1999). Public relations in three Asian cultures: An analysis. *Journal of Public Relations Research, 11*(4), 271–292. https://doi.org/10.1207/s1532754xjprr1104_01

Sriramesh, K., & Vercic, D. (2009). A theoretical framework for global public relations research and practice. In K. Sriramesh & D. Vercic (Eds.), *The global public relations handbook: Theory, research and practice* (2nd ed., pp. 3–21). Routledge.

Sriramesh, K., & Vercic, D. (2019). *The global public relations handbook: Theory, research and practice* (3rd ed.). Routledge.

Storie, L. K. (2015). Lost publics in public diplomacy: Antecedents for online relationship management. *Public Relations Review, 41*(2), 315–317. https://doi.org/10.1016/j.pubrev.2015.02.008

Sweetser, K. D., & Brown, C. W. (2010). An exploration of Iranian communication to multiple target audiences. *Public Relations Review, 36*(3), 238–248. https://doi.org/10.1016/j.pubrev.2010.03.005

Taylor, M., & Kent, M. L. (2014). Dialogic engagement: Clarifying foundational concepts. *Journal of Public Relations Research, 26*(5), 384–398.

Taylor, M., Kent, M. L., & White, W. J. (2001). How activist organizations are using the Internet to build relationships. *Public Relations Review, 27*(3), 263–284.

Toledano, M., & Avidar, R. (2016). Public relations, ethics, and social media: A cross-national study of PR practitioners. *Public Relations Review, 42*(1), 161–169. https://doi.org/10.1016/j.pubrev.2015.11.012

Toledano, M., & McKie, D. (2013). *Public relations and nation building: Influencing Israel* (1st ed.). Routledge New Directions in PR & Communication Research.

Transparency International. (2019). *Wasta: How personal connections are denying citizens opportunities and basic services.* www.transparency.org/en/news/wasta-how-personal-connections-are-denying-citizens-opportunities-services

Vercic, D., Grunig, L. A., & Grunig, J. E. (1996). Global and specific principles of public relations: Evidence from Slovenia. In H. M. Culbertson & N. Chen (Eds.), *International public relations: A comparative analysis* (pp. 31–66). Lawrence Erlbaum Associates.

Vora, N., & Koch, N. (2015). Everyday inclusions: Rethinking ethnocracy, kafala, and belonging in the Arabian peninsula: Everyday inclusions. *Studies in Ethnicity and Nationalism, 15*(3), 540–552. https://doi.org/10.1111/sena.12158

Watkins, B., & Lewis, R. (2014). Initiating dialogue on social media: An investigation of athletes' use of dialogic principles and structural features of Twitter. *Public Relations Review, 40*(5), 853–855. https://doi.org/10.1016/j.pubrev.2014.08.001

20 The European School of Public Relations

Origins, Main Traits, and Theoretical Contributions

Chiara Valentini and Vilma Luoma-aho

Introduction

Public relations theory is often developed to meet the current communication needs of organizations and the societies around them (Ihlen & Fredriksson, 2018). Evolving with the practice (Brunner, 2019; Toth & Dozier, 2018), theoretical developments in public relations are highly influenced by US cultural norms and professional contexts (Sriramesh & Vercic, 2020). However, other theoretical efforts have emerged from across the world, contributing to the body of public relations knowledge (van Ruler & Vercic, 2004). This chapter presents the main underpinnings of several European theoring efforts, offering an overview of the main assumptions of the theories, models, and thinking pertaining to public relations. These shared foundations, we argue, are the basis of the European School of Public Relations (ESPR).

Europe is bordered by the Arctic Ocean to the north, the Atlantic Ocean to the west, the Mediterranean Sea to the south, and Asia to the east. Only 27 of the 44 countries in the continent are part of the European Union. These 27 countries are increasingly joining resources to develop an EU research agenda (see e.g., Horizon Europe), yet the historical, cultural, societal, political, and economic differences across European countries affect the practice and development of public relations both academically and professionally (Verhoeven et al., 2020). Moreover, the variety of languages spoken in Europe contributes to the emergence of language-specific academic traditions that may remain unavailable to outsiders.

Rather than focusing on diversity, this chapter will focus on the common epistemological roots and their impact for theorizing efforts in Europe. Such work is timely; ESPR theories have often been developed as alternatives to mainstream public relations theories, which have fallen short to explain, predict, or govern organization-public relationships in complex organizations and/or situations. The fresh approaches of the ESPR may prove valuable to understand phenomena that do not fit normative theoretical principles, which may be of use to culturally diverse societies during societal challenges, such as pandemics, wars, and economic crises.

DOI: 10.4324/9781003141396-23

The European School of Public Relations: Genesis, Premises and Core Assumptions

Far from being a complete and defined set of thoughts, the ESPR is defined by the intellectual traditions shared by European scholars in the fields of public relations, strategic communication, corporate communication, and organizational communication. Stemming from the history of conflicts between neighboring countries, European social theorists specializing in communication (see for e.g., Habermas and Luhmann) aimed to solve societal problems by better understanding how communication can contribute to the development of a better society and individuals. As the genesis of these sub-communication disciplines is the same, so are their research trajectories, which investigate organizational, societal, and stakeholder impacts.

In Europe, as in many other parts of the world, the emergence of communication sciences as an academic discipline has produced several sub-specializations in specific internal, external, mediating, and moderating elements of human-to-human, human-to-machine, and human-to-organization interactions. Yet, in Europe, and most likely in other parts of the world, these have not developed into distinct and segregated fields or created what Craig (1999, p. 124) described as an increasing "theoretical tension," but rather they have lively dialogues among them and between communication and not-communication disciplines.

For ESPR scholars, it is natural to bridge and redefine existing theoretical assumptions to explain, predict, and understand public relations problems. Yet, part of this dialogical-dialectical disciplinary approach (Craig, 1999) is dialoguing with existing public relations literature. The ESPR does not disregard "classical" public relations theories[1] such as relationship management theory, excellence theory, etc., a priori. But, when classical public relations theories and theoretical propositions are employed by European scholars, they are often reexamined and further developed (Brunner, 2019) based on European perspectives and historical developments. Thus, they change and evolve in response to new observations and empirical validations. A critical mindset to re-examining propositions and theories is common among ESPR scholars (Valentini, 2021b) whose research agenda aims to address, explain, and/or solve professional, societal, and stakeholder challenges. Because professional, societal, and stakeholder problems have become increasingly complex and intertwined, a critical mindset in public relations theorizing has been considered superior to normative thinking in addressing emergent problems without falling short, or conventional in answering important questions.

What Is the ESPR Proposing?

Given the genesis and core premises of the ESPR, three main assumptions emerge as distinctive. First, ESPR scholars prefer to embrace the notions of complexity and paradoxes as "normal aspects" of social realities considering the critical mindset described earlier (Tench et al., 2017). Overall, there is skepticism of simplistic, extreme positivist views and normative principles regarding, for example, what professionals should do and what excellence— as described in the excellence theory—in public relations means. Although not all phenomena can be fully understood, as paradoxes are common in today's global, hypermodern culture, they are considered in theorizing efforts. By accepting paradoxes and the potential challenges associated with every suggestion for excellent communication, scholars are deinstitutionalizing established principles of excellence in public relations. At the same time, although complex findings are challenging to turn into practical managerial implications, they resonate globally among practitioners.

Second, within the ESPR, communication and relationships are assumed to be two sides of the same coin (Vercic et al., 2001), as communication is "a form of behavior and at the same time . . . the essence of any kind of relations" (van Ruler & Vercic, 2004, pp. 4–5). Thus, when strategizing about communication, professionals think about the impact on stakeholder relationships and implications for society. This contrasts with the US mainstream relationship management understanding (see for e.g., Ledingham, 2021), where communication has a marginal role as an antecedent or a dimension/factor of relationship management. To understand public relations problems, European scholars begin with studying the essence of communication in different interactional situations (van Ruler, 2018), including stakeholder and societal relationships. That is, they study communication as a constitutive, mediating, and persuasive element that defines social realities with or without organizations. This understanding has shifted public relations focus from organizations' problems to global and societal problems from multiple points of view, including a broader understanding of the diverse stakeholder expectations, building trust and legitimacy, and ultimately contributing to the common good of societies, not just to organizations' or clients' interests (Canel & Luoma-aho, 2019).

Third, ESPR scholars tend to assume that public relations is driven by four characteristics: reflectiveness, managerialism, operationalization, and education (van Ruler & Vercic, 2004). Reflectiveness involves reflection on societal standards and values and bringing these reflections to the attention to organizations. Managerialism involves cultivating relationships and mutual understandings through a managerial approach driven by theoretical soundness and clear instruments for measuring communication value. Operationalization involves helping organizations to address stakeholders and societal concerns. Finally, education involves helping all members of an organization to become communicators and to understand stakeholders and societal needs.

The Field of Public Relations: A Holistic Communication Discipline and Profession

European scholars have traditionally employed a holistic approach to study different public relations phenomena, applying a broader set of social, cultural, economic, and political theories than a standard education in public relations in the US normally includes. Many European scholars, particularly those of older generations, have been trained in fields other than communication sciences (e.g., applied linguistics, journalism, foreign languages and literature, social sciences, political sciences, business, and economics)[2]. Younger generations of scholars acknowledge that borrowing theoretical thinking from other communication and non-communication disciplines enables public relations to be positioned in different contexts and situations in different manners, thus adding value to the public relations function. An example of such theoretical cross-fertilization is the *communication value circle* theorizing that communication provides professional value through enabling tangible assets, building intangible assets, ensuring flexibility, and adjusting strategy (Zerfass & Viertmann, 2017).

Much like in the US, European professionals have fulfilled several roles and functions beyond the narrow definition of public relations as a message-crafting activity, which characterized most European public relations practices of the first half of the 20th century. In Europe, terms like *organizational communication, communication management, corporate communication* or *strategic communication* (Falkheimer & Heide, 2014; van Ruler & Vercic, 2004) are preferred, perhaps because the term *public relations* often connotes propaganda and image creation. Even within the scholarly community, there is a preference for terms such as *strategic communication, organizational communication*, and *corporate communication*. From an epistemological point of view, names carry specific meanings, identify specific elements of a profession, and reveal how it is perceived by practitioners and the general public. Thus, the choice of any term is not casual nor without implications. It indicates how professionals and academics want to be perceived by stakeholders and the general community, and the approach they take in practicing or theorizing on communication. When scholars and practitioners discuss the field and its contributions, they often refer to holistic management/orchestration of communication in organizations and among stakeholders.

This is also apparent within the ESPR, which tends to theorize less about the distinctive aspects of communication functions and more about the shared elements. In the European academic community, this field focuses "on understanding, exploring and analyzing their different practices and their impact on organizations, publics and stakeholders and societies" (Valentini, 2021a, p. 7).

Even the object of public relations is often very broad, extending beyond what the literature defines as key stakeholders. Particularly in the latest decade of ESPR work, there is an increasing interest in widening the object of public relations in theorizing efforts, as public relations professionals are "asked to perform a number of very different organizing activities at social, cultural, political, economic and interpersonal levels" (Valentini, 2021a, p. 10). This is another reason why, epistemologically and methodologically, European public relations scholars borrow and adapt insights from other disciplines, particularly the European disciplines of corporate communication,

communication management, organizational communication, strategic communication, and, to some extent, marketing communication disciplines.

Dark Side of Public Relations Theory

For most European countries, the World Wars and their propaganda led communication theorists to focus on rhetoric traditions and postwar societal reconstruction (see, Watson, 2015). However, there are also negative forms of public relations and disinformation in Europe, which public relations theory reflects upon (Pamment et al., 2018). Recent work has focused on negative forms of engagement, complaints, and the strength of the emotion associated with them (e.g., Lievonen et al., 2018; Ruppel & Einwiller, 2021) or dark forms of communication related to sustainability and corporate social responsibility (Siano et al., 2017; Valentini & Kruckeberg, 2018; Vollero et al., 2016).

For the Nordic and western European countries with strong public sectors, public relations theories are heavily intertwined with public sector communication (Canel & Luoma-aho, 2019), relying deeply on the work of European sociologists (Ihlen & Fredriksson, 2018). Additionally, according to their missions, public sector organizations should operate in accordance with the best interests of citizens and society. Yet, this is the sector in which, historically, the "propaganda machine" was employed by public relations professionals. The dark side of public relations is still present today in the war-torn Eastern European countries (Hejlová & Klimeš, 2019; Koudelková et al., 2015), where crisis communication may turn into unethical influencing, or "black PR," mixing less ethical practices with new theories (Gryzunova, 2020, p. 201).

On some level, scholars view fighting disinformation similarly to the call for postwar theorizing to rebuild society through the strategic use of communication. To address phenomena pertaining to black PR or disinformation, European scholars have worked in close collaboration with governments and multinational organizations to help them become more antifragile and better able to survive problems and challenges (Canel & Luoma-aho, 2019; Pamment et al., 2018). Pamment et al. (2018) note that communication professionals are centrally located to prepare their organizations to become aware of, identify, and counter attempts to influence information. Despite some dark sides, distinct bright traits of the European School of Public Relations have emerged, which are next addressed in more detail.

Main Traits of the European School of Public Relations

Four overlapping major traits can be identified that characterize the thinking shared by most scholars on the European continent: 1) a focus within public relations inquiry on concerns facing society at large, 2) a focus on the responsibility of professionals and organizations to act and impact society,

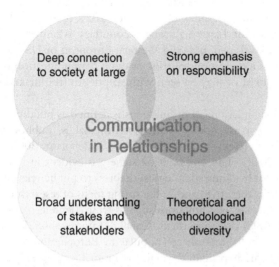

Figure 20.1 Areas of Focus for the European School of Public Relations

3) broad consideration of stakes and social actors, and 4) theoretical and methodological diversity in theorization and conceptualization of public relations. All these develop in tandem, where progress in one shapes the others: for example, any societal change reflects on changes in stakeholders' demands and stakes, the levels, forms and types of responsibilities, and affect the diversity of research efforts. Figure 20.1 illustrates the relations between these four traits with the overall understanding of communication in relationships that characterizes the ESPR. The following sections elaborate on these four overlapping traits.

Deep Connection to Society at Large

European public relations theory has a strong connection to its surrounding society and understanding of the contribution of communication to society at large. As van Ruler and Vercic summarize,

> The common US-oriented approach to the field focuses on "public" as managing "publics"—those concerned people who act to solve a problem they face—while in some European countries at least, the roots of public relations science and practice seem to be much more based on public as in and for the "public sphere."
>
> (2004, p. 3)

Often, European professionals and scholars conceive of the public relations profession as a profession aiming to relate with the larger context of society, labelled the "public sphere" (Bentele & Notthaft, 2008; Vercic et al., 2001).

"Communication as a social institution highly depends on the development of the public sphere" (Kashirskikh & Zverev, 2021, p. 31) and the other way around. Yet, in some Eastern European countries, where the public sphere remains underdeveloped, utilizing Western European or US-based theories may backfire, as expectations of trust or open communication by organizations may not exist or may be seen with skepticism (Kashirskikh & Zverev, 2021).

One of public relations' core functions is defined as building, enhancing, and maintaining trust among social systems, that is, publics, institutions, and organizations (Bentele, 1994; Bentele & Seidenglanz, 2008; Valentini & Kruckeberg, 2011). This emphasis on society is evident in both the European tradition of bridging sociological theories to public relations (see, e.g., Ihlen & Fredriksson, 2018) and in the strong focus of research on intangible assets that enable societal functions such as trust (Bentele, 1994; Bentele & Seidenglanz, 2008) or engagement (Canel & Luoma-aho, 2019).

Theories on collaboration are popular in Europe, and even traditional media relations are explained through the mutual connections and dependencies of different actors in society. For instance, the German scholars Bentele et al. (1997) developed the *Intereffication Model* (from the Latin words *inter* and *efficare*, meaning "to mutually enable") to explain the mutual dependencies, orientations, and influences between journalists and public relations in liberal-democratic societies. It also shows that the activities of public relations professionals and journalists are only possible when the other side exists and cooperates. Early US studies on relationships between public relations professionals and journalists portray the scenario as antagonistic (e.g., Kopenhaver et al., 1984; Ryan & Martinson, 1988; Shin & Cameron, 2004). However, different studies (e.g., Niejens & Smit, 2006; Valentini & Muzi Falcone, 2008) show that, in a European context, these two communication professions are "Siamese twins" (Bentele & Nothhaft, 2008, p. 34), have a "structural coupling" relationship (Luhmann, 1987), and can normally achieve their respective communicative objectives, such as publicity for particular topics or changes of attitude (Bentele & Nothhaft, 2008).

Societal interdependence is also visible in the work and contribution of the Danish scholar Holmström (1998, 2004, 2005), who epistemologically bases her reflections on the function of public relations on Luhmann's system thinking and a reflective paradigm. From this perspective, the role of public relations is organizational legitimization, interrelated with different and changing forms of societal coordination. Holmström's thinking has contributed to the development of a research agenda on public relations' role in organizations' social license to operate and CSR (e.g., Cho et al., 2020; Hurst et al., 2020). Furthermore, the reflective approach to public relations approach is not just a normative ideal, as van Ruler and Vercic (2004) showed. Most European professionals believe that the main role of public relations is to continuously adjust decisions (i.e., to bridge between organizational and societal interests) based on society's changing norms and values. This concern is still high on the agenda of top communication professionals, as underlined by the annual reports of the European Communication Monitor (see Verhoeven et al., 2020).

Overall, at both the professional and academic levels, there is a strong understanding of the Habermasian public sphere (Katus, 2004; Raupp, 2004, 2011) and how communication can contribute to and constitute a society that aligns with the Communicative Constitution of Organization (CCO) perspective (Romenti & Illia, 2013; Valentini et al., 2016; Wehmeier & Winkler, 2013). Accordingly, public relations is often situated as a societal phenomenon rather than an organizational one, and it is studied as something that impacts social realities.

Strong Emphasis on Responsibility

Given its main societal orientation, ESPR and its theorizing efforts are driven by a strong focus on responsibility. Responsibility is taken as a starting point for organizational legitimacy, not an added function or contribution. European scholars have co-edited the leading CSR volume in public relations (see Ihlen et al., 2011), and a special emphasis on ethics in public relations is noticeable among European scholars' thinking (Einwiller & Carroll, 2020). Further, most of the crisis communication literature from Europe includes responsibility beyond corporate losses (e.g., Einwiller & Carroll, 2020; Frandsen & Johansen, 2017; Ruppel & Einwiller, 2021).

Understanding the European contribution to the study of responsibility in public relations contexts requires looking at the different responsibility-related concepts used by European scholars, including accountability, reflectiveness, opacity, transparency, and citizenship. Cross-disciplinary work is the norm, rather than the exception, and contributing to literature beyond public relations is typical. Indeed, European scholars were among the first to examine the financial value of CSR to market performance (see, e.g., Helmig et al., 2016) as well as looking at the potential backfiring effects (Einwiller et al., 2019). In addition, European scholars have examined the ideal match of organizations and their corporate citizenship attempts (Ihlen et al., 2011; Timonen & Luoma-aho, 2010) as well as the new forms of media, including transparency of sponsored content (Borchers & Enke, 2020; Ikonen et al., 2017) and authenticity of organizations' collaborations with influencers (Reinikainen et al., 2020). Theoretically, this has led to new theories that include responsibility as a key component, such as *relationship expectation theory* (RET; Olkkonen & Luoma-aho, 2015, 2021).

Responsibility also pertains to technology. Capriotti and Moreno (2007) were among the first to discuss whether online CSR initiatives were interactive, and they noted that companies were mostly using their websites for promotional purposes, not dialogue with stakeholders. More recently, European scholars have helped expand the understanding of responsibility to the digital realm (Valentini et al., 2022). For example, with the advent of artificial intelligence and its use by professionals and organizations, responsibility has become a key element to be addressed, and communication plays an important role in stakeholder participation, comprehensiveness, and responsiveness as well as multivocality (Buhmann et al., 2019). Others, such as Gregory and Halff (2020) and Bourne and Edwards (2021), have called for organizations to admit the social cost of big data and the public relations it drives. They call for public relations to better consider stakeholders' choices for accessing, using, aggregating, storing, reusing, transacting, and even trading their own data. In addition, they call for public relations professionals to return control of the digital data collected by organizations to stakeholders, or "consumer-citizens."

Overall, responsibility to stakeholders and society at large is seen as a form of professional accountability in the ESPR, or, as van Ruler (2015) suggests with the notion of reflective practitioners, a reflective, holistic aspect of public relations practices. It also pertains to decisional, social, and performative organizational aspects, including reflection at the team level and with organizational partners and alliances. Accountability and its maintenance are integral parts of all relationships between the public relations profession and stakeholders and society. The role of communication in this process is central; it enables the multi-way diachronic process of constructing meaning, which is highly relevant for public relations theory and practice.

Broad Understanding of Stakes and Stakeholders

Given the deep connection to society and great attention to responsibility, European public relations theory acknowledges a much broader definition of the stakes and who can be understood as a stakeholder beyond the typical primary stakeholders in US research. For instance, the environment is often considered a legitimate stakeholder in public relations initiatives.

European scholars also prefer to address stakeholders instead of publics, as publics tend to act in response to problems they face, whereas stakeholders—as groups or entities with tangible and intangible interests—have duties and rights toward organizations and societies. Those rights include influencing the directions of organizations and leaders, their policies, and actions beyond when there is a problem. Indeed, European scholars acknowledge the central role of stakeholders in deciding the strategic direction of organizations (Zerfass & Viertmann, 2017). Often, European public relations theories acknowledge that communication is no longer organization-centric, but stakeholder-centric (see, e.g., Luoma-aho & Vos, 2010).

Originating from network analysis and the theory of social capital (Ihlen & Fredriksson, 2018; Luoma-aho, 2016), European scholars were among the first to discuss different types of stakeholders in the context of public relations: advocating faith-holders (Luoma-aho, 2015) and corporate-attacking negative stakeholders, or hateholders (Gruber et al., 2020; Lievonen et al., 2018; Ruppel & Einwiller, 2021). Building on actor-network theory, which explains how non-human influences (e.g., IT mergers, natural environments) may birth unexpected contexts, situations, and stakeholder groups for organizations and how these shape public relations (Luoma-aho & Paloviita, 2010), European scholars have introduced the idea of non-human stakeholders to public relations theory (Somerville, 2021). Moreover, European scholars have theorized about the role of disinformation (Ihlen et al., 2019), fake stakeholders (or fakeholders; Luoma-aho, 2015), and their effect on organizational legitimacy, and understanding the future changes that technology (Luoma-aho & Badham, 2023) and mediatization (Pallas & Fredriksson, 2013) bring to communication is of central importance.

To study this wide set of stakes and stakeholders, some ESPR scholars have advanced the notion of "arenas" where different voices meet to discuss and interpret events and issues occurring in society (e.g., Frandsen & Johansen, 2017; Luoma-aho & Vos, 2010; Valentini et al., 2016). Such work focuses on continuous interactions rather than messages with a one-time influence and effectiveness. In addition, the concept of arenas shifts the focus from a corporation's own network to broader ones. It also rests on one of the main assumptions of the ESPR: that communication constitutes an element of social reality. Arenas are communicatively constituted, and thereby, so are the interactions that take place among social actors. Anyone, at any time, is capable of defining and offering their own interpretation of events to a wide set of publics, who can, in turn, re-define their meanings.

Based on these underpinnings, Luoma-aho and Vos (2010) suggest that we have actually moved away from communication that is organization-centric and toward issue-centric thinking. Issue arenas, they note, are the online and offline places where societal dialogue occurs, and meanings are assigned. Based on issue arena theory, those individuals or organizations that are able to engage the arena early on are in better strategic positions as they can contribute to who is accepted to the dialogue and how communication follows (Luoma-aho & Vos, 2010). Similarly, Johansen (2018) speaks about rhetorical arenas as social spaces that open when a crisis arises and multiple voices communicate about it. The concept, however, has been applied to various situations when different opinions and ideas are shared and discussed. These spaces are rhetorical in that they are communicatively constructed and maintained through rhetorical moves. Recent European research shows that the concept of rhetorical arena is particularly relevant to study the role of employees in organizational communications. These have been found to be a central stakeholder group when investigating how issues are communicatively constructed and reconstructed in arenas (Frandsen & Johansen, 2017).

Theoretical and Methodological Diversity

European public relations theory has much inherent diversity at the epistemological, ontological, and methodological levels (Jelen, 2008; Pasadeos et al., 2011; Valentini, 2020) as well as in the roots of theories. Epistemologically, public relations theorization in the ESPR has been characterized by a dominant hermeneutic view that focuses on interpretation and understanding of the societal phenomena that affect organizations, stakeholders, and publics as well as society at large. Rather than speaking about public relations as an isolated function of organizations, the European view on public relations theory follows a "hermeneutic circle," understanding the whole from its parts and each individual part by its reference to the whole. As explained earlier, European public relations theory integrates all forms of communications and relationships (Falkheimer & Heide, 2014) and adopts a holistic view of communication. In addition, there may be a preference for subjective ontology, as phenomena are studied in and for a specific context. When European scholars analyze public relations phenomena, they often investigate the context, its interdependencies, and contingencies. Moreover, there is a strong focus on diverse types of organizations beyond businesses and for-profit entities. Another difference is the focus on macro (i.e., societal) and meso (i.e., organizational) level aspects, as opposed to micro-level activities and results that support professional management functions, which often receive more attention from Anglo-American theorists. Overall, European public relations theory addresses organizations and societies as coupled elements (van Ruler & Vercic, 2004).

Ontologically speaking, ESPR research is clearly influenced by interpretivism and social interpretivism, leading to a preference for qualitative empirical studies. For instance, some of the first scholars interested in public relations from the Nordic region were those educated in applied linguistics. It follows that their early research into public relations was highly influenced by their educational background. The language-based roots of public relations is evidenced in studies articulating an understanding of public relations as a rhetorical tradition (e.g., Ihlen, Frandsen, and Johansen's work) or a constituting element of social reality (van Ruler, 2018).

Critical, cultural, social, postmodern, technological, and feminist perspectives, which have long been fringe in public relations theory, have become quite important contributions to the discipline. This is also due to the work of European scholars and their friends working in European universities or abroad, such as Edwards (2018), Hodges (2006), Fawkes (2015), L'Etang (2007), L'Etang et al. (2016), Pieczka (2018), Ihlen and Heath (2019), and Frandsen and Johansen (2013). Although European scholars are also engaging with functionalist studies, a more balanced and diverse range of paradigms seems apparent, especially compared with the US research tradition in public relations, which still tends to rely heavily on behavioralism, with strong emphases on functionalism (Wehmeier & Winkler, 2013), managerial issues (Valentini, 2021b), and applied research (Ihlen & Verhoeven, 2012). European scholars seem to be braver in regard to venues and research approaches other than classical surveys, content analyses, and interviews, which are the dominant research methods in the international public relations field (e.g., Jelen-Sanchez, 2018; Valentini, 2020). Catellani (2012) has been a pioneer in applying Umberto Eco's semiotics learning to study environmental and CSR communications in a public relations context. Likewise, Maier's (2012) multi-modality approach has enriched the potential to study different communication formats in public relations studies, and more recently studies borrowing from visual communication (e.g., Valentini et al., 2018) have contributed to expand public relations knowledge.

As the ESPR relies on theoretical foundations and epistemological, ontological, and methodological positions that borrow from the diverse cultures that characterize Europe, it remains less cohesive and more fragmented in terms of public relations practices than its US counterpart whose cultural, educational, and professional amalgamation efforts have produced a much more homogenous set of values (van Ruler & Vercic, 2004). This is important to consider when reflecting on the standpoints taken by European scholars.

Concluding Reflections

The ESPR reflects the future of the public relations theorizing on several levels. Although Europe's 44 countries differ greatly, there are some common assumptions that underpin the theoretical efforts of European scholars. These assumptions have shaped and are shaping European public relations theory. The four traits outlined in this chapter that link different theoretical trajectories are: 1) a deep connection to society, 2) a strong emphasis on responsibility, 3) a broad understanding of stakes and stakeholders, and 4) wide theoretical and methodological diversity. While individually not unique to European theory, taken together, these traits are the basis for the ESPR.

As cross-collaborations among international scholars and mobility have increased over the last decade, the ESPR's influence has spread beyond Europe, particularly to Australia/Oceania and South America, where scholars have welcomed some of the ESPR's thinking as alternatives to the classical public relations theories developed by US scholars. Globally, theorizing on societal public relations has increased, with more studies conducted on social activism and community engagement (see for e.g., Johnston & Taylor, 2018) as well as responsibility and accountability due in part to early European scholars' work. Indeed, responsibility in businesses and organizations is a largely European concept, and European scholars remain at the forefront of research addressing new forms of responsibility that arise from technological developments in the field of public relations. In addition, European scholars have taken a critical approach to CSR, examining its fit, potential harm, and challenges. As public relations theory in Europe is constructed in an environment of dynamic change and ongoing construction of meanings, the ESPR has developed a broad understanding of stakes, which has been helpful beyond Europe. Stakeholder thinking has become the norm globally, and as digitalization continues, we predict that arena thinking will also become a global starting point. Moreover, the more complex organizations and networks become, the more agency non-human stakeholders and influences can gain, increasing the need for knowledge on broader stakes. To gain an understanding of such complexities, we argue that interdisciplinary approaches, such as those adopted by the ESPR, are needed at the theoretical and methodological levels.

Overall, the ESPR has contributed to increased critical thinking in the discipline, as European scholars or scholars at European universities have shown great interest in challenging established assumptions to develop (original) European theory (Jelen-Sanchez, 2018; Valentini, 2020, 2021b). It has continuously contributed to the contextualization of existing theory for specific national environments and situations, thus helping to empirically validate or re-define global public relations theories.

Far from being a set way of thinking about public relations theory, the ESPR is offering a multidisciplinary and multi-vocal take on current global challenges. Perhaps it has not contributed to legitimizing public relations' identity, but it has demonstrated the broader value of public relations to society. The ESPR has also contributed to public relations theory by situating public relations thinking among ethical, sustainable, and society-oriented disciplines and professions. The ESPR does not promote a normative understanding of public relations (e.g., Heath, 2018; Kruckeberg & Starck, 1988) but embraces contradictions and paradoxes and accepts them as part of dynamic interactions with stakeholders through an agile approach (van Ruler, 2015). Furthermore, the disciplinary dialogues that characterize the ESPR reduce tension among communication sub-disciplines (Craig, 1999) and help scholars focus on the real purpose of public relations theorizing: to solve global problems by establishing, nurturing, and managing mutual and beneficial relationships with diverse stakeholders for organizations and clients. The ESPR holds potential to become a thought leader in the next decades, as responsibility and diversity questions are gaining ground globally. The ESPR calls for more globally diverse debates on public relations theory and practice.

A final warning: some scholars may disagree with the overview offered in this chapter. For some, it may be too reductive, not fully capturing the scholarly reality in Europe. This chapter does not claim to represent all European scholars' endeavors, but we argue that it addresses a large portion. Given the diversity of European traditions within the ESPR, further analyses are needed to better understand specific regions and nations, and it is hoped that this chapter can serve as a starting point.

Notes

1   For a discussion of "classical" public relations theory, see Valentini (2021b).
2   For an overview of the history of public relations education in Europe, see Watson, 2015.

References

Bentele, G. (1994). Öffentliches Vertrauen—normative und soziale Grundlage für public relations. In W. Armbrecht & U. Zabel (Eds.), *Normative aspekte der public relations: Grunlegende Fragen und Perspektiven, Eine Einführung* (pp. 131–158). Westdeutscher Verlag.

Bentele, G., Liebert, T., & Seeling, S. (1997). Von der Determination zur Intereffikation. Ein integriertes Modell zum Verhältnis von Public Relations und Journalismus. In G. Bentele & M. Haller (Eds.), *Aktuelle Entstehung von Öffentlichkeit: Akteure, Strukturen, Veränderungen* (pp. 225–250). UVK.

Bentele, G., & Nothhaft, H. (2008). The intereffication model: Theoretical discussions and empirical research. In A. Zerfass, B. van Ruler, & K. Sriramesh (Eds.), *Public relations research: European and international perspectives and innovations* (pp. 33–47). VS Verlag für Sozialwissenschaften.

Bentele, G., & Seidenglanz, R. (2008). Trust and credibility—prerequisites for communication management. In A. Zerfass, B. van Ruler, & K. Sriramesh (Eds.), *Public relations research: European and international perspectives and innovations* (pp. 49–62). VS Verlag für Sozialwissenschaften.

Borchers, N. S., & Enke, N. (2020). Influencer und Meinungsführer als Herausforderung für die Unternehmenskommunikation. In A. Zerfass, M. Piwinger, & U. Röttger (Eds.), *Handbuch Unternehmenskommunikation* (pp. 1–19). Springer Gabler. https://doi.org/10.1007/978-3-658-03894-6_12-1

Bourne, C., & Edwards, L. (2021). Critical reflections on the field. In C. Valentini (Ed.), *Public relations: Handbooks of communication science* (Vol. 27, pp. 601–614). De Gruyter Mouton.

Brunner, B. R. (2019). *Public relations theory: Applications and understanding.* Wiley-Blackwell.

Buhmann, A., Paßmann, J., & Fieseler, C. (2019). Managing algorithmic accountability: Balancing reputational concerns, engagement strategies, and the potential of rational discourse. *Journal of Business Ethics, 163*(2), 265–280. https://doi.org/10.1007/s10551-019-04226-4

Canel, M.-J., & Luoma-aho, V. (2019). *Public sector communication: Closing gaps between citizens and public organizations.* Wiley-Blackwell.

Capriotti, P., & Moreno, A. (2007). Corporate citizenship and public relations: The importance and interactivity of social responsibility issues on corporate websites. *Public Relations Review, 33*(1), 84–91. https://doi.org/10.1016/j.pubrev.2006.11.012

Catellani, A. (2012). Pro-nuclear European discourses: Socio-semiotic observations. *Public Relations Inquiry, 1*(3), 285–311. https://doi.org/10.1177/2046147X12448610

Cho, M., Park, S. Y., & Kim, S. (2020). When an organization violates public expectations: A comparative analysis of sustainability communication for corporate and nonprofit organizations. *Public Relations Review, 47*(1), 101928. https://doi.org/10.1016/j.pubrev.2020.101928

Craig, R. (1999). Communication theory as a field. *Communication Theory, 9*(2), 119–161. https://doi.org/10.1111/j.1468-2885.1999.tb00355.x

Edwards, L. (2018). *Understanding public relations: Theory, culture, society.* Sage.

Einwiller, S., & Carroll, C. (2020). Negative disclosures in corporate social responsibility reporting. *Corporate Communications: An International Journal, 25*(2), 319–337. https://doi.org/10.1108/CCIJ-05-2019-0054

Einwiller, S., Lis, B., Ruppel, C., & Sen, S. (2019). When CSR-based identification backfires: Testing the effects of CSR-related negative publicity. *Journal of Business Research, 104*, 1–13. https://doi.org/10.1016/j.jbusres.2019.06.036

Falkheimer, J., & Heide, M. (2014). From public relations to strategic communication in Sweden: The emergence of a transboundary field of knowledge. *Nordiccom Review*, *35*(2), 123–138. https://doi.org/10.2478/nor-2014-0019

Fawkes, J. (2015). *Public relations ethics and professionalism: The shadow of excellence.* Routledge.

Frandsen, F., & Johansen, W. (2013). Public relations and the new institutionalism: In search of a theoretical framework. *Public Relations Inquiry*, *2*(2), 205–221. https://doi.org/10.1177/2046147X13485353

Frandsen, F., & Johansen, W. (2017). *Organizational crisis communication: A multivocal approach.* Sage.

Gregory, A., & Halff, G. (2020). The damage done by big data-driven public relations. *Public Relations Review*, *46*(2), 101902. https://doi.org/10.1016/j.pubrev.2020.101902

Gruber, M., Mayer, C., & Einwiller, S. (2020). What drives people to participate in online firestorms? *Online Information Review*, *44*(3), 563–581. https://doi.org/10.1108/OIR-10-2018-0331

Gryzunova, E. (2020). Hybridity of crisis communication professional discourse in Russia. In K. Tsetsura & D. Kruckeberg (Eds.), *Strategic communications in Russia: Public relations and advertising* (pp. 193–205). Routledge.

Heath, R. L. (2018). Fully functioning society. In R. L. Heath & W. Johansen (Eds.), *The international encyclopedia of strategic communication* (pp. 641–649). Wiley-Blackwell.

Hejlová, D., & Klimeš, D. (2019). Propaganda stories in Czechoslovakia in the late 1980s: Believe it or not? *Public Relations Review*, *45*(2), 217–226. https://doi.org/10.1016/j.pubrev.2018.08.005

Helmig, B., Spraul, K., & Ingenhoff, D. (2016). Under positive pressure: How stakeholder pressure affects corporate social responsibility implementation. *Business & Society*, *55*(2), 151–187. https://doi.org/10.1177/0007650313477841

Hodges, C. (2006). "PRP culture": A framework for exploring public relations practitioners as cultural intermediaries. *Journal of Communication Management*, *10*(1), 80–93. https://doi.org/10.1108/13632540610646391

Holmström, S. (1998). *An intersubjective and a social systemic public relations paradigm.* Roskilde University Publishers. www.susanne-holmstrom.dk/SH1996UK.pdf

Holmström, S. (2004). The reflective paradigm. In B. van Ruler & D. Verčič (Eds.), *Public relations and communication management in Europe: A nation-by-nation introduction to public relations theory and practice* (pp. 121–133). De Gruyter Mouton.

Holmström, S. (2005). Reframing public relations: The evolution of a reflective paradigm for organizational legitimization. *Public Relations Review*, *31*(4), 497–504. https://doi.org/10.1016/j.pubrev.2005.08.008

Hurst, B., Johnston, K. A., & Lane, A. B. (2020). Engaging for a social license to operate (SLO). *Public Relations Review*, *46*(4), 101931. https://doi.org/10.1016/j.pubrev.2020.101931

Johansen, W. (2018). Rhetorical arena. In R. L. Heath & W. Johansen (Eds.), *The international encyclopedia of strategic communication* (pp. 1321–1329). Wiley-Blackwell. https://doi.org/10.1002/9781119010722.iesc0155

Johnston, K. A., & Taylor, M. (2018). *Handbook of communication engagement.* Wiley-Blackwell.

Ihlen, O., Bartlett, J. L., & May, S. (2011). *Handbook of communication and corporate social responsibility.* Wiley-Blackwell.

Ihlen, O., & Fredriksson, M. (2018). *Public relations and social theory: Key figures, concepts and developments* (2nd ed.). Routledge.

Ihlen, O., Gregory, A., Luoma-aho, V., & Buhmann, A. (2019). Post-truth and public relations: Special section introduction. *Public Relations Review, 45*(4), 101844. https://doi.org/10.1016/j.pubrev.2019.101844

Ihlen, O., & Heath, R. L. (2019). Ethical grounds for public relations as organizational rhetoric. *Public Relations Review, 45*(4), 101824. https://doi.org/10.1016/j.pubrev.2019.101824

Ihlen, O., & Verhoeven, P. (2012). A public relations identity for the 2010s. *Public Relations Inquiry, 1*(2), 159–176. https://doi.org/10.1177/2046147X11435083

Ikonen, P., Luoma-aho, V., & Bowden, S. (2017). Transparency for sponsored content: Analysing codes of ethics in public relations, marketing, advertising and journalism. *International Journal of Strategic Communication, 11*(2), 165–178. https://doi.org/10.108 0/1553118X.2016.1252917

Jelen, A. (2008). The nature of scholarly endeavors in public relations. In B. van Ruler, A. T. Vercic, & D. Vercic (Eds.), *Public relations metrics: Research and evaluation* (pp. 36–59). Routledge.

Jelen-Sanchez, A. (2018). Experiencing public relations as an academic discipline: What do scholarly views and public research tell us? In E. Bridgen & D. Vercic (Eds.), *Experiencing public relations: International voices* (pp. 6–25). Routledge.

Kashirskikh, O., & Zverev, S. (2021). The forms and shapes of today's communication as a field, as a discipline, and as a social institution in Russia: Communication development as a result of society's modernization. In K. Tsetsura & D. Kruckeberg (Eds.), *Strategic communications in Russia: Public relations and advertising* (pp. 29–44). Routledge.

Katus, J. (2004). Intermezzo: Civil society and public relations. In B. van Ruler & D. Vercic (Eds.), *Public relations and communication management in Europe: A nation-by-nation introduction to public relations theory and practice* (pp. 387–392). De Gruyter Mouton.

Kopenhaver, L. L., Martinson, D. L., & Ryan, M. (1984). How public relations practitioners and editors in Florida view each other. *Journalism & Mass Communication Quarterly, 61*(4), 860–884. https://doi.org/10.1177/107769908406100419

Koudelková, P., Strielkowski, W., & Hejlová, D. (2015). Corruption and system change in the Czech Republic: Firm-level evidence. *DANUBE: Law, Economics and Social Issues Review, 6*(1), 25–46. https://doi.org/10.1515/danb-2015-0002

Kruckeberg, D., & Starck, K. (1988). *Public relations and community: A reconstructed theory.* Praeger.

Ledingham, J. A. (2021). Relationship management: Status and theory. In C. Valentini (Ed.), *Public relations: Handbooks of communication sciences* (Vol. 27, pp. 415–432). De Gruyter Mouton.

L'Etang, J. (2007). *Public relations: Concepts, practice and critique.* Sage.

L'Etang, J., McKie, D., Snow, N., & Xifra, J. (2016). *The Routledge handbook of critical public relations.* Routledge.

Lievonen, M., Luoma-aho, V. L., & Bowden, (2018). Negative engagement. In K. A. Johnston & M. Taylor (Eds.), *The handbook of communication engagement* (pp. 531–548). Wiley-Blackwell.

Luhmann, N. (1987). *Soziale systeme: Grundriss einer allgemeinen Theorie.* Suhrkamp.

Luoma-aho, V. (2015). Understanding stakeholder engagement: Faith-holders, hate-holders and fakeholders. *Research Journal of the Institute for Public Relations, 2*(1), 1–28. https://instituteforpr.org/wp-content/uploads/updated-vilma-pdf.pdf

Luoma-aho, V. (2016). Social capital theory. In C. E. Carroll (Ed.), *The Sage encyclopedia of corporate reputation* (pp. 759–762). Sage.

Luoma-aho, V., & Badham, M. (2023, forthcoming). *Handbook of digital corporate communication.* Edward Elgar.

Luoma-aho, V., & Paloviita, A. (2010). Actor-networking stakeholder theory for corporate communications. *Corporate Communications: An International Journal, 15*(1), 47–69. https://doi.org/10.1108/13563281011016831

Luoma-aho, V., & Vos, M. (2010). Towards a more dynamic stakeholder model: Acknowledging multiple issue arenas. *Corporate Communications: An International Journal, 15*(3), 315–331. https://doi.org/10.1108/13563281011068159

Maier, C. D. (2012). Multimodality in corporate communication. In C. A. Chapelle (Ed.), *The encyclopedia of applied linguistics.* Wiley & Sons. https://doi.org/10.1002/9781405198431.wbeal0843

Niejens, P., & Smit, E. G. (2006). Dutch public relations practitioners and journalists: Antagonists no more. *Public Relations Review, 32*(3), 232–240. https://doi.org/10.1016/j.pubrev.2006.05.015

Olkkonen, L., & Luoma-aho, V. (2015). Broadening the concept of expectations in public relations. *Journal of Public Relations Research, 27*(1), 81–99. https://doi.org/10.1080/1062726X.2014.943761

Olkkonen, L., & Luoma-aho, V. (2021). Public relations and expectation theory: Introducing relationship expectation theory (RET) for public relations. In C. Valentini (Ed.), *Public relations: Handbooks of communication science* (Vol. 27, pp. 541–562). De Gruyter Mouton.

Pallas, J., & Fredriksson, M. (2013). Corporate media work and micro-dynamics of mediatization. *European Journal of Communication, 28*(4), 420–435. https://doi.org/10.1177/0267323113488487

Pamment, J., Nothaft, H., Twetman, H., & Fjällhed, A. (2018). *Countering information influence activities: A handbook for communicators.* Swedish Civil Contingencies Agency. www.msb.se/RibData/Filer/pdf/28698.pdf

Pasadeos, Y., Lamme, M. O., Gower, K., & Song, T. (2011). A methodological evaluation of public relations research. *Public Relations Review, 37*(2), 163–165. https://doi.org/10.1016/j.pubrev.2011.01.007

Pieczka, M. (2018). Critical perspectives of engagement. In K. A. Johnston & M. Taylor (Eds.), *The handbook of communication engagement* (pp. 549–568). Wiley-Blackwell.

Raupp, J. (2004). The public sphere as central concept of public relations. In B. van Ruler & D. Vercic (Eds.), *Public relations and communication management in Europe: A nation-by-nation introduction to public relations theory and practice* (pp. 309–316). De Gruyter Mouton.

Raupp, J. (2011). Organizational communication in a networked public sphere. *Studies in Communication Media, 1,* 15–36. https://doi.org/10.5771/2192-4007-2011-1-71

Reinikainen, H., Munnukka, J., Maity, D., & Luoma-aho, V. (2020). "You really are a great big sister"—parasocial relationships, credibility, and the moderating role of audience comments in influencer marketing. *Journal of Marketing Management, 36*(3–4), 279–298. https://doi.org/10.1080/0267257X.2019.1708781

Romenti, S., & Illia, L. (2013). Communicatively constituted reputation and reputation management. In C. E. Carroll (Ed.), *The handbook of communication and corporate reputation* (pp. 183–196). Wiley.

Ruppel, C., & Einwiller, S. (2021). Pleasant hostility: Disidentified consumers' emotional and behavioral reactions to a brand crisis. *Journal of Consumer Behaviour, 20*(1), 186–200. https://doi.org/10.1002/cb.1866

Ryan, M., & Martinson, D. L. (1988). Journalists and public relations practitioners: Why the antagonism? *Journalism & Mass Communication Quarterly, 65*(1), 131–140. https://doi.org/10.1177/107769908806500118

Shin, J. H., & Cameron, G. T. (2004). Conflict measurements: Analysis of simultaneous inclusion in roles, values, independence, attitudes, and dyadic adjustment. *Public Relations Review, 30*(4), 401–410. https://doi.org/10.1016/j.pubrev.2004.08.001

Siano, A., Vollero, A., Conte, F., & Amabile, S. (2017). More than words: Expanding the taxonomy of greenwashing after the Volkswagen scandal. *Journal of Business Research, 71*, 27–37. https://doi.org/10.1016/j.jbusres.2016.11.002

Somerville, I. (2021). Public relations and actor-network theory. In C. Valentini (Ed.), *Public relations: Handbooks of communication science* (Vol. 27, pp. 525–540). De Gruyter Mouton.

Sriramesh, K., & Vercic, D. (2020). *The global public relations handbook: Theory, research, and practice* (3rd ed.). Routledge.

Tench, R., Vercic, D., Zerfass, A., Moreno, A., & Verhoeven, P. (2017). *Communication excellence: How to develop, manage and lead exceptional communications.* Palgrave Macmillan.

Timonen, L., & Luoma-aho, V. (2010). Sector-based corporate citizenship. *Business Ethics: A European Review, 19*(1), 1–13. https://doi.org/10.1111/j.1467-8608.2009.01575.x

Toth, E. L., & Dozier, D. M. (2018). Theory: The ever-evolving foundation for why we do what we do. In *Fast forward: Foundations + future state: Educators + practitioners* (pp. 71–77). Commission for Public Relations Education.

Valentini, C. (2020). Trust research in public relations: An assessment of its conceptual, theoretical and methodological foundations. *Corporate Communications: An International Journal, 26*(1), 84–106. https://doi.org/10.1108/ccij-01-2020-0030

Valentini, C. (2021a). Public relations and social influence: Understanding the roots of a contested profession. In C. Valentini (Ed.), *Public relations: Handbooks of communication sciences* (Vol. 27, pp. 3–19). De Gruyter Mouton.

Valentini, C. (2021b). Mapping public relations theory: Concluding reflections and future directions. In C. Valentini (Ed.), *Public relations: Handbooks of communication sciences* (Vol. 27, pp. 615–627). De Gruyter Mouton.

Valentini, C., & Kruckeberg, D. (2011). Public relations and trust in contemporary global society: A Luhmannian perspective of the role of public relations in enhancing trust in social systems. *Central European Journal of Communication, 4*(1), 91–107. http://cejsh.icm.edu.pl/cejsh/element/bwmeta1.element.desklight-dd7146cd-6a11-46a7-9826-3570aa147f71

Valentini, C., & Kruckeberg, D. (2018). "Walking the environmental responsibility talk" in the automobile industry: An ethics case study of the Volkswagen environmental scandal. *Corporate Communications: An International Journal, 23*(4), 528–543. https://doi.org/10.1108/CCIJ-04-2018-0045

Valentini, C., & Muzi Falcone, T. (2008). *Lo specchio infranto: Come i relatori pubblici ei giornalisti italiani percepiscono la propria professione e quella dell'altro.* Luca Sossella Editore.

Valentini, C., Romenti, S., & Kruckeberg, D. (2016). Language and discourse in social media relational dynamics: A communicative constitution perspective. *International Journal of Communication, 10*, 4055–4073. https://ijoc.org/index.php/ijoc/issue/view/12

Valentini, C., Romenti, S., Murtarelli, G., & Pizzetti, M. (2018). Digital visual engagement: Influencing purchase intentions on Instagram. *Journal of Communication Management, 22*(4), 362–381. https://doi.org/10.1108/JCOM-01-2018-0005

Valentini, C., van Zoonen, W., & Elving, W. J. L. (2022). CSR Communication in corporate social media: An empirical investigation of European companies' use of social media between 2012 and 2020. In O. Niininen (Ed.), *Social media for progressive public relations* (pp. 73–89). Routledge.

van Ruler, B. (2015). Agile public relations planning: The reflective communication scrum. *Public Relations Review, 41*(2), 187–194.

van Ruler, B. (2018). Communication theory: An underrated pillar on which strategic communication rests. *International Journal of Strategic Communication, 12*(4), 367–381. https://doi.org/10.1080/1553118X.2018.1452240

van Ruler, B., & Vercic, D. (2004). *Public relations and communication management in Europe: A nation-by-nation introduction to public relations theory and practice.* De Gruyter Mouton.

Vercic, D., van Ruler, B., Bütschi, G., & Flodin, B. (2001). On the definition of public relations: A European view. *Public Relations Review, 27*(4), 373–387. https://doi.org/10.1016/S0363-8111(01)00095-9

Verhoeven, P., Zerfass, A., Verčič, D., Moreno, Á., & Tench, R. (2020). Strategic communication across borders: Country and age effects in the practice of communication professionals in Europe. *International Journal of Strategic Communication, 14*(1), 60–72. https://doi.org/10.1080/1553118X.2019.1691006

Vollero, A., Palazzo, M., Siano, A., & Elving, W. (2016). Avoiding the greenwashing trap: Between CSR communication and stakeholder engagement. *International Journal of Innovation and Sustainable Development, 10*(2), 120–140. https://doi.org/10.1504/IJISD.2016.075542

Watson, T. (2015). *Western European perspectives on the development of public relations: Other voices.* Springer.

Wehmeier, S., & Winkler, P. (2013). Expanding the bridge, minimizing the gaps: Public relations, organizational communication, and the idea that communication constitutes organization. *Management Communication Quarterly, 27*(2), 280–290. https://doi.org/10.1177/0893318912469772

Zerfass, A., & Viertmann, C. (2017). Creating business value through corporate communication. *Journal of Communication Management, 21*(1), 68–81. https://doi.org/10.1108/JCOM-07-2016-0059

21 Public Relations Theory in Latin American Culture and Context

A Post-Colonialist Perspective

Juan-Carlos Molleda and
Ana-María Suárez-Monsalve

Introduction

The contemporary transformations that have emerged in business organizations to adjust to market dynamics as well as the demands of globalization and the neoliberal economic model—for internationalization, alliances, business expansion, migration, networking, and many other changes in contemporary society—require a more active and critical role from the public relations professional. Latin American public relations professionals can influence political and economic decisions to further and implement changes. Processes of political change, communication strategies, and strategic public relations that stimulate social interrelations and address the challenges experienced in Latin America (Suárez-Monsalve, 2022; Suárez-Monsalve & Athaydes, 2021; Molleda & Suárez, 2005; Molleda, 2001; Suárez, 2017).

The countries of the region, to a variety of degrees, face frail and mistrusted political systems, limited industrialization, a widening gap between the rich and the poor, a weak civil society dependent on inconsistent and opaque governmental decisions, and erratic compliance and enforcement of the law (Informe Latinobarómetro, 2021). The COVID-19 pandemic has aggravated these problems, and the post-pandemic world does not look promising for many of these countries. According to the 2021 UN *World Economic Situation and Prospects (WESP)*, "Latin America and the Caribbean will face a fragile and uneven recovery as the COVID-19 crisis may leave lasting scars on the region's economies" (¶ 1). This outlook will likely increase poverty and inequality in many countries of the region, worsening social tensions and distrust in government and other institutions, including the private sector.

Strategic communicators and public relations professionals must transcend the interests of managers and government officials to serve the interests of society, assuming our role as part of the social conscience of organizations (Molleda, 2001). In many organizations and programs, the practice of public relations in Latin America centers on social and communitarian concerns

DOI: 10.4324/9781003141396-24

to support societal progress (Molleda, 2001; Molleda et al., 2017). Studies show that professionals in this region understand that they have an explicit commitment to both organizations and the interests of their audiences (Suárez-Monsalve, 2021; Álvarez et al., 2021; Suárez, 2017). Likewise, they intervene in advancing local communities and the country where they operate, aiming for social betterment and market stability with organizational resources and multisector partnerships (Molleda et al., 2017; Moreno et al., 2015). Many professionals in the region see themselves as agents of change and champions of freedom, justice, harmony, equality, and human dignity, using communication to reach agreements, consensus, and convergent attitudes between organizations and their internal and external stakeholders (Molleda & Suárez, 2005).

Considering the challenging nature of the evolving overall context of Latin America as it relates to public relations practice and theory, this chapter explores the central assumptions of post-colonialism as a theoretical framework to inform the study and practice of our disciplineEurasian communication, media, and public relations scholars—i.e., Central and Eastern Europe, Russia, and Central Asia—have also compared post-socialist environments to postcolonial contexts. This offers the potential for comparative research with contexts of relevant historic, political, and sociological characteristics, as argued by Minielli et al. (2021) fundamentally, these calls are focused on the conscious, active, and engaged recognition of the impacts that the cultural hegemony of the West (or the Global North) had and has on numerous communities. Therefore, this chapter has the potential to encourage research and education collaboration with Eurasian scholars, educators, and professionals.

Antecedents of a Critical-Analytical Theory for Public Relations in Latin America

The evolution of communication studies helps understand the introduction and development of public relations in the region. In Latin America, communication studies under the functionalist approach, derived from the research and theories of U.S. scholars such as the "founding fathers" of communication in the first half of the 20th century, dominated the influence in the academy (Nixon, 1984; Krohling-Kunsch, 2011). However, after the 1960s a critical school of thought was born, based on questioning the power of the media, the Frankfurt School, as well as the birth of a Latin American culturalist school that conceptualized communication from the identity of native peoples, rural communities, worldviews of the earth, nature, and cultural practices. This evolution of the culturalist school impacted the nascent professional education programs in public relations, which were brewing in communication schools and colleges. This impact generated an initial expression of the profession with a social focus in the region (Suárez-Monsalve, 2022; Marqués de Melo, 2015).

The International Center for Advanced Communication Studies in Latin America (CIESPAL is the Spanish acronym), created in 1959 during the X General Conference of UNESCO in Paris, promoted social communication with an emphasis on alternative communication media for the service of the Latin American society. From that center, critical theory guided the foundation of the communication school as a scientific discipline in the region (CIESPAL, 2020). Since its inception, CIESPAL contributed with approaches to the management of communication in organizations and the connection of human, social, and organizational relationships to respond to the needs of Latin American peoples.

Since the 1970s, a critical view has been established—a way to understand the forms and expressions of communication, including public relations—more through the lens of culture than through the lens of the mass media as a process of identity recognition from communicational processes. Between 1970 and 1980, the discussion of two perspectives of communication schools became more acute: the instrumental line established in functionalist and pragmatic theories, and the innovation and appropriation, sometimes called experimental because it explores new forms of communication and relationship between communities, guided by critical theories and culturalist thought (Torres, 2015). The inspiration for critical pedagogy proposed by Paulo Freire (2011) with his works "Education as a practice of freedom," published for the first time in 1964, and "Pedagogy of the oppressed" (2005) with a first edition in 1970, triggered important reflections on the contents in the curricula to educate Latin American communication professionals in emerging areas and in traditional social (mass) communication.

When it was created in 1978, the Latin American Association of Researchers in Communication [ALAIC] (2020) sought to disseminate the conceptual and academic advances of authors from the region, as well as the research and scientific production of Argentina, Brazil, Chile, Peru, and Colombia (Krohling-Kunsch, 1997). However, economic problems throughout the region in the 1980s produced a retraction of the production of academic research and publications. After 1990, the integration of the Latin American culturalist school was consolidated with a strong discussion of interdisciplinarity. Thus, ALAIC promotes work groups with different approaches to academic and scientific study on communication and culture. Among these, the Working Group on Organizational Communication and Public Relations exposes research and academic advances in public relations and communication management in organizations (ALAIC, 2020).

Previous research has evaluated the social role of public relations professionals and their role in the Latin American socio-economic, political, and cultural context (Molleda, 2001; Suárez, 2003). However, it has become evident that the characteristics of Latin American countries, in a singular way, vary in terms of public relations performance, particularly due to the training offered in each country, which in some is much more instrumental than analytical-critical.

In the logic of Latin American culture, the development of public relations is a replica of the colonial processes of scientific knowledge: the theories and practices have been adopted, without question, from the theories and practices of the United States and Europe, fundamentally (Sadi & Méndez, 2015). This theoretical and practical dependence has meant that public relations are not explored from the economic, cultural, political, social, and environmental needs of their own people.

The epistemology of public relations is rooted in the theories of communication, the social and human sciences, as well as the sciences of management and modern administration. There are few studies that delve into the origins of public relations linked to causes of liberation and independence, research that is necessary to guide public relations scholars and professionals.

The development of communication as part of the social and human sciences has been historically approached, with a functionalist perspective, based on the process and elements of communication and deepening the role that this process fulfills in society. The critical approach to communication, for its part, is based on questioning the role that these communication processes play in maintaining established power (i.e., information production and distribution, the role of traditional and digital mass media, and the generation of public opinion and public influence).

However, only in the 21st century have there been some advances in thinking about public relations theories from a postcolonial perspective in the Latin American context. There is a call from communication intellectuals, researchers, and academics to shed the dominant theoretical influences in the analyses and move to a more indigenous, critical, and analytical understanding of knowledge, the tensions between theory and practice, and the influence of academia in the industry. They are motivated to think, analyze, and build their own knowledge of the communication disciplines oriented by the recognition of historical identity and external influences, but also by their own productions of thought in communication and, therefore, of public relations.

Advances in and Influence of the Postcolonial Perspective
of Public Relations

In the review of the literature on public relations that includes postcolonial theories, there are articles and book chapters with topics related to theories of resistance in public relations (Dutta, 2018); national identity in postcolonial democracies and the definition of the interests of the public (Gaither & Curtin, 2018); the theoretical and empirical exploration of public relations, society, and culture (Hodges, 2011); and colonial rhetoric (Primack, 2020; Munshi et al., 2017). With regard to studies based on Latin American countries, some publications address education and practice of relations public in

Brazil (Molleda et al., 2009), the economic and political implications in professional practice in Colombia (Molleda & Suárez, 2005), and ethnographic and cultural studies in Mexico (Hodges, 2011).

For this chapter, an initial review of the literature in peer-reviewed journals about postcolonial theories used in public relations was conducted, which will be further explored in later studies with other specialized publications. This search yielded 29 results. Only one article included the concept of postcolonialism in the title (Munshi & Kurian, 2005), and four articles included theories of critical analysis that question the role of public relations in multiculturalism (Yeo & Pang, 2016), nation building (Lee, 2016), and historiography (Sarabia-Panola & Sisonb, 2016). These articles also include discussions on education that perpetuate the colonialist condition (Munshi & Kurian, 2005; Munshi et al., 2017; Ławniczak, 2009); indigenous movements (Dutta & Elers, 2020); feminist, ethnic, and communitarian activism (Ciszek, 2015; Munshi-Kurian et al., 2019); the center-periphery relationship of the theoretical practices (Patwardha & Bardhanb, 2014; Bilowol & Doan, 2015); and reflections of public relations (L'Etang, 2014; Petelin, 2005; Fawkes, 2015; Hiu & Choy, 2018).

These publications coincide with an analytical concern for acting with responsibility and the commitment of professionals with a critical and ethical attitude toward the established power and the defense of the rights of vulnerable publics or communities. Likewise, the conclusions of these articles call on professionals to make substantial transformations in organizations, acting with critical awareness to stop the strategies that perpetuate colonialism with discourses, practices, narratives, and interventions of corporations that maintain the privileges of economic and political elites. Also, some articles with a functionalist approach develop themes about the tensions between local and global affairs, as well as education and the economic-political crisis for the practice of public relations.

This body of knowledge indicates that there is an intellectual production directly or indirectly addressing postcolonialism as a subject of reflective and analytical interest in the field of public relations. It is aimed at linking sociocultural criticism in the practice in relation to issues such as national identity, implications of the political-economic context, cultural influences, and social resistance movements.

Some of the Latin American scholars who construct the historiographic analysis of Latin American public relations are Ferrari (2012), Ferrari and Fraça (2011), and the contributions of professionals from the region in Watson (2014) with the compilation of historical perspectives from Central America, the Caribbean, and South America in the book *Latin American and Caribbean perspectives on the development of public relations*. A first approach about the influences of postcolonialism in the evolution of public relations explains how globalization has been a positive factor for the growth of the practice and particularly in the industry of agencies and consultancies. However, a small group of holding companies dominates the global market, with networks that integrate the most relevant actors around the world (Molleda et al., 2018), overshadowing local and national agencies. The supply of national public relations firms is observed to unequally dispute the service market, because the presence of foreign agencies from the hegemonic groups of the global industry is increasing each time (Suárez-Monsalve, 2021).

Central Assumptions of Post-Colonial Theories

Historically, public relations in Latin America has been associated with a functionalist and pragmatic approach to communication studies and practices. Nevertheless, in recent decades there have been studies with a critical approach that question professional pragmatism (Krohling-Kunsch, 2011; Molleda et al., 2018; Sadi, 2013).

Postcolonial theories have their origin in the concept of colonialism and coloniality. Colonialism is studied as a form of power and territorial, economic, political, and cultural domain. For Castro-Gómez (2005), Marxist social theory informed colonialism as a phenomenon. In this theory, the bourgeoisie would revolutionize social relations, as it would break with the feudal organization and religious power. This break with the past was derived from the expansion of European empires over the territory known in the 15th century as "the New World." The expansion of the market generated a new international commercial, scientific, and technological dynamic that accelerated the modernization process for the centers of European power.

Marx and Engels in "The Communist Manifesto" (1997) (originally published as a pamphlet in 1848) attributed to the bourgeoisie the ability to transform the instruments of production and, therefore, the relations of production. However, this revolutionary process apparently was not conceived possible in the colonies, as there were no favorable conditions for social classes to organize because they were subject to the development of the empires that dominated them.

In this sense, the individuals of Spanish origin who came to conquer and colonize the peoples of these western territories—which were later called the Americas—were representatives of the nascent European bourgeois classes who did not have the capacity to understand the forms of social organization, cultural beliefs and values, political structures, and economic systems of the indigenous original peoples of these lands.

Between the 15th century and the 18th century, with the end of the Middle Ages and the beginning of the modern age, the expansion of the world market and industrialization made the emergence of new social classes possible. The new social classes were no longer subject to a feudal and servile system and emerged as groups with roles and benefits derived from the provision of resources of the Spanish and Portuguese colonies in Latin America (Castro-Gómez, 2005; Castells, 2012; Grosfoguel, 2006). Thus, roles of commercial, social, cultural, religious, and political intermediation were constituted as nascent expressions of the later functions of public relations;

that is, the exchanges between interest groups in the social dynamics of modernity.

The empires' international trade system—fed with the resources obtained from their colonies—made possible the growth of consumption especially of products obtained from the colonized territories in different parts of the world. This also promoted the accelerated development of navigation, terrestrial transport systems, forms of communication, and the exploitation and domination of nature at the service of this development and the desire for wealth. The world market promoted the emergence of large industry and this, in turn, expanded its reach and scope (Castro-Gómez, 2005). The changes derived from the commercial exchange promoted the consumption of exotic products of the so-called West Indies and trade facilitated to know other forms of life and identify the cultural expressions of the peoples in the colonies. The interests of mediation before the political and economic power needed interpreters of interests, symbolic practices and forms of communication and information that relate to the later roles of the profession, which were recognized as such in the following centuries.

In the 1800s, the independence from the Spanish and Portuguese empires of countries in the region led to problems of social organization that continued to be dominated by Creole elites interested in maintaining hierarchical organization models, like those inherited from the empires that governed them. Creole elites had the same interest in wealth, low collective popular consciousness, and forces of power by dependence on world finance capital and used persuasive propaganda techniques to seize and maintain control. Networks of wealthy families that have controlled the political and economic systems in the "Northern Triangle" of Guatemala, El Salvador, and Honduras, for instance, continue to exert great influence after 500 years, brewing inequality and lack of social mobility with subsequent poverty, violence, and northward migration ("Central America's elite," 2021). However, these families seem to be losing political influence, which may force them to see and praise the benefits of transparent and efficient governance.

From Marx's perspective, colonialism was not a phenomenon worthy of consideration by itself, but a collateral effect of European expansion around the world. Ethnic and racial discrimination were considered as pre-capitalist and pre-modern phenomena typical of societies still dominated by the old feudal regime (Castro-Gómez, 2005). These forms in which power is expressed determined social relations and mark the differences of interests and the system of domination over ethnic groups and minorities. These forms of communication and interaction are still expressed in contemporary public relations practices—for example, the relations of North American corporations in the mining sectors, agricultural inputs, and computer services, which establish forms of economic, cultural, communicational, and productive dominance in Central and South America (Bravo et al., 2018).

The reference to postcolonialism has been interpreted as a period after colonialism, but it does not recognize that forms of colonial rule still persist in the world. Postcolonialism is a stance critical to the diversities of domination modalities that persist in the world in forms of relationship between cultures and societies, which is important for public relations because of the critical review of the impacts of the profession on postmodern societies and in the reflection on the need for change to promote more human relations between organizations and audiences.

Postcolonial studies emerged at the end of the 20th century and began to show that colonialism was not only an economic phenomenon and a sociopolitical organization, but that it also had epistemic implications involving the human sciences. For this reason, Castro-Gómez (2005) points out that another dimension must be understood: coloniality, as this phenomenon is cognitively and symbolically recognized. In this dimension, he points out, the human sciences and modern social sciences contributed to creating the representations of the "other"—oriental, black, Indian, peasant—and to maintaining the imagery of the colonizer and the colonized. In public relations practices, the impact on economic negotiations with corrupt state powers that dominate in countries with extreme poverty and social inequality can be observed in the articulation of discourses that represent corporate power over indigenous communities in the region. Public relations campaigns strategically draw on dominant discourses to persuade audiences about the benefits of products that sometimes are harmful or not beneficial to health, or that are tested in vulnerable communities in this region.

The discussions derived from the decolonization processes in Africa, Asia, and the Caribbean territories, which were still dominated by British and French empires, deepen theoretical positions. One category of these studies focuses on epistemic representation, politics, subalternity, the human and social sciences with colonial and Eurocentric origin, and the emergence of new nation-states (Said, 2010; Guha, 1997; Bhabha, 2007; Chakravorty Spivak, 2003).

Another line of studies questions the relationship between modernity-coloniality-capitalism in conversation with social movements and new political subjectivities (Mignolo, 2009). It also includes cultural studies, feminism, and decolonial historiographies, as well as the Group of Latin American Subaltern Studies (Lander, 1993), de-colonialism (Castro-Gómez, 2007), and the proposal of the decoloniality of knowledge (Quijano, 2000). The analyses of Frantz Fannon (1983), Stuart Hall (2017), Aimé Césaire (2000), Paul Gilroy (1997), and Michel Rolph Trouillot (2017) addressed the colonial heritage in the history of Latin America and the problem of insertion into world capitalism, racism, and exotic representations of subaltern peoples.

The theoretical discussion of public relations in recent years has presented new studies that question the relationship of discourses that rely on exoticism used by public relations, including case studies on the actions of corporations in territories with a history of prolonged colonization (Gaither & Curtin, 2018; Dutta & Elers, 2020; Primack, 2020; Patwardhana & Bardhanb, 2014). Critical theory has also inspired other ways of analyzing and understanding the role of professionals in highly demanding contexts (Suárez, 2015) and the transformation of campaigns of activists with the use of new digital tools (Munshi-Kuriana et al., 2019).

The make-up of Latin America or the Americas as a territory is the product of a pattern of world power. The axis of this pattern is colonial domination with a heavily Eurocentric rationality. By "Eurocentrism" we mean the narrative about the world based solely on the European reality. In this narrative, Europe is—or has always been—simultaneously the geographical center and the culmination of the temporal movement. In this context of Eurocentric power, the arrival of what is known as the Americas generated an understanding of the world that marked a division between conquerors and conquered. This understanding of relationships also produced a rational logic of domination of some over others, implying a physical and intellectual superiority (conquerors) over the inferiors (conquered). This classification of the world's population through the lens of superior and inferior races was imposed as a pattern of power, which was expressed continuously and progressively in the realms of labor, production, capital, and the market.

The divisions between the groups supporting "white" power and the mestizo, black, indigenous, and minority groups such as the Roma population, is a constant of the 19th and 20th centuries. In Latin America, the conformation of the population is mestizo, the hybridization both genetic and cultural, generates a pattern of constant behavior of privilege by a white minority that has dominated the majority of mestizo, Afro-Latino, indigenous, and Roma population.

Today's globalization is part of that secular process of domination of colonial, modern, and Eurocentric capitalism. The United States has also exerted influence in the region after the Second World War, especially in the economy, security, and politics; however, the uninterrupted European influence continues to be prominent, particularly in scientific knowledge and in the logics of global financial power.

To understand the academic and scientific knowledge that guides the world today, it is necessary to consider the facts that have historically marked the exercise of economic, political, and cultural power in which public relations is practiced. In other words, understanding the connection between two historical facts is necessary to understand imperialism in the geopolitical logic of knowledge. The economic geopolitical model can be used to reflect on the geopolitics of knowledge because, just as it is difficult to think about economic models ignoring capitalism today, it is also difficult to think about epistemic models ignoring the framework of modern epistemology (the Euro-Western modernity) that has informed our thinking about the world.

Post-Colonial Theories: Need for Adaptation to Professional Practice, Education, and Research

In the review of the literature that expresses postcolonial points of view, the history of public relations proposes a perspective from a position other than that of the elites and dominant powers (Weaver et al., 2006). This change of focus allows us to approach the realities and logic of subaltern peoples. The region is traditionally seen in the periphery and not in the center of politics, the economy, and culture. This view allows us to consider the ability to listen to other, not traditionally dominant voices and understand cultural logics without judging from a position of privilege (corporate, institutional, business) but rather from the horizontality offered by understanding cultural hybridity in a condition of equal knowledge, rights, and duties, with access to dignified living conditions and freedom (Dutta, 2018; Dutta-Bergman, 2006; Dutta & Elers, 2020). This encourages people who practice public relations to be authentic, conscious, and purposeful to influence the construction of national identity in countries that have been subjected to imperial and colonial rule in modern logic, for their transformation into a postmodern perspective.

Also, public relations professionals contribute to this critical awareness in traditionally powerful organizations and institutions, to act in a fair, comprehensive, and sensitive manner to previously dominated groups, promoting freedom of thought and action for the optimization of relationships and exchanges. Public relations professionals must be intercultural themselves to communicate effectively with stakeholders and interact with cultural, ideological, and geographic diversity in the current era of multicultural globalization (Lee, 2016).

Only in this way can public relations be ethical and socially responsible, if they recognize the diversity of stakeholders, flatten hierarchy, and consider the resistance of peripheral publics (Munshi & Kurian, 2005). One of the ways to change the dominance traditionally imposed by the centers of power (geopolitically located in the Global North, with a comprehensive logic of the Western World, Eurocentric, and modern) is education, deontological orientations, and self-awareness of public relations as a field of scientific knowledge.

The Latin American reality induces a practice of public relations more committed to gender equality, education of and engagement with the public, and access to job opportunities. This is due to the high rates of social inequity, the increase in unemployment, and the few opportunities in education. Coherent public relations committed to these realities contributes to generating dialogue between the multiple actors that influence decisions in organizations and society.

The call to consider "the Global South" refers to new logics of understanding about national identities that do not depend on the dominant paradigms. For example, reconsider the priorities of development, relationship with nature, and appropriation and use of the territory not marked by the interests of the "Global North;" that is, by the interests of developed countries that are territorially in the north, which continue with the exploitation of resources in Latin American territories, in Africa, and in some Asian countries.

Therefore, it is necessary to delve into a theory of public relations that considers the logic of the political, economic, cultural, environmental, and social contexts of Latin America. That is the contribution of this chapter, to contribute to a theory of public relations that emerges from reflections on Latin American reality and intellectual evolution and critique.

Theoretical and Professional Line-of-Action of Public Relations in Latin America

With a postcolonial approach, public relations can contribute reflections and practices that balance social justice and equal opportunities while listening to groups that have been on the fringes of political and economic decisions. Some of the most sensitive social issues that public relations professionals can influence within their organizations are, for example, the free expression of diversity, the recognition of multiculturalism, and the well-being of migrant populations. They can achieve this with immediate organizational responses and actions, as well as effective communication through social media. They can minimize adverse effects on the organization's reputation in turbulent times by promoting timely and authentic actions that meet the expectations of stakeholders and a variety of audiences. Public relations professionals must also strive to generate social innovation by joining think tanks and ultimately overcoming the limitations of primarily tactical operations to guide communicational and relational strategic thinking that truly helps transform Latin American society.

This route of reflection and practice should be oriented toward reconstructing the historical narrative of public relations in the region, understanding the influences on the origin as a profession, analyzing the context variables in which their practice originated, as well as teaching. This historiographic analysis should be considered with a critical-analytical approach to find the autochthonous features, the needs of society in each of the countries of the region, as well as the categories that are common and those that differ, recognizing the intercultural diversity of Latin America.

In addition to this historiographic analysis, reflection on daily activities should deontologically guide professional practice in response to one's own needs, shedding foreign practices and building a know-how in its own context, considering potentialities such as autochthonous needs, with identity of nation and region. This reflection must be done with the analysis of cases that delve into the center-periphery tensions, subaltern groups, modernity-postmodernity, and centers of domination and dominated peoples, to find legitimizing practices of new forms of colonialism, as well as liberating proposals.

Likewise, public relations in Latin America should contribute to the construction of a regional narrative, discourse that builds the understanding of the nations making up the region, and narratives that promote self-knowledge and the appreciation of the Latin American essence. The content of the media and the mediations produced to bring interested groups closer together are written and designed from a narrative that respects the dignity, freedom, and diversity of nations, which will allow a better understanding of the history, contemporaneity, and transformative future of the Latin American peoples.

We have developed the following seven propositions to articulate a postcolonial public relations perspective in a Latin American context:

Proposition 1: Public relations professionals must develop a critical theoretical-practical approach in line with the complex challenges of the region. This perspective should be based on the historical theoretical analyses of the foundation of the nations that are part of this region. This approach should consider the political, economic, and cultural national/regional evolution to understand the past, present, and future as a nation and as a region (integration and cultural hybridity).

Proposition 2: The critical approach allows public relations professionals to assume social roles committed to reducing poverty, economic inequality, increase political participation, and strengthened cultural identity through organizational resources and multisector partnerships.

Proposition 3: The social role practiced with commitment allows the professional to influence political, economic, and social decision scenarios, leading discussions, proposing projects and policies, and building national and regional societies that self-manage development appropriate to nature, territorial, and cultural wealth.

Proposition 4: The leadership of topics, discussions, projects, and actions—based on the commitment to the social, analytical, and critical role of the professional—builds the foundation to insert the public relations profession transformative collective force against political apathy and in favor of intentional actions for social progress. Public relations professionals act in power scenarios, and a critical approach helps them influence power to transform the dominant-dominated dynamic toward an equitable and fair relationship among social groups.

Proposition 5: Professionals who work in private organizations must act with a critical conscience and recognize the corporate actions that have perpetuated coloniality in Latin America. This legitimization of new colonialist forms is the product of the exploitation of resources, dominance with economic and technological power, and cultural imperialism in national and regional markets.

Proposition 6: The academic community of public relations must strengthen teaching with a critical and social approach with critical historiography of development in Latin America. They must teach about the role of public relations in national and Latin American identity, as well as foster an innovative, creative, and purposive spirit to influence the political, economic, and cultural sectors with transformational leadership.

Proposition 7: Public relations research in Latin America should propose new theories, based on decolonial thinking that guides professional practice and the construction of national and regional discourses and stories with social and critical awareness to transform Latin American development.

Conclusions

Postcolonial theories are important to the study of public relations in Latin America because they guide reflection on specific knowledge base and practices in historical and contemporary contexts. Promoting critical theoretical analyses in public relations contributes to the understanding of the social and cultural changes derived from globalization and the hegemony of the neoliberal economic model. It also can help to understand the transition from modernity to postmodernity that is expressed in people's relationships with diverse cultural manifestations, values, and beliefs; ideological expressions; and social and organizational practices.

The postcolonial perspective contributes to the understanding of public relations and its role in defending the rights of diverse groups that have traditionally been subject to both economic and cultural domination. The studies articulating the postcolonial perspective guide the reflection of professional practice for all types of organizations and may help redirect their actions in a conscious and proactive way to balance the interests among social groups and consider the value of multiculturalism, cultural narratives, history, geopolitics, and ethical standards.

References

Álvarez-Nobell, A., Molleda, J. C., Moreno, A., Athaydes, A., Suárez-Monsalve, A. M., & Herrera, M. (2021). Comunicación estratégica y relaciones públicas en América Latina: crisis del COVID-19 en la gestion de comunicación, ciberseguridad, situación de las mujeres, retos éticos y nuevas competencias. Resultados de una encuesta en 20 países. EUPRERA.

Asociación Latinoamericana de Investigadores en Comunicación. (2021). *Grupos Temáticos.* Asociación Latinoamericana de Investigadores en Comunicación, ALAIC. Retrieved from https://www.alaic.org/es/

Bhabha, H. K. (2007). *El lugar de la cultura.* Manantial.

Bilowol, J., & Doan, M. A. (2015). Multinational corporations' role in developing Vietnam's public relations industry through corporate social responsibility. *Public Relations Review, 41*(5), 825–832.

Bravo, V., Molleda, J. C., Giraldo-Davila, A. F., & Botero-Montoya, L. H. (2018). Chiquita Brands, its illegal payments to paramilitary groups in Colombia, and the transnational public relations crisis that followed. In B. Brunner & C. Hickerson (Eds.), *Cases in public relations: Translating ethics into action* (pp. 343–348). Oxford University Press.

Castells, M. (2012). *Comunicación y poder.* Siglo XXI.

Castro-Gómez, S. (2005). *La postcolonialidad explicada a los niños*. Instituto Pensar, Universidad Javeriana, Editorial Universidad del Cauca.

Castro-Gómez, S., & Rosfroguel, R. (2007). *El giro decolonial: Reflexiones para una diversidad epistémica más allá del capitalismo global*. Siglo del Hombre Editores.

Central America's elite, blood and money: The influence of the region's most powerful families is on the wane. (2021, April 3–9). *The Economist* (digital edition).

Centro Internacional de Estudios Superiores de Comunicación para América Latina. (2021). *Nuestra historia*. www.ciespal.org/historia/

Césaire, A. (2000). *Discourse on colonialism*. Monthly Review Press.

Chakravorty Spivak, G., & Giraldo, S. (2003). ¿Puede hablar el subalterno? *Revista Colombiana de Antropología*, *39*, 297–364. Retrieved from: https://www.redalyc.org/articulo.oa?id=105018181010

Ciszek, E. (2015). Bridging the gap: Mapping the relationship between activism and public relations. *Public Relations Review*, 41(4), 447–455.

Dutta-Bergman, M. J. (2006). U.S. public diplomacy in the Middle East: A critical cultural approach. *Journal of Communication Inquiry*, *30*(2), 102–124.

Dutta, M. J. (2018). On Spivak: Theorizing resistance in public relations. In Ø. Ihlen & M. Fredriksson (Eds.), *Public relations and social theory: Key figures, concepts and developments* (pp. 374–393). Routledge.

Dutta, M. J., & Elers, S. (2020). Public relations, indigeneity and colonization: Indigenous resistance as dialogic anchor. *Public Relations Review*, 46(1), 101852.

Fannon, F. (1983). *Los condenados de la tierra*. Fondo de Cultura Económica. Retrieved from www.lahaine.org

Fawkes, J. A. (2015). Jungian conscience: Self-awareness for public relations practice. *Public Relations Review*, 41(5), 726–733.

Ferrari, M. A. (2012) Relaciones Públicas en Chile: entre los modelos importados y la búsqueda de su identidad. In: Vercic, D. & Sriramesh, K. *Relaciones Públicas Globales. Teoría investigación y práctica* (307–335). Editorial UOC.

Ferrari, M. A. & Fraça, F. (2011). *Relaciones públicas: naturaleza, función y gestion en las organizaciones contemporáneas*. 1a. ed. La Crujía.

Freire, P. (2005). *Pedagogía del oprimido*. Siglo XXI Editores.

Freire, P. (2011). *La educación como práctica de la libertad*. Siglo XXI Editores.

Gaither, T. K., & Curtin, P. A. (2018). Articulating national identity in postcolonial democracies: Defining relations and interests through competing publics. In J. Johnstone & M. Piecksa (Eds.), *Public interest communication: Critical debates and global contexts* (pp. 113–132). Routledge.

Gilroy, P. (1997) Diaspora and the detours of identity. In Woodward, K. (Ed.), *Identity and difference* (pp. 299–346). Sage Publications and The Open University.

Grosfoguel, R. (2006). La descolonización de la economía política y los estudios postcoloniales: Transmodernidad, pensamiento fronterizo y colonialidad global. *Tabula Rasa*, *4*, 17–46.

Guha, R. (1997). *Dominance without hegemony: History and power in colonial India*. Harvard University Press.

Hall, S. (2017). *Estudios culturales 1983: una historia teorética*. Paidós.

Hiu, C., & Choy, Y. (2018). Online political public relations as a place-based relational practice: A cultural discourse perspective. *Public Relations Review*, *44*(5), 752–761.

Hodges, C. (2011). Public relations in the postmodern city: An ethnographic account of PR occupational culture in Mexico City. In L. Edwards & C. Hodges (Eds.), *Public relations, society and culture: Theoretical and empirical exploration*. Routledge.

Informe Latinobarómetro. (2021). Retrieved April 29, 2022, from www.latinobarometro. org/latContents.jsp

Krohling-Kunsch, M. (1997). *Relações públicas e modernidade: Novos paradigmas na comunicação organizacional.* Summus.

Krohling-Kunsch, M. (2011). Comunicação organizacional e relações públicas: Perspectivas dos estudos Latino-Americanos. *Revista Internacional de Relaciones Públicas, 1*(1), 69–96.

Lander, E. (1993). *La colonialidad del saber: Eurocentrismo y ciencias sociales. Perspectivas latinoamericanas.* Consejo Latinoamericano de Ciencias Sociales, CLACSO.

Ławniczak, R. (2009). Re-examining the economic roots of public relations. *Public Relations Review, 35*(4), 346–352.

Lee, M. (2016). Constructing the nation through negotiating: An outcome of using grounded theory. *Public Relations Review,* 42(2), 298–305.

L'Etang, J. (2014). Public relations and historical sociology: Historiography as reflexive critique. *Public Relations Review, 40*(4), 654–660.

Marqués de Melo, J. (2015). O campo científico de comunicação na América Latina: Perspectiva Histórica. In C. Bolaño, D. Crovi, & G. Cimadevilla (Eds.), *La contribución de América Latina al campo de la comunicación: Historia, Enfoques teóricos, epistemológicos y tendencias de la investigación.* ALAIC.

Marx, C., & Engels, F. (1997). *El manifiesto comunista.* Akal.

Mignolo, W. (2009). La idea de América Latina: La derecha, la izquierda y la opción decolonial. *CyE, 1*(2). http://biblioteca.clacso.edu.ar/ar/libros/secret/CyE/CyE2/09idea.pdf

Minielli, M. C., Lukacovic, M. N., Samoilenko, S. A., Finch, M. R., & Uecker, D. (2021). *Media and public relations in post-socialist societies.* Lexington Books.

Molleda, J. C. (2001). International paradigms: The Latin American school of public relations. *Journalism Studies, 2*(4), 513–530.

Molleda, J. C., Athaydes, A., & Hirsch, V. (2009). Public relations in Brazil: Practice and education in a South American context. In K. Sriramesh & D. Vercic (Eds.), *The global public relations handbook, revised and expanded edition: Theory, research, and practice* (pp. 797–820). Routledge.

Molleda, J. C., Moreno, Á., & Navarro, C. (2017). Professionalization of public relations in Latin America: A longitudinal comparative study. *Public Relations Review, 43*(5), 1084–1093.

Molleda, J. C., & Suárez, A. M. (2005). Challenges in Colombia for public relations professionals: A qualitative assessment of the economic and political environments. *Public Relations Review, 31*(1), 21–29.

Molleda, J. C., Suárez, A. M., Athaydes, A., Sadi, G., Hernández, E., & Valencia, R. (2018). Influences of postcolonialism over the understanding and evolution of public relations in Latin American. In E. Bridgen & D. Vercic (Eds.), *Experiencing public relations international voices.* Routledge.

Moreno, Á., Molleda, J. C., Athaydes, A., & Suárez, A. M. (2015). *Latin American communication monitor 2014–2015: Excelencia en comunicación estratégica, trabajo en la era digital, social media y profesionalización. Resultados de una encuesta en 18 países.* EUPRERA.

Munshi, D., & Kurian, P. (2005). Imperializing spin cycles: A postcolonial look at public relations, greenwashing, and the separation of publics. *Public Relations Review, 31*(4), 513–520. https://doi.org/10.1016/j.pubrev.2005.08.010

Munshi, D., Kurian, P., & Xifra, J. (2017). A "story" in history: Challenging colonialist public relations in novels of resistance. *Public Relations Review, 43*(2), 366–374.

Munshi-Kurian, A., Munshi, D., & Kurian, P. (2019). Strategic interventions in sociology's resource mobilization theory: Reimagining the #MeToo movement as critical public relations. *Public Relations Review*, *45*(5), 101788.

Nixon, R. B. (1984). Historia de las Escuelas de Periodismo. *Chasqui*, Enero–Marzo. 13–19.

Petelin, R. (2005). Editing from the edge: De-territorializing public relations scholarship. *Public Relations Review*, *31*(4), 458–462.

Patwardhana, P., & Bardhanb, N. (2014). Worlds apart or a part of the world? Public relations issues and challenges in India. *Public Relations Review*, *40*(3), 408–419.

Primack, A. J. (2020). You are not the father: Rhetoric, settler colonial curiosity, and federal Indian law. *Review of Communication*, *20*(1), 27–46.

Quijano, A. (2000). Colonialidad del poder, eurocentrismo y América Latina. In *La colonialidad del saber, eurocentrismo y ciencias sociales: Perspectivas latinoamericanas*. Consejo Latinoamericano de Ciencias Sociales–CLACSO.

Sadi, G. (2013). Algunos aportes del pensamiento crítico en Relaciones Públicas. *Dircom*, *100*, 23–28.

Sadi, G., & Méndez, V. (2015). Una aproximación histórica al dominio intelectual de las relaciones públicas: Tensiones paradigmáticas en su construcción disciplinar. *Revista Internacional de Relaciones Públicas*, V(10), 47–66.

Said, E. (2010). *Orientalismo*. De Bolsillo.

Sarabia-Panola, Z., & Sisonb, D. M. (2016). We are what we teach: The impact of persuasive communication on Philippine PR history and contemporary PR education. *Public Relations Review*, *42*(5), 801–811.

Suárez, A. M. (2017). Ciudadanías y rol social de los comunicadores y relacionistas públicos en Colombia: Aportes para la discusión según el Latin American communication monitor (LCM) 2014–2015. *Comunicación*, *36*, 27–48.

Suárez, A. M. (2015). Políticas de recuperación de ciudad, una mirada crítica a las estrategias de comunicación e imagen turística de Medellín y Río de Janeiro. In J. Osorio & E. Rozo (Eds.), *Turismo y cultura: Retos y perspectivas en América Latina*. Universidad Externado de Colombia.

Suárez, A.M. (2003). Responsabilidad social de la comunicación corporativa: Acción dinámica en la transformación social. *Anagramas, rumbos y sentidos de la comunicación*, *2*, 91–98.

Suárez-Monsalve, A. M. (2021). Aportes para discutir en enfoque de las capacidades en la gestión de la comunicación: Aplicación en Colombia. *Comunicacao, Midia e Consumo*, *18*(53), 558–580.

Suárez Monsalve, A. M. (2009). Estrategias de comunicación para crear alianzas. *Anagramas Rumbos y sentidos de la comunicación*, *7*(14), 93-104.

Suárez-Monsalve, A.-M. (2022). Evolution of the public relations profession in Latin America: A brief review of the development of public relations in Latin American countries. *Public Relations Inquiry*, *11*(2), 257–274. https://doi.org/10.1177/2046147X221081175

Suárez-Monsalve, A. M., & Athaydes, A. (2021). Nuevas ciudadanías y nueva capacidad de influencia en decisiones estratégicas. *Organicom*, *18*(37), 84–99.

Torres, W. (2015). Investigar la comunicación y formar comunicadores hoy: Una conversación con Jesús Martín Barbero. In C. Bolaño, D. Crovi Druetta, & G. Cimadevilla (Eds.), *La contribución de América Latina al campo de la Comunicación: Historia, enfoques teóricos, epistemológicos y tendencias de la investigación*. ALAIC.

Trouillot, M. R. (2017). *Silenciando el pasado: el poder y la producción de la historia*. Comares.

UN World Economic Situation and Prospects (WESP). (2021). *In Latin America and the Caribbean: Fragile and uneven economic recovery expected, warns new UN report.* www.cepal. org/en/pressreleases/latin-america-and-caribbean-fragile-and-uneven-economic-recovery-expected-warns-new-un

Watson, T. (2014). *Latin American and Caribbean perspectives on the development of public relations. Other voices.* Palgrave.

Weaver, C. K., Motion, J., & Roper, J. (2006). From propaganda to discourse (and back again): Truth, power, the public interest, and public relations. In J. Letang & M. Pieczka (Eds.), *Public relations: Critical debates and contemporary practice.* Lawrence Erlbaum Associates.

Yeo, S. L., & Pang, A. (2016). Asian multiculturalism in communication: Impact of culture in the practice of public relations in Singapore. *Public Relations Review, 43*(1), 112–122.

22 Inviting an *Ubuntu*-Based Approach to Public Relations Theory Building in Sub-Saharan Africa

Prisca S. Ngondo and Anna Klyueva

The COVID-19 pandemic and the subsequent public health crisis have dramatically altered the way organizations and people communicate around the globe, highlighting the demand for a more empathetic and culture-sensitive approach. While Western countries struggled to find the right messaging that would reconcile individual liberties and collective safety, many countries in Sub-Saharan Africa (SSA) communicated about and justified their stay-at-home orders, limits on travel, curfews, social distancing, mask-wearing, and vaccinations within the context of a common African philosophy—*Ubuntu*. Emphasizing common humanity, *Ubuntu* was used as a shared philosophical basis to bring people together for a common purpose—to protect each other in the fight against COVID-19. Pandemic communication strategies in many SSA countries were based on a quintessential *Ubuntu*-based principle—"a protected person is a protected person through other protected people" (Sulcas, 2020, para. 25). The pandemic demonstrated that *Ubuntu* could also be useful in Western individualistic societies, especially in contexts where the notion of community is amplified and brought the concept of *Ubuntu* to the forefront of many communication domains, including public relations.

Ubuntu is an African cultural humanist philosophy popularized in the Western world by Archbishop Desmond Tutu and Nelson Mandela in the wake of the anti-apartheid movement of the 1980s. *Ubuntu* has been written about extensively by communication and media scholars such as Christians (2004), Tavernaro-Haidarian (2018), and Metz (2015) among others, although many of them focused heavily on media ethics. Yet, *Ubuntu* has been notably missing from mainstream public relations discussions, despite it being a familiar concept in the public relations scholarship. In 2011, Mersham et al. presented a case for public relations theory building on the African continent in which they postulated that such theories must give indigenous epistemologies, specifically the African philosophy of *Ubuntu*, a central position. Mbigi (1997) suggested using the *Ubuntu* philosophy

Author Note
Correspondence concerning this chapter should be addressed to Prisca S. Ngondo, School of Journalism and Mass Communication, Texas State University. Email: psngondo@txstate.edu

DOI: 10.4324/9781003141396-25

as a foundation for organizational culture in South African management practices, arguing that its focus on reconciliation and harmony provides a solid basis for relationship building. Holtzhausen et al. (2003) identified the *Ubuntu* model of public relations in South Africa, asserting that it builds on "African participative practices that represent a sincere attempt to build relationships between management and employees" (p. 335). Surprisingly, this model did not gain traction in the public relations literature.

While there are discussions about the need to develop Afro-centric public relations theory (Mersham et al., 2011; Steyn & Niemann, 2014), there is no pan-African public relations school of thought. Thus, re-introducing overlooked uniquely African concepts such as *Ubuntu* may provide guidance on the direction for public relations theory development in SSA. This shared African philosophy can differentiate itself from Western approaches to public relations and contribute unique perspectives derived from the common values and cultural diversity of the continent. *Ubuntu* builds on the ideas of harmony and reconciliation, espousing values such as inclusiveness, tolerance, mutual understanding, transparency, negotiation, and consensus-building (Fuse et al., 2010; Tavernaro-Haidarian, 2018). The limited public relations research across SSA indicates that practitioners recognize these values as important to practice, yet they are not fully explored and reflected in African public relations scholarship (Holtzhausen et al., 2003; Mersham et al., 2011; Natifu & Zikusooka, 2014; Skinner & Mersham, 2009).

This chapter proposes bringing *Ubuntu* to the forefront of public relations theory building in SSA toward original conceptualizations of public relations approaches. By exploring philosophical values and cultural assumptions shared by diverse countries representing the region, the discussion underscores the African worldview and indigenous forms of communication embedded in local public relations practices, such as storytelling and the palaver tree. To contextualize the argument put forth, the chapter begins by briefly highlighting the socio-political environment, state of public relations education, and media landscapes in SSA countries. The chapter continues with an overview of public relations in SSA, paving the way for the discussion of an *Ubuntu*-based perspective, and concludes with recommendations on how and what can be done to advance SSA theory development.

Public Relations in SSA: Background, Education, and Media Landscape

SSA is one of the most diverse and complex regions in the world, with a mixed and entangled indigenous population and a legacy of colonial influences from Europe, Asia, and the Arab world (Mersham et al., 2011). SSA consists of 46 African countries that are geographically located, fully or partially, south of the Sahara Desert (excluding Sudan). It contrasts with North Africa, considered a part of the Arab world. Somalia, Djibouti, Comoros, and Mauritania are geographically part of SSA but also part of the Arab world (World Bank, 2015).

Generally, SSA is considered the most impoverished region in the world, still suffering from the legacies of colonial conquest and occupation, neo-colonialism, inter-ethnic conflict, and political strife. The region contains many of the least developed countries globally, such as Benin, Mozambique, Malawi, and Burundi (New World Encyclopedia, 2021). However, over the last ten years, the region has experienced appreciable economic growth due to its plentiful mineral and energy resources (Adedoyin et al., 2021), prompting rapid development of the communication industry in SSA nations, including public relations. Growing professionalization of public relations indicates the maturing of the field, simultaneously highlighting the accumulation of specialized knowledge and the need for theory development.

Access to public relations education and the structure of media landscape, both of which influence the development and professionalization of public relations, differ vastly amongst countries in SSA. While aspiring public relations practitioners in some SSA countries have full access to public relations undergraduate and graduate degrees, others must rely on weekend workshops, short courses, or on-the-job training. For example, in Zimbabwe, public relations has been seen as a mass communication, journalism, or marketing appendage and is still fighting to establish itself as a standalone profession and degree program (Ngondo & Klyueva, 2020). Several Kenyan universities offer degrees in communication and public relations, while the Public Relations Society of Kenya (PRSK) offers public relations-related workshops, master classes and bootcamps (PRSK, 2022). Public relations education in Ghana offers training at the diploma level, with a curriculum dominated by Western approaches (Thompson, 2018). Nigerian universities also offer formal courses of study in public relations. However, to receive accreditation from the Nigerian Institute for Public Relations (NIPR), which is required for practicing public relations in the country, a practitioner need not have a specialized degree (Molleda & Alhassan, 2006). Historically, South African public relations degree programs were modeled after the theoretically inclined European model, while some followed the more skills-based American model (Niemann-Struweg & Meintjes, 2008). Public relations education offerings in South Africa range from certificates to doctoral degrees (Niemann-Struweg & Meintjes, 2008), positioning South Africa as a leader in the SSA public relations industry (De Beer et al., 2013).

The highlighted countries offer a glimpse into the state of education in SSA. Varying degrees of access to formal public relations education among SSA countries create critical implications for public relations as practitioners join the profession with educational backgrounds dominated by marketing, journalism, and media studies.

The communication industry infrastructure and media landscapes also differ country by country. For example, Kenya enjoys a vibrant media scene, considered one of the most competitive and sophisticated in the region. Its media landscape is characterized by a combination of state and privately owned media outlets, with some operating beyond the nation's borders (BBC, 2019). However, Reporters Without Borders (RSF) observed that Kenya experienced a weakening of media freedom in recent years due to security concerns and the political situation. Although Zimbabwe is home to one of the oldest newspapers in Africa (*The Herald* dates back to the 1890s), its media is mostly state-owned and tightly controlled through draconian laws and regulations (BBC, 2017). Other countries such as Nigeria, South Africa, and Ghana now have independent media operating freely. The proliferation of civil society organizations and private media in these countries allows for more scrutiny of business practices, leading to a demand for public relations practitioners to guide strategic information dissemination and relationship building (Thompson, 2015).

Media access is key to the functioning of public relations and its theory development (Mersham et al., 2011). Although media organizations in many SSA countries are state-funded and state-controlled, high mobile phone penetration has resulted in social media being the main source of media content and consumption in recent years (Moore, 2018). This type of access has far-reaching implications for public relations and communication management in SSA, as mobile phones are typically the only technology people have to access information, share their opinions, and interact with the media (Mersham et al., 2011). The communication infrastructure and the region's media landscape in conjunction with limited access to formal public relations education shape public relations practice and theory development in SSA, defining its direction.

Public Relations in SSA: An Overview

Although there have been numerous research studies discussing public relations in Africa in the last ten years, research is still fragmented and lacks emphasis on the local socio-cultural contexts (Ngondo & Klyueva, 2020). In fact, of the 46 SSA countries, only a handful of nations have been studied in connection with public relations: Kenya (e.g., Kiambi & Nadler, 2012), South Africa (e.g., Benecke & Verwey, 2020; Holtzhausen et al., 2003; Tindall & Holtzhausen, 2011, etc.), Nigeria (e.g., Akoje & Rahim, 2014; Molleda & Alhassan, 2006; Ukonu et al., 2018), Ghana (e.g., Anani-Bossman, 2021; Wu & Baah-Boakye, 2014), Uganda, Mauritius, Guinea, and Tanzania (Kayuni & Tambulasi, 2012; van Heerden & Rensburg, 2005), and more recently Zimbabwe (Muchena, 2017, 2018; Ngondo, 2019; Ngondo & Klyueva, 2020; Oksiutycz & Nhedzi, 2018, among others). As it stands, the research agenda of SSA public relations (with a notable exception of South Africa) has been dominated by the Western perspective, specifically by the excellence theory and models of public relations practice as explicated by numerous studies.

It is important to acknowledge the inequality in representing public relations research and the profession from the African continent. As the most developed country of SSA with a stable government, democratic tradition, and established public relations education system, South Africa is the most researched African nation. The public relations research literature in South Africa is diverse and multifaceted, covering nation-building (Chaka, 2014), activism (Benecke & Verwey, 2020), dialogic theory (Benecke & Oksiutycz, 2015), public relations roles theory (van Heerden & Rensburg, 2005), excellence theory (Tindall & Holtzhausen, 2011), relationship building (Steyn et al., 2004), and CSR (Skinner & Mersham, 2008) among others. According to Holtzhausen et al. (2003), normative public relations models are irrelevant for the South African context and, in general, South African public relations scholarship aligns more with a European reflective approach and a strategic communication management view of public relations (De Beer et al., 2013). Surprisingly, South African scholarship has been dominating the research agenda without a wider influence on SSA public relations development. For other SSA nations, the excellence theory has been the main backdrop for many studies (Anani-Bossman, 2021; Kiambi & Nadler, 2012; Ngondo & Klyueva, 2020; Tindall & Holtzhausen, 2011; Thompson, 2018; van Heerden & Rensburg, 2005; Wu & Baah-Boakye, 2014).

Although this chapter deals with SSA as a whole, we acknowledge that each country is unique, as not all African countries have the same ecological, political, media, economic, or cultural structures. Persistent national and subnational diversity among SSA countries, particularly ethnolinguistic and religious diversity, are among the factors that affect communication patterns (Gershman & Rivera, 2018). While the full extent of diversity within SSA cannot be fully captured in one chapter, scholars have acknowledged that the philosophy of *Ubuntu* represents an African worldview, a unifying guiding principle with potential for a powerful influence on public relations research and practice across SSA (Kayuni & Tambulasi, 2012; Natifu & Zikusooka, 2014).

Public Relations in SSA: Toward an *Ubuntu* Perspective

Ubuntu is a uniquely African concept that can be translated as "a person is a person through other people" or more commonly as "I am because we are" (Chibba, 2013). Some scholars argue that the term originated in South Africa; however, its variations are present in many other SSA nations (Sambala et al., 2020). Chibba (2013) postulated that *Ubuntu* encompasses numerous sets of values that have their roots in various African cultures. In Zimbabwe, it is known as *unhu*, in Malawi as *uMunthu*, in Kenya and Tanzania as *utu*, and in Mozambique as *vumuntu* (Chibba, 2013; Mangena, 2016).

Ubuntu is generally associated with South Africa and the post-apartheid construction of South African identity. South African theologian Desmond Tutu propagated the term as a foundational principle of humanist philosophy during his time as the chairman of the Truth and Reconciliation Committee (Mboti, 2015). The South African government used *Ubuntu* values in its post-apartheid national branding and the country's moral regeneration (McDonald, 2010). Nelson Mandela hosted a Moral Summit in 1992, where the Moral Regeneration Movement (MRM) was formalized. The MRM was created under the "spirit of *Ubuntu*" and tasked to rebuild and sustain moral communities while fighting against immoral behavior in the public organizations and the community. The infusion of *Ubuntu* was meant to work in tandem with building a post-apartheid South Africa. In fact, MRM leaders argued that *Ubuntu* values were crucial for establishing a national consciousness targeted at rebranding and redefining South Africa and likened the movement to how some Asian countries branded themselves using Confucianism (McDonald, 2010).

The African moral theory of *Ubuntu* is based on the communal worldview, where the community comes ontologically before individuals (Christians, 2004). The translated meaning of *Ubuntu* as "I am because we are" presents a drastic contrast to Descartian/Western "I think therefore I am," highlighting the juxtaposition between understandings of human behavior as fundamentally individual or fundamentally social. Christians (2004) argued that the philosophy of *Ubuntu* represents the "communitarian consciousness" (p. 237) and serves as a remedy to individualistic liberalism. It presumes that human identity is constituted through the social realm. The communitarian nature of *Ubuntu* is expressed through the awareness of interdependence among members of the community (Matolino, 2020), including organizations and its publics. Building on the ideas of harmony and reconciliation and espousing values such as inclusiveness, tolerance, mutual understanding, transparency, negotiation, and consensus-building, *Ubuntu* demonstrates its emphasis on the nurturing of relationships (Tavernaro-Haidarian, 2018; van Niekerk, 2013), a fundamental notion for public relations.

Inclusiveness

Inclusiveness is expressed through respect for all humans and human dignity. Kamwangamalu (1999, p. 25) conceptualized *Ubuntu* as a notion of "humanity toward others." According to Shutte (2001, p. 12), *Ubuntu* finds harmony in diversity and human reliance on "relations with others to exercise, develop, and fulfill those capacities that make one a person." In other words, because people are primarily other-oriented rather than selfish, the fulfillment of humanity in *Ubuntu* philosophy is only possible by considering those around them, embracing their differences, and helping them develop. Because the ideals of *Ubuntu* highly value the inclusion of diverse perspectives through communication, its application to public relations is a natural fit. In the context of *Ubuntu*, for example, employee communication must focus on diversity and inclusion because humans are intrinsically valuable and every conversation has an important social effect such as fostering mutual understanding and harmony (Davis, 2021; Mangaliso, 2001).

Tolerance

Inclusiveness and tolerance go hand-in-hand. A traditional approach to discourse that invites diverse opinions is highly valued as communities get together to deliberate and explore solutions. Tolerance is promoted via dialogue and the celebration of diversity. According to Blankenberg (1999), the dialogue "becomes a process of learning for both 'facilitator' and 'participant'" (p. 46). Public relations tactics that invite genuine participation and engagement with opportunities to be heard would reflect this *Ubuntu* value. For example, Mangaliso (2001) argued that traditional ceremonies and corporate rituals, although may seem trivial to the Western observer, quite often serve as an opportunity to foster community and a sense of belonging in the SSA context.

Transparency

Transparency is another foundational value of *Ubuntu*. While the term transparency commonly conveys honesty and integrity, it can also be interpreted as similar to accountability through greater public disclosure and discourse. According to *Ubuntu*, government and community leaders are stewards of the community's well-being and wealth; hence they must be transparent and also accountable. Accountability and transparency yield trust and credibility, essential to public relations professionals. Mbendera (2020) argued that economic and political corruption in African countries could be attributed to the loss of *Ubuntu* values, such as transparency.

Consensus-Building

In *Ubuntu*, consensus-building emphasizes non-competitive forms of decision making that favor unanimous, consensus-oriented rather than majoritarian agreement (Metz, 2015; Wiredu, 1996). All members of the community have an opportunity to voice their opinions and contribute to the decision-making process arrived at "by consensus, incorporating both majority and minority viewpoints" (Blankenberg, 1999, 46). In some communities and families, deliberations may last for as long as a compromise is not found, seeking all participants of the dialogue to agree with the outcome (Tavernaro-Haidarian, 2018). Because the *Ubuntu* philosophy regards collective decision making as the most appropriate tool for facing complex social challenges, its values become particularly relevant in crisis communication contexts, for example during the COVID-19 pandemic (Tavernaro-Haidarian, 2021). Communication efforts to educate about safe COVID-19 behavior showed that the most influential global communication strategies were those that centered around collective decision making and other-regard (Wilson, 2020). Focus on meaning-making, humanity, empathy, and consensus-building allowed overcoming partisanship in fostering safe behavior during the pandemic (Soy, 2020).

Harmony, reconciliation, and consensus-building are at the heart of *Ubuntu* and are enacted through communication, especially in the form of storytelling that is central to the practice of *Ubuntu* values (Davis, 2021).

Ubuntu *and Storytelling*

Storytelling can be defined as the iterative telling of narratives as individuals construct knowledge together to understand the past, share the present, and shape the future (McPhee & Zaug, 2009). In SSA, several storytelling traditions enable the practice of *Ubuntu*: the griot tradition (Davis, 2021) and the palaver tree tradition (Fuse et al., 2010). The griot tradition of storytelling is one of the most studied forms of traditional African indigenous communication. The griot is a cast of bards, poets, and storytellers who recount traditional knowledge and accounts of historical events, and also can be used as orators or spokesmen on one's behalf (Sopova, 1999). The griots were historically employed by the king to use storytelling to negotiate diplomacy and reconciliation. The palaver tree is a traditional African institution of debate and consensus-building with democratic potential. Sopova (1999) described the palaver as "an assembly where a variety of issues are freely debated and important decisions concerning the community are taken" (p. 42). The purpose of such an assembly is to achieve consensus and resolve conflicts in certain situations. It is called "palaver" because the participants usually gather in the shade of the palaver tree (a baobab tree). In fact, if the purpose of the palaver tree meeting is to resolve a dispute, participants may bring a griot to help their case. Both the griot tradition and the palaver tree tradition represent mechanisms of indigenous storytelling that remain relevant in SSA today.

Kent (2015) acknowledged the importance of storytelling for public relations, as communication does far more for organizations than just transmitting the information. Heritage (1997) contended that organizations are talked into being through iteration of interconnected stories, their discussion of directions and priorities, vision and mission statements. Storytelling, therefore, is important to the practice of *Ubuntu* values because it allows the introduction of different narratives within the story. Because *Ubuntu* highly values the inclusion of diverse perspectives in the creation of narratives, it is important to focus on storytelling. In other words, in *Ubuntu* storytelling is a tool to ensure that every conversation has an important social impact, such as unity and mutual understanding (Mangaliso, 2001). For example, Kenyan communities have used cultural practices and traditions such as talking drums, moonlight storytelling, folktales, village square gatherings, and sporting activities to communicate and build community relations since the advent of human civilization (Ngonyo & Ramakrishna, 2016). Storytelling and *Ubuntu* culture also provide an opportunity for knowledge sharing and training, by making the conveying and retaining of practical knowledge memorable (Bekalu & Eggermont, 2015; Davis, 2021).

Public Relations the *Ubuntu* Way

The goal of *Ubuntu*-based public relations is to create and maintain harmony and reconciliation in society and between organizations and their publics. This can be achieved by incorporating *Ubuntu* values such as inclusivity, tolerance, transparency, and consensus-building into the organization's relationship-building and communication practices. Because public relations rests on the interdependence of communication and relationships, a culture-focused public relations approach must embrace the indigenous forms of communication and appreciate the intricacies of *Ubuntu*-driven relationships.

An *Ubuntu*-based approach to public relations is different from the organization-centric Western approach that emphasizes individual rights and power in the communication process (see Table 23.1). *Ubuntu's* focus on community is also different from the societal perspective espoused by the European school of thought that focuses on "how public relations works, what it does in, to and for organizations, publics, or in the public arena, e.g., society at large" (Ihlen & van Ruler, 2007, p. 247). The societal view also underscores the role of public relations in the restructuring of social relations and in the power struggle organizations engage in. The organization-centric view acknowledges culture as an important factor and cultural awareness as an important skill for consideration of local cultural practices around the world (Choi & Cameron, 2009). However, it is often instrumental and lacks appreciation for the indigenous forms of communication.

As a uniquely African concept, *Ubuntu* is based on the communal worldview, in which the community comes first, the individual—second (Christians, 2004). The practice of *Ubuntu*-based public relations in SSA is intertwined and deeply rooted in the pre-colonial past (see Table 22.1 for comparisons), informed by *Ubuntu's* canon of "relating well with others" and seeing the connections that one has with many (Natifu & Zikusooka, 2014). Therefore, public relations research that embraces *Ubuntu* allows public relations to be understood by an Afro-centric worldview instead of the dominant US/Western conceptual worldview. As Rensburg (2008) argued, it's important to acknowledge "distinct lifestyles, knowledge systems and cultures which justify African paradigms" (p. 255) for an African public relations perspective to take shape.

For an *Ubuntu*-based approach to public relations to take root and flourish requires intentional effort from researchers and practitioners to search for and apply *Ubuntu*-informed practices and values. To move the research agenda forward, there are three ways in which *Ubuntu* can facilitate public

Table 22.1 Exploring *Ubuntu* Assumptions

Western-Based		Ubuntu-Based	
Values	*Assumptions*	*Values*	*Assumptions*
Transparency and honesty/truth telling	Individualism	Transparency	Communitarianism Accountability and community well-being
Two-way communication	Persuasion and mutual benefit	Inclusiveness	Human dignity, humanity toward others
Mutual understanding	Organization-centric	Tolerance and harmony	Dialogue Storytelling
Symmetry Reciprocal strategic reflection		Consensus-building	Participative non-competitive decision making Storytelling

relations theory development in SSA: actively researching, practicing, and educating about *Ubuntu* values in public relations.

Educating About Ubuntu *in Public Relations*

One of the key elements for infusing *Ubuntu* philosophy into the understanding and practice of public relations in SSA is the access to formalized public relations education with a focus on local experiences. However, a major obstacle in developing locally grounded approaches necessary to guide public relations education is the availability of teaching materials, textbooks, and research publications, which are currently dominated by U.S.-based resources (Thompson, 2018).

In addition to the lack of contextualized educational resources, a limited number of professional public relations associations offer public relations training. For example, in Nigeria, practitioners have legal requirements to practice public relations only with the certification from the professional organization NIPR (Molleda & Alhassan, 2006). Despite a more formalized Nigerian public relations practice and education structure, there is still very little literature addressing public relations theory and practice locally (Otubanjo & Amujo, 2013). Conversely, in Uganda, in the absence of formal public relations education, public relations is understood from a culturally constructed *Ubuntu* viewpoint meaning public relations is everybody's business and predominantly concerned with relating well with internal and external publics (Zikusooka, 2002). However, practitioners associated with the professional organization Public Relations Association of Uganda (PRAU) view public relations from a more Western perspective as a management function that fosters mutually beneficial relationships. This juxtaposition highlights the need for a more intentional approach to public relations education in SSA that would emphasize culturally grounded approaches.

Practicing Ubuntu in Public Relations

Cultural realities impact how public relations is practiced in various regions, so looking beyond Western concepts, which oftentimes tend to be impractical in non-Western settings, is important. This is particularly relevant for African public relations practitioners who are continuously tasked to work and communicate at both the local intercultural and international level as Africa forges forward as an emerging economy (Mersham et al., 2011). Through the lens of *Ubuntu*, public relations can be characterized by deeply communal relations and reciprocal moral obligations, and practitioners are expected to engender a public service ethos to serve as a conduit for thoughtful and constructive processes of democratic deliberation, often through the palaver process.

In terms of practical applications of *Ubuntu* public relations, co-creation of meaning and communication in African communities occurs via traditional and indigenous forms of communication and storytelling, such as gatherings under the palaver tree. Scheid (2011) described palaver as a metaphor for a physical, social, and psychological space for open communication where "persons can be integrated into the life and expectations of their communities" (p. 18). While the communication practice originated as a physical space for community gatherings under the ancestral baobab tree, metaphorically, this space is more often psychological. The *Ubuntu* approach and the palaver tree tradition suggest that an organization considers itself a part of the community and prioritizes consensus-building and mutual understanding. Being part of the community also means that an organization considers itself equal to community members, disregarding power structures (Fuse et al., 2010; Sopova, 1999).

This is particularly evident through CSR. For example, in Malawi, there is a common understanding among local and internationally connected organizations that *Ubuntu* is primarily about giving back to the community. Kayuni and Tambulasi (2012) reported that because CSR programs are dependent on the existing cultural context, CSR can enhance the values of *Ubuntu* as it is fundamentally about the community's well-being. *Ubuntu* influences and facilitates CSR activities in Malawian organizations and these organizations acknowledge that they are interconnected with the communities they operate in because the communities' concerns directly impact their operations and existence in those spaces. This example further highlights the need for more applied case studies that document the interrelationship between public relations practices, palaver tree, and *Ubuntu*.

Researching Ubuntu *in Public Relations*

While *Ubuntu* is considered a widely practiced philosophy in many SSA countries, its application in public relations scholarship has been under-documented. The philosophy of *Ubuntu* found a broader application in management, journalism, and media ethics, yet there are very few applications of it found in the public relations literature. In this chapter, we argue that *Ubuntu* not only can inform the development of Afro-centric public relations approaches but also augment the existing public relations theories, such as relationship management and dialogue.

An *Ubuntu*-based approach to public relations embraces values of inclusiveness, tolerance, transparency, and consensus building, therefore, highlighting the importance of relationship building and dialogue. To move forward the research agenda, scholars could start first by investigating relationship building from the *Ubuntu* perspective. Viewing relationship building through the lens of *Ubuntu* offers a glimpse into the potential of Afro-centric public relations theory development that future studies should address.

Van Niekerk (2013) stated that *Ubuntu* is about nurturing relationships through a commitment to harmony and reconciliation. Mersham et al. (2011) argued that traditional African views of communication are built on the principles of humanism and communalism, according to which one becomes a person through building and maintaining harmonious relations with others within their community. In this sense, an individual considers their interests only in relation to the interests of the community. At the same time, Blankenberg (1999) explained, *Ubuntu* is not opposed to individualism. In *Ubuntu* culture, accountability is still an individual responsibility despite its focus on community well-being. Thus, the individual becomes the center of the shared life. Such views connect *Ubuntu*-based communication to the co-creational approach of public relations, which sees the publics [communities] as co-creators of meaning and communication, allowing them to arrive at shared meanings, interpretations, and goals (Botan & Taylor, 2004).

One way to develop *Ubuntu*-based public relations theories is to examine indigenous forms of communication and their application in public relations, such as the palaver tree and its relevance to dialogue. Relationship building in *Ubuntu* is achieved through participative practices that invite diversity and tolerance to promote dialogue. Focus on consensus building is central in SSA participative communication practices because consensus can only be achieved through discourse that invites multifarious opinions to deliberate and problem solve. Storytelling is important to the practice of *Ubuntu* because it allows incorporating different narratives within a story. In other words, since *Ubuntu* values diverse voices, storytelling becomes the tool that helps incorporate such diverse opinions. Thus, storytelling as a tool for dialogic communication and consensus building is another SSA cultural phenomenon to explore in order to propel SSA public relations theory forward.

Further, in *Ubuntu*, consensus building is about the process that seeks all participants of the dialogue to agree with the outcome by emphasizing tolerance, inclusiveness, and transparency. Consensus building is also the process that often occurs under the palaver tree. The palaver communication process possesses the following three uniquely African characteristics relevant to the practice of public relations: 1) time as "a servant to the process" (*Hakuna Matata*), 2) all-inclusive participation, and 3) and systemic treatment of problems. These characteristics are embedded in traditional forms of storytelling that need further conceptualizations and investigation. Historically, the application of Western perspectives and theories to the investigation of African public relations undervalued the importance of indigenous storytelling and its application to public relations. Studying the palaver tree communication process will further help us cement the value and the need of Afro-centric public relations perspectives.

Public relations scholars are yet to appreciate the value of the *Ubuntu* philosophy to knowledge creation about the discipline in SSA countries. The relevance of *Ubuntu* and palaver tree practices to public relations is expressed through their emphasis on community and collectivity (Mersham et al., 2011). Focusing public relations research in SSA on *Ubuntu* will help facilitate the shift from "I think therefore I am" to "I am because we are." Rather than treating *Ubuntu* as a prescriptive set of norms and guidelines, scholars are invited to the idea of *Ubuntu* public relations as an internalized attitude of relationality.

Potential Challenges of Ubuntu

The incorporation of *Ubuntu* into public relations practices is not without its challenges. Scholars of *Ubuntu* have highlighted the contradictory nature of *Ubuntu* and capitalism, thanks to which the public relations industry blossoms. For instance, traditional Western management systems that have been adopted in Africa assume that self-interest is the ultimate determinant of behavior, while *Ubuntu* advocates for suppression of self-interest. The importance placed on profit-making challenges traditional African community values (Sambala et al., 2020). The subsequent inequality, poverty, unemployment, and fractured family unit make it difficult for communities to organize and achieve common goals as outlined by *Ubuntu*.

There is also conflict between culturally grounded values of *Ubuntu* and Africa's colonial past that affect current political systems and social norms (Kayuni & Tambulasi, 2012). African politicians tend to dismiss traditional cultural practices as outdated, yet rural Africans find it hard to accept the imported ideas of how government and community should communicate and problem-solve (Sopova, 1999). However, McDonald (2010) believes *Ubuntu* and capitalism can still work in unison among locals who still have not given up on communal principles.

Furthermore, globalization and Western influences continue to shape African societal norms that deviate from the traditional pan-African values of communitarianism (Sambala et al., 2020). This deviation highlights a tension between human behavior as fundamentally social (*Ubuntu*) or fundamentally individual (Western). In Western approaches to public relations, organizations are at the center of the communication process, making decisions predominantly for their benefit (e.g., excellence theory, relationship building theory, stakeholder theory). In *Ubuntu*-based approaches, organizations are part of the communities, and they both contribute to the conversation (see Table 23.1). Nonetheless, the application of *Ubuntu* has been valuable in CSR, for example, where both viewpoints invest in the community's well-being and find value in the mutually beneficial relationship between organization and community.

Conclusion

To be clear, *Ubuntu* is not a substitution of existing theories and models of public relations. It is about placing more emphasis on storytelling, harmony, and reconciliation. Culture plays a crucial role in public relations because public relations is a communication function, while communication itself is a cultural phenomenon. Therefore, applying Western theoretical thought without regard for particularities of local contexts and cultures overlooks the need for public relations theories to be applied differently due to the difference in societal systems and philosophical backgrounds (Ayish, 2003; Hofstede, 1980; Kriyantono & McKenna, 2017). On the one hand, it is important to acknowledge that African philosophical beliefs and indigenous forms of outreach that underpin public relations exist. Conversely, there are no public relations theories that embody African communication culture and value systems. To answer the question of whether there could be an exclusively African public relations approach, we reiterate that *Ubuntu* is a common African philosophical approach and stress its special role in communication and public relations throughout Africa.

The heightened awareness of global diversity presents the need of developing public relations theories that are based on indigenous epistemologies and culture-focused conceptualizations, such as *Ubuntu*. Although SSA communities have various cultures and local wisdom, in general, they have common characteristics that cannot be easily tested within a Western framework, such as *ubuntism* and collectivity (Mersham et al., 2011). Therefore, incorporating and emphasizing uniquely African communication concepts and the African worldview may facilitate the development of the African public relations school of thought by presenting a normative, value-based perspective as a basis for future public relations theory building in the African context. In other words, a conscious effort is needed to foster an African school of thought by incorporating *Ubuntu* and related concepts to be applied and tested in SSA public relations scholarship.

References

Adedoyin, F. F., Ozturk, I., Agboola, M. O., Agboola, P. O., & Bekun, F. V. (2021). The implications of renewable and non-renewable energy generating in Sub-Saharan Africa: The role of economic policy uncertainties. *Energy Policy, 150*, 112–115. https://doi.org/10.1016/j.enpol.2020.112115

Akoje, T. P., & Rahim, M. H. A. (2014). A comparative analysis of codes of ethics in Nigeria, United Kingdom, United States of America, India and Russia. *Jurnal Komunikasi-Malaysian Journal of Communication, 30*(2), 221–238. https://doi.org/10.17576/jkmjc-2014-3002-12

Anani-Bossman, A. A. (2021). An empirical investigation of public relations roles: A case study of the financial service sector of Ghana. *Corporate Reputation Review*, 1–12. https://doi.org/10.1057/s41299-021-00114-8

Ayish, M. I. (2003). Beyond western-oriented communication theories a normative Arab- Islamic perspective. *Javnost-The Public, 10*(2), 79–92. https://doi.org/10.1080/13183222.2003.11008829

BBC. (2017, November 21). Zimbabwe profile—media. *BBC.com*. www.bbc.com/news/world-africa-14113511

BBC. (2019, July 24). Kenya profile—media. *BBC.com*. www.bbc.com/news/world-africa-13681344

Bekalu, M. A., & Eggermont, S. (2015). Aligning HIV/AIDS communication with the oral tradition of Africans: A theory-based content analysis of songs' potential in prevention efforts. *Health Communication, 30*(5), 441–450. https://doi.org/10.1080/10410236.2013.867004

Benecke, D. R., & Oksiutycz, A. (2015). Changing conversation and dialogue through LeadSA: An example of public relations activism in South Africa. *Public Relations Review, 41*(5), 816–824. https://doi.org/10.1016/j.pubrev.2015.06.003

Benecke, D. R., & Verwey, S. (2020). Social representation of PR activism: Perceptions of early career public relations professionals in South Africa. *Public Relations Review, 46*(5), 101978. https://doi.org/10.1016/j.pubrev.2020.101978

Blankenberg, N. (1999). In search of a real freedom: Ubuntu and the media. *Critical Arts: A South-North Journal of Cultural & Media Studies, 13*(2), 42–65. https://doi.org/10.1080/02560049985310121

Botan, C. H., & Taylor, M. (2004). Public relations: State of the field. *Journal of Communication, 54*(4), 645–661.

Chaka, M. (2014). Public relations (PR) in nation-building: An exploration of the South African presidential discourse. *Public Relations Review, 40*(2), 351–362. https://doi.org/10.1016/j.pubrev.2013.11.013

Chibba, S. (2013, September 19) *Ubuntu is about relationships*. Brand South Africa. https://brandsouthafrica.com/ubuntu-is-about-relationships/

Christians, C. G. (2004). Ubuntu and communitarianism in media ethics. *Ecquid Novi: African Journalism Studies, 25*(2), 235–256. https://doi.org/10.1080/02560054.2004.9653296

Choi, Y., & Cameron, G. T. (2009). Overcoming ethnocentrism: The role of identity in contingent practice of international public relations. *Journal of Public Relations Research, 17*, 171–189. https://doi.org/10.1207/s1532754xjprr1702_6

Davis, C. B. (2021). *Organizational storytelling in the African context*. Paper presented at North Central Evangelical Missiological Society Conference.

De Beer, E., Steyn, B., & Rensburg, R. (2013). The Pretoria school of thought: From strategy to governance and sustainability. In K. Sriramesh, A. Zerfass, & J. N. Kim (Eds.), *Public relations and communication management: Current trends and emerging topics*. Routledge.

Fuse, K., Land, M., & Lambiase, J. J. (2010). Expanding the philosophical base for ethical public relations practice: Cross-cultural case application of non-Western ethical philosophies. *Western Journal of Communication*, 74(4), 436–455. https://doi.org/10.1 080/10570314.2010.492823

Gershman, B., & Rivera, D. (2018). Subnational diversity in Sub-Saharan Africa: Insights from a new dataset. *Journal of Development Economics*, 133, 231–263. https://doi. org/10.1016/j.jdeveco.2018.01.003

Heritage, J. (1997). Conversation analysis and institutional talk: Analyzing data. In D. Silverman (Ed.), *Qualitative research: Theory, method and practice* (pp. 161–182). Sage.

Hofstede, G. (1980). Motivation, leadership, and organization: Do American theories apply abroad? *Organizational Dynamics*, 9(1), 42–63. https://doi. org/10.1016/0090-2616(80)90013-3

Holtzhausen, D. R., Petersen, B. K., & Tindall, N. T. (2003). Exploding the myth of the symmetrical/asymmetrical dichotomy: Public relations models in the new South Africa. *Journal of Public Relations Research*, 15(4), 305–341. https://doi.org/10.1207/ S1532754XJPRR1504_02

Ihlen, Ø., & van Ruler, B. (2007). How public relations works: Theoretical roots and public relations perspectives. *Public Relations Review*, 33(3), 243–248. https://doi. org/10.1016/j.pubrev.2007.05.001

Kamwangamalu, N. M. (1999). Ubuntu in South Africa: A sociolinguistic perspective to a Pan-African concept. *Critical Arts: A South-North Journal of Cultural & Media Studies*, 13(2), 24–42. https://doi.org/10.1080/02560049985310111

Kayuni, H. M., & Tambulasi, R. I. C. (2012). Ubuntu and corporate social responsibility: The case of selected Malawian organizations. *African Journal of Economic and Management Studies*, 3, 64–76. https://doi.org/10.1108/20400701211197285

Kent, M. L. (2015). The power of storytelling in public relations: Introducing the 20 master plots. *Public Relations Review*, 41(4), 480–489. https://doi.org/10.1016/j. pubrev.2015.05.011

Kiambi, D. M., & Nadler, M. K. (2012). Public relations in Kenya: An exploration of models and cultural influences. *Public Relations Review*, 38(3), 505–507. https://doi. org/10.1016/j.pubrev.2012.01.007

Kriyantono, R., & McKenna, B. (2017). Developing a culturally relevant public relations theory for Indonesia. *Jurnal Komunikasi: Malaysian Journal of Communication*, 33(1), 1–16. https://doi.org/10.17576/jkmjc-2017-3301-01

Mangaliso, M. P. (2001). Building competitive advantage from Ubuntu: Management lessons from South Africa. *Academy of Management Executive*, 15(3), 23–33. https://doi. org/10.5465/ame.2001.5229453

Mangena, F. (2016). African ethics through Ubuntu: A postmodern exposition. *Journal of Pan African Studies*, 9(2), 66–81.

Matolino, B. (2020). Ubuntu: A traditional virtue ethics contribution to economic and social development in Southern Africa. In K. Ogunyemi (Ed.), *African virtue ethics traditions for business and management* (pp. 12–29). Edward Elgar Publishing.

Mbendera, R. (2020). Ubuntu ethical values and Africa's quest for a better home. *American Journal of Humanities and Social Sciences Research*, 4(8), 177–187.

Mbigi, L. (1997). *Ubuntu: The African dream in management*. Knowledge Resources.

Mboti, N. (2015). May the real Ubuntu please stand up? *Journal of Media Ethics*, 30(2), 125–147.

McDonald, D. A. (2010). Ubuntu bashing: The marketisation of "African values" in South Africa. *Review of African Political Economy*, 37(124), 139–152.https://doi.org/ 10.1080/03056244.2010.483902

McPhee, R. D., & Zaug, P. (2009). The communicative constitution of organizations. In L. Putnam & A. Nicotera (Eds.), *Building theories of organization: The constitutive role of communication* (pp. 21–44). Routledge.

Mersham, G., Skinner, C., & Rensburg, R. (2011). Approaches to African communication management and public relations: A case for theory-building on the continent. *Journal of Public Affairs, 11*(4), 195–207. http://doi.org/10.1002/pa.413

Metz, T. (2015). African ethics and journalism ethics: News and opinion in light of Ubuntu. *Journal of Media Ethics, 30*(2), 74–90. https://doi.org/10.1080/23736992.2015.1020377

Molleda, J. C., & Alhassan, A. D. (2006). Professional views on the Nigeria institute of public relations' law and enforcement. *Public Relations Review, 1*(32), 66–68. https://doi.org/10.1016/j.pubrev.2005.10.008

Moore, C. (2018, January 11). *5 predictions for PR in Africa in 2018.* www.prweek.com/article/1454367/5-predictions-pr-africa-2018

Muchena, E. (2017). An existential phenomenological analysis of public relations practice as a strategic management function in selected organisations in Harare (Zimbabwe). *IOSR Journal of Humanities and Social Sciences, 22,* 58–65.

Muchena, E. (2018). An investigation into the role played by public relations in selected public institutions in Harare, Zimbabwe. *The International Journal of Humanities and Social Studies, 6*(9), 64–72.

Natifu, B., & Zikusooka, A. (2014). Ubuntu, professionalism, activism, and the rise of public relations in Uganda. In S. J. Burton & J. L'Etang (Eds.), *Pathways to public relations: Histories of practice and profession* (pp. 224–238). Taylor & Francis.

New World Encyclopedia. (2021). *Sub-Saharan Africa.* www.newworldencyclopedia.org/entry/Sub-Saharan_Africa

Ngonyo, M. H., & Ramakrishna, C. (2016). Assessment of public relations practitioners' perception on their own professional practice in Kenya. *Assessment, 55,* 49–56.

Ngondo, P. S. (2019). An exploratory study: Digital and social media use by Zimbabwean public relations practitioners. *Public Relations Journal, 12*(3).

Ngondo, P. S., & Klyueva, A. (2020). Exploratory study of public relations roles in Zimbabwe. *Public Relations Review, 46*(5), 101961. https://doi.org/10.1016/j.pubrev.2020.101961

Niemann-Struweg, I., & Meintjes, C. (2008). The professionalism debate in South African public relations. *Public Relations Review, 34*(3), 224–229. https://doi.org/10.1016/j.pubrev.2008.03.029

Oksiutycz, A., & Nhedzi, A. (2018). Zimbabwean communication agencies: Current state and future prospects. *Communicare: Journal for Communication Sciences in Southern Africa, 37*(1), 94–117.

Otubanjo, O., & Amujo, O. (2013). 150 years of modern public relations practices in Nigeria. *Global Media Journal: Pakistan Edition, 6*(1), 1–26.

Public Relations Society of Kenya. (2022). *CPD/training.* www.prsk.co.ke/prsk-training-calendar-2021/

Rensburg, R. (2008). Public relations research and evaluation in Africa. In B. van Ruler, A. T. Vercic, & D. Vercic (Eds.), *Public relations metrics: Research and evaluation* (pp. 252–63). Routledge.

Sambala, E. Z., Cooper, S., & Manderson, L. (2020). Ubuntu as a framework for ethical decision making in Africa: Responding to epidemics. *Ethics & Behavior, 30*(1), 1–13. https://doi.org/10.1080/10508422.2019.1583565

Scheid, A. F. (2011). Under the palaver tree: Community ethics for truth-telling and reconciliation. *Journal of the Society of Christian Ethics, 31*(1), 17–36.

Shutte, A. (2001). *Ubuntu: An ethic for a new South Africa.* Cluster Publications.

Skinner, C., & Mersham, G. (2008). Corporate social responsibility in South Africa: Emerging trends. *Society and Business Review, 3*(3), 239–255. https://doi.org/10.1108/17465680810907314

Skinner, C., & Mersham, G. (2009). The nature and status of public relations practice in Africa. In K. Sriramesh & D. Vercic (Eds.), *The global public relations handbook: Theory, research and practice* (pp. 284–311). Routledge. https://doi.org/10.4324/9780203889374.ch14

Sopova, J. (1999). In the shade of the palaver tree. *UNESCO Courier, 52*(5), 42.

Soy, A. (2020, October 8). Coronavirus in Africa: Five reasons why Covid-19 has been less deadly than elsewhere. *BBC.* www.bbc.com/news/world-africa-54418613

Steyn, B., & Niemann, L. (2014). Strategic role of public relations in enterprise strategy, governance and sustainability—a normative framework. *Public Relations Review, 40*(2), 171–183. https://doi.org/10.1016/j.pubrev.2013.09.001

Steyn, E., de Beer, A. S., Steyn, T. D., & Schreiner, W. N. (2004). Enron and Saambou Bank in South Africa: A case study of insufficient relationship management. *Public Relations Review, 30*(1), 75–86. https://doi.org/10.1016/j.pubrev.2003.11.007

Sulcas, A. (2020, August 5). Show your solidarity and just wear that mask already—it's Ubuntu. *Daily Maverick.* www.dailymaverick.co.za/article/2020-08-05-show-your-solidarity-and-just-wear-that-mask-already-its-ubuntu/

Tavernaro-Haidarian, L. (2018). *A relational model of public discourse: The African philosophy of Ubuntu.* Routledge.

Tavernaro-Haidarian, L. (2021). I am because we are: A relational approach to journalism. In L. Price, W. Wyatt, & K. Sanders (Eds.), *Routledge companion to journalism ethics* (pp. 93–100). Routledge.

Thompson, E. E. (2015). Public relations technology in a nascent democracy—the case of Ghana. In K. Ansu-Kyeremeh, A. Gadzekpo, & M. Amoakohene (Eds.), *Communication theory and practice in Ghana: A critical appraisal* (pp. 71–84). University of Ghana Readers.

Thompson, E. E. (2018). Public relations education in an emerging democracy: The case of Ghana. *Journal of Communication Management, 22*(4), 476–489. https://doi.org/10.1108/JCOM-04-2018-0038

Tindall, N. T., & Holtzhausen, D. R. (2011). Toward a roles theory for strategic communication: The case of South Africa. *International Journal of Strategic Communication, 5*(2), 74–94. https://doi.org/10.1080/1553118X.2011.561075

Ukonu, M. O., Anyadike, D. O., & Okoro, N. M. (2018). Issues in the evolution of public relations in Nigeria. *The Journal of International Communication, 24*(1), 37–54.

van Heerden, G., & Rensburg, R. (2005). Public relations roles empirically verified among public relations practitioners in Africa. *Communicare: Journal for Communication Sciences in Southern Africa, 24*(1), 69–88.

van Niekerk, J. (2013). *Ubuntu and moral value* [Unpublished doctoral dissertation, University of the Witwatersrand].

Wilson, S. (2020). Three reasons why Jacinda Ardern's Coronavirus response has been a masterclass in crisis leadership. *The Conversation.* https://theconversation.com/three-reasons-why-jacinda-arderns-coronavirus-response-has-been-a-masterclass-in-crisis-leadership-135541

Wiredu, K. (1996). *Cultural universals and particulars: An African perspective.* Indiana University Press.

World Bank. (2015). *Sub-Saharan Africa.* https://elibrary.worldbank.org/doi/abs/10.1596/978-1-4648-0483-0_ch2_SSA

Wu, M. Y., & Baah-Boakye, K. (2014). Public relations in Ghana: Professionalism and impacts of globalization. *China Media Research, 10*(3), 15–23.

Zikusooka, A. (2002). *The role of the public relations association of Uganda (PRAU) in demystifying public relations in Uganda* [unpublished bachelor's thesis, Makerere University, Kampala]. https://doi.org/10.9781137404299.0015

Section 4

Applications of Theory

23 Health Communication Theory in Public Relations

Sarah A. Aghazadeh and Linda Aldoory

Introduction

One way that public relations contributes to society is by influencing how individuals, organizations, and public institutions make important health decisions and grapple with health challenges. We consider health campaigns and other forms of public health messages as health communication, which is an integral body of knowledge linked to public relations. The relationship between health communication and public relations is a symbiotic one, where both fields can benefit from valuable and applied research and both fields use similar theories to design messages that affect health outcomes. As early as 2004, Botan and Taylor considered the utility of public relations theory for applied communication contexts, such as health communication. Several theories used in health communication can be applied to public relations planning and implementation, where variables such as self-efficacy and perceived threat can be message design factors that have impact on health.

In many studies, however, these theories were used to only focus on cognitive processing and assume a clear, linear relationship between a message and outcomes such as attitudes, behavioral intent, and behavioral outcomes. Also, the most common research methods used to test the prevailing health communication theories rely on short-term effects, such as perceived behavioral intent. While this is not negative in and of itself, it does show limitations in the ability of past research to help explain multiple, complex health behaviors and limits how public relations messages and campaigns can be developed.

This chapter surveys three prevailing health communication theories that have informed public relations over the last few decades, analyzes the assumptions underlying these theories, and considers how beneficial these theories are for health public relations efforts. The theories included for analysis are social learning theory/social cognitive theory (SLT/SCT), health belief model (HBM), and theory of planned behavior/reasoned action (TPB/TRA). Research on the theories has shaped a variety of past and present health campaigns and communication interventions while providing valid

DOI: 10.4324/9781003141396-27

information on how audiences process and respond to health messages. They have provided some promising pathways for public relations.

However, the prevailing approach to health communication in public relations is individualistic, positivist, and cognitive focused. This approach fails to consider the role of culture and community, and it neglects sustainable measures, such as resilience against future health risks. In addressing these limitations, we propose that health communication in public relations should consider a socio-ecological model (SEM) for research. SEM has been used in health research and health communication studies (Figueroa, 2017), as well as in public relations research (Aldoory & Toth, 2021). It takes into consideration organizational, societal, and interpersonal relations for individual health behavior change. What we propose is to use the SEM, but with a distinct goal: to design health messages and health communication efforts in public relations that contribute to community health, health empowerment, and social change for health equity.

This chapter walks readers through the intersections of health communication and public relations and proposes an alternative perspective that gives context for future research. First, we offer definitions and examples of health communication research in public relations. Then, we describe the three prevailing health communication theories that have been used in public relations. We critique them and pay particular attention to limitations in the body of knowledge. We end the chapter by explaining the socio-ecological model and how it can contribute to health communication in public relations.

Defining Public Relations for Health Communication Purposes

Public relations has been defined in various ways and with various goals in mind. For our purposes in this chapter, we consider public relations to include strategic communication planning in order to influence health outcomes. This general framework can include organizational settings as well as community settings, and it can include relationship building, such as between a health system and a physician or patient, as well as advocacy such as with health prevention campaigns. Scholars have interrogated public relations' role in addressing a variety of public health issues and assisting public health entities (Wise, 2001). Aldoory and Austin (2011) married the two fields to present *health public relations* as a burgeoning area of study that requires attention to understand how people think about, comprehend, and make decisions about their health and the efforts to communicate for improved health outcomes.

Health communication can refer to the "multifaceted and multidisciplinary field" that focuses on the sharing of health information, messages, and ideas to promote health across a variety of contexts, groups of people, and levels of society (Schiavo, 2014, p. 5). The National Cancer Institute (2004) presented a definition of health communication as "the study and use of communication strategies to inform and influence individual and community decisions that enhance health" (p. 2). Similarly, Maibach and Holtgrave (1995) defined *public health communication* specifically as the "use of communication techniques and technologies to (positively) influence individuals, populations, and organizations for the purpose of promoting conditions conducive to human and environmental health" (pp. 219–220). Ultimately, health communication seeks to understand how people make health decisions to inspire positive health outcomes.

What Health Communication Looks Like in Public Relations

As the disciplinary name implies, health communication is specific to health topics, and its domain is "usually problem-based, focusing on identifying, examining, and solving health care and health promotion problems" (Kreps et al., 1998, p. 2). Health communication scholars are often interested in predicting and changing behavior (Green et al., 2020), which include a range of intervention points such as patient-provider communication and mass media messages. Essentially, health communication has contributed a vast array of knowledge about how to predict and persuade for behavioral changes particularly at the campaign and message-levels.

The public relations research and theory that has focused on health has often emphasized the role of mass media (Grunig et al., 2006) and issues management (Heath, 2018). Thus, public relations has a foundational interest in understanding how media and organizations influence health topics. Health organizations share science and health information and draw attention to specific health issues within communities and society (Hoskig, 2020; Lynch, 2017). For instance, Park and Reber (2010) investigated how health organizations (American Cancer Society, American Heart Association, and the American Diabetes Association) used research to communicate with publics; authors found that these organizations often drew on arguments that portrayed health as a societal responsibility.

Public relations research on health has also turned to well-known public relations theories to explain health perceptions and health outcomes. Relationship management theory has been used to detect how health organizations develop health messages to change a public's trust, control mutuality, and satisfaction, which are variables of relationship management theory, to affect their health. One study, for example, analyzed how African American adults perceived their relationships with healthcare providers and used relationship management theory to detect the importance of the role of control and trust in health relationships (Stanley et al., 2019). Another example was a focus group study that explored how relationship management theory explained the process of different health organizations working together for HIV prevention (Aldoory et al., 2015). There are also studies that use the situational theory of publics to dig into the variables of that theory—public's level of involvement, problem recognition, and constraint recognition—but in health contexts (Aldoory et al., 2018, 2010).

Public relations scholarship has also contributed to crisis and risk studies that investigate and theorize about how publics, government entities, and organizations manage health threats. For example, Kim and Liu (2012) explored public and private sector responses to the 2009 H1N1 pandemic via quantitative content analysis of social media and traditional communication materials from federal health agencies (e.g., CDC) and corporations (e.g., pork producers). The authors found that federal agencies often instructed publics about how to protect health and manage risk. Theoretical implications for the situational theory of crisis communication (SCCT) included operationalizing instructing information and adjusting information while offering two new crisis response strategies (enhancing and transferring) (Kim & Liu, 2012). As another example, Veil and Anthony (2017) conducted a case study about the Federal Emergency Management Agency's (FEMA) formaldehyde trailer crisis, where FEMA's Hurricane Katrina trailers set up to support people affected by the natural disaster exposed residents to dangerous levels of formaldehyde. This study found that FEMA's previous Hurricane Katrina response failures created a lack of trust from stakeholders and illustrated how crises can negatively impact an organization's social capital/network to the point where they cannot effectively respond to future health challenges (Veil & Anthony, 2017).

Health Communication Theories Useful to Public Relations

One main way that public relations and health communication intersect is in the use of theory. There are certain well-tested health communication theories that are useful for public relations goals and used frequently by public relations scholars. We selected three health communication theories because they are the most well-tested health behavior theories and focused on principles that can guide campaign planning, execution, and evaluation. Their primary focus on health outcomes helps public relations efforts to stay focused on public health as well as individual outcomes. The three theories explicated here are social learning theory/social cognitive theory, the health belief model, and theory of planned behavior/reasoned action.

Social Learning Theory/Social Cognitive Theory

Social learning theory/social cognitive theory (SLT/SCT) outlines the important relationships between cognitive, environmental, and behavioral factors that influence learning processes (Parcel & Baranowski, 1981). The theory posits that people learn through direct and indirect experience—through rewards, punishments, and observation (Bandura, 1977). An important premise of this pair of theories is that people can learn from the behavior of others through vicarious experiences (Bandura, 1977, 1998). This set of theories was revolutionary in the ways it turned away from solely personality-based and internal motivators as the primary influencers of behavior and toward expectancies and incentives as environmental influencers (Bandura, 1977; Rosenstock et al., 1988). The theories also highlighted publics as central actors in determining the outcome of communication efforts and focused on the importance of self-efficacy, or the self-belief that one can do something, in enacting behaviors (Bandura, 1998; Rosenstock et al., 1988). When applied to health, these theories can provide a breadth of explanation about how people interpret internal and external information sources to make health decisions. These theories have been applied to a range of health topics, including college binge-drinking (Durkin et al., 2005) and the effects of role models for persuasive health messaging (Bosone et al., 2015).

Health Belief Model

The health belief model (HBM) helps explain and understand preventive health behavior (Rosenstock, 1974). This model blossomed from health professionals' concerns and interests in making people aware about health risks and informing them about how they could reduce those risks (Green et al., 2020). HBM is based on four central variables: perceived susceptibility, perceived severity, perceived barriers, and perceived benefits (Green et al., 2020). Essentially, this theory questions the extent to which people believe they have a serious risk, that they can make change at reasonable cost/barriers, and that they can do so for a positive outcome (Carpenter, 2010; Rosenstock et al., 1988). HBM was later modified to include self-efficacy (Green et al., 2020). The HBM has informed the creation of health campaigns (Sundstrom et al., 2018) and been applied to pressing contemporary questions, such as how online communities influence medication adherence for chronic conditions (Willis, 2018).

Theory of Planned Behavior / Reasoned Action

The theory of planned behavior and theory of reasoned action help to explain a person's intention to enact a particular behavior in a given situation (Ajzen, 1991). This pair of theories started as the theory of reasoned action (TRA) and then evolved into the theory of planned behavior (TPB). TRA assumed that people can decide to take an action and then act (volitional control), which limited its applicability because of the important differences between actual and perceived control (Ajzen, 2020). Thus, TPB added the variable of perceived behavioral control (Madden et al., 1992). Ajzen (1991) likened perceived behavioral control to Bandura's (1977) self-efficacy and claimed that "perceived behavioral control, together with behavioral intention, can be used directly to predict behavioral achievement" (p. 184). In TPB, intentions are influenced by three factors: attitude toward behavior (belief that performing behavior will produce a certain outcome), subjective norm (perception of social expectation to perform the behavior or not), and perceived behavioral control (Ajzen, 1991, 2020). People form their beliefs based on a variety of experiences, social interactions, and media messaging (Yzer, 2017). Essentially, these theories outline how attitude and subjective norms influence behavioral intention and, then, behavior (Madden et al., 1992).

Contributions to Public Relations Research

These prevailing health communication theories have proved useful to public relations because they help answer a range of questions about how to engage publics in messages and campaigns that focus on health issues and behavior change. Public relations researchers can look to the health communication principles for designing best practices in communication. For instance, Aldoory et al. (2018) conducted interviews with content developers and a content analysis of Text4Baby text messages to understand how communicators constructed messages to encourage women to engage in their prenatal healthcare. Researchers explored the message-level considerations of health communication theories (such as HBM, SCT, and TPB) to engage publics and influence their involvement in the issue as categorized by the situational theory of publics (STP). They found that the communicators created messages related to risk, social norms, and resources and that communicators faced a host of challenges when attempting to incorporate theory into health messaging (Aldoory et al., 2018). As another example, Sundstrom et al. (2018) used the HBM to inform a cervical cancer prevention/human papillomavirus (HPV) vaccination promotion effort and engage a community in this health issue. Before implementing the campaign, this research identified how various media outlets share information about cervical cancer and HPV, how people perceive that information, and how new communication messages and strategies could address the variables of HBM (i.e., perceived susceptibility, perceived barriers, and perceived benefits) (Sundstrom et al., 2018). The campaign then targeted college-aged women in South Carolina through a combination of traditional and new media and an awareness event to ultimately influence preventive behaviors and intentions (Sundstrom et al., 2018). These examples show how health communication theories can address public relations problems related to informing and engaging a variety of publics and constituents affected by a particular health issue.

Critique of Prevailing Health Communication Theories

The three health communication theories described here have much in common. First, they are the most well-known and well-tested health communication theories and the most used by public relations scholars who study health. Second, all of them have independent variables that focus on cognitive processing (or how a person processes and understands information), and the dependent variables are behavioral in nature. Third, they use the same core constructs: perceived threat, self-efficacy, and perceived social norms. Finally, the theories are grounded in value expectancy, or the assumption that a person will gain a worthwhile outcome because of a particular behavior or behavior change.

However, the prevailing theories are grounded in linear assumptions about how a message can directly make a health change, and the theories are relatively blind to contextual factors that may affect the relationship between communication factors and behavioral outcomes. The health risks that we grapple with today are more complex and interconnected than ever before. Borders are fluid, goods and services move easily between and among various regions, and culture can be exchanged across time and space. Similarly, risky health behaviors, such as tobacco and alcohol use, and communicable diseases can also be easily shared (Pang & Guindon, 2004). Pang and Guindon (2004) outline globalization as encompassing an important communication component that affects health: "Perhaps the most profound changes that have taken place during the past 10 years have come through the globalization of ideas and information, facilitated through the revolution in information technology" (p. s13). The COVID-19 global pandemic has proven the fluidity and complexity of health risks today. This is further exacerbated by digitization, which has increased the availability and sharing of health information and misinformation (Gold et al., 2019).

Our post-pandemic world will need new explanations for health and communication that reflect the fluid, digitized, and complex relationships between messages and desired health outcomes. Changes in climate, governance, health status, economics, or any other part of life can have rippling physical, mental, and emotional health consequences. For instance, climate change impacts the spread of infectious diseases, food insecurity, and mental distress related to natural disasters and displacement (Patz et al., 2014). Health concerns can evolve into health crises that are compounded by public uncertainty and frustration about the unknown and confusing details of health challenges (Nowak & Greenwell, 2021). The global, digital, and dynamic health context necessitates a move away from only considering individual factors or concepts and moving toward an examination of the integrative constellation of factors that impact communication and health. We argue that theory must acknowledge social determinants of health and interlocking influences amidst adversity, alongside individual and cognitive factors. Health is multifaceted and influenced by a variety of environmental and social factors in addition to individual ones. Individual and cognitive explanations do not fully account for the complex, intersectional ways that people experience the world and how myriad factors influence someone's health and decisions. Furthermore, social and digital media have changed the information landscape. The fragmentation and synergy of traditional and new media messaging impact the effectiveness of health campaigns and desired health outcomes. We need to adapt current theory to meet the demands of contemporary health communication contexts. Thus, we propose an alternative framework for understanding health communication in public relations.

Alternative Framework: A Socio-ecological Model

History and Background

A socio-ecological model (SEM) takes a contextual and holistic approach to understanding health and communication. The main premise of the approach is that several domains or factors at social, individual, institutional and ideological levels will impact health and behavior change (Aldoory & Toth, 2021; Figueroa, 2017). A push toward a socio-ecological approach to understanding health started decades ago with scholars and the Centers for Disease Control and Prevention (CDC) calling for the individual medical and health education approaches to consider people's environments and contexts (Crawford, 1979; McLeroy et al., 1988). This call was born not only from a need for more holistic and effective health systems and services, but also from the desire to avoid blaming people for their health issues (Crawford, 1979; McLeroy et al., 1988). As Crawford (1979) explained, "What must be questioned is both the effectiveness and the political uses of a focus on lifestyles and on changing individual behavior without changing social structure and processes" (p. 256). Scholars developed different levels of influences on health outcomes (Bronfenbrenner, 1977; McLeroy et al., 1988) and considered how those levels interplay with one another in the context of social and individual life.

The SEM is a visual representation of these levels of influence on health. The levels in the model include: 1) individual/intrapersonal, 2) interpersonal, 3) institutional/organizational, 4) community, and 5) public policy (McLeroy et al., 1988). These five levels are helpful for explaining health communication in public relations. Please see Figure 23.1 for a visual representation of the SEM for health communication in public relations. While the visual is a two-dimensional rendering, what it suggests is a synergistic and often interdependent relationship between different systems of influence on individual health. For example, policy makers may create a law about wearing seat belts, which would ultimately affect many individuals who would be motivated to then wear seat belts. However, there must also be a change in social norms to influence more individuals to wear seat belts, which is how community interacts with individuals. Organizational may come into play in terms of insurance companies with incentives, or car companies who install seat belts. While of course the individual still has autonomy in their health decision making, the multiple influences on them to decide is highlighted visually here.

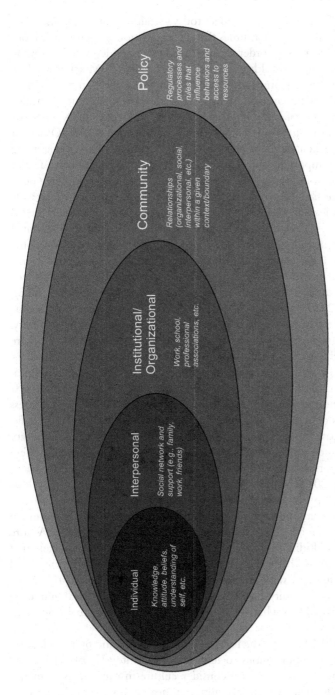

Figure 23.1 Socio-Ecological Model for Health Communication in Public Relations

Source: Adapted from McLeroy et al. (1988)

Note: The figure shows the socio-ecological levels as described by McLeroy et al., 1988 within a generic socio-ecological shape. (Figure also informed by CDC, n.d.; Krug, Dahlberg et al., 2002.)

Contributions of SEM to Public Relations

Assumptions of this SEM better reflect today's health public relations. First, a socio-ecological approach assumes that a constellation of factors is important to study and know in order to more realistically understand how public relations can impact health outcomes. For instance, SEM acknowledges social determinants that impact health. *Healthy People 2020* presented five key areas that organize some of the many determinants that influence health including economic stability, education, social and community context, health and health care, and neighborhood/built environment (Office of Disease Management and Prevention, 2020, para. 10). These organizing categories raise important questions that go beyond individual attitude and behavior when promoting health. For instance, how can we encourage people to eat more fruits and vegetables when they live in a food desert? Or when they work multiple jobs and do not have time to prepare fresh meals?

Second, desired outcomes from this model are no longer individual behaviors, but instead are sustainable processes, such as resilience and community health. Resilience, or the ability to rebound after disruptive events (Buzzanell, 2010), is a paradigmatic shift in understanding how to collectively manage disaster and promote community health (Wulff et al., 2015). As Buzzanell (2010) explained, "The construction of resilience is a collaborative exchange that invites participation of family, workplace, community, and interorganizational network members" (p. 9). Communities are where researchers and practitioners can build resilience and address issues of collective concern. This idea of resilience can be integrated into socio-ecological approaches to theory building.

Third, community-based and relational methods are needed to address multiple levels of analysis for a more holistic version of inquiry and praxis. Community-based participatory research (CBPR) looks to community members to guide research and theory building to address issues that affect their lived experiences and includes a range of participatory/engagement levels (Hacker, 2013; Minkler, 2005). At its core, CBPR is about developing a relationship between researchers and a community (Hacker, 2013), and health fields have notably adopted such an approach to meet the unique needs of underserved communities and address health inequities. A core benefit is the multidisciplinary and methodological diverse parameters that CBPR allows for in that it is an approach to research that can be employed by any discipline and with any appropriate method (Hacker, 2013; Minkler, 2005). A community-based approach also allows for critical, inductive analysis that can add to what we already know about individual cognitions that impact health.

Fourth, the SEM centers the role of culture in health and public relations. It provides more opportunities to understand the interplay of culture and health and how messages should consider culture in each of its elements, from visual to textual. A focus on culture in health also acknowledges how social norms can embody harmful pressures, for instance, body shaming and exercise addiction. Moran et al. (2016) identified Dutta's (2008) culture centered approach (CCA) as an ecological one that integrates a variety of levels. Such approaches also connect to the importance of understanding the many geographical, identity-based, and experience-based cultures and subcultures of which people are a part and how those memberships influence health communication. Furthermore, CCA's explication of culture and health transcends cultural sensitivity approaches to health communication, which seek to adapt existing messages and perspectives to make them acceptable in a particular cultural context. Instead, CCA approaches seek the necessary systemic and structural changes to better suit and respect a given community's culture (Dutta, 2007).

Finally, from a socio-ecological perspective, a central component is to act and make changes that lead to better health outcomes at the societal level. These changes can be made via public policy, changes to institutions and systems, and changes to cultural norms and values. In building healthy communities and engaging in community centered research, there should also be opportunities for community members to participate in policy creation (Wulff et al., 2015). In many public health contexts, such as pandemics and outbreaks, policy interventions help get treatments and resources to communities quickly (Figueroa, 2017). Particularly when communities experience inequitable harm from such health crises and challenges, it is imperative that societal and policy responses be enacted to mitigate health disparities and provide resources for underserved communities. However, as Golden and Earp (2012) explained, "the calls for multilevel interventions that better incorporate social, institutional, and policy approaches to health promotion have gone largely unheeded" (p. 368), meaning there is more work to be done to realize these societal-level goals. These societal and policy goals overlap with public relations approaches to issues management, which take into account the life cycle and stages that issues take on, particularly how media, community members, local leaders, and researchers can draw attention to health issues of communal concern and mobilize people to take action to address them (Botan & Taylor, 2004). Table 23.1 provides an explanation of each of these contributions of SEM to health public relations, alongside potential purposes, important factors, and health topics to consider in future research.

Applied Case Using SEM in Health Public Relations

One well-known health topic associated with SEM is violence prevention to address the various forms and intentional harm that threaten communities (e.g., intimate partner violence, suicide prevention, sexual violence, etc.) (Krug, Dahlberg et al., 2002). Researchers have found value in the model for violence prevention efforts, as SEM addresses the complex reasons

Table 23.1 Future Socio-ecological Research Areas for Health Public Relations

Future Research Area	Future Research Purposes	Important Factors/ Variables	Example Health Topics
Contextualizing individual health issues within socio-ecological model (SEM) levels	Explore how social determinants of health impact beliefs and health behaviors Create communication efforts that balance individual agency with systemic/social constraints Consider how every level of SEM influences individual health behavior	Social determinants of health Interplay between levels of SEM Systemic factors that influence individual and community health issues (e.g., politics, healthcare resources, etc.) Constraints and agency	Chronic diseases (e.g., diabetes and heart disease), addiction (e.g., opioid misuse), violence and suicidality
Sustainable processes/ resilience	Understand how communities can withstand events that disrupt everyday life and threaten health Determine how to best prepare for collective health disruptions	Community Social institutions Perceived collective risk and threat	Natural disasters, pandemics, political violence
Community-based participatory research	Encourage community support to address health issues Build relationships between organizations and individuals that can be leveraged for improved health outcomes	Interpersonal relationships and group dynamics Mutually beneficial relationships Health empowerment	Nutrition, health literacy, mental health, homelessness
Culture	Understand how health public relations influences and is influenced by culture(s) at the various SEM levels (interpersonal, organizational/ institutional, community, and policy) Explore how culture at various levels of SEM shapes health perceptions and behaviors Consider systemic changes to complement culture in relation to health needs	Social norms Global health Health systems Health campaigns	Overexercise and disordered eating, employee health and organizational culture, sexual health

Future Research Area	Future Research Purposes	Important Factors / Variables	Example Health Topics
Societal change	Use PR efforts for improved health policy Advocate for institutional changes that address health inequities along the lines of race, gender, status, etc. Promote access to health services Consider how to leverage and attend to health issue life cycles for societal change	Health equity Health promotion Political system	Healthcare policy (e.g., Affordable Care Act), health mandates, federal agency health initiatives

and accessibility issues that contribute to violence and harmful outcomes (Allchin et al., 2019). SEM approaches integrate policy, community, family, relationship, and individual levels of intervention and communication to ultimately influence individual health decision making and community health. One case of using SEM is when the CDC applied a socio-ecological approach to developing messages and communication about how violence prevention is interrelated with people's social lives (CDC, n.d.; Krug, Mercy et al., 2002). The Domestic Violence Prevention Enhancements and Leadership Through Alliances, Focusing on Outcomes for Communities United with States, or DELTA FOCUS, serves as an example of using SEM in communicating to publics about a particular problem to encourage behavioral change. DELTA FOCUS (2002–2013) included various prevention levels that addressed multiple goals, such as changing social and gender norms related to violence, including men and boys in prevention efforts, and mobilizing entire communities for violence prevention (CDC, 2018). Campaign elements used to address these goals include sharing partners' best practices for prevention and messages, helping connect partner organizations to each other, and garnering national attention for the health issue (CDC, 2018). Ultimately, this program provided large-scale support at societal and community levels to promote messages that impacted individual behaviors (CDC, 2018).

Conclusion

Health communication and public health have begun to transcend the limitations of focusing on individual behavior irrespective of the broader environment and context (Green et al., 2020). While this chapter focuses on the role of health communication in public relations, some of these distinctions highlight crucial areas of health communication theory and public health to which public relations has or can contribute. For instance, attention to issues management and mass media opens up opportunities for public relations to fulfill its role as "a technique for changing the culture or the environment for individual decision making" (Ratzan, 2001, p. 211). A reciprocal relationship exists between public health and public relations particularly because public relations can help public health bodies effectively fulfill their purposes of improving population health (Wise, 2001). We can conceptualize public relations and health communication as two related disciplines that often have overlapping objectives—to draw attention to important health issues; involve groups, organizations, and communities in addressing health issues that matter to them; and improve health through persuasive messaging and information sharing.

A SEM for health public relations can help theory and practice address a range of complex, difficult, and culturally rooted dilemmas including homelessness, sexual health, and a variety of other taboo topics. It can also help organizations, public health entities, and communities navigate complex health crises (Nowak & Greenwell, 2021) and build communities that can more easily recover from life-altering health concerns such as pandemics. With more holistic and multi-level theories that account for relationship building, preparation, prevention, and sustainability, public relations researchers and practitioners who are interested in improving health outcomes will have more varied tools in their toolkits that better suit today's health reality.

References

Ajzen, I. (1991). The theory of planned behavior. *Organizational Behavior and Human Decision Processes, 50*(2), 179–211. https://doi.org/10.1016/0749-5978(91)90020-T

Ajzen, I. (2020). The theory of planned behavior: Frequently asked questions. *Human Behavior & Emerging Technology, 2*(4), 314–324. https://doi.org/10.1002/hbe2.195

Aldoory, L., & Austin, L. (2011). Relationship building and situational publics: Theoretical approaches guiding today's health public relations. In T. L. Thompson, R. Parrott, & J. F. Nussbaum (Eds.), *The Routledge handbook of health communication* (2nd ed., pp. 132–145). Routledge.

Aldoory, L., Bellows, D., Boekeloo, B. O., Randolph, S. M. (2015). Exploring use of relationship management theory for cross-border relationships to build capacity in HIV prevention. *Journal of Community Psychology, 43*(6), 687–700. https://doi.org/10.1002/jcop.21755

Aldoory, L., Kim, J. N., & Tindall, N. (2010). The influence of perceived shared risk in crisis communication: Elaborating the situational theory of publics. *Public Relations Review, 36*(2), 134–140. https://doi.org/10.1016/j.pubrev.2009.12.002

Aldoory, L., Roberts, E. B., Bushar, J., & Assini-Meytin, L. C. (2018). Exploring the use of theory in a national text message campaign: Addressing problem recognition and constraint recognition for publics of pregnant women. *Health Communication, 33*(1), 41–48. https://doi.org/10.1080/10410236.2016.1242034

Aldoory, L., & Toth, E. (2021). *The future of feminism in public relations and strategic communication: A socio-ecological model of influences.* Rowman & Littlefield.

Allchin, A., Chaplin, V., & Horwitz, J. (2019). Limiting access to lethal means: Applying the social ecological model for firearm suicide prevention. *Injury Prevention, 25,* i44–i48. http://dx.doi.org/10.1136/injuryprev-2018-042809

Bandura, A. (1977). *Social learning theory.* Prentice-Hall.

Bandura, A. (1998). Health promotion from the perspective of social cognitive theory. *Psychology & Health, 13*(4), 623–649. https://doi.org/10.1080/08870449808407422

Bosone, L., Martinez, F., & Kalampalikis, N. (2015). When the model fits the frame: The impact of regulatory fit on efficacy appraisal and persuasion in health communication. *Personality and Social Psychology Bulletin, 41*(4), 526–539. https://doi.org/10.1177/0146167215571089

Botan, C., & Taylor, M. (2004). Public relations: State of the field. *Journal of Communication, 54*(4), 645–661. https://doi.org/10.1111/j.1460-2466.2004.tb02649.x

Bronfenbrenner, U. (1977). Toward an experimental ecology of human development. *American Psychologist, 32*(7), 513–531. https://doi.org/10.1037/0003-066X.32.7.513

Buzzanell, P. M. (2010). Resilience: Talking resisting and imagining new normalcies into being. *Journal of Communication, 60,* 1–14. https://doi.org/10.1111/j.1460-2466.2009.01469.x

Carpenter, C. J. (2010). A meta-analysis of the effectiveness of health belief model variables in predicting behavior. *Health Communication, 25*(8), 661–669. https://doi.org/10.1080/10410236.2010.521906

Centers for Disease Control and Prevention. (2018). *The DELTA FOCUS program: Intimate Partner violence is preventable.* www.cdc.gov/violenceprevention/deltafocus/index.html

Centers for Disease Control and Prevention. (n.d.). *The socio-ecological model: A framework for violence prevention.* www.cdc.gov/violenceprevention/pdf/sem_framewrk-a.pdf

Crawford, R. (1979). Individual responsibility and health politics in the 1970s. In S. Reverby & D. Rosner (Eds.), *Health care in America: Essays in social history* (pp. 247–268). Temple University Press.

Durkin, K. F., Wolfe, T. W., & Clark, G. A. (2005). College students and binge drinking: An evaluation of social learning theory. *Sociological Spectrum, 25*(3), 255–272. https://doi.org/10.1080/027321790518681

Dutta, M. (2007). Communicating about culture and health: Theorizing culture-centered and cultural sensitivity approaches. *Communication Theory, 17*(3), 304–328. https://doi.org/10.1111/j.1468-2885.2007.00297.x

Dutta, M. (2008). *Communicating health: A culture-centered approach.* Polity.

Figueroa, M. E. (2017). A theory-based socioecological model of communication and behavior for the containment of the Ebola epidemic in Liberia. *Journal of Health Communication, 22*(Sup 1), 5–9. https://doi.org/10.1080/10810730.2016.1231725

Gold, R. S., Auld, M. E., Abroms, L. C., Smyser, J., Yom-Tov, E., & Allegrante, J. P. (2019). Digital health communication common agenda 2.0: An updated consensus for the public and private sectors to advance public health. *Health Education & Behavior, 46*(Sup 2), 124–128. https://doi.org/10.1177/1090198119874086

Golden, S. D., & Earp, J. A. (2012). Social ecological approaches to individuals and their contexts: Twenty years of health education & behavior health promotion interventions. *Health Education & Behavior: The Official Publication of the Society for Public Health Education, 39*(3), 364–72. https://doi.org/10.1177/1090198111418634

Green, E. C., Murphy, E. M., & Gryboski, K. (2020). The health belief model. In K. Sweeny, M. L. Robbins, & L. M. Cohen (Eds.), *The Wiley encyclopedia of health psychology* (pp. 211–214). John Wiley & Sons, Inc. https://doi.org/10.1002/9781119057840.ch68

Grunig, J. E., Grunig, L. A., & Dozier, D. M. (2006). The excellence theory. In C. H. Botan & V. Hazleton (Eds.), *Public relations theory II* (pp. 21–62). Lawrence Erlbaum Associates.

Hacker, K. (2013). *Community-based participatory research*. Sage.

Heath, R. L. (2018). Issues management. In R. L. Heath & W. Johansen (Eds.), *The international encyclopedia of strategic communication* (pp. 814–828). John Wiley & Sons, Inc.

Hoskig, K. (2020). Raising community awareness: The role of public relations in health communication. In M. L. Weekes (Ed.), *Improving use of medicines and medical tests in primary care* (pp. 215–234). Springer.

Kim, S., & Liu, B. F. (2012). Are all crises opportunities? a comparison of how corporate and government organizations responded to the 2009 flu pandemic. *Journal of Public Relations Research*, *24*(1), 69–85. https://doi.org/10.1080/1062726X.2012.626136

Kreps, G. L., Bonaguro, E. W., & Query, J. L. (1998). The history and development of the field of health communication. In L. D. Jackson & B. K. Duffy (Eds.), *Health communication research* (pp. 1–15). Greenwood Press.

Krug, E. G., Dahlberg, T. T., Mercy, J. A., Zwi, A. B., & Lozano, R. (2002). *World report on violence and health*. World Health Organization. https://apps.who.int/iris/bitstream/handle/10665/42495/9241545615_eng.pdf?sequence=1

Krug, E. G., Mercy, J. A., Dahlberg, L. L., & Zwi, A. B. (2002). The world report on violence and health. *Lancet*, *360*(9339), 1083–1088. https://doi.org/10.1016/S0140-6736(02)11133-0

Lynch, J. (2017). Public relations in health and risk communication. In J. Nussbaum (Ed.), *Oxford research encyclopedia of communication*. Oxford University Press. https://doi.org/10.1093/acrefore/9780190228613.013.216

Maibach, E., & Holtgrave, D. R. (1995). Advances in public health communication. *Annual Review of Public Health*, *16*(1), 219–238. https://doi.org/10.1146/annurev.pu.16.050195.001251

McLeroy, K. R., Bibeau, D., Steckler, A., & Glanz, K. (1988). An ecological perspective on health promotion programs. *Health Education Quarterly*, *15*(4), 351–377. https://doi.org/10.1177/109019818801500401

Moran, M. B., Frank, L. B., Zhao, N., Gonzalez, C., Thainiyom, P., Murphy, S. T., & Ball-Rokeach, S. J. (2016). An argument for ecological research and intervention in health communication. *Journal of Health Communication*, *21*(2), 135–138. https://doi.org/10.1080/10810730.2015.1128021

National Cancer Institute. (2004). *Making health communication programs work: A planner's guide, pink book*. www.cancer.gov/publications/health-communication/pink-book.pdf

Nowak, G., & Greenwell, M. (2021). A promising but difficult domain: Complex health-related crises and academic-professional collaboration. In Y. Jin, B. H. Reber, & G. Nowak (Eds.), *Advancing crisis communication effectiveness: Integrating public relations scholarship with practice* (pp. 79–91). Routledge.

Madden, T. J., Ellen, P. S., & Ajzen, I. (1992). A comparison of the theory of planned behavior and the theory of reasoned action. *Personality and Social Psychology Bulletin*, *18*(1), 3–9. https://doi.org/10.1177/0146167292181001

Minkler, M. (2005). Community-based research partnerships: Challenges and opportunities. *Journal of Urban Health: Bulletin of the New York Academy of Medicine*, *82*(Sup 2), ii3–ii12. https://doi.org/10.1093/jurban/jti034

Office of Disease Management and Prevention. (2020). Social determinants of health. *Healthy People.gov*. Retrieved February 19, 2021, from www.healthypeople.gov/2020/topics-objectives/topic/social-determinants-of-health

Pang, T., & Guindon, G. E. (2004). Globalization and risks to health. *EMBO Reports*, *5*(Sup 1), s11–s16. https://doi.org/10.1038/sj.embor.7400226

Parcel, G. S., & Baranowski, T. (1981). Social learning theory and health education. *Health Education*, *12*(3), 14–8. https://doi.org/10.1080/00970050.1981.10618149

Park, H., & Reber, B. H. (2010). Using public relations to promote health: A framing analysis of public relations strategies among health associations. *Journal of Health Communication*, *15*(1), 39–54. https://doi.org/10.1080/10810730903460534

Patz, J. A., Frumkin, H., Holloway, T., Vimont, D. J., & Haines, A. (2014). Climate change: Challenges and opportunities for global health. *Journal of the American Medical Association*, *312*(15), 1565–1580. https://doi.org/10.1001/jama.2014.13186

Ratzan, S. C. (2001). Health literacy: Communication for the public good. *Health Promotion International*, *16*(2), 207–214. https://doi.org/10.1093/heapro/16.2.207

Rosenstock, I. M. (1974). The health belief model and preventive health behavior. *Health Education Monographs*, *2*(4), 354–386. https://doi.org/10.1177/109019817400200405

Rosenstock, I. M., Strecher, V. J., & Becker, M. H. (1988). Social learning theory and the health belief model. *Health Education Quarterly*, *15*(2), 175–183. https://doi.org/10.1177/109019818801500203

Schiavo, R. (2014). *Health communication: From theory to practice*. Jossey-Bass.

Stanley, S. J., Chatham, A. P., Trivedi, N., & Aldoory, L. (2019). Communication and control: Hearing the voices of low-income African American adults to improve relationships with healthcare providers. *Health Communication*, *35*, 1633–1642. https://doi.org/10.1080/10410236.2019.1654177

Sundstrom, B., Brandt, H. M., Gray, L., & Young Pierce, J. (2018). It's my time: Applying the health belief model to prevent cervical cancer among college-age women. *Journal of Communication Management*, *22*(2), 161–178. https://doi.org/10.1108/JCOM-06-2016-0044

Veil, S. R., & Anthony, K. E. (2017). Exploring public relations challenges in compounding crises: The pariah effect of toxic trailers. *Journal of Public Relations Research*, *29*(4), 141–157. https://doi.org/10.1080/1062726X.2017.1355805

Willis, E. (2018). Applying the Health Belief Model to medication adherence: The role of online health communities and peer reviews. *Journal of Health Communication*, *23*(8), 743–750. https://doi.org/10.1080/10810730.2018.1523260

Wise, K. (2001). Opportunities for public relations research in public health. *Public Relations Review*, *27*(4), 475–487. https://doi.org/10.1016/S0363-8111(01)00102-3

Wulff, K., Donato, D., & Lurie, N. (2015). What is health resilience and how can we build it? *Annual Review of Public Health*, *36*(1), 361–374. https://doi.org/10.1146/annurev-publhealth-031914-122829

Yzer, M. (2017). Theory of reasoned action and theory of planned behavior. In P. Rössler, C. A. Hoffner, & L. Zoonen (Eds.), *The international encyclopedia of media effects* (pp. 1955–1962). https://doi.org/10.1002/9781118783764.wbieme0075

24 Relationship Management Theory

Its Past, Present, and Future

Eyun-Jung Ki, Yi-Hui Christine Huang, and Tugce Ertem-Eray

Reviewing the first nine years of articles published in *Public Relations Review*, Ferguson (1984, 2018)[1] pointed out the lack of a theory or paradigm in public relations and presented three foci that offered opportunities for theory development: social responsibility and ethics, social issues and issue management, and public relationship. Out of these three foci, Ferguson (1984) claimed that shifting the focus of public relations to the relationship between an organization and its public could accelerate the possibility of theory development. Since her call, the primary role of public relations has changed from crafting communication materials to managing the relationship between an organization and its publics (Botan & Taylor, 2004). As the name of the field reflects, public relations deals with relationships with publics. The shift was the logical step for the discipline to move forward.

Relationship management has been consistently dominant in the public relations scholarship over the past three decades. For example, Sallot et al. (2003) discovered that relationship management is the second most frequently used theory after excellence theory in the public relations scholarship. In a bibliometric study, Ki et al. (2019) analyzed a total of 78,345 citations from 1,139 articles published in six public relations journals[2] from 2010 to 2015 and discovered that relationship management has been the largest category in the most-cited works list. Ledingham (2003) originally claimed that relationship management is a general theory of public relations based on Littlejohn's (1989) eight functions of theory. Recently, Ledingham (2021) identified relationship management as "a normative theory of public relations seeking to benefit publics, to provide guidelines for dealing with crisis, to encourage benefit for society, and to do so not only efficiently but also ethically" (p. 428).

Empirical studies added more evidence that a positive relationship between an organization and its publics contributes to organizational effectiveness such as enhancing corporate reputation (Bridges & Nelson, 2000), resolving conflicts between the organization and its publics (Huang, 1997), and so on. With the popularity and importance of relationship management in the public relations discipline, scholars have conducted systematic literature reviews to understand its state of the art. For example, Ki and

DOI: 10.4324/9781003141396-28

Shin (2015) analyzed the content of published articles on the topic of relationship management between 1984 and 2004. Huang and Zhang (2015) reviewed empirical research published from 2000 to 2011. In addition to confirming the steady growth of relationship management research, Huang and Zhang found two main streams of relationship management research in terms of authorship and research themes. These are explained further in the theoretical background section that follows. Cheng (2018) performed a comprehensive analysis of 156 studies published in 1998–2016 and categorized them into five clusters: antecedents, outcomes, mediation, process, and structure of organization-public relationships (OPRs).

Although these studies examined academic articles from different periods and with various focuses, relationship management research has been continuously at the center of the scholarship and evolved in the field. Despite the rising trend of relationship management research, however, there are several discrepancies, including definitions, naming, dimensions, methodological rigor, and so forth (e.g., Huang & Zhang, 2013; Huang & Zhang, 2015; Ki & Shin, 2015). For example, Broom et al. (1997) criticized the lack of conceptual consensus and methodological rigor. Reviewing a decade's worth of relationship management articles, Huang and Zhang (2015) concluded that the problems still persist, stating that "the naming of OPR and its contents remains unresolved and inconclusive" (p. 2). Moreover, a dynamic process of the relationship between an organization and its publics within diverse contexts is often neglected (Ki & Shin, 2015). Most of the previous studies have measured relationship state at the point of data collection. This one-time data collection does not represent the dynamic of the relationship.

Therefore, this chapter is written with the intention to limit the confusion about relationship management by discussing its key elements, its development, and future directions. The remainder of this chapter is divided into four sections: 1) comparison between relationship management and organization-public relationships; 2) three relationship stages: antecedents of relationship, relationship cultivation strategies, and relationship outcomes; 3) criticisms of relationship management; and 4) future directions.

Theoretical Background

Relationship Management vs. Organization-Public Relationships

There has been some confusion between the terms *relationship management* and *organization-public relationships* (OPRs), which have often been used interchangeably among scholars. Some widely cited works have defined relationship management as "effectively managing organizational-public relationships around common interests and shared goals, over time, results in mutual understanding and benefit for interacting organizations and publics" (Ledingham, 2003, p. 190), adding that "relationship management theory specifies how to build toward symmetry (managing organizational-public relationships around common interests and shared goals) and when to apply that approach (over time)" (Ledingham, 2003, p. 192). In recent work, Ledingham (2021) conceptualized relationship management as "a normative theory of public relations seeking to benefit publics" (p. 428). As these popular definitions articulate, relationship management covers the entire process of initiating, developing, and cultivating relationship among all the parties involved.

On the other hand, OPR is the state of a relationship between an organization and publics. The definition of OPRs by Broom et al. (2000) is "the patterns of interaction, transaction, exchange, and linkage between an organization and its publics" (p. 18). This definition is one of the most commonly adopted in the field because it emphasizes what an organization and its public actually do to build the relationship. Ledingham and Bruning (1998) refer to OPR in terms of broad relational consequences, as "the state which exists between an organization and its key publics in which the actions of either entity impact the economic, social, political, and/or cultural well-being of the other entity" (p. 62). Other scholars treat OPR as relational outcomes: "the degree that the organization and its publics trust one another, agree on who has rightful power to influence, experience satisfaction with each other, and commit oneself to one another" (Huang, 1998, p. 12). Some scholars specifically define OPR according to the types of publics examined. For example, Men and Stacks (2014) defined the organization–employee relationship as "the degree to which an organization and its employees trust one another, agree on who has the rightful power to influence, experience satisfaction with each other, and commit oneself to the other" (p. 307). While OPR can measure the state or quality of the relationship between the parties involved, the concept does not represent the entire process of relationship management.

As outlined in these definitions, relationship management is a more comprehensive and inclusive theory that covers the *entire process* of relationship from beginning to end. By contrast, OPR primarily refers to the *quality* of the relationship between an organization and its public. Measuring OPR as an effect of a public relations program might have contributed to the confusion between relationship management and OPR. Moreover, as many studies using a relational approach have focused on measuring relationship quality between an organization and its publics, researchers tend to use OPR to refer to relationship management. Although the definitions of OPR and relationship management are wide-ranging, scholars seem to be in consensus for the composition of relationship management stages.

Relationship Stages

Broom et al. (1997) originally proposed three stages of the relationship management: 1) antecedents of relationship, 2) relationship cultivation strategies, and 3) relationship outcomes. These stages cover the process of relationship management in a comprehensive manner. All or some of these stages have been applied as a framework or a model of studies in relationship management.

Stage 1: Antecedents of Relationship

Antecedents of relationship are the conditions or reasons to consider establishing a relationship between two parties. Broom et al. (1997) explained the antecedents of relationship as "social and cultural norms, collective perceptions and expectations, needs for resources, perceptions of uncertain environment, and legal/voluntary necessity," specifically "sources of change, pressure, or tension on the system derived from the environments" (Broom et al., 1997, p. 94). At this stage, an organization should identify the publics it needs to develop a relationship with.

A core element of relationship management is publics. Without a public, there is no relationship to build or manage. Publics are groups that are formally or informally affected by an organization or vice versa (Grunig & Hunt, 1984). In most cases, an organization has multiple publics who are not just groups of individuals but also other organizations such as government, local businesses, media, industry and so on. Therefore, in this phase, an organization should identify its publics, including groups of individuals and other organizations that can affect or be affected by the life of the organization. To determine the target publics, an organization should analyze its environments and establish communication objectives for the target publics. Antecedents of relationships articulate the conditions, motivations, and/or reasons organizations need to build relationships with their specified publics (Broom et al., 1997). This preparation stage is when the organization identifies what is required to consider to form a relationship.

Compared with the other stages, antecedents have been investigated less often than the other stages. Although some studies claimed to examine antecedents, what they actually measured was either relationship cultivation strategies (e.g., Men & Stacks, 2014) or relationship outcomes (e.g., Jiang, 2012). One exception is Seltzer and Zhang (2010), who exclusively explicated the concept of relational antecedents by differentiating the distal (enduring individual, organizational, and environmental factors) and proximal antecedents (situational individual and organizational behaviors and interactions). They confirm that relational antecedents are actual motives for individuals to form a relationship with organizations, such as social/cultural expectations and risk reduction. Another exception is Bortree (2015), who explored the role of antecedents in the relationship between volunteers and nonprofit organizations. She found that volunteers had certain motivations—values, understanding, career, social, protective, and enhancement—and the organization had to meet these expectations to form a favorable relationship.

Stage 2: Relationship Cultivation Strategies

Once an organization has identified target publics and its communication goals, it should implement activities to achieve these goals. The organization's action is relationship cultivation strategies, which were originally called relationship maintenance strategies. Grunig (2006) replaced the word *maintenance* with *cultivation* to reflect the dynamic process of relationship. These strategies are what practitioners or organizations do on a regular basis at the program level to make better relationships with their publics. Drawn from the interpersonal relationship literature, scholars in public relations (e.g., Grunig & Huang, 2000; Hon & Grunig, 1999) developed relationship cultivation strategies that are applicable to a public relations setting. The six strategies that are deemed to be most effective are access, positivity, openness, sharing of tasks, networking, and assurances. (Definitions and examples of each strategy can be found at Ki and Hon (2012).) Grunig and Huang (2000) broadly grouped potential strategies into two categories, *symmetry* (disclosure, assurances (assurances of legitimacy), participation in mutual networking; sharing of tasks; integrative strategy; cooperation; unconditional constructive; win–win or no deal) and *asymmetry* (distributive strategy; competing; avoiding; accommodating; and compromising).

A few studies have explored relationship cultivation strategies in various settings. For example, Bortree (2010) tested the effect of relationship cultivation strategies on the organization-adolescent relationship. Ki and Hon (2008) developed a reliable and valid measure of relationship cultivation strategies on membership organization-member relationship. Then, Ki and Hon (2009) investigated the causal relationship between six relationship cultivation strategies (access, openness, sharing of tasks, networking, assurances) and relationship outcomes in membership organization setting. Both studies empirically confirmed the significant effect of cultivation strategies on relationship quality across different organizations.

As new communication platforms have become more prevalent, scholars have investigated how organizations cultivate relationships with their publics in venues such as websites and social media (Kelleher, 2009; Waters et al., 2009). Ki and Hon (2006) examined the nature of how *Fortune 500* companies have enacted relationship cultivation strategies on their websites through content analysis. The sampled websites most frequently used openness strategies, followed by access.

Studies on relationship cultivation strategies are meaningful to understand how organizations apply each strategy. However, they are limited in measuring the success of these strategies. Relationship quality outcomes, which are often called organization-public relationship, are the measure of relationship cultivation strategy success.

Stage 3: Relationship Quality Outcome

The last stage of relationship management is *relationship quality outcome*, defined as an "organization's goal achievement or consequences that are produced by effective relationship cultivation strategies" (Grunig & Huang, 2000). The terms *relationship quality outcomes* and *organization-public relationships* have been used interchangeably because both terms are the outcome of relationship cultivation strategies or public relations programs. In the first two decades since relationship management emerged as a central component in the discipline, scholars have endeavored to develop and improve relationship quality outcome measures (e.g., Ferguson, 1984; Grunig & Huang, 2000; Hon & Grunig, 1999; Huang, 2001a, 2001b; Ki & Hon, 2007a, 2007b). By reviewing the articles published on the topic of relationship management during 2000–2011, Huang and Zhang (2015) identified two primary clusters—Ledingham and Bruning scale and Grunig and his collaborators' scale—of relationship outcome measures.

CLUSTER #1: LEDINGHAM AND BRUNING SCALE

The first cluster is mainly developed and refined by Ledingham, Bruning, and their collaborators. First, Ledingham et al. (1997) identified a set of relationship dimensions composed of 17 variables: investment, commitment, trust, comfort with relational dialectics, cooperation, mutual goals, interdependence/power imbalance, performance satisfaction, comparison level of the alternatives, adaptation, non-retrievable investment, shared technology, summate constructs, structural bonds, social bonds, and intimacy. Their most popular relationship scale consists of personal, professional, and community relationship (Ledingham & Bruning, 1998). In their studies, they measured organization-public relationships as publics' attitudes. They stated that the members of publics expect the organization to satisfy the needs of personal, professional, and community relationships (Bruning & Ledingham, 1999). Bruning and Ledingham (1998) also established a multiple-item scale of relationship dimension that includes trust, openness, involvement, investment, and commitment. They treated OPR as an independent variable that affects the public's attitudes, evaluations, and behaviors.

CLUSTER #2: RELATIONSHIP MEASURES

The second cluster defines organization-public relationship based on multi-dimensional relationship outcomes. Huang (1997) developed a four-dimensional relationship measure including control mutuality, satisfaction, trust, and commitment. She later published this measure as Organization Public Relationship Assessment (OPRA) (Huang, 2001a). Based on Huang's relational dimensions, Hon and Grunig (1999) published *PR Relationship Measurement*, a report for the Institute for Public Relations.

With a full measurement items' availability and easy access to the report, scholars have intensively applied and refined Hon and Grunig's scale across different settings and contexts (Jo, 2006). In these studies, relationship was treated as a perception about the relationship between an organization and its publics. Huang and Zhang (2015) confirmed that these four measures—control mutuality, satisfaction, trust, and commitment—were the most frequently used variables in the field, and trust is the most emphasized variable among these four. Scholars who adopted this four-dimensional scale conceptualized OPR as the states of the relationship between an organization and its publics. This measurement reached acceptable level of reliability (.70 or higher) across the studies (Huang & Zhang, 2015). Researchers have shown its reliability and validity and used it to expand and refine the theory (see Table 24.1).

Criticisms of Relationship Management

With robust interest, the relationship management theory has been criticized (e.g., Heath, 2013), and some points should be addressed to make relationship management a solid public relations paradigm.

First, most studies have measured only the public's perspective. The scholarship has emphasized that the purpose of relationship building is for mutual benefits and relationship is two-way (Ledingham, 2003). However, almost all the studies have measured only one side (the public's side) of the relationship perception. There are some exceptions (e.g., Chandler, 2014; Lee et al., 2017; Men, 2012; Men et al., 2017; Plowman, 2013; Wiggill, 2014). Measuring the perception of only one party does not portray a complete picture of the relationship.

Second, conceptual clarity and methodological rigor of the theory have been criticized (Huang & Zhang, 2015; Ki & Shin, 2015). Broom et al. (1997) pointed out that relationship management lacks thorough conceptualization and methodology as it tends to be informed by intuition.

Last, some measurement issues exist. For example, trust is a key measure of OPR (Grunig & Huang, 2000), and indeed it is one of the most frequently used and important measures of relationship quality. However, Cheng (2018), pointed out that trust measure has an issue because scholars often assume that trust exists between an organization and its publics. However, scholars have overlooked the situation that parties may never trust or have no intention to engage with each other (Dutta, 2014). Although distrust is often treated as the opposite of trust, these two are different (Shen, 2017).

Future Directions

As the term *public relations* implies, our field concerns the relationship of an organization with its stakeholder publics. Thus, relationship management will continue to be paramount as long as our field exists. Without it, the field itself will suffer an identity crisis. Accordingly, what do we need to do to strengthen our field and keep moving forward?

The past and present often point to roads we should take to move forward. We have several opportunities and directions in front of us. First, the relational turn can be our next paradigm. Driven by the expansion of

Table 24.1 Reliabilities of Relationship Dimensions

Studies	Reliability
Hyojung Park and Bryan H. Reber (2011)	trust (α = .84), control mutuality (α = .68), commitment (α = .84), and satisfaction (α = .88)
Minjeong Kang (2013)	trust (α = .92), control mutuality (α = .90), commitment (α = .74), and satisfaction (α = .95)
Trent Seltzer and Weiwu Zhang (2011)	trust, satisfaction, commitment, and control mutuality for both the Democratic Party (alphas of .93, .93, .94, and .78 respectively) and for the Republican Party (alphas of .91, .92, .93, and .79, respectively)
Patricia A. Curtin et al. (2011)	Cronbach's alphas for each construct ranged from (α = .88) for commitment to (α = .95) for satisfaction
Denise Sevick Bortree (2011)	trust (α = .81), control mutuality (α = .83), commitment (α = .81), and satisfaction (α = .83)
Linjuan Rita Men (2011)	Organization-employee relationship (ranged from .70 to .87)
Eyun-Jung Ki and Linda Hon (2012)	control mutuality (α = .92), satisfaction (α = .91), trust (α = .92), commitment (α = .89)
Alessandro Lovari et al. (2012)	trust (α =.91), control mutuality (α =.82), commitment (α = .91), and satisfaction (α = .91).
Hongmei Shen and Jeong-Nam Kim (2012)	trust (α = .80), control mutuality (α = .68), commitment (α = .86), and satisfaction (α = .91)
Tiffany Derville Gallicano et al. (2012)	Cronbach's alphas for each construct ranged from .88 for commitment to .95 for satisfaction.
Yi-Hui Christine Huang (2012)	Sample 1—Cronbach's alpha coefficient for OPR .85 Sample 2—Cronbach's alpha coefficient for OPR .85
Michel M. Haigh and Frank Dardis (2012)	trust (α = .89), commitment (α = .89)
Richard D. Waters and Denise Sevick Bortree (2012)	Cronbach alpha values ranged from a low of α = .76 for communality to a high of α = .85 for trust.
Hua Jiang (2012)	Quality of employee-organization relationships = .98
Linjuan Rita Men and Wan-Hsiu Sunny Tsai (2013)	trust (α = .95), satisfaction (α = .95), and commitment (α = .96)
Hyung Min Lee and Jong Woo Jun (2013)	A test revealed a high internal consistency among the measurement items (Cronbach's .86).
Hyunmin Lee and Hyojung Park (2013)	trust (α = .93), control mutuality (α = .72), commitment (α = .93), satisfaction (α = .95)
Adam J. Saffer et al. (2013)	trust (α = .87), control mutuality (α = .75), satisfaction (α = .94), and commitment (α = .90)
Seow Ting Lee and Mallika Hemant Desai (2014)	Organization-Media Relationship Index (Cronbach's 0.954)
Linjuan Rita Men and Wan-Hsiu Sunny Tsai (2014)	trust (α = .74), control mutuality (α = .92), commitment (α = .81), and satisfaction (α =.89)
Linjuan Rita Men and Don Stacks (2014)	trust (α = .89), control mutuality (α = .93), commitment (α =.91), and satisfaction (α = .96)
Linjuan Rita Men (2014)	trust (α =.89), control mutuality (α =.93), commitment (α =.91), and satisfaction (α =.96).
Erich J. Sommerfeldt and Michael L. Kent (2015)	control mutuality (α = .85), trust (α = .88), commitment (α = .84), and satisfaction (α = .85).
Linjuan Rita Men (2015)	trust (α = .89), control mutuality (α = .93), commitment (α = .91), and satisfaction (α = .96).

(Continued)

Table 24.1 (Continued)

Studies	Reliability
Linjuan Rita Men and Wan-Hsiu Sunny Tsai (2015)	trust (α = .74), control mutuality (α = .92), commitment (α = .81), satisfaction (α = .89)
Linjuan Rita Men and Hua Jiang (2016)	trust (α = .83), control mutuality (α = .93), commitment (α = .86), and satisfaction (α = .95)
Geah Nicole Pressgrove and Brooke Weberling McKeever (2016)	Reliability measures were well above accepted cut-off (exceeding .87).
Linjuan Rita Men and Wan-Hsiu Sunny Tsai (2016)	trust (α = 0.92) and satisfaction (α = 0.93)
Soojin Kim et al. (2017)	control mutuality (α = .86), trust (α = .87), commitment (α = .79), and satisfaction (α = .88)
Yeunjae Lee (2017)	trust (α = .90), control mutuality (α = .90), commitment (α = .91), and satisfaction (α = .92)
Minjeong Kang and Minjung Sung (2017)	trust (α = .90), satisfaction (α = .77), commitment (α = .89), and control mutuality (α = .89)
Linjuan Rita Men and Sidharth Muralidharan (2017)	trust (China: α = .73; the United States: α = .90), satisfaction (China: α = .89; the United States: α = .90), commitment (China: α = .90; the United States: α = .87)
Hongmei Shen (2017)	trust: Study 1 (α = .88) and Study 2 (α =. 92); distrust: Study 1 (α = .86) and Study 2 (α = .85); control mutuality: Study 1 (α = .68) and Study 2 (α = .79); commitment: Study 1 (α = .70) and Study 2 (α = .83); satisfaction: Study 1 (α = .91) and Study 2 (α = .93)
Seow Ting Lee and Amanda Kee (2017)	The Cronbach's alpha for the six dimensions ranged between .85 and .92.
Ji Young Kim and Jinhyon K. Hammick (2017)	trust (α = .82)
Diana C. Sisson (2017)	trust (α = .90), commitment (α = .86), control mutuality (α = .92), and satisfaction (α = .89)
Virginia S. Harrison et al. (2017)	trust (α = .91), control mutuality (α = .90), commitment (α = .87), and satisfaction (α = .75)
Yi-Ru Regina Chen (2017)	trust (α = .89), commitment (α = .82), control mutuality (α = .87), satisfaction (α = .87)
Daewook Kim (2018)	trust (α = .89), satisfaction (α = .83), commitment (α =.89), control mutuality (α = .91)
Linjuan Rita Men and Katy L. Robinson (2018)	trust (α = .92), control mutuality (α = .94), commitment (α = .91), and satisfaction (α = .96)
Linjuan Rita Men et al. (2018)	trust (α = .96) and satisfaction (α = .94)
Nicole Lee and Trent Seltzer (2018)	trust (α = .80), commitment (α = .82), satisfaction (α = .87) control mutuality (α = .55)
Trent Seltzer and Nicole Lee (2018)	trust (α = .94), commitment (α = .93), satisfaction (α = .95), and control mutuality (α = .91)
Wan-Hsiu Sunny Tsai and Rita Linjuan Men (2018)	trust (α =.92), satisfaction (α = .93), and commitment (α = .90)
Zifei Fay Chen et al. (2019)	control mutuality (α = .76), trust (α = .92), commitment (α = .94), and satisfaction (α = .96)
Yeunjae Lee et al. (2019)	trust (α = .88), control mutuality (α = .94), commitment (α = .93) and satisfaction (α = .94)

Studies	Reliability
Alan Abitbol and Miglena Sternadori (2019)	commitment (Nike: α = .86; Under Armor: α = .84; Google: α = .87; Microsoft: α = .89); satisfaction (Nike: α = .86; Under Armor: α = .86; Google: α = .87; Microsoft: α = .94); trust (Nike: α = .87; Under Armor: α = .88; Google: α = .90; Microsoft: α = .93); control mutuality (Nike: α = .81; Under Armor: α = .83; Google: α = .88; Microsoft: α = .88)
Minjeong Kang and Minjung Sung (2019)	trust (α = .90), satisfaction (α = 77), commitment (α = .89), and control mutuality (α = .89)
Linjuan Rita Men et al. (2019)	satisfaction (α = .86) and commitment (α = .79)
Tom Kelleher et al. (2019)	trust (α = .92), satisfaction (α = .92), commitment (α = .92), and control mutuality (α = .92)
Ganga S. Dhanesh and Gaelle Duthler (2019)	trust (six items), commitment (four items), satisfaction (four items), and control mutuality (four items) (α=.93)
Yufan Qin and Linjuan Rita Men (2019)	trust (α = .85), satisfaction (α = .88), control mutuality (α = .83), and commitment (α = .87)
Lan Ni et al. (2019)	control mutuality (α = .87), trust (α = .93)
Yeunjae Lee (2020)	trust (α = .81), control mutuality (α = .86), commitment (α = .82), and satisfaction (α = .86)
Nicholas Browning et al. (2020)	Study 1—trust (α = .95), control mutuality (α = .95), commitment (α = .95), satisfaction (α = .96) Study 2—trust (α = .94), control mutuality (α = .94), commitment (α = .93), satisfaction (α = .95)

technology, the paradigm shift now underway from communication management to relationship management is appearing in all levels of communication, from the local to global. In communicative settings, dialogic engagement actively connects individuals to one another, which builds enduring interpersonal relationships and abundant social capital. Accordingly, we must consider the structure, dynamics, and outcome of relationships in the interpersonal, community, and global contexts.

At the interpersonal level, communication studies have shown how individuals connect with neighbors, fellow churchgoers, and other community members to broaden and deepen their interpersonal bonds (Hampton et al., 2011; Huang, 2000). Ellison et al. (2011) demonstrated how connected individuals foster interpersonal relations and create social capital in the digital environment.

At the community level, political communication research indicates that citizens form networks to advance community goals. For instance, online discussion about community matters and offline engagement about politics can enhance citizen perceptions of improved community relations and generate a sense of belonging (Gil de Zúñiga et al., 2012). Indeed, according to Kim and Ball-Rokeach (2006), citizen participation provides an essential element for creation and growth of a civic community. Ganesh and Zoller (2012) stressed that in the long run, fostering citizenship and democracy requires online dialogic engagement. This paradigm shift to relationship management likewise affects commerce. For instance, Boyd (2003) pointed out that the continuous interchange between business and consumers in online transactions produces social capital in the form of trust.

At the global level, numerous communication studies have examined the development of international or interregional relations and their contribution to conflict avoidance and regional stability. For example, diplomats and ordinary citizens may form public diplomacy networks that engage in dialogue that cultivate international relationships and understanding (Park & Lim, 2014). Stohl and Stohl (2007) found that flexible, dynamic networks of government actors from different regions can help combat regional terrorism. According to Foot (2001), networks of professional actors with different cultural backgrounds are especially useful for detecting the early signs of regional conflicts resulting from ethnic divisions.

At whatever level, this turn toward relationship management arises from the growing dependence of mutually satisfactory and trusting relationships on ideals regarding the social role and symmetrical worldviews of public relations advocated by the management perspective. A key facilitator of this trend is the constantly increasing potential of digital media to expand organization public relationship from a local context to the global context (Huang et al., 2017).

Relationship building and management in the interpersonal, community, business, and global communicative contexts bring with them a relational turn in other domains of communication studies, including public relations. Whereas prior public relations studies analyzed the delivery or exchange of information—a functional approach—new public relations research is gradually shifting to the cultivation of relationship quality, advancing new relational hermeneutics to interpret the formation and development of organization-public relationship in the digital era. Thus, examination of relationships, already an important concept in communication studies in the 1990s (Fitzpatrick, 1994), is drawing even closer to the center of communication research (Zaharna, 2016).

The relational turn in public relations scholarship has an ontological divide. The first ontological divide concerns statist versus process/dynamics. On the one hand, scholars who adhere to the statist ontology see relations or connectivity as cultural and social capital (Slaughter, 2009) and types of power resources. The other perspective asserts that relations come before states and processes and analyzes how such processes constitute the states.

No matter which stance is taken, however, the nature of communication has changed. That is, it is no longer a linear or one-way causal relationship. On the contrary, two-way, reciprocal relations substitute the traditional ontology of communication, in which information dissemination or exchange explains the reality. Namely, we observe a paradigm shift from linear flow, information-focused communication to reciprocal and relationship-oriented communication.

The second divide concerns determinism and co-determinism. Two perspectives exist in the literature. One perspective advocates a version of social determinism that emphasizes how relations are determined by organizations instead of individuals or stakeholders. Another version tends to study how social structures interact with agency (i.e., stakeholders or individuals). For example, Huang et al. (2020) explicated the role of the degree of democracy through the lens of the cultural-institutional perspective and found that the degree of democracy would interact with individual's perceived government's responsiveness to influence people's institutional trust.

Moreover, the ontological commitment ingrained in the social role of public relations in different worldviews such as conservative, radical, or ideal, also affects how scholars position the role of relations between an organization and its publics. We indeed observe that this relational turn would offer new conceptual tools in reconstructing public relations both on theoretical and applied planes. It would thus break free from the stagnation of debates from different theoretical perspectives that are based upon incompatible ontological stances, such as critical and interpretative against positivist and normative conceptualizations of the power asymmetry between an organization and its publics. The outcome: a "relational turn" will probably develop into a new field of relational public relations.

Given these ontological divides, we contend that public relations theorists ought not to define this field in any universal way but to observe, describe, compare, etc., them as they are, with all their diversity and complexity. Although different theoretical perspectives still hold their own ontological and epistemological positions, it is evident that a relational turn underlies the changes observed in these theoretical perspectives in public relations research.

Public relations research in the last decade, be it originally from management, rhetorical, or even critical perspectives, seems to converge and evolve along this line of theorization. In essence, the line of relational theorizing assumes changes and transformation in the ontological and epistemological status of an organization, its publics, and their relations. Refocusing on organization-public relationships and on their constitution and effects affords us a new form of describing, understanding, and explaining organization, stakeholder, public relations, social and cultural phenomena as relational facts.

In a nutshell, moving from the "classical" paradigm to this "relational" successor responds to the digital era's "horizontalized" and "fragmentized" phenomenon. To sum up, co-creator, co-worldview, and co-producers of social processes are the key concepts in the relational shift in public relations scholarship. In essence, the tension between "autonomous" and "relational" conceptions of public relations manifests itself no less in the contemporary debate on "reciprocal public relations." As such, both organizations and publics are not only bound by abstract right, but also—and more fundamentally—by underlying principles of proper behavior.

To expand our understanding of relationship management, we should conduct studies that take advantage of an immense but underused resource—social media and big data. Relationship management studies have primarily used self-reported survey data (Cheng, 2018). Self-reported data relies on the respondents' subjective memories, perceptions, and/or opinions. This does not mean that self-reported data has less value. We continue to collect data through survey or experiment. However, enormous data are available at our fingertips. Social media data or big data will help us to analyze the actual conversation between an organization and its publics.

Notes

1   This conference paper was finally published as a journal article almost 30 years later. *See* Ferguson, M. A. (2018). Building theory in public relations: Interorganizational relationships as a public relations paradigm. *Journal of Public Relations Research, 30*(4), 164–178.

2   The six journals they examined are *Journal of Public Relations Research, Journalism & Mass Communication Quarterly, Public Relations Review, Corporate Communication: An International Journal, Journal of Communication Management,* and *International Journal of Strategic Communication.*

References

Abitbol, A., & Sternadori, M. (2019). Championing women's empowerment as a catalyst for purchase intentions: Testing the mediating roles of OPRs and brand loyalty in the context of femvertising. *International Journal of Strategic Communication, 13*(1), 22–41. https://doi.org/10.1080/1553118X.2018.1552963

Bortree, D. S. (2010). Exploring adolescent–organization relationships: A study of effective relationship strategies with adolescent volunteers. *Journal of Public Relations Research, 22*(1), 1–25. https://doi.org/10.1080/10627260902949421

Bortree, D. S. (2011). Mediating the power of antecedents in public relationships: A pilot study. *Public Relations Review, 37*(1), 44–49. https://doi.org/10.1016/j.pubrev.2010.11.002

Bortree, D. S. (2015). Motivations of publics. In E.-J. Ki, J.-N. Kim, & J. A. Ledingham (Eds.), *Public relations as relationship management: A relational approach to the study and practice of public relations* (pp. 144–158). Routledge.

Botan, C. H., & Taylor, M. (2004). Public relations: State of the field. *Journal of Communication, 54*(4), 645–661. https://doi.org/10.1111/j.1460-2466.2004.tb02649.x

Boyd, J. (2003). The rhetorical construction of trust online. *Communication Theory, 13*(4), 392–410. https://doi.org/10.1111/j.1468-2885.2003.tb00298.x

Bridges, J. A., & Nelson, R. A. (2000). Issues management: A relational approach. In J. A. Ledingham & S. D. Bruning (Eds.), *Public relations as relationship management: A relational approach to the study and practice of public relations* (pp. 95–115). LEA.

Broom, G. M., Casey, S., & Ritchey, J. (1997). Toward a concept and theory of organization-public relationships. *Journal of Public Relations Research, 9*(2), 83–98. https://doi.org/10.1207/s1532754xjprr0902_01

Broom, G. M., Casey, S., & Ritchey, J. (2000). Concept and theory of organization-public relationships. In J. A. Ledingham & S. D. Bruning (Eds.), *Public relations as relationship management: A relational approach to the study and practice of public relations* (pp. 3–22). LEA.

Browning, N., & Sweetser, K. S. (2020). How media diet, partisan frames, candidate traits, and political organization-public relationship communication drive party reputation. *Public Relations Review, 46*(2), 1–17. https://doi.org/10.1016/j.pubrev.2020.101884

Browning, N., Lee, E., Park, Y. E., Kim, T., & Collins, R. (2020). Muting or meddling? Advocacy as a relational communication strategy affecting organization–public relationships and stakeholder response. *Journalism & Mass Communication Quarterly, 97*(4), 1026–1053. http://doi.org/10.1177/1077699020916810

Bruning, S. D., & Ledingham, J. A. (1998). Organization-public relationships and consumer satisfaction: The role of relationships in the satisfaction mix. *Communication Research Reports, 15*(2), 198–208. https://doi.org/10.1080/08824099809362114

Bruning, S. D., & Ledingham, J. A. (1999). Relationships between organizations and publics: Development of a multi-dimensional organization-public relationship scale. *Public Relations Review, 25*(2), 157–170. https://doi.org/10.1016/S0363-8111(99)80160-X

Chandler, C. S. (2014). Investor relations from the perspective of CEOs. *International Journal of Strategic Communication, 8*(3), 160–176. https://doi.org/10.1080/15531 18X.2014.908296

Chen, Y.-R. R. (2017). Perceived values of branded mobile media, consumer engagement, business-consumer relationship quality and purchase intention: A study of WeChat in China. *Public Relations Review, 43*(5), 945–954. https://doi.org/10.1016/j. pubrev.2017.07.005

Chen, Z. F., Hong, C., & Occa, A. (2019). How different CSR dimensions impact organization-employee relationships. The moderating role of CSR-culture fit. *Corporate Communications: An International Journal, 24*(1), 63–78. https://doi.org/10.1108/ CCIJ-07-2018-0078

Cheng, Y. (2018). Looking back, moving forward: A review and reflection of the organization-public relationship (OPR) research. *Public Relations Review, 44*(1), 120–130. https://doi.org/10.1016/j.pubrev.2017.10.003

Curtin, P. A., Gallicano, T., & Matthews, K. (2011). Millennials' approaches to ethical decision making: A survey of young public relations agency employees. *Public Relations Journal, 5*(2), 1–22.

Dhanesh, G. S., & Duthler, G. (2019). Relationship management through social media influencers: Effects of followers' awareness of paid endorsement. *Public Relations Review, 45*(3), 101765. https://doi.org/10.1016/j.pubrev.2019.03.002

Dutta, M. J. (2014). Public relations in a global world: Culturally centering theory and praxis. *Asia Pacific Public Relations Journal, 14*(1/2), 21–31.

Ellison, N. B., Steinfield, C., & Lampe, C. (2011). Connection strategies: Social capital implications of Facebook-enabled communication practices. *New Media & Society, 13*(6), 873–892. https://doi.org/10.1177/1461444810385389

Ferguson, M. A. (1984). *Building theory in public relations: Interorganizational relationships.* Paper presented at the Association for Education in Journalism and Mass Communication.

Ferguson, M. A. (2018). Building theory in public relations: Interorganizational relationships as a public relations paradigm. *Journal of Public Relations Research, 30*(4), 164–178. https://doi.org/10.1080/1062726X.2018.1514810

Fitzpatrick, K. R. (1994). *Who's in charge? Balancing public relations and legal counsel in a crisis.* National Emergency Training Center.

Foot, K. A. (2001). Cultural-historical activity theory as practice theory: Illuminating the development of conflict-monitoring network. *Communication Theory, 11*(1), 56–83.

Gallicano, T. D., Curtin, P. A., & Matthews, K. (2012). I love what I do, but . . . A relationship management survey of millennial generation public relations agency employees. *Journal of Public Relations Research, 24*(3), 222–242. https://doi.org/10.10 80/1062726X.2012.671986

Ganesh, S., & Zoller, H. M. (2012). Dialogue, activism, and democratic social change. *Communication Theory, 22*(1), 66–91. https://doi.org/10.1111/j.1468-2885.2011.01396.x

Gil de Zúñiga, H., Jung, N., & Valenzuela, S. (2012). Social media use for news and individuals' social capital, civic engagement and political participation. *Journal of Computer-Mediated Communication, 17*(3), 319–336. https://doi.org/10.1111/j.1083-6101.2012.01574.x

Grunig, J. E. (2006). Furnishing the edifice: Ongoing research on public relations as a strategic management function. *Journal of Public Relations Research, 18*(2), 151–176. https://doi.org/10.1207/s1532754xjprr1802_5

Grunig, J. E., & Huang, Y.-H. (2000). From organizational effectiveness to relationship indicators: Antecedents of relationships, public relations strategies, and relationship outcomes. In J. A. Ledingham & S. D. Bruning (Eds.), *Public relations as relationship management: A relational approach to the study and practice of public relations* (pp. 23–53). LEA.

Grunig, J. E., & Hunt, T. T. (1984). *Managing public relations.* Holt, Rinehart and Winston.

Haigh, M. M., & Dardis, F. (2012). The impact of apology on organization – public relationships and perceptions of corporate social responsibility. *Public Relations Journal, 6*(1), 1–16.

Hampton, K. N., Lee, C.-J., & Her, E. J. (2011). How new media affords network diversity: Direct and mediated access to social capital through participation in local social settings. *New Media & Society, 13*(7), 1031–1049. https://doi.org/10.1177/1461444810390342

Harrison, V. S., Xiao, A., Ott, H. K., & Bortree, D. (2017). Calling all volunteers: The role of stewardship and involvement in volunteer-organization relationships. *Public Relations Review, 43*(4), 872–881. https://doi.org/10.1016/j.pubrev.2017.06.006

Heath, R. L. (2013). The journey to understand and champion OPR takes many roads, some not yet well traveled. *Public Relations Review, 5*(39), 426–431. https://doi.org/10.1016/j.pubrev.2013.05.002

Hon, L. C., & Grunig, J. E. (1999). *Guidelines for measuring relationships in public relations.* Institute for Public Relations.

Huang, Y.-H. (1997). *Public relations strategies, relational outcomes, and conflict management strategies* [Unpublished doctoral dissertation, University of Maryland].

Huang, Y.-H. (1998, August 5–8). *Public relations strategies and organization–public relationships.* Paper presented at the annual conference of the Association for Education in Journalism and Mass Communication.

Huang, Y.-H. (2001a). OPRA: A cross-cultural, multiple-item scale for measuring organization-public relationships. *Journal of Public Relations Research, 13*(1), 61–90. https://doi.org/10.1207/S1532754XJPRR1301_4

Huang, Y.-H. (2001b). Values of public relations: Effects on organization-public relationships mediating conflict resolution. *Journal of Public Relations Research, 13*(4), 265–301. https://doi.org/10.1207/S1532754XJPRR1304_01

Huang, Y.-H. (2012). Gauging an integrated model of public relations value assessment (PRVA): Scale development and cross-cultural studies. *Journal of Public Relations Research, 24*(3), 243–265. https://doi.org/10.1080/1062726X.2012.671987

Huang, Y.-H., & Zhang, Y. (2013). Revisiting organization–public relations research over the past decade: Theoretical concepts, measures, methodologies and challenges. *Public Relations Review, 39*(1), 85–87. https://doi.org/10.1016/j.pubrev.2012.10.001

Huang, Y.-H., Lu, Y., Kao, L., Choy, C. H. Y., & Chang, Y.-T. (2020). Mainframes and mandarins: The impact of internet use on institutional trust in East Asia. *Telecommunications Policy, 44*(2), 101912. https://doi.org/10.1016/j.telpol.2020.101912

Huang, Y.-H., & Zhang, Y. (2015). Revisiting organization–public relationship research for the past decade. In E.-J. Ki, J.-N. Kim, & J. A. Ledingham (Eds.), *Public relations as relationship management: A relational approach to the study and practice of public relations* (pp. 3–27). Routledge.

Huang, Y.-H., Wu, F., & Huang, Q. (2017). Does research on digital public relations indicate a paradigm shift? An analysis and critique of recent trends. *Telematics and Informatics, 34*(7), 1364-1376. https://doi.org/10.1016/j.tele.2016.08.012

Huang, Y.-H. (2000). The personal influence model and Gao Guanxi in Taiwan Chinese public relations. *Public Relations Review, 26*(2), 219-236. https://doi.org/10.1016/S0363-8111(00)00042-4

Jiang, H. (2012). A model of work–life conflict and quality of employee–organization relationships (EORs): Transformational leadership, procedural justice, and family-supportive workplace initiatives. *Public Relations Review, 38*(2), 231–245. https://doi.org/10.1016/j.pubrev.2011.11.007

Jo, S. (2006). Measurement of organization–public relationships: Validation of measurement using a manufacturer–retailer relationship. *Journal of Public Relations Research, 18*(3), 225–248. https://doi.org/10.1207/s1532754xjprr1803_2

Kang, M. (2013). Effects of the organization-public relational gap between experiential and expected relationship outcomes. Relational gap analysis. *Journal of Communication Management, 17*(1), 40–55. https://doi.org/10.1108/13632541311300142

Kang, M., & Sung, M. (2017). How symmetrical employee communication leads to employee engagement and positive employee communication behaviors. The mediation of employee-organization relationships. *Journal of Communication Management, 21*(1), 82–102. https://doi.org/10.1108/JCOM-04-2016-0026

Kang, M., & Sung, M. (2019). To leave or not to leave: the effects of perceptions of organizational justice on employee turnover intention via employee-organization relationship and employee job engagement. *Journal of Public Relations Research, 31*(5–6), 152–175. https://doi.org/10.1080/1062726X.2019.1680988

Kelleher, T. (2009). Conversational voice, communicated commitment, and public relations outcomes in interactive online communication. *Journal of Communication, 59*(1), 172–188. http://dx.doi.org/10.1111/j.1460-2466.2008.01410.x

Kelleher, T., Men, R. L., & Thelen, P. (2019). Employee perceptions of CEO ghost posting and voice: Effects on perceived authentic leadership, organizational transparency, and employee-organization relationships. *Public Relations Journal, 12*(4), 1–23.

Ki, E.-J., & Hon, L. C. (2006). Relationship maintenance strategies on fortune 500 company web sites. *Journal of Communication Management, 10*(1), 27–43. https://doi.org/10.1108/13632540610646355

Ki, E.-J., & Hon, L. C. (2007a). Reliability and validity of organization-public relationship measurement and linkages among relationship indicators in a membership organization. *Journalism & Mass Communication Quarterly, 84*(3), 419–438. https://doi.org/10.1177/107769900708400302

Ki, E.-J., & Hon, L. C. (2007b). Testing the linkages among the organization–public relationship and attitude and behavioral intentions. *Journal of Public Relations Research, 19*(1), 1–23. https://doi.org/10.1080/10627260709336593

Ki, E.-J., & Hon, L. C. (2008). A measure of relationship cultivation strategies. *Journal of Public Relations Research, 21*(1), 1–24. https://doi.org/10.1080/10627260802520488

Ki, E.-J., & Hon, L. C. (2009). Causal linkages between relationship cultivation strategies and relationship quality outcomes. *International Journal of Strategic Communication, 3*(4), 242–263. https://doi.org/10.1080/15531180903218630

Ki, E.-J., & Hon, L. C. (2012). Causal linkages among relationship quality perception, attitude, and behavior intention in a membership organization. *Corporate Communications: An International Journal, 17*(2), 187–208. https://doi.org/10.1108/13563281211220274

Ki, E.-J., Pasadeos, Y., & Ertem-Eray, T. (2019). Growth of public relations research networks: A bibliometric analysis. *Journal of Public Relations Research, 31*(1–2), 5–31. https://doi.org/10.1080/1062726X.2019.1577739

Ki, E.-J., & Shin, J. (2015). The status of organization-public relationship research through an analysis of published articles between 1985 and 2013. In E.-J. Ki, J.-N. Kim, & J. A. Ledingham (Eds.), *Public relations as relationship management: A relational approach to the study and practice of public relations* (pp. 28–45). Routledge.

Kim, D. (2018). Examining effects of internal public relations practices on organizational social capital in the Korean context. Mediating roles of employee-organization relationships. *Corporate Communications: An International Journal, 23*(1), 100–116. https://doi.org/10.1108/CCIJ-01-2017-0002

Kim, Y.-C., & Ball-Rokeach, S. J. (2006). Community storytelling network, neighborhood context, and civic engagement: A multilevel approach. *Human Communication Research, 32*(4), 411–439. https://doi.org/10.1111/j.1468-2958.2006.00282.x

Kim, J. Y., & Hammick, J. K. (2017). Effects of corporate online communication on attitude and trust: Experimental analysis of Twitter messages. *Public Relations Journal, 11*(2), 1–19.

Kim, S., Tam, L., Kim, J.-N., & Rhee, Y. (2017). Determinants of employee turnover intention. Understanding the roles of organizational justice, supervisory justice, authoritarian organizational culture and organization employee relationship quality. *Corporate Communications: An International Journal, 22*(3), 308–328. https://doi.org/10.1108/CCIJ-11-2016-0074

Ledingham, J. A. (2003). Explicating relationship management as a general theory of public relations. *Journal of Public Relations Research, 15*(2), 181–198. https://doi.org/10.1207/s1532754xjprr1502_4

Ledingham, J. A. (2021). Relationship management: Status and theory. In C. Valentini (Ed.), *Public relations in handbooks of communication science* (pp. 415–432). De Gruyter Mouton.

Ledingham, J. A., & Bruning, S. D. (1998). Relationship management in public relations: Dimensions of an organization-public relationship. *Public Relations Review, 24*(1), 55–65. https://doi.org/10.1016/S0363-8111(98)80020-9

Ledingham, J. A., Bruning, S. D., Thomlison, T. D., & Lesko, C. (1997). The applicability of interpersonal relationship dimensions to an organizational context: Toward a theory of relational loyalty a qualitative approach. *Journal of Organizational Culture, Communications and Conflict, 1*(1), 23.

Lee, Y. (2017). Exploring the impacts of relationship on employees' communicative behaviors during issue periods based on employee position. *Corporate Communications: An International Journal, 22*(4), 542–555. https://doi.org/10.1108/CCIJ-03-2017-0022

Lee, Y. (2020). A situational perspective on employee communicative behaviors in a crisis: The role of relationship and symmetrical communication. *International Journal of Strategic Communication, 14*(2), 89–104. https://doi.org/10.1080/1553118X.2020.1720691

Lee, S. T., & Desai, M. H. (2014). Dialogic communication and media relations in nongovernmental organizations. *Journal of Communication Management, 18*(1), 80–100. https://doi.org/10.1108/JCOM-07-2012-0059

Lee, H., & Jun, J. W. (2013). Explicating public diplomacy as organization–public relationship (OPR): An empirical investigation of OPRs between the us embassy in Seoul and South Korean college students. *Journal of Public Relations Research*, 25(5), 411–425. https://doi.org/10.1080/1062726X.2013.795863

Lee, S. T., & Kee, A. (2017). Testing an environmental framework for understanding public relations practitioners' orientation toward relationship management. *Journal of Public Relations Research*, 29(6), 259–276. https://doi.org/10.1080/10627 26X.2017.1408465

Lee, Y., Kim, K. H., & Kim, J.-N. (2019). Understanding the impacts of issue types and employee–organization relationships on employees' problem perceptions and communicative behaviors. *Corporate Communications: An International Journal*, 24(3), 553–568. https://doi.org/10.1108/CCIJ-12-2018-0127

Lee, H. & Park, H. (2013). Testing the impact of message interactivity on relationship management and organizational reputation. *Journal of Public Relations Research*, 25(2), 188–206. https://doi.org/10.1080/1062726X.2013.739103

Lee, N., & Seltzer, T. (2018). Vicarious interaction. The role of observed online communication in fostering organization-public relationships. *Journal of Communication Management*, 22(3), 262–279. https://doi.org/10.1108/JCOM-11-2017-0129

Lee, N., Seltzer, T., & Callison, C. (2017). Relationship building in the craft beer industry: A study of public relations within the growing artisanal and locavore movements. *Public Relations Journal*, 11(2), 1–20.

Littlejohn, S. W. (1989). *Theories of human communication*. Waveland Press.

Lovari, A., Martino, V., & Kim, J.-N. (2012). Citizens' relationships with a municipality and their communicative behaviors in negative civic issues. *International Journal of Strategic Communication*, 6(1), 17–30. https://doi.org/10.1080/1553118X.2011. 634870

Men, L. R. (2011). How employee empowerment influences organization–employee relationship in China. *Public Relations Review*, 37(4), 435–437. https://doi. org/10.1016/j.pubrev.2011.08.008

Men, L. R. (2012). Revisiting the continuum of types of organization-public relationships: From a resource-based view. *Public Relations Journal*, 6(1), 1–19.

Men, L. R. (2014). Why leadership matters to internal communication: Linking transformational leadership, symmetrical communication, and employee outcomes. *Journal of Public Relations Research*, 26(3), 256–279. https://doi.org/10.1080/10627 26X.2014.908719

Men, L. R. (2015). Employee engagement in relation to employee–organization relationships and internal reputation: Effects of leadership communication. *Public Relations Journal*, 9(2). http://www.prsa.org/Intelligence/PRJournal/Vol9/No2/

Men, L. R., Ji, Y. G., & Chen, Z. F. (2017). Dialogues with entrepreneurs in China: How start-up companies cultivate relationships with strategic publics. *Journal of Public Relations Research*, 29(2–3), 90–113. https://doi.org/10.1080/10627 26X.2017.1329736

Men, L. R., & Jiang, H. (2016). Cultivating quality employee-organization relationships: The interplay among organizational leadership, culture, and communication. *International Journal of Strategic Communication*, 10(5), 462–479. https://doi.org/10.1080/155 3118X.2016.1226172

Men, L. R., & Muralidharan, S. (2017). Understanding social media peer communication and organization–public relationships: Evidence from China and the United States. *Journalism & Mass Communication Quarterly*, 94(1) 81–101. https://doi. org/10.1177/1077699016674187

Men, L. R., & Robinson, K. L. (2018). It's about how employees feel! Examining the impact of emotional culture on employee–organization relationships. *Corporate Communications: An International Journal, 23*(4), 470–491. https://doi.org/10.1108/CCIJ-05-2018-0065

Men, L. R., & Stacks, D. (2014). The effects of authentic leadership on strategic internal communication and employee-organization relationships. *Journal of Public Relations Research, 26*(4), 301–324. https://doi.org/10.1080/1062726X.2014.908720\

Men, L. R., Sung, Y., & Yue, C. A. (2019). Relational antecedents of employee engagement: A test of the investment model predictions. *Public Relations Journal, 12*(3), 1–29.

Men, L. R., & Tsai, W.-H. S. (2013). Toward an integrated model of public engagement on corporate social networking sites: Antecedents, the process, and relational outcomes. *International Journal of Strategic Communication, 7*(4), 257–273. https://doi.org/10.1080/1553118X.2013.822373

Men, L. R., & Tsai, W.-H. S. (2014). Perceptual, attitudinal, and behavioral outcomes of organization–public engagement on corporate social networking sites. *Journal of Public Relations Research, 26*(5), 417–435. https://doi.org/10.1080/1062726X.2014.951047

Men, L. R., & Tsai, W.-H. S. (2015). Infusing social media with humanity: Corporate character, public engagement, and relational outcomes. *Public Relations Review, 41*(3), 395–403. https://doi.org/10.1016/j.pubrev.2015.02.005

Men, L. R., & Tsai, W.-H. S. (2016). Public engagement with CEOs on social media: Motivations and relational outcomes. *Public Relations Review, 42*(5), 932–942. https://doi.org/10.1016/j.pubrev.2016.08.001

Men, L. R., Yang, A., Song, B., & Kiousis, S. (2018). Examining the impact of public engagement and presidential leadership communication on social media in China: Implications for government-public relationship cultivation. *International Journal of Strategic Communication, 12*(3), 252–268. https://doi.org/10.1080/15531 18X.2018.1445090

Ni, L., Xiao, Z, Liu, W., & Wang, Q. (2019). Relationship management as antecedents to public communication behaviors: Examining empowerment and public health among Asian Americans. *Public Relations Review, 45*(5), 101835. https://doi.org/10.1016/j.pubrev.2019.101835

Park, S. J., & Lim, Y. S. (2014). Information networks and social media use in public diplomacy: A comparative analysis of South Korea and Japan. *Asian Journal of Communication, 24*(1), 79–98. https://doi.org/10.1080/01292986.2013.851724

Park, H. & Reber, B. H. (2011). The organization-public relationship and crisis communication: The effect of the organization-public relationship on publics' perceptions of crisis and attitudes toward the organization. *International Journal of Strategic Communication, 5*(4), 240–260. https://doi.org/10.1080/1553118X.2011.596870

Plowman, K. D. (2013). Creating a model to measure relationships: U.S. army strategic communication. *Public Relations Review, 39*(5), 549–557. https://doi.org/10.1016/j.pubrev.2013.07.001

Pressgrove, G. N., & McKeever, B. W. (2016). Nonprofit relationship management: Extending the organization-public relationship to loyalty and behaviors. *Journal of Public Relations Research, 28*(3–4), 193–211. https://doi.org/10.1080/1062726X.2016.1233106

Qin, Y., & Men, R. L. (2019). Exploring negative peer communication of companies on social media and its impact on organization-public relationships. *Public Relations Review, 45*(4), 101795. https://doi.org/10.1016/j.pubrev.2019.05.016

Saffer, A. J., Sommerfeldt, E. J., & Taylor, M. (2013). The effects of organizational Twitter interactivity on organization–public relationships. *Public Relations Review, 39*(3), 213–215. https://doi.org/10.1016/j.pubrev.2013.02.005

Sallot, L. M., Lyon, L. J., Acosta-Alzuru, C., & Ogata Jones, K. (2003). From aardvark to zebra: A new millennium analysis of theory development in public relations academic journals. *Journal of Public Relations Research*, *15*(1), 27–90. https://doi.org/10.1207/ S1532754XJPRR1501_2

Seltzer, T., & Lee, N. (2018). The influence of distal antecedents on organization-public relationships. *Journal of Public Relations Research*, *30*(5–6), 230–250. https://doi.org/10 .1080/1062726X.2018.1542598

Seltzer, T., & Zhang, W. (2010). Toward a model of political organization–public relationships: Antecedent and cultivation strategy influence on citizens' relationships with political parties. *Journal of Public Relations Research*, *23*(1), 24–45. https://doi.org/10.1 080/1062726X.2010.504791

Seltzer, T., & Zhang, W. (2011). Debating healthcare reform: How political parties' issue-specific communication influences citizens' perceptions of organization-public relationships. *Journalism & Mass Communication Quarterly*, *88*(4), 753–770. https://doi. org/10.1177/107769901108800405

Shen, H. (2017). Refining organization–public relationship quality measurement in student and employee samples. *Journalism & Mass Communication Quarterly*, *94*(4), 994– 1010. https://doi.org/10.1177/1077699016674186

Shen, H., & Kim, J.-N. (2012). The authentic enterprise: Another buzz word, or a true driver of quality relationships?. *Journal of Public Relations Research*, *24*(4), 371–389. https://doi.org/10.1080/1062726X.2012.690255

Sisson, D. C. (2017). Control mutuality, social media, and organization-public relationships: A study of local animal welfare organizations' donors. *Public Relations Review*, *43*(1), 179–189. https://doi.org/10.1016/j.pubrev.2016.10.007

Slaughter, A.-M. (2009). America's edge: Power in the networked century. *Foreign Affairs*, 94–113. http://www.jstor.org/stable/20699436

Sommerfeldt, E. J., & Kent, M. L. (2015). Civil society, networks, and relationship management: Beyond the organization–public dyad. *International Journal of Strategic Communication*, *9*(3), 235–252. https://doi.org/10.1080/1553118X.2015.1025405

Stohl, C., & Stohl, M. (2007). Networks of terror: Theoretical assumptions and pragmatic consequences. *Communication Theory*, *17*(2), 93–124. https://doi. org/10.1111/j.1468-2885.2007.00289.x

Tsai, W.-H. S., & Men, L. R. (2018). Social messengers as the new frontier of organization-public engagement: A WeChat study. *Public Relations Review*, *44*(3), 419–429. https://doi.org/10.1016/j.pubrev.2018.04.004

Waters, R. D., & Bortree, D. S. (2012). Advancing relationship management theory: Mapping the continuum of relationship types. *Public Relations Review*, *38*(1), 123–127. https://doi.org/10.1016/j.pubrev.2011.08.018

Waters, R. D., Burnett, E., Lamm, A., & Lucas, J. (2009). Engaging stakeholders through social networking: How nonprofit organizations are using Facebook. *Public Relations Review*, *35*(2), 102–106. https://doi.org/10.1016/j.pubrev.2009.01.006

Wiggill, M. N. (2014). Donor relationship management practices in the South African non-profit sector. *Public Relations Review*, *40*(2), 278–285. https://doi.org/10.1016/j. pubrev.2013.10.005

Zaharna, R. (2016). Beyond the individualism–collectivism divide to relationalism: Explicating cultural assumptions in the concept of "relationships". *Communication Theory*, *26*(2), 190–211. https://doi.org/10.1111/comt.12058

25 Media Relations

Research, Theory, and the Digital Age

Xiaomeng Lan and Spiro Kiousis

Introduction

Media relations, one of the most important functions of public relations and a key area of interest for public relations researchers (Shaw & White, 2004; Supa, 2014; Verčič & Verčič, 2016), involves establishing and maintaining mutually beneficial relationships with the media (Supa & Zoch, 2009). Public relations practitioners have long worked with news media to communicate important messages to a broad array of publics and stakeholders. In fact, the earliest form of public relations as we understand it today is said to have involved the efforts to influence press coverage of organizations and individuals (Grunig & Hunt, 1984). In a historical examination of public relations, Cutlip (1994) noted that public relations as a distinctive professional field emerged in the mid-19th century in the United States, when publicists and press agents were hired on a large scale by industry, the public sector, causes, and individuals and started exerting its "great though unmeasured force" on American economic, political, and social life (p. xvi). After more than 100 years of development, public relations today has gone well beyond simple publicity and using all means to gain access to the news media (Verčič & Verčič, 2016; Zoch & Molleda, 2006), and there is a growing recognition that successful public relations requires integration of strategic management of media relations (Lieber & Golan, 2011; Supa, 2014; Supa & Zoch, 2009; Zerfass et al., 2016).

Media relations is considered critically important to organizations, as, at its best, it can contribute to organizational legitimacy, with the news media serving as an authoritative third party to establish higher credibility in comparison to messages that originate from the organization itself, such as advertisements (Carroll, 2010; Gilpin, 2008). News media are found to be one of the major sources from which the public learns about organizations, their activities, and their connections to matters of public interest, and therefore the media impact perceptions of organizational reputation (Carroll & McCombs, 2003; Deephouse, 2000; Einwiller et al., 2010; Meijer & Kleinnijenhuis, 2006; Ragas, 2013b; Vogler & Eisenegger, 2020). As media relations works to affect news-making processes, particular interests of

DOI: 10.4324/9781003141396-29

organizations are expected to draw the public's attention or even to be perceived as in the public interest (Raupp, 2017; Shoemaker & Reese, 1996).

News media can also serve as an important information intermediary that brings company-initiated information, such as financial disclosures, to key stakeholders, helping decrease information asymmetry and assisting them in making investment decisions (Bushee et al., 2010; Call et al., 2021). For nonprofit organizations in particular, the media can help drive broader awareness and donor support (Waters, 2013; Wenger & Quarantelli, 1989). Legislators, too, rely on news media to communicate with their constituents and compete for public attention (Grimmer, 2010). In the public health arena (whose vital importance has been highlighted by the COVID-19 pandemic), some scholars have called attention to the dire need for health agencies and their public information officers to develop better media relations strategies, as media can make important health information and recommendations accessible to a wider range of publics and thus advance public health solutions (Avery & Kim, 2009; J. M. White & Wingenbach, 2013).

Good media relations can bring benefits for news media too. Journalists are constantly looking for trusted sources of news and information, and public relations can be such a source, providing the media information that is easier and cheaper to use in a news story than that from other sources—what Gandy (1982) called "information subsidies" (Cameron et al., 1997; Reese, 1991; Shoemaker & Reese, 1996).

Despite the strategic importance of media relations for public relations and for the media, previous research has largely focused on the tactical aspects of media relations rather than situating it in a strategic context (Lieber & Golan, 2011; Supa, 2014; Supa & Zoch, 2009; Taylor, 2000). "Tactical" areas of interest have included the working relationship between public relations practitioners and journalists (e.g., Cameron et al., 1997; Zoch et al., 2014), qualities of news releases and factors determining newsworthiness and journalists' news decisions (e.g., Morton & Warren, 1992; Zoch & Supa, 2014), and, more recently, the use of digital tools for media relations purposes (e.g., Callison, 2003; Kent & Taylor, 2003; Zerfass & Schramm, 2014).

At the same time, this field lacks a theoretical underpinning that could speak to the strategic core of media relations and help establish parameters needed for measuring and evaluating the value of media relations. Supa (2014) noted that researchers have often relied on established theories developed in other fields to investigate media relations, theories including gatekeeping (Shoemaker, 1991; D. M. White, 1950), agenda-setting (McCombs & Shaw, 1972, 1993), agenda-building (McCombs, 2004; Weaver & Elliott, 1985), and framing (Entman, 1993; Scheufele, 1999).

The rise of social media and mobile technology over the last decade is drastically changing the media landscape and media relations practice, putting yet more pressure on academia to advance theory and research in this field. With the plethora of new communication channels, organizations can now bypass the news media—who have long been characterized as the "gatekeepers" (D. M. White, 1950) of the information publics receive—and directly communicate with stakeholders (Saffer, 2013; Verčič & Verčič, 2016; Zerfass et al., 2016). At the same time, citizens and groups are taking advantage of the expansion of the digital media to become creators, publishers, and distributors of news and information, contributing to a mix of voices in the public sphere (Habermas et al., 1974; Holtzhausen & Zerfass, 2015; Sweet et al., 2013; Taylor, 2009a). Here a fundamental question emerges: What does all this mean for public relations academics? Perhaps no better answer to this question exists than that given by Supa (2014), who suggested what media relations research with a *strategic* focus would be like:

> What is lacking is a substantial body of literature that addresses the big picture issues that media relations practitioners face. Those issues, including how to best integrate media relations as a strategic function in public relations programs, how to best measure and evaluate the discrete function of media relations, how to best incorporate new communication platforms as a tool of media relations with different media audiences, as well as larger field issues such as development of theory in media relations should be some of the areas that researchers look to as they continue to better understand the media relations function.
>
> (pp. 10–11)

This is the context within which the present chapter reviews the academic understanding of media relations and theories that have a bearing on this field. This chapter also attends to the broad question of what would be expected of media relations in a digital age. In particular, this chapter draws attention to a theory that can potentially serve as the foundation for a strategically focused research paradigm for media relations: the theory of agenda-building.

Traditional Media Relations Research

Much of the academic understanding of media relations is built around the questions of how it is practiced or how it should be practiced. The practice of media relations encompasses a variety of activities, including maintaining media contacts, studying what journalists will find newsworthy about their organizations, crafting information subsidy materials to be sent to a newsroom, and responding to journalists' interests in the organization (Ryan, 2013; Zoch & Molleda, 2006). Research into such aspects of media relations practice forms a major foundation of today's understanding of this "most practiced function of public relations" (Verčič & Verčič, 2016).

The Public Relations Practitioner-Journalist Relationship

The crux of media relations is the relationship between public relations practitioners and journalists, which has received much attention from researchers in the last six decades (see Cameron et al., 1997). One often-studied aspect of the relationship is how the two groups of professionals view each other (DeLorme & Fedler, 2003; Ryan & Martinson, 1988; Supa & Zoch, 2009). Findings from these studies tend to conclude that journalists are more likely to have an attitude of distrust and low esteem regarding public relations practitioners, and this unfavorable perception is "more profound in the abstract than in the specific experience of journalists" (Cameron et al., 1997, p. 118). By comparison, public relations practitioners generally have a more positive view of journalists (Supa, 2014).

Belz et al. (1989) explained this disparity by revealing that journalists see public relations practitioners negatively because they seem to be self-interested advocates who have hidden agendas, withhold information, and compromise ethics. These views may have multiple causes, including public relations' rooting in the practice of press agentry and publicity (Gower, 2008), public relations practitioners' reported unprofessional practices (Ryan & Martinson, 1988), journalists' belief that their work is more important to society than is public relations (Sallot, 1990), and the news media's gate-keeping power over public relations materials (Nicolai & Riley, 1972). Practical suggestions have been made on the public relations practitioners' side to improve the relationship, frequently emphasizing ethics and professional standards (Bowen, 2016; Wells & Spinks, 1999), understanding of routine journalistic practices and values (Pang, 2010; Zoch & Molleda, 2006), and a legitimate supply of information that is truthful and fair (Larsson, 2009; Ryan, 2013). Another often-cited reason is a sense of resentment among media people who find themselves forced to engaged with public relations practitioners, as their own resources are stretched due to the 24-hour news cycle and the economic pressures brought on by the competition from new media (Obermaier et al., 2018; Sterne, 2010).

Studies on the relationship between public relations practitioners and reporters in non-Western countries, although very limited in number, have also suggested an interdependency between the two professions (Pharr & Krauss, 1996; Shin & Cameron, 2003; Sriramesh et al., 1999; Wu, 2011). The two groups tend to develop private and personal relationships in Eastern Asian societies such as Japan, Korea, and Taiwan, and their interactions are usually more informal and implicit than in the U.S. (Shin & Cameron, 2003; Wu, 2011). For example, in Japan, journalists and public relations people often engage in "nomunication," which means informal communication while drinking ("nomu") (Sriramesh et al., 1999).

Information Subsidies and the Source-Reporter Perspective

The information subsidy, which is defined as "source-controlled, pre-packaged materials provided to journalists in an attempt to influence and respond to the priorities found in the news" (Ragas, 2013a, p. 219), is one of the most important concepts applied to media relations. It suggests that media relations is a two-way process (Bowen, 2016; Neijens & Smit, 2006), since, as Einwiller et al. (2010) reasoned, while public relations professionals need the news media to reach their stakeholders and to foster organizational reputations, the news media often depend on public relations practitioners for content that is of interest to their audiences.

Media sociologist Herbert Gans (1979), in his analysis of *CBS Evening News*, *NBC Nightly News*, *Newsweek*, and *Time*, found that news is shaped by "the knowns," or the sources on which a newsroom relies. Gandy (1982) expanded this view by describing the relationship between a newsroom and its sources as one of mutual need. Public relations practitioners serve as a source through their provision of information subsidies such as news releases, statements, and news conferences, and consequently influence media coverage (Burns, 1998; Cameron et al., 1997; Saffer, 2013). Taylor (2009b) considered information subsidy a "guiding metaphor" with which to characterize the public relations-media relationship, as it explains how professionals from the two fields "work together to create news content" (p. 24). In fact, researchers trying to capture the various factors affecting media content have documented public relations as one such influence (Reese, 2019; Shoemaker & Reese, 1996, 2014).

From the perspective of the source-reporter relationship, Cameron et al. (1997) considered public relations professionals to act as a "boundary-spanner" between the press and the organization's management. To fulfill their media relations responsibilities, practitioners need to relate their organizations' worldviews and interests to the news media and their audiences, and also to relate news media's and the publics' concerns and values to their organizations. Yang et al.'s (2016) comparison of the codes of ethics adopted by 66 public relations and journalism professional associations provides some insight into the basic values the two professions share—and those they do not. The findings suggest that professionalism, moral standards, and expertise were valued by both groups. However, public relations codes of ethics emphasized advocacy, clients' rights, and relationships, while journalism's codes promoted the values of society, social justice, and human rights. The study then called for public relations practitioners to align their values with the journalists', as an ethical public relations practice should serve the public's and society's interests.

With the development of new media, professional journalism's gatekeeping control is threatened (Reese & Shoemaker, 2016), whereas public relations practitioners have more alternative means to communicate with stakeholders (Callison, 2003; Meraz, 2009; Zerfass et al., 2016). This has placed stress on journalists, giving rise to what Waters et al. (2010) called the "media catching" pattern of media relations, where public relations practitioners increasingly interact with journalists by responding to their information requests rather than by merely pitching organizational stories.

Source Credibility and Newsworthiness

Another stream of media relations literature has centered on the qualities of information subsidy materials, particularly news releases, to determine what factors might affect their acceptance by journalists (Cameron et al., 1997; Zoch & Supa, 2014). The news release (or press release) is one of the most common communication materials written by public relations professionals (Wilcox et al., 2015). Traditionally, news releases are sent to a media gatekeeper such as a print journalist or a producer of a television program to deliver a strategic message from an organization that the media will, ideally, publish or broadcast (Daugherty, 2013; Martinelli, 2021).

Researchers have examined several factors that may influence the likelihood of the news release actually being disseminated to the public via the news. One of them is source credibility (Gans, 1979; Powers & Fico, 1994), defined by Reich (2011) as the extent to which a source is perceived by journalists as credible. Gaziano and McGrath (1987) observed that credibility has more to do with perceived fairness, lack of bias, and good faith, and less to do with perceived accuracy or reliability of information, suggesting that the perceived quality of the source matters more than the information. That being the case, building a trust relationship with media is essential for a would-be source to be effective (McQuail, 2010).

Other research has identified a broad spectrum of factors—or news values—that make a news release "newsworthy," thereby increasing its chances of consideration by journalists selecting or preparing material for publication (for reviews, see Cameron et al., 1997; Harcup & Deirdre, 2017; Zoch & Supa, 2014). Some factors frequently reported to be associated with journalists' selections include exclusivity or exclusive content (Schultz, 2007), timeliness (Walters & Walters, 1992), magnitude or significance (Berkowitz, 1990), relevance or cultural proximity (Brighton & Foy, 2007), bad news or negative overtone (Harcup & Deirdre, 2001), and unexpectedness or surprise (Bednarek, 2016).

Theory and Effects of Media Relations

In his review of the academic literature on media relations, Supa (2014) concluded that this area's theoretical development is still lacking. As a result, scholars continue to use theories and hypotheses from other areas of research to help explain the fundamental issues, including the evaluation and measurement of the effects of media relations. The theories of gatekeeping, framing, agenda-setting, and agenda-building are particularly relevant for media relations, as they connect the audience and effects side of communication studies with the shaping and control of content (Shoemaker & Reese, 2014). These theories provide a structure for studying the interrelated processes relevant to larger issues in media relations, including how media coverage and public opinion are shaped by media relations efforts, how information subsidies are constructed and positioned to more effectively engage media gatekeepers, and how different actors in the public sphere (including media outlets, organizations, governments, policy makers, and the general public) interact with and influence each other (Habermas et al., 1974; Ihlen, 2008; Sommerfeldt, 2013).

Gatekeeping Theory

Much of the understanding of media relations in a pre-Internet era rests on the premise that the media served a gatekeeping function (Grunig & Hunt, 1984; Taylor, 2000). Lewin (1947) originally used the metaphor "gatekeepers" to refer to the decision makers who make food choices at certain decision points, or "gates," along the "channel" by which food gets from its source to the family table. The concept of gatekeepers determining which items enter and move through the channel was then applied to the context of news selection by D. M. White (1950), who examined how a newspaper editor—whom he called "Mr. Gates"—decided which news items provided by wire services would be published. Reese and Ballinger (2001) argued that White's gatekeeper model provides a useful and realistic conceptual frame for analyzing media content, even though its focus on gatekeepers' news "selection" overlooks other influences on the production of media content, such as routinized judgments and message structure.

Shoemaker and Reese (2014) considered White's study to inaugurate the tradition of examining the criteria media decision makers use to select information. Subsequent studies further explored the factors involved in the gatekeeping process, looking beyond the individual preferences of journalists and editors to include even factors outside the journalism profession. Shoemaker (1991) returned to Lewin's holistic approach and considers the multitude of influences from societal, institutional, organizational, routine, and individual practices in gatekeeping channels that collectively affect the production of media messages that reach the public. These influences were further formalized into a "hierarchy of influences" model, in which public relations is considered to be an important social institutional factor that could exert influence on the production of news or media agendas (Reese, 2001; Shoemaker & Reese, 1996).

Framing Theory

Framing theory gained currency through the early work of sociologist Erving Goffman (1974), for whom frames are abstract models, principles, or organizational patterns that people can use to identify and interpret otherwise confusing situations. This sociological theory later became important in a variety of research fields concerned with how individuals, groups, and societies construct, perceive, and communicate meanings about reality (e.g., Benford & Snow, 2000; O'Keefe & Jensen, 2007; Pan & Kosicki, 1993; Reese et al., 2001). According to Tewksbury and Scheufele (2009), communication scholars are particularly interested in two types of framing processes—how frames are constructed and socially negotiated (what they called "frame building") and how framing affects audiences (or "frame setting," including how audiences receiving a frame come to interpret an issue or event).

Examining framing in communicating texts, Entman (1993) summarized the concept with a simple sentence: "Framing essentially involves selection and salience" (p. 52). According to him, frames "select and call attention to particular aspects of the reality described, which logically means that frames simultaneously direct attention away from other aspects" (p. 54). The frames thereby shape the perspective from which the receiver of the message perceives the reality and can be used strategically "to promote a particular problem definition, causal interpretation, moral evaluation and/or treatment recommendation" (p. 52).

Hallahan (1999) applied framing theory to public relations, seeing their connection in the strategic creation of messages to focus special attention on some aspects over others and to help establish common frames of reference—themes or arguments that can be considered by publics when they discuss an issue or event of mutual concern. Focusing on message framing in political communication and political public relations in particular, Hallahan (2011) argued that framing can be viewed as a tool of relationship building and political reconciliation by helping develop mutual perspectives among key political stakeholders, including governments, political candidates, voters, constituents, and special interest groups.

With regard to framing's effects within the media relations context, Raupp (2017) argued that "framing as a dimension of media effects occurs when journalists adopt the strategic frames or frame elements from the frame sponsors" (p. 6). Zoch and Molleda (2006) also incorporated framing in their media relations process model, highlighting the importance of strategic framing in the process of creating information subsidies.

Agenda-Setting Theory

As one of the most prominent theories of media effects (Potter, 2011), agenda-setting concerns the ability of the news media to influence the audience's perception of which issues or topics are important (McCombs & Reynolds, 2002). Without explicitly referring to agenda-setting, Cohen (1963) is widely credited with identifying the process by noting that "[The press] may not be successful much of the time in telling people what to think, but it is stunningly successful in telling its readers what to think about" (p. 13). In the seminal empirical study of the agenda-setting hypothesis, McCombs and Shaw (1972) found a correlation between the campaign issues emphasized in media content and the issues voters used in deciding how to vote during the 1968 presidential campaign. They then used the agenda-setting metaphor by reasoning that "Readers learn not only about a given issue, but also how much importance to attach to that issue from the amount of information in a news story and its position. . . . The mass media may well determine the important issues—that is, the media may set the 'agenda' of the campaign" (p. 176).

One important expansion of the theory is the differentiation between object agenda-setting and attribute agenda-setting. According to McCombs and Shaw (1993), an *agenda* is an abstract term that can potentially be applied in many settings to refer to various communication concepts that are competing for attention. Media coverage could influence the priority assigned to certain objects—such as issues, political candidates, organizations, foreign nations, events, and problems—to tell people *what to think about*. The news can also tell people *how to think about it* by influencing second-level "attribute agendas" (Golan & Wanta, 2001; McCombs et al., 1997). McCombs (1997b) further developed the theory by linking attribute agenda-setting to framing theory, arguing that framing is "the selection of a restricted number of thematically related attributes for inclusion on the media agenda when a particular object is discussed" (p. 37).

In addition to the transfer of objects and attributes saliency, scholars have explicated a third level of agenda-setting based on social network theory and the perspective of social network analysis (Guo, 2012, 2013; Guo et al., 2012). Network agenda-setting hypothesizes that when objects and/or attributes occur together within an agenda, the likelihood of those objects and attributes being jointly seen as salient increases (Guo et al., 2012; Schweickart et al., 2016). These combinations could be pairs, triads, or even entire systems of elements.

Agenda-Building Theory and the Effects of Media Relations

Agenda-building is an important macro-level implication of agenda-setting (Bryant & Miron, 2004). While agenda-setting's focus is on the transfer of salience between news media and public opinion, the agenda-building model expands the scope of inquiry to include the sources who "set" the media's agenda and the policy agenda (Burns, 1998; Rogers & Dearing, 1988). Lang and Lang (1983) considered "agenda-building—a more apt term than agenda-setting—[as] a collective process in which media, government, and the citizenry reciprocally influence one another" (pp. 58–59). From the public relations perspective, Schweickart et al. (2016) emphasized the strategic nature of agenda-building and defined it as "the process by which strategic communication efforts are made on behalf of a variety of stakeholders by public relations practitioners to influence the news media, the public, or other stakeholders either directly or indirectly" (p. 364).

Some public relations researchers think of agenda-building as one of the more robust and applicable theoretical frameworks for studying media relations and its effects (Lieber & Golan, 2011). The broader concept of agenda-building explicates the role of public relations in the social processes of salience formation around issues in the media, public, and policy agendas. It also provides an empirically viable structure with which the effectiveness of media relations is best understood. Information subsidies as important manifestations of public relations' agenda-building efforts are an ideal medium for measuring how messages are strategically framed and how priorities are communicated to influence media content (Grimmer, 2010; Kiousis et al., 2016). The agenda is treated as a list of objects (e.g., issues and candidates), attributes of the objects (e.g., issue frames and candidates' characteristics), or association networks of the objects or attributes that are viewed at a point in time ranked in a hierarchy of importance (Rogers & Dearing, 1988). Agendas in source information subsidies, media coverage, public opinion, and/or legislators' communication are compared to determine the likely patterns of salience transfer. To the extent that the agenda of source information subsidies aligns with that of the news media, public opinion, and/ or policymaking, the agenda-building effects of the media relations efforts occur (Raupp, 2017).

The core idea of agenda-building has been applied to a wide variety of contexts in which the agendas of different social actors and institutions were studied, substantively adding to the knowledge of the possible effects of media relations. Types of information subsidies studied have included government and presidential communications in various forms (press releases, speeches, statements, press briefings, tweets, YouTube videos, or Facebook posts) (Albishri et al., 2019; Parmelee, 2014; Ragas & Kiousis, 2010; Schweickart et al., 2016; Wanta & Foote, 1994), political ads produced by candidates and activist groups during election campaigns (Kiousis et al., 2009; Ragas & Kiousis, 2010), state-sponsored media publications (as information subsidies of government) (Cheng et al., 2016; Zhang et al., 2017), policymakers' press releases (Grimmer, 2010), as well as corporate news releases, shareholder letters, and CEOs communications on social media or in interviews (Kiousis et al., 2007; Lan et al., 2020; Ragas, 2012).

For organizations, effective media relations can also have an impact on their reputation, a topic that has attracted much attention from public relations researchers (DiStaso, 2012; Kim et al., 2015; Kiousis et al., 2007; Meijer & Kleinnijenhuis, 2006). Based on the agenda-building hypotheses, Kim et al. (2015) found a strong attribute (reputation dimensions, in this case) agenda-building influence of corporate press releases on media coverage and online customer reviews. The results suggest that news releases may be used strategically to shape media portrayals and public perceptions of organizational reputation.

Conclusion: Media Relations in the Digital Age

The tremendous expansion of communications in the digital age and the rise of alternative information intermediaries such as bloggers, experts, and other online opinion leaders (Bushee et al., 2010) has challenged public relations people to think about media relations from new perspectives. The news media that media relations traditionally deals with are now one among a multitude of possible influence agents that shape public opinion and policy (Perloff, 2017). Whereas before the Internet, media relations existed between public relations practitioners and journalists, in the digital age, media relations should be expanded to include a variety of individuals, groups, and organizations (Lahav & Zimand-Sheiner, 2016), who themselves act as producers of content or actively participate in online discussions and communities to generate network effects that move public opinion (Thompson, 2020). The lessening of news media's intermediary role between organizations and publics in the new media ecosystem (Anderson, 2013) has challenged the linearity of the traditional media relations process, which is characterized by public relations' reliance on news media as a channel for distribution and amplification of messages. There is a need for a more participative approach to media relations that factors in the networked connections and sharing of influence among the organizations, journalists, customers, and other publics and citizens.

In keeping with all these developments, the agenda-building perspective suggests that a broader array of voices should be monitored in the salience formation, transfer, and exchange processes (Kiousis & Ragas, 2016), and it is thus an apt concept that we believe can serve as the foundation for a strategically focused research paradigm for media relations in the digital age. However, the scholarship in this area still needs to be developed. Kiousis and Ragas (2016) observed that most of the agenda-building studies had focused on the relationship between sources and news media in the development of news content, and they tended to describe the balance of power in such relationships in favor of sources, particularly those in government or authoritative capacities. Future research should examine the relative influence of a larger variety of stakeholders and constituencies, for example, politicians, political parties, corporations, journalists, bloggers, interest groups, opinion leaders, and nations. In a similar vein, Professor Spiro Kiousis (as cited in Schmierbach et al., 2022) introduced the concept "agenda sharing" to recognize the power of alternative voices in shaping the agendas of the stakeholders that media relations ultimately works to influence.

The agenda-building perspective also suggests that media relations in a fragmented and networked new media environment (Gilpin et al., 2010) should focus on the mutual shaping and co-construction of meaning with all kinds of stakeholders (Holtzhausen & Zerfass, 2015). This involves a process that generates communication, negotiation, and consensus regarding the priorities the stakeholders should focus on. Such consensus is particularly significant in a society where meanings, ideologies, and values are constantly contested. Public relations practitioners can work to build consensus and win wider support among stakeholders to make a better environment for the organization. The effectiveness of media relations, therefore, can be reflected in the extent to which an organization's priorities become priorities in other stakeholders' agendas (González-Arteaga et al., 2016; McCombs, 1997a).

In the consensus-building process, the social networks of the individuals, the groups, and the organizations are considered an important factor—as Klandermans (1988) argued, "consensus is not created by convincing individual after individual; rather, groups of individuals linked by social networks learn to move together" (p. 193). This points to the value of network agenda-building (or third-level agenda-building), which looks at the transfer of salience when elements co-occur across agendas (Guo & McCombs, 2011; Guo & Zhang, 2020; Kiousis & Ragas, 2016). As more communication today takes place in the networked public sphere (Ausserhofer & Maireder, 2013; Reese & Shoemaker, 2016), the network agenda-building model can provide public relations scholars and practitioners with a more sophisticated way to gauge the effectiveness of media relations.

Looking ahead, media relations is a fertile area of inquiry that may help answer questions of strategic importance for public relations. These include how organizations can build an optimal multi-level, multi-channel, and multimedia framework of media relations; how to monitor and evaluate the dynamics and changes in such frameworks in a timely manner; and—despite the difficulties—how to foster consensus on shared values and promote cohesiveness among the constituents of the framework. Agenda-building, in turn, can help advance knowledge in the arena of media relations, which is so crucial to understanding communication in the digital age.

References

Albishri, O., Tarasevich, S., Proverbs, P., Kiousis, S. K., & Alahmari, A. (2019). Mediated public diplomacy in the digital age: Exploring the Saudi and the U.S. governments' agenda-building during Trump's visit to the Middle East. *Public Relations Review*, *45*(4), 1–14. https://doi.org/10.1016/j.pubrev.2019.101820

Anderson, C. W. (2013). *Rebuilding the news: Metropolitan journalism in the digital age.* Temple University Press.

Ausserhofer, J., & Maireder, A. (2013). National politics on Twitter: Structures and topics of a networked public sphere. *Information, Communication & Society*, *16*(3), 291–314. https://doi.org/10.1080/1369118X.2012.756050

Avery, E. J., & Kim, S. (2009). Anticipating or precipitating crisis? Health agencies may not be heeding best practice advice in avian flu press releases. *Journal of Public Relations Research*, *21*(2), 187–197. https://doi.org/10.1080/10627260802557449

Bednarek, M. (2016). Voices and values in the news: News media talk, news values and attribution. *Discourse, Context & Media*, *11*, 27–37. https://doi.org/10.1016/j.dcm.2015.11.004

Belz, A., Talbott, A. D., & Starck, K. (1989). Using role theory to study cross perceptions of journalists and public relations practitioners. *Journal of Public Relations Research*, *1*(1–4), 125–139. https://doi.org/10.1207/s1532754xjprr0101-4_7

Benford, R. D., & Snow, D. A. (2000). Framing processes and social movements: An overview and assessment. *Annual Review of Sociology*, *26*(1), 611–639. https://doi.org/10.1146/annurev.soc.26.1.611

Berkowitz, D. (1990). Refining the gatekeeping metaphor for local television news. *Journal of Broadcasting & Electronic Media*, *34*(1), 55–68. https://doi.org/10.1080/08838159009386725

Bowen, S. A. (2016). Clarifying ethics terms in public relations from A to V, authenticity to virtue: BledCom special issue of PR review sleeping (with the) media: Media relations. *Public Relations Review*, *42*(4), 564–572. https://doi.org/10.1016/j.pubrev.2016.03.012

Brighton, P., & Foy, D. (2007). *News values.* Sage.

Bryant, J., & Miron, D. (2004). Theory and research in mass communication. *Journal of Communication, 54*(4), 662–704. https://doi.org/10.1111/j.1460-2466.2004.tb02650.x

Burns, J. E. (1998). Information subsidies and agenda building: A study of local radio news. *Atlantic Journal of Communication, 6*(1), 90–100. https://doi.org/10.1080/15456879809367337

Bushee, B. J., Core, J. E., Guay, W., & Hamm, S. J. (2010). The role of the business press as an information intermediary. *Journal of Accounting Research, 48*(1), 1–19. https://doi.org/10.1111/j.1475-679X.2009.00357.x

Call, A. C., Emett, S. A., Maksymov, E., & Sharp, N. Y. (2021). Meet the press: Survey evidence on financial journalists as information intermediaries. *Journal of Accounting and Economics, 73*(2–3). http://dx.doi.org/10.2139/ssrn.3279453

Callison, C. (2003). Media relations and the Internet: How fortune 500 company Web sites assist journalists in news gathering. *Public Relations Review, 29*(1), 29–41. https://doi.org/10.1016/S0363-8111(02)00196-0

Cameron, G. T., Sallot, L. M., & Curtin, P. A. (1997). Public relations and the production of news: A critical review and theoretical framework. *Annals of the International Communication Association, 20*(1), 111–155. https://doi.org/doi.org/10.1080/23808985.1997.11678940

Carroll, C. E. (2010). Should firms circumvent or work through the news media? *Public Relations Review, 36*(3), 278–280. https://doi.org/10.1016/j.pubrev.2010.05.005

Carroll, C. E., & McCombs, M. E. (2003). Agenda-setting effects of business news on the public's images and opinions about major corporations. *Corporate Reputation Review, 6*(1), 36–46. https://doi.org/10.1057/palgrave.crr.1540188

Cheng, Z., Golan, G. J., & Kiousis, S. (2016). The second-level agenda-building function of the Xinhua news agency: Examining the role of government-sponsored news in mediated public diplomacy. *Journalism Practice, 10*(6), 744–762. https://doi.org/10.1080/17512786.2015.1063079

Cohen, B. C. (1963). *The press and foreign policy.* Princeton University Press.

Cutlip, S. M. (1994). *The unseen power: Public relations: A history.* Lawrence Erlbaum Associates.

Daugherty, E. L. (2013). Media release. In R. L. Heath (Ed.), *Encyclopedia of public relations* (2nd ed.). Sage.

Deephouse, D. L. (2000). Media reputation as a strategic resource: An integration of mass communication and resource-based theories. *Journal of Management, 26*(6), 1091–1112. https://doi.org/10.1016/S0149-2063(00)00075-1

DeLorme, D. E., & Fedler, F. (2003). Journalists' hostility toward public relations: An historical analysis. *Public Relations Review, 29*(2), 99–124. https://doi.org/10.1016/S0363-8111(03)00019-5

DiStaso, M. W. (2012). The annual earnings press release's dual role: An examination of relationships with local and national media coverage and reputation. *Journal of Public Relations Research, 24*(2), 123–143. https://doi.org/10.1080/1062726X.2012.626131

Einwiller, S. A., Carroll, C. E., & Korn, K. (2010). Under what conditions do the news media influence corporate reputation? The roles of media dependency and need for orientation. *Corporate Reputation Review, 12*(4), 299–315. https://doi.org/10.1057/crr.2009.28

Entman, R. M. (1993). Framing: Toward clarification of a fractured paradigm. *Journal of Communication, 43*(4), 51–58. https://doi.org/10.1111/j.1460-2466.1993.tb01304.x

Gandy, O. H. (1982). *Beyond agenda-setting: Information subsidies and public policy.* Ablex.

Gans, H. J. (1979). *Deciding what's news: A study of CBS evening news, NBC nightly news, newsweek and time.* Pantheon Books.

Gaziano, C., & McGrath, K. (1987). Newspaper credibility and relationships of newspaper journalists to communities. *Journalism Quarterly, 64*(2–3), 317–345. https://doi.org/10.1177/107769908706400205

Gilpin, D. R. (2008). Narrating the organizational self: Reframing the role of the news release. *Public Relations Review, 34*(1), 9–18. https://doi.org/10.1016/j.pubrev.2007.08.005

Gilpin, D. R., Palazzolo, E. T., & Brody, N. (2010). Socially mediated authenticity. *Journal of Communication Management, 14*(3), 258–278. https://doi.org/10.1108/13632541011064526

Goffman, E. (1974). *Frame analysis: An essay on the organization of experience.* Harvard University Press.

Golan, G., & Wanta, W. (2001). Second-level agenda setting in the New Hampshire primary: A comparison of coverage in three newspapers and public perceptions of candidates. *Journalism & Mass Communication Quarterly, 78*(2), 247–259. https://doi.org/10.1177/107769900107800203

González-Arteaga, T., de Andrés Calle, R., & Chiclana, F. (2016). A new measure of consensus with reciprocal preference relations: The correlation consensus degree. *Knowledge-Based Systems, 107*, 104–116. https://doi.org/10.1016/j.knosys.2016.06.002

Gower, K. (2008). US corporate public relations in the progressive era. *Journal of Communication Management, 12*(4), 305–318. https://doi.org/10.1108/13632540810919774

Grimmer, J. (2010). A Bayesian hierarchical topic model for political texts: Measuring expressed agendas in Senate press releases. *Political Analysis, 18*(1), 1–35. https://doi.org/10.1093/pan/mpp034

Grunig, J. E., & Hunt, T. (1984). *Managing public relations.* Holt, Rinehart & Winston.

Guo, L. (2012). The application of social network analysis in agenda setting research: A methodological exploration. *Journal of Broadcasting & Electronic Media, 56*(4), 616–631. https://doi.org/10.1080/08838151.2012.732148

Guo, L. (2013). Toward the third level of agenda-setting theory: A network agenda-setting model. In T. J. Johnson (Ed.), *Agenda setting in a 2.0 world: News agendas in communication* (pp. 112–133). Routledge.

Guo, L., & McCombs, M. E. (2011). *Network agenda setting: A third level of media effects.* Paper presented at the 61st Annual Conference of the International Communication Association.

Guo, L., Vu, H. T., & McCombs, M. E. (2012). An expanded perspective on agenda-setting effects: Exploring the third level of agenda setting. *Revista de Comunicación, 11*(11), 51–68.

Guo, L., & Zhang, Y. (2020). Information flow within and across online media platforms: An agenda-setting analysis of rumor diffusion on news websites, Weibo, and WeChat in China. *Journalism Studies, 21*(15), 2176–2195. https://doi.org/10.1080/1461670X.2020.1827012

Habermas, J., Lennox, S., & Lennox, F. (1974). The public sphere: An encyclopedia article (1964). *New German Critique*(3), 49–55. https://doi.org/10.2307/487737

Hallahan, K. (1999). Seven models of framing: Implications for public relations. *Journal of Public Relations Research, 11*(3), 205–242. https://doi.org/10.1207/s1532754xjprr1103_02

Hallahan, K. (2011). Political public relations and strategic framing. In J. Strömbäck & S. Kiousis (Eds.), *Political public relations: Principles and applications* (pp. 177–212). Routledge.

Harcup, T., & Deirdre, O. N. (2001). What is news? Galtung and Ruge revisited. *Journalism Studies*, *2*(2), 261–280. https://doi.org/10.1080/14616700118449

Harcup, T., & Deirdre, O. N. (2017). What is news? News values revisited (again). *Journalism Studies*, *18*(12), 1470–1488. https://doi.org/10.1080/1461670X.2016.1150193

Holtzhausen, D., & Zerfass, A. (2015). Strategic communication: Opportunities and challenges of the research area. In D. Holtzhausen & A. Zerfass (Eds.), *The Routledge handbook of strategic communication* (pp. 3–17). Routledge.

Ihlen, Ø. (2008). Mapping the environment for corporate social responsibility: Stakeholders, publics and the public sphere. *Corporate Communications: An International Journal*, *13*(2), 135–146. https://doi.org/10.1108/13563280810869578

Kent, M. L., & Taylor, M. (2003). Maximizing media relations: A Web site checklist. *Public Relations Quarterly*, *48*(1), 14–18.

Kim, J. Y., Kiousis, S., & Xiang, Z. (2015). Agenda building and agenda setting in business: Corporate reputation attributes. *Corporate Reputation Review*, *18*(1), 25–36. https://doi.org/10.1057/crr.2014.18

Kiousis, S., Kim, S.-Y., McDevitt, M., & Ostrowski, A. (2009). Competing for attention: Information subsidy influence in agenda building during election campaigns. *Journalism & Mass Communication Quarterly*, *86*(3), 545–562. https://doi.org/10.1177/107769900908600306

Kiousis, S., Popescu, C., & Mitrook, M. (2007). Understanding influence on corporate reputation: An examination of public relations efforts, media coverage, public opinion, and financial performance from an agenda-building and agenda-setting perspective. *Journal of Public Relations Research*, *19*(2), 147–165. https://doi.org/10.1080/10627260701290661

Kiousis, S., & Ragas, M. (2016). Implications of third-level agenda building for public relations and strategic communication. In L. Guo & M. McCombs (Eds.), *The power of information networks: New directions for agenda setting* (pp. 161–174). Routledge.

Kiousis, S., Ragas, M. W., Kim, J. Y., Schweickart, T., Neil, J., & Kochhar, S. (2016). Presidential agenda building and policymaking: Examining linkages across three levels. *International Journal of Strategic Communication*, *10*(1), 1–17. https://doi.org/10.1080/1553118X.2015.1090441

Klandermans, B. (1988). The formation and mobilization of consensus. *Research in Social Movements, Conflicts and Change*, *1*, 173–196.

Lahav, T., & Zimand-Sheiner, D. (2016). Public relations and the practice of paid content: Practical, theoretical propositions and ethical implications. *Public Relations Review*, *42*(3), 395–401. https://doi.org/10.1016/j.pubrev.2016.02.003

Lan, X., Tarasevich, S., Proverbs, P., Myslik, B., & Kiousis, S. (2020). President Trump vs. CEOs: A comparison of presidential and corporate agenda building. *Journal of Public Relations Research*, *32*(1–2), 30–46. https://doi.org/10.1080/1062726X.2020.1719494

Lang, G. E., & Lang, K. (1983). *The battle for public opinion: The president, the press, and the polls during Watergate*. Columbia University Press.

Larsson, L. (2009). PR and the media: A collaborative relationship? *Nordicom Review*, *30*(1), 131–147. https://doi.org/10.1515/nor-2017-0143

Lewin, K. (1947). Frontiers in group dynamics II. Channels of group life: Social planning and action research. *Human Relations*, *1*(2), 143–153. https://doi.org/10.1177/001872674700100201

Lieber, P. S., & Golan, G. J. (2011). Political public relations, news management, and agenda indexing. In J. Strömbäck & S. Kiousis (Eds.), *Political public relations: Principles and applications* (pp. 54–74). Routledge.

Martinelli, R. (2021). *The evolving world of public relations: Beyond the press release.* The Pennsylvania University Press.

McCombs, M. E. (1997a). Building consensus: The news media's agenda-setting roles. *Political Communication, 14*(4), 433–443. https://doi.org/10.1080/105846097199236

McCombs, M. E. (1997b). New frontiers in agenda setting: Agendas of attributes and frames. *Mass Communication Review, 24*(1–2), 32–52.

McCombs, M. E. (2004). *Setting the agenda: The mass media and public opinion.* Polity.

McCombs, M. E., Llamas, J. P., Lopez-Escobar, E., & Rey, F. (1997). Candidate images in Spanish elections: Second-level agenda-setting effects. *Journalism & Mass Communication Quarterly, 74*(4), 703–717. https://doi.org/10.1177/107769909707400404

McCombs, M. E., & Reynolds, A. (2002). News influence on our pictures of the world. In J. Bryant & D. Zillmann (Eds.), *Media effects: Advances in theory and research* (2nd ed., pp. 1–18). Lawrence Erlbaum Associates.

McCombs, M. E., & Shaw, D. L. (1972). The agenda-setting function of mass media. *Public Opinion Quarterly, 36*(2), 176–187. https://doi.org/10.1086/267990

McCombs, M. E., & Shaw, D. L. (1993). The evolution of agenda-setting research: Twenty-five years in the marketplace of ideas. *Journal of Communication, 43*(2), 58–67. https://doi.org/10.1111/j.1460-2466.1993.tb01262.x

McQuail, D. (2010). *McQuail's mass communication theory* (6th ed.). Sage.

Meijer, M. M., & Kleinnijenhuis, J. (2006). Issue news and corporate reputation: Applying the theories of agenda setting and issue ownership in the field of business communication. *Journal of Communication, 56*(3), 543–559. https://doi.org/10.1111/j.1460-2466.2006.00300.x

Meraz, S. (2009). Is there an elite hold? Traditional media to social media agenda setting influence in blog networks. *Journal of Computer-Mediated Communication, 14*(3), 682–707. https://doi.org/10.1111/j.1083-6101.2009.01458.x

Morton, L. P., & Warren, J. (1992). News elements and editors' choices. *Public Relations Review, 18*(1), 47–52. https://doi.org/10.1016/0363-8111(92)90020-Y

Neijens, P., & Smit, E. (2006). Dutch public relations practitioners and journalists: Antagonists no more. *Public Relations Review, 32*(3), 232–240. https://doi.org/10.1016/j.pubrev.2006.05.015

Nicolai, R. R., & Riley, S. G. (1972). The gatekeeping function from the point of view of the PR man. *Journalism Quarterly, 49*(2), 371–373. https://doi.org/10.1177/107769907204900222

Obermaier, M., Koch, T., & Riesmeyer, C. (2018). Deep impact? How journalists perceive the influence of public relations on their news coverage and which variables determine this impact. *Communication Research, 45*(7), 1031–1053. https://doi.org/10.1177/0093650215617505

O'Keefe, D. J., & Jensen, J. D. (2007). The relative persuasiveness of gain-framed loss-framed messages for encouraging disease prevention behaviors: A meta-analytic review. *Journal of Health Communication, 12*(7), 623–644. https://doi.org/10.1080/10810730701615198

Pan, Z., & Kosicki, G. M. (1993). Framing analysis: An approach to news discourse. *Political Communication, 10*(1), 55–75. https://doi.org/10.1080/10584609.1993.9962963

Pang, A. (2010). Mediating the media: A journalist-centric media relations model. *Corporate Communications: An International Journal, 15*(2), 192–204. https://doi.org/10.1108/13563281011037955

Parmelee, J. H. (2014). The agenda-building function of political tweets. *New Media & Society, 16*(3), 434–450. https://doi.org/10.1177/1461444813487955

Perloff, R. M. (2017). *The dynamics of political communication: Media and politics in a digital age* (2nd ed.). Routledge.

Pharr, S. J., & Krauss, E. S. (1996). *Media and politics in Japan.* University of Hawai'i Press.

Potter, W. J. (2011). Conceptualizing mass media effect. *Journal of Communication, 61*(5), 896–915. https://doi.org/10.1111/j.1460-2466.2011.01586.x

Powers, A., & Fico, F. (1994). Influences on use of sources at large US newspapers. *Newspaper Research Journal, 15*(4), 87–97. https://doi.org/10.1177/073953299401500410

Ragas, M. W. (2012). Issue and stakeholder intercandidate agenda setting among corporate information subsidies. *Journalism & Mass Communication Quarterly, 89*(1), 91–111. https://doi.org/10.1177/1077699011430063

Ragas, M. W. (2013a). Agenda building during activist shareholder campaigns. *Public Relations Review, 39*(3), 219–221. https://doi.org/10.1016/j.pubrev.2013.03.007

Ragas, M. W. (2013b). Agenda-building and agenda-setting theory: Which companies we think about and how we think about them. In C. E. Carroll (Ed.), *The handbook of communication and corporate reputation* (pp. 151–165). John Wiley & Sons.

Ragas, M. W., & Kiousis, S. (2010). Intermedia agenda-setting and political activism: MoveOn. org and the 2008 presidential election. *Mass Communication and Society, 13*(5), 560–583. https://doi.org/10.1080/15205436.2010.515372

Raupp, J. (2017). Public relations: Media effects. In P. Rössler, C. A. Hoffner, & L. van Zoonen (Eds.), *The international encyclopedia of media effects* (pp. 1–9). John Wiley & Sons, Inc.

Reese, S. D. (1991). Setting the media's agenda: A power balance perspective. *Annals of the International Communication Association, 14*(1), 309–340. https://doi.org/10.1080/23808985.1991.11678793

Reese, S. D. (2001). Understanding the global journalist: A hierarchy-of-influences approach. *Journalism Studies, 2*(2), 173–187. https://doi.org/10.1080/14616700118394

Reese, S. D. (2019). Hierarchy of influences. In T. P. Vos, F. Hanusch, D. Dimitrakopoulou, M. Geertsema-Sligh, & A. Sehl (Eds.), *The international encyclopedia of journalism studies* (pp. 1–5). John Wiley & Sons.

Reese, S. D., & Ballinger, J. (2001). The roots of a sociology of news: Remembering Mr. Gates and social control in the newsroom. *Journalism & Mass Communication Quarterly, 78*(4), 641–658. https://doi.org/10.1177/107769900107800402

Reese, S. D., Gandy, J. O. H., & Grant, A. E. (2001). *Framing public life: Perspectives on media and our understanding of the social world* (3rd ed.). Lawrence Erlbaum Associates.

Reese, S. D., & Shoemaker, P. J. (2016). A media sociology for the networked public sphere: The hierarchy of influences model. *Mass Communication and Society, 19*(4), 389–410. https://doi.org/10.1080/15205436.2016.1174268

Reich, Z. (2011). Source credibility and journalism: Between visceral and discretional judgment. *Journalism Practice, 5*(1), 51–67. https://doi.org/10.1080/17512781003760519

Rogers, E. M., & Dearing, J. W. (1988). Agenda-setting research: Where has it been, where is it going? In J. Anderson (Ed.), *Communication yearbook 11* (pp. 555–593). Sage.

Ryan, M. (2013). Media relations. In R. L. Heath (Ed.), *Encyclopedia of public relations* (2nd ed.). Sage.

Ryan, M., & Martinson, D. L. (1988). Journalists and public relations practitioners: Why the antagonism? *Journalism Quarterly, 65*(1), 131–140. https://doi.org/10.1177/107769908806500118

Saffer, A. (2013). *Intermedia agenda building of the blogosphere: Public relations role in the network.* Institute of Public Relations. https://instituteforpr.org/wp-content/uploads/Intermedia-Agenda-Building-of-the-Blogosphere-FINAL.pdf

Sallot, L. M. (1990). *Public relations and mass media: How professionals in the fields in Miami and New York view public relations effects on mass media, themselves, and each other.* Paper presented at the Paper presented at the annual meeting of the Association for Education in Journalism and Mass Communication.

Scheufele, D. A. (1999). Framing as a theory of media effects. *Journal of Communication, 49*(1), 103–122. https://doi.org/10.1111/j.1460-2466.1999.tb02784.x

Schmierbach, M., McCombs, M., Valenzuela, S., Dearing, J. W., Guo, L., Iyengar, S., Kiousis, S., Kosicki, G. M., Meraz, S., & Scheufele, D. A. (2022). Reflections on a legacy: Thoughts from scholars about agenda-setting past and future. *Mass Communication and Society, 25*(4), 500–527. https://doi.org/10.1080/15205436.2022.2067725

Schultz, I. (2007). The journalistic gut feeling: Journalistic doxa, news habitus and orthodox news values. *Journalism Practice, 1*(2), 190–207. https://doi.org/10.1080/17512780701275507

Schweickart, T., Neil, J., Kim, J. Y., & Kiousis, S. (2016). Time-lag analysis of the agenda-building process between White House public relations and congressional policymaking activity. *Journal of Communication Management, 20*(4), 363–380. https://doi.org/10.1108/JCOM-01-2016-0001

Shaw, T., & White, C. (2004). Public relations and journalism educators' perceptions of media relations. *Public Relations Review, 30*(4), 493–502. https://doi.org/10.1016/j.pubrev.2004.08.004

Shin, J.-H., & Cameron, G. T. (2003). The interplay of professional and cultural factors in the online source-reporter relationship. *Journalism Studies, 4*(2), 253–272. https://doi.org/10.1080/1461670032000074829a

Shoemaker, P. J. (1991). *Gatekeeping: Communication concepts 3.* Sage.

Shoemaker, P. J., & Reese, S. D. (1996). *Mediating the message* (2nd ed.). Longman.

Shoemaker, P. J., & Reese, S. D. (2014). *Mediating the message in the 21st century: A media sociology perspective.* Routledge.

Sommerfeldt, E. J. (2013). The civility of social capital: Public relations in the public sphere, civil society, and democracy. *Public Relations Review, 39*(4), 280–289. https://doi.org/10.1016/j.pubrev.2012.12.004

Sriramesh, K., Kim, Y., & Takasaki, M. (1999). Public relations in three Asian cultures: An analysis. *Journal of Public Relations Research, 11*(4), 271–292. https://doi.org/10.1207/s1532754xjprr1104_01

Sterne, G. D. (2010). Media perceptions of public relations in New Zealand. *Journal of Communication Management, 4*(1), 4–31. https://doi.org/10.1108/13632541011017780

Supa, D. W. (2014, September 17). *The academic inquiry of media relations as both a tactical and strategic function of public relations.* Institute for Public Relations. https://instituteforpr.org/academic-inquiry-media-relations-tactical-strategic-function-public-relations/

Supa, D. W., & Zoch, L. M. (2009). Maximizing media relations through a better understanding of the public relations-journalist relationship. *Public Relations Journal, 3*(4), 1–28.

Sweet, M., Pearson, L., & Dudgeon, P. (2013). @IndigenousX: A case study of community-led innovation in digital media. *Media International Australia, 149*(1), 104–111. https://doi.org/10.1177/1329878X1314900112

Taylor, M. (2000). Media relations in Bosnia: A role for public relations in building civil society. *Public Relations Review, 26*(1), 1–14. https://doi.org/10.1016/S0363-8111(99)00026-0

Taylor, M. (2009a). Civil society and rhetorical public relations process. In R. L. Heath, E. L. Toth, & D. Waymer (Eds.), *Rhetorical and critical approaches to public relations II* (pp. 76–91). Routledge.

Taylor, M. (2009b). Protocol journalism as a framework for understanding public relations–media relationships in Kosovo. *Public Relations Review, 35*(1), 23–30. https://doi.org/10.1016/j.pubrev.2008.12.002

Tewksbury, D., & Scheufele, D. A. (2009). News framing theory and research. In J. Bryant & M. B. Oliver (Eds.), *Media effects: Advances in theory and research* (3rd ed., pp. 17–33). Routledge.

Thompson, G. (2020). *Post-truth public relations: Communication in an era of digital disinformation*. Routledge.

Verčič, D., & Verčič, A. T. (2016). The new publicity: From reflexive to reflective mediatisation. *Public Relations Review, 42*(4), 493–498. https://doi.org/10.1016/j.pubrev.2015.07.008

Vogler, D., & Eisenegger, M. (2020). CSR communication, corporate reputation, and the role of the news media as an agenda-setter in the digital age. *Business & Society*, 1–30. https://doi.org/10.1177/0007650320928969

Walters, L. M., & Walters, T. N. (1992). Environment of confidence: Daily newspaper use of press releases. *Public Relations Review, 18*(1), 31–46. https://doi.org/10.1016/0363-8111(92)90019-U

Wanta, W., & Foote, J. (1994). The president-news media relationship: A time series analysis of agenda-setting. *Journal of Broadcasting & Electronic Media, 38*(4), 437–448. https://doi.org/10.1080/08838159409364277

Waters, R. D. (2013). Tracing the impact of media relations and television coverage on US charitable relief fundraising: An application of agenda-setting theory across three natural disasters. *Journal of Public Relations Research, 25*(4), 329–346. https://doi.org/10.1080/1062726X.2013.806870

Waters, R. D., Tindall, N. T., & Morton, T. S. (2010). Media catching and the journalist–public relations practitioner relationship: How social media are changing the practice of media relations. *Journal of Public Relations Research, 22*(3), 241–264. https://doi.org/10.1080/10627261003799202

Weaver, D., & Elliott, S. N. (1985). Who sets the agenda for the media? A study of local agenda-building. *Journalism Quarterly, 62*(1), 87–94. https://doi.org/10.1177/107769908506200113

Wells, B., & Spinks, N. (1999). Media relations: Powerful tools for achieving service quality. *Managing Service Quality: An International Journal, 9*(4), 246–256. https://doi.org/10.1108/09604529910273193

Wenger, D., & Quarantelli, E. L. (1989). *Report series #19: Local mass media operations, problems and products in disasters*. University of Delaware Disaster Research Center.

White, D. M. (1950). The "gate keeper": A case study in the selection of news. *Journalism Quarterly, 27*(4), 383–390. https://doi.org/10.1177/107769905002700403

White, J. M., & Wingenbach, G. (2013). Potential barriers to mass media coverage of health issues: Differences between public information officers and journalists regarding beliefs central to professional behaviors. *Journal of Public Relations Research, 25*(2), 123–140. https://doi.org/10.1080/1062726X.2013.758582

Wilcox, D. L., Cameron, G. T., & Reber, B. H. (2015). *Public relations: Strategies and tactics* (11th ed.). Pearson Education, Inc.

Wu, M.-Y. (2011). Comparing media relations in Japan, South Korea, Taiwan, and the United States: A metaresearch analysis. *China Media Research, 7*(1), 5–16.

Yang, A., Taylor, M., & Saffer, A. J. (2016). Ethical convergence, divergence or communitas? An examination of public relations and journalism codes of ethics. *Public Relations Review*, *42*(1), 146–160. https://doi.org/10.1016/j.pubrev.2015.08.001

Zerfass, A., & Schramm, D. M. (2014). Social media newsrooms in public relations: A conceptual framework and corporate practices in three countries. *Public Relations Review*, *40*(1), 79–91. https://doi.org/10.1016/j.pubrev.2013.12.003

Zerfass, A., Verčič, D., & Wiesenberg, M. (2016). The dawn of a new golden age for media relations?: How PR professionals interact with the mass media and use new collaboration practices. *Public Relations Review*, *42*(4), 499–508. https://doi.org/10.1016/j.pubrev.2016.03.005

Zhang, T., Kim, J. Y., Schweickart, T., Myslik, B. A., Khalitova, L., Golan, G. J., & Kiousis, S. (2017). Agenda-Building role of state-owned media around the world: 2014 Hong Kong protest case. *Journal of Public Relations Research*, 1–17. https://doi.org/10.1080/1062726X.2017.1396988

Zoch, L. M., & Molleda, J.-C. (2006). Building a theoretical model of media relations using framing, information subsidies, and agenda-building. In C. H. Botan & V. Hazleton (Eds.), *Public relations theory II* (pp. 279–309). Lawrence Erlbaum Associates.

Zoch, L. M., & Supa, D. W. (2014). Dictating the news: Understanding newsworthiness from the journalistic perspective. *Public Relations Journal*, *8*(1), 1–28.

Zoch, L. M., Supa, D. W., & VanTuyll, D. R. (2014). The portrayal of public relations in the era of Ivy Lee through the lens of the New York Times. *Public Relations Review*, *40*(4), 723–732. https://doi.org/10.1016/j.pubrev.2014.02.002

26 The Implications of Character Assassination and Cancel Culture for Public Relations Theory

Sergei A. Samoilenko and James M. Jasper

Introduction

Because public relations theory needs to understand how value-driven social changes and new technologies affect the development of new practices, it requires new epistemologies. Public relations theory should take a closer look at the reputational challenges posed by character assassination campaigns and cancellation strategies, the former of which is being facilitated by a new generation of manipulated media and the latter of which is being driven by the increased expectations of diverse cross-cultural publics. This chapter thus introduces two innovative concepts—*character assassination* and *cancel culture* (cancellation)—to public relations theory.

Character assassination (CA) is a strategic effort to discredit an individual or group target via subversive communication (Samoilenko, 2021a; Samoilenko et al., 2020; Shiraev et al., 2022). Changes in the capacity and use of new information technologies have created new forms of disinformation smear campaigns that employ altered imagery, deepfakes, and other manipulated media generated by artificial intelligence (AI). AI-generated media are the quintessential compromising imagery, commonly used to destroy reputations by exploiting the topics of inappropriate behavior, sex (adultery), drug usage, and age-related incompetency (Samoilenko & Suvorova, 2023). Moreover, AI can be weaponized in malicious political and ideological contests to blackmail a target, engage in trolling, or exert pressure on whistleblowers and investigative journalists (India Today, 2018).

Cancel culture (CC) emerged in the United States and other Western post-industrial societies, seeking social change in line with liberal perspectives on sexual and gender identities, family structures, racial justice, and related topics (Norris & Inglehart, 2019; Norris, 2021). But canceling has been used just as often by rightwing groups trying to silence their ideological opponents (Pascale, 2019). In the United States, there are two popular views of CC: it is perceived either as a way to promote social justice or as a social media mobbing practice used to censor and punish dissenting voices (Vogels et al., 2021). CC is enacted via different cancellation strategies, including public shaming, deplatforming, and doxing. Such strategies

DOI: 10.4324/9781003141396-30

are commonly used by activist groups to put pressure on policymakers and corporate brands.

Both CA and cancellation practices have been brought to prominence by the rise of digital activism linked to the ongoing value-driven conflicts in Western societies. Today, organizations and corporate brands are under constant pressure to respond to emergent social, political, and environmental issues (Proulx, 2021; Swant, 2021). They often risk cancellation in the form of shaming and boycott for failing to articulate their position on current events or to take a political stand in a timely manner (Bakhtiari, 2020; Pietsch, 2022). As noted by Coombs and Holladay (2020), stakeholders can even push management to change their behavior by threatening to harm the corporate image of their company. Amid the ongoing Russia-Ukraine war, for example, pressure from public opinion and shaming strategies applied by political strategists and digital activists—among other factors— have prompted many Western companies to suspend operations in Russia (Satariano, 2022).

This chapter engages in a comprehensive discussion of CA and CC, explaining their implications for strategic communication, issues management, crisis communication, and reputation management. It concludes by advocating for a paradigmatic shift toward more culture-sensitive and humanistic perspectives of public relations in the context of recent technological developments and the growing role of networked online communities and digital activism.

Character Assassination

On the Concept

Award-winning Indian journalist Rana Ayyub became a target of CA after she spoke to the BBC and Al Jazeera about how India was bringing shame on itself by protecting those who sexually abuse children. The campaign against her started with a series of fake tweets, edited to appear as though they had come from her verified Twitter account, that made such statements as "I hate India," "I hate Indians," and "I love Pakistan." After that, her personal details were made public and a deepfake pornographic video, showing a naked woman whose face had been replaced with Ayyub's headshot, was released on WhatsApp. The information campaign targeting Ayyub resulted in a lynch mob against her in India (Ayyub, 2018).

Character assassination (CA) refers to the deliberate destruction of reputation through character attacks (Icks & Shiraev, 2014). It is understood as both the process of communication and the outcome of this process (e.g., a damaged reputation). Character attacks can take various forms, including verbal assaults, rumors, negative campaign ads, cartoons, and tweets. The concept was originally used to describe political smear campaigns and negative ads that targeted opponents. For example, during the 2004 presidential campaign, John Kerry's heroism as a Swift Boat commander during the Vietnam War was questioned by a group of Vietnam U.S. Navy veterans and former prisoners of war. The group produced a series of television ads and a book, *Unfit for Command*, to discredit Kerry's military record and condemn his subsequent antiwar activities; their efforts contributed to his defeat in the presidential election (Seiter & Gass, 2010).

Subversive rhetoric is argued to be among the fundamental motivations for human interaction (Fisher, 1970). Character attacks are inherent to polemics in liberal democracies (Walton, 1999) and instrumental to achieving goals and winning political contests (Benoit et al., 2007). Benoit (2020) considers a persuasive attack on character to be relevant when it exposes wrongdoing, informs voters, or influences consumer decisions.

Essentially, *character* is a matter of public perception. It is a public image of accepted ethical standards and social functions assigned to a public figure by public opinion at a given point of time (Walton, 1999). Character is also a moral profile that the environment demands at present (Bruner, 1990). Importantly, a character attack is a persuasive attack targeting public opinion (Benoit, 2020). CA aims to alter the way character is perceived and judged by others. A noticeable public attack on the moral standing of a political or corporate leader inevitably triggers social evaluation and a judgment of the individual's reputation. When someone's reputation comes under attack, audiences may change their opinion about the target regardless of whether the allegations are true or false. The perception of character is thus a subjective knowledge structure (Boulding, 1973) that is discussed and agreed upon by different interpretive communities. Next, we will discuss three cardinal perspectives on CA.

Theoretical Perspectives on CA

There are three main perspectives on CA. These are embodied in the rhetorical (Benoit & Glantz, 2017; Benoit & Stein, 2021; Keohane, 2020), sociopsychological (Shiraev, 2014), and sociocultural traditions (Samoilenko, 2020b, 2021a), respectively.

Rhetoricians and argumentation scholars classify character attacks as a form of *ad hominem* argument that is perceived as either a logical fallacy (Copi, 1961) or a rhetorical strategy (van Eemeren, 2010). The distinction is that the latter perspective considers that there are certain contexts where it is both effective and appropriate to deploy such attacks (Benoit, 2017; Walton, 1998).

Political psychologists study the motivations of the so-called "pragmatic attacker" and the reasons why an attacker chooses certain strategies. They have found that CA can be an effective means of creating uncertainty among voters (Skaperdas & Grofman, 1995) or swaying undecided voters during an election cycle (Sigelman & Shiraev, 2002). Psychological research also studies the ways in which audiences process information about targets and react to character attacks and scandals (Shiraev, 2014).

The sociocultural perspective takes issue with the rhetorical and psychological perspectives, arguing that their functional view of CA often disregards scenarios of mutual influence, where multiple actors engage simultaneously in attack and defense (Samoilenko, 2020b). Hence, these perspectives are often unable to capture the transactional complexity of character attacks and responses. The sociocultural perspective fills the gaps left by the functional views by addressing issues and events in the context of intergroup or institutional logic and explain the history of relationships between attackers, targets, and their multiple audiences.

Lately, CA has been conceptually linked to a number of social theories, including persuasive attack theory (Benoit, 2017), systems theory (Samoilenko, 2020a), structuration theory (Samoilenko, 2020b), root theory (Simmons, 2021), and the cocreational model (Samoilenko, 2021b). Social scientists have discussed CA in connection with stigma communication (Smith & Eberly, 2021), public shaming (Stephenson, 2021), face and impression management (Samoilenko, 2020a), Burke's approach to framing (Schumacher-Rutherford & Muddiman, 2021), and Bourdieu's field theory (Samoilenko, 2020b).

CA is an emergent topic in public relations research. Scholars have investigated the use of character attacks as framing strategies in geopolitical conflicts (Samoilenko et al., 2017), the attacks on corporate CEOs traits during corporate crises (Seiffert-Brockmann et al., 2018), and the application of inoculation strategies against character attacks (Compton et al., 2021). Originally, the term *character assassination* was applied to individuals (Icks & Shiraev, 2014). Later contributions argued for a more inclusive use of CA and applied it in a broader way to collectives such as corporations (Coombs & Holladay, 2020) and even nations (Aspriadis et al., 2020). Next, we examine five constituent elements of reputational attacks, illuminating their complexity.

CA Typology and Methods

CA scholars consider how attacker, target, audience, media, and context interact to determine the effectiveness and longevity of attacks (Icks et al., 2020). These puzzle pieces are usually discussed together when assessing the probability of reputational crisis and public outrage following a character attack.

The Attacker

The character attacker aims to trigger a public reaction and thereby undermine the social standing of the subject. An attacker may act out of sheer malice or because they want to exact revenge for an injustice. In most cases, however, the destruction of a target's reputation is itself a means of achieving a strategic goal, such as the elimination of a rival in a power contest or the improvement of the attacker's own chances of success. A character attack can be an effective means of alarming voters (Riker, 1996) or preventing defections (Doron & On, 1983). Political actors also employ character attacks to force a target to expend time, energy, and resources on responding, as well as to divert the public's attention from a debated issue or to promote the attacker's agenda at the target's expense (Shiraev, 2014).

The Target

A CA target is typically a prominent individual who has achieved high social status, fame, or some other form of public recognition. Attackers may attack a target's personality, status or affiliation, past behavior and statements, and current beliefs and views. The outcome of a CA attempt is generally observed as damage to the target's reputation (Helm, 2005). The impact of a precarious issue or risk on reputation is assessed in terms of declining confidence in leadership, erosion of public trust, and other tangible and intangible losses (Coombs, 2019). This may result not only in damage to the target's public standing, but also in his or her loss of social capital, or the "network of more or less institutionalized relationships of mutual acquaintance and recognition" (Bourdieu & Wacquant, 1992, p. 119). It should be noted that attacks on individuals and organizations are often intertwined, as organizations and even nations are often personified by—and perceived through—the public image of their leaders (Simons, 2020). Character attacks on individuals and groups may overlap when individuals are targeted because they represent a particular ideology or cause.

The Medium/Media

It is critical to understand the role of both traditional and social media in situations involving CA. Today's media provide a hospitable environment for CA, which is amplified by the negative effects of mediatization, such as content simplification, personalization, and the production of click-bait content favoring conflict and negativity (Downey & Stanyer, 2013; Esser & Matthes, 2013). In the United States, the development of niche media, cable news with attitude (like Fox News and MSNBC), tabloid journalism, and television entertainment with a person-centered focus have normalized personal ridicule and justified character attacks on political actors (Lichter & Farnsworth, 2020). Social media help promote misperceptions about public figures during political campaigns (Garrett, 2019), serving to scale up calculated *reputational warfare* strategies online (Rosamond, 2020).

The Audience

Public opinion is crucial in CA-related scenarios, as a target's reputation is damaged when various publics see it that way, regardless of the truth and relevance of the allegations. In political contexts, uncivil and relevant negative messages are the most powerful (Fridkin & Kenney, 2011). Receptiveness to such messages is associated with one's level of political knowledge, trust in government, and gender or related personal factors (Sigelman & Kugler, 2003). Under the cocreational model, a public is understood as an "interpretative community" engaged in a process of developing a shared understanding of its relationship with a group or organization (Botan, 2018, p. 59). Publics have agency to attend to or ignore the attacker's allegations, as well as to take sides and actively participate in online discussions, thereby cocreating the course and outcomes of initial CA campaigns (Samoilenko, 2021b).

The Context

Character attacks take place in political, social, and cultural contexts that are characterized by social norms, cultural traditions, and embedded moral codes (Poushter, 2014). In the United States, there is an ideological divide between the two main political parties as to what is offensive or morally acceptable (Schaffer, 2021). It also matters to what extent potential targets are protected by libel and slander laws. For example, "Right to be Forgotten" legislation, in force mainly in the European Union, allows individuals to shield their online browser histories from search engines (Brock, 2016). Introducing such a law in the United States, meanwhile, could be considered to infringe on the free flow of information. Similarly, character attacks launched in different historical epochs feature different moral and cultural standards (Icks & Shiraev, 2014).

The types and methods of character attacks include: a) anonymous lies and other deception strategies, b) well-timed revelations of embarrassing facts, c) deliberate misquoting and quoting out of context (including the use of unfortunate photographs), d) silencing a target by denying them the opportunity to respond to allegations, e) erasing from public memory by eliminating any record of good deeds and achievements, and f) name-calling and other forms of stigmatized labeling (via nicknames, demonization, ridiculing memes, etc.). The latter category includes attaching labels of mental illness or sexual deviance (Icks & Shiraev, 2014; Samoilenko, 2016).

Scholars have tested this typology or referred to it in their studies of television news containing character attacks in the context of geopolitical conflict (Samoilenko et al. 2017); Internet memes about political candidates prior to the 2016 U.S. presidential election (Seiffert-Brockmann, 2020); Donald Trump's strategic use of nicknames (Johnson, 2021); and populist Italian politician Matteo Salvini's social media communication (Berti & Loner, 2021). The scholars who first elaborated this typology later revised it (see Samoilenko, 2016, 2020a; Shiraev et al., 2022). Icks et al. (2020) expanded on the original work by classifying character attacks based on their scope, timing, momentum, direction, and opacity. Shiraev et al. (2022) identified three cardinal CA media strategies: provocation, contamination, and obliteration. These strategies seek to seek to produce highly mediated scandals, spread falsehoods, or purge the public memory of the target's accomplishments.

CA accompanies political and social conflicts, especially when unresolved ideological and moral issues are involved. According to moral conflict theory (Pearce & Littlejohn, 1997), ideological conflicts become aggravated when incommensurate values mix with political and economic factors and become entrenched in debates around critical social issues (e.g., abortion, gun control, climate change, etc.). Factions then resort to character attacks to invalidate arguments and delegitimize their opponents. Such behavior is emblematic of *cancel culture*, a social trend that was brought to prominence by Twitter activists of the social movement campaigns #MeToo and #BlackLivesMatter.

Cancel Culture and Cancellation Strategies

In October 2017, newspapers reported that several women had accused Harvey Weinstein, the famous film producer who co-founded the entertainment company Miramax, of sexual harassment, assault, and rape. The allegations were soon supported by the testimonies of other women in the film industry who had had similar experiences with Weinstein. In less than two weeks, Weinstein went from being the most powerful Hollywood mogul to being dismissed from his own company, rejected by his wife, and expelled from the Motion Picture Academy and the board of directors of the Producers Guild of America. The #MeToo campaign provoked the "Weinstein Effect," a global movement denouncing misogynic behavior and sexual harassment and holding certain powerful male figures to account (NPR, 2017).

Cancel Culture as Social Trend

Cancel culture (CC) is an extreme form of character assassination, in which efforts are made not only to criticize and stigmatize the target but at the same time to exclude them from public media arenas. It was brought to prominence by the viral hashtag campaigns #MeToo and #BlackLivesMatter, both of which called for social justice and strived to mobilize supporters around a fundamental social issue: sexual abuse and racism, respectively. The #MeToo movement has had a particular impact on global society, increasing awareness of sexual harassment in the workplace and prompting thousands of organizations to adopt harassment policies and enhance employee harassment training (Boyle & Cucchiara, 2018).

Some see CC as an effective method of social justice because it involves the public shaming and subsequent humiliation of individuals who have—in the eyes of public opinion—committed a moral transgression. CC critics indicate that, in addition to public embarrassment, publicly shamed individuals may be excluded from their professional and social circles and lose the ability to support their families (Mishan, 2020).

CC is often compared to the traditional practice of boycotting, or the withdrawal from any relations with someone as a punishment or protest. The latter may include the refusal to vote for corrupt politicians or use certain corporate goods and services in protest of their political or corporate wrongdoing. Although most boycotts aim to reduce demand for a company's product, they may have a larger impact on that company's reputation as one strategic player after another joins the boycott (Jasper, 1997, chapter 11; Seidman, 2015). CC, however, is not merely about ceasing to listen to a toxic person or distancing oneself from an offensive social behavior. It involves destroying a target psychologically, delegitimizing them socially, and silencing them.

Cancellation Strategies

In both democratic and authoritarian societies, the imposition and regulation of moral standards is often outsourced to moral crusaders and entrepreneurs (Eder, 1985). Research has linked the use of CC strategies to the actions of networked activists (Bouvier & Machin, 2021; Felaco et al., 2022). Indeed, Norris (2021) defines CC as "collective strategies by activists using social pressures to achieve cultural ostracism of targets (someone or something) accused of offensive words or deeds" (p. 4). Reeves and Ingraham (2020), however, argue that moral surveillance and policing are not a grassroots practice so much as a political technology used to manage others' conduct by marginalizing certain forms of behavior. In any case, while the notion of CC might be new, its methods of social pressure, stigmatization, and ostracism have been employed for centuries (Smith & Eberly, 2021).

The cancellation process has two phases: *calling out* and *canceling*. The *first* phase starts with public callouts and online criticism to raise public awareness of someone's socially unacceptable actions. Edwards (2022) describes canceling out as a form of public humiliation that involves "publicly identifying something that someone has said or done that is wrong" (p. 16). The author compares public callouts to a public performance "where people can demonstrate their wit or resentment" (p. 16). Ultimately, calling out can be seen as a simple form of *ad hominem* attack on character (Walton, 1998).

The *second* phase, canceling, goes further, asking that a "called out" person or behavior be punished. Importantly, canceling is a rhetorical technique used by rightwing as well as leftwing groups. It does not always succeed, especially when targets can mobilize their own supporters to demonize the accusers in turn (Brown et al., 2020). Canceling is enacted via two key strategies: public shaming and silencing.

Public shaming is a form of punishment, the main feature of which is humiliating and disgracing a person (Norlock, 2017). Many problems have obvious victims, especially environmental degradation and climate change, but the villains are less apparent. Activists therefore engage in "naming and shaming" to draw attention to problems by creating villains who are responsible for them (Seidman, 2016). This can include trying to prove which corporation caused an issue like pollution. Activists may also seek to shame big companies for such behavior as working with suppliers who use child labor or threatening natural resources through their mining activities. Shaming mobilizes members of the community to unite in righteous anger against the shamed person and expose collective representations of right and wrong (Stephenson, 2021). It works best against companies that care about their reputations, usually those that sell products directly to the public rather than to other companies.

Today, activists may organize Twitter hashtag campaigns to cancel people "who wouldn't otherwise be brought to justice because they are protected by their wealth, power or privilege" (Edwards, 2022, p. 12). They seek to bring social pressure to bear on individuals for their morally offensive actions and delegitimize views, perspectives, and conventions deemed to represent sexist, racist, patriarchal, or hegemonic values. Publicly accused and shamed persons are often excluded from their social or professional circles, and even dismissed from their positions.

Silencing is a strategy aimed at preventing an individual from expressing and defending an unpopular view. Popular methods of silencing include deplatforming and doxing. *Deplatforming* refers to the practice of blocking— or attempting to block—an individual from speaking because of their moral or political views by taking away their platform, which may include speaking venues or websites (Simpson & Srinivasan, 2018). *Doxing* refers to disclosing and posting online private or identifying information with the goal of ruining a target's reputation, getting a target dismissed from his or her job, etc. This crowdsourced grassroots practice often uses a combination of human and artificial intelligence to search for and publish the name, phone numbers, email addresses, physical addresses, photos, and affiliations of a target (Shen, 2017).

Social media, particularly Twitter and Instagram, allow like-minded activist networks to mobilize and conceive new strategies within gated communities and echo chambers (Wanless & Berk, 2021). Online tweets are amplified via traditional news media, including journalists, commentators, and other opinion leaders (Marwick & Lewis, 2017). Moral outrage in the form of anger, contempt, and disgust is the driving force behind cancellation campaigns (Ginther et al., 2021). Outrage discourse provokes highly emotional responses from social media followers in the form of anger, disappointment, or a sense of moral righteousness.

Recent studies demonstrate that activists' strategies have been successfully appropriated by state and corporate agencies, which use astroturfing to promote their business and ideological products (Keller et al., 2020). In such scenarios, digital communications that elicit outrage discourse may strengthen the agendas and ideologies of governments and lobbying groups.

The Relationship Between CA and CC

There are obvious similarities between CA and cancellation strategies. While attacks on character are present at the initial stage of CC campaigns, the cancellation process represents a more uncompromising form of *character work* (Jasper et al., 2020). This is designed to establish the essence of an individual or group—or the natural consequence of doing so—and apply various forms of psychological pressure and coercion to mark and stigmatize the target before banning it from the interpretative community, thereby denying its agency as "the narrative being" (Fisher, 1984).

All strategic rhetoric involves the construction of character tropes: heroes whom we admire and support, victims whom we pity, minions whom we ridicule. Cancellation strategies focus on a fourth character: villains (Jasper et al., 2020). The logic of cancellation, like much CA, calls for instantaneous consequences on the grounds that the target is too evil to be allowed to remain in an organization or public sphere. Even though there may be a door left open for their redemption and conversion, they must be seen as so powerful and so threatening that it is urgent to mobilize against them. Cancellation is a powerful technique precisely because punishment is imposed before the person's character can be fully assessed.

Character work has always been the essence of protest activism (Jasper et al., 2018). There must be acknowledged victims to establish the existence of a social problem. Identifying a villain, meanwhile, helps to arouse indignation. The heroes are usually implicit: elected politicians and social movements typically compete for credit, sometimes alongside journalists, who see themselves as heroic crusaders. There are often strategic dichotomies to be navigated, such as how movements can take advantage of the compassion due to victims while still projecting the strength needed to be full citizens and successful protestors (Jasper, 2014).

Established social-movement organizations devote considerable effort to their choice of targets and accusations against them (even if they are not above exaggerations and distortions for rhetorical effect), while individuals on social media often forgo such research. The two processes seem to produce different targets: activist groups target organizations such as government units or corporations, while individuals on social media go after other individuals. Mistakes are easier to make in the latter case, which is perhaps one reason that many are uneasy with CC.

In an age of social media, political and corporate leaders are becoming increasingly susceptible to scandals and reputational crises due to increased visibility, the 24/7 news cycle, and the speed of unfolding events (Rivera & Karlsson, 2017). Corporations and their leaders are increasingly expected to change with the zeitgeist of a generation and follow new trends in transparency and accountability (Holland & Salvo, 2012). More than ever before, they are called upon to take stances on issues related to the environment, human rights, gender, and politics (George-Parkin, 2019). These factors interfere with traditional crisis management strategies, making it harder for organizations to control for reputational risks.

Implications for Public Relations

The concepts of character assignation and cancel culture enrich public relations theory by offering valuable insights for the areas of strategic communication, issues management, crisis communication, and reputation management.

First, the sociocultural perspective of CA underscores the importance of the *cocreational model of strategic communication,* which explains the socially constructed nature of contemporary strategic communication campaigns (Botan, 2018; Samoilenko, 2021b). This approach sees CA as being socially constructed through interactions between multiple interpretive communities across multiple contexts and digital platforms. Contemporary subversive campaigns are strategic enterprises that involve journalists, bloggers, activist groups, competitors, and other active investors based on their capacity to amplify the effects of destructive messages. This conceptual marriage helps us better understand how strategic attackers seek to influence public opinion and persuade members of different interpretive communities to side with them in their transgressional efforts. Importantly, this perspective argues that publics have agency to act independently and are the primary determinants of whose reputation deserves disgracing and ostracism.

Second, CA and CC research has implications for developing new approaches to *issues management* to the extent that it focuses on the causes and effects of moral outrage in response to issues, events, and conversations concerning gender, race, identity, and other relevant topics. There is a growing trend of corporate CEOs taking a stand on political issues and speaking on matters affecting society (Schaeffer, 2019). However, a corporate response that misses the mark can tarnish a company's image for years. In the context of CC, issues management is critical because it involves proactive attempts to identify and resolve high-priority issues that present imminent challenges to organizations (Heath, 2018; Xiong et al., 2019). Staying in tune with developing social trends regarding gender, ethnicity, and sexuality allows organizations to associate themselves with the zeitgeist during times of social change.

Third, as noted by Coombs and Holladay (2020), one of the strongest links between CA and *crisis communication* is the *challenge crisis,* or situations where stakeholders claim that an organization and its leadership are acting in an irresponsible or immoral manner (Lerbinger, 1997). When risk that an organization must manage in public view is handled improperly, a paracrisis can escalate into a full-fledged reputational crisis (Chen et al.,

2022). Moreover, situational crisis communication theory can provide valuable information on responding to reputational crises and scandals caused by strategic CA campaigns (Coombs, 2019). This discussion is also relevant to emergent scholarship on *scansis* situations, or those at the intersection of scandal and crisis (Coombs & Tachkova, 2019). Another point of intersection is research on *brandjacking*—that is, appropriating individual and corporate identities or hijacking the conversation around another's brand or reputation (Langley, 2014).

Finally, an area of public relations that holds particular promise is reputation management through inoculation against CA (Compton et al., 2021). Compton (2020) argues that inoculation-informed campaigns offer a preemptive, protective reputational management strategy. By identifying common strategies used to make character attacks, inoculation messages can help to spot fallacies and respond with logic (Cook et al., 2017). A relevant framework here is *image prepare*, a conceptual model elaborated by Compton (2016) to protect against reputational challenges by making preemptive use of the rhetorical strategies used in image repair theory (see Benoit, 2014).

Conclusion and Future Directions

Historically, public relations theory has invested in producing instrumental knowledge to protect power structures against issues and reputational challenges (Grunig, 1992; Ledingham & Bruning, 1998). Lately, however, the idea of omnipotent communication management has declined due to the impact of globalization, the growing role of social media movements and participatory online culture, and declining trust in traditional institutions, among other things (Botan, 2018; Yang & Saffer, 2019).

This chapter supports a paradigmatic shift toward more culture-sensitive and humanistic perspectives on public relations in the context of power redistribution from traditional institutions to empowered citizens and networked online communities. The sociocultural view stimulates new ways of thinking about theory and its applications across several disciplines (Craig, 1999). The discussion of both CA and CC through the lens of *reflexive sociology* (Lizardo, 2010) offers the depth and heuristic potential required to understand both communication phenomena as micro-level processes taking place within larger social structures. On this view, CA and cancellation strategies can be seen as tools for bringing public persuasion and pressure to bear on hegemonic structures—and thus as forces of social change. At a micro level, they serve as rhetorical devices in competition- and conflict-driven situations. At a macro level, issues and crises created by attacks on public image and social ostracism produce tectonic cultural shifts.

The sociocultural approach provides a means of making sense of CA practices in the political context of intergroup or institutional logic. A potential direction for future research is to link the sociocultural perspective of CA to the large body of literature on social conflict. Structurational divergence

(SD) theory provides an explanation of institutional positionings in which incompatible sets of institutional rules and meanings create unresolved conflict between individuals and social groups (Ford et al., 2022; Nicotera, 2015).

SD theory has primarily been discussed in organizational contexts. However, it is instrumental to analyzing situations where power struggles lead to unresolved political and social conflicts becoming locked in "hamster wheel" situations. In such situations, the opposing sides often form entrenched ideological camps with insulated spheres of discourse; they then vilify and demonize other ideological groups, often through strategic CA. As these camps cannot learn from any external viewpoint, their ideologies become increasingly polarized and the initial ideological conflict even more intractable, leading to another SD cycle (Dimock & Wike, 2020). Conflict theory offers a unique theoretical lens on CA and CC through which to examine ideological and cross-cultural differences in moral conflicts and their implications for public relations theory.

References

Aspriadis, N., Takas, E., & Samaras, A. N. (2020). Country reputation assassination during the Greek memorandum re-negotiations. In S. A. Samoilenko, M. Icks, J. Keohane, & E. Shiraev (Eds.), *Routledge handbook of character assassination and reputation management* (pp. 236–250). Routledge.

Ayyub, R. (2018, November 21). I was the victim of a deepfake porn plot intended to silence me. *The Huffington Post*. https://bit.ly/3uQ8DDy

Bakhtiari, K. (2020, September 29). Why brands need to pay attention to cancel culture. *Forbes*. https://bit.ly/37HOWUV

Benoit, W. L. (2014). *Accounts, excuses, apologies: A theory of image restoration strategies*. (2nd ed.). State University of New York Press.

Benoit, W. L. (2017). Criticism of actions and character: Strategies for persuasive attack. *Extended Relevant Rhetoric, 8*. https://bit.ly/2Y0rqvC

Benoit, W. L. (2020). Character assassination and persuasive attack on CBS's face the nation. In S. A. Samoilenko, M. Icks, J. Keohane, & E. Shiraev (Eds.), *Routledge handbook of character assassination* (pp. 295–307). Routledge.

Benoit, W. L., Brazeal, L., & Airne, D. (2007). *A functional analysis of televised U.S. senate and gubernatorial campaign debates*. Communication Studies Faculty Publications, Paper 7. http://scholarworks.umt.edu/communications_pubs/7

Benoit, W. L., & Glantz, M. (2017). *Persuasive attack on Donald Trump in the 2016 Republican primaries*. Lexington Books.

Benoit, W. L., & Stein, K. A. (2021). Character assassination on Judge Brett Kavanaugh in his 2018 supreme court confirmation hearing. *Journal of Applied Social Theory, 1*(3), 7–30.

Berti, C., & Loner, E. (2021). Character assassination as a right-wing populist communication tactic on social media: The case of Matteo Salvini in Italy. *New Media & Society*. https://doi.org/10.1177/14614448211039222

Botan, C. H. (2018). *Strategic communication: Theory and practice*. Wiley-Blackwell.

Boulding, K. E. (1973). *The image: Knowledge in life and society*. University of Michigan Press.

Bourdieu, P., & Wacquant, L. J. D. (1992). *An invitation to reflexive sociology*. University of Chicago Press.

Bouvier, G., & Machin, D. (2021). What gets lost in Twitter "cancel culture" hashtags? *Discourse and Society*, *32*(3), 307–327.

Boyle, D., & Cucchiara, A. (2018, December). *Social movements and HR: The impact of #MeToo* [White Paper]. Cornell Center for Advanced Human Resource Studies. https://bit.ly/31TbTRX

Brock, G. (2016). *The right to be forgotten: Privacy and the media in the digital age*. I. B. Tauris.

Brown, S., Brison, N., & Bennett, G. (2020). Corporate social marketing: An analysis of consumer responses to Nike's campaign featuring Colin Kaepernick. *Global Sport Business Journal*, *8*(1), 33–50.

Bruner, J. S. (1990). *Acts of meaning*. Harvard University Press.

Chen, F., Coombs, W. T., & Holladay, S. J. (2022). Paracrisis and crisis guidance from situational crisis communication theory. In Y. Jin & L. Austin (Eds.), *Social media and crisis communication* (pp. 118–129). Routledge.

Compton, J. (2016). Inoculating against a losing season: Can inoculation-informed public relations strategies protect fan loyalty? *International Journal of Sport Communication*, *9*, 1–12.

Compton, J. (2020). Inoculation against/as character assassination. In S. A. Samoilenko, M. Icks, J. Keohane, & E. Shiraev (Eds.), *The Routledge handbook of character assassination* (pp. 25–35). Routledge.

Compton, J., Wigley, S., & Samoilenko, S. (2021). Inoculation theory and public relations. *Public Relations Review*, *47*(5). https://doi.org/10.1016/j.pubrev.2021.102116

Coombs, W. T. (2019). *Ongoing crisis communication. Planning, managing, and responding* (5th ed.). Sage.

Coombs, W. T., & Holladay, S. (2020). Corporate character assassination and crisis communication. In S. A. Samoilenko, M. Icks, J. Keohane, & E. Shiraev (Eds.), *Routledge handbook of character assassination* (pp. 225–235). Routledge.

Coombs, W. T., & Tachkova, E. R. (2019). Scansis as a unique crisis type: Theoretical and practical implications. *Journal of Communication Management*, *23*(1), 72–88.

Copi, I. M. (1961). *Introduction to logic*. Macmillan.

Cook, J., Lewandowsky, S., & Ecker, U. K. H. (2017). Neutralizing misinformation through inoculation: Exposing misleading argumentation techniques reduces their influence. *PloS One*, *12*(5). https://doi.org/10.1371/journal.pone.0175799.

Craig, R. T. (1999). Communication theory as a field. *Communication Theory*, *9*, 119–161.

Dimock, M., & Wike, R. (2020, November 13). *America is exceptional in the nature of its political divide*. Pew Research Center. https://pewrsr.ch/3CpSaWR

Doron, G., & On, U. (1983). A rational choice model of campaign strategy. In A. Arian (Ed.), *The elections in Israel, 1981* (pp. 213–231). Ramot Publishing.

Downey, J., & Stanyer, J. (2013). Exposing politicians' peccadilloes in comparative context: Explaining the frequency of political sex scandals in eight democracies using fuzzy set qualitative comparative analysis. *Political Communication*, *30*(3), 495–509.

Eder, K. (1985). The "new social movements": Moral crusades, political pressure groups, or social movements? *Social Research*, *52*(4), 869–890.

Edwards, S. B. (2022). *Cancel culture*. Special reports. Abdo Publishing.

Esser, F., & Matthes, J. (2013). Mediatization effects on political news, political actors, political decisions, and political audiences. In H. Kriesi, S. Lavenex, F. Esser, J. Matthes, M. Bühlmann, & D. Bochsler (Eds.), *Democracy in the age of globalization and mediatization* (pp. 177–201). Palgrave Macmillan.

Felaco, C., Nocerino, J., Parola, J., & Tofani, R. (2022). I correct or canceling you: Political correctness and cancel culture on social media—the case of Twitter communication in Italy. In G. Punziano & A. Delli Paoli (Eds.), *Handbook of research on advanced research methodologies for a digital society* (pp. 708–725). IGI Global.

Fisher, W. R. (1970). A motive view of communication. *Quarterly Journal of Speech*, *56*(2), 131–139.

Fisher, W. R. (1984). The narrative paradigm: In the beginning. *Journal of Communication*, *34*, 74–89.

Ford, J. L., Zhu, Y., & Barrett, A. K. (2022). Structurational divergence, safety climate, and intentions to leave: An examination of health care workers' experiences of abuse, *Communication Monographs*, *89*(1), 1–24.

Fridkin, K. L., & Kenney, P. (2011). Variability in citizens' reactions to different types of negative campaigns. *American Journal of Political Science*, *55*, 307–325.

Garrett, R. K. (2019). Social media's contribution to political misperceptions in U.S. presidential elections. *PLoS One*, *14*(3), e0213500.

George-Parkin, H. (2019, February 5). Why companies need to get comfortable with taking a stand on social issues. *FN*. https://bit.ly/3C7gdti

Ginther, M. R., Hartsough, L. E. S., & Marois, R. (2021). Moral outrage drives the interaction of harm and culpable intent in third-party punishment decisions. *Emotion*. https://doi.org/10.1037/emo0000950

Grunig, J. E. (1992). *Excellence in public relations and communication management*. Lawrence Erlbaum Associates.

Heath, R. L. (2018). Strategic issues management organizations operating in rhetorical arenas. In Ø. Ihlen & R. L. Heath (Eds.), *The handbook of organizational rhetoric and communication* (pp. 385–400). Wiley.

Helm, S. (2005). Designing a formative measure for corporate reputation. *Corporate Reputation Review*, *8*, 95–109.

Holland, D., & Salvo, D. (2012). *Change management: The new way: Easy to understand; powerful to use.* Xlibris.

Icks, M., & Shiraev, E. (2014). *Character assassination throughout the ages.* Palgrave-MacMillan.

Icks, M., Shiraev, E., Keohane, J., & Samoilenko, S. A. (2020). Character assassination: Theoretical framework. In S. A. Samoilenko, M. Icks, J. Keohane, & E. Shiraev (Eds.), *Routledge handbook of character assassination and reputation management* (pp. 11–24). Routledge.

India Today. (2018, November 21). *I was vomiting: Journalist Rana Ayyub reveals horrifying account of deepfake porn plot.* https://bit.ly/3oWraKL

Jasper, J. M. (1997). *The art of moral protest.* University of Chicago Press.

Jasper, J. M. (2014). *Protest: A cultural introduction to social movements.* Polity Press.

Jasper, J. M., Young, M., & Zuern, E. (2018). Character work in social movements. *Theory and Society*, *47*, 113–131.

Jasper, J. M., Young, M. P., & Zuern, E. (2020). *Public characters: The politics of reputation and blame.* Oxford University Press.

Johnson, T. (2021). Sleepy Joe? Recalling and considering Donald Trump's strategic use of nicknames. *Journal of Political Marketing*. https://doi.org/10.1080/15377857.2021.1939572

Keller, F. B., Schoch, D., Stier, S., & Yang, J. H. (2020). Political astroturfing on Twitter: How to coordinate a disinformation campaign. *Political Communication*, *37*(2), 256–280.

Keohane, J. (2020). The rhetorical and ethical implications of character assassination in the age of McCarthy. In S. A. Samoilenko, M. Icks, J. Keohane, & E. Shiraev (Eds.), *Routledge handbook of character assassination* (pp. 269–281). Routledge.

Langley, Q. (2014). *Brandjack: How your reputation is at risk from brand pirates and what to do about it*. Palgrave Macmillian.

Ledingham, J. A., & Bruning, S. D. (1998). Relationship management and public relations: Dimensions of an organization–public relationship. *Public Relations Review, 24,* 55–65.

Lerbinger, O. (1997). *The crisis manager: Facing risk and responsibility*. Lawrence Erlbaum.

Lichter, R. S., & Farnsworth, S. (2020). Late night TV humor and the culture of ridicule. In S. A. Samoilenko, M. Icks, J. Keohane, & E. Shiraev (Eds.), *The Routledge handbook of character assassination and reputation management*. Routledge.

Lizardo, O. (2010). Beyond the antinomies of structure: Levi-Strauss, Giddens, Bourdieu, and Sewell. *Theory and Society, 39*(6), 651–688.

Marwick, A., & Lewis, R. (2017). *Media manipulation and disinformation online*. Data and Society Research Institute. https://bit.ly/36rjv0b

Mishan, L. (2020, December 3). The long and tortured history of cancel culture. *The New York Times*. https://nyti.ms/3LZq5dM

Nicotera, A. M. (2015). Damned if I do and damned if I don't: How structurational divergence strips actors of agency. *Management Communication Quarterly, 29*(3), 493–498.

Norlock, K. J. (2017). Online shaming. *Social Psychology Today, 33,* 187–197.

Norris, P. (2021). Cancel culture: Myth or reality? *Political Studies*. https://doi.org/10.1177/00323217211037023

Norris, P., & Inglehart, R. (2019). *Cultural backlash*. Cambridge University Press.

NPR. (2017, November 4). Why "the Weinstein effect" seems like a tipping point. *NPR*. https://n.pr/37tureB

Pascale, C.-M. (2019). The weaponization of language: Discourses of rising right-wing authoritarianism. *Current Sociology Review, 76*(6), 989–917.

Pearce, W. B., & Littlejohn, S. W. (1997). *Moral conflict: When social worlds collide*. Sage.

Pietsch, B. (2022, March 8). A list of companies still doing business in Russia circulated. McDonald's, Coca-Cola and Starbucks soon pulled out. *The Washington Post*. https://wapo.st/37BG572

Poushter, J. (2014, April 15). *What's morally acceptable? It depends on where in the world you live*. Pew Research Center. https://pewrsr.ch/3s3tQIG

Proulx, M. (2021, April 8). *A brand's values must withstand the pressure of politics*. Forrester. https://bit.ly/3O0Po19

Reeves, J., & Ingraham, C. (2020). Character assassins and moral entrepreneurs: Social media and the regulation of morality. In S. A. Samoilenko, M. Icks, J. Keohane, & E. Shiraev (Eds.), *Routledge handbook of character assassination* (pp. 366–378). Routledge.

Riker, W. H. (1996). *The strategy of rhetoric: Campaigning for the American constitution*. Yale University Press.

Rivera, K., & Karlsson, P. (2017, June 6). CEOs are getting fired for ethical lapses more than they used to. *Harvard Business Review*. https://goo.gl/Z2Nz7H

Rosamond, E. (2020). From reputation capital to reputation warfare: Online ratings, trolling, and the logic of volatility. *Theory, Culture & Society, 37*(2), 105–129.

Samoilenko, S. (2016). Character assassination. In C. Carroll (Ed.), *The Sage encyclopedia of corporate reputation* (pp. 116–118). Sage.

Samoilenko, S. A. (2020a). Character assassination in the context of mediated complexity. In K. Sriramesh & D. Verčič (Eds.), *The global public relations handbook: Theory, research, and practice* (3rd ed.). Routledge.

Samoilenko, S. A. (2020b). Character assassination as a structurational phenomenon. In S. A. Samoilenko, M. Icks, J. Keohane, & E. Shiraev (Eds.), *Routledge handbook of character assassination* (pp. 45–62). Routledge.

Samoilenko, S. A. (2021a). Character assassination: The sociocultural perspective. *Journal of Applied Social Theory*, *1*(3), 186–205.

Samoilenko, S. A. (2021b). The cocreational view of character assassination. In C. H. Botan (Ed.), *The handbook of strategic communication* (pp. 76–90). Wiley.

Samoilenko, S. A., Erzikova, E., Davydov, S., & Laskin, A. (2017). Different media, same messages: Character assassination in the television news during the 2014 Ukrainian crisis. *International Communication Research Journal*, *52*(2), 31–55.

Samoilenko, S. A., & Icks, M., Keohane, J., & Shiraev, E. (Eds.). (2020). *Routledge handbook of character assassination and reputation management*. Routledge.

Samoilenko, S. A., & Suvorova, I. (2023). Artificial intelligence and deepfakes in strategic deception campaigns: The U.S. and Russian experiences. In E. Pashentsev (Ed.), *The Palgrave handbook of malicious use of AI and psychological security*. Palgrave Macmillan.

Satariano, A. (2022, March 12). Shaming Apple and texting Musk, a Ukraine minister uses novel war tactics. *The New York Times*. https://nyti.ms/37BPJXg

Schaeffer, L. (2019, October 2). Consumers expect the brands they support to be socially responsible. *Business Wire*. https://bwnews.pr/3ncNbV2

Schaffer, K. (2021, August 17). *How Americans feel about "cancel culture" and offensive speech in 6 charts*. Pew Research Center. https://pewrsr.ch/3GIT7fe

Schumacher-Rutherford, A., & Muddiman, A. (2021). The bullying pulpit: The audience effects of a partisan character-attacking speaker. *Journal of Applied Social Theory*, *1*(3), 31–61.

Seidman, G. W. (2015). Divestment dynamics: Mobilizing, shaming, and changing the rules. *Social Research*, *82*(4), 1015–1037.

Seidman, G. W. (2016). Naming, shaming and changing the world. In S. Vallas & D. Courpasson (Eds.), *The Sage handbook of resistance* (pp. 351–366). Sage.

Seiffert-Brockmann, J. (2020). Character assassination by memes: Mosquitos versus elephants. In S. A. Samoilenko, M. Icks, J. Keohane, & E. Shiraev (Eds.), *Routledge handbook of character assassination* (pp. 402–421). Routledge.

Seiffert-Brockmann, J., Einwiller, S., & Stranzl, J. (2018). Character assassination of CEOs in crises—questioning CEOs' character and values in corporate crises. *European Journal of Communication*, *33*(4), 413–429. https://doi.org/10.1177/0267323118763860

Seiter, J. S., & Gass, R. H. (2010). Aggressive communication in political contexts. In T. A. Avtgis & A. S. Rancer (Eds.), *Arguments, aggression, and conflict: New directions in theory and research* (pp. 217–240). Routledge.

Shen, W. (2017). Online privacy and online speech: The problem of the human flesh search engine. *Penn Law: Legal Scholarship Repository*. https://bit.ly/3rmo2bV

Shiraev, E. (2014). Character assassination: How political psychologists can assist historians. In M. Icks & E. Shiraev (Eds.), *Character assassination throughout the ages* (pp. 15–36). Palgrave Macmillan.

Shiraev, E., Keohane, J., Icks, M., & Samoilenko, S. A. (2022). *Character assassination and reputation management: Theory and applications*. Routledge.

Sigelman, L., & Kugler, M. (2003). Why is research on the effects of negative campaigning so inconclusive? Understanding citizens' perceptions of negativity. *The Journal of Politics*, *65*(1), 142–160.

Sigelman, L., & Shiraev, E. (2002). The rational attacker in Russia? Negative campaigning in Russian presidential elections. *The Journal of Politics*, *64*(1), 45–62.

Simmons, S. (2021). Root narrative theory and character assassination. *Journal of Applied Social Theory*, *1*(3), 158–185.

Simons, G. (2020). The role of propaganda in the character assassination of world leaders in international affairs. In S. A. Samoilenko, M. Icks, J. Keohane, & E. Shiraev (Eds.), *Routledge handbook of character assassination and reputation management* (pp. 163–180). Routledge.

Simpson, R., & Srinivasan, A. A. (2018). No platforming. In J. Lackey (Ed.), *Academic freedom* (pp. 186–209). Oxford University Press.

Skaperdas, S., & Grofman, B. (1995). Modeling negative campaigning. *American Political Science Review, 89*(1), 49–61.

Smith, R, & Eberly, R. A. (2021). Advancing research on character assassination and stigma communication: A dynamics of character. *Journal of Applied Social Theory, 1*(3), 134–157.

Stephenson, S. (2021). A ritual civil execution: Public shaming meetings in the post-Stalin Soviet Union. *Journal of Applied Social Theory, 1*(3), 112–133.

Swant, M. (2021, April 19). Silence is not an option: Research shows consumers expect CEOs to take a stand on political issues. *Forbes.* https://bit.ly/3vcJhxU

van Eemeren, F. H. (2010). *Strategic maneuvering in argumentative discourse.* John Benjamins.

Vogels, E. A., Anderson, M., Porteus, M., Baronavski, C., Atske, S., McClain, C. Auxier, B., Perrin, A., & Ramshankar, M. (2021, May 19). *Americans and "cancel culture": Where some see calls for accountability, others see censorship, punishment.* Pew Research Center. https://pewrsr.ch/3Dh4YiZ

Walton, D. N. (1998). *Ad hominem arguments.* University of Alabama Press.

Walton, D. N. (1999). Ethotic arguments and fallacies: The credibility function in multi-agent dialogue systems. *Pragmatics and Cognition, 7*(1), 177–203.

Wanless, A., & Berk, M. (2021). *The changing nature of propaganda: Coming to terms with influence in conflict.* Routledge.

Xiong, Y., Cho, M., & Boatwright, B. (2019). Hashtag activism and message frames among social movement organizations: Semantic network analysis and thematic analysis of Twitter during the #MeToo movement. *Public Relations Review, 45*(1), 10–23.

Yang, A., & Saffer, A. J. (2019). Embracing a network perspective in the network society: The dawn of a new paradigm in strategic public relations. *Public Relations Review, 45*(4), https://doi.org/10.1016/j.pubrev.2019.101843

27 Strategic Issues Management

A Rhetorical Theoretical Perspective on Contestable Questions of Place

Damion Waymer and Robert L. Heath

The concept of (strategic) issues management came into public relations and management theory literature in the 1970s (Harlow, 1976), gained momentum during the 1980s (Crable & Vibbert, 1985), and matured in the 1990s (Heath, 1997) and the 2000s (Heath & Palenchar, 2009). The period consisting of the last decades of the 20th century, often referred to as the age of activism, was one of the most robust in US history (Foley, 2013). Public relations practitioners were caught off guard by challenges that private sector, non-profit, and government policy preferences created legitimacy gaps between what large organizations did and said and what critics preferred. Robust examination and criticism by stakeholders of large organizations' actions resulted in claims that this period represents a business and government era without soul (Taylor, 1992).

Public skepticism that large organizations were not addressing vital issues led to the emergence of issues management, and the discipline and practice resulted in a multidimensional intelligence for examining private sector, governmental, and activist policy preferences and (in)actions and the related communication processes.

Issues are inherently rhetorical (textual, discursive, multivocal) and were postulated to be contestable questions of fact, value, or policy. Over time, issues management expanded to include issues of identity and identification. Now, as a conceptual update, this chapter adds and discusses another issue type of contestable matter: place. Place is defined as a portion of physical, digital, or socially constructed space available or designated for or being used by someone. As a concept, place allows us to advance our understanding and knowledge of issues management practice and theory because it enables us to address more fully pressing contemporary issues. As organizations battle to establish and maintain legitimacy, questions of who gets to define what place is, its parameters, and who is welcome or is excluded from a place are central to a range of contemporary issues including communicative debates surrounding illegal immigration, whether Critical Race Theory should be taught in K–12 schools, or debates surrounding Confederate soldier memorial removal for example. We conceptualize, explicate, and interrogate the role of place in issues management and provide directions for future research on and application of the concept.

DOI: 10.4324/9781003141396-31

This chapter begins by revisiting SIM's foundations by providing an overview of its connections to organizational rhetorical theory (see Ihlen & Heath, 2018).

Revisiting SIM's Rhetorical Roots

In *Public Relations Theory II*, Heath (2006a) examined the rhetorical underpinnings of SIM, emphasizing its discursive bias (versus systems and information theory) centered on the underpinning problematics of text, societal decision making, intelligence (Gardner, 1983), and decision-making outcomes hampered by mutually beneficial relationships (see also Heath, 2021). That chapter explored three topics: "the definition and theoretical underpinnings of issues and issues management; the implications of these underpinnings for future research and theory development; and a discussion of the implications of theory and research for the practice of issues management in conjunction with public relations and public affairs" (p. 65). It emphasized the strategic challenges of legitimacy and legitimacy gaps as shared issues positions and Corporate Social Responsibility (CSR) challenges.

That chapter also emphasized how traditional public relations had been heavily orientated to reputational (image) and relationship perspectives, whereas public policy battles were natural rhetorical disputes. That chapter drew heavily upon the paradigm of rhetoric advanced by Aristotle and Isocrates. Aristotle (1954) noted how the operational integrity of civil society is contingent on three types of issue disputation: deliberative (variations of expedience; just/unjust policy), forensics (guilt/innocence), and epideictic (praise/blame, systematic moral judgment). Both ancient Greek scholars, but especially Isocrates (1929), reasoned that rhetoricians' textual, argumentative skills strategically enact civic responsibility by determining the stasis (turning point) of issues (see Marsh, 2010). By public argument, communities operate through co-created narratives that strategically depend on disputatious resolutions of controversies of fact, value, identity, identification, and place.

The Greek paradigm of rhetoric expected people (and later, organizations) to "speak" in public as deliberative means by which societies and communities make collective decisions, decisions of collective interest and benefit. By that means, choices and actions preferred by citizens could be judged to achieve legitimacy. Stances of legitimacy in these contexts presume issue debate and gaps between what is expected of individuals and organizations. Hence, issues are inherently discursive, dialogic matters of disputation, contention, contestable matters. The most legitimate intelligence and strategic quest of issues management is the constitution of deliberative democracy: "As stewards of democracy, organizations can play a pivotal role in fostering environments, the infrastructures and collaborative processes, that allow and even facilitate collective decision making as well as blend the private sphere (individualism) and the public sphere (collectivism)" (Heath et al., 2013, p. 271).

Such is the case whether rhetoric, processually and contextually, is deliberative or instrumental. Instrumental rhetoric is more focused on specific outcomes, such as guilt convictions (including claims that certain organizations foster global warming) or the establishment of innocence (demonstrating claims that they do not). Deliberation consists of agonistic processes of convincing (Shanahan et al., 2018). By this processual approach, society and community are inherently rhetorically dynamic: a discursive characteristic of place as ever changing and demanding.

One noted organizationally and rhetorically rooted theory is the fully functioning society theory (FFST)—(see Heath, 2006b)—which is a framework that can be used to help scholars and practitioners understand, research, critique, and theorize public relations in society systematically. On FFST, Heath stated:

> A rhetorical perspective is vital (or for some, a European sociological perspective) because we must have a theory-based systematic way to understand, research, and critique the role of public relations in forming and responding to ideas—competing and convergent shared social realities that can broadly be interpreted as zones of meaning. In public relations, communication is about something; ideas and meaning count.
> (Heath, 2006b, p. 93)

Ideas and meaning not only count, but they are central to understanding SIM's role in society and its theorizing. By responding to claims about FFST, we account for the increasing pressure on firms to address social issues (Coombs & Holladay, 2017) and to provide directions for theory development and research. Furthermore, in this chapter we critique public relations and its role in forming and responding to society's competing and convergent shared social realities by highlighting and unpacking the interlocking and interdependent nature of identity, identification, and place.

Four of those five contestable matters, considered to be foundational SIM stones, have been discussed in SIM literature for years. For example, scholars (Brooks & Waymer, 2009) have studied contestable questions of fact (which competing entity is the "true" owner of mining rights in Venezuela), contestable questions of value (steroid use in baseball is bad and violates the integrity and legitimacy of the game—see Boyd, 2009), contestable questions of policy (a personal care corporation that manufactures flushable wipes challenged city-initiated policy bans on the product—see Waymer & Heath, 2019), contestable questions of identity (emotions and gender are linked to the intersectionality of marginalized stakeholder identities—see Madden, 2019), and identification (Black, U.S. Civil Rights Era activists' rhetoric equally addressed identification and solidarity of the group as it did racism—see Heath, 2012). The fifth contestable matter, place, has been implied, but is far less explored. After a review of the four established SIM concepts, this chapter will emphasize the need, rationale, and implications of discussing place to continue to flesh out the rhetorical logics of SIM.

Establishing a Conceptual Foundation for "Place"

As established previously, from its inception, the logic of rhetorical disputation informed SIM by focusing on arguable, propositional matters of fact, value, and policy (Heath, 1997). As information, fact achieves its importance for decision making through critical examination (metaphysics and epistemology) addressed as choice: what do we know and with what certainty? Value debates examine the moral and ethical choices (what is right, wrong, good or bad) that inform policy based on available moral judgment. Policy debates contest which organizational and individual actions are legitimate expressions of shared fact and value, considering what should or should not be done, legal or illegal. To these three constructs Heath and Palenchar (2009) added identity, as one might consider what it means to be "American" as a contestable question of identity to ponder. Influenced by the heritage of Kenneth Burke (Burke, 1969b/1950), identification was added to the list (see Heath & Palenchar, 2009), as some might consider identification as a contestable question. To elucidate, consider in 2021, U.S. citizens turned insurgent and stormed the U.S. Capitol Building—a hallowed place of government—in protest of the presidential election whereby then-President Donald Trump was not reelected. A rallying cry for these insurgents was that they identified themselves as "patriots" fighting for the soul of a nation (Jaffe et al., 2021). How is what constitutes identity and identification as a patriot a matter of deliberative rhetoric?

Primarily, the focus on identity (and image) was the result of realizing that both the constitutive nature/character of an organization as well as that of human individuals are contestable matters, especially during a crisis or a reputational battle (Heath & Palenchar, 2009). Despite the fact that critical rhetorical scholars question the level and extent that organizations are able to create, shape, and influence said identities without revealing and making tacit their self-interest (see Boyd & Waymer, 2011), organizational identification remains powerful. As such, organizations often seek to create, shape, and influence the identities of workers (associates) and consumers (clients), and organizations also leverage SIM within marketing efforts as organizations use product, service, or locational appeals to ask customers and other stakeholders to intertwine their identities with the organization. Consider what it means to be an Apple product user. Consider how the notion of "homecoming" at U.S. universities is rooted in drawing alumni back to a physical campus location while engendering loyalty and identification from current students, faculty, and community residents.

In recent times, scholars have begun to extend the application of identity in issues management beyond the realm of crisis and reputational battle. Among others, Madden (2019) argued that emotions and gender can make the issues management paradigm more inclusive by speaking directly to issues, such as sexual assault, that are linked intricately to the intersectionality of marginalized stakeholder identities.

Stated simply, principles, as contestable matters of identification, become embedded in the constitution of organizations based on the logics of identification. Furthermore, identity and identification are both conditions of community, reputation, crisis, risk, and place. For instance, what is (are) the identity(ies) of employees working for and at this organization (a place) and how well and in what ways do they identify with one another? Issues of identity have been raised in many "places." Such topics as issues, for instance, have been examined as conditions of legitimacy in the military (who should be allowed to join U.S. military combat units), the workplace (gender pay disparity issues in U.S.), and places of education. As such, all three concepts of identity, identification, and place are relevant when discussing, analyzing, or critiquing organizations. The same logic of relevance can be understood intersectionally to ripple through all aspects of society. These factors include employment, consumption, memberships, neighborhoods, professional association, activist associations, national origin, race, and ethnicity, and rhetorical theory provides substantiation for such a claim. In sum, the discussion up to this point underscores how interlocking and interdependent identity, identification, and place are, and how they are essential to matters of conflict management, social justice, and even civil society. All of these rhetorical contestations are characterized by the stasis of choice, which is confounded by and yields to the problematics of textuality (Heath et al., 2021). The key elements of such collective decision making are those inherent to rhetorical argumentation (fact, value, policy) expanded to include identity, identification, and place. These concepts are interdependent and interpenetrating. Fact and value are foundational, implying and allowing strategic policy that is often relevant to identity, identification, and place.

Now, as an update, this chapter adds and details the issue type, place.

Strategic Foundations and Assessments of Place

SIM can be thought of as the strategic resource management of finite community resources based on facts, values, policies, identities, identifications and place. In the classical, modern, postmodern rhetorical traditions, these factors are as relevant to one another and the rights and responsibilities of association as they were in ancient Greece (see Ihlen & Heath, 2018). The essential quality of societal issues is their agonism as stasis (Davidson, 2018). Accordingly, organizations, communities, and societies are not static but ever changing and changed through discourse. Such change is not only discursive, but more likely its discursiveness is affected by terministic changes in place. Consider, if place is space available or designated for or being used by someone, then what defines appropriate Internet communication and how have such protocols changed over time? Persons once regarded workplace email as an open, yet private, internal communication medium, but today persons often carefully craft email messages in fear that their professional downfall is but one forwarded email away. Such changes in place and how it is perceived might be "natural" or human made, material or symbolic. Such views underscore the nature of communities as rhetorical arenas, as ongoing, never-ending discourse and deliberation, as constitutive agonism. Agonistically, rhetorical investigation of issues constitutes collective efforts to reduce decision uncertainty. The important point, however, is that such rhetorical argumentation never ends. It is the deliberative state and constitutive character of society and community.

Two premises of FFST's original premises are especially relevant to this chapter and to the prospect that SIM is a constitutive, communitarian intelligence.

> Premise: Society is a complex of collectivities engaged in variously constructive dialogue and power resource distribution through meeting socially constructed and shared norm-based expectations whereby individuals seek to make enlightened choices in the face of risk, uncertainty, and reward/cost ambiguity.
>
> (Heath, 2006b, p. 107)

> Premise: Through collective and individual voices in varying degrees of dialogue, what can be or may be seen as partisan causes need to be put into public discourse in ways that give the evidence, facts, identifications, and policy choices full potential for responsible and reflective review.
>
> (Heath, 2006b, p. 108)

In addition to restating the foundational pillars of SIM, these themes and premises, when carefully unpacked, extend the rhetorical theory of SIM by emphasizing place as a rhetorical problem. It is not only context and arena but the meaning of relevant facts, values, policies, identities, and identifications that both shape and constitute place.

To unpack this claim, imagine in U.S. society the historic importance of South(ern) as place. The South as place defined issues regarding people, property, privilege, and power that included privileged White (male and Christian) identity and identification. Such place continues to be problematic, as is evident in the battle over Confederate epideictic honors, including statues and place names (Heath & Waymer, 2019). Should USA military bases be named for military personnel and government figures who sought to break the union, especially to protect chattel slavery? As the South has been a place that carefully separated races as White Christian heritage, White ministers such as Lee (2019) and Christian social critics such as Jones (2020) have argued for the constitution of racial harmony as social justice. White Christian evangelism is place (or arena of contest) for assessing moral justice regarding human persons' identity, values, and identification. Such judgment has implications far beyond the physical place of pulpit and pew, to the places of everyday life. In contestable matters of legitimacy, one could aspire that morality dominated materiality, but the opposite seems true in this example; when that occurs, it imperils the full functioning of society.

A Rhetorical Theory Case for Place in SIM

Botan and Taylor (2004) mused about "how one area of public relations— issues management—may be able to make a theoretic/conceptual contribution to the broader field of communication, particularly in applied areas such as health, risk and political communication" (p. 646). To them, issues management is a "strategic core" more than "peripheral technical skills" (p. 654). Arguably it is an intelligence by which societies and communities create shared zones of meaning needed for collective resource management. The covariant nature of issues and publics made the difference as rationale for collaborative decision making as the life cycle of issues (Crable & Vibbert, 1985). Issues, by this logic, are subject to the paradoxes of collective decision making. "Issues management can serve these areas because it focuses on the common core of all applied communication—publics— and on the role of communication in building relationships with them" (Botan & Taylor, 2004, p. 657). Such relationship building, as society and community, presumes discursive means by which issues of facts, values, policies, identities, identifications, and place are investigated and interrogated as problems searching for resolution and solution. If we take organization to be both as broad and narrow as possible, Botan and Taylor's (2004) conclusion is provocative: "Axiologically, issues management explains and improves organization—public communication and subsequent relationship building" (p. 685). Thus, organization, as agonistic organizing, is provocative to place in issues management.

In a similar vein, Hess (2011) emphasized the critical turn of analyzing "the types and locations worthy of rhetorical examination" (p. 127). Specific to place, one can emphasize the nature of vernacular and narrative context advocacy. Such critical analysis not only investigates strategic processes but the assumptions about processes in context, vernacular and context advocacy. Instrumental to such analysis is the understanding that how arguments are invented and deployed is both constitutive and oppositional. Arguments are contextually relevant to the nature of place and vital to its constitutiveness. Emphasizing context as process, "It follows that in situ rhetoric refers to naturally occurring rhetoric that is accessed, documented, and interpreted as it occurs in the moment of rhetorical invention" (Endres et al., 2016, p. 516). The rhetoric of place has the parallel qualities of being unique to specific situations but is as universal as places are universal. "In situ rhetoric is an all-encompassing sensual experience that happens in a particular time and place and through particular bodies" (Endres et al., 2016, p. 516).

Such theory presumes layers of issues discourse by topic, theme, or problem. Such layers can also be interpreted as narratives: narratives of society, community, organizations, stakeholder groups, stakeseeker groups, and eventually to individuals who are embedded intersectionally in other layers/ groups. The discourse of specific social justice events, such as Black Lives Matter protests, can be unpacked as such layers and by stakeholders' critical perspectives, but they are also contextualized as place in related discourses, such as legislative discourse. One of many issues management problems occurs as levels of discourse are disjointed, incoherent to one another, and frustrated as higher power levels refute, reject, or dismiss lower levels. "Do you hear us now?" is more than a chant, and it is more than a Doritos corporate-sponsored commercial in support of Black Lives Matter (Doritos, 2020); it is an issues management monitoring and communication misjudgment. Arguably it is place: Do you hear us on social media, in our workplaces, in the streets where police offices murder Black persons, or in society writ large? As policy rests on and/or advocates the higher levels of place rhetoric, the problematic consequences of careful deliberation are narrative infidelity and coherence: "You love our music; you love our culture, but do you love us? . . . We sing songs, and you didn't listen" (Doritos, 2020). Black Lives Matter activists, in these statements, highlight the lack of fidelity and coherence in the narrative: actions displayed are not congruent (celebrating Black music and culture, yet standing by idly when brutality against Black lives is committed).

Arguments relevant to issues are contextual of place, about place, reflective of place, and expressive of place. Such wrangles over place are wrangles over power and control. A corporativist view of SIM presumes that corporate institutions engage, even define place, as a means of shaping power and control to their advantage, even if by engagement and collaboration. Place is discourse, shapes discourse, and emerges as and through discourse. Such discourse emphasizes identity and identification. Such discourse is the manifestation of collective self-interests. Protests of police violence against citizens are as much an expression of place as they are a definition of place(s). By this logic ideology(ies) expresses place as constitutive of those in it and those who express and seek to achieve it.

The narrative logics of place facilitate society and community as the rationale for organizations of all types to exist, operate, gain/lose resources, and engage agonistically. Especially relevant to businesses, one can question whether organizations bend society to serve them or whether they bend to serve societal interests. That is a place issue, one that is multivocal and multitextual (think of word clouds possible through analysis of social media discourse). Corporations cannot decide their policy preferences unilaterally; legitimacy standards, license to operate, and gaps occur regarding the rationale for reward preferred by the company and those granted/allowed by society and community. (See Heath, 2006a.)

The Texuality of Place

Place is textual. As Burke (1960) argued, language allows the enactment of ideas, identities, and identifications. "It is by this realm, the realm of [hu] man's many languages, that our complex civilizations are built up, with their many isms, ologies, and ographies, uniting the individual economic plants in wider economic units variously cooperating and variously at odds with one another" (p. 6). Society and community are symbolic action, variously coherent narratives, that unifies and divides. It is important to presume that language is not used for the purposes of communication per se, but other strategic purposes and outcomes, such as organizing, creating community, shaping society, defining place, and reflecting the symbolic action of place. In civil rights and social justice discourse, for instance, placing a statue of a Confederate general in a public square, such as the lawn of a courthouse, is both a statement about that place and a reflection of the place in the evaluative textuality of the statue. To act in the name of freedom is to take it as identity, gain identification, and define place. Thus, the U.S. states (southern) that created a confederacy did so in the name of freedom, a purpose, definition of action, and motive that had teleological implications to the endurance of the Union. The freedom of white supremacy presumed the absence of freedom for chattel slaves. The enactment of one person's freedom was the expression of another's oppression.

An essential theme in the unpacking of the rhetorical implications of place, Burke (1969a) reasoned, is motive: "Any complete statement about motives will offer *some kind of* answers to these five questions: what was done (act), when or where it was done (scene), who did it (agent), how he did it (agency), and why (purpose)" (p. xv, italics in original). Situation, context, is scene. Scene is place. Acts are interpreted and critically judged as they express (are in ratio to scene) by an agent (actor), doing or saying (agency) something with purpose. To backfill or back track interpretations and critical judgment, purpose as intended outcome or effect presumes the quality of the act, by the agent's agency.

As predominantly White, European populations in the USA celebrated freedom by enacting Independence Day on July 4th each year, abolitionist Frederick Douglass used an antislavery association meeting (July 5, 1852) to point out that in the midst of celebrations of freedom, four million people lived in chattel slavery (Heath & Waymer, 2009). At the same time, cries for freedom from "northern tyranny and aggression" were rising in southern states and would lead to secession. Scene-act ratios worked to express definitions, motivations, identities, identifications, values, facts, and purpose into a coherent clash of interests. Particularly relevant to SIM's foundations in rhetorical theory, the textuality of issues as contestable matters can be found as ambiguities: "What we want is *not terms that avoid ambiguity*, but *terms that clearly reveal the strategic spots at which ambiguities naturally arise*" (Burke, 1969a, p. xviii, italics in original). At such point, transformations can occur that have implications for issues planning, monitoring, CSR, and issue communication. Freedom cannot long be the absence of oppression in the name of oppression. Such ambiguities of scene-act presume that text used by an agent motivates counter agent (counter narrative).

Before continuing this dramatistic (a Burkean concept) analysis of symbolic action relevant to issues management, a discussion of sub*sta*nce will help. The key root is *sta*, which centers terms such as *statement, existence, subsistence, stage, state, station, contrast*, and many more including a key term used previously, *stasis*. It also is fundamental to *transubstantiation, constitution, situation, constitutive*, and *consubstantiality*. On this last concept, consubstantiality is vital to community as the place for and beneficiary of rhetoric: "To identify A with B is to make A 'consubstantial' with B" (Burke, 1969b, p. 21).

Notice, as well, how those words and their relatives are scenic terms and in ratio, action-purpose terms. The important reasoning about this concept leads to the conclusion that substance is the statement about the essence of a word (or scene): what it means or what it does not mean. The south is not the north. To understand issues of place, per se, we are referring "to an attribute of the *thing's* context, since that which supports or underlies a thing would be a part of the thing's context" (Burke, 1969a, p. 23). Key terms count in association and as clusters. "When taking their stand *in* Dixie, they are also taking their stand *for* Dixie" (Burke, 1969a, p. 24, italics in original).

By extension, taking a stand on the reality (fact) of climate change expresses a value and policy stance on the topic, which can foster identity and identification. Thus, climate change as place (scene) presumes an act by agents using agency with purpose. And its issue nature is both its contestability and the fact that change and non-change cannot both exist as defensible logic.

Ironically, climate change is as much place as is Black Lives Matter and Blue Lives Matter. As issues discourse, however, opponents of climate change cannot agree with those who believe it is true. Likewise, exponents of Black Lives Matter and Blue Lives Matter can take on identities, achieve identification, that address the quality of place because both propositions can not only be true but in unison create constructive motives on behalf of life and well-being of all people. Thus, they define (constitute) community as consubstantiation. By this logic, it is possible to find concurrence in opposition by understanding the joining sub*sta*nce as opposed (literally and figuratively) to the opposing sub*sta*nce. As issues monitoring, analysis, and discursive communication, the search for identification is a search for "either/or" or "both/and" logics. Opponents can be transformed (by transubstantiation) into allies.

Scenes suppose corresponding acts as the relationship between the container and the thing contained (Burke, 1969a). Acts presume that agents use agency consonant with purpose in scene, context, place. So, in theatric productions the "scenery" for a drama is likely to be different from a comedy. We understand that issue communication rhetorically begins by setting, or defining, scene. How the scene is set, scenery designed and painted, will foretell the narrative that will unfold. (Thus, climate change icon Greta Thunberg sailed to the USA rather than taking an airplane.) "From the motivational point of view, there is implicit in the quality of a scene the quality of the action that is to take place within it" (Burke, 1969a, pp. 6–7). Thus, discursively we have the scene of a trial for murder, the raising of a monument in honor of a person, or analogically, the playing of a game; basketball is different than football. Merely seeing the "place" predicts the meaning one is likely to experience.

Such discussions of place as an issue management challenge presume the normative ability to co-create society as shared norm-based expectations that withstand responsible and reflective review. Issues management is a search for community capability for making collective decisions, decisions of collective benefit. One person speaking (statement) and another responding (counterstatement) constitute the agonistic paradigm of collective self-governance whereby issues resolution constitutes enacted citizenship (Ihlen & Heath, 2018). This communitarian orientation constitutes means by which organizations' and other voices (publics as discourse partners) discursively shape and share community. According to Edwards (2006), rhetorical societal engagement

> seems to be broader in context of its societal function in that the specific reality and identification go beyond the connection of publics and organization, to the community (of which the organization is a part) as a whole. This is a particularly important distinction when companies become involved in social issues that extend beyond the public-organization relationship.
>
> (p. 844)

A fully functioning society creates community that addresses partisan causes by responsible and reflective review. Collectives, the shaping, instantiation, consubstantiation, and transubstantiation of community, co-socially construct shared norm-based legitimacy expectations. Meaning constitutes place as shared fact, values, policies, identities, and identifications.

Constitutive Approach to Place in SIM

Text rhetorically constitutes place, including organizations of all types as places with unique identities and identifications (simply, seller presumes buyer, educator presumes student—and vice versa). Textually, communication constitutes organizations. In the case of SIM, voices of all types of organizations are relevant to the collective discursive formation of societal narratives: Corporations, non-profits, issue-oriented activists, governmental agencies, and professional associations for example. Although advocates of this paradigm realize that organizations organize to communicate, they also presume that communication constitutes organization.

Without communication that influences outcomes, organizations cannot formulate strategic plans and achieve the information, networks, systems, structures, balance, strategic adjustment, and identifications they need to organize. For this reason, place has a multidimensional role in SIM. Such management plans must fit with dominant textual narratives of each society. Fundamentally, place is defined by political economy, which constitutes resource management, shared interest, and social justice. Issues-oriented place is defined by regulatory, legislative, and judicial principles. The assumption, for instance, that free market society is self-regulating, presumes inherently a balance between free market players, government, and the public interest that is constantly agonistic. Generically, rhetorical strains occur over legitimacy battles regarding how corporations seek to bend society to serve their interests, versus how society seeks to bend market-driven corporations to serve the public interest.

Quality of Place as Issue

For decades issues regarding the quality of place have existed, particularly coinciding with activist rhetoric and social movement agitation over issues such as environmental quality, atomic energy safety, and worker rights (pay and safety) following WW II. Urban planning is also included in the list of places as issues. Battles occur as water resources, especially to cities, are changed, and periodically degraded—as what occurred in Flint, Michigan. Disaster mitigation and emergency management provide opportunities to contest issues that define community quality and provide means for protecting public and private interests. Debates recur as to quality, low-cost housing, as well as structural access to health care. Debates evaluate the quality of schools and educational opportunity. Transportation systems are a contestable aspect of the quality of place. FFST presumes the need to create communities and organizations that are good places to live and work.

Persona of Place

Organizations use place to speak for them; that is true, for instance, when publicly traded businesses include glossy, flattering pictures of corporate activities, happy employees, tantalizing/appealing products, and satisfied customers. Personae of place address marketing issues, such as ski/snowboarding resorts or vacation spots as well as tourism and nation branding. Such personae of place argue for the quality of place as good places to recreate, vacation, work, and live.

Places of memorializing serve epideictically to set and demonstrate values essential to the quality of community and society. Washington, D.C., pays complex homage to Presidents Washington, Jefferson, and Lincoln. Its museums interrogate the stasis of issues such as the complex heritage, identity, identification, and status of African Americans and Native Americans. It also pays homage to military personnel who died during the Vietnam War, highly contentious at the time, as government policy, and now as lasting memory of those who served.

Persona of place has substantial implications for issues of restoration and recovery, for health and safety, and invitational rhetoric. Governments brand themselves, as do private corporations seeking resources that legitimize licenses to operate. Places of infamy are also preserved as value statements, as in the case of Belchite, Spain (near Zaragoza), and Corbera d'Ebre, Spain: cities left in ruins by the Spanish Civil War. Similarly, Oradour-sur-Glane, France, serves as place persona recalling Nazi vindictive destruction.

Personae of place address issues of policy, strategic planning and management, legitimacy, identity, and identification. They focus critical attention on facts and values intended to rhetorically argue for the quality of place as good places to work and live.

PLACE AS RHETORIC

The concept of place as rhetoric presumes the processual rationale offered by place to justify the need, agency, and purpose of rhetoric as societal benefit: "A processual view of rhetoric relates to the 'when' dimension of context" (Sillence & Golant, 2018, p. 100). At what moments in the history of place is discourse demanded to reduce uncertainty, consider value, discuss and decide upon policy, understand and advance identity, encourage and accomplish identification? Consider the following.

Civil rights activists strategically picked places where marches would occur. The objective was to take the fight to the opponents. Rather than marching on Washington, voter rights advocates such as John Lewis picked dangerous places where backlash from White persons who were against Black persons acquiring voting rights was most likely to affirm the cause of the marchers. Thus, these were places of high quality rhetorically and symbolically. Edmund Pettus Bridge was one such place. Theophilus Eugene "Bull" Connor was a White man and prominent Alabama commissioner of public safety. He had a reputation for hatred and violence, which was put on public trial on that bridge (place) as the world watched, via television, John Lewis' head being broken as the result of bludgeoning by police.

Place as Metaphor   Setting the ground for such analysis, Waymer (2018) reemphasized that "metaphor is inherent to the nature of language and thought" (p. 245). By that reasoning, "metaphor is means by which materiality is connected to language" (p. 245). Because rhetoric, including metaphor, constitutively blends the material and symbolic, "institutionalism is complex because it brings together the symbolic and material" (Sillence & Golant, 2018, p. 97). Schools, national parks, seacoasts, pipelines, or solar panel farms: all of these have metaphorical implications for facts, policies, values, identities, and identifications that constitute community. To elucidate this point, consider the following metaphors used to describe various places in the U.S.: the Rust Belt, the Bible Belt, the Sun Belt, Silicon Valley, Hollywood (also known as Tinseltown), or even "blighted" inner cities (see Waymer, 2009), and more. All these metaphors for place conjure images in one's mind about the issues that shape and even constitute these locations and how they are to be debated, deliberated, defended, and managed.

Directions for Future Research

The study of issues management qua issues management emerged at a time when large commercial organizations and governments were being critically interrogated. Such events demonstrate the processual rhetorical efforts to achieve agentic dynamism, deliberative democracy. Surely large organizations seek to constitute the societies and communities where they operate, derive their license to operate, and in which they have various kinds of responsibility. But this is a multivocal, agonistic enterprise. Identities and relationships are interdependent and interpenetrating. They are constituted by communication. Are they constituted to the mutual benefit of all?

Over the 50 years of this robust multi-discipline, it has generated answers and raised questions. The quality of community and society is the endpoint. Until that moment, issues will be addressed in pursuit of the better, the best, but likely never the perfect. The discipline's future depends on the continued refinement of factors essential to understanding and achieving the morally responsible co-management of the human condition.

Place provides a useful avenue to explore the theoretical and practical applications of issues management—that is the strategic use of communication to influence matters of public policy. Consider the following: When we see university leaders make policy statements mandating that in-person, on-campus instruction should occur regardless of employees' health and safety concerns during the COVID-19 pandemic, we witness the rhetorical power of place in their various justifications (financial consequences of not being on campus—that is a question of fact; perceptions of students having a lower-quality educational experience—question of value; or inability for students to build a strong connection with the university—question of identification). By examining contestable questions of place, we can explore the myriad ways that SIM's foundational stones coalesce and interpenetrate. Yet, by using rhetorical theory (FFST), we also can unpack hegemonic ways place can be used to advance the interests of organizations at the expense of less powerful stakeholders (workplaces requiring employees to work in hazardous conditions) or conversely, how activists strategically leverage place to challenge more powerful organizational actors (civil rights activists choosing places of significance to advance their aims). Thus, place analysis allows researchers to examine issues more holistically, hopefully leading to more robust theorizing and application.

Conclusions

Rhetorical argumentation is the overriding principle of the discipline. Also, rather than thinking of it as centric to any type of organization, especially a business, SIM is a collective intelligence for managing facts, values, policies, identities, identification, and place, not for the benefit of a business or an industry, but a community and its societal textuality. Such efforts are strategic and aspirational; they are relevant to efforts to co-create the substance of place that can justify (and deny) organizational legitimacy needs as stakeholder expectations.

Thus, we can imagine White European migrants coming into a place eventually called Iowa (a name derived from the Ioway native people). Virgin land gave way to farming and related commercial activities. Identities and identifications arose as did the shared facts, values, and policies that legitimatized communities and societies as place. Regulations came into play that legitimized landownership, agricultural activities, commercial activities, and communities, including infrastructures and educational institutions that often originated in mission to serve the agricultural, mechanical, and intellectual interests of citizens, and including current efforts to foster social justice. Animal health, crop production, and food safety were compelling issues. Thus, states (mere constructions of human imagination and vocabulary) become constituted by co-developed (but not necessarily mutually beneficial) standards of legitimacy. Via this chapter, we made clear the concept of place and its status as a foundational pillar in the SIM rubric, and we hope that we have provided strong evidence to support the position that ideas and meaning not only count, but they are central to understanding the role of SIM in society, public relations' role in society, and SIM theorizing.

References

Aristotle. (1954). *Rhetoric* (W. R. Roberts, Trans.). Modern Library.

Botan, C. H., & Taylor, M. (2004). Public relations: State of the field. *Journal of Communication, 54*, 645–661.

Boyd, J. (2009). 756*: The legitimacy of a baseball number. In E. L. Toth, R. L. Heath, & D. Waymer (Eds.), *Rhetorical and critical approaches to public relations II* (pp. 154–169). Routledge.

Boyd, J., & Waymer, D. (2011). Organizational rhetoric: A subject of interest(s). *Management Communication Quarterly, 25*, 474–493. https://doi.org/10.1177/0893318911409865

Brooks, K. P., & Waymer, D. (2009). Public relations and strategic issues management challenges in Venezuela: A discourse analysis of Crystallex international corporation in Las Cristinas. *Public Relations Review, 35*, 31–39. https://doi.org/10.1016/j.pubrev.2008.11.002

Burke, K. (1960, November). The brain beautiful. *Bennington College Bulletin*, 4–7.

Burke, K. (1969a/1945). *A grammar of motives*. University of California Press.

Burke, K. (1969b/1950). *A rhetoric of motives*. University of California Press.

Coombs, W. T., & Holladay, S. J. (2017). Social issue qua wicked problems: The role of strategic communication in social issues management. *Journal of Communication Management, 21*(2), 79–95.

Crable, R. E., & Vibbert, S. L. (1985). Managing issues and influencing public policy. *Public Relations Review, 11*, 3–16.

Davidson, S. (2018). Organizational rhetoric in deeply pluralistic societies: The agonistic alternative. In Ø. Ihlen & R. L. Heath (Eds.), *Handbook of organizational rhetoric and communication* (pp. 301–314). Wiley Blackwell.

Doritos. (2020). *Do you hear us now? #AmplifyBlackVoices.* www.youtube.com/watch?v=pqMgoNXxRGU&feature=emb_logo

Edwards, H. H. (2006). A rhetorical typology for studying the audience role in public relations communication: The Avon 3-day disruption as exemplar. *Journal of Communication Management, 56*(4), 836–860.

Endres, D., Hess, A., Senda-Cook, S., & Middleton, M. K. (2016). *In situ* rhetoric: Intersections between qualitative inquiry, fieldwork, and rhetoric. *Culture Studies, 16*(6), 511–524.

Foley, M. S. (2013). *Front porch politics: The forgotten heyday of American activism in the 1970s and 1980s.* Hill and Wang.

Gardner, H. (1983). *Frames of mind: The theory of multiple intelligences.* Basic Books.

Harlow, R. F. (1976). Building a public relations definition. *Public Relations Review, 2*(4), 34–42.

Heath, R. L. (1997). *Strategic issues management: Organizations and public policy challenges.* Sage.

Heath, R. L. (2006a). A rhetorical theory approach to issues management. In C. Botan & V. Hazleton (Eds.), *Public relations theory II* (pp. 63–99). Lawrence Erlbaum Associates.

Heath, R. L. (2006b). Onward into more fog: Thoughts on public relations' research directions. *Journal of Public Relations Review, 18*(2), 93–114.

Heath, R. L. (2012). Was Black rhetoric ever anything but race in public relations? The challenge of the rhetoric of identity. In D. Waymer (Ed.), *Culture, social class, and race in public relations: Perspectives and applications* (pp. 225–244). Lexington Books.

Heath, R. L. (2021). Immovable objects/irresistible forces: Intelligences of sociopolitical decision making. *Public Relations Review.* https://doi.org/10.1016/j.pubrev.2021.102013

Heath, R. L., & Palenchar, M. J. (2009). *Strategic issues management: Organizations and public policy challenges* (2nd ed.). Sage.

Heath, R. L., & Waymer, D. (2009). Activist public relations and the paradox of the positive: A case study of Frederick Doublass' "fourth of July address". In R. L. Heath, E. L. Toth, & D. Waymer (Eds.), *Rhetorical and critical approaches to public relations II* (pp. 195–215). Routledge.

Heath, R. L., & Waymer, D. (2019). Public relations intersections: Statues, monuments, and narrative continuity. *Public Relations Review, 45*(5). https://doi.org/10.1016/j.pubrev.2019.03.003

Heath, R. L., Waymer, D., & Ihlen, Ø. (2021). Rhetorical theory of public relations. In C. Valentini, P. J. Schulz & P. Cobley (Eds.), *Public relations: Handbooks of communication science* (Vol. 27, pp. 361–379). De Gruyter Mouton.

Heath, R. L., Waymer, D., & Palenchar, M. J. (2013). Is the universe of democracy, rhetoric, and public relations whole cloth or three separate galaxies? *Public Relations Review, 39*, 271–279.

Hess, A. (2011). Critical-rhetorical ethnography: Rethinking the place and process of rhetoric. *Communication Studies, 62*(2), 127–152.

Ihlen, Ø., & Heath, R. L. (2018). *Handbook of organizational rhetoric and communication.* Wiley Blackwell.

Isocrates. (1929). *Antidosis* (G. Norlin, Trans). Loeb Classical Library, Harvard University Press.

Jaffe, G., Lamothe, D., & Tate, J. (2021, January 15). Conspiracy theories and a call for patriots entice veterans at the capitol. *The Washington Post*. www.washingtonpost.com/national-security/military-veterans-capitol-riots-protests/2021/01/15/7774da50-5763-11eb-a817-e5e7f8a406d6_story.html

Jones, R. P. (2020). *White too long: The legacy of white supremacy in American Christianity*. Simon & Schuster.

Lee, R. W. (2019). *A sin by another name: Reckoning with racism and the heritage of the South*. Convergent.

Madden, S. (2019). The issue of issues management: Considering the emotional and gendered core of issues. *Public Relations Inquiry, 8*(3), 299–317.

Marsh, C. (2010). *Classical rhetoric and modern public relations: An isocratean model*. Routledge.

Shanahan, F., Vogelaar, A. E., & Seele, P., (2018). Persuasion in organizational rhetoric: Distinguishing between instrumental and deliberative approaches. In Ø. Ihlen & R. L. Heath (Eds.), *Handbook of organizational rhetoric and communication* (pp. 329–343). Wiley Blackwell.

Sillence, J. A. A., & Golant, B. D. (2018). A theory of organization as context for, and as constituted by, rhetoric. In Ø. Ihlen & R. L. Heath (Eds.), *Handbook of organizational rhetoric and communication* (pp. 95–110). Wiley Blackwell.

Taylor, B. (1992). Crime? Greed? Big ideas? What were the 80s about? *Harvard Business Review*. https://hbr.org/1992/01/crime-greed-big-ideas-what-were-the-80s-about

Waymer, D. (2009). Liberty and justice for all? The paradox of governmental rhetoric. *Communication Quarterly, 57*, 334–351. https://doi.org/10.1080/01463370903107170

Waymer, D. (2018). Spades, shovels, and backhoes: Unearthing metaphors in organizational rhetoric. In Ø. Ihlen & R. L. Heath (Eds.), *Handbook of organizational rhetoric and communication* (pp. 245–256). Wiley Blackwell.

Waymer, D., & Heath, R. L. (2019). Political public relations, corporate citizenship, and corporate issues management. In J. Strömbäck & S. Kiousis (Eds.), *Political public relations: Concepts, principles and applications* (2nd ed., pp. 250–269). Routledge.

28 A Theoretic Perspective on the Evolution of Ethics for P.R. Theory

Shannon A. Bowen

Introduction and Evolution

Ethics in public relations has always been a challenging, difficult terrain, complicated by occasional setbacks, such as notable deceptions at Enron (Sims & Brinkman, 2003) or Toyota (Bowen & Zheng, 2015) and numerous others. To say that ethics in public relations is a difficult topic is an understatement, as much of the history of public relations is fraught with unethical activities, strategies, and tactics in pursuit of a goal based on self-interest alone. Philosophers define self-interest as a decision-making maxim that is unethical and eventually self-defeating.

Moral philosophy is, perhaps, the greatest challenge and final frontier of public relations theory development because of the difficulties posed not only by ethical problems but also by the inherent capacity in communication for misinterpretation, misleading information, omission and commission, and dishonesty. Because of the challenging and often contentious nature of this final frontier, those who study ethics in public relations must also boldly go forward into epistemological territory that often forces many practitioners to retreat. Moral courage is often required of those who would seek to speak about ethics, particularly at the intersection of governments, propaganda, public information, diplomacy, public affairs, crisis management, warfare, and the many domains that comprise public relations theory and practice.

Public relations ethics was once derided as an oxymoron. Cynics argued that ethical communication on a professional basis on behalf of an organization or client was an impossibility or "window dressing," pointing to evidence of dishonest communication in the development of public relations practice. Precious few scholarly, theory-based studies of public relations ethics existed until study of public relations ethics became more common. In recent years, the topic has developed and received expanded attention, in theory and research, and has grown substantially by being based in normative moral philosophy. Because of the historically rocky start of public relations ethics, the demand for theory-driven inquiry is heightened in importance.

DOI: 10.4324/9781003141396-32

Terminology and Evolution

An assessment of the theoretical development of ethics in public relations requires an understanding of the terminology related to moral philosophy, the intellectual pursuit that explores ethics in a systematic and analytical manner. There are three broad areas of inquiry in moral philosophy: meta-ethics, normative ethics, and applied ethics.

Metaethics is the study of how ethics and morals are understood epistemologically, seeking to determine what morality is and what constructs create moral understanding. Metaethics is a broad area of study ranging from ontology to linguistics, moral psychology, analytical and anthropological approaches to questions of moral abstraction, such as, "What is morality itself?" *Normative ethics* is the study of ideal ethical solutions to problems, using philosophical approaches to determine the basis for consistent and good ethical decisions. Norms or ideal ethics help define what is right or wrong behavior across a type or class of actions, such as honesty versus dishonesty. Normative ethics excels in applying theory to decisions and understanding what values should be considered in determining the basis for making an ideal decision such as duty, justice, or public good. *Applied ethics* is a descriptive practice of applying ethics to real-world scenarios or using ethics to understand real cases. Applied ethics can be useful in best-case applications, deconstructing what happened in an instance, or making recommendations for confronting future dilemmas common in public relations and communication management contexts.

As one may expect, each of the major approaches to moral philosophy contains numerous schools and varying perspectives, such as consequence or principle, to enlighten ethical questions. Moral philosophies are largely based on analytical reasoning, seeking to apply a logical framework to ethical situations that can help to standardize considerations in terms of consistency. Moral philosophers diverge on the purpose of the field at that point, some preferring to define the ethical in terms of outcomes, others in terms of virtue, and others in terms of moral law, principle, or right or wrong.

The evolution of ethical theory in public relations is paradoxically both ancient and nascent. Although little is known about public relations activities in the ancient world, we do have evidence that these activities were used with strategic intent thousands of years ago. However, the modern field of public relations, based on strategic management and communication theory, has grown and expanded into a vibrant part of the larger "relational" communication discipline (Eadie, 2022).

The purpose of this chapter is not to thoroughly recount public relations history; yet, with the maturation of public relations as a young professional field and academic discipline, a focus on ethics emerged. Therefore, offering an overview of the development of ethical theory often involves some concurrent connection with historical developments and changes in the field of public relations. One can view this theoretical development of ethics in public relations as comprised of numerous time periods, some studied more than others: ancient, Catholicism and Christian propagation, Gutenberg era, Enlightenment, New World and Revolution, Industrial Revolution, press agentry and muckraking periods, wartime propaganda, professionalization, issues management and corporate social responsibility, the excellence theory, and the rational era in which we currently reside. These truncated markers on the roadmap of time can in no way capture the entire complexity of ethical development of an emerging field, but they can allow illustration of turning points in theory along that intellectual path.

Professionalism

The post-World War II years saw the rise of public relations visionaries as counselors in public opinion, such as John W. Hill (Heath & Bowen, 2002). Hill operated as a counselor rather than a hired communicator, and he was known for firing clients who would not follow ethical advice and arguably influenced the entire profession to focus on ethics (Heath & Bowen, 2002). It is arguable that this time period of refocus on veracity, away from propaganda toward an ethical counselor role, was crucial in the development of public relations as a profession because professions must have an established code of ethics or ethical guidelines and norms to which members ascribe (Sullivan, 1965; Wright & Turk, 2007).

From the late 1970s to the turn of the millennium researchers studied relationships, dialogue, symmetry, and ways of helping public relations contribute to the overall effectiveness and strategic management of an organization. The scholarly literature of public relations was still relatively new and growing from professionally oriented publications such as *PR Quarterly* to academic journals such as *Public Relations Review*, established in 1975. Having an academic, scholarly body of knowledge is another trait of a profession, yet in this time few studies focused on ethics in the field, largely due to the field trying to define its boundaries.

Issues Management, Moral Development, and Ethical Conscience

As early as 1983 scholars began to turn serious study to development of public relations professionals' codes of ethics in the field (Kruckeberg, 1993; Wright, 1993), paradigms of ethics applied to communication questions (Wright, 1982), power and internal communication (Wright, 1995), and how ethical behavior could lead to more involvement in strategic management for the function (Bivins, 1980). Scholars (Heath, 1990, 1992, 1997) from both issues management and rhetorical perspectives argued that acting as an ethical voice arguing for truth was the highest calling of a public relations professional. Situational ethics, untrained and unstudied, was often the norm for practitioners (Pratt, 1991).

Notable at this time, Wright (1985) applied moral development theory to public relations professionals and found that they became less consequentialist (situational or utilitarian) in their thinking and more principle-based (deontological) as their levels of experience grew. Similarly, Bivins (1989, 1992) found that a systems model of ethics in public relations failed to offer an adequate baseline for the profession and that texts covered ethics in a superficial fashion if at all (Bivins, 1989). These scholars and a handful of others like them showed us not only what ethics could be as a moral conscience for public relations and organizations, but also how woefully underprepared most were to step into that role (Curtin et al., 2011; Neil & Weaver, 2017).

Excellence Theory, Relationships, and Moral Philosophy Forays

At this point, theories such as the excellence theory (Grunig, 1992a) began to include ethics as a component of symmetrical, dialogic decision making and conflict resolution important to the overall effectiveness of an organization and the functions' contributions toward that goal through strategic management. By the turn of the millennium, the next generation of scholars pursued specific elements of ethics within the excellence theory, relationship management, organization public relationships, contingency theory, power relations, or strategic issues management. The enormous scandal and fall of Enron corporation despite its 65-page code of ethics document (Bowen, 2010a) highlighted the importance of ethics, and these studies became more commonplace in the literature of public relations.

More studies specific to ethics emerged within the academic journals of public relations and closely related fields such as media ethics or business ethics, including replications and new explorations of applied moral philosophy. For the last three decades, scholars have emerged who study public relations ethics specifically or exclusively. Still, metaethical questions such as how we know what constitutes ethical communication are rare within public relations (Grunig, 1992b). One must turn to moral philosophy to understand specific taxonomy needed in tracing more modern theoretical developments such as the application of normative moral philosophy to public relations.

Approaches to Moral Philosophy

There are numerous approaches and schools of thought within moral philosophy, as part of the ancient and well-developed discipline of philosophy. Within moral philosophy, normative approaches can range from humanistic to pragmatic, to analytical or rational. Philosophy generally eschews the selfish, prudential self-interest or zero-sum game approach of "winner takes all" as a short-lived and unethical approach to complex problem solving. Because of the depth of moral philosophy literature, it is normally condensed into three main approaches to ethical thought, each with a different measurement for determining that which is ethical: virtue ethics (character), utilitarianism (consequentialism/outcomes), and deontology (principle/rights). The ethical standard of each approach differs in what it considers valuable, therefore familiarity with each paradigm offers the ability to conduct staggeringly different forms of moral analyses.

Virtue Ethics

Virtue ethics sought living the good life, based on Aristotle's *a priori* concept of "that which is—in itself—good" (Aristotle, 1910/322 BCE, p. 270). Rhetorical scholars based in the Platonic, Socratic, and Aristotelian traditions (sometimes termed "classicism") have applied virtue ethics in the broad sense to public relations practice. Socrates and his student Plato figure prominently in this approach to ethics. Plato's *Apology* credits Socrates as saying, "The unexamined life is not a life worth living for a human being" (p. 38a1). Socrates's statement requires analytical examination and places a burden of worth on human beings alone, achieving a moral determination not required of other beings. A love of wisdom is also central to this philosophy in which self-examination, reflection, consideration of achieving good, and a worthy life and as a pleasurable intellectual exercise are considered the ethical goals by which one is judged. This philosophy tends to focus on the individual level of character rather than the organizational level.

Aristotle refined the virtue approach to ethics into a formal system of logical reasoning. Aristotle required hypothetical logical reasoning and the time to engage in conscious moral deliberation to create choice. Choice, combined with habituation or praxis, created a life of virtue, in this view. Aristotle's ethics are sometimes called Nicomachean ethics, in reference to his son who transcribed his lectures into several books, the earliest documents we have on ethics (Aristotle, 1910/322 BCE). A notable sociologist Habermas, sought to apply virtue ethics to the discourse as "communicative action" or rhetorical argument in pursuit of truth based on discursive reflection (Habermas, 1982, 1984).

Perhaps best recognized among rhetorical public relations scholars is Robert L. Heath, who spent much of his career arguing that public relations professionals should be a voice to argue for truth, persuasively and compellingly, on the public stage. Thereby an audience would judge not only the character of the rhetor but also the truth of the argument. Heath (2001) termed this approach the *rhetorical enactment approach*.

As arguing for truth or a definition or interpretation of an issue or problem, and defining perspectives on its ethical or correct resolution, this perspective forms much of the theoretical basis of strategic issues management and public affairs research (Heath, 2005, 2006). Much of the virtue perspective research (Pearson, 1989a, 1989b) has been based on dialogue and argument to arrive at an ethical understanding (Kent & Taylor, 2002). Other scholars (Coombs, 1999; Place, 2021) have sought to apply a virtue-based ethics to communication, prioritizing feminist values such as care. However, many philosophers discredit this approach as inherently biased, preferential, and non-analytical, explaining its infrequent use in moral philosophy.

Rather than providing guidance on how one should act, virtue ethics emphasizes human flourishing and living a life of virtue or acting as a virtuous person would act. With the notable exception of rhetorical scholars, as applied in issues management (Heath & Palenchar, 2009), this approach to ethics has gained little traction in modern communication theory research. The vagueness of the proposition of creating human flourishing, combined with the time and reflection necessary, make virtue ethics rather impractical as a framework for applied ethics in the discipline. Therefore, public relations scholars have more often investigated other moral frameworks.

Consequentialism and Utility-Based Reasoning

Perhaps as a response to the highly individualistic approach of virtue ethics, a group or consequence-based reasoning appeared in communication scholarship. In ancient philosophy, Aristotle discussed the term *telos* (Greek: τέλος): meeting the end purpose, aim, or goal of a decision, later developed into teleological philosophy, or consequentialist-based reasoning. Well-known forms of teleology include hedonism and utilitarianism essentially holding that morally right actions are those decisions that produce the best consequences.

How one defines "best" consequences separates the numerous and varied approaches to consequentialism. For example, in utilitarianism, one seeks to maximize the utility of a decision, or what consequence it creates, to determine whether the act is ethical or not (Gorovitz, 1971). In act utilitarianism, it may be to create the greatest amount of happiness or good in one specific and detailed situation, or in rule utilitarianism to serve the greatest good for most people (i.e., vaccination requirement). Act utilitarianism examines the utility of consequences of an act in all specificity for creating maximum good outcomes and minimum harms. Rule utilitarianism also serves a majority interest but examines a class or type of action, looking at prior history and creating good outcomes from that class of actions as though it were a rule for all. There are drawbacks to majority-based solutions, such as disenfranchising a minority, reinforcing a status quo, equating humans with numbers, ignoring moral principle, or attempting to accurately predict dynamic future outcomes. Nonetheless these theories have been tested in public relations, equating the field as serving the public interest (Grunig, 1993, 2000), yet the search for more thorough ethical routes continued.

Professionalism has long been a standard for ethics in public relations. According to Parkinson (2001), professions include recognition or licensing standards that must have: "1). a clear definition of what acts are prohibited to those in the profession; 2). a unique set of skills and knowledge, and

3). recognition or identification of the professional or ethical obligations a member of the profession must meet" (p. 28). Applying this test of professionalism shows that the public relations industry, in most of the world, fails to meet the standard of a profession due to using unenforceable codes of ethics, a lack of licensing, no prosecution of offenses, or holding vague or conflicting ethical standards. However, licensing and codes of ethics, even if enforceable, are no panacea for a field as broad and nebulous as communication. What is defined as public relations is difficult to draw boundaries around, unlike medicine or law, as communication happens across all fields of endeavor. It is further complicated by marketing promotions, lobbying, governmental public affairs, news media, and other types of public communication in which influence and persuasion are difficult to define. However, some principled approaches to ethics have been proposed in quasi-professional "best practices" or case studies. For example, Parsons (2004) recommended pillars of public relations: veracity, non-maleficence, beneficence, confidentiality, and fairness (p. 21). These pillars or principles of public relations are primarily consequentialist but appear to see a deontological, principled basis prioritizing veracity or truth telling as a basis for ethics.

Perhaps more problematically, professionalism as a standard for ethics in public relations falls into the consequentialist paradigm and therefore holds other philosophical contradictions, such as equating people with numbers or reinforcing a majority-focused status quo, which oppresses minority opinion. Operating under the standards of professionalism often leads to ignoring greater moral obligations to principle and acting as a pure advocate for a client or position, akin to an attorney (c.f., Fitzpatrick & Bronstein, 2006). The advocacy model is problematic because the public relations person acts as a promoter of a certain view or how they define the public good or public interest, rather than as a moral agent seeking to reveal truth and further veracity independently of a client's interests (Bowen, 2006).

Approaches to studying whether public relations produces the greatest good for the greatest number, while minimizing harm, are utilitarian in nature but judged upon the outcome of creating professionalism across the field (Parsons, 2004). Professionalism often relies on prohibitive and somewhat simplistic codes of ethics that usually specify unethical acts in the absence of offering analytical understanding of the reasoning behind such prohibition (Parkinson, 2001). Further, standards of professionalism that rely simply on professional norms or codes of ethics have been roundly critiqued by philosophers because they often do not offer the amount of moral autonomy (Bivins, 2006) or analytical reasoning needed to resolve complex moral dilemmas and understand the principles behind such tenets.

Ideal-based, normative codes of ethics have been argued to be useful in unifying ethical understanding and priorities in a global setting (Kruckeberg, 1996). Kruckeberg and Starck (2001) also observed that a consequentialist approach to ethics termed *communitarianism* uses the standards of the community and tradition to seek guidance in ethical behavior. Although communitarianism is not a primary school of thought within moral philosophy, it has been applied in public relations theory by several scholars. The public relations function is concerned with community stakeholders and relationships with various publics, leading researchers (K. A. Leeper, 1996; R. Leeper, 2001) to conclude that a community-based ethic was quite relevant to the field. This approach sees consequences from the stakeholder view rather than only an organizational or management standpoint, offering a broad and inclusive perspective of consequences and potential outcomes.

As public relations theory developed toward a business-oriented, strategic management function, business ethics began to play a more prominent role in the literature of public relations. Based upon a decade-long, three-country grant study from the International Association of Business Communicators (IABC), the excellence study (Dozier et al., 1995) created a theory of nine "generic" (cross-organization type, size, culture, and national boundaries) principles that inspired public relations to contribute maximally to organizational effectiveness. Ethics was not an explicit part of this formula for excellence but was assumed to be a part of symmetrical dialogue in a larger, but rather vague, teleological approach.

However, in 1996, the excellence team (Vercic et al., 1996) acknowledged that assuming inherent ethics was a mistake by omission. They (Vercic et al., 1996) published a chapter that corrected the lack of ethics in the original principles, indicating that ethics should be a stand-alone principle of excellence in public relations. Follow-up empirical and conceptual research (Bowen, 2004, 2005) indicated that ethics was indeed the tenth "generic" principle of excellence and, based on how ethics was used in the executive-level of organizations, located it in the principle-based philosophy of deontology.

Deontology and Principle-Based Reasoning

Deontology is the primary form of non-consequence-based ethical decision making, created in the late 1700s by eminent philosopher Immanuel Kant, refining virtue ethics with rationality, a universal standard, and responsibility (Ward, 2019). Deontology seeks to make decisions based on the underlying moral principle to be upheld and is highly focused on individual rights and moral autonomy. Beck (1963) argued that deontology offered "the most important ethical theory of modern times" (p. xiii). Therefore, applying such an influential theory to public relations was a natural extension of moral philosophy to the growing body of knowledge in the field. Deontology also compensates for the vagueness and lack guidance in virtue ethics, and the lack of completeness and principle in consequentialist reasoning.

Moral autonomy is required in deontological ethics, meaning that the decision-maker must be able to objectively analyze based on reason and moral principle alone without being subjected to other concerns that would constrain options. This approach holds that preferential treatment of consequences would bias the decision-making process, leading to a loss of autonomy or rationality, meaning that no ethical decision could possibly result. Because all people are equally capable of autonomous, rational analyses, all people are equally obligated to act ethically.

Moral principles are "maxims" that are thought to be *universal*, meaning that they apply to all people equally, in all like situations, across time, and space (with exclusions for children, animals, and the mentally incapacitated). To ascertain what universal moral principle applies in each situation, one must rationally consider the three tenets of this philosophical approach, known as the three tests of the categorical imperative: 1) duty to uphold universal moral principle, 2) dignity and respect for humanity, and 3) good intention. A rational basis is of utmost importance in the consideration of these factors. No special or additional consideration is given to the self or the organization making the decision (as contrasted with utilitarianism), but consequences are not eschewed—just equally contemplated based on rationality.

Kant (1793/1974) wrote, "There can be no will without an end in view" (p. 25), but the consequences involved are not a deciding factor, just one consideration among many to consider rationally. To base a decision on consequences, in Kant's view, would invite a level of bias toward selfish goals that would disallow an ethical decision. The lack of bias in this approach lends it an epistemology of fairness, giving rise to the theory of justice (Rawls, 1971) that is also a part of deontology. Rationally determining a correct course of action should be done from an objective standpoint, ruling out preferential treatment, biases, self-interest alone, and other sources of influence that would make the decision less than objective (Rawls, 1971).

Kant's categorical imperative implies that every rational person is categorically obligated and has an imperative to consider the ethics of their decision due to their moral autonomy—and to do what all other rational agents would also do. The categorical imperative's three tests are as follows:

Duty—Act on that maxim that one could will [desire to become] as a universal law in all similar situations for all time. In other words, this is Kant's test that helps to identify a universal moral principle underlying the specific situation, while stripping away socio-centric context such as bias, prejudice, selfishness, and cultural norms. (Kant, 1785/1964; Schneewind, 1992)

Radical equality—Always treat others as end in themselves rather than a means to an end. By virtue of the rationality inherent in the human intellect, Kant held that all decision makers are therefore equal and equally obligated to uphold the moral law, be they educated or uneducated, aristocratic or commoner, male or female. This view of everyone being equal was radical in Kant's time (Sullivan, 1989). Kant was the first philosopher to situate morality within the self rather than lawmakers, arbiters, or institutions. (Sullivan, 1994)

Intent or good will—Act on the maxim [reason] of good will alone. Kant's third and final form of the categorical imperative test is arguably the highest bar of ethics to pass because it tests the intention of the decision maker. (Kant, 1785/1964)

Assessing the intention of others is often a difficult task that should be fact based and undertaken with objective moral autonomy. Even assessing one's own intention may require deep reflection and thoughtful analysis, as well as the freedom to engage in moral deliberation (Sullivan, 1989). Kant (1963/1930) explained, "If our conduct as free agents is to have moral goodness, it must proceed solely from a good will" (p. 18). For public relations, actions to promote the self, organization, or other interests would not be considered ethical because only satisfying the moral law is a reason to act.

The three forms of the categorical imperative are used *together* to analyze decision options and to determine the ethicality of a decision. The be considered ethical under deontology, a decision must affirmatively pass all three forms of the categorical imperative test. Only then can a decision maker be confident that a reasoned analysis of moral principle has been satisfied and the action is ethical (O'Neill, 1992).

Applying Deontology to Public Relations: A Reasoned Approach

Deontology suits public relations theory particularly well (Paquette et al., 2015). Kant's philosophy advises that one consider the dignity and respect of humanity (stakeholders and publics) through treating them never as means to an end but ends of value in and of themselves. This understanding holds that all people have intrinsic worth and value equal to that of others and should not be "used" as simply a means to accomplishing the decision maker's own ends, a relationship-building perspective. By basing decisions on his conception of a good moral will alone, a decision maker rules out decisional bias sources such as greed, bias, selfishness, prejudice, or culture/tradition. The decision maker can see clearly what is required when a standard of good will is used to make decisions, and any inclination toward duplicity would render the decision unethical. In stakeholder terms, the application of good intention provides a basis for making ethical choices related to not only the organization itself, but also all types of stakeholders and public relationships regardless of power or influence. Ethics has been described as a "pre-cursor" to other variables in building organization-public relationships (Bowen et al., 2016) and a way to create shared value (Chen et al., 2018).

Respecting stakeholders as a moral principle allows the decision maker to contemplate the values of these groups more objectively and clearly and how they would see the ethics of a decision the public relations manager may implement. Then these views can be respected and taken into view in strategic management when forming the organization's decision alternatives, including only the options which maintain duty, respect and dignity, and good will toward stakeholders inside and outside the organization. Those rights and responsibilities should resonate well with both members of the stakeholder community and anyone considering messaging, issues, or policies related to them. It is important to note that one must have access to information from many perspectives and maintain open lines of communication to build understanding.

Deontology has been applied in public relations more than other ethics paradigms, with the rationale being that public relations professionals prefer deontological reasoning over other approaches (Pratt, 1991; Pratt et al., 1994) or that at higher career levels they become more deontological (Bowen, 2002; Wright, 1985) and use Kantian reasoning in approaching complex problems and counseling executives on ethics (Bowen, 2009; Neill & Drumright, 2012). Public relations scholars have developed visual representations (boxes, pyramids, decision trees, and flowcharts) that help to implement a deontological analysis for those new to the philosophy (c.f., Bowen, 2005; Bowen & Gallicano, 2013; McElreath, 1997; Tilley, 2005). In an epistemological works on ethics in public relations, the valuable pro-social role of communication as creating social understanding and helping to resolve conflict was highlighted (Bowen, 2010b). This role involves a high level of moral autonomy, the highest amount of rational objectivity, and a will to consider respect, duty, and intention before self-interest, profit, or other biased motives. In an ideal or normative sense, public relations can authentically create good through acting as a conduit for problem solving, generating understanding on multiple sides of an issue.

As this philosophy has grown in understanding and importance in the field, rational approaches to acting as a moral conscience, a counselor in ethics, and a "conscience officer" or an engagement officer emerged (Bowen, 2008; Curtin et al., 2011; Neill & Drumright, 2012). In a challenge to the old idea that all actions must be mutually beneficial in public relations, new research showed that perspective was often in conflict with ethical truth, using climate change to illustrate the moral analysis of Kantian principle in combination with an issues management approach (Bowen & Heath, 2020). The purpose of public relations, then, is not advocacy, or mutual benefit (satisficing) but creating ethical decisions as a third, "tri-analytic" vantage (Bowen & Coombs, 2020). This new approach is not preferential or biased in favor of a one-sided client cause or an organization-management interpretation, but it is a third, rational-objective view. The tri-analytic public relations professional sees each perspective for analysis but is objective and morally autonomous in search of truth or ethical principle alone.

Conclusions and Future

In analyzing the development of ethics in public relations, there has been a steady but not constant evolution of more ethical inclusion, consideration, and theory in the field. Ethical drawbacks have been influenced by power struggles of various kinds, world wars, revolutions in the literal sense and the equality sense, and numerous scandals. However, tracing the broad evolution of ethics in the field shows that the ship of ethics normally corrects itself even after practically capsizing. Those with moral agency and ethical intention normally return to studying ethics in the field and having some influence on the practice of communication being based on ethical standards, autonomy, and moral philosophy.

In the future, public relations ethics will be challenged in myriad unpredictable ways. These challenges will come in the forms of loss of privacy rights, information warfare, AI warfare, political division, recession, pandemics, over-crowding, famine, violence, information suppression, natural disasters, climate change, and the crises, scandals, and collapses borne of selfishness. The future communication environment is one that is surrounded in habitable areas with instantaneous worldwide communication, no longer subject to editing, fact-checking, and gatekeeping as we understand them in mass communication theory. In this vortex of unfiltered information, critical thought, varying levels of media literacy, and verifying information will be of vital importance. Numerous scholars, many cited in this chapter, have offered rigorous analytical decision-making tools (c.f., Bowen & Gallicano, 2013) that can aid in the proactive analysis of moral dilemmas in this information environment. New approaches continue to be developed in both normative and specialized topics of ethics.

Social media can easily be manipulated through applying big data and artificial intelligence (AI), as nefarious players already know through their use of chat bots, deepfakes, and online influence agents bent on undermining truth. For the public relations professional, ethics will no longer be "nice to have" but will be the essential building block upon which *any* communication exists. Without credibility and trustworthiness, information is simply noise and distraction to be dismissed or ignored, misleading misinformation, or deceptive disinformation. Mumby (2013) observed, "All communication is relational and contextual" (p. 117), but in the atomized digital world determining those relationships and contexts is more difficult than ever before. With critical and credible composition, information becomes communication of value to the receiver. Public relations scholars and professionals must embrace the role of ethical counsel, examining principles carefully and advising based on reason, tri-analytic autonomy, and truth.

How do we achieve this goal? Thinking critically and studying rational critical thought are essential practices. Learning philosophy, also known as the love of reason, can help to overcome the future challenges we face. Critical thought has become more important than ever in a crowded or "polluted" information environment (Kahan, 2017). Therefore, rational, analytic philosophy is the cornerstone of ethical reasoning in a complex world. Other forms of moral reasoning have worth but are normally not stand-alone approaches to guide public relations professionals through the maze of responsibilities, competing interpretations, and post-truth claims that we must face. Only reason based on solid analytics can protect public relations from an unethical descent into the influence-peddling maelstrom of propaganda and "spin."

Rational, rigorous, and well-reasoned analyses are explainable, understandable, and speak to not only fairness but a respect for the equality and worth of the individual. Rising above influence to employing rational moral philosophy is a normative ethical obligation that will allow public relations to contribute to society. It can enhance public discussion, building understanding, equality, and increased organizational responsibility, fostering ethical rectitude across all areas of the function—and society.

References

Aristotle. (1910/322 BCE). *Nicomachean ethics*. Routledge.

Beck, L. W. (1963). Foreword. In L. W. Beck (Ed.), *Immanuel Kant's lectures on ethics* (pp. ix–xiv). Hackett.

Bivins, T. H. (1980). Ethical implications of the relationship of purpose to role and function in public relations. *Journal of Business Ethics, 8*(1), 65–73.

Bivins, T. H. (1989). Are public relations texts covering ethics adequately? *Journal of Mass Media Ethics, 4*(1), 39–52.

Bivins, T. H. (1992). A systems model for ethical decision making in public relations. *Public Relations Review, 18*(4), 365–383.

Bivins, T. H. (2006). Responsibility and accountability. In K. Fitzpatrick & C. Bronstein (Eds.), *Ethics in public relations: Responsible advocacy* (pp. 19–38). Sage.

Bowen, S. A. (2002). Elite executives in issues management: The role of ethical paradigms in decision making. *Journal of Public Affairs, 2*(4), 270–283.

Bowen, S. A. (2004). Expansion of ethics as the tenth generic principle of public relations excellence: A Kantian theory and model for managing ethical issues. *Journal of Public Relations Research, 16*(1), 65–92.

Bowen, S. A. (2005). A practical model for ethical decision making in issues management and public relations. *Journal of Public Relations Research, 17*(3), 191–216.

Bowen, S. A. (2006). Autonomy in communication: Inclusion in strategic management and ethical decision-making, a comparative case analysis. *Journal of Communication Management, 10*(4), 330–352.

Bowen, S. A. (2008). A state of neglect: Public relations as "corporate conscience" or ethics counsel. *Journal of Public Relations Research, 20*(3), 271–296.

Bowen, S. A. (2009). What communication professionals tell us regarding dominant coalition access and gaining membership. *Journal of Applied Communication Research, 37*(4), 418–443.

Bowen, S. A. (2010a). Almost a decade a later: Have we learned lessons from inside the crooked E, Enron? *Ethical Space: The International Journal of Communication Ethics, 7*(1), 28–35.

Bowen, S. A. (2010b). The nature of good in public relations: What should be its normative ethic? In R. L. Heath (Ed.), *The Sage handbook of public relations* (pp. 569–583). Sage.

Bowen, S. A., & Coombs, W. T. (2020). Ethics in crisis communication. In F. Frandsen & W. Johansen (Eds.), *Crisis communication* (pp. 539–557). De Gruyter.

Bowen, S. A., & Gallicano, T. D. (2013). A philosophy of reflective ethical symmetry: Comprehensive historical and future moral approaches and the excellence theory. In K. Sriramesh, A. Zerfass, & J. N. Kim (Eds.), *Public relations and communication management: Current trends and emerging topics* (pp. 193–209). Routledge.

Bowen, S. A., & Heath, R. L. (2020). Intelligences in strategic issues management: Challenging the mutually beneficial relationship paradigm. *Partecipazione e Conflitto: The Open Journal of Sociopolitical Studies, 13*(2), 1–20. https://doi.org/10.1285/i20356609v13i2p1002

Bowen, S. A., Hung-Baesecke, C. J., & Chen, Y. R. (2016). Ethics as a pre-cursor to organization-public relationships: Building trust before and during the OPR model. *Cogent Social Sciences, 2.* http://dx.doi.org/10.1080/23311886.2016.1141467

Bowen, S. A., & Zheng, Y. (2015). Auto recall crisis, framing, and ethical response: Toyota's missteps. *Public Relations Review, 41*(1), 40–49. www.sciencedirect.com/science/article/pii/S036381111400160X

Chen, Y.-R. R., Hung-Baesecke, C.-J. F., Bowen, S. A., Zerfass, A., Stacks, D. W., & Boyd, B. (2018). The role of leadership in shared value creation from the public's perspective: A multi-continental study. *Public Relations Review*, 101749. https://doi.org/10.1016/j.pubrev.2018.12.006

Coombs, W. T. (1999). Information and compassion in crisis responses: A test of their effects. *Journal of Public Relations Research, 11*(2), 125–142.

Curtin, P. A., Derville-Gallicano, T., & Matthews, K. (2011). Millennials' approaches to ethical decision-making: A survey of young public relations agency employees. *PR Journal, 5*(2), 1–22. www.instituteforpr.org/files/uploads/IPRRC_13_Proceedings.pdf

Dozier, D. M., Grunig, L. A., & Grunig, J. E. (1995). *Manager's guide to excellence in public relations and communication management.* Lawrence Erlbaum Associates.

Eadie, W. F. (2022). *When communication became a discipline.* Lexington Books.

Fitzpatrick, K., & Bronstein, C. (Eds.). (2006). *Ethics in public relations: Responsible advocacy.* Sage.

Gorovitz, S. (Ed.). (1971). *Utilitarianism, with critical essays.* Bobbs-Merrill.

Grunig, J. E. (1993). Public relations and international affairs: Effects, ethics and responsibility. *Journal of International Affairs, 47,* 138–162.

Grunig, J. E. (2000). Collectivism, collaboration, and societal corporatism as core professional values in public relations. *Journal of Public Relations Research, 12*(1), 23–48.

Grunig, J. E. (Ed.). (1992a). *Excellence in public relations and communication management.* Lawrence Erlbaum Associates.

Grunig, L. A. (1992b). Toward the philosophy of public relations. In E. L. Toth & R. L. Heath (Eds.), *Rhetorical and critical approaches to public relations* (pp. 65–91). Lawrence Erlbaum Associates.

Habermas, J. (1982). A reply to my critics (T. McCarthy, Trans.). In J. Thompson & D. Held (Eds.), *Habermas: Critical debates* (pp. 219–283). MIT Press.

Habermas, J. (1984). *The theory of communicative action: Reason and the rationalization of society* (T. McCarthy, Trans., Vol. 1). Beacon Press.

Heath, R. L. (1990). Effects of internal rhetoric on management responses. *Journal of Applied Communication Research, 18,* 153–167.

Heath, R. L. (1992). Critical perspectives on public relations. In E. L. Toth & R. L. Heath (Eds.), *Rhetorical and critical approaches to public relations* (pp. 37–61). Lawrence Erlbaum Associates.

Heath, R. L. (1997). *Strategic issues management: Organizations and public policy challenges.* Sage.

Heath, R. L. (2001). A rhetorical enactment rationale for public relations: The good organization communicating well. In R. L. Heath (Ed.), *Handbook of public relations* (pp. 31–50). Sage.

Heath, R. L. (2005). Rhetorical theory. In R. L. Heath (Ed.), *Encyclopedia of public relations* (Vol. 2, pp. 749–752). Sage.

Heath, R. L. (2006). A rhetorical theory approach to issues management. In C. Botan & V. Hazleton (Eds.), *Public relations theory II* (pp. 63–99). Lawrence Erlbaum Associates.

Heath, R. L., & Bowen, S. A. (2002). The public relations philosophy of John W. Hill: Bricks in the foundation of issues management. *Journal of Public Affairs, 2*(4), 230–246.

Heath, R. L., & Palenchar, M. J. (2009). *Strategic issues management: Organizations and public policy challenges* (2nd ed.). Sage.

Kahan, D. M. (2017). "Ordinary science intelligence": A science-comprehension measure for study of risk and science communication, with notes on evolution and climate change. *Journal of Risk Research, 20*(8), 995–1016.

Kant, I. (1785/1964). *Groundwork of the metaphysic of morals* (H. J. Paton, Trans.). Harper & Row.

Kant, I. (1793/1974). *On the old saw: That may be right in theory, but it won't work in practice* (E. B. Ashton, Trans.). University of Pennsylvania Press.

Kant, I. (1963/1930). *Lectures on ethics* (L. Infield, Trans.). Hackett Publishing.

Kent, M. L., & Taylor, M. (2002). Toward a dialogic theory of public relations. *Public Relations Review, 28*(1), 21–37.

Kruckeberg, D. (1993). Universal ethics code: Both possible and feasible. *Public Relations Review, 19*(1), 21–31.

Kruckeberg, D. (1996). Transnational corporate ethical responsibilities. In H. M. Culbertson & N. Chen (Eds.), *International public relations: A comparative analysis* (pp. 81–92). Lawrence Erlbaum Associates.

Kruckeberg, D., & Starck, K. (2001). Public relations and community: A reconstructed theory revisited. In R. L. Heath (Ed.), *Handbook of public relations* (pp. 51–60). Sage.

Leeper, K. A. (1996). Public relations ethics and communitarianism: A preliminary investigation. *Public Relations Review, 22*(2), 163–179.

Leeper, R. (2001). In search of a metatheory for public relations: An argument for communitarianism. In R. L. Heath (Ed.), *Handbook of public relations* (pp. 93–104). Sage.

McElreath, M. P. (1997). *Managing systematic and ethical public relations campaigns* (2nd ed.). Brown & Benchmark.

Mumby, D. K. (2013). *Organizational communication: A critical approach.* Sage.

Neill, M. S., & Drumright, M. E. (2012). PR professionals as organizational conscience. *Journal of Mass Media Ethics: Exploring Questions of Media Morality, 27*(4), 220–234.

Neil, M. S., & Weaver, N. (2017). Silent & unprepared: Most millennial practitioners have not embraced role as ethical conscience. *Public Relations Review, 43*(2), 337–344. http://dx.doi.org/10.1016/j.pubrev.2017.01.002

O'Neill, O. (1992). Vindicating reason. In P. Guyer (Ed.), *The Cambridge companion to Kant* (pp. 280–308). Cambridge University Press.

Paquettea, M., Sommerfeldt, E. J., & Kent, M. L. (2015). Do the ends justify the means? Dialogue, development, communication, and deontological ethics. *Public Relations Review, 41*, 30–39.

Parkinson, M. (2001). The prsa code of professional standards and member code of ethics: Why they are neither professional or ethical. *Public Relations Quarterly, 46*(3), 27–31.

Parsons, P. J. (2004). *Ethics in public relations: A guide to best practice.* Kogan Page.

Pearson, R. (1989a). Beyond ethical relativism in public relations: Coorientation, rules, and the idea of communication symmetry. In J. E. Grunig & L. A. Grunig (Eds.), *Public relations research annual* (Vol. 1, pp. 67–86). Lawrence Erlbaum Associates.

Pearson, R. (1989b). *A theory of public relations ethics* [Doctoral dissertation, Ohio University].

Place, K. R. (2021). People are more than just a statistic: Ethical, care-based engagement of marginalized publics on social media. *Journal of Media Ethics,* 1–13. https://doi.org /10.1080/23736992.2021.1937175

Pratt, C. B. (1991). Public relations: The empirical research on practitioner ethics. *Journal of Business Ethics, 10,* 229–236.

Pratt, C. B., Im, S. H., & Montague, S. N. (1994). Investigating the application of deontology among U.S. public relations practitioners. *Journal of Public Relations Research, 6*(4), 241–266.

Rawls, J. (1971). *A theory of justice.* Harvard University Press.

Schneewind, J. B. A. (1992). Autonomy, obligation, and virtue: An overview of Kant's moral philosophy. In P. Guyer (Ed.), *The Cambridge companion to Kant* (pp. 309–341). Cambridge University Press.

Sims, R. R., & Brinkman, J. (2003). Enron ethics (or, culture matters more than codes). *Journal of Business Ethics, 45*(3), 243–256.

Sullivan, A. J. (1965). Values of public relations. In O. Lerbinger & A. J. Sullivan (Eds.), *Information, influence, and communication: A reader in public relations* (pp. 412–439). Basic Books.

Sullivan, R. J. (1989). *Immanuel Kant's moral theory.* Cambridge University Press.

Sullivan, R. J. (1994). *An introduction to Kant's ethics.* Cambridge University Press.

Tilley, E. (2005). The ethics pyramid: Making ethics unavoidable in the public relations process. *Journal of Mass Media Ethics, 20*(4), 305–320.

Vercic, D., Grunig, L. A., & Grunig, J. E. (1996). Global and specific principles of public relations: Evidence from Slovenia. In H. M. Culbertson & N. Chen (Eds.), *International public relations: A comparative analysis* (pp. 31–65). Lawrence Erlbaum Associates.

Ward, K. (2019). *The development of Kant's view of ethics.* Wiley Blackwell.

Wright, D. K. (1982, April). The philosophy of ethical development in public relations. *IPRA Review, 22.*

Wright, D. K. (1985). Can age predict the moral values of public relations practitioners? *Public Relations Review, 11*(1), 51–60.

Wright, D. K. (1993). Enforcement dilemma: Voluntary nature of public relations codes. *Public Relations Review, 19*(1), 13–20.

Wright, D. K. (1995). The role of corporate public relations executives in the future of employee communications. *Public Relations Review, 21*(3), 181–198.

Wright, D. K., & Turk, J. V. (2007). Public relations knowledge and professionalism: Challenges to educators and practitioners. In E. L. Toth (Ed.), *The future of excellence in public relations and communication management: Challenges for the next generation* (pp. 571–588). Lawrence Erlbaum Associates.

29 Theoretical Models for Corporate Social Media Use

Alvin Zhou and Linjuan Rita Men

Introduction

The evolution of social media has transformed the practice of public relations and corporate communication. The norm where companies dominate corporate speak with one-way information flow has been challenged by the social media era. With social media platforms providing the unique interactive, conversational, personal, decentralized, and communal features, publics are increasingly connected and empowered in their interactions with organizations. Publics are not passive message receivers; instead, they are enabled to be active communicators, content creators, and distributors (Men & Tsai, 2014). In this active communication, social media has brought forth both opportunities and challenges for corporate communication practice. On the one hand, social media provides organizations optimal tools to conduct two-way conversations and engage in and build relationships with today's digital savvy publics. On the other hand, the viral nature of social media poses challenges for organizations' online reputation management and risk communication. How organizations should capitalize on the unique characteristics of social media to contribute to public relations effectiveness remains a critical question for both scholars and practitioners.

While scholars start to employ normative theories such as the dialogic theory to characterize the effective use of corporate social media for organizational purposes, some emerging interdisciplinary theoretical frameworks have recently risen to prominence to provide more pragmatic guidance for the practice. This chapter evaluates this area of research, by: 1) reviewing the definition of social media and how it has changed the practice of corporate communication, 2) providing a comprehensive review of relevant literature and theories related to corporate social media use, 3) critically examining some widely held assumptions about social media, and 4) suggesting areas for future researchers to advance theorization in corporate social media use.

DOI: 10.4324/9781003141396-33

Corporate Social Media Use

Social Media: Definition and Characteristics

Numerous definitions exist for social media, but most of them contend that it is a distinct category and a prime example of the computer-mediated communication technologies that spawned from the era of Web 2.0. In contrast to its predecessor, Web 1.0, where content creation was limited to very few and only one-way communication channels such as website portals were available for passive information consumption, Web 2.0 emphasizes user-generated content, interactive media, and social networks (Allen, 2013; Cormode & Krishnamurthy, 2008). For example, a popular definition from Kaplan and Haenlein (2010) states that social media are "Internet-based applications that build on the ideological and technological foundations of Web 2.0, and that allow the creation and exchange of user generated content" (p. 62).

In the context of corporate social media use, the "user" in "user generated content" can refer to both corporations and their stakeholders. Corporations can broadcast messages on social media to their online followings, while regular people can post their reactions or voice their opinions for everyone to see. Therefore, in terms of public relations practice, social media has facilitated two-way symmetrical communication, which was hailed as the desired form of organization-public communication even before the rise of social media (J. Grunig, 1992). Though some scholars have questioned the value of this two-way ideal in recent scholarship (e.g., Valentini, 2015), it is still a matter of fact that social media, compared to previous communication technologies, grant organizational stakeholders more communication power than ever before, and this interactive form of organization-public communication significantly deviates from traditionally one-way public relations practice of years past. In fact, Solis and Breakenridge (2009) hold that social media renews the legitimacy of the public relations profession for corporations, as social media management has swiftly become one of the most important job responsibilities for practitioners as found by recent industry surveys (Meganck et al., 2020). In this sense, the Internet age and especially the rise of corporate social media have transformed the public relations profession, altered its research agenda, and prompted more theoretical models that incorporated the factor of computer mediation.

Social Media Use By and in Corporations

Although social media seems so ubiquitous now, it is important to consider its rise against the historical backdrop and recognize that corporate social media use is still a relatively new phenomenon. Prior to the Internet age, which encompasses Web 1.0 and Web 2.0, corporate communication had been limited to traditional media such as television, radio, and newspaper. Journalists previously acted as gatekeepers to traditional media channels, which made the practice of media relations such as media pitching an important—if not paramount—part of public relations practice (Waters et al., 2010). From this view, the practice of using social media to directly communicate and listen to the mass public is quite neoteric.

Often, public relations researchers and practitioners consider organizational blogging as the earliest example of corporate social media use. Starting with employees casually blogging in semi-official capacities, organizational blogs became a full-blown communication strategy for corporations in the mid-2000s, and scholars have since recognized the potential of using social media to build mutually beneficial organization-public relationships (e.g., Kelleher & Miller, 2006; Yang & Lim, 2009). Social networking sites such as Facebook and Twitter, which digitalized personal relationships and later started hosting organizational presences, soon accelerated the adoption of social media by corporations (boyd & Ellison, 2007; McCorkindale, 2010; Utz, 2009). More than a decade later, consumers expect large corporations to have a social media presence where they can directly engage with organizational representatives (Men & Tsai, 2013, 2014), and some resourceful corporations have started adopting internal social media for employee communication (e.g., Men et al., 2020a; Sievert & Scholz, 2017).

The following review and analysis concern social media platforms such as blogs, Facebook, Twitter, LinkedIn, Instagram, YouTube, Reddit, Snapchat, social messaging apps (e.g., WeChat, WhatsApp), and other enterprise social media developed in-house for employees' internal use. Most empirical studies in this realm focused on one specific social media platform; however, the theoretical models are platform-agnostic.

Theoretical Frameworks for Corporate Social Media Use

A survey of recent public relations scholarship on corporate social media use suggests the following theoretical frameworks to be among the most used. However, since the study of corporate social media use is still a nascent area in public relations research, we do not claim it to be an exhaustive list. New and interdisciplinary theoretical frameworks left uncovered by this review continue to be employed by emerging research, and many of them have shown promising directions at theorizing corporate social media use, such as the organizational listening framework (Borner & Zerfass, 2018; Macnamara, 2019).

Dialogic Communication

What dialogue and dialogic communication mean in public relations continues to be a topic contentiously discussed among academic researchers. There are two streams of research that have taken the word *dialogue* in slightly different directions, the first focusing on the enactment of dialogue as communication ethics for public relations practice, and the second focusing on the employment of communication strategies by public relations practitioners to make use of the Internet's dialogic potential (Zhou & Xu, 2021). Many consider the first stream of inquiries as organization-public dialogue's philosophical roots and the latter as its specific empirical case (Sommerfeldt & Yang, 2018; Taylor & Kent, 2014). In this review, we will focus on the latter, as it closely pertains to the topic of corporate social media use.

Kent and Taylor (1998) articulated an optimistic view that the Internet (i.e., corporate websites at that time), as a communication tool, has the potential to help organizations build and sustain dialogues with stakeholders, since the mediated space afforded by the technology allows organizations to engage with publics in open, honest, risky, and synchronous discussions. To achieve the Internet's dialogic potential, they suggested five communication strategies that spawned two decades of empirical research in digital media and dialogic communication. The five communication strategies, named "dialogic principles," are: 1) dialogic loop, which contends that corporations' websites should establish feedback channels where stakeholders can provide feedback and organizations can address concerns in a back-and-forth manner; 2) useful information, which emphasizes that corporate websites should include information of general value to their concerned publics; 3) return visit generation, which states that corporations should encourage stakeholders to revisit their sites, since relationship building is not a one-time conduct but needs sustained communication; 4) ease of interface, which requires corporate websites to be easy to load and intuitive to navigate for all types of stakeholders and hardware setups; and 5) visitor conservation, which discourages designs that might unintentionally lead visitors astray and away from the corporate website.

These five strategies, suggested for website communication, have since been adjusted and adopted by empirical research on corporate social media use (see summaries in Ao & Huang, 2020; McAllister-Spooner, 2009; Morehouse & Saffer, 2018; Wirtz & Zimbres, 2018). For example, an early content analysis conducted by Rybalko and Seltzer (2010) coded the presence and absence of dialogic features on corporate Twitter accounts' profiles and found that corporations with and without dialogic orientations presented different types of Twitter messages. For mobile communication, McCorkindale and Morgoch (2013) found Fortune 500 mobile websites to be more customer-centric and to feature more dialogic principles. Comparative studies in this area have revealed that corporations adhered to the dialogic suggestions to various degrees on different social networking sites, one example being that corporate pages on Facebook usually employed more dialogic principles than their Twitter counterparts (e.g., D. Kim et al., 2014). Recently, with the industry's increasing pursuit of digital engagement indicators such as likes and retweets, some studies have linked these outcomes with dialogic principles. For example, results from Men et al. (2018) show that not all dialogic principles positively contribute to desirable engagement outcomes, as the return visit generation negatively affects the number of shares and reactions on Facebook. However, the link between dialogic principles and engagement indicators remains unclear, as some recent empirical analyses seem to suggest that the relationship varies across study contexts and media platforms (e.g., Gálvez-Rodríguez et al., 2018; Yue et al., 2019).

Overall, these studies have shown that a corporation's online communication does not fully realize social media's potential for dialogic communication. These findings are corroborated by evidence across cultural backgrounds as well (e.g., Al-Kandari et al., 2019; Qu, 2020). Thus, researchers have argued that more critical and innovative scholarship should be undertaken to further theorize or conceptually reconsider the dialogic communication framework for corporate social media use (Chen et al., 2020; Sommerfeldt & Yang, 2018). Scholars have considered adding new measures to capture different communication strategies employed by corporations, such as the message's level of social presence, media vividness, and linguistic features (e.g., W. Liu et al., 2020; Men et al., 2018), while other scholars have investigated why dialogic communication fails to take place in corporate settings by examining the role of digital media, suggesting revisions to dialogic principles and providing new communication strategies (e.g., Pang et al., 2018; Zhou & Xu, 2021, 2022).

Public Engagement

The use of the term *engagement* (see the "Engagement in Digital Communication" chapter) has seen a dramatic increase in recent public relations research. One of its most formal and theoretically robust definitions provided by Johnston (2018) referred to engagement as "a dynamic multidimensional relational concept featuring psychological and behavioral attributes of connection, interaction, participation, and involvement, designed to achieve or elicit an outcome at individual, organization, or social levels" (p. 19).

Engagement can be a state, where consistent corporate efforts lead to an engaged stakeholder community and an engaged society at the collective and social level (e.g., Men et al., 2020a). Engagement can be a process, where corporations use communication strategies to interact with stakeholders to achieve cognitive, affective, and behavioral outcomes at the individual level, which include but are not limited to the social media likes, shares, and comments (e.g., Men & Tsai, 2016). Engagement can be carried out by organizations to achieve communal outcomes and change public behavior, where studies consider corporate agency in changing their business environment (e.g., Johnston & Lane, 2018). Engagement can also be carried out by stakeholders as a response to corporate social media messages (e.g., Men et al., 2018). Therefore, compared to dialogue, this new paradigm seems to encourage and accommodate a more diverse and dynamic understanding of the corporate communication process.

At the current stage, most empirical public relations studies on corporate social media rely on the engagement framework to examine individual-level consequences of organization-public communication. Instead of dissecting how corporations craft social media messages—the apparent emphasis of studies using the dialogic communication framework—many engagement studies on corporate social media use have inquired how consumers and stakeholder groups react to those efforts. For example, Men and Tsai (2014), among the first to connect the public engagement concept to the public relations literature, showed how consumer engagement behaviors including reactive message consumption (e.g., reading corporate social media posts) and proactive content contributing (e.g., posting comments, uploading product-related pictures) can contribute to organization-public relationships as the central relational outcome. Though public engagement seems to contribute less to the behavioral outcome of public advocacy, their study, along with others (e.g., Kang, 2014; Paek et al., 2013), recognized the importance of corporate social media engagement for relationship building with publics.

In terms of public engagement's antecedents, studies have suggested that stakeholders' traits that are usually not controllable by organizations, such as their media dependency and community identification, can affect public engagement (Men & Tsai, 2013). However, corporations do have the ability to motivate stakeholders for engagement through their digital channels. For example, social presence has been regularly examined as an important way for corporations to cultivate public engagement (e.g., Tsai & Men, 2017). Message characteristics and the authenticity and transparency communicated on social media can also influence stakeholder engagement outcomes (e.g., Ji et al., 2019; Ott & Theunissen, 2015).

Aforementioned literature considered engagement as something stakeholders do (at the behavioral level) or feel (at the attitudinal level) in reaction to corporations' messages. Another line of research examines engagement as something corporations do on digital media to stakeholders or their general business environment. Though early studies concerning non-profit, health-related, or governmental organizations have found positive outcomes of stakeholder engagement on social media (e.g., Guidry et al., 2017; Smitko, 2012), recent studies on corporate social media use have highlighted potential risks. For example, social media engagement can sometimes be detrimental to reputation and online word-of-mouth when corporate engagement efforts with social issues do not align with stakeholder expectations (e.g., Ji et al., 2017), and its effect seems to be contingent upon the communication dynamics and relational networks among stakeholders that are somewhat out of corporate control (Xu & Zhou, 2020). More discussion will be devoted to this topic in later sections.

Use and Gratification, and Parasocial Interactions

Both derived from early communication studies on traditional media use (i.e., television), theories on uses and gratification and parasocial interactions have also been applied to corporate social media use. In contrast to the previously discussed dialogic communication and public engagement, these two frameworks are very much audience centric. They answer questions as to why people consume information—in our case corporate media—and what effects it has on those audiences.

Not all stakeholders follow or consume corporate social media. People consume media to satisfy their needs, as the uses and gratifications theory contends (Katz et al., 1973). In corporate communication, those needs could be gaining more knowledge about the company, sharing information regarding the company, providing feedback to the company, seeking companionship and social interaction, or simply relaxing. The communication management paradigm in public relations, with models such as situational theory of problem solving (STOPS) and social-mediated crisis communication (SMSS) (Jin et al., 2014; J.-N. Kim & J. Grunig, 2011), provides a utilitarian examination on publics' communicative actions and focuses on stakeholder intentions such as information seeking and information sharing. Research has shown that in serious situations like corporate crises, the need for transparent information will peak among corporate stakeholders, and companies should employ social media to swiftly and transparently communicate their responses (e.g., B. F. Liu et al., 2019). Gratifications also drive various use of mobile technologies when companies communicate their corporate social responsibilities (Cheng et al., 2019).

However, corporate social media use has been increasingly characterized by gratifications that do not involve concrete information. This is evident through the rise of relationship marketing and some recent cases where corporate accounts became social media sensations, such as Wendy's Twitter personality and Nike's Colin Kaepernick campaign where corporate social media accounts chitchat with other organizations in a witty fashion or publicly engage in social issues that are beyond their profit-making areas. In these cases, stakeholders were drawn to corporate social media accounts to have a communal celebration on certain issues or viral content, and the corporate social media role as information provider has dramatically diminished. To understand this phenomenon of entertaining gratification, scholars usually consider parasocial interactions as its important relational antecedent.

Parasocial interactions denotes audiences' intimate and personal relationships with corporate characters (Horton & Wohl, 1956; Thorson & Rodgers, 2006). Research in this area asserts that the creation of parasocial relationships takes repeat interactions between corporations and stakeholders, and that corporations need to put consistent and prolonged investment into their social media management to achieve a high degree of relational commitment (Eyal & Dailey, 2012; Tsai & Men, 2017). Organizational authenticity and social presence also come into play in the development of parasocial relationships, since a personable and agreeable corporate character established through social media content creation is critical in initiating parasocial interactions (Men & Tsai, 2015).

Channel Selection and Media Affordances

Another prominent line of research on corporate social media use focuses on the selection of media platforms and its subsequent effects on corporate communication. In a nutshell, it addresses questions such as what social media practitioners use, whether the medium is the message, and how channel choice affects corporate communication.

Distinct differences among media channels have been noted since early public relations media buying research (Schwartz & Glynn, 1989). With the proliferation of social media platforms developed by various technology companies, the landscape of digital public relations has been flooded with numerous channels for organization-public communication. Sommerfeldt et al.'s study (2019) on public relations channel repertoire (i.e., the practice of using a combination of media channels) found that the selection of media channels varies across public relations units, for instance those who are responsible for employee communication are more likely to use sharing platforms such as Facebook. However, in practice, companies usually follow organizational publics in terms of their channel selections to reach as many relevant stakeholders as possible. It seems to be a given that large corporations need to establish online representations on major social media platforms that reach billions of users such as Twitter. However, the ongoing phenomenon of audience fragmentation also means that different digital media channels might capture different user populations (Webster & Ksiazek, 2012), and this presents an issue of company-platform fit for corporate social media use. For example, TikTok predominantly reaches Generation Z, a specific demographic group that might be hard for some corporations to reach on other platforms, but Generation Z might also be the demographic group that possesses little value for certain corporations. Therefore, corporations need to strategically evaluate social media platform demographics to determine channel use.

Other than demographics and channel repertoire, another line of scholarly inquiries on social media channel selection focuses on the effect of platforms themselves. Studies on crisis communication have shown that websites and Facebook continue to be the media channels most desired by information-seeking publics (Park et al., 2019). And compared to blogs, stakeholders respond more positively to crisis responses communicated by mass-mediated social media platforms such as Twitter (Schultz et al., 2011). These studies examine specific social media platforms employed by public relations practitioners and have considerable practical implications. However, one important issue that has not been addressed in these studies is why existing social media channels differ on a theoretical level.

A line of recent research adopts the affordance framework in psychology and human-computer interaction to dissect why public relations outcomes differ across various social media platforms (e.g., Fu & Zhang, 2019). By differentiating communication channels in terms of their action possibilities—for example, Twitter affords greater anonymity but less network association than Facebook, scholars are now pinpointing what theoretical constructs underlying the design of social media platforms are driving cross-channel differences. Studies in this area have connected the affordance framework with the dialogic theory (Zhou & Xu, 2021, 2022) and the engagement framework (Chewning, 2018) discussed earlier, and this provides a promising new direction in which to theorize social media's effect on corporate communication.

Specific Contexts of Corporate Social Media Use

Corporations employ social media in two broad contexts: external public communication and internal communication. Most of the research is conducted in the area of public communication, which encompasses issues such as marketing communication, crisis communication, corporate social responsibility communication, and advocacy communication. These communication programs are built to influence external stakeholders such as governments, stockholders, consumers, and business partners. Another important context of corporate social media use that has been gaining steam in the past decade is internal communication. As a fast-growing area of public relations research and practice (Men & Bowen, 2017; Tkalac Verčič et al., 2012), internal communication pertains to the use of internal social media in building communities, internal relationships, and employee engagement (Men et al., 2020b; Weber & Shi, 2017).

It has been argued that organizational use of internal social media enhances open communication, encourages two-way interactions between management and employees, and fosters employee collaboration, connection, and community building (Leonardi et al., 2013). A growing number of recent studies have provided ample evidence that links corporate internal social media use to perceived organizational transparency (Men et al., 2020a), employee organizational identification (Madsen, 2016; Men et al., 2020a), a sense of community among employees (Laitinen & Sivunen, 2020; Uysal, 2016), employee engagement (Haddud et al., 2016; Men et al., 2020a; Sievert & Scholz, 2017), employee-organization relationships (Men et al., 2020b), and pro-social behaviors such as organizational citizenship behavior (Madsen, 2016) and innovation (Gode et al., 2019).

However, risks, challenges, and barriers also exist for organizations' internal social media use, just as in external. Researchers have pointed out potential risks and challenges associated with protection of intellectual property and privacy, distractions from work, fear of loss of control from management, erosion of employee work-life boundaries, employee self-censoring in posting, and lack of participation on internal social media (Ewing et al., 2019; Madsen, 2017; Men et al., 2020a).

Is Social Media Good for Corporate Public Relations?

If we take one step back and evaluate the body of literature that has been reviewed, it becomes obvious that most research takes an optimistic view on corporate social media use. By connecting the digital practice with positive outcomes such as improved online word-of-mouth, relational outcomes, and enhanced stakeholder engagement in theoretical models, our existing knowledge seems to be built upon the assumption that social media is good for corporate public relations. This assumption may need to be critiqued as we move forward theory-building in corporate public relations research. Specifically, two emerging themes in public relations literature on social media practice are calling for a more critical analysis of this unquestioned underlying presupposition.

First and foremost, empirical and real-world evidence on the effectiveness of using social media for relationship building remains elusive (Sommerfeldt & Yang, 2018). As the development of social media coincides with the relational turn of public relations ethics (i.e., the relationship management paradigm and the dialogic theory), some scholars have been repeatedly making one central argument about social media's "potential" to help corporations build relationships with key publics. Meanwhile, although studies have built linkages between actual corporate social media usage and various positive outcomes, most of them used cross-sectional designs. These studies use observational data and can hardly identify causal relationships that are testable in experimental settings.

As Valentini (2015) argued, "The use of social media is not necessarily as beneficial to either organizations or publics as has been depicted" by the literature (p. 175). This "social media is good for public relations" assumption needs more scholarly inquiries. To investigate this question, scholars may compare relational outcomes between two similar companies wherein one organization used, and one did not use, social media or employ a longitudinal design that explores how the establishment of social media presence changed desirable outcomes.

A more theoretically elevated investigation on this topic can ask how computer mediation changes organization-public relationship building. This question concerns multiple research disciplines including public relations, interpersonal communication, and computer-mediated communication, but it has not been extensively addressed. And it seems a natural fit and a great opportunity for public relations scholars to contribute theories back to the broader study of digital media and communication technology.

Second, the increasing polarization among issue publics, where stakeholder groups' cognitive beliefs on social and political issues grow apart and their affective attitudes toward each other become more hostile, has brought more risks to corporate social media use, especially for the communication of corporate social responsibility and corporate advocacy. Social media provides direct communication channels between corporations and their stakeholders but subsequently exposes businesses to unfiltered user feedback.

The feedback, taking forms as comments and reposts, are often situated in a socially mediated discourse that is affective, political, and polarizing. For example, corporate social media accounts trying to engage in issues such as anti-racism and anti-sexism have had mixed results (Ciszek & Logan, 2018; Xu & Zhou, 2020). This conundrum could get more prevalent with time, as many previously nonpolitical issues engaged by corporations, such as environment protection and education equity, might be co-opted and polarized by political parties in the future. This problem exists independently from whether a said corporation uses social media, but due to the fact that most existing social media platforms afford an unprecedented level of transparency and visibility, the potential risk of engaging in polarized issues will multiply when corporations employ social media. These factors, compounded with the upward trend of stakeholders actively demanding corporations take stands on important social issues, renders social media a volatile space. Corporations are thus advised to be more cautious, vigilant, deliberative, and strategic in their social media use in terms of issue-related communication.

Looking Ahead: Future of Corporate Social Media Research

As public relations research on social media moves into its third decade, there are some notable future directions for theoretical development, informed by technological advances and business practices, that are of particular interest for corporations. There has been a push for a general normative theory of social media in public relations (e.g., Kent & Li, 2020), but here, we consider ways forward that are more positive, concrete, and can help us reconsider focal concepts in existing public relations research.

Theoretical approaches to understanding social media in public relations are bound to be fragmented, as different research designs will apply theoretical frameworks of different scales, macro, meso, or micro, to the studied phenomenon. However, development is much required on theorizing mediation, i.e., mechanisms of how exactly corporate social media use affects public relations and organizational effectiveness. Future efforts are also needed to further define digital relationships (Lock, 2019), especially taking into account varied emerging digital platforms with unique affordances and channel features (e.g., TikTok, Clubhouse), the ever-evolving digital media landscape, and the changing nature of social media publics with Gen-Z and upcoming generations entering the digital space.

Another area that demands more scholarly attention and exploration in the future, which has been a standing issue in practice and under-researched, is the development of social media models for measurement and evaluation. For instance, other than the widely used metrics of likes, shares, retweets, comments, and sentiment, what else should be measured? How do corporate social media engagement efforts connect to the bottom line and business outcomes? How can traditional communication measurement models of output, outtake, and outcomes be applied to the digital context?

Finally, with AI-powered platforms (e.g., chatbots) increasingly used by companies (e.g., Men et al., 2022), research should keep pace to theorize automated relationships and unlock the potential of artificial intelligence and other emerging technologies (e.g., virtual reality, smart work-from-home technologies) for corporate communication purposes.

References

Al-Kandari, A. A., Gaither, T. K., Alfahad, M. M., Dashti, A. A., & Alsaber, A. R. (2019). An Arab perspective on social media: How banks in Kuwait use Instagram for public relations. *Public Relations Review, 45*(3), 101774. https://doi.org/10.1016/j.pubrev.2019.04.007

Allen, M. (2013). What was Web 2.0? Versions as the dominant mode of internet history. *New Media & Society, 15*(2), 260–275. https://doi.org/10.1177/1461444812451567

Ao, S. H., & Huang, Q. S. (2020). A systematic review on the application of dialogue in public relations to information communication technology-based platforms: Comparing English and Chinese contexts. *Public Relations Review, 46*(1), 101814. https://doi.org/10.1016/j.pubrev.2019.101814

Borner, M., & Zerfass, A. (2018). The power of listening in corporate communications: Theoretical foundations of corporate listening as a strategic mode of communication. In S. Bowman, A. Crookes, S. Romenti, & Ø. Ihlen (Eds.), *Advances in public relations and communication management* (pp. 3–22). Emerald Publishing Limited.

boyd, d., & Ellison, N. B. (2007). Social network sites: Definition, history, and scholarship. *Journal of Computer-Mediated Communication, 13*(1), 210–230. https://doi.org/10.1111/j.1083-6101.2007.00393.x

Chen, Y.-R. R., Hung-Baesecke, C.-J. F., & Chen, X. (2020). Moving forward the dialogic theory of public relations: Concepts, methods and applications of organization-public dialogue. *Public Relations Review, 46*(1), 101878. https://doi.org/10.1016/j.pubrev.2019.101878

Cheng, Y., Chen, Y.-R. R., Hung-Baesecke, C.-J. F., & Jin, Y. (2019). When CSR meets mobile SNA users in Mainland China: An examination of gratifications sought, CSR motives, and relational outcomes in natural disasters. *International Journal of Communication, 13*, 319–341.

Chewning, L. V. (2018). Virtual engagement: A theoretical framework of affordances, networks, and communication. In K. A. Johnston & M. Taylor (Eds.), *The handbook of communication engagement* (pp. 439–452). Wiley-Blackwell.

Ciszek, E., & Logan, N. (2018). Challenging the dialogic promise: How Ben & Jerry's support for Black Lives Matter fosters dissensus on social media. *Journal of Public Relations Research, 30*(3), 115–127. https://doi.org/10.1080/1062726X.2018.1498342

Cormode, G., & Krishnamurthy, B. (2008). Key differences between Web 1.0 and Web 2.0. *First Monday, 13*(6). https://doi.org/10.5210/fm.v13i6.2125

Ewing, M., Men, L. R., & O'Neil, J. (2019). Using social media to engage employees: Insights from internal communication managers. *International Journal of Strategic Communication, 13*(2), 110–132. https://doi.org/10.1080/1553118X.2019.1575830

Eyal, K., & Dailey, R. M. (2012). Examining relational maintenance in parasocial relationships. *Mass Communication and Society, 15*(5), 758–781. https://doi.org/10.1080/15205436.2011.616276

Fu, J. S., & Zhang, R. (2019). NGOs' HIV/AIDS discourse on social media and websites: Technology affordances and strategic communication across media platforms. *International Journal of Communication*, *13*, 181–205.

Gálvez-Rodríguez, M. D. M., Sáez-Martín, A., García-Tabuyo, M., & Caba-Pérez, C. (2018). Exploring dialogic strategies in social media for fostering citizens' interactions with Latin American local governments. *Public Relations Review*, *44*(2), 265–276. https://doi.org/10.1016/j.pubrev.2018.03.003

Gode, H. E., Johansen, W., & Thomsen, C. (2019). Employee engagement in generating ideas on internal social media: A matter of meaningfulness, safety and availability. *Corporate Communications: An International Journal*, *25*(2), 263–280. https://doi.org/10.1108/CCIJ-03-2019-0024

Grunig, J. E. (Ed.). (1992). *Excellence in public relations and communications management*. Lawrence Erlbaum Associates.

Guidry, J. P., Jin, Y., Orr, C. A., Messner, M., & Meganck, S. (2017). Ebola on Instagram and Twitter: How health organizations address the health crisis in their social media engagement. *Public Relations Review*, *43*(3), 477–486. https://doi.org/10.1016/j.pubrev.2017.04.009

Haddud, A., Dugger, J. C., & Gill, P. (2016). Exploring the impact of internal social media usage on employee engagement. *Journal of Social Media for Organizations*, *3*(1), 1–22.

Horton, D., & Wohl, R. R. (1956). Mass communication and para-social interaction: Observations on intimacy at a distance. *Psychiatry*, *19*(3), 215–229. https://doi.org/10.1080/00332747.1956.11023049

Ji, Y. G., Chen, Z. F., Tao, W., & Li, Z. (2019). Functional and emotional traits of corporate social media message strategies: Behavioral insights from S&P 500 Facebook data. *Public Relations Review*, *45*(1), 88–103. https://doi.org/10.1016/j.pubrev.2018.12.001

Ji, Y. G., Li, C., North, M., & Liu, J. (2017). Staking reputation on stakeholders: How does stakeholders' Facebook engagement help or ruin a company's reputation? *Public Relations Review*, *43*(1), 201–210. https://doi.org/10.1016/j.pubrev.2016.12.004

Jin, Y., Liu, B. F., & Austin, L. L. (2014). Examining the role of social media in effective crisis management: The effects of crisis origin, information form, and source on publics' crisis responses. *Communication Research*, *41*(1), 74–94. https://doi.org/10.1177/0093650211423918

Johnston, K. A. (2018). Toward a theory of social engagement. In K. A. Johnston & M. Taylor (Eds.), *The handbook of communication engagement* (pp. 19–32). Wiley-Blackwell.

Johnston, K. A., & Lane, A. B. (2018). Building relational capital: The contribution of episodic and relational community engagement. *Public Relations Review*, *44*(5), 633–644. https://doi.org/10.1016/j.pubrev.2018.10.006

Kang, M. (2014). Understanding public engagement: Conceptualizing and measuring its influence on supportive behavioral intentions. *Journal of Public Relations Research*, *26*(5), 399–416. https://doi.org/10.1080/1062726X.2014.956107

Kaplan, A. M., & Haenlein, M. (2010). Users of the world, unite! The challenges and opportunities of social media. *Business Horizons*, *53*(1), 59–68. https://doi.org/10.1016/j.bushor.2009.09.003

Katz, E., Blumler, J. G., & Gurevitch, M. (1973). Uses and gratifications research. *Public Opinion Quarterly*, *37*(4), 509. https://doi.org/10.1086/268109

Kelleher, T., & Miller, B. M. (2006). Organizational blogs and the human voice: Relational strategies and relational outcomes. *Journal of Computer-Mediated Communication*, *11*(2), 395–414. https://doi.org/10.1111/j.1083-6101.2006.00019.x

Kent, M. L., & Li, C. (2020). Toward a normative social media theory for public relations. *Public Relations Review, 46*(1), 101857. https://doi.org/10.1016/j.pubrev.2019.101857

Kent, M. L., & Taylor, M. (1998). Building dialogic relationships through the world wide web. *Public Relations Review, 24*(3), 321–334. https://doi.org/10.1016/S0363-8111(99)80143-X

Kim, D., Kim, J.-H., & Nam, Y. (2014). How does industry use social networking sites? An analysis of corporate dialogic uses of Facebook, Twitter, YouTube, and LinkedIn by industry type. *Quality & Quantity, 48*(5), 2605–2614. https://doi.org/10.1007/s11135-013-9910-9

Kim, J.-N., & Grunig, J. E. (2011). Problem solving and communicative action: A situational theory of problem solving. *Journal of Communication, 61*(1), 120–149. https://doi.org/10.1111/j.1460-2466.2010.01529.x

Laitinen, K., & Sivunen, A. (2020). Enablers of and constraints on employees' information sharing on enterprise social media. *Information Technology & People.* https://doi.org/10.1108/ITP-04-2019-0186

Leonardi, P. M., Huysman, M., & Steinfield, C. (2013). Enterprise social media: Definition, history, and prospects for the study of social technologies in organizations. *Journal of Computer-Mediated Communication, 19*(1), 1–19. https://doi.org/10.1111/jcc4.12029

Liu, B. F., Xu, S., Lim, J. R., & Egnoto, M. (2019). How publics' active and passive communicative behaviors affect their tornado responses: An integration of STOPS and SMCC. *Public Relations Review, 45*(4), 101831. https://doi.org/10.1016/j.pubrev.2019.101831

Liu, W., Xu, W., & Tsai, J.-Y. (2020). Developing a multi-level organization-public dialogic communication framework to assess social media-mediated disaster communication and engagement outcomes. *Public Relations Review, 46*(4), 101949. https://doi.org/10.1016/j.pubrev.2020.101949

Lock, I. (2019). Explicating communicative organization-stakeholder relationships in the digital age: A systematic review and research agenda. *Public Relations Review, 45*(4), 101829. https://doi.org/10.1016/j.pubrev.2019.101829

Macnamara, J. (2019). Explicating listening in organization-public communication: Theory, practices, technologies. *International Journal of Communication, 13*, 5183–5204.

Madsen, V. T. (2016). Constructing organizational identity on internal social media: A case study of coworker communication in Jyske bank. *International Journal of Business Communication, 53*(2), 200–223. https://doi.org/10.1177/2329488415627272

Madsen, V. T. (2017). The challenges of introducing internal social media—the coordinators' roles and perceptions. *Journal of Communication Management, 21*(1), 2–16. https://doi.org/10.1108/JCOM-04-2016-0027

McAllister-Spooner, S. M. (2009). Fulfilling the dialogic promise: A ten-year reflective survey on dialogic Internet principles. *Public Relations Review, 35*(3), 320–322. https://doi.org/10.1016/j.pubrev.2009.03.008

McCorkindale, T. (2010). Can you see the writing on my wall? A content analysis of the fortune 50's Facebook social networking sites. *Public Relations Journal, 4*(3), 1–13.

McCorkindale, T., & Morgoch, M. (2013). An analysis of the mobile readiness and dialogic principles on fortune 500 mobile websites. *Public Relations Review, 39*(3), 193–197. https://doi.org/10.1016/j.pubrev.2013.03.008

Meganck, S., Smith, J., & Guidry, J. P. (2020). The skills required for entry-level public relations: An analysis of skills required in 1,000 PR job ads. *Public Relations Review, 46*(5), 101973. https://doi.org/10.1016/j.pubrev.2020.101973

Men, L. R., & Bowen, S. (2017). *Excellence in internal communication management*. Business Expert Press.

Men, L. R., O'Neil, J., & Ewing, M. (2020a). Examining the effects of internal social media usage on employee engagement. *Public Relations Review, 46*(2), 101880. https://doi.org/10.1016/j.pubrev.2020.101880

Men, L. R., O'Neil, J., & Ewing, M. (2020b). From the employee perspective: Organizations' administration of internal social media and the relationship between social media engagement and relationship cultivation. *International Journal of Business Communication*. https://doi.org/10.1177/2329488420949968

Men, L. R., & Tsai, W.-H. S. (2013). Beyond liking or following: Understanding public engagement on social networking sites in China. *Public Relations Review, 39*(1), 13–22. https://doi.org/10.1016/j.pubrev.2012.09.013

Men, L. R., & Tsai, W.-H. S. (2014). Perceptual, attitudinal, and behavioral outcomes of organization–public engagement on corporate social networking sites. *Journal of Public Relations Research, 26*(5), 417–435. https://doi.org/10.1080/1062726X.2014.951047

Men, L. R., & Tsai, W.-H. S. (2015). Infusing social media with humanity: Corporate character, public engagement, and relational outcomes. *Public Relations Review, 41*(3), 395–403. https://doi.org/10.1016/j.pubrev.2015.02.005

Men, L. R., & Tsai, W.-H. S. (2016). Public engagement with CEOs on social media: Motivations and relational outcomes. *Public Relations Review, 42*(5), 932–942. https://doi.org/10.1016/j.pubrev.2016.08.001

Men, L. R., Tsai, W.-H. S., Chen, Z. F., & Ji, Y. G. (2018). Social presence and digital dialogic communication: Engagement lessons from top social CEOs. *Journal of Public Relations Research, 30*(3), 83–99. https://doi.org/10.1080/1062726X.2018.1498341

Men, L. R., Zhou, A., & Tsai, W.-H. S. (2022). Harnessing the power of chatbot social conversation for organizational listening: The impact on perceived transparency and organization-public relationships. *Journal of Public Relations Research, 34*(1–2), 20–44. https://doi.org/10.1080/1062726X.2022.2068553

Morehouse, J., & Saffer, A. J. (2018). A bibliometric analysis of dialogue and digital dialogic research: Mapping the knowledge construction and invisible colleges in public relations research. *Journal of Public Relations Research, 30*(3), 65–82. https://doi.org/10.1080/1062726X.2018.1498343

Ott, L., & Theunissen, P. (2015). Reputations at risk: Engagement during social media crises. *Public Relations Review, 41*(1), 97–102. https://doi.org/10.1016/j.pubrev.2014.10.015

Paek, H.-J., Hove, T., Jung, Y., & Cole, R. T. (2013). Engagement across three social media platforms: An exploratory study of a cause-related PR campaign. *Public Relations Review, 39*(5), 526–533. https://doi.org/10.1016/j.pubrev.2013.09.013

Pang, A., Shin, W., Lew, Z., & Walther, J. B. (2018). Building relationships through dialogic communication: Organizations, stakeholders, and computer-mediated communication. *Journal of Marketing Communications, 24*(1), 68–82. https://doi.org/10.1080/13527266.2016.1269019

Park, S., Boatwright, B., & Avery, E. J. (2019). Information channel preference in health crisis: Exploring the roles of perceived risk, preparedness, knowledge, and intent to follow directives. *Public Relations Review, 45*(5), 101794. https://doi.org/10.1016/j.pubrev.2019.05.015

Qu, Y. (2020). Engaging publics in the mobile era: A study of Chinese charitable foundations' use of WeChat. *Public Relations Review, 46*(1), 101815. https://doi.org/10.1016/j.pubrev.2019.101815

Rybalko, S., & Seltzer, T. (2010). Dialogic communication in 140 characters or less: How Fortune 500 companies engage stakeholders using Twitter. *Public Relations Review, 36*(4), 336–341. https://doi.org/10.1016/j.pubrev.2010.08.004

Schultz, F., Utz, S., & Göritz, A. (2011). Is the medium the message? Perceptions of and reactions to crisis communication via twitter, blogs and traditional media. *Public Relations Review, 37*(1), 20–27. https://doi.org/10.1016/j.pubrev.2010.12.001

Schwartz, D. F., & Glynn, C. J. (1989). Selecting channels for institutional public relations. *Public Relations Review, 15*(4), 24–36. https://doi.org/10.1016/S0363-8111(89)80062-1

Sievert, H., & Scholz, C. (2017). Engaging employees in (at least partly) disengaged companies. Results of an interview survey within about 500 German corporations on the growing importance of digital engagement via internal social media. *Public Relations Review, 43*(5), 894–903. https://doi.org/10.1016/j.pubrev.2017.06.001

Smitko, K. (2012). Donor engagement through Twitter. *Public Relations Review, 38*(4), 633–635. https://doi.org/10.1016/j.pubrev.2012.05.012

Solis, B., & Breakenridge, D. (2009). *Putting the public back in public relations: How social media is reinventing the aging business of PR.* FT Press.

Sommerfeldt, E. J., & Yang, A. (2018). Notes on a dialogue: Twenty years of digital dialogic communication research in public relations. *Journal of Public Relations Research, 30*(3), 59–64. https://doi.org/10.1080/1062726X.2018.1498248

Sommerfeldt, E. J., Yang, A., & Taylor, M. (2019). Public relations channel "repertoires": Exploring patterns of channel use in practice. *Public Relations Review, 45*(4), 101796. https://doi.org/10.1016/j.pubrev.2019.101796

Taylor, M., & Kent, M. L. (2014). Dialogic engagement: Clarifying foundational concepts. *Journal of Public Relations Research, 26*(5), 384–398. https://doi.org/10.1080/1062726X.2014.956106

Thorson, K. S., & Rodgers, S. (2006). Relationships between blogs as EWOM and interactivity, perceived interactivity, and parasocial interaction. *Journal of Interactive Advertising, 6*(2), 5–44. https://doi.org/10.1080/15252019.2006.10722117

Tkalac Verčič, A., Verčič, D., & Sriramesh, K. (2012). Internal communication: Definition, parameters, and the future. *Public Relations Review, 38*(2), 223–230. https://doi.org/10.1016/j.pubrev.2011.12.019

Tsai, W.-H. S., & Men, L. R. (2017). Social CEOs: The effects of CEOs' communication styles and parasocial interaction on social networking sites. *New Media & Society, 19*(11), 1848–1867. https://doi.org/10.1177/1461444816643922

Utz, S. (2009). The (potential) benefits of campaigning via social network sites. *Journal of Computer-Mediated Communication, 14*(2), 221–243. https://doi.org/10.1111/j.1083-6101.2009.01438.x

Uysal, N. (2016). Social collaboration in Intranets: The impact of social exchange and group norms on internal communication. *International Journal of Business Communication, 53*(2), 181–199. https://doi.org/10.1177/2329488415627270

Valentini, C. (2015). Is using social media "good" for the public relations profession? A critical reflection. *Public Relations Review, 41*(2), 170–177. https://doi.org/10.1016/j.pubrev.2014.11.009

Waters, R. D., Tindall, N. T. J., & Morton, T. S. (2010). Media catching and the journalist–public relations practitioner relationship: How social media are changing the practice of media relations. *Journal of Public Relations Research, 22*(3), 241–264. https://doi.org/10.1080/10627261003799202

Weber, M. S., & Shi, W. (2017). Enterprise social media. In C. R. Scott, L. K. Lewis, J. R. Barker, J. Keyton, T. Kuhn, & P. K. Turner (Eds.), *The international encyclopedia of organizational communication* (pp. 600–606). Wiley.

Webster, J. G., & Ksiazek, T. B. (2012). The dynamics of audience fragmentation: Public attention in an age of digital media. *Journal of Communication, 62*(1), 39–56. https://doi.org/10.1111/j.1460-2466.2011.01616.x

Wirtz, J. G., & Zimbres, T. M. (2018). A systematic analysis of research applying "principles of dialogic communication" to organizational websites, blogs, and social media: Implications for theory and practice. *Journal of Public Relations Research, 30*(1–2), 5–34. https://doi.org/10.1080/1062726X.2018.1455146

Xu, S., & Zhou, A. (2020). Hashtag homophily in twitter network: Examining a controversial cause-related marketing campaign. *Computers in Human Behavior, 102*, 87–96. https://doi.org/10.1016/j.chb.2019.08.006

Yang, S.-U., & Lim, J. S. (2009). The effects of blog-mediated public relations (BMPR) on relational trust. *Journal of Public Relations Research, 21*(3), 341–359. https://doi.org/10.1080/10627260802640773

Yue, C. A., Thelen, P., Robinson, K., & Men, L. R. (2019). How do CEOs communicate on Twitter? A comparative study between fortune 200 companies and top startup companies. *Corporate Communications: An International Journal, 24*(3), 532–552. https://doi.org/10.1108/CCIJ-03-2019-0031

Zhou, A., & Xu, S. (2021). Digital public relations through the lens of affordances: A conceptual expansion of the dialogic principles. *Journal of Public Relations Research, 33*(6), 445–463. https://doi.org/10.1080/1062726X.2022.2046585

Zhou, A., & Xu, S. (2022). Computer mediation vs. dialogic communication: How media affordances affect organization-public relationship building. *Public Relations Review, 48*(2), 102176. https://doi.org/10.1016/j.pubrev.2022.102176

Conclusion

30 Reflections on the Evolving Theories of Public Relations

Maureen Taylor

Botan and Sommerfeldt's *Public Relations Theory III* offers a space to reflect on over three decades of efforts to develop, test, and extend public relations theory. I read the initial book, Botan and Hazleton *Public Relations Theory* (1989), as a first-year master's student at Purdue University. This book made me want to be a part of public relations scholarship, and I am certain that it inspired others in their journey to theorize about public relations.

Writing the concluding chapter of this volume is both a challenge and a gift given by my advisor, Carl H. Botan, and my advisee, Erich Sommerfeldt. It is a challenge because who doesn't still remember writing for their advisor? Almost everything I know about scholarly writing I learned from Carl H. Botan. And writing for Erich Sommerfeldt is challenging as well because I made him rewrite his dissertation chapters several times when they were already pretty solid. But writing this conclusion chapter is also a gift because it allows me the time and space to organize my observations of the evolution of public relations theory. This final chapter of *Public Relations Theory III* is not meant to be a history lesson about the field, but the arguments that it seeks to make about the evolution of public relations theory and possible future directions need to be historically contextualized. Please indulge me in a short summary of my perceptions of the history of theory building in public relations, the roles that the chapters across the first two *Public Relations Theory* books have played, and how *Public Relations Theory* III will play in the evolving story of public relations theory.

Introduction and Chapter Overview

It would not be an understatement to say that when Botan and Hazleton's *Public Relations Theory* (1989) was published the field of public relations lacked its own set of strong conceptual frameworks. Botan and Hazleton argued that public relations was an applied social science and that "we should be able to apply communication theory to explain and predict public relations practice, and use public relations practice as a site for the development of communication theory" (p. xiii). Botan and Hazleton treated public relations as a context that was both informed by communication theory and

DOI: 10.4324/9781003141396-35

could also contribute to it. They did not call for any one unified theory of public relations and featured many different approaches in Botan and Hazleton's 1989 book, including two-way symmetrical communication (Grunig, 1989), rhetoric (Cheney & Dionisopoulos, 1989), game theory (Murphy, 1989), and a wide range of persuasion theories (Anderson, 1989; Cline et al., 1989; Hamilton, 1989; Johnson, 1989; Van Leuven, 1989). Dominant theories and research themes in the 1980s were agenda setting, persuasion, and information subsidies—reflecting the mass communication roots of public relations scholars and the interest in studying *how the profession worked through media and how public relations communication could be influential in different contexts.* A lot of these chapters fell into what Botan and Taylor (2004) would later describe as the functional approach, which "sees publics and communication as tools or means to achieve organizational ends" (p. 651). The term *functional* is not meant to denigrate the contributions, but merely to describe that a lot of the early work that public relations drew upon was organizational centric and treated publics as something to be changed by communication.

By the 1990s, there was interest in public relations as a management function. Excellence theory was treated by many as a paradigm to explain which organizational behaviors and communication would facilitate ethical public relations. During this time, scholars sought out ways to show how organizations were creating balanced, two-way symmetrical relationships with publics. Excellence theory asked questions about *how public relations management decisions were made and communicated to publics.*

By the time that Botan and Hazleton's *Public Relations Theory II* (2006) was published, the field looked a lot different. Excellence theory was still being advanced as a general theory about the value of public relations to organizations (Grunig et al., 2006). But other theories were emerging because excellence theory could not answer questions about how internationalization and technology, like the Internet, changed how organizations communicated with publics. An organization cannot have balanced symmetrical communication through a website! By the late 1990s and early 2000s, the field was looking at contingency theory, relationship management, and dialogic communication as alternative lenses through which to theorize about public relations. Theories of sociology, dialogue, and civil society provided conceptual frameworks that opened larger social possibilities of what public relations could achieve. Research in the 2000s reflected what Botan and Taylor termed the "cocreational approach," which recognizes publics as "cocreators of meaning and communication as what makes it possible to agree to shared meanings, interpretations, and goals" (p. 652). In contrast to focusing on only organizational goals, cocreational perspectives emphasize the value of relationships and cocreated meaning, even when there is disagreement.

By the 2010s to 2020s, after the publications of *Public Relations Theory II*, public relations theory continued to evolve with more calls to consider the societal contributions of public relations. European scholars advocated for sociological theory as a basis of considering public relations' roles in organizations and society. Public relations theory both critiqued power and studied how it was created by public relations communications. The social network perspective, critical and social theory, and engagement emerged as theories showing *the contributions of public relations to society*. The evolution was additive, not radical, and older theories were integrated into new theorizing and research.

This brief history no doubt misses many trends and themes, but it shows that over time, public relations has moved away from more functional approaches to more cocreational approaches. This chapter is the final anchor of the book, and my assigned task was to reflect on the theories, identify potential gaps, and humbly identify future directions for theory building. For me, the three books of *Public Relations Theory* (Botan &Hazleton, 1989, 2006; Botan & Sommerfeldt, 2023) provide the roadmap for my research agenda in public relations and embody the past, present, and the still-unwritten evolving future of public relations theory.

This book is personal. Carl H. Botan was my advisor at Purdue and mentor for the last 30 years, and Erich Sommerfeldt was my first public relations doctoral advisee at the University of Oklahoma. The list of contributors and university affiliations reads like a network map of where the field has been and where it is going. This book showcases *five generations* of public relations scholars that began with Botan and includes Sommerfeldt's doctoral student, Stephanie Madden, co-authoring with her doctoral student, Mikayla Pevac. I read the chapters like a genealogy story of how public relations concepts and theories have evolved. The family story is not just an American story. This book is more global in contributors, showing that we've come quite far and that we have a lot to celebrate in public relations theory.

To reflect on the book and the general state of the field of public relations theory, this final chapter is comprised of three sections. The first section provides a bird's eye view of discussion of the some of the theories conceptualized in the field and in this book. The second section steps back to interrogate some of the assumptions underlying the body of knowledge in public relations. This section also poses questions for discipline-wide discussions about public relations theory in general. The final section identifies potential ways forward for theory building over the next decades.

Evolving Public Relations Theories

From a Theory Desert to a Theory Buffet

My first observation is that *Public Relations Theory III* contains a buffet of theories ranging from considerations about individual level ethics (Bowen, 2023) and practices to public relations communication shaping relationships in large networks (Saffer & Yang, 2023). Chapters advance theory building from rhetorical, quantitative, and critical perspectives. A student could pick up this volume and have several theories to apply to a research context. Additionally, after reading the book, students will have a better visualization of how public relations contributes to society. This book is beneficial because it brings a dozen theories together in one place for comparison, and some chapters are fulfilling the challenge from *Public Relations Theory II* to stimulate debates about the field. For instance, Sommerfeldt and Iannacone's (2023) chapter provides an interesting challenge to some of the assumptions advanced in the Ki et al. (2023) chapter on relationship management. Saffer and Yang (2023) also critique OPR. Kent's (2023) conceptualization of dialogue is quite different from how Dhanesh and Avidar (2023), Chen et al. (2023), and Zhou and Men (2023) suggest we study dialogue. Waymer and Heath (2023), Saffer and Yang (2023), and Madden and Pevac (2023) approach issues management a bit differently as well. Nothhaft and Zerfass's (2023) chapter pretty much challenges many of the foundational claims in the other chapters! *Public Relations Theory III* provides a buffet of theories to answer questions about a broader conceptualization of public relations than the earlier books. Such debates are now possible, meaning that the discipline is maturing.

The theory buffet, however, is still sourced from other fields, and the verdict is out as to whether this is a good or bad situation for theory building in public relations. While many scholars have bemoaned the interdisciplinarity of public relations and argued for the creation of theories unique to public relations, Nothhaft and Zerfass (2023) make the argument that public relations theory happened because scholars were trying to create theory out of practice, and having multidisciplinary approaches and theories is the natural part of being an applied communication discipline. Their chapter argues not for public relations theories' uniqueness but for accepting that we are a part of other fields because of the complexity of public relations practice. They note:

> All applied communication disciplines claim the key concepts that give organizational prestige: strategic outlook, value creation and accountability, ethical high ground, co-creation, dialogue, relationships, and authenticity. The result is not only a bewildering disciplinary landscape. The result is a belief that any commitment to public relation's *own agenda* might mean a lost opportunity, a potential loss of territory.

Nothhaft and Zerfass believe that a "postdisciplinary shake-up would impact" the respectability of the field and "that intra-disciplinary sophistication will count less, utility more." Their critique of the field for trying to create distinctive theories provides a counterbalance to the rest of the chapters of the book. I encourage readers to look at this chapter before reading other chapters and then to revisit Nothhaft and Zerfass's chapter after finishing the book. Regardless of where you land in the interdisciplinary, intradisciplinary, or post-disciplinary debate, we know that there are more diverse theories today. And many of the theories come with an ethical component.

Ethical Assumptions Are Embedded in Public Relations Theories

A second observation is that many of the theories conceptualized in this book have, at their core, ethical dimensions. That's different from the functional theories of past *Public Relations Theory* books. The societal turn that supported the development of engagement, dialogue, critical, feminist, and cultural theories proceeds from the acknowledgement that what we say and do matters a great deal. Organizations have important roles to play in society, but individuals, groups, networks, and social movements also provide key information and discourses that shape society. While influence is a desired outcome of public relations communication, ethical practice should always be grounded in what Bowen (2023) noted, "Rising above influence to employing rational moral philosophy is a normative ethical obligation that will allow public relations to contribute to society, public discussion for understanding, equality, and increased organizational responsibility as a whole, fostering ethical rectitude across all areas of the function" (Chapter 29).

Likewise, dialogic theory and engagement theory have at their core assumptions of ethics, respect, and a positive orientation to others. For example, dialogic theory from both Buberian (Kent & Taylor, 2002) and Bakhtinian (Capizzo, 2018) approaches take ethical concepts and apply them to practice. Similarly, in engagement theory, ethics is inherent in the approach (Johnston & Taylor, 2018a). Scholars are working to identify and support ethical systems of public relations. For instance, Kent (2023) argues that "dialogue is based on two key ideas: a body of rules or practices for interacting with other people in an ethical and uplifting manner, and the assumption of a potentially ongoing relationship of mutual respect" (Chapter 9). Ethics in public relations theories transcends considering the organizational level as the ultimate end of public relations, and ethics can also be applied at the societal level. Waymer and Heath's chapter makes a compelling argument for the theory of place for understanding how public relations contributes to a fully functioning society. The chapters in Section 3 provide insights into how we can apply theory to make society a better place for all. Whereas Nothhaft and Zerfass might say that this approach "wastes energy chasing the *appearance* of academic respectability" (Chapter 15), I believe public relations has a positive role in society. But I am also swayed by the idea of agonism as a framework for thinking about ethical public relations practice. The agonist approach provides a "conceptual framework for understanding a constructive role for forms of public relations practice that enable transparent rhetorical rivalries as well as acting as a catalyst for tangible contributions to the public good" (Davidson, 2016, p. 147). Waymer and Heath's chapter makes a solid ethical argument for public relations in society without ever using the term *ethics* in the text. Theory building has moved from being about individual and organizational ethics to theorizing about societal ethics. Indeed, the social aspect of communication is another theme in *Public Relations Theory III*.

Situating the Practice Within Culture, Social, Economic, Place, and Political Contexts

A third theme that is evident in evolving public relations theory is the need to reflect context. Edwards and Ihlen (2023) remind us that "all public relations work is implicated in wider social, political, and economic arrangements, and those arrangements in turn underpin its function as a location of dominance or resistance, or where power is in flux" (Chapter 13). Contextual factors such as culture, social relationships, economics, place, and politics situate public relations practices across the world. Several of the chapters in this book (Aghazadeh & Aldoory, 2023; Chen et al., 2023; Dhanesh & Avidar, 2023; Liu & Austin, 2023; Ni & Sha, 2023; Ngondo & Klyueva, 2023) explore this theme and remind us that public relations practice is situated in larger contexts that may ultimately influence the outcome of communication and relationships more than our messaging.

Public Relations Theory III provides a clear answer to Ihlen and van Ruler (2007), who asked, "What does public relations do in, to, and for society?" In the 15 years since that question, it has become clearer what public relations contributes to society. One of the more recent trends in public relations scholarship and theory building has been to situate public relations practice in wider social frameworks, rather than organizational contexts. Motion and Leitch (2015) envisioned a future where public relations contributed to "the democratic, deliberative and decision-making roles of civil society" (p. 148). Public relations could make this contribution by preparing organizations to engage with stakeholders and by preparing stakeholders to engage with organizations. One example of this can be in found in Waymer and Heath's chapter that has flipped issues management from being a mostly organization-centric approach to a more activist, place-centered use of communication to cocreate meaning in society. The consideration of context in public relations theory has set the stage for theorizing about engagement and relationships. For example, Chen et al. (2023) applied their shared Chinese cultural heritage to explore how dialogic communication, crisis management, and corporate social responsibility (CSR) theory are enriched when considered in a Chinese context. Theories will be adapted and changed when scholars across the world use them. Theories will also be changed when applied to digital contexts.

Digital Engagement in Theory Building

A fourth observation is the almost overwhelming focus of public relations theorizing about digital communication. The chapters by Johnston (2023) and Zhou and Men (2023) conceptualize digital engagement and argue for future research agendas. Engagement is also implicitly and explicitly situated in the Chon et al. (2023), Saffer and Yang (2023), Pang et al. (2023), Sellnow et al. (2023), and Lui et al. (2023) chapters. Contributors to this book base their theories on different levels of and types of communication engagement and often the type of engagement is around social media. Zhou and Men (2023) ask, "Is social media good for corporate public relations?" Their answers are thoughtful and prompt questions that may drive theory development.

I like the concept of engagement and have published on the topic (Taylor & Kent, 2014; Johnston & Taylor, 2018a, 2018b; Taylor, 2018). Yet, looking at the chapters, I must ask, "Is digital engagement enough to provide the insights needed to extend our theorizing of engagement?" Public relations practice occurs in evolving media eco systems, and the eco systems are constantly changing. I don't remember many articles studying engagement on the mediums of television, radio, or print. To be fair, those were not high-engagement mediums, but the point needs to be raised. If we reduce public relations to digital public relations, and we use digital data to test our theories, we are missing a lot of public relations communication. All social media communication is not public relations. All public relations communication is not digital.

Recent research using big data and data mining provide unique insights into digital behaviors created by public relations (Zhou, 2019). But the questions to be asked are: *What is the importance of knowing an organization's digital network? What does a loosely connected group of people mean for social stability or social change? Is a public just a group of people who follow certain people or organizations on a platform? Is commenting or sharing a post valid evidence of engagement?* When we only study the digital side of public relations, we have narrowed our assumptions about cocreated meaning, relationships, engagement, and the possibility of broader theory building. Public relations theory and practice may be overly optimistic about the value of social media to accomplish organizational or activist objectives. That's why we need to critically review the assumptions that we are making in our research and theorizing.

Holding Up a Mirror to the Assumptions Underpinning Public Relations Theories

The chapters in *Public Relations Theory III* and the previous two books provide a large enough sample for us to "hold up a mirror" to reflect on our field. One of the best ways to reflect on the theories that guide public relations scholarship is to examine the assumptions that many of our theories are based upon. These implicit assumptions are important to make explicit because they influence theory building.

Assumption 1: Public Relations Theory Informs Public Relations Practice

Nothhaft and Zerfass noted that many of the research articles published in public relations or strategic communication journals have little or no relevance to practitioners. Fields that are applied or practice-based have challenges when it comes to theory building. Normative theories are supposed to theorize about the best way to do something, while positive theories describe how something is done. Theory is supposed to guide practice, and practice is supposed to inform theory. In an applied field like public relations, there should be close relationships between practitioners and scholars.

What is the relationship between public relations practitioners and scholars? If I had to rate the quality of the interaction among those who practice public relations and those who study it, I would have to give the quality of the interaction a low score. Some of our research, including theories, have little application to the field. Byrne (2008) observed that "much of the research to date concludes that practitioners see the work of academics in the field adding little or no value to them due to issues surrounding utility and accessibility" (p. 21). The groups have different priorities. Academics seek to develop and extend theories by adding new variables or refining existing scales. Much of the research is what Kuhn (1970) named "mopping up," which creates a lot of derivative research. The frequent use of statistics to look for differences between conditions means that many of the papers published in our field could not be picked up by a practitioner and used in their next day's work. Structural equation modelling, scraping big data from social media, and panel surveys may not hit the mark when it comes to providing tangible, usable competencies to those who work in the profession.

That observation is doubly true for communication professionals working across the world. Many practitioners cannot access or may not want to read our journals (Cheng & de Gregorio, 2008). They may not have access to professional associations that are supposed to serve as a bridge between practitioners and scholars. Even when there are professional associations, the exchanges may not be creating the kind of cross fertilization of ideas that was originally envisioned. Indeed, most of the information exchange between scholars and practitioners is in the form of practitioners taking surveys about current practices and competencies. Theory is rarely the topic of discussion. Because our insights in public relations are drawn from current and past practice, this means that academic understanding of public relations practice is looking in the *rear-view mirror,* watching what has been done rather than shaping future practices based on insight from theory building.

Assumption 2: Publics Are Active and Empowered

Public relations theories are still based on assumptions of an aware or active public (stakeholders) who are interested in influencing organizations. Chon et al. (2023) lay out the history, foundational assumptions, and future directions of the situational theory of problem solving (STOPS). This line of research places publics at the center of theorizing. Situational theories suggest that organizations need to "invest resources to identify them [publics] and prioritize strategic publics with whom organizations should build, cultivate, and maintain relationships" (Chapter 5).

Madden and Pevac (2023) share an example of local activist publics and how they used social media to create social change in a US college town. There are lots of case studies in the public relations literature that celebrate small-scale activism. The Internet and social media allow both activist organizations and corporations to build public support and mobilize resources. Over time, we can see that publics (or in some cases networks) have evolved, but social change is elusive. A public is more than people who follow an account or share social media content. We put a lot of stock in people to hold organizations accountable when in many countries, there is little to no accountability to the public from organizations or government.

Assumption 3: The Media Matter

Throughout *Public Relations Theory I, II,* and *II,* there have been chapters about public relations and the media. Agenda setting, agenda building, and now agenda sharing theories seek to explain and predict how all types of organizations use public relations to gain or modify media attention. Lan and Kiousis (2023) argue that organizations need to build an "optimal multilevel, multi-channel, and multimedia framework of media relations" and that organizations need "to monitor and evaluate the dynamics and changes in such frameworks in a timely manner, and—despite the difficulties—how to foster consensus on shared values and promote cohesiveness among the constituents of the framework" (Chapter 25). But these media (and public relations theories) are still based on assumptions of a media function that publishes credible information that holds government and organizations accountable. Whereas many scholars have pointed to media integration and mergers as a problem for civil society, there are many nations where the media have always been controlled by the government, political parties, or a few powerful families. The traditional assumption of earned media being a credible way to reach publics may have some limitations. For instance, sponsored content has grown on websites and cable channels. The line between news, entertainment, and advertising has become blurred. Misinformation and disinformation have become both intended and unintended parts of the media ecosystem, but public relations has not yet theorized about these trends.

Assumption 4: Public Relations Practitioners Are Empowered to Act

As an applied social science, public relations studies the people who practice public relations. We afford practitioners an important place in our theorizing, probably more than other fields. Public relations theories are still based on assumptions that individual practitioners are credible organizational leaders who have the opportunity, knowledge, responsibility, and agency to shape organizational behavior.

Public relations theories still believe that an individual public relations employee or department can influence organizational decisions. Scholars have called public relations practitioners "counselors" and describe them as being the "conscience of organizations." This attribution of agency to practitioners means that we theorize them as change agents and moral agents. Yet, most have little or no training in ethics to guide them (Chapter 28) and instead fall back on situational ethics and organizational norms if and when they get to make important decisions. That is, they fall back on comfortable ethical frameworks when they get to be in the room when decisions are made. Surveys of practitioners across the world remind us that many of them are not included in the highest levels of organizational decision making and thus lack agency and empowerment.

Yet, in some situations, practitioners may be empowered. Molleda and Suárez-Monsalve (2023) call for a postcolonial approach where public relations practitioners tackle some of the most sensitive social issues that public relations professionals can influence within their organizations. They argue that public relations practitioners can work for the free expression of diversity, the recognition of multiculturalism, and the well-being of migrant populations. Social issues may be one way to empower practitioners to guide their organization's discourse in a fully functioning society (Heath, 2006).

Assumption 5: Western Public Relations Theories Are Transferable to Other Contexts

While public relations is practiced in various forms across the world, most of the research reflects a Western perspective. There has been a lot of work considering social, political, cultural, and economic contexts when theorizing, but even with those efforts the theories of public relations are still very Western oriented. Many public relations theories are based on individualist, capitalist, corporate, media-focused, or organization-centric assumptions. This makes sense because these are the cultural and philosophical values of people raised in Western societies. But there is so much more that we can learn from importing the values of other cultures into theory building.

Ngondo and Klyueva (2023) put forth a compelling case for *Ubuntu* as a framework for public relations theory building, noting "the communitarian nature of *Ubuntu* is expressed through the awareness of interdependence among members of the community" (Chapter 23). Ubuntu calls for harmony, reconciliation, inclusiveness, tolerance, mutual understanding, transparency, negotiation, and consensus-building.

Likewise, Molleda and Suárez-Monsalve call for public relations researchers in Latin America to propose new theories based on decolonialized thinking that guides professional practice and the construction of national and regional discourses and stories with social and critical awareness to transform Latin American development. Ni and Sha argue that "a holistic examination of culture should also be expanded to more areas of research in the organizational and professional settings" (Chapter 7). We need new theories reflecting diverse cultural and social contexts to make public relations theory more useful across the globe.

Conclusions: Where Are We Now, and Where Are We Going?

If you made it to this conclusion chapter, then I hope you will agree that the diversification of public relations theories is a positive sign. Theories are tools to understand and explain phenomena. Theories set the boundaries of a field, and they delineate which questions can be asked and answered (Kuhn, 1970). Applied social science fields, like public relations, often borrow and adapt existing theories in the early years. Over time, new theories are generated by scholars, and the domain becomes more focused and specialized. It is through specialization that disciplinary boundaries are set until new questions are raised that need new theories.

Not only has the diversity of theories grown since *Public Relations Theory I*, but so has the diversity of the people theorizing about public relations. There were a total of 26 authors in *Public Relations Theory I*, with female contributors comprising 15% of the authors. All but one of the contributors was US-based. Ron Pearson was from Canada, but he earned his doctorate in the US. In *Public Relations Theory II*, there were 29 contributors, and 31% of them were female. Three of the contributors worked at universities outside of the United States. In *Public Relations Theory III*, nearly 60% of the contributors are female, and approximately one-third of all contributors are working outside the United States at institutions in Germany, Australia, Hong Kong, United Kingdom, Norway, Columbia, Singapore, United Arab Emirates, Israel, and Finland. Moreover, many of the scholars contributing to *Public Relations Theory III* were born and received their early education in places such as China, Korea, Turkey, India, Tajikistan, Zimbabwe, Italy, and Denmark.

Kuhn (1970) noted that fields of research are dominated by paradigms. Paradigms are powerful in that they identify the questions that can be asked and the methods that can be used to generate knowledge in a field. In *The Structure of Scientific Revolutions*, Kuhn is credited with observing *the answers that you get depend upon the questions that you ask.*

I am going to add another part to that observation: "*the answers you get depend on who asks the questions.*" Identity matters, as the chapters in Section 3: Race, Gender, and Identity provide readers with diverse perspectives on how public relations can reify or challenge societal norms. Logan reflects on the Public Relations Theory series and notes, "The inclusion of this chapter in this volume testifies to the extent that critical cultural scholarship has raised the prominence of race and identity as key public relations concerns" (Chapter 18). In this book, Logan draws on critical race theory to note that public relations scholarship about race and ethnicity has heightened awareness of the different experiences of white and non-white practitioners. We also know more about how those who do not conform to heteronormativity or have fluid racial identities are often marginalized. Although CRT is not a public relations discipline specific theory, it can be applied to questions, industry assumptions, norms, processes, and structures that influence the practice and thus influence theory building, especially at the organizational and societal level.

The cultural backgrounds of theorists matter a great deal as well. Theorists who have lived in fragile or quickly evolving (or devolving) social, political, and economic contexts can see firsthand how Western-based theories might fail to explain public relations practice in their home country. Molleda and Suárez-Monsalve (2023) describe public relations practice in Latin America as helping to support societal progress. They want a public relations practice that embodies explicit commitments to serve both the organization's and the public's interests. "Many professionals in the region see themselves as agents of change and champions of freedom, justice, harmony, equality, and human dignity, using communication to reach agreements, consensus, and convergent attitudes between organizations and their internal and external stakeholders" (Chapter 22).

The chapters in this book are the culmination of nearly 35 years of thinking about public relations theories. We now have theories that have been created by public relations scholars, and when we import other theories, we do so while recognizing that they are complementary to our own theories. The field is at an interesting ontological point. Ki's (2023) chapter observes that we are "moving from the 'classical' paradigm to this 'relational' successor respond[ing] to the digital era's 'horizontalized' and 'fragmentized' phenomenon. To sum up, co-creator, co-worldview, and co-producers of social processes are the key concepts in the relational shift in public relations scholarship" (Chapter 16).

The recent trend toward thinking about dissensus and agonism raises important questions that need to be answered not only by public relations scholars but by society as well. I am one of the many scholars who has argued for a consensus-based understanding of public relations. The theories of dialogue, engagement, and civil society provide great frameworks for thinking about larger contributions of public relations to society. But I also now see the value of consensus–dissensus as future debates in the field, as public relations seeks to make contributions to society.

As I look at the chapters of *Public Relations Theory III*, I am pleased with where we are as a discipline. Yes, we have borrowed concepts from other fields, but that's all right because we are theorizing about a complex practice. The chapters in this book show that there is a significant body of knowledge that helps explain and predict the inputs and outcomes of public relations communication. The field is tackling big questions, and I think you will agree that we see public relations theory and practice as an integral part of the communication ecosystems of the 21st century. I look forward to seeing where the field will be in *Public Relations Theory IV*, and I encourage each reader of this book to make their contributions to theory building.

References

Aghazadeh, S. A., & Aldoory, L. (2023). Health communication theory in public relations. In C. H. Botan & E. J. Sommerfeldt (Eds.), *Public relations III*. Lawrence Erlbaum Associates.

Anderson, R. (1989). Reassessing the odds against finding meaningful behavioral change in mass media health promotion campaigns. In C. H. Botan & V. Hazleton (Eds.), *Public relations theory* (pp. 309–321). Lawrence Erlbaum Associates.

Botan, C. H., & Hazleton, V. (1989). *Public relations theory*. Lawrence Erlbaum Associates.

Botan, C. H., & Hazleton, V. (2006). *Public relations theory II*. Lawrence Erlbaum Associates.

Botan, C. H., & Sommerfeldt, E. (2023). *Public relations theory III*. Lawrence Erlbaum Associates.

Botan, C. H., & Taylor, M. (2004). Public relations: The state of the field. *Journal of Communication, 54*(4), 645–661.

Bowen, S. A. (2023). A theoretic perspective on the evolution of ethics. In C. H. Botan & E. J. Sommerfeldt (Eds.), *Public relations III*. Lawrence Erlbaum Associates.

Byrne, K. (2008). The value of academia: Variance among academic and practitioner perspectives on the role of public relations academics. *Asia Pacific Public Relations Journal, 9*(2008), 17–34.

Capizzo, L. (2018). Reimagining dialogue in public relations: Bakhtin and open dialogue in the public sphere. *Public Relations Review, 44*(4), 523–532.

Chen, Y. R. R., Hung-Baesecke, & Cheng, Y. (2023). Public relations theory development in China: In the areas of dialogic communication, crisis communication, and CSR communication. In C. H. Botan & E. J. Sommerfeldt (Eds.), *Public relations III*. Lawrence Erlbaum Associates.

Cheney, G., & Dionisopoulos, G. N. (1989). Public relations? No, relations with publics: A rhetorical–organizational approach to contemporary corporate communications. In C. H. Botan & V. Hazleton (Eds.), *Public relations theory* (pp. 135–157). Lawrence Erlbaum Associates.

Cheng, I. H., & de Gregorio, F. (2008). Does (linking with) practice make perfect? A survey of public relations scholars' perspectives. *Journal of Public Relations Research, 20*(4), 377–402.

Chon, M. J., Tam, L., Lee, H., & Kim, J.-N. (2023). Situational theory of problem solving (STOPS): A foundational theory of publics and its behavioral nature in problem solving. In C. H. Botan & E. J. Sommerfeldt (Eds.), *Public relations III*. Lawrence Erlbaum Associates.

Cline, C. G., McBride, M. H., & Miller, R. E. (1989). The theory of psychological type congruence in public relations and persuasion. In C. H. Botan & V. Hazleton (Eds.), *Public relations theory* (pp. 221–239). Lawrence Erlbaum Associates.

Davidson, S. (2016). Public relations theory: An agonistic critique of the turns to dialogue and symmetry. *Public Relations Inquiry, 5*(2), 145–167.

Dhanesh, G., & Avidar, R. (2023). Culture and dialogic theory in public relations: The Middle Eastern context. In C. H. Botan & E. J. Sommerfeldt (Eds.), *Public relations III*. Lawrence Erlbaum Associates.

Edwards, L., & Ihlen, O. (2023). Social theory in public relations: Insights and directions. In C. H. Botan & E. J. Sommerfeldt (Eds.), *Public relations theory III*. Lawrence Erlbaum Associates.

Grunig, J. E. (1989). Symmetrical presuppositions as a framework for public relations theory. In C. H. Botan & V. Hazleton (Eds.), *Public relations theory* (pp. 17–44). Lawrence Erlbaum Associates.

Grunig, J. E., Grunig, L. A., & Dozier, D. M. (2006). The excellence theory. In C. H. Botan & V. Hazleton (Eds.), *Public relations theory II* (pp. 21–62). Lawrence Erlbaum Associates.

Hamilton, P. K. (1989). Application of a generalized persuasion model to public relations research. In C. H. Botan & V. Hazleton (Eds.), *Public relations theory* (pp. 323–334). Lawrence Erlbaum Associates.

Heath, R. L. (2006). Onward into more fog: Thoughts on public relations' research directions. *Journal of Public Relations Research, 18*(2), 93–114.

Ihlen, Ø., & van Ruler, B. (2007). How public relations works: Theoretical roots and public relations perspectives. *Public Relations Review, 33*, 243–248.

Johnson, D. (1989). The coorientation model and consultant roles. In C. H. Botan & V. Hazleton (Eds.), *Public relations theory* (pp. 243–263). Lawrence Erlbaum Associates.

Johnston, K., & Taylor, M. (2018a). *The handbook of communication engagement*. Wiley Blackwell.

Johnston, K., & Taylor, M. (2018b). Engagement as communication: Pathways, possibilities and future directions. In K. Johnston & M. Taylor (Eds.), *Handbook of communication engagement* (pp. 1–16). Wiley-Blackwell.

Kent, M. L. (2023). Dialogic theory in public relations. In C. H. Botan & E. J. Sommerfeldt (Eds.), *Public relations theory III*. Lawrence Erlbaum Associates.

Kent, M. L., & Taylor, M. (2002). Toward a dialogic theory of public relations. *Public Relations Review, 28*(1), 21–37.

Kuhn, T. (1970). *The structure of scientific revolutions*. University of Chicago Press.

Liu, B., & Austin, L. (2023). Digital crisis communication theory: Current landscape and future trajectories. In C. H. Botan & E. J. Sommerfeldt (Eds.), *Public relations III*. Lawrence Erlbaum Associates.

Logan, N. (2023). Critical race theory, identity and public relations. In C. H. Botan & E. J. Sommerfeldt (Eds.), *Public relations III*. Lawrence Erlbaum Associates.

Madden, S., & Pevac, M. (2023). Agenda building through community building: Theorizing place and digital space in grassroots activist public relations. In C. H. Botan & E. J. Sommerfeldt (Eds.), *Public relations III*. Lawrence Erlbaum Associates.

Motion, J., & Leitch, S. (2015). Critical discourse analysis. In J. L'Etang, D. McKie, N. Snow, & J. Xifra (Eds.), *The Routledge handbook of critical public relations* (pp. 142–150). Routledge.

Murphy, P. (1989). Game theory as a paradigm for the public relations process. In C. H. Botan & V. Hazleton (Eds.), *Public relations theory* (pp. 173–192). Lawrence Erlbaum Associates.

Ngondo, P. S., & Klyueva, A. (2023). Inviting an Ubuntu-based approach to public relations theory building in Sub-Saharan Africa. In C. H. Botan & E. J. Sommerfeldt (Eds.), *Public relations III*. Lawrence Erlbaum Associates.

Ni, L., & Sha, B. L. (2023). Development of intercultural public relations theory. In C. H. Botan & E. J. Sommerfeldt (Eds.), *Public relations III*. Lawrence Erlbaum Associates.

Nothhaft, H., & Zerfass, A. (2023). Public relations in a postdisciplinary world: On the impossibility of establishing a constitutive PR theory within the tribal struggles of applied communication disciplines. In C. H. Botan & E. J. Sommerfeldt (Eds.), *Public relations III*. Lawrence Erlbaum Associates.

Saffer, A. J., & Yang, A. (2023). Applying the network perspective to public relations theory and practice. In C. H. Botan & E. J. Sommerfeldt (Eds.), *Public relations theory III*. Lawrence Erlbaum Associates.

Sellnow, T., Sellnow, D. D., Johansson, B., Lane, D. R., & Seeger, M. W. (2023). The IDEA model theoretical framework: An explication of risk communication as engaged public relations. In C. H. Botan & E. J. Sommerfeldt (Eds.), *Public relations III*. Lawrence Erlbaum Associates.

Taylor, M. (2018). Reconceptualizing public relations in an engaged society. In K. Johnston & M. Taylor (Eds.), *Handbook of communication engagement* (pp. 103–114). Wiley-Blackwell.

Taylor, M., & Kent, M. L. (2014). Dialogic engagement: Clarifying foundational concepts. *Journal of Public Relations Research, 26*(5), 384–398.

Van Leuven, J. (1989). Theoretical models for public relations campaigns. In C. H. Botan & V. Hazleton (Eds.), *Public relations theory* (pp. 193–202). Lawrence Erlbaum Associates.

Waymer, D., & Heath, R. L. (2023). Strategic issues management: A rhetorical theoretical perspective on contestable questions of place. In C. H. Botan & E. J. Sommerfeldt (Eds.), *Public relations III*. Lawrence Erlbaum Associates.

Zhou, A. (2019). Bring publics back into networked public relations research: A dual-projection approach for network ecology. *Public Relations Review, 45*(4), 101772.

Zhou, A., & Men, R. (2023). *Theoretical models for corporate social media use.*

Index

Printed in the United States
by Baker & Taylor Publisher Services